WORLD PHILOSOPHY

WORLD PHILOSOPHY

Essay-Reviews
of
225 Major Works

2

Third century B.C. - A.D. 1713

Edited by
FRANK N. MAGILL

Associate Editor
IAN P. McGREAL
Professor of Philosophy
California State University
Sacramento

SALEM PRESS
Englewood Cliffs, N.J.

Library of Congress Catalog Card Number: 82-060268

Complete Set: ISBN 0-89356-325-0
Volume II: ISBN 0-89356-327-7

First Printing

Some of the material in this work also appears in *Masterpieces of World Philosophy in Summary Form* (1961)

PRINTED IN THE UNITED STATES OF AMERICA

CHRONOLOGICAL LIST OF TITLES
IN VOLUME TWO

WORLD PHILOSOPHY

WORLD PHILOSOPHY

TAO TE CHING

Author. Unknown (but erroneously attributed to Lao Tzu, born c. 600 B.C.)
Type of work: Metaphysics, ethics, political philosophy
First transcribed: Late third century B.C.

PRINCIPAL IDEAS ADVANCED

Tao, *the way, is the nameless beginning of things, the universal principle underlying everything, the supreme, ultimate pattern, and the principle of growth.*

If a man takes possession of the tao, *the universal principle, he becomes a Sage fit for ruling the world.*

By observing Nature man learns to follow Nature's way, the tao.

The man who possesses tao *must hide his power and appear soft and weak, for he who shows his power is without power; and the soft overcomes the hard.*

To attain tao *a man must return to the state of infancy, avoid action, and preserve the breath, the life-force, by breath control.*

Perhaps more than any other ancient Chinese text this work has been a center of philological dispute through the centuries. The first question is its authorship. Legend has identified a Li Erh of the seventh century B.C. as the writer, but more reliable historical records yield only a Li Erh of the fourth century B.C. who could not have done the things attributed to him by numerous hagiographical accounts, including having been born with a beard and having taught Confucius for a period. It seems that while the historical Li Erh (or another person named Tsung, of the third century B.C.) may have actually expounded some of the ideas in this work, the story is pure fiction that the legendary Li Erh (known as Lao Tan, or Lao Tzu) composed this book all by himself shortly before he vanished beyond the mountains on the back of a blue water buffalo. In fact the *Tao Te Ching* as it has come down to us contains many telltale features which point to its collective authorship; most probably it was not written by any single author, but has grown into its present shape.

An understanding about the authorship of this work is important for a proper grasp of the central ideas behind the eighty-one short but epigrammatic and sometimes cryptic chapters in this work. For however poetically integrated these ideas may be around the central theme of a mystic quietism that dates as far back as the dawning of Chinese history, there are passages in this book alluding to the many different schools of thought that contended for intellectual dominance in the early Warring States period (fifth to third century B.C.). The voice (or voices, hereafter called the "Taoist") speaking behind these epigrams is arguing against the Legalists (some call them Realists), the Confucians, and the Mohists, but the voice also seems to borrow some of the arguments of its rivals. The borrowings are possibly due both to the coexistence of these arguments, as part of the common knowledge of the intellectuals at the time this book was first put together, and to the subsequent interpolations of commentaries that became hopelessly enmeshed with the original text.

A vague notion of the *"tao"* existed among the proto-philosophical ideas in ancient China long before any Taoist, or Mohist, or Confucian expounded their respective views on this concept. It stemmed, apparently, from an early effort of the Chinese mind to search into the mystery of the universe and to discover the reason, if any, behind things. To name the unnamable, the Chinese borrowed this term, *tao*, or the "Way." The ambiguous nature of this term allows it to serve several doctrines. Hence to Confucius *tao* means the sage-king's way to social harmony; to Mo Ti, *tao* means the way to ample supply of staple foods and a populous state, and to Mencius, *tao* means the way to moral (and spiritual) perfection. But to a Taoist, *tao* could mean all these and more.

Throughout this work (and particularly in Chapter XXV), *tao* is described as the nameless beginning of all things, even prior to Heaven and Earth. *Tao* is unchanging and permeates everything; hence, *tao* must be a kind of constant, universal principle that underlies all phenomena. *Tao* has always existed and has no beginning of itself; hence, it must be comparable to the First Cause. Everything in the universe patterns itself after the dictates of a higher being, such as man patterning his ways after those of Heaven. But *tao*, being supreme, follows itself. Hence, it suggests the Ultimate Pattern. *Tao* "is so of itself," without any outside force or influence. Above all, *tao* is "always so" because it is the dynamic principle of change. It dictates the rhythm of growth and decay, but since it is itself the principle of growth it remains constant.

This is a frontal attack against the Legalist. The Legalist divides phenomena into rigid categories, and he demands that the rigidity of his system be maintained at all costs because he sees no other essence of anything except its name. The Taoist points out, in Chapter I, that the named are but the manifestations of essence. They are only the crust. What lies behind them is the real essence which is the source of all mysteries of the universe. In its application, the Taoist argument thus refutes the Legalist's emphasis on rules and regulations as the essential order of things.

As the First Cause and the Ultimate Pattern, *tao* possesses infinite power without being powerful. It does not force anything to follow its way; yet everything by virtue of being itself will of itself follow *tao*, just as water will ultimately flow downward. Any interruption of this Ultimate Pattern can be only temporary. Why, then, should a ruler employ force, as the Legalist insists he must, in order to conquer and reign over the world? Violence contrived by man is against *tao*; if only the king possesses *tao*, all the world will obey him; even Heaven and Earth will bless him and come to his aid.

The Taoist speaks metaphorically of *tao*, identifying it as the secret of all secrets, but he also goes on to suggest a way of comprehending *tao*. Since *tao* is the unchanging universal principle that dwells in everything, then everything in its original state reflects *tao*. In man the original state of existence, his infancy, comes closest to this idea. If man does not tamper with his heart (mind), so that his heart remains untainted, he has the best chance of comprehending this mysterious universal principle. Unspoiled, the *tao* in a tree trunk is as great and as efficacious as the *tao* filling the universe, so long as the tree trunk remains an "uncarved block." If carved, the block of wood becomes a few ordinary articles of daily use. But if man takes possession of the universal principle within an "uncarved block," he becomes a Sage fit for ruling the world.

Like the Confucians, the Taoist also talks about the Sages. But the Taoist Sage is not one who studies the classics, disciplines himself according to the rules of propriety, and preaches constantly to the rulers to be benevolent (as is recommended in Confucius' *Lun Yü*). On the contrary, the Taoist Sage has little use for words, because the words of *tao* are "simple and flavorless." He does not occupy himself with such useless motions as seeking audience with the rulers or teaching students, activities which kept the Confucians and the Mohists busy, because "*tao* never does, and yet through it all things are done." The life of the people becomes proportionately impoverished as Confucian rituals and decorum multiply; thieves and bandits redouble at the same rate as the laws are promulgated. The Taoist Sage "does nothing," and the people of themselves behave properly. The anti-intellectual attitude of the Taoist leads him to stress non-activity because only by refraining from useless motions can the state of the "uncarved block" be preserved.

Clearly Nature in its primeval stage is the best example of the "uncarved block." Consequently, unspoiled Nature is regarded by the Taoist as the best place to observe the revelation of the universal principle or *tao*. By observing Nature man learns to follow Nature's way, the way of *tao*. This acceptance of the way of Nature as inevitable and regular and normal leads to an attitude of resignation. It is not a negative attitude undertaken with a deep sigh of regret, but a joyful acceptance of what is the perfect pattern of things and events. The Taoist does not hesitate to discourage man's efforts to undo what Nature has done. He regards such efforts as useless even should man, out of his ignorance and perversion, attempt to disobey the universal principle revealed in Nature. *Tao* is like an immense boat that drifts freely and irresistibly according to its own will, the Taoist says, and thus man does well in avoiding butting his head uselessly against this huge boat, and by riding along in it. In this idea is found the seed of the Chinese concept that the strongest is he that makes use of his enemy's strength—a concept that finds its prosaic expression in the theory of Chinese boxing. Behind this concept lies the reason why the Taoist respects whatever appears to be soft, weak, and yielding.

The multiple metaphors in this work comparing the nature of *tao* to the secret, the "dark," and the "mysterious," are not merely poetic embellishment, but revelations of the strand of primitive quietism in Taoism. Among the proto-philosophical ideas of ancient China there is the notion of *yin-yang* (negative-positive, or female-male), a pair of mutually complementary forces that are at work in and behind all phenomena. The *yin* force or element is characterized as passive, receiving, and meek (at least in appearance). Yet like the idea of the female or mother, *yin* also possesses the potential of infinite creation. Hence the *yin* principle is closer to *tao*. *Tao* is compared to "a ravine that receives all things" and, therefore, has "unlimited power." In consonance with the *yin* characteristics, the man who possesses *tao* (a Sage) must hide his power, for he who shows his power is really without power. A Taoist Sage appears to be soft and weak because it is the "soft that overcomes the hard, and the weak, the strong," and because *tao* itself is unostentatious; *tao* "produces, clothes, and feeds" all beings without claiming mastery over them, yet everything submits itself to *tao*. For the same reason the Taoist praises the infant who is soft and weak and yet is most strong because in him the universal essence is not dissipated and the harmony of *yin* and *yang* is still perfect.

In this concept lies the Taoist relativity of attributes. To a Taoist nothing is absolute except *tao* itself. Without "short," there cannot be "long." Thus, a Taoist dismisses the validity of the Dialecticians' effort to distinguish the white of a white horse from the white of a white jade. In doing so he also dismisses the Confucian effort to distinguish good from bad as useless trifling. Just as "long and short" have nothing to do with the essence of things, death and life are also two manifestations of what is so of itself (natural). To treasure the good, to prefer the rich, and to cherish life are equally meaningless, equally foolish to one having arrived at *tao*.

Since there is no real difference between acting and not acting, he who does nothing accomplishes most. This concept of non-activity, coupled with the idea that he who "moves not" endures the longest, strengthens the Taoist belief in quietism.

Throughout this book there are repeated hints at a process of attaining *tao*. The Taoist urges man to retain his untainted and untampered heart, and to return to a state of infancy, desirable because of its undissipated essence. The expression for "essence" here is *ch'i*. Generally understood as "gaseous matters," *ch'i* in ancient Chinese cosmology is closely tied in with "spirit" as distinguished from "physical substance." In man, *ch'i* is identified with breath as separate from flesh and bones. The Taoist regards man's *ch'i* as part of the universal *ch'i*, or man's life-force. Hence, to avoid dissipation man must attempt to preserve his life-force, and this effort turns out to be a process of breath control. Indeed the subsequent development of magical Taoism shows many features parallel to the esoteric Indian yoga. And practitioners of Taoist magic can always cite certain passages from this work for authority. For instance, there is at least one line (in Chapter LV) which tends to support the practice of sexual hygiene as a means of achieving *tao*.

Mysticism thickens around the Taoist when he claims that neither poisonous insects nor wild animals can harm the infant, or that by fixing one's gaze in meditation one can achieve longevity. Three aspects are involved in these claims. First, the Taoist actually believes in a certain kind of yoga practice to prolong this life on earth. Second, in the Taoist vocabulary, the word longevity may mean endurance. That which endures in man is his essence, being part of the universal essence. Man may die, but so long as he does not lose his essence, he actually endures. The manifestation of his essence may take different forms, such as a tree or a rock, but his essence remains unchanged, hence his longevity. Third, by promoting life-nurture, the Taoist stood opposed to another school of thought prevailing at that time. Led by a philosopher named Yang Chu, this school advocated total gratification of man's physical senses as the real goal of life and the road to salvation, a doctrine clearly contrary to the Taoist emphasis on quietism.

To be with *tao* is to be free, so the *Tao Te Ching* tells us. Such a man is free because he has the infinite power which enables him to do whatever he pleases while he stays within *tao*. Metaphysically this freedom should mean spiritual emancipation and salvation—a liberation of man from the bondage of his limited orbit in this earthly world. But it can readily be seen how a man with political ambitions or a magical bent of mind could make use of this theory. Thus, we read in this book the mystic references to "travels in spirit" which take a man with *tao* through space and time to ethereal realms. It has been suggested that this book must have had a southern Chinese origin as some passages in it allude to a southern setting; that is, to the south of the Yangtze River. That region was rich in shamanistic tradition, and a book of southern songs, collected at about the same time as the *Tao Te Ching*, contains descriptions of similar "spirit travels." It seems quite certain that these supernatural feats were part of the shamanistic belief common in the Warring States period along the middle reaches of the Yangtze River. The shamans induced trances with prayers and dances as well as through concentration and yoga-like hypnotism. Later in magical Taoism there appears a True Man, a Taoist adept at having acquired the powers to perform these superhuman feats.

As we have suggested, the *Tao Te Ching*, like most Chinese classics originating during the Warring States period, was intended to serve more as a political manual than as a purely metaphysical treatise. However, the metaphysical speculations in this book are provocative enough to have inspired many developments—some occult, some seriously philosophical—in the history of Chinese thought. The cult of nature is one of them.

Nature in the *Tao Te Ching* is amoral because it is one manifestation of the universal essence. Nature does not house more *tao* than an infant or a tree trunk, yet Nature by its grandeur has a special appeal to the Taoist. The unchanging mountains, as contrasted with the changing affairs of man, symbolize for the Taoist the principle of nonactivity, and a calm lake expresses the idea of quietude. A profound appreciation of Nature, at once aesthetic and mystic, stems from this Taoist attitude and forms the basis of a cult of nature that has played an important role in Chinese poetry and art. In philosophy, the cult of nature became the native stock upon which Indian Mahayana Buddhism was grafted to bear the fruits of Chinese Ch'an (Zen) Buddhism.

Nature also has its violent moods. Its wild destructive forces must have been the inspiration behind the passage in the *Tao Te Ching* that refers to Heaven and Earth as unkind because "they treat all beings like straw dogs," or expendable sacrificial objects. But kindness has no place in *tao* which is "always so" and unchanging. The Taoist making the above remark is not criticizing Nature but rather is stating an actuality. This attitude has encouraged many people to embrace a political absolutism which they justify and defend with the claim that they have attained *tao*.

The esoteric elements in Taoism encouraged the accumulation of magical formulas and alchemy, and through the years they influenced a large area in Chinese folk religion. A city of Taoist gods has been constructed. A Taoist clerical and lay tradition and a library of Taoist scriptures have grown to impressive proportions.

The *Tao Te Ching* deserves credit as an enduring expression of basic Chinese philosophy. The belief in the existence of a universal principle, having received such eloquent and poetic expressions in this book, leads contemplative minds to search for the profound and the true in Nature and in man himself.
—*K.Y.H.*

PERTINENT LITERATURE

Lao Tzu. *The Way of Life: Lao Tzu*. Edited and translated by R. B. Blakney. New York: New American Library, 1955.

R. B. Blakney was for a long time a Christian missionary in China and had studied the *Tao Te Ching* for thirty years before rendering it into English. Because of its low-cost Mentor paperback edition and the author's fascinating writing style, it has become a most popular translation of the *Tao Te Ching*. In addition to translating the text, Blakney has written a long introduction and extensive paraphrases or comments under each poem (called "chapter" by other scholars).

Blakney consciously rejects *tao* as impersonal and calls it "proto-personal." With straightforwardness, he equates *tao* with the medieval conception of

Godhead or Godness. He then calls his readers' attention to the saying of Jesus Christ, "I am the way. . . ." The identification of the Way of God, according to Blakney, has gained biblical support. Blakney may not be mistaken in this view; yet his theme is very misleading. If we interpret *tao* as God or as a Divine being, this is to force Chinese culture to be as religious as the Hebrew and the Hindu traditions. Such an interpretation will undermine the humanistic spirit of Chinese culture and the naturalistic flavor of Taoism. After all, there are striking differences between *tao* and God. First, *tao* is the embodiment of the principle of *wu-wei* or non-action, while God (as recorded in the *Old Testament*) is a deity of tremendous action. Second, a Christian prays to God, but a Taoist never prays to *tao*, which is never an object for worship. Third, Christians often talk about "the will of God," but Chinese people never speak of "the will of Tao." In short, *tao* is far from being a personal deity or a "proto-personal" being, as Blakney wants it to be. As to some philosophers' concept of God as a metaphysical principle, such a principle is not much different from *tao*; yet the use of "God" in this sense is a violation of the ordinary use of language and thus may lead to confusion in our understanding of a different culture. Accordingly, the God-*tao* analogy is highly misleading and blocks the way to the understanding of Taoism.

The second topic concerns the label "mysticism." Blakney in his introduction regards Yang Chu as the first Chinese mystic and Chuang Chou as the second one. No doubt, from his viewpoint, the *Tao Te Ching* is a great classic of mysticism rather than a masterpiece in philosophy. The problem with Blakney's viewpoint is although religion has been an important cultural force in the West, it does not follow that it should possess the same weight in a non-Western culture. Nevertheless, the label "mysticism" is not entirely mistaken provided that we make a distinction between "religious mysticism" and "aesthetic mysticism" and apply the latter only to Taoism. Chinese culture is predominantly aesthetic and naturalistic. If we link mysticism to Chinese culture, we should be careful enough to make a distinction between the experience of a Christian mystic who had a union with God and the experience of a naturalistic poet who was self-forgettingly intoxicated with the radiance of the sunset. Only through this distinction can we grasp the unique nature of the *Tao Te Ching* as different from a religious scripture.

Blakney's contribution to the study of the *Tao Te Ching* is substantial and significant. His refreshing style certainly should encourage many students to continue serious studies of this masterpiece. His interpretation remains a cardinal example of how Chinese culture can be sympathetically understood by a religionist in Western culture.

Welch, Holmes. *The Parting of the Way: Lao Tzu and the Taoist Movement.* London: Methuen, 1958.

Holmes Welch's book is written with a dual purpose: to promote the understanding of Taoism as an important component of Chinese culture and to present the philosophy of Lao Tzu with a consideration of its relevance to the contemporary world. About one fourth of this book (Part Two) is devoted to an exposition of the central themes of the *Tao Te Ching*.

Welch starts with the concept of *wu-wei* (inaction, non-action, and so on) which is the answer offered by Lao Tzu to the social and political problems of his time. *Wu-wei*, in Welch's interpretation, "does not mean to avoid all action, but rather all hostile, aggressive action." What is important is not the action itself, but the attitude behind the action. The attitude behind *wu-wei* is the ideal of *tz'u*—love in the sense of compassion and pity: "For the Christian love is the mainspring of action: for the Taoist it is ostensibly what makes inaction effective." Another implication of the principle of *wu-wei* is timeliness in action. With such a wisdom, one is able to solve a problem before it comes into being. A government of *wu-wei* is to rule by noninterference, together with the abolishment of capital punishment.

The next topic is the concept of "Uncarved Block" (*p'u*), which is one of the most common symbols in the *Tao Te Ching*. *P'u* means wood in its natural form before any craftsman works on it. This signifies the original state of human consciousness which is free from hostility and aggressiveness. What is further implied in this symbol is the near absence of desires, since primitive consciousness knows very little about social vanity or ambition of any kind. In addition, this symbol implies the rejection of public opinion. The Uncarved Block, as Welch sums up, is described by Lao Tzu as "blank, childlike, untutored, dark, nameless," and "to reach it is to 'know oneself,' to 'return to the root from which we grew.'"

The third and last theme in Welch's treatment is the concept of *tao*. Like R. B. Blakney, Welch relies heavily on his Christian background and knowledge of mysticism in his interpretation. The criticism of Blakney can also apply, at least in part, to Welch. Nevertheless, Welch is quite aware of interpretations on a naturalistic and humanistic basis. Consequently he is free from the mistake of turning *tao* into a personal deity. For him, *tao* can be conceived as "the laws of nature, the God that exists by the argument from design; not identical with the universe and yet at work everywhere with it." In addition, "Tao is impersonal, 'unkind,' and beyond the reach of prayer." Then, because of his affinity with Christian mysticism, Welch cites the cases of such well-known mystics as St. Angela, St. Teresa, St. John of the Cross, and the authors of the *Upanishads*, emphasizing the similarities between mystical experience and sexual ecstacy. When he comes back to the *Tao Te Ching*, he could not find anything of the same kind because this Chinese classic does not offer any sexual imagery. Still, Welch attempts to establish Taoism as a form of mysticism. To regard Taoism as mysticism, however, is an error, for Chinese culture is fundamentally naturalistic and humanistic. The *Tao Te*

Ching is a product of this culture and should be studied as a form of humanistic naturalism or naturalistic humanism.

In the main, in spite of some methodological inadequacies, Welch's book will continue to appeal to both scholars and laymen alike. His comprehensive knowledge of American culture and substantial background in Christianity has made his book attractive to the American general reader. It is a rare intellectual accomplishment by a Western scholar in promoting intercultural understanding and spiritual development for the contemporary world.

Wing-tsit Chan. *The Way of Lao Tzu (Tao Te Ching)*. New York: Bobbs-Merrill, 1963.

In Wing-tsit Chan's book we find substantial scholarship comprising painstaking research in history, philology, and philosophy. In addition to a translation which has synthesized recent scholarly discoveries in textual subtleties, Chan has provided three well-organized and clearly written informative essays: (1) The Philosophy of Tao, (2) Lao Tzu, the Man, and (3) *Lao Tzu, the Book*.

Chan's interpretation of *tao* is a naturalistic one which is truthful to the character of Chinese culture. After a philological introduction, Chan exposes the metaphysical meanings of *tao* by quoting key passages from the text. Then he presents Han Fei's interpretation of *tao* as the unification of all principles operating in the universe. The concept "Tao as non-being," as Chan explains, is positive in character, although its linguistic form is negative. He then proceeds to analyze the concept of *wu-wei*, which is also positive in nature. In doing so, he is able to link metaphysics and theory of life together. In fact, from *wu* (non-being) to *wu-wei* (non-action), Chan sees a clear logical unity which has escaped many earlier scholars. Again, Chan cites many key passages from the text in the course of his explication. In the main, *wu-wei* is interpreted as "taking no artificial action, noninterference, or letting things take their own course." Chan's naturalistic interpretation is not alone, for he finds a similar viewpoint in the writings of Joseph Needham, who has equated *tao* with the Order of Nature.

After an exposition of the concept of *tao*, Chan explains other concepts of the text. First, *te* is interpreted as "Tao endowed in the individual things." Then he considers symbols such as "water," "the infant," "the female," "the valley," and "the uncarved block." As Chan rightly puts it, they are used as models or symbols for a life according to *tao*; they symbolize the life of simplicity. In addition, "weakness" is cherished as a virtue, of which "water" and "the female" are exemplars.

Scholars have in the past usually emphasized the striking differences between Lao Tzu and Confucius. Chan does the opposite in order to correct the impression that the two are irreconcilable. After an exposition of their common points, Chan rightly concludes that "It is because of these and other similarities that Taoism and Confucianism run harmoniously parallel throughout Chinese history so that every Chinese is at once a Taoist and a Confucianist."

In addition, Chan has compared Lao Tzu with Chuang Tzu in terms of both differences and similarities. He has also commented on how the *Tao Te Ching* influenced Neo-Taoism, Buddhism, and Neo-Confucianism. He clarifies the distinction between philosophical Taoism and the Taoist religion by an exposition of the origin and development of the latter. In his conclusion, Chan points out that Taoist thinking is still alive among Chinese people today, in spite of the absence of a Taoist school, a book, a theory, or a single Taoist philosopher in the last thousand years.

In the main, Chan's book represents the most accomplished scholarship in the study of the *Tao Te Ching* available in English. It is a rewarding resource, essential for understanding Chinese culture and its philosophy.—*J.S.W.*

ADDITIONAL RECOMMENDED READING

Chang Ch'i-chün. *Lao Tzu che hsueh (The Philosophy of Lao Tzu)*. Taipei, Taiwan: Chêng Chung Book Company, 1969. A logically clear exposition by a leading Chinese scholar of the philosophical system implicit in the *Tao Te Ching*.

Chang Chung-yüan. *Creativity and Taoism: A Study of Chinese Philosophy, Art, and Poetry*. New York: Julian Press, 1963. An interpretation of some practical and cultural aspects of Taoism. There is no sharp demarcation between Philosophical Taoism and the Taoist religion.

Chen, Ellen Marie. *Tao, Nature, Man: A Study of the Key Ideas in the Tao Te Ching*. Fordham University Thesis, 1966. Interesting thesis interpreting *tao* as Mother Nature.

Creel, H. G. *Chinese Thought: From Confucius to Mao Tsê-tung*. Chicago: University of Chicago Press, 1953. The doctrine of Taoism clearly summed up with thought-provoking discussion; lucidly written.

Fung Yu-lan. *A History of Chinese Philosophy*. Translated by Derk Bodde. Princeton, New Jersey: Princeton University Press, 1952-1953. Best history of Chinese philosophy available in English, containing a good summary of the philosophy of the *Tao Te Ching* in Chapter VIII.

Lau, D. C., tr. *Tao Te Ching*. Middlesex, England: Penguin Books, 1963. The translation is done with care, objectivity, and scholarship. The long introduction and lengthy appendix are very informative.

Lin Yutang, ed. and tr. *The Wisdom of Laotse*. New York: Modern Library, 1948. A very readable translation of the *Tao Te Ching*, interspersed with selections from the *Chuang Tzu* which serve as a kind of commentary on the text.

Waley, Arthur. *The Way and Its Power: A Study of the Tao tê Ching and Its*

Place in Chinese Thought. London: George Allen & Unwin, 1934. An authoritative translation with a scholarly introduction on historical and linguistic questions. The view that *Tao Te Ching* is primarily a dialogue between quietists and realists (legalists) is too narrow.

Wu, Joseph. "Understanding Taoism: A Chinese Philosopher's Critique," in *Clarification and Enlightenment: Essays in Comparative Philosophy*. Washington, D.C.: University Press of America, 1978. This essay contains a criticism of some serious misconceptions about the *Tao Te Ching*, together with an original interpretation of the theory of *wu-wei* as "disinterested action."

THE GREAT LEARNING

Author: Attributed to Tseng Tzu (disciple of Confucius, c. fifth century B.C.),
   or Tzu Ssu (grandson of Confucius)
Type of work: Ethics, political philosophy
Compiled: c. end of first century B.C.

PRINCIPAL IDEAS ADVANCED

The purpose of the Ta Hsüeh *is to teach man to know the great virtue, to love the people, and to pursue the highest good.*

To make the great virtue prevail and to bring peace to the world man must first cultivate himself; only then can he cultivate his family, his state, and the world.

To cultivate oneself one must rectify the heart, but that involves making thoughts sincere, and that in turn involves extending knowledge by the investigation of things.

The pursuit of knowledge is to continue until man achieves moral excellence.

The investigation of things is an intuitive comprehension of the essence of things.

There are three principles of the art of government: the ruler should cultivate his own moral stature; he should make use of wise and moral men; and he must esteem what is right above what is profitable.

Among the dozen or so great books that have exercised a controlling influence on the Chinese mind since ancient times is one called the *Li Chi*, or the *Book of Rites*. The editor of this work, Tai Sheng (c. first century B.C.), gathered together a number of treatises whose authorship he did not take pains to clarify. Most of the chapters deal with the various types of rites—from the arrangement of the most important imperial shrine to the funeral of a plain citizen—and their philosophical import. A few of these chapters, however, treat some quite fundamental philosophical problems not at all connected with any ritual. The *Ta Hsüeh* (*Great Learning*) is one of the latter, having been removed from the *Book of Rites*, annotated, and installed as one of four most important Confucian classics by the Sung dynasty philosopher, Chu Hsi (1130-1200). These four books are, Confucius' *Analects*, the *Meng Tzu*, the *Great Learning*, and the *Doctrine of the Mean* (*Chung Yung*). The last named is also a chapter of the *Book of Rites*. After Chu Hsi these four books became the primers given to every schoolboy, as well as the principal texts upon which the candidates for civil service were examined. The ideas in these books as interpreted by Chu Hsi constituted a durable intellectual orthodoxy that curtailed effectively the Buddhist influence on the Chinese mind and maintained a dominance in Chinese thought until modern times.

It is not difficult to see why this short work, which up to most recent times every schoolboy learned by heart, was used as a basic guide to man's self-cultivation. Within its ten short chapters, the author outlines a complete theory on how to bring to reality the Confucian ideal of man's life. He describes the process of making "man" worthy of his name out of an existence in ignorance. He teaches man how to attain the ideal goal of being man, which is self-perfection, in order to prepare himself for the supreme task of bringing peace and order to the world.

The very opening paragraph of the book puts forth the gist of the *Great Learning*: to teach man to know the great virtue, to love the people, and to pursue the highest good as his ultimate goal. Immediately after this statement, the reader is told that pursuing the highest good to perfect himself individually is actually the first step, whence man proceeds to influence all people with his personal virtue until the principle of great virtue is understood and accepted by all. When this condition obtains, a utopian state will exist on earth.

The author explains in greater detail the process of making the great virtue prevail. Man must first cultivate himself to perfection, then put his own house in order, then bring the same harmonious order to the state, and finally extend the same influence to all corners of the world so that there will be universal peace and prosperity. For achieving this perfection, the author urges man to "rectify his heart [mind]." However, this cannot be done unless he traces this process back to its very beginning in the following order: make his thoughts sincere, extend his knowledge, and investigate things. The last is, therefore, the real beginning of man's self-cultivation.

Two problems already emerge. One is a linguistic question on the order of the last two steps. The original language could mean either "to obtain knowledge is for the purpose of understanding things," or "investigating things in order to extend knowledge." Even leaving this problem aside, the second problem remains, namely, the exact meaning of the phrase, "investigation of things." The text goes no further to explain this point, and two diametrically opposed schools of thought center their arguments precisely on this phrase.

The school headed by Chu Hsi (whose annotations, as we have noted, have become orthodox) believes in a dualism of principle and matter. As each being contains its own principle, the mind of man can comprehend the universe only after he has investigated all the principles of all things. Chapter V of the *Great Learning*, according to Chu Hsi, deals with this question. But as the entire chapter is lost except for two fragmentary phrases, Chu Hsi's annotation becomes the only authoritative conjecture. Chu says that the student must start from the principles of limited things already known to him and "search exhaustively for all the principles of all things." After a lengthy period of such concentration, the student would "suddenly penetrate" the universal principle and then his knowledge would become complete. Chu Hsi's opponents tend to entertain a monistic view and regard the universal principle as indivisible. They therefore see no value in investigating the outside world, but urge man to search within his own mind for an understanding of the universal principle.

Without going into details about this debate that lasted for centuries, it seems reasonable and acceptable to arrive at an understanding of this problem on the basis of several other key ideas in the *Great Learning*. One of these ideas is the notion of "the end" of the process of pursuing knowledge.

It has been noted that the end of this process is stated in the opening paragraph as "the highest good." To know the end of this process is important because without knowing where to stop, man would go on searching for knowledge, drifting and getting confused and being led astray by his contact with and involvement in the outside world. Consequently, he would never attain the "complete knowledge." Thus we see that the pursuit of knowledge continues until the attainment of extreme moral excellence. The *Great Learning* does not urge man to keep on accumulating objective facts and data which, as the author of this work rightly hints, are endless and confusing.

Also, in the beginning paragraph we find some elaboration on the importance of "knowing where to stop." To know where to stop, it is said, precedes the fixation of the object of pursuit. Having fixed the object of pursuit, man then and only then can achieve the peace of mind (or quiescence, or calm) which is a necessary condition for deliberation. Without deliberation, no knowledge can be obtained. Thus, without knowing where to stop in the process of pursuing knowledge, there can be no possibility of man's ever acquiring knowledge.

The next key idea is the notion of "root and branches." This is not merely a notion of a fixed order of things—for the root precedes the branches—it is a recognition of the distinction between the principal and the adjunct, or between the essence and its extension. The overriding principle upheld in the *Great Learning* is that man must distinguish the root from the branches when he approaches anything, acquiring knowledge being no exception. To know a thing is to know its essence, and he who has learned of the essence of things possesses "complete knowledge." The author of this work considers knowledge of the distinction between the essence and the outward features of things to be the central theme of the *Great Learning*. The underlying assumption is that knowledge of phenomena is not true knowledge.

A third key idea lies in the term "peace of mind" or "quiescence." We have noted that the attainment of quiescence is necessary to acquiring knowledge. This state of mind is directly linked to the theory of "rectifying the heart [mind]." The author stresses the importance of maintaining an undisturbed mind, free from anger, anxiety, sorrow, and even the feeling of fond attachment. Only after he has succeeded in ridding his mind of all prejudices which ordinary people erroneously call knowledge, can man expect to reach true knowledge or complete knowledge. A rectified mind is a mind immune to emotional influences. Such a mind comes close to the Taoist's "empty mind," whose approach to knowledge is intuitive rather than investigative.

The author demands that man "make his thought sincere" in order to rectify his mind. Sincere thought means thought of concentration. The thought of a distracted mind cannot be sincere. When applied to the practical level of understanding, the author here is advising man to keep his mind on the object when he seeks knowledge of it. Metaphysically, the author seems to assume that knowledge can be attained only by maintaining an ever-present mind, which is still an intuitive approach to knowledge.

Another application of the idea of "making one's thought sincere" is the author's injunction that an ideal man would be careful about his action and speech even, and especially, when he is alone. When alone, man must consider himself "watched by ten eyes and pointed at by ten fingers." As a moral admonition, the author urges man to behave according to one moral standard by which he could face the world as well as himself. But as an elaboration of the notion of sincerity, the author here advocates a unity of man's being. Man's mind and his behavior are one, his inner thought and outer expression cannot contradict each other because anyone "knowing" him could see his inner self which no amount of pretension can hide. The underlying assumption here is that there is a unity of reality. The moment one perceives even a fraction of what is real and essential, he has perceived the whole.

Examining the above key ideas together, we are quite assured that what the author means by "investigation of things" is, basically, an intuitive comprehension of the essence of things which lies beyond deceptive appearances. In order to arrive at such intuitive comprehensions, man must prepare his mind for the task by "emptying his mind" of all biases and by insuring undivided concentration. Having grasped the essence of things, man stops any further pursuit of knowledge because his knowledge is already complete, and because he has reached the highest good, which is also supreme moral excellence. The wise, in other words, is also the morally good. We see how the author applies the whole theory to politics and develops a theory of the exemplar.

The final goal of self-cultivation being the maintenance of a peaceful and prosperous world, the author never loses sight of the application of his principles to politics at every point. Each of the ten chapters develops one step in the process from "investigation of things" to "bringing peace to the world." The last chapter, dealing with the art of government, occupies half of the *Great Learning*.

Three principles of the art of government are discussed in this work. The first is that people of themselves will do exactly what the ruler does. People will follow their ruler as long as the latter is "sincere"; that is to say, as long as the ruler keeps his words and deeds in agreement and consistent. In the remote past some rulers were said to have been benevolent, and other kings violent, but the people followed them equally until the sovereign proved himself to be inconsistent in that he demanded his subjects to be moral while he himself exhibited no moral scruples. People always imitate their leaders. This premise is parallel to Mo Ti's teaching in the *Mo Tzu*. Therefore, if the ruler himself sets an example, he will function as the yardstick against which the conduct of his people will be measured. The *Great Learning* cites a number of historical cases to prove that the taste and value-standard of a nation change along with what the royal court upholds. The Confucian doctrine of rule by moral magnetism (see the *Meng Tzu*) thus finds another exponent in the author of this work. The ruler seeking the best way to run his state is always asked to examine his own conduct and to cultivate his own moral stature.

The second principle is to be able to recognize and make use of wise and moral men. From the sovereign down to the village chief, if the head can use good men as his assistants and expel the bad elements from positions of influence, the state will be well governed. In this effort the ruler must be "sincere"; he must not seek the good and capable merely because they are useful but because he "likes them more than he can say." He must be genuinely fond of these people and hate those who cannot practice the same principle. A minister who is jealous of others as good as he is must be removed and exiled to the "land of the barbarians and never allowed to return."

The third principle is the esteem of what is right above what is materially profitable. The ideas of righteousness and profit were made the basis for the political philosophy of Mencius, and the *Great Learning* here reaffirms the same principle by instructing the ruler to value moral excellence above material gain. A moral ruler attracts people and commands their respect. When people flock around the ruler, his domain extends. As his domain extends, the wealth of the nation also grows, and the king has no need to be concerned with any insufficiency of material supplies. It is not that the *Great Learning* disregards the solvency of a state. Rather, it stresses the importance of "accumulating wealth in the right way."

Such a morally magnetic ruler is one who appears in the eyes of his people under a paternal halo. The *Great Learning* metaphorically calls him "people's parent" and advises him to "like what the people like and hate what the people hate." What is unclear about the last statement is how it can be reconciled with the exemplar theory which sees the people as "followers" and not as the ones to make decisions. If the ruler is to observe only what the people want, then how is he to function as an exemplar?

The answer seems to lie in the confusion about a basic understanding of human nature that disturbed the philosophical world of ancient China and was not clarified even within the Confucian orthodoxy. Confucius himself was silent on this point, and his sayings merely suggest faith in the teachability of man. According to Confucius, man can be and needs to be cultivated toward the good. Mencius, the second standard-bearer of Confucianism, insisted on the innate goodness of human nature, but he did not neglect the need for self-cultivation, either. Hsün Tzu, the third great Confucian philosopher whose doctrines are said to have influenced the *Great Learning* more than did the two earlier philosophers, held a diametrically opposed view. He said that man has undesirable propensities which, if uncurbed, will inevitably lead man to evil. On the question as to what the ruler should do for the people, the *Great Learning* reflects all three views in different passages. When it says that people follow only examples above them, the book accepts Hsün Tzu's views. When it advises the ruler to love what the people love, the book takes Mencius' theory. But in most instances the book appears to stay with Confucius himself in holding that people can be taught to follow the good, so that the responsibility of the ruler is teaching by demonstration, using himself as an example. Consequently, the cycle appears to be as follows: At first people are ignorant and seek only to meet their basic needs, which are neither good nor bad. They follow the good example of a ruler and cultivate their moral senses until the atmosphere (moral customs) of the nation becomes good. When they have attained this moral discipline, they know, generally, what is good and what is bad. Hence the ruler loves what the people love and hates what the people hate.

The influence of the key ideas in this book, however underdeveloped and ill-defined they may be in the original text, can hardly be exaggerated. After Chu Hsi, the Chinese people for the past one thousand years have used these ideas in molding the nation's ideology. Self-cultivation, explained exactly in Chu Hsi's terms, was upheld by all orthodox educators up to the very end of the nineteenth century. And self-education, explained with some variation, is still a living idea among the Marxist as well as the rightist Chinese theorists today. An authoritative pamphlet written by the Chinese Communist leader Liu Shao-ch'i (elected Chairman of the People's Republic of China in 1959), instructs the youth of the nation to "set their thoughts sincere" and "watch over their behavior when alone" in order to become good communists. The whole "cadre" theory in the Marxist frame, urging the good and capable to set themselves us as exemplars, is so congenial with the exemplar theory in the *Great Learning* that it won the nation overnight without encountering any resistance.—*K.Y.H.*

PERTINENT LITERATURE

Hughes, E. R., ed. and tr. "The 'Great Learning,'" in *Chinese Philosophy in Classical Times*. New York: E. P. Dutton, 1942.

E. R. Hughes remarks that the *Great Learning* first appeared as part of the *Book of Rites*, a collection compiled at the end of the first century, B.C. For 1200 years the work received no special attention, but during the Sung era it was made one of the Four Books regarded as the classic expressions of the "Great Tradition," the others being the *Analects*, the *Mencius*, and the

Chung Yung (the *Doctrine of the Mean*). Hughes's theory concerning the authorship of the *Great Learning* is that it was compiled by a court tutor "during Shang Yang's later years" (perhaps about 330 B.C.) as a guide to the Confucian faith and as a criticism of the new materialism. In any case, by Sung times the work was in radical disorder, but the Sung scholars made a rearrangement (which Hughes modifies).

Hughes describes the *Great Learning* as a "text-book," something to be learned by heart in sections and expounded on by the teacher. When the *Great Learning* begins with a statement of its theme—that of making clear each person's "abiding-place" so that the moral personality can be developed and used to make a new people in a spirit of highest goodness—reference is made to the importance of extending one's knowledge. Such extension consists (according to Hughes's translation) in "appreciating the nature of things." (Fung Yu-lan in his *A History of Chinese Philosophy* translates the same passage as "This extension of knowledge lay in the investigation of things.") Hughes prefers the term "appreciating" to "investigation" because the term in question, *ko*, is used, he argues, more in the sense of the artist's "appreciate" than the scientist's "investigate." The "things" to be appreciated (the word *wu* is used) are, Hughes explains, not exclusively material things but anything at all that might became an object of thought—an event, a tradition, a doctrine, and so on.

The word "appreciating" does seem to be more in the spirit of the *Ta Hsüeh*, which aims at developing and strengthening the right attitudes, the right spirit with regard to things, thereby encouraging a harmony within the self that would affect families and eventually the state, resulting in "the Great Society . . . at peace." The moral task was to bring each self "to flower"; such an outcome would be the "root" ("the essential thing," Hughes suggests), and the knowledge, acquired through appreciation, would consist, therefore, in "knowing the root." Knowing the root involves cultivating the self and making "supreme endeavours," as Hughes puts it. The cultivation of the self involves being careful not to deceive oneself and working for "the rectification of the mind"—which, once again, entails seeing things as they are, keeping one's emotions under control, and appreciating the order of things.

Once the self is cultivated, the *Great Learning* says, one is rid of the prejudices that interfere with appreciating the worth of others—even of those that in ignorance one hates. Consequently, one is in a position to be part of a harmonious family. If the family is "human-hearted" (Hughes's translation of *jen*; others use the term "humane" in this context), then the country will become human-hearted. Such a country would be in harmony within itself and such harmony would contribute toward a state of universal peace. (The right spirit within the individual and the family affects society as a whole.)

The "true" man realizes the power of moral personality and hence "possesses"—wins over and positively affects—others, thereby acquiring the "soil," the "wealth," and "the means for governing." Hughes translates *yi* as "justice" in rendering into English the claim that the human-hearted man uses wealth to expand the individual self (instead of using individuals as tools for the expansion of wealth) and thereby achieves justice and affects others so that they are also devoted to justice. (Hughes explains that his use of the term "justice" is in the Platonic sense such that justice involves equity and fair dealing.)

If one uses Hughes's terminology, the point of the *Great Learning* emerges as a moral injunction: So learn yourself and so develop yourself as to become a human-hearted person: one properly appreciative of things, one in control of oneself and in harmony within oneself and with others, one who is just in understanding and in action, and thereby a person of goodness and peace able to bring others, the family, and the state to a similar condition.

Fung Yu-lan. *A History of Chinese Philosophy*. Vol. I. Translated by Derk Bodde. Princeton, New Jersey: Princeton University Press, 1952.

Fung Yu-lan discusses the *Great Learning* under the heading, "Confucians of the Ch'in and Han Dynasties" (Chapter XIV of Volume I). He reminds the reader that this work, the *Ta Hsüeh*, is one of the Four Books that together formed the classical basis of Chinese education. Although it is a short work, it has had a "tremendous influence," Fung writes—as has another short work, also one of the Four Books, the *Chung Yung* (*Doctrine of the Mean*).

Fung remarks that the Neo-Confucianist Sung philosopher Chu Hsi (1130-1200) believed the *Great Learning* to have been written by Tseng Tzu; however, another Sung scholar, Wang Po (1197-1274), believed it to have been written by Tzu Ssu, Confucius' grandson. Fung regards both of these statements as the expression of surmises unsupported by evidence.

The opening sentence of the *Great Learning* is translated by Fung as follows: "What the Great Learning teaches is: clearly to exemplify illustrious virtue, to love the people, and to rest in the highest good." (It is interesting to compare this rendering to that given by E. R. Hughes: "The Way (*Tao*) of learning to be great consists in shining with the illustrious power of moral personality (*te*), in making a new people, in abiding in the highest goodness.")

Like Hughes, Fung comments on his translation of the Chinese expressions *chih chih*, which Fung translates as "extension of knowledge" (as does Hughes), and *ko wu*, which Fung translates as "investigation of things" (as compared to Hughes's "appreciation of the nature of things"). According to Fung, these two phrases have provoked many interpretations and intensive controversy. In fact, the conflict between the Sung and Ming schools centered for the most part on the interpretation of *chih chih* and *ko wu*. (The characters differ in the *chih chih* phrase.)

Fung argues that since the *Ta Hsüeh* states three ends and eight steps toward the attaining of those ends, the entire process beginning with what Fung calls "the investigation of things," the interpretation made by Hsün Tzu, which emphasizes comprehensive knowledge and its transforming effect, should be followed.

Fung draws the parallels between the progression given in the *Great Learning*—from cultivation of the person through that of the home and empire—and the progressions mentioned in the *Hsün Tzu* and *Mencius*. (The quotation from the Mencius uses the metaphor of the root: "The root of the empire is in the state. The root of the state is in the family. The root of the family is in the individual.") The idea that if the ruler is correct and virtuous, the people will emulate him is also found in the *Hsün Tzu*, Fung shows. (There is also a suggestion of this idea in the *Chung Yung*.)

Other ideas stressed in the Great Learning to which there are parallels in other classics are that the cultivation of the self requires rectifying the mind; to be rectified, the mind must concentrate and allow no self-deception; by concrete examples, such as that of the care a loving mother gives her child, one learns of such virtues as sincerity; inward thought should be the same as outward conduct; sincerity comes from knowing where to rest, and knowing where to rest comes from extension of knowledge whereby one comprehends that things have their root and their branches; but, finally, the extension of knowledge depends on being correct about the root and the branches, and being correct requires the investigation of things.

By following the progression of thought in the *Great Learning*, Fung argues in effect, one learns that the kind of knowledge that will correct the mind and bring about sincerity and the cultivation of the individual is what he calls "the investigation of things."—*I.P.M.*

ADDITIONAL RECOMMENDED READING

Chan Wing-tsit, comp. and tr. *A Source Book in Chinese Philosophy*. Princeton, New Jersey: Princeton University Press, 1963. An excellent presentation of the *Great Learning* in its entirety, with illuminating comments. Chan comments at length on the influence of the commentator Chu Hsi (1130-1200), who affected the entire course of Chinese thought by his brilliant commentaries and synthesizing efforts; he is the philosopher responsible for bringing together the four books as the "Four Books" of Chinese learning. Chu Hsi's commentary is included.

Hackett, Stuart C. *Oriental Philosophy: A Westerner's Guide to Eastern Thought*. Madison: University of Wisconsin Press, 1969. Although Hackett has little to say about the *Great Learning*, he provides a synoptic view of Eastern thought that is helpful in orienting oneself while reading the more intensive studies of such scholars as Hu Shih, E. R. Hughes, Fung Yu-lan, Arthur Waley, and Wing-tsit Chan (Chan puts his family name last).

Koller, John M. *Oriental Philosophies*. New York: Charles Scribner's Sons,

1970. A clear and responsible survey of Oriental thought and religion from the beginnings of Indian philosophy through the Buddhist and Chinese philosophies, ending with the Neo-Confucians and, finally, Mao Tsê-tung.

DE RERUM NATURA

Author: Lucretius (Titus Lucretius Carus, c. 98-55 B.C.)
Type of work: Ethics, metaphysics, philosophy of nature
First transcribed: First century B.C.

PRINCIPAL IDEAS ADVANCED

Nothing is ever generated from nothing; nature consists of atoms moving in void.

Atoms naturally move downward, but when some swerve from their course, collisions occur; free will in human beings is a similar phenomenon.

Everything in nature is different from every other thing; the number of atoms of each shape is infinite, although the shapes of atoms are not infinite in number.

Sensed qualities are produced by combinations of atoms of various shapes, sizes, and weights.

The soul is composed of atoms; hence, at death the soul dies with the body.

Lucretius' *De rerum natura* (*On the Nature of Things*), by general agreement the greatest didactic poem in any language, is an exposition of the philosophy of Epicurus (about 340-270 B.C.). No divergence of doctrine, however minute, is to be found between Lucretius and his master.

After an invocation to Venus, symbolic of the loveliness, fruitfulness, and peace of nature, Lucretius eulogizes Epicurus as the deliverer of mankind from the superstitious terrors of religion: "When human life lay foul before the eyes, crushed on the earth beneath heavy religion, who showed her face from the regions of heaven, glowering over mortals with horrible visage, first a Greek man dared to lift mortal eyes against her and to stand up to her; neither stories of gods nor thunderbolts nor heaven with menacing growl checked him, but all the more they goaded the spirited manliness of his mind, so that he longed to be first to break through the tight locks of nature's portals. Thus the lively force of his mind prevailed, and he journeyed far beyond the flaming walls of the world and traversed the whole immensity with mind and soul, whence victorious he reports to us what limit there is to the power of each thing, and by what law each has its boundary-stone set deep. And so religion in turn is cast down under foot and trampled; the victory exalts us to heaven." (This is, of course, a great exaggeration of Epicurus' place in the history of free thought.)

Men make themselves miserable through fear of divine caprice in this life, and of hellfire after it. Lucretius argued that the one comes from ignorance of the workings of nature, the other from the false belief in an immortal soul. The cure for both is understanding of materialist philosophy. "Thus of necessity this terror of the mind, these darknesses, not the rays of the sun nor the bright arrows of daylight will disperse, but nature's aspect and her law."

You may think, says Lucretius to Memmius (the Roman official to whom the poem is dedicated), that the materialist philosophy is unholy. Not so: "On the contrary, that very religion has very often given birth to criminal and impious deeds." For instance, the sacrifice of Iphigenia by her father. "*Tantum religio potuit suadere malorum!*—so much of evil has religion been able to put over!"

The first law of nature is: "Nothing is ever generated from nothing, by any divine force." This Lucretius takes to be amply proved by experience. If something could come from nothing, then anything could beget anything, or things would pop up out of season, or grown men and trees would appear all at once. The observed regularity of birth and growth implies fixed seeds of all things, or in other words sufficient causes of all that happens. Nor can anything disappear into nothing; if it could, then already in the infinity of time nothing would be left. "By no means then do any of the things that are seen perish utterly; since Nature refashions one thing out of another, nor permits anything to be born unless aided by the death of something else."

Nature consists of atoms ("seeds," "beginnings"—Lucretius does not use the Greek word) too small to be seen, but nevertheless real; the winds, odors, heat, and cold show that real things can be invisible, while the drying of wet clothes and the gradual wearing away of rings and stones proves that the things we can see are made of tiny particles. Since things move, there must be void space for them to move in. Visible objects contain much void, as is proved by differences in density and by the free passage through apparently solid objects of heat and sound, of water through rocks, and of food through the tissues of the body. Besides atoms and void, there is no third kind of thing; everything else that has a name is either an essential or accidental property of these two.

Atoms are absolutely solid, containing no void within them, hence internally changeless. If they were not, there would be no large-scale objects left by now, for all would have been pulverized in infinite time. Moreover, if things were infinitely divisible, then the sum of things and the least thing would be equal, both containing an equal, since infinite, number of parts—an absurd situation (says Lucretius).

After refuting (what he takes to be) the rival theories of Heraclitus, Empedocles, and Anaxagoras, Lucretius proceeds to prove that the universe is infinite in space. Suppose it were not: then if you went to the edge of it and shot an arrow, what would happen? Either the arrow would stop, because there was something beyond to stop it, or it would not, and again there would be space beyond the presumed boundary. The number of atoms in infinite space is also infinite, for since their general tendency is to fly apart, a finite number in infinite space would have so spread out by now that the average density would be near zero, which is against observation. There is no center to the world, and no antipodes. (All the ancient atomists continued to hold that the earth is a flat disc, even though schools such as the Pythagoreans and Aristotelians, less scientific in their general principles, had long known better.)

Book I concludes with a famous passage, more applicable to the progressive nature of science than to the fossilized dogmas of Epicureanism: "These things you will learn thus, led on with little trouble; for one thing will grow clear from another, nor will blind night snatch away the road and not let you perceive Nature's ultimates. Thus things will kindle lights for things."

The proem to Book II is the longest ethical passage in the poem, depicting the peaceful serenity of the Epicurean's life, contrasted with the troubled existence of the unenlightened, who in getting and spending lay waste their powers.

Atoms move either by their own weight or by blows from other atoms. Left to themselves, atoms move "downward" (what down means in an infinite, centerless universe we are not told), all at the same speed, faster than light, because the void offers no resistance. No atom, then, would ever have hit another, if it were not for the fact that "at quite an uncertain time and at uncertain places they push out a little from their course." Thus one hits another, the second a third, and so on. Lucretius also employs this "swerve," which is supposed to occur not just "in the beginning" but even now, to account for free will in human beings—in the same way, and as irrelevantly, as some philosophers now try to buttress free will with Heisenberg's uncertainty principle. (Both are irrelevant because whatever we mean by free will, we certainly do not mean capriciousness.)

Everything in nature is different from every other thing: each lamb knows its own mother, one blade of wheat is not exactly like the next. The atoms too differ in their shapes. Lightning, though it is fire, "consists of more subtle and smaller figures." Honey is sweet because, being made of smooth and round bodies, it caresses the tongue and palate, while the hooked atoms of wormwood tear them. (According to atomism, all the senses are varieties of touch.) The *shapes* of atoms are not infinite in number. If they were, Lucretius infers, there would have to be some that were of enormous size. However, the number of atoms of each shape is infinite. Not every kind of particle can link with every other—that would produce monstrosities.

All combustibles contain particles capable of tossing fire abroad. Anything, such as a fruit, that has color, taste, and smell, must contain at least three kinds of constituent atoms. But no atom *by itself* has color, savor, or odor; the properties of atoms are simply solidity, size, shape, and weight. Colors and the other sensed qualities are products of atomic *arrangements*. If colors were embedded in the ultimate constituents of matter, we should be unable to account for their rapid changes without violating the principle nothing-from-nothing. (This is the main point of superiority of ancient atomism to the other schools of "physics.") Lucretius has another argument: since color, as we know, is not essentially bound up with the shape of a thing, if atoms

were themselves colored, we should expect all visible things to exist in all possible colors, "even black swans!"

Nor are individual atoms endowed with consciousness. For (1) sense depends on vital motions, and hence depends on birth; (2) heavy blows can produce unconsciousness, which ought not to happen if consciousness were independent of atomic arrangements; (3) pain is the result of a disturbance, but an atom cannot be (internally) disturbed; for (4) otherwise we should be led to all sorts of absurdities, such as that not only a man but his semen would be conscious.

Lucretius makes brilliant use of the atomistic principle that just as an indefinitely large number of meanings can be conveyed by rearranging the few letters of the alphabet, "so also in things themselves, when motion, order, position, and figure are changed, the things also are bound to be changed."

There are other worlds, like this one, in the infinite universe. Indeed, the vastness and complexity of the universe is itself proof that the whole is not governed by gods: it would be too much for them. Or, if you assume intellects adequate for the task, it then becomes inexplicable why there is evil and confusion in the world.

Growth and decay pertain to worlds as much as to individuals. The vital powers of this earth are wearing out. "Indeed, already the broken and effete earth has difficulty in creating little animals, though it once created all the kinds at once, and gave birth to the huge bodies of wild beasts."

Lucretius distinguishes between the mind (*animus, mens*) which is what thinks in us, and the soul (*anima*), which is the vivifying principle: "seeds of wind and hot vapor, which take care that life shall stay in the limbs." Both, of course, are made of atoms, "extremely subtle and minute." They form a unity: "Mind and soul are joined to each other and form one nature, but the chief, so to speak, that which rules the whole body, is the Reason. . . . It is situated in the middle region of the chest." Besides atoms of wind, air, and hot vapor, the mind also contains a fourth, unnamed kind of atom, "than which nothing finer or more mobile exists." This "very soul of the whole soul" has to be postulated to account for consciousness, which *is* the motion of this superfine substance. (Lucretius is a consistent materialist; consciousness is not for him an unexplained product of atomic motions, distinct from them, but, like color, an "accident" of atoms of a certain kind in a certain arrangement. In other words, consciousness is an atomic process.)

Souls differ in their compositions: lions have more heat, deer more wind, oxen more air. Men differ from one another likewise, their temperaments depending on the makeup of their souls. But Lucretius is quick to add: "So tiny are the traces of the natures, which Reason could not dispel from us, that nothing prevents us living a life worthy of the gods."

The soul particles are few in number compared to those of the flesh, as we know from our inability to sense very slight stimuli.

It follows from the atomic nature of the soul that it is dispersed at death; hence consciousness ceases. Lucretius deems this point so important that he reinforces it with a multitude of observations. Lucretius points out that understanding grows with the body and decays with it; that the soul is affected by bodily diseases, besides having some of its own; that mental ills can be cured by material medications; that "dying by pieces" in paralysis, and the twitches of recently severed limbs, show that the soul is divisible and therefore destructible; that there must be *some* soul-fragments left in the body after death, to account for the generation of worms in the corpse; that if the soul is immortal, we should remember our past existences (to the ancients, the immortality of the soul implied preexistence as much as life *post mortem*), and to reply that it loses its memory at the shock of birth "is not, I think, to stray very far from death." Animals have souls appropriate to their bodily constitutions; this is odd on the transmigration hypothesis, even if restricted to intraspecies reincarnations. And it is not only incomprehensible, but ridiculous, that souls should queue up to get into a body. In general, each thing has its appointed place: that of the soul is the body. If the soul were immortal, there would be a tremendous grotesqueness in its being so intimately linked with a mortal thing (as Lucretius contends elsewhere, there could never have been any centaurs, because the disparity in growth rates between the limbs of equine and human beings render them incompatible). Immortal things are so because they cannot be assaulted (atoms), or because they offer no resistance to blows (void), or because there is no room for them to scatter; none of these applies to the soul.

Thus fears of hell are foolish. "Death, therefore, is nothing to us, nor does it concern us in the least, inasmuch as the nature of the mind is held to be mortal. And just as we felt no ill in time gone by when the Carthaginians came from all quarters to the attack, when all things under the high shore of heaven shook and trembled in horror at the fearful tumult of war, and it was in doubt to which of them would fall the rule of all things human by land and sea—so, when we shall not exist, when there shall have been a parting of body and soul by whose union we are made one, you may know that by no means can anything happen to us, who will then not be, nor move our feeling; not if earth is confounded with sea and sea with sky."

The theory of vision in atomism is that objects constantly throw off "idols" or "semblances," very thin films, of which the snake's discarded skin furnishes an example. Such "idols" enter the eye and jostle the atoms of the mind, resulting in vision. The less said about this doctrine—which, as ancient critics pointed out, cannot even explain why we cannot see in the dark, or how we can get the "idol" of an elephant into our eye—the better. Though we may remark that while the Epicurean theory is patently false and ridiculous, its ancient rivals are unintelligible.

All perceptions are true, according to the Epicureans, even those in imagination and dreams—which are perceptions of finer idols that enter the body otherwise than through the eyes. It is in inferences from perception that errors arise. Epicurus consequently held that the gods really do exist, since they are perceived in dreams. They live in the peaceful spaces between the worlds, in "quiet mansions that winds do not shake, neither do clouds drench them with rainstorms nor the white fall of snow disturb them, hardened with bitter frost; ever a cloudless sky covers them, and smiles with light widely diffused." The gods are, in short, ideal Epicureans. The mistake of men is in their false inferences that these beings trouble themselves with *us*, or even know of our existence. *True* (Epicurean) religion consists in taking these blessed beings as models and making one's own life, as far as possible, like theirs.

In discoursing of perception and imagination, Lucretius takes the opportunity to state another important principle of materialist philosophy, the denial of purposive causation. One must not suppose that our organs were created *in order to* perform their appropriate functions: this is "back-to-front perverse reasoning, for nothing at all was born in the body so that we might be able to use it, but what is once born creates its own use."

This book concludes with a discussion of sex, genetics, and embryology, containing the magnificent (but misguided) denunciation of the passion of love as "madness." It is best (we are told) not to fall in love at all; but if you do, you can still be saved if only you will open your eyes to "all the blemishes of mind and body of her whom you desire."

The world was not created by the gods. Suppose they set out to create a world, where could they get the plan for it otherwise than through observation of nature? We are to understand the origin of the world this way: "So many beginnings of things, of many kinds, already from infinite time driven on by blows and by their own weights, have kept on being carried along and hitting together, all trying to unite in all ways, creating whatever conglomerations were possible among them, so that it is no wonder that they have fallen into those dispositions also and come through those passages by which the present sum of things is carried on by renewal." But even if we knew nothing of this concourse of atoms, we ought still to reject the hypothesis of divine creation, on account of the many evils in the world. Most of the earth is uninhabitable sea, mountain, and desert; what can be lived in requires laborious clearing and cultivation, the fruits whereof are uncertain. Why are there wild beasts, diseases, untimely deaths, the helplessness of human infancy?

The world is young, for discoveries—such as the Epicurean philosophy— are still being made. The heavy earth-seeds came together and squeezed out the smoother and rounder which went to make sea, stars, sun, and moon. Lucretius gives five alternative explanations of the revolutions of the heavens; one is free to take his choice, as long as gods are not introduced. The sun and moon are about the size they appear to be (whatever that may mean).

First bushes appeared on the earth's surface, then trees, then, by spontaneous generation, birds and beasts. "Wherever there was an opportune spot, wombs grew, grasping the earth with their roots." Many monsters (though no centaurs) came out of them; in the end, all perished except those few that were capable of feeding and protecting themselves and begetting offspring. (While this account contains the notion of survival of the fittest, it is hardly an improvement over the fantasies of Empedocles, and distinctly inferior to the evolutionary speculations of Anaximander, who in the sixth century B.C. had already freed himself from the prejudice of fixity of species.)

Lucretius next proceeds to a reconstruction of the history of civilization. This passage, which has nothing to do with atomist principles, is a marvel of shrewd deduction, confirmed in almost all its details by modern anthropology and archaeology. His principle of reasoning is that certain discoveries could not have been made unless others had preceded them; for example, woven textiles must have come after iron, which is necessary for making various parts of the loom. (Of course he was mistaken—but the method is promising.)

Fire came first, and made possible stable family relationships and the development of human sympathy. "Then too neighbors began to join in friendship, anxious neither to harm nor be harmed among themselves." Language arose in these primitive societies, first as mere animal cries, but developing by the assignment of conventional names. Then kings and cities, and property and gold. Then revolts against absolute rulers, leading to the rule of law. Religion, unfortunately, also arose.

Metallurgy was discovered accidentally: first that of copper, silver, and gold, later bronze and iron.

Though this account, quite unlike most ancient philosophies, shows a knowledge of technology and of the idea of progressive development, Lucretius did not consider material progress an unalloyed blessing. Life was on balance no more secure in his day than in times of savagery; then one might be eaten by a wild beast, but one did not have looting armies to contend with. Then one might have poisoned oneself through ignorance; but for Lucretius the danger was that someone else might poison you very skillfully. Lucretius the materialist wrote: "Thus the race of men labors always in vain, and uses up its time of life in idle cares, truly because it has not learned what the limit of getting is, nor at all how far true pleasure can increase. And this, little by little, has raised life up to the height and stirred up from below the great tides of war."

Book VI consists of miscellaneous Epicurean "explanations" of phenomena such as thunder, lightning, and earthquakes, the natural causes of which need to be understood lest they provide material for religion to frighten us with. The poem, left unfinished at its author's death, ends abruptly after a translation of Thucydides' description of the plague at Athens in the second year of the Peloponnesian War.—*W.I.M.*

PERTINENT LITERATURE

Latham, R. E. "Introduction," in Lucretius' *Lucretius: The Nature of the Universe*. Baltimore: Penguin Books, 1951.

In his Introduction to his translation of Lucretius, R. E. Latham emphasizes that the perspective expressed by *On the Nature of the Universe* (or: *On the Nature of Things*) developed in a particular type of social milieu. The city-state ideals of liberty, democracy, and national self-sufficiency had lost their attractiveness in a context characterized by despotism and economic and social disorder. The gods retained their institutions without inspiring genuine confidence. Plato and Aristotle seemed no longer relevant. In this setting, Epicurus "preached his gospel of salvation by common sense."

Latham finds the Epicureanism Lucretius expounds "the simplest of all philosophies." It holds, Latham notes, that all the knowledge we have is gained through sensory experience. (How we could know this is so, if it were true—how its being true is compatible with its being known—is not explained.) Nevertheless, things are not quite as we perceive them but as we would perceive them were our sensory capacities greater. Since physical objects are perceived, Latham continues, Lucretius concludes that they exist. That wind also exists, but is not perceived visually, does not, for Lucretius, give grounds for supposing that something exists which is immaterial, or radically different from physical objects. Rather, Latham explains, Lucretius suggests that one can form a picture of the wind as comprised of physical particles, albeit particles too small to be perceived, like smaller versions of flecks of dust in a shaft of sunlight. Enough of such tiny particles beating upon a branch would account for the branch's movements. (A picture so used becomes, in effect, a model which is conceived as a large-scale representation isomorphic with the microstates it represents and renders intelligible.) Thus, Latham notes, Lucretius endeavors to explain whatever exists by reference to (sometimes very small) physical objects, plus space conceived as the absence of objects.

As Latham explains, this requires Lucretius, in all consistency, to adopt particular sorts of positions on a wide variety of issues. He views the mind, for example, as a set of very mobile particles; these particles form patterns in accord with images which, caused by physical objects, impinge upon them. And, Latham continues, Lucretius supposes that the only thing that is good is pleasurable sensation. Thus Lucretius embraces mind-body materialism in metaphysics and hedonism in ethics. Further, Latham notes, Lucretius denies the existence of God and of any intelligent cause of order in the universe, thinking any such view to be a delusion, and he rejects both polytheism and monotheism.

These Epicurean dogmas, Latham suggests, of course have a history, and Lucretius' positions have their historical predecessors. His materialism resembles, and is influenced by, the atomism of the fifth century B.C. writers Leucippus and Democritus. But, Latham contends, one can understand Lucretius without tracing his historical debts. The positions of Epicurus, and so the positions of Lucretius, can be understood as an effort to hold only positions compatible with all knowledge being gained through sensory perception, expressed without any qualifications concerning such extensions of the senses as telescopes and microscopes and the other instruments of science provide—without qualification, that is, save the qualification concerning the acuteness of our senses, noted above.

Epicurus and Lucretius believed that the pagan deities existed, Latham admits, but they had little interest in them; essentially, these philosophers were enemies of the religion of their day with its omens and taboos. Rather, nature itself, without purpose or mind, but orderly and beautiful, received their religious emotions.

In one respect, Latham notes, the Epicurean system seems to involve a metaphysical claim. Lucretius asserts that human beings have freedom of choice. He reasons, Latham in effect suggests, that since human beings, according to this view, are entirely comprised of atoms, if their movements are simple functions of the movements of these atoms, and if these movements are entirely determined, then there is no movement (and so no action) that is other than determined. Hence, it must be the case that (influenced by human choice) some atoms, some times, must swerve somewhat from the path to which they were otherwise ordained.

Nevertheless, Latham tells us, the system is purely materialistic. When ideas or worries are given spatial location in the breast, this is to be construed literally. (Whether claims ascribing spatial location to mental states are coherent can be, and has been, doubted, but this is not our question here.) Further, Latham continues, the same applies to his claim that the source of all thought is composed of heat, air, and wind, plus an unnamed further element, and is located in the breast. The same mixture, although less concentrated, Lucretius conceives to be diffused throughout the limbs; here, too, Latham suggests, we are to take Lucretius literally.

Latham suggests that Lucretius holds that the truth about the nature of things is not hard to discern, and not very different from what it appears to the unaided senses to be. This, Latham contends, aids the expression of his views in pictorial language. And, as distinctions not based on sensory experience are not, for Lucretius, such that it is part of the human essence to make them, Lucretius will at least be free from the temptation to regard such distinctions, being abstract, as therefore being universal or self-evidently true.

Cochrane, Charles N. *Christianity and Classical Culture*. New York: Oxford University Press, 1944.

Charles N. Cochrane sets the thought of Epicurus, as expressed by Lucretius, in its historical context. He reports that in the society to which Lucretius presented Epicurus' thought (Epicurus' dates are 341-270 B.C., Lucretius' dates are 99-55 B.C.) traditional restraints had been thrown aside. The members of the aristocracy, Cochrane tells us, sought new forms of experience and allowed themselves the fullest range of luxury and vice; they sought pleasure in decadence. For others, Cochrane notes, who were not aristocrats, bread and circuses provided a substitute for rich banquets. All in all, Cochrane says, there was "a riot of sensationalism and emotionalism" which promoted political competition and social disintegration.

Cochrane informs us that Lucretius presents "the gospel of Epicurus" to this "distracted world." Lucretius, in Cochrane's opinion, expounds Epicurus charmingly and persuasively with an intent to show the way out of the reigning anarchy. Cochrane sees Lucretius as trying to elicit an order and understanding that rested on a system of thought which could serve as a basis for human life.

He notes that Lucretius traces the cause of the evils and sufferings of his day to belief in the traditional pagan gods. He regards these evils as prompted by a desire to obtain the favor or escape the anger of these beings, who were thought not only to exist but also to control the fate of human beings. Thus, he reports, Lucretius holds that human ills result from hopes and fears which are unreasonable, being based on mistaken views about the world. Lucretius desires to replace such views by an Epicurean science for which ultimate reality—that which depends for its existence on nothing external to or distinct from itself—contains only simple material atoms moving in the void. As Cochrane suggests, such a world is not one in which there is need to placate or propitiate autocratic but invisible rulers of our destinies. As replacement for prior religious aspirations, emancipation from terror of the invisible is offered.

Lucretius insists, Cochrane continues, that such emancipation will not be produced by following desires, but by following reason. More carefully, it will be produced by a rational patterning of one's life in which one seeks the concrete satisfactions of life in the usual human relationships rather than in concourse with the gods. The criterion for satisfactions, Cochrane notes, is, for Lucretius, presence of individual pleasure and absence of individual pain.

As Cochrane presents it, Lucretius' recommendation involves submitting unprotestingly to the mechanical laws in accordance with which nature operates and which are discoverable by observation. This doctrine depends, Cochrane says, on not having concern for the morrow—it involves cutting "the nerve of effort." While he describes Lucretius' purpose in terms of "salvation through enlightenment," he also suggests that the Lucretian perspective provides not a stimulant but a sedative whose purpose was to provide a cure for the ills of imperial society.

This, Cochrane continues, involved Lucretius in seeking for solutions to "the Roman problem" (of decadent disorder), not in Roman, but in Greek thought. This problem was ultimately moral and psychological. To solve it, Cochrane suggests, Lucretius relies on a Greek science which provides his basis for developing an ethic. (The science in question, of course, was Greek atomism in which the world is conceived as comprised of indivisible material atoms in a void.) Lucretius thus not only views nature as mechanistic and as not run by deities, but also views both society and individual as nondivine, removing the aura of mystery from both. In so doing (no doubt with the scientific atomism in mind), Cochrane contends that Lucretius sponsors a sort of moral atomism in which there is no adequate restraint on private choice and no satisfactory ground for social and political cohesion. While hardly anarchistic in intent, Lucretius' (and Epicurus') perspective, Cochrane feels, puts society under suspicion of being the cause of dissatisfactions not present in persons who are uninfluenced by an organized empire. It made nonpolitical ends the aim of human action and found the state to be no more than an economic expedient. This, Cochrane suggests, involved a repudiation of the Roman past and the rejection of a distinctively Roman future.

Lucretius, Cochrane concludes, was the first to appeal only to (a conception of) reason and nature in an attempt to solve the Roman problem, and he thus focused the dispute on principles rather than prejudices; in effect, he issued a challenge to alternative systems of thought to answer his arguments, if possible, on similar terms—a challenge, Cochrane asserts, that Cicero accepted.—*K.E.Y.*

ADDITIONAL RECOMMENDED READING

Bevan, E. R. *Stoics and Sceptics*. New York: Oxford University Press, 1913. An older work by a Gifford Lecturer and first-rate scholar.

Bréhier, Émile. *The Hellenistic and Roman Age*. Translated by Wade Baskin. Chicago: University of Chicago Press, 1965. A discussion of Epicureanism and Roman and Greek philosophy generally.

Cornford, F. M. *Principium Sapiente*. Edited by W. K. C. Guthrie. New York: Harper & Row Publishers, 1965. Subtitled "A Study of the Origins of Greek Philosophical Thought," with many references to Lucretius.

De Witt, Norman W. *Epicurus and His Philosophy*. Cleveland: Meridian Books, 1967. De Witt argues that Epicureanism is an important bridge between Greek philosophy and Christianity.

Latham, R. E. "Lucretius," in *The Encyclopedia of Philosophy*. Edited by Paul Edwards. Vol. V. New York: Macmillan Publishing Company, 1967. A brief discussion of Lucretius' views with a short bibliography.

Rose, H. J. *Religion in Greece and Rome*. New York: Harper and Brothers, 1959. A general discussion of the varieties of Greek and Roman religion.

DISCOURSES and MANUAL

Author: Epictetus (c. 65-c. 135)
Type of work: Ethics
First transcribed: c. 120

PRINCIPAL IDEAS ADVANCED

The good life is a life of inner tranquillity which comes from conforming to nature—to reason and to truth.

To achieve the good life a man must master his desires, perform his duties, and think correctly concerning himself and the world.

To master desire one has only to bring desire to the level of facts; only what is within a man's power should be of concern to him.

Every man has a duty to others because each man is a citizen of the world, one of its principal parts.

To discover one's duty one should be skilled in elementary logic, in the art of disputation, and in the right use of names.

So far as is known, Epictetus left no philosophical writings. The *Discourses* (or *Diatribes*) is a transcription of some of his lectures made by a pupil, Arrian. Originally there were eight books, of which only four are known to us. The *Manual* (or *Encheiridion*), a condensed selection from the *Discourses*, was also composed by Arrian. The *Manual* is a good résumé of Epictetus' main doctrines, but the *Discourses* is rewarding for the vivid picture it calls up of Epictetus as a teacher. It catches the vigor and warmth of a wise and witty man in the act of expounding his philosophy informally. He wore his technical equipment lightly as he answered questions concerning practical difficulties, pointed out dangers in contemporary customs, and delivered short homilies suggested by current events.

For Epictetus, the goal of philosophy is not so much to understand the world as to achieve the good life, which, for him, consisted in inner tranquillity. The Stoics, of whom he was a representative, had a well-developed philosophy of nature, based on the Heraclitean doctrine that Logos or Reason governs all change. They were also competent logicians. But their chief interest lay in personal ethics, in which they applied a knowledge of physics and logic. Inner serenity, they held, consists in conforming to nature, or, which is the same thing, following reason, or, again, discovering and living by the truth. Epictetus alluded to logic from time to time, but only rarely mentioned philosophy of nature. When he spoke of philosophy, he meant "philosophy of life." In his view, the philosopher is the wise man.

Three stages in the achievement of the good life were noted by Epictetus. The first has to do with mastering one's desires, the second with performing one's duties, and the third with thinking correctly concerning one's self and the world. He complained that students are prone to neglect the first two, which are the most important, and to overvalue the third, because students are less concerned with achieving moral excellence than with gaining a reputation as disputants. As a result, the world is flooded with vain, passionate, fault-finding fellows who have so little self-mastery that a mouse can frighten them to death; yet they boast the name of philosopher.

Epictetus put the mastery of desires first because he regarded the main business of philosophy to be the achievement of a tranquil mind. In his view, all perturbations are the result of a disproportion between our wills and the external world. The natural man supposes that happiness is possible only when the external world comes up to his expectations. The philosopher knows that this condition rarely exists, that if we build on any such hope, we are doomed to endless sorrow, which in turn leads to envy and strife. Instead of trying to bring the world up to our desires we should bring our desires to the level of actuality. Happily, this is quite within the realm of possibility because our wants are in our power, as external things are not.

In effect, the philosopher tells himself that things which are not in his power are matters of indifference, and all that matters is the use he can make of them. He may be exiled—that he cannot prevent—but does any man hinder him from going with smiles? He must die—but must he die lamenting? His leg may be fettered—but not even Zeus can overpower his will.

Epictetus recognized the difference between saying these things and doing them, and he sought various means of inculcating the habits of self-mastery. A man should daily write and meditate on extreme situations, such as how to comport himself if a tyrant puts him to torture. When enjoying anything, he should form the habit of calling up contrary appearances; for example, when embracing his child, let him whisper, "Tomorrow you will die." To overcome passions, such as anger, let each one keep a day-book in which he writes down every offense. Such are the concerns in which the philosopher ought to employ most of the time he has for thinking. "Study not to die only, but also to endure torture, and exile, and scourging, and, in a word, to give up all which is not your own." Without such practice, a man will not be prepared when unexpected trials descend upon him.

Epictetus liked to speak of the "handles" which things present to us. "Everything has two handles, the one by which it may be borne, the other by which it may not." He cited the example of a man whose brother uses him unjustly: if the man thinks of the injustice, he will not bear it; if he thinks of him as a brother, he will.

This illustration affords a good transition to the second of Epictetus' main concerns—namely, duty. It was an important part of his teaching that man is not a detached entity, but part of a whole. In a passage which is quite similar to one in the writings of St. Paul (I Corinthians XII), he compares man to one of the organs of the human body: "Do you know that as a foot is no longer a foot if it is detached from the body, so you are no longer a man if you are separated from other men? For what is a man? A part of a state, of that which first consists of gods and men; then of that which is called next to it, which is a small image of the universal state." The whole duty of man is inscribed here. Man is, as Epictetus liked to say, "a citizen of the world," and not one of the subservient parts—like the lower animals—but "one of the principal parts, for you are capable of comprehending the divine administration and of considering the connection of things." The lower creatures fulfill their functions without knowing what they do. It is the prerogative of man to understand the "connection of things." And in these connections lie his duties.

"Duties," Epictetus said, "are universally measured by relations." Among the most important for the ordinary person he listed: "engaging in public business, marrying, begetting children, venerating God, taking care of parents, and generally, having desires, aversions, pursuits of things and avoidances, in the way in which we ought to do these things, and according to our nature." The Cynics, who were in some respects the predecessors of the Stoics, used to oppose nature to society and to make a great issue of obeying the former and flouting the latter. That the Stoics of Epictetus' day should see their way to including society as part of nature is noteworthy.

But Epictetus was not ready simply to follow conventional conceptions as to what our duties are. The view that man was a citizen of the cosmos before he was a citizen of Rome has important implications. One of these is that all men, in virtue of possessing reason, are "sons of Zeus." Another is that all men are brothers. To the slave-owner, he said, "Will you not bear with your own brother, who has Zeus for his progenitor, and is like a son from the same seeds and of the same descent from above? . . . Will you not remember who you are, and whom you rule, that they are kinsmen, that they are brethren by nature, that they are the offspring of Zeus?" Conversely, the fact that a man happened to wear the emperor's crown was, in itself, no reason for obeying him. One must examine the stamp on the coin, whether it be that of a Trajan—gentle, sociable, tolerant, affectionate—or that of a Nero—passionate, resentful, violent.

As we have duties toward our fellows, so, said Epictetus, we have duties toward the gods: "to have right opinions about them, to think that they exist, and that they administer the All well and justly; and you must fix yourself in this principle, to obey them, and yield to them in everything which happens, and voluntarily to follow it as being accomplished by the wisest intelligence." Epictetus spoke of the place appointed to an individual as being like the role assigned an actor. The actor should not complain about the role—whether it is the part of a lame man or of a magistrate. "For this is your duty, to act well the part that is given to you; but to select the part belongs to another."

In another figure, he spoke of God as resembling a trainer of wrestlers who matches his athletes with suitable partners in order to bring out the best in them. Difficulties, in other words, are designed to test our souls. "For what purpose? you may say. Why, that you may become an Olympic conqueror; but it is not accomplished without sweat." Again he varied the figure: "Every man's life is a kind of warfare, and it is long and diversified. You must observe the duty of a soldier and do everything at the nod of the general."

Some of these thoughts seem far removed from the ideal of inner tranquillity which Epictetus had for his ultimate goal. "Give me a man who cares how he shall do anything, not for the obtaining of a thing." Such a passage seems close to the view which urges duty for duty's sake. But Epictetus also said that faithfulness is accompanied by the consciousness of obeying God and performing the acts of a wise and good man. What higher peace is there, he asked, than to be able to say, "Bring now, O Zeus, any difficulty that thou pleasest, for I have means given to me by thee and powers for honoring myself through the things which happen"?

The third stage in the education of a philosopher, in Epictetus' program, concerns the discipline of logic and disputation. Because right thinking is a prerequisite both to the rational control of appetite and to discovering one's duty to God and man, it is imperative that every man should study to avoid "deception and rashness of judgment." But how far formal logic is necessary for this purpose was, for Epictetus, an open question. Mostly, logic was useful in debating with sophists and rhetoricians—and with Epicureans. A knowledge of elementary fallacies seemed to him sufficient for most purposes.

Of the problems which arise in connection with moral judgments, three were particularly noticed by Epictetus. The first had to do with right names. If man's duty is prescribed by relations, it is important to see things as they are. "Does a man bathe quickly? Do not say that he bathes badly, but that he bathes quickly." The right name puts the thing in the right light. Like Confucius in his *Analects*, Epictetus urged his disciples to consider what is meant by "father," "son," "man," and "citizen." Right names disclose true relations.

Similarly, inferences should be studied, so that we may not conclude from a proposition more than it really says. Epictetus used as an example the inference, "I am richer than you are, therefore I am better than you." This is invalid. Nothing follows necessarily from the premise except judgments of the order, "I have more possessions than you." Epictetus explained the function of inference as establishing assent, and that of critical thinking as teaching us to withhold assent from what is uncertain.

Finally, it was necessary to learn the art of testing whether particular things are good. According to Epictetus, all men are by nature endowed with common moral conceptions, such as the conceptions of the good and the just; but nature does not teach us to apply these in detail. A man begins to be a philosopher when he observes that people disagree about what is good or when he casts about for some rule by which he may judge between them. There is no simple rule; but there is what Epictetus called "the art of discussion," which draws out the consequences of a man's conception so that he may see whether it agrees or conflicts with what he really wants. If it is maintained that pleasure is the good, ask such questions as these: "Is the good something that we can have confidence in?" Yes. "Can we have confidence in what is insecure?" No. "Is pleasure insecure?" Yes. Here is our answer: pleasure is not the good. Epictetus supposed that his art of discussion was the same as Socrates' dialectic, and he advised his pupils to read Xenophon's *Symposium* in order to see Socrates in action and "how many quarrels he put an end to."

Socrates was one of those held to be "saints" by the later Stoics. Another was Diogenes the Cynic. These men were, in Epictetus' view, "messengers from Zeus to men about good and bad things, to show them that they have wandered and are seeking the substance of good and evil where it is not."
—*J.F*

PERTINENT LITERATURE

Bonhöffer, Adolf. *Epictet und die Stoa*. Stuttgart, Germany: Verlag von Ferdinand Enke, 1890.

—————— . *Die Ethik das Stoikers Epictet*. Stuttgart, Germany: Verlag von Ferdinand Enke, 1894.

Having originated during the decline of the Greek city-states about 300 B.C., Stoicism concluded its career as the almost unchallenged philosophy of Imperial Rome. Only fragments remain from the writings of the old Stoics (Zeno, Cleanthes, Chrysippus), and historians have asked how far the late Stoics (Seneca, Epictetus, Marcus Aurelius) adhered to the original teachings of the school. It is well known that the middle Stoics (Panaetius and Posidonius, who influenced Cicero) were eclectic: that is, they combined Stoicism with Platonism and Aristotelianism. Adolf Bonhöffer, in what remains to this day the only comprehensive study of Epictetus, argues that, although Seneca and Marcus Aurelius were eclectic, this was not the case with Epictetus, who was well-grounded in the writings of the founders, especially Chrysippus, and who remained faithful to Stoic principles on such fundamental matters as the nature of the soul and the definition of the human good.

Bonhöffer's two volumes are parts of an essentially single work, one part dealing with psychology, the other with ethics. The first volume consists largely in an examination of the vocabulary used by different Stoic writers in their account of the soul. As opposed to the Platonists and the Aristotelians, Zeno and his followers distinguished eight parts of the soul (the ruling-part, the five external senses, speech, and procreation). In keeping with their primitive materialism, they held that the ruling part (*hegemonikon*) of each soul is pure fire, but that in the other parts of the soul this active element is mixed with the grosser elements that make up the several bodily organs. In this way, orthodox Stoics, including Epictetus, were able to maintain the soul's essential unity throughout its various functions of knowing, willing, and feeling. The *hegemonikon* perceives by means of the sense and wills according to bodily impulses and desires.

The second volume is a detailed exposition of Epictetus' moral teachings, with notes and appendixes comparing his teachings with those of other Stoics. According to Bonhöffer, Epictetus' entire moral doctrine follows from three theses: (1) every creature strives for its own natural good; (2) because man's essence lies in his soul, his natural good is moral or spiritual; (3) undeveloped when he comes into the world, man must use discipline to achieve his natural good. Thus, although Epictetus shared the teleological orientation that characterized Greek philosophy as a whole, he conceived man's good in such a way that the distinction between happiness and virtue tended to disappear. Virtue was looked on as being its own reward.

Actually, virtues in the traditional sense (wisdom, justice, courage, temperance) found no place in Epictetus' teaching. There is, in Stoicism, no conflict between rational and irrational parts of the soul. Every individual, whether wise or foolish, strives necessarily for the satisfaction of his desires. The general notions, good and evil, are innate to rational beings; but only the wise, that is, persons trained in Stoic philosophy, know how to apply them correctly. Once a person understands what is his natural good, he will do what is right by the same necessity with which he formerly did what was wrong. Thus, according to Epictetus, virtue is no more difficult than vice.

Many accounts of Epictetus' teaching never get past the first stage in the philosopher's training; that is, the mastery of desire, neglecting what he has to say about duties. R. D. Hicks, for example, interprets Epictetus as urging his hearers to hold aloof from domestic cares, and says that Epictetus "is marked out amongst Stoics by his renunciation of the world." Not so Bonhöffer, who places his main emphasis on the second stage, which, he says, follows naturally from the first in that, when man's soul is freed from desires of the wrong sort, those desires most proper to its divine nature demand to be realized. Such desires lead a person out of himself and initiate duties— toward self, toward the gods, and toward one's fellows. Although in the providence of God each person has his special calling, most will marry, become parents, perform temple rites, manage property, and hold public office.

According to Bonhöffer, Zeno and his early disciples, although they believed that the wise man ought to play an active part in society, were prevented from putting their principles into practice because existing institutions fell too far short of their ideas as to what constituted natural society. Epictetus' disciples were not burdened with unrealistic expectations. For this philosopher, the eternal *logos* is manifest not merely in nature but in custom as well. The philosopher does everything that his worldly counterpart is called upon to do, but he does it not for the sake of wealth or honor or power, but out of love for his fellow man and in obedience to the gods.

In connection with religious duties, Bonhöffer discusses Epictetus' theology, which, in spite of occasional pantheistic and polytheistic expressions, was essentially theistic. The divine principle which orders nature as a whole and in its several parts was, for Epictetus, a personal God, who thinks, feels, and wills the same as men do, who takes a fatherly interest in each of his creatures, and with whom men may commune. Bonhöffer's only problem is how, with these exalted thoughts, Epictetus could take the temple cult as seriously as he did. Presumably he did not do so merely out of deference to the ignorant masses, because, as Epictetus himself pointed out, the common man, who prays and sacrifices with worldly ends in view, can never arrive at peace with the gods.

The distinction between the common man and the philosopher was fundamental to the Stoics, some of whom went to the extreme of saying that the common man can do nothing right and that the sage can do nothing wrong.

That, says Bonhöffer, was meant to be taken with a grain of salt. Whatever claim they may have made for Socrates or Diogenes, whom they held up as models, neither Zeno nor any major Stoic ever claimed to have reached perfection, but only that as Stoics they were on the right path and were progressing toward the goal.

More, Paul Elmer. "Epictetus," in *Hellenistic Philosophies*. Princeton, New Jersey: Princeton University Press, 1923.

The works of Epictetus have not been neglected by English and American scholars, as the number of translations into English attests. Apart from introductory notices that sometimes accompany these translations, however, Epictetus' thought is usually dealt with in conjuction with that of other Roman Stoics. Paul Elmer More's chapter is a noteworthy exception. As one of a series of volumes called *The Greek Tradition*, in which More traces the relation between Platonism and other post-Socratic philosophies up to their eventual merging in patristic Christianity, *Hellenistic Philosophies* is concerned with what More calls the Socratic heresies—Epicureanism, Stoicism, Neoplatonism, and Pyrrhonism.

The self-sufficiency of Socrates, so greatly admired by his contemporaries, rested, according to More, on three distinct principles: intellectual skepticism, spiritual affirmation, and belief in the identity of virtue and knowledge. Plato preserved the combination, but rival schools left out one or another of the theses. The Stoics, who were impressed with Socrates' optimistic endurance of suffering, failed to see that it was his skepticism that made this optimism possible, and burdened themselves with a dogmatic philosophy of nature which was both materialistic and deterministic.

More finds Epictetus worthy of special study because, although primarily a moralist, he sought to preserve the teachings of Zeno and the old Stoics about nature and the human soul. Plato, with his dualism of spirit and matter, had maintained that the just man is happy while enduring real evils. Zeno, rejecting the dualism, held that for the wise man there are no real evils. Epictetus tried to combine Zeno's metaphysical monism with the ethical dualism demanded by the cry of suffering and the voice of conscience. In doing so, however, he landed in two contradictions: that the world is totally good, yet human experience is full of evil; and that all things are fatally determined, yet man's will is free.

More maintains that Epictetus wavered between two ethical theories, one humanistic, the other naturalistic. Working in the former vein, he treated human good and evil as quite real. As rational beings, men are endowed by nature with the ideas of good and of right, and through experience they learn that some things are harmful and some actions inappropriate. It is right for man, as a living creature, to act in ways that preserve and enhance his life; similarly, it is right for man, as a social being, to uphold human institutions and to assist his neighbor in times of need. In this way, Epictetus combined a sense of social responsibility with the egoistic pursuit of happiness. He did so, however, without allowing any place for sympathy or fellow-feeling; for, true to his tradition, he could not long forget that men are parts of nature and that what seems bad of a finite creature is ultimately indifferent; or, to take the lofty view, "partial ill is universal good." In the end, Epictetus' naturalism prevailed over his humanism, leading him to the same mood of resignation which characterizes the *Bhagavad Gītā*: "Without attachment, lay thy hand to thy peculiar work."

The second contradiction arises, like the first, out of Epictetus' attempt to affirm moral categories in a nonmoral universe—this time the categories of freedom and responsibility. More recognizes that Plato himself had a problem bequeathed to him by Socrates' insistence that virtue is identical with knowledge: how to escape the conclusion that what we call man's will is identical with his most recent impression. According to More, Plato avoided determinism by affirming a transcendent element in the soul that enables man to bring a higher order of truth to bear upon his transient impressions. Superficially, Epictetus did the same thing when he located freedom in the power of reason to give or to withhold assent; but, says More, the reason appealed to by the Stoics contains no transcendent element, being no more than a congeries of impressions acting one on the other, so that "when erroneous opinions affect it concerning things good and evil, there is necessity upon us to act unreasonably."

Certainly Epictetus did not want his students to lapse into moral indifference of the ordinary sort: the pangs of self-reproach were among the sanctions which he used to steer them away from trivial pursuits. Yet at a deeper level all this becomes indifferent; for the good consists in tranquility, and this consists in willing that things be as the divine will has ordered. Thus, at last, Epictetus' moral teachings were swallowed up in adoration. "What else can a lame old man like me do but chant the praise of God? If indeed I were a nightingale, I should sing as a nightingale; if a swan, as a swan; but as I am a rational creature I must praise God. This is my task." This, More points out, is the language not of a philosopher but of a divine; and he quotes the poem by Herbert of Cherbury, "Of all the creatures both in sea and land, only to Man has Thou made known thy ways." Nevertheless, says More, we have to remember that the Being whom Epictetus worshiped was "only a subtle form of matter," that the Providence which he praised was "only another name for mechanical law," and that the rational element in man was "nothing more than a glimmering flame of the universal fire"; and, doing so, we can only lament the estrangement between philosophy and religion which could have been avoided had this noble sect been able to throw off the tyranny of metaphysics.—*J.F.*

ADDITIONAL RECOMMENDED READING

Arnold, E. V. *Roman Stoicism*. Cambridge: Cambridge University Press, 1911. A systematic approach, with no special treatment of individual philosophers.

Epictetus. *Epictetus*. Locb Classical Library. Translated by W. A. Oldfather. Cambridge, Massachusetts: Harvard University Press, 1925. Greek and English text, with an introduction to Epictetus' life and teaching, and a bibliography.

Hicks, R. D. *Stoic and Epicurean*. New York: Charles Scribner's Sons, 1910. See Index, under "Epictetus."

Rist, J. M., ed. *The Stoics*. Berkeley: University of California Press, 1978. Articles by different scholars dealing with problems in Stoicism.

MEDITATIONS

Author: Marcus Aurelius (Marcus Aurelius Antoninus, 121-180)
Type of work: Stoic ethics
First transcribed: Latter half of the second century

PRINCIPAL IDEAS ADVANCED

Nature is one, the divine substance, God or Reason, so that virtue for man consists in being in harmony with the way of Nature.

Virtue is the highest good.

The ideal Stoic wills to control himself in those respects in which control is possible—in desiring, believing, and responding.

Man's freedom, in a world in which all events are determined, is his power to assent or dissent to the course of events.

Nothing that is according to Nature can be evil; hence, death is not evil, nor are the ordinary misfortunes of life.

Many great works of literature and philosophy give us nothing of the sense of the persons who composed them. In the process of composition the author abstracts from his experience and his thought and, under the disguise of style, creates an immortal work in which the idiosyncratic features of his own vulnerable person are lost. But now and then, as we read, we close the gap of centuries, even of style, and come mind to mind and spirit to spirit with one who, though long dead, made such a mark in history and letters that it is as though he were making that mark still—yet responding as a person of flesh and feeling to the challenges of the world. Such a figure, at once emperor and philosopher, man of history and vulnerable man, is Marcus Aurelius; and his peculiar immortality is made possible by the personal record of his thoughts, the *Meditations.*

He was a stoic. To some modern readers the term *stoic* calls up the picture of one who, in the midst of life's threatening adventures, stands unmoved by either pleasure or pain. To be stoical is to be one who endures, one who may suffer but who refuses to be moved by suffering.

Perhaps Marcus Aurelius was, in this sense, stoical; surely he survived the treacherous debaucheries of Lucius Aurelius Verus with whom he shared his empire, the rebellious uprisings of powerful tribes, famine and flood, the deaths of his children—but for one, who became a tyrant—and the threat of Christianity. Perhaps he also had to tolerate faithlessness in his wife—but of that we have no word from him, and rumors may be false.

But he was more than a stoic. He was a Stoic, one fallen heir to a great philosophic tradition initiated by Zeno of Cyprus and expanded and continued by Chrysippus, Panaetius, Posidonius, Seneca, and Epictetus. What is central to Stoicism is not a stonelike stubbornness in a world of suffering, but a strengthening faith in the way of Nature. Nature is one, the substance of God; and God is a divine fire which periodically consumes all things. But although the divine conflagration turns all things and persons to fire—thus effectively uniting all in the purest form possible—things and persons will exist in the next cycle of existence; the cycles of existence and conflagration will succeed each other forever. Virtue for man is in willing to be in harmony with the way of Nature. Pleasure and pain are irrelevant, if the only good is Nature's way and obedience to that way. Thus, the stoical attitude is the consequence of a dedication to the Stoical ideal; it is not itself the essence of that ideal.

So conceived, Stoicism can be recognized as being close in spirit to Taoism, the philosophy and religion of ancient China, in which obedience to the *tao*, the *way* of the universe, is the highest virtue. Stoicism, like Taoism, involved the belief that Nature, since it is the matter of God, works only toward the good—although the Chinese did not identify the cosmic power as fire or as God. Finally, to fix the idea of Stoicism, it is helpful to distinguish between Stoicism and Epicureanism. Although both the Stoics and the Epicureans fostered a life of moderation in which the passions would be controlled by will and reason, the Epicureans regarded pleasure as the highest good— although, contrary to common belief, they did not endorse a program of wine, women, and song but, rather, a life of moderation in which the desire for peace and contemplation would take precedence over the desire for gratification of the senses. For the Stoics, virtue itself was the highest good, although it was generally believed that a modest kind of happiness would be the virtuous man's natural reward. Although there are other important differences, one can come to understand the essential distinction between Stoicism and Epicureanism by realizing that for the Stoics virtue was the highest good, while for the Epicureans happiness was the highest good and virtue only the means.

In Stoicism, and particularly in the later philosophy as exemplified in the *Meditations*, the ethical elements received more emphasis than the metaphysical. The early philosophy was, strangely, a pantheistic materialism— since it held that God is fire, and all Nature is God—but later Stoics were not interested in developing these ideas, and insofar as fire was mentioned it was in a metaphorical, rather than a metaphysical, way.

The Stoic ethics is not complicated; it is more an expression of dedication to Nature's way and to the control of the self than it is a specific guide to the complexities of life. The wise man, the one who becomes the ideal Stoic, is one who wills to control himself in those respects in which control is possible: in desiring, believing, and responding—and he is one who (like the Epicurean) refuses to be affected, in his desires or attitudes, by matters beyond his control or unworthy of his concern.

Nevertheless, although the ethics of Stoicism is not complicated, problems develop in connection with the metaphysical ground of the ethics. If all nature

tends toward the good, and if all events are causally determined—as the
Stoics believed—how is it possible for man to err, and how can man be held
responsible for his actions? The Stoics were unanimous in giving assent to
the claim that man is morally responsible and that his responsibility involves
his freedom, and they were generally united in adhering to a strict determinism. The answer which won most favor among the Stoics, and which seems
to be influential in the thinking of Marcus Aurelius, is that despite the fact
that, causally speaking, events could not be other than they are, in the act
of assenting or dissenting man plays a critical role in the course of events;
and it is in that moment of assent or dissent that man shows his freedom and
acquires his responsibility. At its most positivistic, this philosophy means that
to attribute moral responsibility to man is simply to attribute to him the
power, in the causal situation, of assenting or dissenting.

Although there are reflections of Stoical philosophy in the *Meditations*, the
work itself is not a philosophic treatise. It is a record of the reflections of a
philosophically tempered ruler, a person with moral sensitivity and intellectual
awareness who never gave up the practice of examining his ideas, his motives,
and his actions with the intention of refining himself. He is a generous and
thoughtful man in his book, an honest man with a sense of his errors—but
throughout the work Marcus seems to be sustained by a strengthening spirit,
the fire or *pneuma* which is the cosmic principle of the universe. Whether or
not the Roman emperor who wrote it ever intended to have it read by anyone
other than himself, the *Meditations* remains an intensely personal philosophic
journal by one of the greatest of the Stoics.

The book begins with expressions of gratitude—to his grandfather Verus
for having taught him to refrain from passion, to his father for having inspired
in him manlike behavior, to his mother for teaching him to be religious and
to "content myself with a spare diet," and to his great-grandfather for having
encouraged him to acquire a good education. Other friends and teachers are
remembered in charming fashion. Marcus shows gratitude for having been
taught to be humble as a prince while at the same time maintaining a sense
of his responsibilities in public matters. He thanks the gods "That I was not
long brought up by the concubine of my father; that I preserved the flower
of my youth. That I took not upon me to be a man before my time, but rather
put it off longer than I needed."

Within a few pages of the beginning of the *Meditations* Marcus Aurelius
writes that nothing is more important than understanding "the true nature
of the world, whereof thou art a part," and he gives himself sober counsel:
"These things thou must always have in mind: What is the nature of the
universe, and what is mine in particular: This unto that what relation it hath:
what kind of part, of what kind of universe it is: And that there is nobody
that can hinder thee, but that thou mayest always both do and speak those
things which are agreeable to that nature, whereof thou are a part."

Again, in Book VI, Marcus writes, "He that seeth the things that are now, hath seen all that either was ever, or ever shall be, for all things are of one kind; and all like one unto another. Meditate often upon the connection of all things in the world, and upon the mutual relation that they have one unto another. For all things are after a sort folded and involved one within another, and by these means all agree well together."

To "meditate often"—this was both the duty and the practice of Marcus Aurelius. Even in the midst of war, while waiting for the next day's battle, he reflected on the "connection of all things" and attempted to understand the relation of himself, a part, to that Nature of which he was a part.

He concerned himself with the problem of evil and considered whether death is evil. His conclusion was that since Nature is the means by which man and God are united, whatever man finds disagreeable is no true evil. He believed both in the justice and intelligence of the creative force in the universe and regarded it as inconceivable that Nature would be so constituted as to allow both the good and the bad to happen to good and bad men "equally and promiscuously. . . ."

His advice to himself was to spend each moment as if it were the last moment in his life. If death comes, he argues, it brings man into the company of the gods—or it brings extinction—and in either case a rational man should not be disturbed. In any event, what one loses at the moment of death is nothing more than the present moment—and it does not seem proper to complain about losing a moment of one's life. Thus he writes, "The time of a man's life is as a point; the substance of it ever flowing, the sense obscure; and the whole composition of the body tending to corruption." But what of it? For one who by the use of philosophy allows his spirit to discipline him, all things that happen are accepted contentedly, and one is assured by the conviction that "nothing that is according to nature can be evil."

It may sometimes seem that the ideal Marcus constructed is beyond reach: in his regard for community, for other men, for the way of Nature in all its manifestations, he constructed a moral pattern for himself (and, by implication, for others) that few men could hope to attain. He enjoins himself always to keep his thoughts on worthy matters, to think only of that which he would be happy to reveal were he asked to state his thoughts; and he charges himself never to act against his will, or against community, or without examination of what he proposes to do; and he vows soberly to "let thy God that is in thee to rule over thee" so that his life might be so ordered that were the trumpet to call retreat from life, he would be ready.

But this Stoic ideal is so carefully considered and presented as the product of personal meditations that it carries with it no hint of moral pride or arrogance. Indeed, if Marcus Aurelius ever supposed he was successful in meeting the ideal, there is no sign of it in his book. For the nobility of his character we have the evidence of the testimony from those who knew him—together with the spirit of the *Meditations*—a philosophic, universe-accepting, strenuous spirit forever exploring Nature for intimations of divine intention.

We are reminded of Emerson's call for self-reliance in Marcus Aurelius' determination "to stand in no need, either of other men's help or attendance, or of that rest and tranquillity, which thou must be beholding to others for." Here again is no insensitive stubbornness but a sign of a faith in the way of Nature.

Marcus argued that if reason is common to men, then reason's law is common law, and from common law can be derived the commonweal which makes the world a city and all men the fellow citizens of it. He placed great faith in reason because he regarded it as an expression of the great ordering breath of God which pervades all Nature. The concern for other human beings fills the *Meditations*, and the spirit is much like that of the Christianity which Marcus never understood.

To live according to nature, to disdain rest and tranquillity, to be ready for death, to take misfortune as nothing evil, to be persistent in one's efforts to live like a man, to be happy as one who has faith in the purposes of God and Nature, to live with the gods and to give allegiance to the god within, to honor reason and to use it as the divine in man whereby he both recognizes and participates in the community of all men, to regard happiness as the consequence of "good inclinations of the soul, good desires, good actions"— this is the genteel, impassioned Stoical philosophy which emerges from the pages of the *Meditations*. The common conception of Stoicism as a philosophy of endurance is destroyed in the face of the fact that Marcus Aurelius' Stoicism is well-balanced, sympathetic, strenuous, idealistic, demanding—a religious call to man to use his highest powers and to control his passions.

But much of the delight of the work comes not from its philosophy— although the Stoicism developed by Marcus Aurelius is in every respect admirable—but from the author's sprightly style which, while communicating the most serious of thoughts, ever reminds us of the presence of the living thinker, a lover of men, action, and nature. Such an aphorism as "That which is not good for the beehive cannot be good for the bee" creates a pleasant image, expresses a sentiment, fixes an idea, and rounds out an argument. Again, reflecting on anger, he writes, "To them that are sick of the jaundice, honey seems bitter; and to them that are bitten by a mad dog, the water terrible; and to children, a little ball seems a fine thing. And why then should I be angry?"

Sometimes you know a man by his heroes. Marcus Aurelius writes: "Alexander, Caius, Pompeius; what are these to Diogenes, Heraclitus, and Socrates? These penetrated into the true nature of things; into all causes, and all subjects: and upon these did they exercise their power and authority. But as for those, as the extent of their error was, so far did their slavery extend." With Marcus Aurelius also the philosopher takes precedence over the soldier and emperor—both in his opinion and in ours.

Throughout all of his actions and reflections Marcus Aurelius was sustained by an unconquerable faith. He wrote that neither time nor place can limit a man's efforts to be a true man; and he regarded true manhood as made possible by reflection on God's ways as shown in the course of Nature and by calm acceptance of all circumstances. Not to accept Nature, for him, was not to accept law; and not to accept law was to be a fugitive from God. Yet to live in accordance with Nature and to accept all things, to act as directed by reason, not passion—this was not a burdensome life, but a happy one: "How happy is man in this his power that hath been granted unto him: that he needs not do anything but what God shall approve, and that he may embrace contentedly, whatsoever God doth send unto him?"

For the Stoic Marcus Aurelius, the answer was clear—and the assurance of his self-reliant faith is alive in his words:

"Herein doth consist happiness of life, for a man to know thoroughly the true nature of everything; what is the matter, and what is the form of it: with all his heart and soul, ever to do that which is just, and to speak the truth."
—*I.P.M.*

PERTINENT LITERATURE

Farquharson, A. S. L. "The Religion of Stoicism," in *Marcus Aurelius, His Life and His World*. New York: William Salloch, 1951.

Most books about Marcus Aurelius are written by historians, concerned mainly with dynastic developments. A. S. L. Farquharson, however, writes from the standpoint of a classical scholar, and the chapter in this biography which sums up Marcus' creed has behind it the years of study which the author devoted to his two-volume edition of the *Meditations*.

That Marcus wrote his *Meditations* while conducting military campaigns suggests to the author that the work is best thought of as a soldier's book, far different in its concerns from Julius Caesar's *Wars*, yet characterized by the same directness, constraint, and old Roman scorn for sentimentality. Life itself is viewed by Marcus as a conflict, a war between flesh and spirit. For example, in the dialogue at the beginning of Book V, the sluggard, slow to leave his warm bed, is reminded that he was not born to feel things but to do things, and that in this regard he is no different from the ant, the spider, and the bee, each of which has its task to perform and in its minute way contributes to the order of the world.

People who complain that Stoicism is too intellectual are mistaken, says Farquharson, if they apply this judgment to Marcus Aurelius, whose philosophy is more of the heart than of the head. Marcus respected learning, and on occasion he lamented the fact that his station prevented him from spending his time with books; but the masters whom he followed, notably Epictetus, did not encourage their followers to give attention to logic and speculation until they had first mastered the art of living. The latter was what Marcus meant when he spoke of philosophy. He says, for example, that the Empire is like a stepmother, to whom he owes dutifulness, but that philosophy is his true mother, to whom he turns for refreshment. What he calls philosophy here and elsewhere is a discipline by means of which he recollects himself from cares and distractions to find strength and quiet through identity with the Divine.

The interest of the *Meditations* for a biographer lies, however, less in Marcus' practice of retirement than in the difference which the practice made in his active life. Like another Stoic, Seneca, Marcus speaks of two cities—the city of one's birth and the universal city of gods and men. As it was his privilege to draw consolation from his higher citizenship when things went wrong, so it was his duty to keep in mind as Rome's chief citizen the common law which governs all rational beings. According to Farquharson, Marcus did this by reinterpreting traditional Roman virtues in the light of the teaching he had received from his masters in philosophy. Many of his maxims, the author points out, do not come from books but from the common stock of human experience, including those which have to do with sorrow and the brevity of life.

Thus, there is nothing unusual in Marcus' treatment of temperance, which, for the common man as well as for the philosopher, rested on the view that there are in man two natures and that the lower must be controlled by the higher. Still, says Farquharson, it was paradoxical that the Stoics, who held that nature is everywhere one and the same and that man's duty is to live according to nature, should also hold that only man's reason may be nurtured and that his appetites must be denied in the severest way.

While regarding Marcus' views on temperance as a weak point, Farquharson finds much to commend in his teaching about justice, which Marcus interpreted as the identification of the individual will with that of the whole. Marcus understood this in two ways. First, taking man as a social animal, he looked upon particular human societies as parts of nature, so that for an individual to perform his social functions is to act justly and follow nature. Second, looking beyond particular societies, Marcus viewed all men as members of a universal brotherhood. The concept had been used already by Roman lawyers in their attempts to adjust Roman rule to the needs of many peoples. What it meant to Marcus is best seen at the opening of Book IX, quoted by Farquharson. "He who acts unjustly is impious. Since universal nature has made men reasonable animals for one another's sake, to help one another according to the worth of each, but nowise to injure, he who transgresses her will plainly is impious towards the eldest of the gods, for universal nature is the nature of all that is."

Courage also consists in rejecting self-will. The soldier's virtue is to obey orders; this is a theme that runs throughout the *Meditations*, nowhere more clearly than in Marcus' frequent discussions of death—nature's final proof of the vanity of self-will. For the Mediterranean world of that period, Farquharson points out, death was a common preoccupation because of its terrors, both physical and spiritual. Marcus reasons his way through both aspects of death, accepting the fact that one must live his death, finding dignity in the thought that the elements of one's body return to nature, and consoling himself with the hope that his ruling spirit will rejoin the mind of the world.

In naming the virtues, Marcus sometimes mentions wisdom and sometimes freedom as the fourth virtue. That he interchanges the two agrees with the doctrine that man, no exception to the rule that everything is determined by immutable law, is free to the degree that his governing principle is purged of mixture with sensation and desire and brought into harmony with the principle which rules the whole. "Remember that your thought is the master of things, and that thought is in your power." The wise knows that sensations are indifferent: it is the judgment which determines whether what comes one's way is good or bad.

One other virtue, not included in the usual four but frequently paired by Marcus with justice, is piety. Farquharson calls it the crown of all the virtues as occupying in Marcus' thought much the same place that happiness holds in other philosophies. Negatively, it is resignation; positively, it is tranquility and joy. Marcus counts himself as one who has attained the former only. To Farquharson, however, he "seems to be the man he desired to be, to possess the joy which is the philosopher's portion."

Bussell, Frederick W. *Marcus Aurelius and the Later Stoics*. Edinburgh: T. & T. Clark, 1910.

Frederick W. Bussell's book is a systematic study of Marcus Aurelius' philosophy. Part I is biographical; Part II outlines the moral and intellectual background of Marcus' times; Part III, comprising two-thirds of the book, is an exposition of his teachings under such headings as "Man as an Agent," "Man and the World," and "Man's Destiny." Bussell is aware that Marcus did not pretend to be a teacher of philosophy and that his concern was to live his philosophy rather than to answer theoretical questions. But the fact that Marcus attached great importance to his understanding of the world, together with that fact that students of the *Meditations* ordinarily approach the book expecting to find a noble philosophy behind a noble life, is Bussell's warrant for subjecting Marcus' doctrine to critical appraisal.

Viewed historically, the *Meditations* documents the moral change that was part of the decline and fall of the Graeco-Roman civilization, when thoughtful men were turning away from the outer world and in upon themselves. By the middle of the next century, Stoicism was all but forgotten and Neoplatonism, with its emphasis on the soul's return to the One, had established itself as the ruling philosophy. Already in Marcus Aurelius, however, Bussell observes a marked tendency in that direction. Committed by school loyalties to Zeno's physical monism, Marcus was led by his good sense and earnestness to think mainly in terms of moral dualism; moreover, in desperate moments he forgot both nature and the world of affairs and affirmed that nothing is real but the self and its impressions.

Although Marcus was open to other influences, he seems to have considered Epictetus his master, a philosopher well-trained in the doctrines of the Old Stoics, who did not let his scholars forget that men find their good by subordinating themselves to the whole of which they are parts. Marcus followed Epictetus' advice and memorized numerous maxims designed to guide would-be philosophers on different occasions. One of these maxims is "Man is made for society." Another is "Everything has a purpose." Bussell combines several maxims syllogisticaly to show man's place in Marcus' universe. "Everything has an end; that for which a thing is born is its end; where the end is, there is the useful and the good relative to that thing; man is born for reciprocity and social life; nothing that is good for the community can be bad for the citizen." In this same context Bussell collects passages which reiterate Marcus' assurance that what is good for the community, the swarm, the universe, has to be good for the citizen, the bee, the man.

The monistic side of Marcus' doctrine provided him with maxims suited to bring peace of mind when he was angry with men or vexed with the gods. It was passive, quietistic. The maxim "Follow Nature" made a virtue of submission and called on men to adore necessity as divine. It was this strain in Marcus' thought that he owed especially to the Stoics.

Practical man that he was, Marcus had a different set of maxims which made it possible for him to govern a huge empire; but this active side of his thought, says Bussell, derived almost entirely from traditions of Roman morality. When Marcus sought a philosophical basis for action, he turned not to the Old Stoics but to those of the Middle school (Panaetius, Posidonius) who had embraced many of the teachings of Plato. Marcus' active philosophy was frankly dualistic. Self-examination and daily contact with men kept before him the fact that whatever sweeping notions the mind may form of the unity of physical nature, the nature of man is divided.

Physical monism and moral dualism both claim objective truth. But from the time of the Sophists, subjective idealism held an appeal for the ancients, and, although rigorously combatted by all except the skeptics, it found a limited place in both Platonism and Stoicism. From Epictetus, Marcus had learned to say, when faced with anything that displeased him, "You are nothing but an impression," and to ask himself whether the impression was in his power. In the power to judge impressions lay the key to the Stoic claim to self-sufficiency: man's true self was his mind, and his mind was his to govern. However, Bussell points out, the road that led the Stoic to freedom increased his distance from other men. They are reduced to objects, and although Marcus knows that men have souls, he finds their inmost selves inaccessible. In principle, he says, every soul should be open to every other; but in practice the man who follows reason must close his ears to what others say. Still, he is haunted on occasion by the question, Can one be sure that the other person is wrong?

Bussell shares the general admiration, or, as he prefers to say, affection, for the man who, in addition to his other cares, struggled so hard to coordinate his thought and his practice; but Bussell thinks that most of what we admire in the man—for example, the satisfaction he found in showing mercy and pity—stems from traits of character and would have appeared had his teachers been Epicureans or even skeptics. Stoic monism and pantheism on the one hand and introversion and a tendency toward mysticism on the other tended to undermine—or would have done so had he allowed it—his Roman sense of honor and of moral obligation.

In Bussell's day the popular philosophies were Hegelian idealism and Spencerian naturalism. Although poles apart, both were monistic and, in Bussell's judgment, incompatible with moral effort and with a true appreciation of human personality. It is not difficult to discern Bussell's disapproval of these philosophies in much of what he has to say about the later Stoics.—*J.F.*

ADDITIONAL RECOMMENDED READING

Birley, Anthony. *Marcus Aurelius*. Boston: Little, Brown and Company, 1966. The story of Marcus' life and work in the light of his Stoic philosophy.

Dodds, E. R. *Pagan and Christian in an Age of Anxiety*. Cambridge: Cambridge University Press, 1965. The culture-crisis in the age of the Antoninus.

Farquharson, A. S. L., ed. *The Meditations of the Emperor Marcus Antoninus*. Oxford: Clarendon Press, 1944. Standard reference work for advanced students.

Sedgwick, Henry D. *Marcus Aurelius*. New Haven, Connecticut: Yale University Press, 1922. A biography composed of letters and other second century documents.

OUTLINES OF PYRRHONISM

Author: Sextus Empiricus (fl. late second and early third centuries)
Type of work: Skeptical criticism
First transcribed: Early third century

PRINCIPAL IDEAS ADVANCED

Skeptical arguments are designed to cure dogmatists of the disease of supposing that knowledge is possible.

The skeptic relies upon appearances, and he avoids the error of passing judgment.

To suppose that it is possible to judge truth and falsity is to ignore the relativity of perception and judgment.

The writings of Sextus Empiricus are the only texts that have survived from the Pyrrhonian skeptical movement of ancient times. The movement takes its name from Pyrrho of Elis (c. 367-275 B.C.), who doubted that there is any way by which one can attain knowledge. He urged that judgment be suspended as to whether any particular assertion is true or false. He argued that to suspend judgment leads to a state of indifference toward the world, and to a kind of inner tranquillity which enables one to live at peace in a troubled world.

The actual school of Pyrrhonian thought began much later, in the first century B.C. It developed out of the extreme skepticism that had been prevalent in the Platonic Academy under Arcesilas (c. 315-c. 241 B.C.) and Carneades (c. 213-c. 129 B.C.). The Academic skeptics developed a series of brilliant arguments to show that nothing can be known; they recommended that one live by probabilities. The Pyrrhonists regarded the Academics as being too dogmatic, and the former maintained their doubts, even about the skeptical contention that nothing can be known. Starting with Aenesidemus (c. 100-c. 40 B.C.), who had been a student at the Academy, the Pyrrhonian movement developed in Alexandria, primarily among medical doctors. Aenesidemus and his successors set forth a series of arguments against various dogmatic philosophies, including the Academic skeptics. The arguments purport to show that every dogmatic attempt to gain knowledge leads to difficulties that cannot be resolved. Instead of seeking knowledge, one should suspend judgment, thus gaining peace of mind.

Sextus Empiricus was one of the last leaders of the Pyrrhonian school. Besides the fact that he was a doctor and a teacher, practically nothing is known about him. His writings—probably copies of lectures—consist of compilations of the arguments that his predecessors had worked out on any and all subjects. The *Outlines of Pyrrhonism* is a summary of the Pyrrhonian position, whereas his other works, *Against the Mathematicians* and *Against the Dogmatists*, are much more detailed expositions of the arguments that the school had developed regarding each particular area in which other philosophers had claimed to have discovered true knowledge. Sextus' writings are veritable storehouses of skeptical arguments designed to confound all other philosophers. Although very repetitious, they contain both good and bad arguments.

In the last chapter of the *Outlines of Pyrrhonism*, Sextus explains the uneven character of his book in answering the question why skeptics sometimes propound arguments which lack persuasion. The skeptic, we are told, is a lover of mankind. He is seeking to cure an ailment called "self-conceit and rashness," from which the dogmatic philosophers suffer. Just as doctors employ remedies of different strengths, depending on the condition of the patient, so, too, the skeptic employs arguments of different strengths depending upon how "sick" the dogmatic philosopher is. If the therapy can succeed with a weak argument, good. If the case is severe, a strong argument is needed. Hence, the Pyrrhonist offered a variety of arguments, good and bad, weak and strong, since his avowed aim was to cure the dogmatist of the disease of supposing that he knew something.

The *Outlines of Pyrrhonism* begins by dividing philosophers into three groups: the dogmatists, such as Aristotle and Epicurus, who say that they have discovered the truth; those such as Carneades, who say it cannot be found; and the Pyrrhonian skeptics who keep seeking for it. The aim of the Pyrrhonian arguments is to cure people from holding either of the first two views. Sextus guards himself from being accused of "secret dogmatism" by saying that the statements in his book are not to be taken as positive assertions of what is true, but only as expressions of what *appear* to him to be matters of fact.

Sextus describes skepticism as the ability or mental attitude which opposes appearances, the objects of sense experience, to judgments that can be made about them, so that suspense of judgment is achieved in which we neither affirm nor deny anything. This state is followed by the state of "quietude," in which we are untroubled and tranquil. The various dogmatic schools of Hellenistic philosophy—the Stoic, the Epicurean, and the Academic—were all looking for "peace of mind," and their theories of knowledge and of the real nature of the universe were intended to lead one to mental peace. The skeptics contend that the dogmatists never achieve peace because they worry about never knowing whether their theories are true. But the skeptic who suspends judgment achieves peace of mind, since he escapes such worry.

If the skeptic suspends judgment about everything, how does he live? Sextus answers by declaring that the skeptic accepts the world of sense experience undogmatically. It seems to the skeptic that he sees certain things, has certain feelings, and so on, but he does not know whether such is really the case. He suspends judgment about all that is not immediately evident to him. Then, without judging, he follows nature and custom, so that—for example—when he seems to be hungry, he eats. He has peace of mind, since he does not judge, and he is guided in his life by his experience, his feelings, and the laws and customs of his society.

To achieve this tranquillity, one must first achieve suspension of judgment. Skeptical arguments are offered by Sextus to encourage such suspension. The first of these is the famous ten tropes, or arguments, of Aenesidemus, which show why we should suspend judgment about whether sense objects really are as they appear to be. (Sextus prefaces these and all the other arguments he sets forth with the disclaimer that he is not asserting dogmatically the exact number, nature, or truth of the arguments, but only that it seems to him that they are a set of arguments.) The ten tropes all deal with difficulties in ascertaining when features of our sense experience belong to real objects existing independently of our perceptions.

First, Sextus points out, different animals experience things differently according to the nature of their sense organs. We cannot tell which animal has the correct experience. Second, even among men, the same object is experienced differently, and we have no basis for deciding which man has the correct experience. Third, the same object affects different senses in different ways. Honey is sweet to the tongue, but sticky to the finger. We cannot tell which quality really belongs to the object. Fourth, our impressions of things vary according to our state of mind or our condition. Fifth, things appear different from different positions. Sixth, we never perceive objects individually, but only together with other objects, so that we never know what they are like by themselves. Seventh, objects look different when decomposed or analyzed than they do whole. We cannot judge which is their true nature. Eighth, everything that we perceive is seen relative to its position in space and time, so we do not know what it is like out of position. Ninth, we regard things differently according to whether they occur frequently or rarely. And tenth, since different nations and cultures have different laws and customs, we cannot judge what things are really right or wrong. These ten tropes should lead us to suspend judgment since they show that our sense impressions vary and are different, and we have no means for deciding which are correct ones.

Sextus follows with five additional tropes, or reasons for suspending judgment, attributed to Agrippa, a skeptic of a century earlier. These are more general reasons for doubting dogmatic contentions. First of all, there is interminable controversy about everything, so we cannot tell who is right. Second, every judgment must be proved, if it is to be accepted as true. But the proof will require a further proof, and so on *ad infinitum*. Third, any judgment is relative to the judge, and may not be true of the thing itself. Fourth, the dogmatists must assume something in order to make judgments, but we cannot tell if these assumptions or hypotheses are true. Fifth, the only way to escape from the infinite regress of proofs of proofs, or from starting with some unwarranted hypothesis, is to employ a circular argument in which something that is to be proved is used as part of the proof itself.

Further sets of tropes are offered, including Aenesidemus' arguments against any dogmatic theory of causation. Then the first book of the *Outlines* concludes with an explanation of skeptical terminology (showing how the skeptics can say what they do without making dogmatic assertions) and with a comparison of other Greek philosophies with Pyrrhonian skepticism.

The second and third books of the *Outlines* show why the skeptic suspends judgment with regard to knowledge claims in various specific disciplines. The second book treats problems of logic and the theory of knowledge, while the third is a collection of arguments about theology, metaphysics, mathematics, physics, and ethics. The second book, and its longer exposition in *Against the Logicians*, has attracted much attention in recent years because of the similarity of some of the views expressed to those of David Hume and of the contemporary logical positivists, analysts, and ordinary language philosophers.

The second book first presents the disturbing problem of whether the skeptic can deal with the arguments of the dogmatists without admitting that he, the skeptic, knows something, namely what the opponents are talking about. After contending that he deals only with what seems to be the dogmatists' views, Sextus turns to what he regards as crucial to any theory of true knowledge, the question whether there is any criterion for judging what is true. Philosophers disagree as to whether there is such a criterion. To settle the dispute, a criterion is needed, but it is not known whether one exists. Further, any proposed criterion of knowledge would have to be judged by another criterion to tell if it were a true one, and that criterion by still another, and so on.

If the dogmatic philosophers insist that man is the judge or criterion of true knowledge, then a problem exists: whether all men or only some are judges of truth. If all, then another criterion is needed to settle disputes among men. If only some, then a criterion is needed to tell which men are proper judges, and under what conditions. The Stoics, for example, claim that the wise man, the Sage, is the judge. But by what standards can one tell *who* is the Sage, and whether what he says is true? Other philosophers say that the criteria are the faculties of sense and reason. But under what conditions are they the criteria? By what standards shall we judge? And whose sense and reason are standards?

It is not even obvious that anything true exists. There is controversy about this matter; so, if somebody asserts that truth exists, he will not be believed unless he offers proof. But is the proof true? Further proof has to be offered. But is *that* true? Unless some criterion of truth can be established, we cannot tell. But how can we ever determine if the criterion is the true one?

Further, one can ask, what sort of truths are they—apparent ones or nonapparent ones? Since there is disagreement about everything (and Sextus appeals to the fact that there have been philosophers who disputed everything), it is not obvious that something is true. If truths are not apparent, some standard is needed for ascertaining what is true, but all of the above difficulties arise when one attempts to apply a standard of truth.

Philosophers, especially the Stoics, maintain that they can gain true knowledge by means of signs or inferences which connect what is obvious or evident with that which is not. What is nonevident, Sextus says, falls into one of three categories: the *temporarily nonevident*, as, for example, that which is on the other side of the wall I am facing; the *naturally nonevident*, those things which can never under any circumstances be perceived, such as the pores in the skin, but which can be inferred from what is evident; and finally, the *absolutely nonevident*, whatever can never be known at all, such as whether the number of stars is odd or even. There is a type of sign, called the "suggestive sign," which connects what is obvious, our immediate experience, with what is temporarily nonevident. Smoke suggests that there is a fire. The skeptic, like anyone else, accepts suggestive signs and acts by them, because this is the natural way of relating present experience to possible future experience. But suggestive signs do not provide true knowledge, only predictions or expectations about the future course of events.

Philosophers hope to gain true knowledge by means of another kind of sign, the "indicative" one. This is defined as "an antecedent judgment in a valid hypothetical syllogism which serves to reveal the consequent." In a syllogism of the form "If A, then B; A, therefore B," A is an indicative sign if it, itself, is evident, if it reveals that B, which is naturally nonevident, is true, and if the syllogism is valid. Sextus offers many arguments against the existence of indicative signs, including the contention that one can determine if a hypothetical syllogism is valid only if one knows whether the consequent is true or false. The consequent in this case is a statement about what is naturally nonevident, which can be revealed only by an indicative sign. Hence, one is always involved in circular reasoning, since it requires knowing what is naturally nonevident to tell if an indicative sign actually exists, and one can tell what is naturally nonevident only by means of indicative signs.

Demonstrative reasoning consists of using signs to reveal conclusions. Hence, similar doubts can be cast as to whether anything at all can be demonstrated or proved. Sextus offers many arguments to show that nothing can be proved, and then, to avoid establishing the negative conclusion, he offers evidence to show that something can be proved. Therefore, one has to suspend judgment on the question.

A very brief criticism is leveled against induction, pointing out that if a general conclusion is drawn from some particular instances, it may be disproved by other cases. If generalizations can properly be made only after a review of *all* particular cases, it is obviously impossible to survey all of the data, and hence, to generalize.

The second book of the *Outlines* examines the claims of various logicians and epistemologists of ancient times, especially the Stoics and Epicureans, and shows reasons for suspending judgment as to whether there is anything that is true, and as to whether there is any method for discovering truths. The third book rapidly surveys the various sciences from theology and metaphysics to mathematics, physics, and ethics, and indicates that in each of these areas the fundamental concepts are meaningless, that the basic principles are open to question, and that, as a result, one must suspend judgment about whether anything can be known in any of these areas.

Though the skeptic accepts the customs of his society, and hence its religious views, undogmatically, Sextus points out that the arguments for the existence of God and for atheism are inconclusive, and that the conceptions of God offered by various philosophers are conflicting and often inconsistent in themselves. Further, various problems, like the problem of evil, cast doubt on the claim that a good, all-knowing deity exists.

With regard to metaphysics and physics, the basic notions, like "cause," "matter," and "body," contain difficulties. We cannot even be sure that anything causes anything else, or that bodies exist. We seem to have no way of gaining indisputable knowledge in this area. And arguments like those of Zeno of Elea, of the fifth century B.C., indicate that paradoxical conclusions can be drawn about the nature of bodies, motion, and so on.

There are also paradoxes with regard to mathematics, such as the odd argument Sextus offers to show that 6 equals 15. The whole equals the sum of its parts. The parts of 6 are 5, 4, 3, 2, and 1. Therefore, 6 equals 15.

The disagreements among philosophers and mathematicians, and the various paradoxical arguments, whether valid or not, that had been developed in ancient times suffice to raise doubts as to whether anything can be known about the world, or about mathematics. Hence, we must again suspend judgment.

When Sextus turns to ethical matters, he points out that philosophers disagree about what is good and bad. There is not even adequate evidence that anything really good or bad exists. The variety of beliefs and opinions about what is good and bad in the various known cultures leads one to suspend judgment about whether there are any objective moral values in the world. (Sextus even points out that some people and some societies condone incest and cannibalism. And who can say that they are wrong?) The skeptic lives undogmatically, not judging whether things are good or bad, but living according to the dictates of nature and society. The skeptic, like others, may suffer from physical pains, but he will avoid the additional mental suffering that results from judging that pains are bad or evil.

The writings of Sextus Empiricus seem to have had little or no influence in their own time and to have been practically unknown during the Middle

Ages. Their rediscovery in the Renaissance greatly influenced many modern thinkers from Michel de Montaigne, onward, for Sextus' writings proved to be a treasurehouse of argumentation on all sorts of subjects. Philosophers such as Pierre Gassendi, George Berkeley, and David Hume, among others, used arguments from Sextus in setting forth their own theories. Pierre Bayle contended that modern philosophy began when arguments of Sextus were introduced on the philosophical scene. The arguments of the skeptic continue to stimulate twentieth century minds caught between the power of faith and the faith in power.—*R.H.P.*

PERTINENT LITERATURE
Brochard, Victor. *Les Sceptiques grecs*. Paris: J. Vrin, 1932.

Victor Brochard's work, first presented to the French Academy of Moral and Political Studies in 1884, was awarded the Victor Cousin Prize. It has remained the most complete study of ancient skepticism, and it contains just about all the information that is known on the subject. Unfortunately, even though the book has been reprinted in French, it has never been translated into English.

Brochard first covers the early indications of skepticism before Socrates, and in Socrates' attitudes. Next he sets forth what we know about the skepticism of Pyrrho of Elis and his disciple Timon of Phlius. A very large section of the book is devoted to the skepticism of the New Academy, Arcesilaus, and Carneades, and then of the more eclectic successors, Philo of Larissa and Antiochus of Ascalon. The last half of the work, more than two hundred pages, deals with the emergence of Pyrrhonism in the philosophy of Aenesidemus, and as presented by Sextus Empiricus. Brochard's portrayal is as definitive as one could wish; and he cites the relevant historical sources for what is known. The book is indispensable for the facts concerning the history of Greek skepticism. However, the work is more than merely a compendium of historical data, for throughout the book, and especially in the conclusion, Brochard offers his interpretation and evaluation of the various kinds of skepticism.

Pyrrhonism, we are told by Brochard, is a radical doctrine. It is pure phenomenalism in logic, and abstention and renunciation in morality. On the other hand, the skepticism of the New Academy is a doctrine of a just man; it presents precepts of conduct and assigns a goal to human life. This evaluation (which is nearly the opposite of that given by Philip P. Hallie) is then carried over by Brochard to modern philosophical theories. Aenesidemus and Sextus are seen as being like David Hume, while Carneades is compared to Immanuel Kant (except that, as Brochard points out, Carneades lacked Kant's serious moral concern). Ancient Pyrrhonism is portrayed as foreshadowing modern empiricism, while the theory of the New Academy—"looking for a middle term between dogmatism, idealism or sensualism, and pure Pyrrhonism"—is described as a view analogous to that of Kant. So, Brochard claims, the real difference between Pyrrhonism and Academic skepticism is very similar to that between modern positivism and the critical philosophy of Kant.

In his lengthy conclusion, Brochard comes to grips with the many attempts to answer skepticism. Pyrrhonism is treated by Brochard as a greater philosophical danger than Academic skepticism until one realizes that the Pyrrhic arguments are either self-refuting or based on fundamental misunderstandings. If the Pyrrhonist really rejects all theories, he reduces himself to a fool, and even a dogmatic fool. The Pyrrhonist cannot escape this conclusion. On the other hand, the Academic skeptic is a proper kind of dogmatist, evaluating matters according to probabilities. Sextus is described as a dogmatic philosopher with no justification for his dogmatism. The Academic skeptics, instead, are portrayed as proposing their views provisionally, judging according to probabilities. This latter feature, for Brochard, puts the Academics, not the Pyrrhonians, into the camp of modern science.

Brochard then goes on to claim that of all the schools in the history of philosophy, the school of the probabilists has been most unjustly treated. From the days of Carneades to the nineteenth century, they have provided some of the most productive views. From these a positive view of science has developed; and this scientific outlook eliminates the fear of the Pyrrhonian critiques of knowledge. Nevertheless, Brochard writes in conclusion, the skepticism of Pyrrho, Carneades, Aenesidemus, and others has played an important role in the development of modern thought.

Sextus Empiricus. *Scepticism, Man and God: Selections from the Major Writings of Sextus Empiricus*. Edited by Philip P. Hallie. Translated by Sanford G. Etheridge. Middletown, Connecticut: Wesleyan University Press, 1964.

Philip P. Hallie asserts that since most of the histories of philosophy and most of the encyclopedia articles are incorrect in their portrayal of Greek skepticism, this work is needed. In fact, he goes on, most discussions are usually antagonistic to skepticism. Hallie proposes that Classical skepticism be recognized as a significant force in Western thought. He puts forth his case in what he called "A Polemical Introduction." Although the Greek skeptics were hardly the first or only doubters, he writes, they were the ones who realized what doubt consists in and to what it leads. The dangerous implications of doubt may account for skepticism's having been ignored by so many thinkers. Further, Hallie contends, there is also a practical problem: that, unfortunately, only one text of Greek skeptical thought exists—the dry and often dull writings of Sextus Empiricus. Hallie hopes that his new and lively translation will make it easier to come into intellectual contact with Greek skepticism.

The basic misconception that appears in almost all accounts of Greek skepticism is that skeptical doubts lead to inaction or lack of feeling. Hallie insists that skepticism, like Stoicism and Epicurianism, was a practical philosophy aiming at happiness; it was not some kind of paralytic anesthesia, but a way of living. The doubting process, for the skeptics, removed the features that made man's intellectual life difficult, and when this was done, a happy every-day life was possible. Classical skepticism, as presented in Sextus, neither maintained that nothing is true nor employed doubting in order to destroy normal life. Once doubt has accomplished its function, doubt itself is elimi-nated, and a practical criterion provides a guide for living.

Hallie next reviews the history of ancient skepticism to show how this misconception developed. He sketches the stages of skepticism, beginning with the pre-Academics, principally Pyrrho of Elis and his disciple Timon. The legends about Pyrrho that appear in Diogenes Laertius picture the early skeptic as indifferent or even apathetic to external events, not even getting out of the way of carts or wild animals, lest he admit he *knew* they were dangerous. A different set of stories about Pyrrho portray him as being mod-erate all the time, even in the face of very dangerous happenings. His student Timon said that Pyrrho was looking for peace of mind. The various tales, however, do not allow for a clear judgment as to what kind of a skeptic Pyrrho was. His student Timon, about whom we have more information, was defi-nitely not indifferent to ordinary events: he was continually attacking other people's beliefs and actions.

After a detailed account of the Academic skeptics, Hallie turns to the movement to which Sextus belonged, the Pyrrhonians. Both the Academics and the Pyrrhonian Aenesidemus organized the skeptical challenge against the dogmatists into systematic sets of arguments. On the more positive side, Aenesidemus described the recollective or suggestive sign as a way we relate immediate experience to other possible events, without having to have gen-uine knowledge. Sextus, the codifier of Pyrrhonism, showed the skeptic as the "inquirer" (the original meaning of skeptic), dealing with the actual prob-lems of people. He showed how one can live without certainty by living according to nature and in harmony with sense experience and with the laws and customs of one's society. Hallie emphasized that the Pyrrhonian skeptics dealt with experience in a positive way, consistent with loving life.

Selections from various portions of *Sextus' Outlines of Pyrrhonian*, as well as his *Adversus Mathematicos*, grouped around the topics skepticism, man, and God, are presented. Much helpful data and interpretation is offered by Hallie in the footnotes. He has tried to show that skepticism should be rec-ognized as an important tradition from ancient times to Michel de Montaigne, Pierre Bayle, David Hume, and Ludwig Wittgenstein.

Stough, Charlotte L. *Greek Skepticism: A Study in Epistemology*. Berkeley: University of California Press, 1969.

Charlotte L. Stough's *Greek Skepticism* is the most recent analysis of Greek skeptical thought. Although there has been a growing interest and concern with various skeptical problems and arguments, there have been few book-length studies, especially in English. Stough has concentrated on four basic kinds of ancient skepticism: early Pyrrhonism, Academic skepticism, the skepticism of Aenesidemus, and the views of Sextus Empiricus. (Of course, the writings of Sextus are a major source of our knowledge of all four of these points of view.) Stough focuses chiefly on those aspects of skeptical views that can be classified as "epistemological"—those that deal with questions of knowledge, belief, experience, perception, and sensation. The metaphysical, ethical, social, political, and theological views of the different kinds of skeptics are largely set aside.

Although Sextus Empiricus figures throughout the book, principally as a source of information, the specific discussion of his views appears in the fifth chapter. What is emphasized as a significant difference in his views from earlier skeptical ones going back to Pyrrho of Elis is Sextus' empiricism—his emphasis on experience. Using material both from his *Outlines of Pyrrhonism* and from his larger work, *Against the Mathematicians*, Stough shows first that Sextus accepted the empiricist axiom that knowledge originates in sensory experience. He held both that experience causes ideas and that it produces their content. Through sensation we receive the content, and through perception we recognize the experience. Our thinking is about images received through experience. Things that we cannot conceive, such as a line without breadth, cannot be reasoned about. Stough contends that Sextus used the claim that ideas are images as a powerful weapon against dogmatists.

Developing the empiricism in Sextus' views further, Stough points to his use of an empirical verification principle to determine whether a given claim is true. To ascertain whether something is true, we have to be able to verify it in experience. At the same time we have to recognize that experiences are affected by various factors. Thus, we can learn about experienced objects, but not about independent "real" objects.

The identification of impressions with phenomena, Stough writes, is a central feature of Sextus' empiricism, a feature not present in the Pyrrhonian theory of Aenesidemus. Using classifications that have been developed by modern empirical thinkers, Stough shows that many difficulties or even inconsistencies result from Sextus' view. When one asks what an impression is of, no referent is left. All that remains is a subject with its private experience. This view is described by Stough as an extreme form of empiricism.

Next Stough deals with Sextus' theory of signs, by which one experience makes another known. Sextus held that only perceptually associative signs are usable. The so-called indicative signs of Stoic theory go beyond experience. So, Stough shows, Sextus' refusal to admit that there could be any signs other than observable conjections, is part and parcel of his empiricism.

Having neatly portrayed Sextus' empiricism, Stough then shows that Sextus' ultimate epistemological position casts doubt on the validity of inductive, empirical inferences. Induction, which has been such a major feature in empiricism since David Hume, is briefly and quickly disposed of by Sextus. (Many of Sextus' points were later raised by Hume.) Sextus then goes on to argue that nothing is true. Sextus' thoroughgoing skepticism, Stough points out, challenged the criterion of truth of Carneades (that of credibility) and of Aenesidemus (general consent). But in order to reject them as well as those of assorted dogmatists, Sextus apparently had to assume that any empirical statement that can be true or false (the only ones worth discussing) makes a claim about the real external world. Sextus' arguments are geared to show that we have no way to verify such claims. This result seems to follow from the assumption that truth must be connected with real existence.

Stough, in her evaluation of Sextus, asserts that if Sextus could only have gotten beyond the earlier skeptical tradition and seen that truth can be about experiences and not "real" existences, he could have been a phenomenalist (maybe the first one before the eighteenth century) and not just a skeptic. Stough argues that as a complete skeptic Sextus would have had to doubt his own views. She then quotes a famous passage showing that Sextus was the culmination of the line of skeptical thinking that began in the fourth century with Pyrrho of Elis:

> And, again, just as it is not impossible for a man who has climbed up to a high place by a ladder to overturn the ladder with his foot after his ascent, so too it is not unreasonable that the Skeptic, after he had proceeded, as it were by a kind of ladder, to construct the above argument proving that there is no such thing as demonstration, should then also do away with this very argument.

—*R.H.P.*

ADDITIONAL RECOMMENDED READING

Bevan, Edwyn R. *Stoics and Sceptics*. Oxford: Clarendon Press, 1913. A literate and scholarly account of the period.

Chisholm, Roderick. "Sextus Empiricus and Modern Empiricism," in *Philosophy of Science*. VIII, no. 3 (July, 1941), pp. 371-384. An examination of Sextus' empirical method.

Mates, Benson. *Stoic Logic*. Berkeley: University of California Press, 1953. Sextus Empiricus is considered, among others, as contributing to the development of Stoic logic.

Patrick, Mary Mills. *The Greek Sceptics*. New York: Columbia University Press, 1929. A substantial account of skepticism.

_____ . *Sextus Empiricus and Greek Scepticism*. Cambridge: D. Bell, 1899. Here the focus is on Sextus within the context of skepticism.

DE PRINCIPIIS

Author: Origen (c. 185-c. 254)
Type of work: Theology and metaphysics
First transcribed: c. 220

PRINCIPAL IDEAS ADVANCED

God is incorporeal, the light, the truth, the good; he knows, and is known, as an intellectual being.

The Trinity is eternal; although the Intellectual Principle (Nous) and the Son are eternally generated by God the Father, they are eternal with him.

The conception of the Holy Spirit is Christianity's unique contribution to religious doctrine.

Every creature within the rational structure of the universe has its position in relation to God as a result of what it merits because of its free action.

Scripture has a threefold meaning: the obvious sense, the essential meaning, and the spiritual meaning.

At first glance it may be hard for the modern reader to see the relevance to philosophical questions of this central systematic work of Origen. Numerous Scriptural references fill the pages, and it is obvious that biblical documents comprise for Origen one major test for the correctness of any theological conclusion. Moreover, the theological issues Origen chooses to consider are concerned with peculiarly Christian doctrine. Yet, to the careful reader, one who can disregard the prejudice of modern forms of expression and argument, the basic philosophical importance of Origen can soon become clear.

In the first place, it seems correct to say that Origen is the first major figure in the Christian era who wrote—in Greek—with full philosophical training and with a full sympathy toward philosophical method. Augustine is sometimes given this credit, but the truth is that before him stands Origen, to whom Augustine owes much. The revived interest in medieval philosophy has ultimately brought students back to a concern with these formative years of the church fathers. In any inquiry into the sources of later philosophy and theology, Origen must be given wide attention. Here is an example of the kind of infusion of Greek philosophical skill into theology which gave Christian thought its unusual theoretical side and has allowed it to develop such close relationships with pagan philosophical interests.

Therefore, as one might suspect, Origen's *De Principiis* (*On the Principles*) subjected him to charges of heresy. The strong philosophical interests and training demonstrated in the past by so many famous theological figures have at times tended to lead them in this direction. If a man feels a strong attraction to philosophy, this is bound to mean that doctrine cannot win at every point.

But since the original Greek text of the *De Principiis* has, for the most part, been lost, these charges are difficult to establish. The elaborated Latin translation by Rufinus contains indications that Origen's work was considerably altered in its rendering, and modern scholarship tends to find Origen not so extreme on some points as has sometimes been charged. It will always be of interest to students of the history of philosophy that Plotinus and Origen had the same philosophical teacher, Ammonius Saccas, who is sometimes said to be the founder of Neoplatonism.

Origen begins by establishing the words and teachings of Christ as a central norm, and his fame as a biblical interpreter is widespread. To develop theological issues along the lines of philosophy, some interpretive scheme had to be devised to make biblical thought and expression amenable to philosophical treatment. Like many a sophisticated follower of religion, Origen was caught between the rough and untechnical nature of biblical expression and the abstract nature of technical and systematic analysis. In response, Origen attempted first of all to establish what can be taken as agreed apostolic teaching, since the church of his time provided for him no single unequivocal set of agreed doctrines.

The *Contra Celsum* (*Against Celsus*) is sometimes thought to be more immediately relevant to philosophy, since Origen wrote it during the time of Philip the Arabian to refute the attack against Christianity by the Greek philosopher Celsus. Actually, it is less philosophical in the systematic sense than the *De Principiis*, since it is in the latter work that Origen develops his principal doctrines. The *Contra Celsum* is rather contrived and often shows philosophical reason at its worst, compiling lists of apparently rational arguments in order to overwhelm an opponent's point. It is true that the *De Principiis* is much more inextricably involved with the details of Christian doctrine, but this fact should bother none but the anti-metaphysical readers.

The opening chapter of the first of the four books is titled "On God." Such a starting point must spring from systematic interests, for the Bible contains little direct discussion of the Divine Nature, and none in technical form. Later philosophy agreed with Origen in beginning immediately with a discussion of the divine attributes, until the modern period began to swing the emphasis away from metaphysics. Origen then discusses the second and third persons of the Trinity and gives an account of the origin of sin or defection. After this he considers man as a rational creature and the doctrine of last things, or eschatology. He ends the book by discussing the nature and function of angels, which to contemporary readers will seem the most artificial use of rational argument. In short, what Origen provides is a vast scheme, beginning with God and including all natural creatures in an account of the beginning and end of the world.

Origen is most concerned to prove God to be incorporeal and to deny any possible physical attributes. His love for the immaterial undoubtedly reflects his Platonic training, and Origen also stresses light symbolism in referring to God, another favorite Platonic sign. Like Augustine, Origen uses "God" as a symbol and norm for truth, but he goes on to place God beyond final human comprehension. Like the "Good" of Plato, God is too bright for direct human vision. God's incorporeality, it turns out, has its primary example in the human intellect, which Origen takes to be equally incorporeal in its operation. God is not seen as a corporeal body is seen; he is known, and he knows, as an intellectual being.

When Origen turns to Christology, we see clearly that his conception of divinity in its highest sense is personal, as is not true in Neoplatonism. The personal relationship of the three members of the Trinity is immediately apparent, and Origen establishes the coeternality of the Father and Son, despite the fact that the Son is said to have been "generated." Any Platonic, and especially Neoplatonic, framework can accept eternal generation as an intelligible concept, so that Origen's philosophical background here helps to set the theological orthodoxy. And just as *Nous*, the Intelligible-World (or Principle), in Plotinus is the source of our natural order, containing the seeds and forms of all things, so the primary function of the Son, as Origen sees it, is to be the Second Person, the divine creative agent for the natural world. The world is not eternal and the three members of the Trinity are coequal and personal in nature. This view radically distinguishes Origen and Plotinus from a basic Neoplatonism, despite the many similarities.

The Son is the truth and life of all things which exist, and Origen goes on to argue that there should be a resurrection of the type which the Son in fact undergoes in order to destroy the bond of death placed on men. But the Son is the Word (*Logos*), the intelligible structure of all things, and as such is not subject to sight but can be revealed only to the understanding. The incorporeality of the Son, and God, is again an overriding concern. Origen also takes the classical position in upholding the necessity of creation. God's omnipotence demands a world to govern and so he has no choice but to create a world through the agency of the second person of the Trinity, his Word.

Origen finds the sources for his doctrine of the Son, the divine intellectual and creative agency, in pagan philosophical views. It is interesting, and somewhat startling, to see that he considers, not the doctrine of the Son, but that of the Holy Spirit to be the unique theological idea in Christianity. No pagan before, Origen believes, had conceived of the Holy Spirit; but such teaching is, he feels, in the Bible, both in the Old and the New Testaments. The Holy Bible is the divine agent, and all rational beings, Origen asserts, partake of Reason. This is not a matter of being a Christian or not. As a measure of the importance Origen gives to the Holy Spirit, he believes that a sin committed against the Son can be forgiven but that a sin against the Holy Spirit cannot.

When Origen turns to discuss what a rational nature is, his famous doctrine of the freedom of the will becomes evident. Every rational creature is capable of earning praise or censure; and thus, if men receive censure for sin, it is not because they were incapable of different action. But among rational creatures Origen lists angels and spiritual powers of wickedness along with men. Angels and the powers of wickedness are also fully free to determine their course. Angels are free to fall, and they remain angels only as a reward for contrived choice of the good.

Every creature within the rational structure has its position because of the merit, or demerit, it has earned. The situation of every creature is the result of his own work and movement. Origen is adamant about keeping the responsibility for the fall of the angels, or the sin of man, away from God. No malignant powers were formed by God in creation, although such irrational forces now exist. They have come into being and now plague the world. Through a fall they were converted into wicked beings and that fall resulted from their own choices. Such a power was formerly holy and happy, and from that state of happiness it fell from the time that iniquity was found in it.

Our world is rationally governed, and it contained only good beings at its creation; but those beings were free to choose their own actions; they included powers and angels far stronger than man. Once such divine powers fell, because their chosen iniquity was discovered, then rational man came to have superior forces—both of good and evil—at play upon him. Man is still free to determine his choices, but not in the easy way that existed before the transformation of some good powers into evil. Spotless purity exists in the essential being of none save the Father, Son, and Holy Spirit; it is an accidental quality in every created thing and thus can easily be lost. Yet it lies within ourselves, in our own human actions, to possess either happiness or holiness.

When Origen comes to discuss the end of the world and the ultimate transformation and restoration of all things, he acknowledges immediately that such questions are not subject to strict definition but must take the form of speculative discussion. The Trinity can be set forth in propositional form: but any account of the end of the world can only be conjecture, despite its obvious basis in Scripture. How things will be after such a day is known with certainty only to God.

There is no rational creature that is not capable of both good and evil. Since not even the devil himself was incapable of good, what we become is the result of our own decisions and not of any inevitable force. But the righteousness of man is only accidental, and it is easy for him to throw it away. Yet God has so constructed the world that no rational creature is compelled by force, against the liberty of his own will, to any course other than that to which the motives of his own mind lead him.

Origen has sketched his position, one which concedes a great deal of the directive powers of each rational individual, but he ends by admitting that his view is only a possible one. Let each reader, he says, determine for himself whether any one of the views he argues can be adopted or not. Origen trusts reason a great deal, and he makes every question of theology a matter for rational discussion; but he does not believe his conclusions to be unavoidable or inevitable.

Perhaps Origen's greatest ability is shown by the way in which he treats Scripture's place in theological argument, a particularly interesting problem in view of his obvious attachment to philosophy and to rational argument on all points. The authority of Scripture as a norm must first be agreed to, Origen says, and in that sense argument is prior to the Scripture's authority. Thus, he first set down the *reasons* which lead us to regard them as divine writings. The wide conversions to Christianity, he argues, attest to the special significance of its Scriptures. Origen argues for the deity of Christ, and thus for the divine inspiration of the Scripture which prophesied him, so that the authority of Scripture in theology really rests upon the prior acceptance of the divinity of Christ. Scripture is not obviously authoritative for Origen, but it becomes so for those who are convinced of Jesus' divine authority, and one can be convinced through a process of reasoning.

Scripture hides the splendor of its doctrines in common and unattractive phraseology, and the inability to see through this is one of the most frequent reasons for rejecting Scriptural passages as valid points in an argument. Thus the central problem is to state the manner in which Scripture is to be read and understood, since its validity is not immediately obvious. Here Origen introduces his famous distinction of the "spiritual meaning" as opposed to the interpretation according to the "mere letter." Origen finds certain mystical economies in the Scriptures, but to see these the words must be properly interpreted. Each individual, Origen insists, ought to receive the threefold meaning of Scripture: first, the obvious sense; second, the "soul," or essential meaning of the words; and third, the hidden wisdom or mystery of God contained in a "spiritual" meaning.

There are, then, esoteric and exoteric meanings in Scripture, and one cannot easily tell which of the three meanings will best fit a passage. Some men are better interpreters of Scripture than others and can divine the esoteric meanings of certain important passages, but the exoteric meaning is easily available, even to simple folk. This being so, not all Scriptural accounts need to be factual. That is not their purpose. Interwoven in the historical accounts are reports of events which did not occur, some which could not have happened, and some which could have happened but did not. The biblical documents are not a pure history of events but were intended to convey meaning and truth on a threefold level, according to the scheme Origen has sketched. They reveal facts about the divine intention which no mere record of events could convey.

Many biblical accounts cannot be believed literally—for example, God walking in paradise in the evening—and when this is so, one knows that a deeper meaning must be sought beneath the literal phrase. Such being the case, the biblical documents are, in themselves, no simple authoritative norm in theological debate, for their normative value depends upon the prior working out, and acceptance of, a rational framework for interpreting the literature. Were the Bible to be taken literally, Origen argues, it would be incredibly irrational. Yet the passages which are true in their historical meaning are much more numerous than those which are interspersed with a purely spiritual signification. The exact reader must be careful to ascertain how far the literal meaning is true, and how far it is impossible. Certainly this places the ultimate norm in the rational judgment of the individual interpreter, since there is nothing obviously literal to compel him.

Thus Origen sets Scripture into a rational framework, making it possible to use it in support of rational theological discussion. A modern reader may at first miss the philosophical importance of Origen's analysis in the *De Principiis*. It is more the way in which Origen treats his material than the material itself that is philosophical. Furthermore, if Origen's approach to Scriptural authority is basically rational, his philosophical interests can be seen even more clearly in his stress upon the freedom of the will. For this is not basically a religious problem but one which a philosophical instinct might regard as important to theological doctrine. Classical philosophy had not laid a great stress on the question of freedom; the contemporary importance of the problem of man's freedom stems from the movement of philosophical minds, such as Origen's, into a religious context which stresses the relation between a creating, ordaining God and all rational beings. Origen's philosophical background makes him sense that rational independence for man depends upon establishing some form of freedom of the will as the basis of independence from God's action. Such independence also solves the theological problem of God's responsibility for sin, which the religious doctrine stresses; and the result is to give to the question of freedom of the will a place of new importance for all succeeding philosophy.—*F.S.*

PERTINENT LITERATURE

Kerr, H. T. *The First Systematic Theologian*. Princeton, New Jersey: Princeton Theological Seminary, 1958.

It is H. T. Kerr's contention that Origen was the first to offer a systematic account of Christian theology. His intent is to show that Christianity was not refuted by the objections placed against it by pagan thinkers, but provided a coherent, intellectually respectable view of the world.

Kerr notes that Origen has been both eulogized and condemned for his efforts. Some have viewed him as the most learned biblical scholar of antiquity and a great biblical and philosophical theologian; others have viewed him as a heretic. Origen lived in a time of deep intellectual conflict between systems of non-Christian and psuedo-Christian thought. Without the benefit of theological precedent, he was a pivotal figure in this debate. Given the historical conditions in which he worked, Kerr suggests, it is not surprising that there has been sharp controversy over the orthodoxy and the value of Origen's thought.

Origen spent the first half of his life in Alexandria, where three religious and philosophical schools of thought were influential. Philo, Plotinus, and Basilides, respectively, represented Hellenistic Judaism, Neoplatonism, and Gnosticism. Christian thought came into contact and conflict with each of these viewpoints, and Origen reacted to each of them. They all tended to be syncretistic, emphasizing common ground and downplaying differences. To some extent this was also true of Alexandrian Christianity and of Origen's thought. Thus Kerr sees Origen endeavoring to make use of elements from each of these viewpoints without sacrificing the uniqueness of Christianity.

Kerr discusses Origen's hermeneutics, noting that Origen shared with Philo the tactic of interpreting the Bible allegorically. While he developed rules by which illegitimate allegorizing could be identified and rejected, his critics charged that by his methods one could make the Scriptures say anything. In any case, allegorization of the Scriptures was Origen's method, according to Kerr, for dealing with Jewish and Greek critics.

With respect to Neoplatonism and Gnosticism, Kerr suggests that Origen's strategy was to use Greek philosophy to show that Christianity was different from and superior to the competing philosophies. The result Kerr describes as a typically Alexandrian mixture of Judeo-Hellenistic monotheism, Gnostic dualism, and Neoplatonic cosmology. Alexandrian thought revolved around the themes of God and creation, humanity and the world, and the path to salvation. Between God and the world, including humanity, a great gulf is fixed. The basic Alexandrian problem was to determine how, exactly, God and the nondivine are related and in what human salvation consists and how it is to be obtained. Fundamentally, Kerr concludes, there was a cosmological question (could God be the creator of a material world containing evil?) and a soteriological question (how can one be delivered from this world?).

Kerr notes that Origen's *De Principiis* is divided into four sections which roughly correspond with these topics: God, the world, humanity, and the Scriptures (Alexandrian topics, except for the last). He also notes some problems concerning the text. The only complete edition we have of it is in a Latin translation prepared by Rufinus. Rufinus took great liberties with the text, as is revealed by comparing his text with the fragments of the Greek text that we have, and by the debate on this matter between Rufinus and Jerome. The translation, in effect, is a modified paraphrase. Besides textual changes caused by manuscript copying, and considering the fact that standards of literary exactness were lower then, there is the further fact that Rufinus was a supporter of Origen. In addition, Kerr continues, Origen's orthodoxy had become suspect, and it was widely accepted that heretics had placed heretical statements into his writings. So Rufinus took his translation task to also include an editing that would bring the text basically in line with orthodox perspective. In any case, Kerr contends, the *De Principiis* is not constructed with thorough systematic rigor, although there is some logical progression and simplicity of structure.

Kerr tells us that, for Origen, the source of knowledge of the good life is Christ—the Word of God who was with Moses and the prophets, and become Incarnate. The apostolic tradition, handed down in the church, presents for Origen a concensus of Christian conviction. This conviction is expressed in the *De Principiis* in terms of one God creating and ordering all things from nothing; whose only begotten Son, Christ Jesus, was actually born and really suffered and died for us, and rose from the dead; who is Trinitarian; who gave each soul not only substance and life, but also a rationality and freedom of its own; and who will reward each soul justly. Kerr's view is that in all of this Origen manifests his acceptance of and dependence on biblical doctrine.

Kerr adds that Origen views the task of interpreting the Bible allegorically as the apostolic method; and Origen says that the Bible contains "mysteries and the images of divine things," using a Neoplatonic phrase which he intends to provide with a Christian meaning.

Kerr notes that while Origen holds that God is incorporeal and noncomposite, and that the Son, although eternally begotten, is not an emanation from the Father, nor a creature who serves as a lesser deity whose lower status allows him to come into contact with matter, still a Greek fragment from the *De Principiis* says that Christ is "an image of God's goodness but not goodness itself." Kerr finds a similar ambivalence concerning the status of the Holy Spirit.

In Kerr's opinion, the *De Principiis* is particularly disappointing, not in what it says about, but by its neglect of, such topics as sin, grace, and reconciliation. Thus, Kerr maintains, while Origen is temporally first among Christian theologians, he did not succeed in providing a full and systematic treatment of Christian theology and left many gaps to be filled in by his successors.

Chadwick, Henry. *Early Christian Thought and the Classical Tradition: Studies in Justin, Clement, and Origen.* New York: Oxford University Press, 1966.

In this study (in Chapters 3 and 4) Henry Chadwick, Regius Professor of Divinity at Oxford University, places Origen's *De Principiis* in the context of his life and thought, summarizes its contents, and examines its presuppositions. According to one account, Origen's parents were Christians and his father became a martyr at Alexandria in A.D. 202. Eusebius, who offers this information, quotes from a letter from Origen's father to his son in which

Origen is encouraged to stand firm in his faith in his hour of trial. In another account, from the anti-Christian Porphyry, Origen was born and educated as a pagan. Chadwick notes that one can reconcile the accounts, if one wishes, by assuming that Origen's parents became converted from Paganism to Christianity sometime after Origen's birth. Further, Chadwick reports that, according to Porphyry, Origen studied under the eclectic Platonist Ammonius Saccas, with whom Plotinus also studied.

In any case, Chadwick tells us, Origen's writings show acquaintance with the works of Plato and the Stoic philosopher Chrysippus (died 206 B.C.), together with a knowledge of the Greek philosophical schools. Origen taught grammar, and then he became a catechist or teacher of converts who desired baptism and required instruction prior to their reception of the rite. In his role as catechist, Origen came to assign the less advanced students to an assistant and to take the more advanced ones himself. At this period of his life (around A.D. 212), Chadwick reports, Origen constructed a synopsis of the Old Testament, using the Hebrew version, adding a transliteration thereof into Greek characters, then adding the standard Greek version used by the churches (the Septuagint), with various other translations. This synopsis, or *Hexapala*, Chadwick explains, was designed for use in debates with Jewish rabbis, who would recognize the authority of the Hebrew text only. Chadwick adds that the *Hexapala* also illustrates Origen's own concern for exposition of the text of the Bible, a concern reflected in the fact that the bulk of his writings consisted of exegetical sermons preached to his congregations, together with commentaries and brief notes on particular texts.

According to Chadwick, Origen combined a concern for the correct interpretation of the biblical text with a desire to find harmony between Christianity and the teachings of Plato, to refute gnostic dualism and determinism, and to articulate a hermeneutic, or set of rules for correct biblical interpretation. One thing these enterprises required, Chadwick notes, was a general statement of Christian doctrine. This was the intent of *De Principiis*; systematic in the sense of trying to state a coherent contrastive view to gnostic thought it is nevertheless an exploratory volume. In it, Chadwick finds, Origen at times reviews alternatives which are open to a Christian without opting for any one view himself. While its first four words are reminiscent of Plato's *Gorgias*, Chadwick maintains that it is not an attempt to synthesize Platonism and Christianity. Instead, he finds it to be a polemic against gnostic doctrines which tries to incorporate whatever positive elements it sees in its object of attack.

Chadwick tells us that in his Preface to *De Principiis* Origen comments that while the Apostles taught clear doctrine which must be accepted by anyone claiming to be a Christian, they often did not state any reasons for the doctrine they taught; and the apostolic doctrine, moreover, is not decisive on various important theological issues. Hence, by way of both rationale and specificity, one may go beyond the apostolic doctrine. Further, Chadwick adds, it was Origen's opinion that where apostolic doctrine has nothing to say, or requires no particular view, the Christian theologian may develop views as seems best.

Chadwick, in an extended summary, explains that the core Christian doctrines are these, according to Origen: one God created the world from nothing, being just and good, and the author of both biblical testaments. Jesus Christ is God's son, who existed prior to his virgin birth, crucifixion, resurrection, and ascension to heaven. The Holy Spirit may or may not have been created, but is of the same rank as the Son: he inspired the biblical authors. The human spirit will go to Heaven or Hell and the dead will rise. How exactly the spirit comes to be embodied is not known. Human beings have freedom of will. There is a Devil, whom most Christians take to be a fallen angel; and there are other angels. The physical world was created at some time and will dissolve at another time. What preceded it, what will succeed it, how angels came to be, is all obscure. The literal, historical sense of a Scriptural text is not its deepest meaning. The task of eliciting the meaning of a text is left to the interpreter; there is no inspired hermeneutic to assist the interpreter of the inspired text. Whether God, and whether human spirits, have some shape or are in some fashion material, is not completely ruled out; nor is the existence of guardian angels or of souls which are embodied in sun, moon, or star.

In contrast to Irenaeus, Chadwick maintains, Origen was quite content that one speculate about matters not set out in the apostolic rule of faith. According to Origen, the limits of human speculative inquiry need not be set at the boundaries of biblical teaching. Still, rational inquiry is not sufficient for knowledge of God. Chadwick adds that Origen claims that God is the uncaused cause, the nonmaterial ground, of everything that exists. Creation stems from an overflow of divine goodness. The initial object of creation is the production of unembodied spirits. As God has always existed, and been good, so unembodied spirits have always existed.

In this aspect of his thought, Chadwick finds, Origen is close to thinkers who have viewed creation as emanation, a sort of overflow of God's existence. Nevertheless, he holds that divine creation is free; God has no needs and is under no necessity to create. That nondivine things exist is not necessitated by God's nature. For if God's nature in some fashion necessarily caused things other than himself to exist, then that God exists would entail that nondivine things exist; and thus that nondivine things not exist would entail that God himself not exist. This position Origen rejects. The dependence of things upon God is one-way, or asymmetrical. Rational, spiritual beings—unembodied spirits—are thus everlasting but dependent.

In this way, Chadwick says, Origen attempts to combine the Christian doctrine of a free creation by God of items dependent on him for their existence, and the Neoplatonic view that God, as perfect, must be changeless.

That dependence without beginning or end relate each creature to God is intended to allow creation from nothing, which might not have occurred, to occur in such a way that God never changes. One theological consequence of this motif, Chadwick remarks, is that the Son is viewed as everlastingly generated by, and so everlastingly subordinated to, the Father.

Chadwick adds that for Origen unembodied spirits who make wrong free choices become embodied as their punishment—spirit (*nous*) thus becomes soul (*psyche*). He tells us that for Origen a soul, or embodied spirit, is located on the chain of being below a pure, or unembodied, spirit, and the assortment of goods and evils that occur in a given human life reflect the moral desert of that person in terms of his or her choices while unembodied. The result is a chain of being from angels through human beings to demons which is created not by sheer divine fiat but by free choice. Each member of the chain bears its own responsibility for its location in the chain.

While Origen holds that becoming embodied is, so to speak, a step down for a spirit, Chadwick emphasizes that this is not, for Origen, because matter is inherently evil since God creates matter from nothing (not out of some previously existing stuff). Origen considers the possibility that matter is eternal and will be transformed in the resurrection, that the material will at some time be entirely destroyed, and that material bodies may be created only as necessary for the education of souls on their way back to being spirits, without deciding between these options. Still, Chadwick notes, Origen is not very enthusiastic about matter. One way in which this expresses itself, Chadwick remarks, is through Origen's view that while marriage is acceptable for Christians, celibacy is preferable.

In these (and other) ways, Chadwick sees Origen attempting to express Christian theology in terms of what he found attractive in his cultural and intellectual environment, Chadwick suggests that Origen was probably not fully successful in this enterprise, although he pursued it with genius and unstinting labor.—*K.E.Y.*

ADDITIONAL RECOMMENDED READING

Cross, F. L. ed. *The Oxford Dictionary of the Christian Church*. London: Oxford University Press, 1958. A standard reference work.

Harnack, Adolf. *History of Dogma*. New York: Dover Publications, 1961.

Kelly, J. N. D. *Early Christian Doctrines*. New York: Harper & Row Publishers, 1959. A more recent work, briefer than Harnack's and first-rate.

Pelikan, Jaroslav. *The Christian Tradition: A History of the Development of Doctrine*. Vol. I. Chicago: University of Chicago Press, 1971. The first volume of a felicitously written history of doctrine, destined to become a classic.

Schaff, Philip. *History of the Christian Church*. Grand Rapids, Michigan:

Eerdmans, 1955. The standard history of the Christian Church for years, and still valuable.

Seeberg, R. *Textbook of the History of Doctrines*. Translated by Charles E. Hay. Grand Rapids, Michigan: Baker, 1966. A recent and much-used text on the history of doctrine.

ENNEADS

Author: Plotinus (c. 204-c. 270)
Type of work: Metaphysics
First transcribed: c. 256

PRINCIPAL IDEAS ADVANCED

Reality is one, and the source of all being is the One, the Divine Unity.
From the One emanates the Divine Mind (Nous), *the Intellectual-Principle.*
The Divine Mind, in turn, spends the creative force of the One in giving rise to the Divine Soul.
The One, Nous, *and the Soul make up the Divine Trinity.*
While lost in the contemplation of the One, the Soul desires to return to its source of being, but in turning away from the One, it creates a lower (and hence, less perfect) order of souls and material objects by forming matter according to the Ideas of the Intellectual-Principle.

Only in recent years has the full importance of Plotinus been widely recognized. Previously, Neoplatonism, of which Plotinus is the greatest representative, and Platonism had not been clearly distinguished. Lacking the original writings to compare, the Middle Ages blended the two forms of thought together without a clear notion of their distinctive qualities. Historical research and the availability of the sources themselves have produced a growing awareness of the distinctiveness of Plotinus' thought and of his unique contributions in the *Enneads.* Its intimate connection with the Platonic tradition is readily admitted by Plotinus himself, but such closeness in origin need not mean similarity, as Plato's famous student Aristotle made clear.

In a strict sense the *Enneads* are unsystematic. Neither Porphyry's ordering of the scattered writings nor scholarly reconstruction of possible temporal sequence can make the writings form any strictly logical order. Plotinus discussed with his students a few very central philosophical problems, each of which he returned to many times, and the *Enneads* represent in content but not in form the consistency of this continual development of certain central themes.

Plotinus' metaphysical interest in the problems of the one and the many is well known, but his central interest in ethics and his fully developed aesthetic theory, which is one of the first to be elaborated, are not always so widely recognized. Most important of all, however, are Plotinus' explorations into philosophical psychology. The soul is central in all Plotinian thought, and he was the first major writer to put the analysis of the soul at the center of philosophical investigation.

The soul in Plato's world held an important place, and Plato devoted considerable time to describing it (in the *Republic* and the *Phaedrus).* Yet somehow "soul" was never reconciled with "form" as a metaphysical principle. Plotinus began where Plato left off, making soul central; and the analysis of it is more direct and extended than Plato's mythical framework could allow. Despite the importance of Plato both as to the problems Plotinus treated and as to style, what many are surprised to find upon reading Plotinus is the large amount of Aristotelianism present, as well as a wide variety of other views. In some sense, Plotinus began with Platonic problems, but his scope takes in almost all previous philosophy.

Just as Plato had a strong interest in sense perception, so also Plotinus was led by the problems of sense perception to consider the soul as of first importance. Soul is intimately related to the body and clearly is combined with it. After considering most known theories of the soul, Plotinus went on to make the soul more perfect than the body in virtue of the soul's greater unity. Soul centralizes perception and is not subject to physical division as the body is.

In Plotinus' philosophy, sensation is only the beginning of knowledge. Above that stands the soul's grasp of intelligible forms. Sensation is dependent upon the soul's close association with a physical body; but, since the soul in virtue of its greater unity stands higher in the order of being than the body, its grasp of intelligible form indicates that something in turn stands above it in the ontological order. This is the Intellectual-Principle, the locus of the intelligible forms of all things and of the principle of thought itself. This principle, which is superior to the soul, is often called the Divine Mind, since it exemplifies the union of universal thought with all of the intelligible forms of thought. This is a level of unity which exceeds that possessed by the soul, just as the soul surpasses that of the physical world.

Physical body, as it looks away from soul's guidance, tends to become sheer disorganized matter; on the other hand, as the body is subject to the soul's direction, it exemplifies harmony and order to the highest degree possible for it. As the soul's attention is absorbed by physical matter, it tends to forget itself and to be overcome with sensual desires; it goes out of itself seeking a multitude of things. But when the soul considers the Intellectual-Principle above it, then it tends to be drawn away from physical concerns and to regain its original and essential integrity, absorbed in contemplation.

The Intellectual-Principle when considered in relation to soul appears as the rational structure of our world order, but in itself it is sheer intellection, involved with no motion or change and retaining no distinction except that between thought and object. All, then, has been hierarchically arranged in the Plotinian metaphysical scheme, beginning with the soul and ascending and descending according to the degree of unity. As far removed from the multiplicity of the physical world as the Intellectual-Principle is, it still embodies the necessity of at least a distinction between thought and its object, as well as the distinctions between the various intellectual forms themselves.

Since unity has operated all along the way to delineate the various structures, Plotinus found himself driven to seek Unity itself, beyond even the division between thought and its object. Such a first principle Plotinus called the One (sometimes the Good), and it stands at the pinnacle of the hierarchy as Unity itself, from which all of the lower gradations of unity are in turn derived. These three central principles, One, Intellectual-Principle, and Soul (body is not given equal status), are nowhere simply defined, but they are refined through constant reference throughout the writings.

Evil was both a moral and a metaphysical problem for Plotinus. The deficiencies which the individual finds in this world are precisely what drove him to seek an order of existence higher than this world. Contrary to much popular opinion, Plotinus did not despise this world. Rather, he regarded the world as the fullest expression of beauty above. The natural world holds all the perfection that its lower order allows, and as such it is the very embodiment and evidence of that from which it descends, its higher origin. Yet this is not necessarily a temporal origin, since Plotinus never questioned the fact that the world is eternal. It is "origin" in the sense of the dependence of the lower orders upon the higher for the power of their existence.

Metaphysically speaking, evil was difficult for Plotinus. Since all must be accounted for by means of one principle which is without defect, the problem is to show how what is essentially perfect can eventually become bad. Plotinus did this through the image of gradually diminishing light and through increasing multiplicity. What is in itself One and perfect (the Divine Unity) as it goes out from itself to create lower orders, becomes in the process increasingly multiple and less perfect, until its final outreach is sheer matter (the negative of being), its moral equivalent, evil.

But the process which leads down from the One to the creation of matter and evil also leads upward. The soul, by looking to itself and discovering its essentially higher nature through its essential difference from its body, grasps the basic distinction which can lead it away from matter toward matter's perfect and unitary source. Seeing the gradations of unity represented in the various levels, the soul may rise by intelligence to the intelligible world and then beyond it, at least momentarily, to the One beyond intellectual distinctions.

The description of the One itself, of course, was an even more difficult problem for Plotinus than accounting for matter and evil. No explanation of evil is ultimately possible in a world which is eternal and whose structure is necessary. But the description of the One is of necessity baffling, and both Plotinus and his interpreters have been painfully aware of this fact. The One as the first principle of all transcends all multiplicity and therefore all distinctions, whereas an intellectual grasp depends upon the presence of at least a minimum of distinction.

Thus, the One may be approached and may be grasped, but neither directly nor intellectually. Here the famous "negative method" comes to its fullest classical use. We may deny qualities inappropriately attributed to the One more easily than we can say what its characteristics are. Indirectly, from the process of denial and of paring away, we come to some grasp of the One, but this is not a discursive understanding. Such an apprehension does not induce conversation, and Plotinus said that if we are tempted to speak about the One, to give it a set of positive characteristics, then silence is more appropriate.

This difficulty leads to what is often called Plotinus' "mysticism." And if the term is used carefully, it is quite accurate as applied to the Plotinian view. Plotinus was not needlessly vague, and surely he did not belittle the powers of reason. Everything discerned is grasped through reason's light. Yet above reason's highest level stands a more ultimate realm, the source of intelligence and all below it, a realm not itself subject to the distinctions which reason requires for its operation. Not that the One is empty (such a thought must wait for a later time); the One is the source of all below it, containing the power of all but without itself being any single thing.

The ethical aims of Plotinus were high. Having devised this hierarchical scheme of the nature of things, each level determined by the multiplicity of its distance from the One, the goal then becomes to raise the soul in its considerations to the highest possible level. To do this, however, in some sense means that the knower must himself become the very level he contemplates. The soul ceases to be like the indefinite multiplicity below and actually becomes what it finds above it. Thus the soul tends not only to become good as it turns from matter and evil; it becomes godlike. Thus, the soul recovers the "essential man."

Beauty has a part in this conversion from the lower to the higher, and Plotinus here admitted his dependence on Plato's analysis of the use of beauty in the *Phaedrus*. The apprehension of beauty draws the soul upward, reminding it of its true self and of the higher levels open to it. Beauty represents purity, and the truly happy and virtuous life is not a thing of mixture; it is an unchanging state. By its nature beauty is present where a diversity has become a unity, which is why the pleasure derived from such beauty is itself essentially an unchanging state.

The whole process is not an easy one. It requires training and discipline. We must learn to cut away and to detach ourselves from multiple concerns. Not that they are in themselves bad or that beauty is not found in the multiplicity of the natural order, but the soul has become aware of something higher and more perfect that is possible to attain. Trained properly, the soul requires no guide for the last steps. The soul that wants the vision of beauty must first make itself beautiful through discipline and order. Action and effort are preparation for achieving a level beyond act. The Good, which is Plotinus' other name for the One, is self-sufficient, and through virtuous effort we also reach a level of essential rest.

Despite the absolute determinism of the natural structure as a whole which is eternal and without alternative, Plotinus still allowed for an area of freedom in human affairs. Some causation is due to environmental factors, but some causes originate from the soul, and this is the area of self-determination. Like Spinoza after him, Plotinus defined a free act as essentially one which springs from the individual's own nature, neither reflecting outside forces nor representing accidental features. It is the soul's clear vision of its own essential nature. Here the soul is guided by the Reason Principle above it, so that fate (freedom's opposite) prevails when action is contrary to reason. Thus Plotinus stands within the tradition: freedom means self-determination guided by rational apprehension of the structure of things.

In the Intellectual-Principle above the soul no spatial distinction can be found, no division, no incompleteness. It is a living intellection as one act within a unity, whereas the soul's intellection is a more multiple and temporal affair. In keeping with the classical idea of perfection, any widespread activity would represent defeat. The various ontological levels are thus characterized by a decreasing activity as well as by an increasing unity the nearer we move toward the One. Not that all activity is missing, but it here becomes fully realized activity.

The inequality within the natural world and the inequality of the various ontological orders all are necessary. They are, in fact, the best expression possible to the One. Gradations and completeness of every possible kind from highest to lowest, from best to worst, are the fullest expression possible for the One as the first principle of all things. Its fullness requires expression, and the widest possible variety actually expresses its perfection best. In this way Plotinus justified the presence of evil in a world which is essentially of good origin. Individual objects or events may be bad, but viewed as a part of the total panorama their place can be seen to be within a necessarily good order.

Following Plato's suggestion in the *Timaeus*, Plotinus developed the view that the natural order is like an organism. As unity "fissures out," it reaches out to the farthermost extent of things and yet embraces all in one system; but with all its differentiation it is still one organized living thing. Not everything can be equal; there must be levels from the highest to the lowest, but the overall scheme is that of the natural order as a living, self-sustaining organism.

In considering love, Plotinus made it clear that, once one has discovered the basic ontological levels and gained control over himself through discipline, there is no reason why the beauties of the natural order may not be enjoyed. Viewed properly as the descendants of yet higher orders, natural beauties may be instructive and are not to be shunned. The usual picture of Plotinus as an ascetic and as rejecting the everyday world is not accurate. One must study and discipline himself for metaphysical insight; but, although the levels above the soul are to be preferred, the natural world and human life are to be enjoyed fully as representing the best possible expression of those higher principles.

"Matter" is perhaps Plotinus' most pressing problem in his effort to see the natural order as good and as being the best expression of the One. Matter seems to be opaque and surd, and the very opposite of the light which represents the One. But Plotinus argued that, although matter is responsible for much evil and distortion, it is necessary to the One's essentially good production, since it furnishes a base for the imprinting of forms. Without matter the world would be insubstantial. Thus, despite its difficult properties, matter is necessary. As necessary to the order, it is in that sense good. This is not so much to explain matter as being in itself good as it is to account for it as necessary to the whole and as being good only in that indirect sense.

In accounting for time Plotinus foreshadows Augustine's famous discussion of time in the *Confessions*. The Intellectual-Principle is not temporal, although time lies, so to speak, self-concentrated there. Soul, on the other hand, must by nature move and produce, and thus soul's activity is the essential origin for time. This is not the soul perceived as a cosmic principle produced immediately by the Intellectual-Principle; this is soul as it turns away from its origin to produce physical structures below it. In the process of producing the other orders below it, soul clothes itself with time. If soul withdrew and turned itself entirely toward its primal unity, time would once again disappear.

Augustine's dependence upon Plotinus for his doctrine of time is one major illustration of the now recognized importance of Plotinus for all medieval philosophy and theology. Since Plato's own writings were unavailable, Plotinus was accepted as the representative of Platonism, with no distinction drawn between Platonism and Neoplatonism. Augustine's debt to Plotinus is heavy, as Augustine acknowledges. Through Plotinus the Neoplatonic strain became extremely influential, particularly since it formed such a natural background for the rapidly developing Christian doctrine. For instance, Plotinus' ontology is based on a trinitarian concept, although the doctrine developed by Christian theologians differs from it in detail.

Spinoza and Hegel are also much in Plotinus' debt, so that in this sense much modern thought is his heir. Wherever soul is stressed as a prime object of philosophical analysis, there is a strong kinship to Plotinus. Wherever reason is powerful but is ultimately to be transcended, there rational mysticism begins and owes a debt to Plotinus. Whenever men are urged to seek their authentic existence and to turn back from multiple pursuits, the philosophical psychology and the metaphysics of Plotinus are not far away.

Contrary to some popular opinion, Plato actually stressed the practical application of philosophy, together with the constant necessity to blend practical skill with philosophical insight. Plato had his moments as a visionary, but when we turn to Plotinus we find that the whole direction of thought is turned this way. Plato described his realm of forms in their perfection, but Plotinus' almost lyrical praise for the purity and repose of his Intellectual-Principle is unrestrained and unqualified. Toward this vision all thought bends, and it is not modified as it is for Plato by the necessity for return to the practical world. Plotinus knew that that vision cannot be sustained, but the return to the sense world is simply a necessity; it is never a goal.

Ethically, then, Plotinus had a single direction: upward and beyond this world's structure. But it would be false to say that this unrelieved goal involves a disparagement of the natural world. Plotinus did not disdain ordinary affairs. He loved nature, but only for what it could tell him about the source of all things and for the guidance it could provide for transcending it.

This is why the apprehension of beauty is such a stirring phenomenon for a Plotinian. Such experience is a taste here of the realm beyond being which the soul seeks. And the sense of beauty is a natural guide in detecting and in separating the higher from the lower orders within nature. Such a sensitivity to hierarchy is absolutely essential, since it is by establishing orders and levels that the mind is able to orient itself and to discern realms even beyond the natural order.

Thus the lover is very close to the philosopher, and philosophy's classical definition (the love of wisdom) fits Plotinus almost perfectly. Plato's *Phaedrus* is important here. Plotinus, like his revered predecessor, found in the phenomenon of love a philosophical key. The philosopher is stirred by love and moved by beauty; both of these experiences teach him to discern the higher from the lower in nature's sphere. Evil is not a question at this point. The natural tendency under the influence of beauty is away from evil's home (matter) and toward beauty's source, the intellectual sphere.

In a rationalistic age, we tend to think of all structures as basically the same and as subject to the same general conditions. Plato described a world of forms different from our world, but Plotinus carried this transcendental tendency much further. In the ascent which the apprehension of beauty has launched, what we soon discover is that each level has laws of its own, until we come finally to the One itself, where even the law of identity does not hold. Below this the Intellectual-Principle has been found to be free of all distinctions, whereas division and partition are the essential elements of every lower order. To learn to read Plotinus is to stretch the mind's natural habits and to learn to think and visualize in new ways. Contrast is the proper method: bodies are exclusively many; the Supreme is exclusively one.

In some genuine sense Plotinus was an evolutionist. That is, since his theory was based upon levels each of which is different in kind from the others, his primary task was to explain how the levels are related; that is, how each lower order came from a higher principle. Plotinus' theory differs from modern evolutionary theory in that this succession is not a temporal affair. The world and all its orders were, for Plotinus, eternal. But each order is derived constantly from its superior, so that if each ontological realm exhibits basically different properties, then an evolutionary theory is required to show how something generated by one level can become unlike its origin in kind. This is also the modern evolutionist's problem.

In some sense this continual attempt to trace the evolutionary cycle, now upward, now downward, is the substance of much of the *Enneads*. Beginning with the soul, Plotinus tried to explain how it could generate something different and inferior to it—physical body. Then the movement of the discourse turns upward to account for the soul's generation by the Intellectual-Principle. Finally, we reach the One, the logical terminus which the delineation of the various realms below requires.

What the modern reader gains from Plotinus is a feeling for the necessary dialectical movement between qualitatively different realms. This constant passage from the One to the Intellectual-Principle and then to the soul takes place all the while a multitude of traditional ethical and epistemological questions are being discussed. Yet, underneath this constant recovering of old ground, the picture of the Plotinian world gradually emerges crystal clear. The reader begins to see how, within such a framework as Plotinus has constructed, Plotinus could hope to deal with practical questions successfully.

In a basic sense, the Plotinian view is a contemplative one, although for reasons already explained it is incorrect to infer from this any aversion to everyday life. In addition to his contemplative quality, Plotinus was surely also speculative. He did not claim to know his doctrines with finality, but he attempted an answer to all of philosophy's most fundamental and comprehensive problems. The scope is breathtaking; and, even in an age not given to the grander views, to grasp what Plotinus saw is still an exhilarating experience that gives life and energy to the philosophical quest.—*F.S.*

PERTINENT LITERATURE
Bréhier, Émile. *The Philosophy of Plotinus*. Translated by Joseph Thomas. Chicago: University of Chicago Press, 1958.

Modern scholars agree in recognizing two perspectives in the *Enneads*: a religious concern for the destiny of the soul and a philosophical need to understand the universe. They differ on where to place the emphasis. Émile Bréhier gives the religious interest priority, but without neglecting the demands of the understanding. Indeed, as he interprets the work, Plotinus' fundamental problem was the perennial one: Can life have meaning in a world determined by intelligible causes? Bréhier reminds his readers that Plotinus took over the architecture of his system from contemporary Neoplatonism, and that the theory of three hypostases was for him a given, much as the theory of evolution was for nineteenth century philosophers of religion. What is of interest, he says, is not the architecture so much as the problems which it posed for a thinker determined to preserve the validity of man's sense of alienation and of the intimations of bliss afforded in moments of ecstasy.

Describing, as he does at some length, the religious milieu of third century Alexandria and Rome, Bréhier uses the story of Ulysses to illustrate the widespread assumption that the human soul is a wanderer seeking its homeland. He points out, however, the difference between the beliefs of popular sacrificial cults, with their mediators, and those of contemplatives who, like Plotinus, sought salvation by means of ascesis and recollection. At the basis of this difference lay the conviction held by the latter that the world order is fixed from eternity. Accepting contemporary astronomical theories, based on regularity and periodicity, they looked for no alteration in the established order, but sought instead to discover a fundamental affinity between the world and man.

A clue to Plotinus' solution is already given in the notion of contemplation, taken not merely as the occupation of the sage but as the nature of reality. Contemplation differs from both sensation and discursive reason. The multiple movements in a dance figure, for example, are apprehended by sight, but their living unity is grasped by the contemplative mind, which, while apprehending the dancer's intention, loses nothing of the richness of the sensations. So with everything in the corporeal world, which reveals itself to contemplation because it is the product of contemplation. Only thought is real, whether at the highest level where thought and its object are identical, or at lower levels down to and including sensible objects.

Plotinus was receptive to the teachings of Plato, and to a lesser extent to those of Aristotle and the Middle Stoics. But, according to Bréhier, there are new elements in his philosophy which make him the forerunner of idealism in the West. For a historian, the question arises: What is the nature and source of those of Plotinus' ideas which did not originate in Greek philosophy?—in other words, the question of the "orientalism of Plotinus." Was Plotinus acquainted with the *Upanishads* and other Indian writings? Bréhier quotes from these at some length and owns himself convinced. "With Plotinus, then, we lay hold of the first link in a religious tradition which is no less powerful basically in the West than the Christian tradition, although it does not manifest itself in the same way. I believe that this tradition comes from India."

Bréhier's book originated as a course of lectures delivered at the Sorbonne in 1921-1922. It differs from most recent books on Plotinus in that it was composed for nonspecialists and also in the zest with which its author pursues his thesis. Notwithstanding all that has been written since, it is still a good book with which to begin one's study of Plotinus.

Armstrong, A. H. *The Architecture of the Intelligible Universe in the Phi-*

losophy of Plotinus. Cambridge: Cambridge University Press, 1940.

Émile Bréhier several times speaks of the architecture of the hypostases, but always to minimize its importance for understanding Plotinus' thought. A. H. Armstrong tries to show that Plotinus' originality lies precisely in the way he modified this conventional design. The book is skeletal, not in the sense of being an outline but in the sense that it leaves out a great deal and concentrates on the main metaphysical questions. The book is divided into three sections: the One, the Intellectual Principle (*Nous*), and Soul.

Armstrong's main contention is that the problems which Plotinus faced were generated by conflicts inherent in the Greek tradition, and that his solutions were drawn from the same source. While admitting that something of the spirit of Indian philosophy seems to be reflected in the *Enneads*, he finds no evidence of direct influence. Unlike many of Plotinus' interpreters, Armstrong is willing to acknowledge the limitations of the Plotinian theory, and he suggests that the study of approximations of his doctrine in previous Greek philosophy makes these limitations intelligible.

Armstrong's method is to focus on ambiguities and inconsistencies in the system—he speaks of testing its joints. His treatment of the One will serve as an example. The first two chapters of this section deal respectively with what he calls the positive and the negative conceptions of the One; not that Plotinus so distinguished them but that they are distinguishable to one who approaches his philosophy in the context of Helenic philosophy. The third chapter, "The One and Spiritual Life," points out the original element in Plotinus' apprehension of the One: namely, his passionate devotion to the Supreme; and he mentions antecedents in Greek thought, notably the Hymn to Zeus by the Stoic Cleanthes.

Central to Armstrong's discussion is his discussion of the term "negative theology," used to designate man's knowledge of the One. Superficially the term asserts the transcendence of the Supreme Principle by denying that its nature can be expressed; but analysis reveals three distinct "roads of negation," each of which leads to a different conception of the Supreme. First is the negative theology of the Pythagorean and Parmenidean tradition, which posits an abstract epistemological and mathematico-metaphysical unity, detached from ethical and religious considerations. Second is the negative theology of positive transcendence, which views the One as the primary reality from which all else proceeds. It is called nonbeing "only because its reality cannot be adequately expressed in terms of the realities that we know." In this aspect the One is properly the object of devotion. Third is the negative theology of the Infinite subject or self, according to which the distinction between subject and object is dissolved and knowledge in the ordinary sense of the word disappears. This last form of negative theology is the one that has suggested oriental borrowing. Armstrong, however, argues that the materials for a theory of the Infinite self are present in the works of Aristotle. In Armstrong's opinion, the three theologies are all present in Plotinus but cannot be reconciled, and he holds that of the three it is the theology of positive transcendence that is implied in his doctrine of emanation and in those passages in which the distinctions between the One, the Intellectual Principle, and Soul are understood as permanent features of reality which are not negated in any mystical trance.

Armstrong does not deny that Plotinus' mystical experience gave vitality to his thought, but he points to the dangers that come from making this experience the basis for metaphysical claims. Two features of the mystical moment are, he says, likely to be confused: one is the simplicity of the experience, in which the consciousness of difference is swallowed up; the other is the sense of transcendence, which carries the conviction that nothing else has any worth. But whatever the significance of the experience, it must, says Armstrong, be taken (as indeed it was taken by Plotinus) as momentary and exceptional, if it is not to dissolve the fabric of philosophy.

Rist, J. M. *Plotinus: The Road to Reality*. Cambridge: Cambridge University Press, 1967.

Although the title might suggest that J. M. Rist's book is an introductory sketch with inspirational overtones, the author warns that it is intended for students far enough advanced to be interested in a detailed discussion of "certain problems in Plotinus' thought." The chapters are separate studies, some of them apparently written as occasional papers. Each deals with a problem arising out of the current literature; but in resolving the problems the author is less concerned with the literature than with passages from the *Enneads* bearing upon them, which he cites at length and attempts to harmonize. A full index of these passages makes the book useful as a commentary.

If there is any doctrinal tendency in Rist's book, it is to emphasize those of Plotinus' sayings which break out of the Hellenic mold and accord with the more personalist and individualist pattern of Judeo-Christian thought. Without underestimating the gulf between Plotinus' One and the other hypostases, Rist reminds us that Plotinus had a great deal to say about the Unspeakable, that he found "traces" of the One throughout the world and, in effect, based his metaphysics on analogical reasoning. Indeed, in contrast to the paradoxical teaching that the One does not "exist," Rist reads Plotinus as saying that the One is "a different kind of being from finite beings, that is, he is infinite being." In somewhat the same way Rist finds evidence to show that the One has knowledge of itself, although knowledge which, because it does not entail duality, cannot be described in finite terms.

Rist finds fault with the traditional view that the process of emanation is "a necessary, unconscious reflex of its primary activity of contemplation." In contrast to Plato, says the author, Plotinus spoke of the One as the maker or creator of everything, of matter as well as of forms. Moreover, Rist maintains that for Plotinus the One is free in the sense of "willing to be what he is," so that even if emanation follows by a kind of necessity from the One's nature, it will be "an act of a kind of free will."

It is usual to regard Plotinus as inconsistent in his teachings concerning matter and evil. Rist's opinion is that there is more consistency than is generally admitted. This appears, he says, if one keeps clear the distinction between the World Soul and the individual souls; for although both are said to descend toward the world of matter, only individual souls are said to be tainted by the contact with matter. Partly the taint is owing to the constitution of individual souls which, experiencing sensations and emotions, are confronted (as the World Soul is not) with the necessity of making choices; but partly it is due to the fact that matter, as sheer negativity, corrupts, by its lack of reality, whatever comes into contact with it.

The problem of man's nature and destiny comes up in several contexts. In a chapter on the sensible object, Rist discusses the problem of the empirical individual, the relation between the Socrates familiar to the Athenians and the personality (or reason-principle) of Socrates, and the further relation in the divine Intellectual Principle between the idea of Socrates and the idea of man. In further chapters on free will and on happiness he deals with the distinction between the higher and lower parts of the soul and with Plotinus' claim that the former resides eternally in the divine Intellectual Principle while the latter is active in the material world. Because most people are unconscious of the activity of the soul's higher part, Plotinus counseled neglect of temporal affairs, both one's own and those of one's fellows. But, says Rist, Plotinus' behavior suggests that he thought himself able to preserve the higher consciousness while active on the lower plane.

In his chapter on mysticism, Rist takes a typological approach, distinguishing monistic and theistic interpretations of the unitive act. In his judgment, Plotinus belongs to the latter type, according to which the soul is surrendered to God but does not lose its identity; nor, according to this view, is the multiplicity of the world held to be an illusion. Thus, Rist rejects Émile Bréhier's attempt to base Plotinus' teaching on Indian sources, citing the orientalist Olivier Lacombe, who denies that anything comparable to the saying, "I am Brahman," can be found in the *Enneads*, "in which the sentiment of the transcendence of the One appears more emphatically."—*J.F.*

ADDITIONAL RECOMMENDED READING

Armstrong, A. H., ed. "Plotinus," in *The Cambridge History of Later Greek and Early Medieval Philosophy*. Cambridge: Cambridge University Press, 1967, pp. 195-268. A review of Plotinus' life and times followed by a discussion of central themes of his philosophy: the One, Intellect, the soul, matter.

Henry, Paul, S. J. Introduction: "Plotinus' Place in the History of Thought," in Plotinus' *The Enneads*. Translated by Stephen MacKenna. London: Faber and Faber, 1942. Useful especially for its study of the vocabulary of Plotinus' mysticism.

Inge, W. R. *The Philosophy of Plotinus*. London: Longmans, Green and Company, 1929. More valuable on the philosophy of religion than on philosophy in general. A standard work.

Lovejoy, Arthur O. *The Great Chain of Being*. Cambridge, Massachusetts: Harvard University Press, 1936. Concerned mainly with the influence of Plotinus' doctrine of the plenitude of being on Western thought.

Merlan, Philip. "Plotinus," in *The Encyclopedia of Philosophy*. Edited by Paul Edwards. Vol. VI. New York: Macmillan Publishing Company, 1967, pp. 351-359. Excellent introduction by a leading authority on Hellenistic philosophy.

Whittaker, Thomas. *The Neoplatonists*. Cambridge: Cambridge University Press, 1928. A history of the entire school. Chapter V, "The Philosophical System of Plotinus," treats his psychology, metaphysics, cosmology, aesthetics, and ethics.

CONFESSIONS

Author: Saint Augustine (Aurelius Augustinus, 354-430)
Type of work: Theology, metaphysics (religious autobiography)
First transcribed: c. 397

PRINCIPAL IDEAS ADVANCED

How can an eternal God be the cause of anything evil?

God is not the cause of evil, for evil has no genuine existence; evil is the absence of the good, the corruption of possibilities, as in the human will.

Only the parts of creation, not the whole, can partake of evil, the privation of the good.

By faith the corruption of the human will is cured.

The question as to what God was doing before he created the world is a senseless question, since "before" the creation would make sense only if God had not created time; God's creative acts are not in time.

The greatest theologian of the disintegrating ancient Roman world, St. Augustine, came to Christian faith partly "from the outside" after a trying spiritual and intellectual pilgrimage. His *Confessions* recounts episodes from a restless life finally blessed by religious peace and certainty. The work opens and closes with ardent praise for God's goodness and mercy. This unique literary classic constitutes a kind of autobiography whose details achieve significance only in the focus of a deeply experienced conversion. After the conversion everything is seen from a new perspective.

The book is the first and most universally read of its special kind of literature. Examples of this type of literature in the modern world are probably best found in aspects of the novel and in straightforward autobiographies. No other Christian writing of its kind has so influenced despairing persons or suggested so wide a range of psychological insights into the human quest after religious meaning in existence. Augustine writes of guilt and forgiveness from the vantage point of one who, threatened by the apparent worthlessness of life and haunted by a terrifying realization of the nature of human egoism, overcomes anxiety through a self-authenticating faith in the Christ of the Cross. In a world of chaos and impending destruction this faith speaks out joyously and compellingly in the *Confessions*.

The psychology of human belief is such that, given any series of experiences, men can reinterpret the significance of any of the earlier items in the light of any later ones. Likewise, men can judge the significance of any later experience in terms of an earlier one. Men's judgments about what is important in their experiences need not follow a simple chronological ordering. Augustine writes like a man who obviously judges that an item in his experience is not only centrally crucial but, in some sense, is finally so. He reports this conversion experience in Book VIII of his *Confessions*. The significance of all items of his experience is to be decided in relation to his achievement of God's "grace"; but *that* experience is final, self authenticating and in principle beyond any possibility of doubt or reinterpretation. That experience is the standard measure of value. Consequently, Augustine's conversion to the Christian faith leads him to reconsider even selected aspects of his earlier life in its light. Among these are his childhood sins including a youthful theft of some pears; his strong sexual appetites which involved him with concubines and produced an illegitimate son; his philosophical "errors" prior to the discovery of his Christian "truth"; and his relations with a beloved Christian mother and half-pagan father.

The *Confessions* includes confidential admissions of a man who seems preoccupied with the problem of human guilt, even inordinately so. Augustine's association of Christian faith with sexual abstinence explains the extent of his guilt feelings though, of course, it does not explain the Christian emphasis on asceticism. So difficult and austere a standard of human conduct, once applied in human practice, may well cause even earlier slight transgressions to appear momentous. Such reasoning may well enable an unsympathetic reader to understand Augustine's otherwise puzzling concern about a childish theft of pears. Given a Christian belief in the basic sinfulness of human acts, even seemingly trivial actions may take on great personal significance—since formerly trivial items making up a great part of a man's personal life will be those very ones over which a convinced Christian will think he should have control. It is as if Augustine wants to say to his readers following his conversion: How sinful man really is may be learned from an examination of seemingly unimportant acts of mine, including those of my childhood.

Two major currents dominate the predominately autobiographical books of the *Confessions* (Books I through IX). One current is an apologetic account of Augustine's intellectual search after comprehension or wisdom among some of the important "schools" popular in fourth century Roman civilization. The other is a current of continuous intellectual rootlessness—a sense of "being taken in" by a philosophical position which proves only temporarily satisfying. There is a description of the reasoned effort to understand the meaning of human existence in philosophical terms which goes side by side with the experienced failure of each tentatively grasped solution. The certainty for which Augustine thirsts is not, we soon learn, to be found in philosophy alone. Faith, and only Christian faith, is able to bring certainty, but the intellectual restlessness continues even after conversion. This restlessness receives serious attention in the contents of Books X through XIII. Nonetheless, even the philosophical quest has altered. Where previously faith was to be judged by reason, now reason is to be employed in a context involving faith.

Augustine's intellectual and spiritual quest lasted from his nineteenth until his thirty-third year. At that age he experienced total conversion to Christianity. He tells how, reading from Cicero, he earlier became interested in religious issues and even turned to the Scriptures without understanding; he "was not such as could enter into it, or stoop my neck to follow its steps." He turned next to the astrologers, hoping in some material mode to discover deity. In the process he became obsessed by the problem of evil.

Teacher of rhetoric, he came to Carthage and, while "for this space of nine years . . . we lived seduced and seducing, deceived and deceiving in divers lusts," sought intellectual clarification among the Manichees, a group of men who thought a kind of divine knowledge was possible. He became disillusioned by a Manichee spokesman, who proved unable to put some of Augustine's doubts to rest and was judged adversely by the seeker. From Carthage, Augustine traveled to Rome. He did this against his mother's entreaties. In Rome he was temporarily attracted to the philosophical Academics, whose chief ability was criticism and whose philosophical tenets tended toward skepticism. Still concerned about evil—which he thought of as a kind of substance—Augustine became a catechumen in the Catholic Church. Moving to Milan, where he was at last joined by his mother, and continuing to live with the concubine who bore him a son, Augustine worried about evil, became attracted to the Platonic philosophers who sensed the ultimate unity of Being, heard St. Ambrose preach, and after a trying emotional episode was converted to Christianity.

The remainder of the *Confessions* is devoted to discussions of specific religious and philosophical topics. Three problems dominate the later books. One is the problem of evil, which had proved such a stumbling block to Augustine's acceptance of the Christian faith. Two others are time and memory, discussed in Books X and XI, respectively. Divorced from the autobiographical nature of the earlier books, Books X through XIII contain some of the most significant of Augustine's intellectual reflections. These books indicate the extensiveness of Augustine's intellectual questioning following his emotional conversion. These books also discuss the biblical notion of the creation of the world, as well as the ways in which Scripture may be interpreted. Only Augustine's treatments of evil, time, and memory can receive consideration in the remainder of this analysis.

Because the Christian faith requires beliefs which do not always seem to meet the demands of reason, Augustine's anguished effort to understand the origin and nature of evil proved a persistent one. His first step involved denying the Manichean dualism which made God finite and evil an objective reality. If evil were real, then God as the cause of all created things would have to contain positive evil. Intellectually, a part of Augustine's development here resulted from his reading of Platonist writers. God is to be viewed as eternal rather than as infinite. Therefore, no spatial or temporal being could be God. Yet the problem of evil remained. How can an eternal God as creator of a temporal-spatial order produce anything evil? The demands of the Christian faith permitted only one solution—the denial that evil is a substance, a genuinely objective existent.

Augustine later confesses: "And I sought 'whence is evil,' and sought in an evil way; and saw not the evil in my very search." There can be no positive evil in the world, according to Augustine's final position on the matter. There is corruption, of course. This includes the corruption of man's will. Yet the perversion of the human will is a human responsibility. God cannot be seen as the cause of such perversion. Corruption is rather the absence of good, a privation and a lack rather than a positively existing thing. It is the failure of parts of the system of Creation to harmonize for which God is not causally responsible. It is doubtful that Augustine's "solution" of the problem of evil is a clearly rational one. Rather it seems to follow from the need of faith to discover a satisfactory position which will not involve denial of God's immutability. Whatever has been caused by God to exist must be good. Evil cannot therefore possess a positive existence. It must be treated as an absence of positive goodness. Because God is a creator—though not of a universe *in* time, since there could have been no time prior to the world's existence—his immutability and absolute goodness exclude the possibility that anything could be evil from God's perspective. The parts alone and not the whole of Creation can include evil as privation. If one's faith demands the denial of genuinely existing evil, clearly, then, whatever corruption may exist results from man's will. This corruption is to be cured, for Augustine, by faith in "my inmost Physician." A position which he defends in other writings is that which argues that God's foreknowledge of events is not incompatible with human freedom; God's foreknowledge of how men will act is not the cause of such action.

Yet Augustine's mental inquiry continued long after his conversion. The philosopher in him would not completely give way to faith. One example is his discussion of the human memory. Although inconclusive, this discussion raises a number of fascinating questions about the phenomena of human mental activity. The fact of faith is that Augustine loves his God. But *what* is it which he loves? He knows this is a unique kind of love, but he desires some clear notion of the nature of its object. He does not love bodily beauty, light, melodies, harmony of time, or the earth, when he loves God. What then can he love? The earth answers when asked: "I am not he"; and heaven, moon, sun, and other created bodies reply only: "He made us." Yet Augustine is certain he loves something when he loves God—"a kind of light, melody, fragrance, meat, embracement of my inner man." Eventually, he seeks the answer within his own consciousness. "And behold, in me there present themselves to me soul, and body, one without, the other within." God made his body, which is the corporeal aspect of his manhood. But his body cannot tell him what he loves when he loves God. It must then be the soul ("mind") by which Augustine can love his God. Mental activity must be the means by which one can know the object of his love in loving God; yet God must exist "beyond" one's own mind. This concern with mental activity ("soul") leads Augustine into his puzzlement over memory.

The memory enables Augustine to recall images rather at will, including images of the different separate senses (touch, hearing, and so forth). He can also recall items from his past personal life. He can combine these images freshly as well as consider future contingent possibilities. "Great is the force of this memory, excessive great, O my God"; so great, Augustine concludes, that it appears bottomless. Though it is by memory that Augustine knows whatever he does know, yet he cannot comprehend the full extent of his self. "Therefore is the mind too strait to contain itself." But how can one get into his own mind? Whatever is known mentally as an image came originally through the senses, as Augustine knows well. Yet he now remembers images even in the dark which are not the objects originally sensed. The memory is also an active capacity which knows reasons, laws, and numbers. It is capable of cognition. His memory recalls notions of truth and falsity. It also contains emotions like desire, joy, fear, and sorrow—which are the four great perturbations of the mind. He knows what he recognizes in naming memory but only by virtue of that which he names. Puzzlingly, Augustine even remembers forgetfulness. Augustine argues that remembering God is much like rummaging in the memory for something temporarily seeming to be lacking and finally saying: "This is it." But one, remembering, can never say, "This is it," unless it is somehow a remembered thing which has been temporarily forgotten. "What then we have utterly forgotten, though lost, we cannot even seek after."

Seeking God in the memory is, for Augustine, something like seeking happiness, if indeed they are not the same. But in seeking, men are "looking" for *something*. If the mind is essential to this search, then *what* is sought after must be like something once known but now forgotten. To say that God resides in memory is to assert that God can be known through the agency of mental activity. Yet God cannot reside in a specific part of memory. It is ultimately a mystery. Loving God is like seeking happiness. The soul ("mind") is nonetheless often tempted to seek knowledge of the object of its love through the senses. But it is obvious that what the eye, ear, nose, tongue, and fingers sense are specific things—bodily things—greatly unlike God. A mind-body dualism is characteristic of Augustine's thought. Though bodily things may be aspects of God's Creation, they are not God. Mental phenomena must be the means by which men can know God. Strangely, however, men do not always love God, at least not consciously. Yet God must somehow reside in memory even when men's mental activities are not searching for him. Coming to know God suggests a discovery. Augustine's moving words express this: "Too late loved I Thee, O Thou beauty of ancient days, yet ever new! too late I loved thee!"

The nature of time also puzzles Augustine. This puzzlement arises partly from Augustine's belief that in some sense God created the world from nothing. Yet on the view that time may be infinite, having no beginning or end, a skeptic may ask what God was doing before he created the world. Augustine refuses to commit himself to the notion of a finitely created spatial-temporal world. If time is infinite, then the world is equally so; and both time and the world yet exist as created by God. God's creative act stands "outside" time. God is therefore eternal rather than infinite. This view probably stems from Plato's influence. As eternal, God contains neither spatial nor temporal parts. God exists in an eternal "present," possessing neither pastness nor futurity.

Augustine attempts to show how this view can prove meaningful through an analysis of the psychology of human time. Men speak of things as past, present, and future. Clearly, the past and future are in some sense nonexistent. They are *not* except in relation to some present. The past is finished and done with; the future is not yet here. Time moves only relative to some present measuring unit. What and where is this present for men? The present as a unit of measurement can in itself have no parts. Yet no unit of time is in principle removed from the possibility of further subdivision. But this suggests that one spatializes time. Yet even the man who is aware of time-movement can measure such movement only in a present. This present cannot itself be measured while operating as the necessary norm of measurement. Analogous to this human present, though absolutely unique, is God's eternity, God's present. Augustine "sees" an eternal God as involving a timeless present containing no temporal subdivisions whatever. God contains all possible reality and yet has neither past nor future. This view is related to Augustine's belief that God has complete knowledge of events, including historical ones— as if all events are somehow immediately, nontemporally available to God.

Speculations like these, plus many others, occur throughout Augustine's *Confessions*. However indecisive is Augustine's handling of such items, they help to make his book the unique work it is.—*W.T.D.*

PERTINENT LITERATURE
O'Meara, John J. *The Young Augustine: The Growth of St. Augustine's Mind Up to His Conversion*. London: Longmans, Green and Company, 1954.

Persons interested in the background of Saint Augustine's life through his thirty-second year (the period covered by the narrative part of the *Confessions*) will find here all the information available, and those who have failed in their attempts to read the *Confessions* should find the going easier after reading *The Young Augustine*. But the book is also of value to students already acquainted with the *Confessions* who want to explore more closely Augustine's philosophical development during the period leading up to his conversion.

As there has been much controversy concerning this development, we shall restrict our attention to the relevant chapters of John J. O'Meara's book.

For nearly a century, historians have debated the accuracy of Augustine's account of his conversion, some arguing that there is a discrepancy between the *Confessions*, written twelve or more years after the event, and the earliest of his extant writings, the *Dialogues*, composed shortly after his retirement from the world. The latter, it is argued, shows that the conversion in his thirty-third year was not to Christianity but to Platonism. According to O'Meara, defenders of the traditional view have frequently accorded less to Neoplatonism than a fair interpretation of both the *Confessions* and the *Dialogues* requires; and it is his opinion that, as a result of the controversy, a more balanced view has emerged: namely, that while Augustine's conversion to Christianity was genuine, he nevertheless "was convinced at the time that Neoplatonism and Christianity were two approaches to the same truth," a belief which he later rejected.

O'Meara's contribution to the debate is twofold. First, on the basis of independent study of the *Dialogues*, he argues that there is no discrepancy between this and the later work. As an example, he cites the dedicatory epistle of the earliest dialogue, in which Augustine refers to his recent conversion, mentioning the same three stages described in the *Confessions*: reading Neoplatonist books, comparing them with the Scriptures, and finally submitting to the words of St. Paul. Other passages in the same vein make it clear that Christianity was given preference to Neoplatonism, although because the *Dialogues* is philosophical rather than theological Christianity did not ordinarily enter into the discussion. Generally, O'Meara reminds us, the literary conventions surrounding the composition of dialogues put their historical accuracy in question, whereas the *Confessions*, which was written for close friends, must be taken as substantially true.

O'Meara's reconstruction of the stages of Augustine's conversion is a further contribution to the debate. Scholars have given varying accounts of which of the Neoplatonist books Augustine read and how he passed from this philosophy to Christianity. Pierre Courcelle, a leading authority, has argued that Ambrose had already effected a synthesis of Christianity and Platonism, and that under his influence Augustine embraced them at the same time. But O'Meara contends that Augustine discovered Platonism by himself and pursued it with enthusiasm before he renewed his interest in Christianity.

The most distinctive feature of O'Meara's reconstruction is the importance he attaches to the writings of the Neoplatonist Porphyry in bringing Augustine to the threshold of Christianity. Scholars agree that the "Platonic books" which Augustine mentions must have included writings of both Plotinus and Porphyry. But O'Meara argues that it was the attention which Porphyry gave to popular cults, with their divine redeemers, which made Augustine receptive to the preaching of Ambrose and revived his interest in the New Testament.

According to O'Meara, Augustine's intellectual conversion to Christianity was completed prior to the intense moral struggle which resulted in his decision to abandon his worldly prospects and accept baptism.

Jordan, Robert. "Time and Contingency in St. Augustine," in *Augustine: A Collection of Critical Essays*. Edited by R. A. Markus. Garden City, New York: Anchor Books, 1972.

Philosophers who comment on Saint Augustine's philosophy of time commonly err, says Robert Jordan, because they take his discussion out of context. As an example, he cites Bertrand Russell, who, condensing and paraphrasing, makes Augustine say that memory, perception, and expectation are all there is to time, and who concludes from this that Augustine meant to substitute subjective time for the time of history and physics. "Subjective time might suffice for a solipsist of the moment," says Russell, "but not for a man who believes in a real past and future, even if only his own."

What Russell fails to notice, says Jordan, is the perspective in which time became important for Augustine. Unlike the Greeks, who discussed time in relation to cosmology, Augustine was concerned with time in a moral and religious context. Because he was interested in time as it concerns man, his discussion naturally appears subjective; but Jordan denies that it is really so.

First, although Augustine is describing psychic or spiritual facts when he discusses time, he does so in an objective manner, examining what could today be called the natural intentionality of the mind. The fact that past and future are experienced in the present and are perceived only in relation to the present leads Augustine to say that time is an extension (*distentio*) of present experience, giving rise to logical and linguistic problems, such as how we can speak of measuring the past if the past no longer exists. But this does not imply that time is essentially subjective and private. Necessarily the evidence is drawn from an examination of consciousness; but, says Jordan, what is *given* to consciousness qualifies as objective evidence.

Second, Augustine's account in Book XI of time as experienced is followed in Book XII by a quite different account. Here, in the context of God's act of creation, Augustine links temporality to change and change to motion and form, denying that unformed matter exists in time and coming near to equating time with measurable successiveness. This account, which resembles that in Aristotle's physics, Jordan does not regard as conflicting with Augustine's earlier account of our experience of time, but as complementing it by revealing the metaphysical foundations for what is there described in psychological terms.

Combining the two accounts, Jordan proposes the following as Augustine's definition: "Time is a relation, with a foundation in successive states of finite or limited being, whose measurement is a cognitive act terminating in the

distentio of the mind." Not time but the measurement of time is a function
of the mind—namely, of the mind's capacity for extending itself to include
what has been and what is yet to be. Time, according to Augustine, does not
exist in an absolute sense. It is a relation, the foundation of which lies in the
finite mode of being that belongs to creatures as such—being that arises out
of nonbeing and tends to nonbeing. This is certainly not a subjective view of
time, as if time depended on "man's measuring glance." Still, Jordan adds,
"the qualitative differences that make time spiritually significant" cannot exist
except for men. Thus, we experience time as opportunity, sometimes also as
a burden, and always, in the last analysis, as a threat.

This is enough to show that, for Augustine, the problem of time is not
merely an intellectual one. The real problem of time is existential: "how to
give creatures an anchorage in reality and a place in history, to give the whole
sensible world meaning and significant being." The second part of Jordan's
article is, therefore, concerned with the question of the unchangeable and
with the mystical element in man's experience. Interestingly, Jordan finds the
key to this experience in the same *distentio* by means of which the mind
measures time. By enabling man to enter into relation with the eternal, it
restrains his own mutability. "The soul is perfected by its object and it is by
changing the object of our attention that we overcome the flux of time."

Cochrane, Charles Norris. *Christianity and Classical Culture: A Study of
Thought and Action from Augustus to Augustine*. Oxford: Clarendon Press,
1940.

This magisterial work attempts to identify the causes of Rome's decline and
fall, as well as to explain why, rather marvelously, the Church did not sink
with the rest of society, but saved itself and much of the achievement of
classical civilization. Charles Norris Cochrane's thesis is that Rome's fall was
an intellectual and moral failure, traceable ultimately to defects inherent in
the classical world view, and that Christianity survived because the Church
Fathers, especially Saint Augustine, succeeded in reconstructing the classical
inheritance on the new foundation provided by the Gospel.

Whatever its defects, says Cochrane, the *Confessions* set a new standard
in autobiography. Marcus Aurelius, in his *Meditations*, recounted his efforts
to realize the Stoic ideal, "remembering that it was his business to exemplify
as far as possible the conventional type of excellence." Augustine, for his
part, was ready "to defy every canon of Classicism in order merely to bear
witness to the truth."

What especially impresses Cochrane is that, in the course of tracing his
development, Augustine learned to think of experience as both continuous
and cumulative, and in this way he overcame the failure of classicism to find
any place in its conceptual system for human individuality. As Cochrane reads

him, Augustine envisaged the self as primarily a will which uses the mental faculties in its efforts to satisfy various wants, developing characteristic dispositions and aptitudes in the process.

From this point of view, Cochrane sees Augustine's narrative of his adolescent adventures as a way of posing the question of how man is to achieve the fullest measure of satisfaction, and of examining three solutions offered by pagan society. The first solution, to try everything and to make the intensity and duration of experience the measure of values, resulted, said Augustine, in the waste of precious energy. It was in this context that he made his famous criticism of the theatre, repudiating the classical attempt to rationalize this form of excitement by pronouncing it cathartic, and arguing that the staging of tragic situations demoralizes the spectator by artificially dissociating emotion from action. The second solution, utilizing literary studies, professed to liberalize men's minds, but it too missed the mark. While recognizing its value as discipline, Augustine complained of the vanity and boredom of studies which exhausted the resources of language on themes such as Dido's love for Aeneas, and which culminated in the professional rhetorician, who, as Augustine said of an oration of his own in honor of the Emperor, must utter lies in order to be applauded by those who knew that he lied. The third solution, religion, which promised to raise experience to a higher plane, failed from its inability to overcome human pride. This was particularly the case with gnosticism, which the young Augustine chose in preference to his childhood faith because of its snob appeal. Later he made the same complaint against Neoplatonism, which, like gnosticism, restricted salvation to "those who know."

Read in the light of Cochrane's analysis, Augustine's decision to abandon the world takes on new depth. Admitting that Augustine needed time to grasp the full implications of his conversion, Cochrane argues nevertheless that even in the early dialogues Augustine had begun to perceive what was amiss in classicism and, in the spirit of Plato, to attempt a fresh synthesis of experience.—*J.F.*

ADDITIONAL RECOMMENDED READING

Brown, Peter R. L. *Augustine of Hippo: A Biography*. Berkeley: University of California Press, 1967. The best recent life.

Findlay, J. N. "Time: A Treatment of Some Puzzles," in *Logic and Language*. Edited by Antony Flew. Garden City, New York: Doubleday & Company, 1965. The author acknowledges that the basic ideas of this article come from Ludwig Wittgenstein. See Wittgenstein, *The Blue and Brown Books*, pp. 26 and 106f. Oxford: Basil Blackwell, 1969.

Gilson, Étienne. *The Christian Philosophy of Saint Augustine*. New York: Random House, 1960. A systematic account of Augustine's philosophy.

O'Connell, Robert J. *St. Augustine's Confessions: The Odyssey of Soul*. Cambridge, Massachusetts: Harvard University Press, 1969. Continuing the debate concerning Augustine's Neoplatonism, O'Connell argues that Augustine was still a Neoplatonist (Plotinian) when he wrote the *Confessions*.

THE CITY OF GOD

Author: Saint Augustine (Aurelius Augustinus, 354-430)
Type of work: Theology
First transcribed: c. 413-426

PRINCIPAL IDEAS ADVANCED

The essential nature of man is will, and no man wills the true God to be God unless he is touched by Divine Grace.

Theology is faith seeking understanding; man has faith in order that he may understand.

History has at its beginning the Creation; at its center, Christ, and, as its consummation, the judgment and transformation.

Because God had foreknowledge, he knew that man's will would be misdirected and that evil would thereby come into the world; but he also knew that through his grace good could be brought from evil.

History is divided by two cities formed by alternative loves: the earthly city by the love of self, and the heavenly city by the love of God.

It has been held that the whole of Christian thought may be seen as variations on the essential positions of two men—St. Augustine and St. Thomas Aquinas. This contention is closely related to another—that the history of philosophy is wisely seen as variations on the work of Plato and Aristotle. It is inevitable that when a religious thinker expresses the content of his faith he will use the most appropriate words, concepts, and even systems available in his culture. Consequently, St. Augustine was a Platonist, St. Thomas was an Aristotelian. Any attempt to gloss over this fundamental difference between these two leading theologians of Christendom is to pervert both.

It was St. Thomas in the thirteenth century who was most influential in establishing Aristotelian empiricism, thereby establishing a momentous division between philosophy and theology. This was quite different from the complete separation of the two to which the Protestant Reformation came in opposing the Roman Catholic synthesis. St. Thomas held that there were certain areas unique to each discipline, while other matters could be properly understood from either perspective. The Trinity and Incarnation, for example, could be known only through revelation; the nature of the empirical world was properly the jurisdiction of philosophy, almost perfectly understood by Aristotle. But God's existence, and to a certain extent his nature, could be known either through revelation or by the processes of natural reason, operating on sense perception. Thus natural theology was strongly defended as a legitimate discipline and a fitting handmaiden of the Church.

St. Augustine, however, writing eight centuries before, drew his inspiration from Plato, strongly tempered by the theology of St. Paul. For Plato, "knowledge" through the senses was inferior to intuitive knowledge, that knowledge of the essential nature of all things without which men perceive only dim shadows in a darkened cave. Coupled with this Platonic distrust of the senses was St. Augustine's preoccupation with the problem of evil and his own personal problems of morality. At first this concern had driven him to the position of Manicheanism, that philosophy holding to a metaphysical dualism of good and evil, and to the inherent evil of matter. Disillusioned by the naïveté of its spokesmen, Augustine turned to Neoplatonism, finding there a suitable explanation of evil in terms of a theistic universe, intuitively understood. "I found there," he said, "all things but one—the *Logos* made flesh."

The significance of this omission rested in Augustine's common confession with St. Paul—"I can will what is right, but I cannot do it. For I do not do the good I want, but the evil I do not want is what I do. . . . Wretched man that I am! Who will deliver me from this body of death?" Truth is not a matter simply of knowledge but of action; to anticipate the existentialists, the problem is not knowing the truth but living the truth. With this awareness came Augustine's baptism of Neoplatonism into the Christian *Weltanschauung*—the result has been called a complete break with all previous understandings of man.

Against the Greek philosophers, Augustine insisted that to know the truth is not necessarily to do the truth, for the essential nature of man is not reason but will. Man is so created that he has no option but to love, to orient his being to some object, principle, person, with an ultimate devotion. This supreme object willed by each person characterizes his total being, giving to him his presuppositions, motivations, rationale, vitality, and goal. There is no man without such a faith, "religion," "god." One does not reason *to* such an object, but reasons *from* it. No man believes in the true God, the God of moral demand, unless he wills so to do; but no amount of persuasion can change an unwilling will. Since man is essentially self-centered, he will always will something other than the true God to be god—man will create god in his own image. Only when man is touched by Divine Grace can he will God alone as true center.

Consequently, there must be no severance of theology and philosophy—there can be no reasoning to faith, to Truth. There can only be reasoning *from* faith. Only from the rightly oriented will, the mind already turned toward the redeeming God, can man discover Truth. The keystone of Augustinianism is this—"I believe in order to understand," or even better, theology is "faith seeking understanding." The same applies to morality, for every "virtue" that makes no reference to God is a vice. This insistence, essentially discounted by Aquinas and much of the medieval period, was revived as an essential proclamation of the Protestant Reformation. Through Kierkegaard it has become an adapted tenet of existentialism.

This understanding is the foundation for Augustine's magnum opus, *The*

City of God. Augustine's writing career was largely consumed in apologetics, in defending orthodox (Nicene) Christianity against its antagonists both within and without the Church. Occasioned by the sack of Rome in 410, *The City of God* arose as an answer to pagan critics who insisted that Christianity was the principal cause of the weakening of the Roman Empire. The reasons documenting this charge ranged from the religious position that avowal of the Christian God had elicited the vengeance of the true pagan gods, to the secular charge that Christian otherworldliness had undermined the internal solidarity of the Empire. With a brilliant display of concerned patience, Augustine produced one of the most detailed, comprehensive, and definitive apologies ever written. Not only are major charges answered, but Augustine deals with every conceivable attack. He answered the critics in terms of the Christian position and defended his answers in detail from the writings of the honored spokesmen of the Empire throughout its history. Augustine's second purpose with this work was to help Christians themselves who had been weakened or perplexed by persecution and by the disastrous events of history.

Yet from this apology emerged what has made this not only a work of historic interest, but also a classic. *The City of God* is one of the first attempts at a theology or philosophy of history. Although Greek concepts of history differed somewhat, they were essentially in agreement that history was cyclic, characterized by an endess round of recurring events. In effect, there was no *telos*, no final goal, toward which history moved. St. Augustine's apology developed the cosmic implications of Christian revelation, defending history as a linear pattern. The Christian God is Triune; that is, God operates in the three eternal modes of Creator-Sustainer, Redeemer, Inspirer. History as the plane of divine activity has as its beginning Creation, as its center point God's redemptive act in Jesus Christ, and continues in the Spirit towards the consummation, the judgment and transformation of all into a new heaven and a new earth. From the perspective of faith the pattern of history is visible and the meaning of life perceivable. Augustine's work set the basic view of much of the Middle Ages and of Western culture as such, and he, perhaps more than any other man, provided the fundamental theology of Christendom.

The situation confronting Augustine was fraught with theological difficulties. He could easily counter petty charges, pointing to the Church as a refuge during the sacking, to Christian teachings as having tempered pagan bloodthirstiness, and to pagan respect for possessions of the Christian God. Equally easy was Augustine's proof of the moral decadence of Rome, a condition and its disastrous consequences long warned against by the Roman orators. Although Augustine may have had an apology of this scope in mind at first, the work, once begun, held vast implications. Involved here were the problems of Divine Providence, the justification of evil in a theistic world, the reconciliation of unmerited suffering, and the meaning of a history interrupted by disasters. Nothing short of a cosmology, a total world view, could do justice to the questions forcing such an apology.

The overarching problem was providence. If God does not know what evils will occur, is he God? If he does know, is God not then either impotent or evil? Augustine answers the first question in the negative—God must have foreknowledge to be God. The problem exists only if one holds that infallible foreknowledge implies necessity. For Augustine, God can know all things without undermining free will, for *the free wills themselves* are included in the order of causes which God foreknows. It is God's knowledge of a thing which gives it not only being but also its specific nature; thus, it is *the very fact* of God's knowledge of man's free will *which makes it free*—it is known as free and not as determined. Freedom does not mean uncaused but self-caused, and it is the very self which God knows even more intimately than the self does. Consequently, God's knowledge of a person is that he will sin, not that he will be forced to sin.

In this manner God's immediate responsibility for evil is met. Yet there is a larger problem, for God still permits man in his freedom to do evil. The Empire provided the framework for Augustine's answer. The Empire, at its beginning, was dedicated to truth, justice, and the good of man—it was blessed by God. But love of liberty became love of domination; desire for virtue became intoxication for pleasure; glory in well-doing became vaunted pride. Herein is portrayed the dilemma of man from the beginning. In the beginning God created all things, and continues to create, for all would relapse into nothingness if he were to withdraw his creative power. All that God created is good, yet mutable, for having been created from nothing, it is absolutely dependent on God. Everything was graduated according to being, and the opposition of contraries serves to heighten the beauty of the universe. It was with the act of creation that time began, for time means movement and change—none of these apply to God. As a result, God's foreknowledge applies to *all* of time, for his eternal envisagement is unchangeable; although God knows what man in his freedom will do, he also knows what he will do to bring from every evil a greater eventual good. It is in knowing all time as present that the evil in each human present is redeemed. For Augustine, everything adds to God's cosmic whole; even sinners beautify the world.

Nothing, however, is evil by nature, for all natures are God-created. Evil can be nothing but privation, lack of good. Only the will, not one's nature, is the source of evil. Both the highest of the angels and Adam became inflated by pride in their God-given capacities, craving to become ends in themselves—"ye shall be as gods." Thus evil entered the world, for men made what was good into an evil by elevating it as the *supreme* good. Sex, for example, is a good, but is made evil when claimed as the center and meaning of life. It is not the thing turned to, but the turning itself, which is evil. Since man is sustained in being by his relation to the Supreme Good, any substitution of a lesser good brings with it an ontic disruption in which man's nature is injured. Although by such action man comes to approximate a nonentity, God does not revoke his nature totally, but sustains man enough for him to be aware of his self-inflicted loss.

The result is a creature frustrated in the conflict between nature and will— "O Lord. Thou hast made us for Thyself, and we are restless until we find our rest in Thee." In first not wanting to will what he could, man now wills to do what he cannot. This is evil as privation—the impotence of an essentially good nature. Since God alone truly is, that alone which is opposed to God is nonbeing; in willing less than fullness of being, man does not create evil but gives to nonbeing the existential status of being. Expressed in another way, sin is living the lie of believing oneself to be self-created, self-sustained, self-dependent. Such confusion establishes the duality, the fall, of creation— death is the most obvious consequence. Evil then has no efficient cause but a deficient one—the will. And as man is insubordinate to God, the "flesh" becomes insubordinate to the will.

In a phrase, evil is misdirected love. At this point Augustine's theory of history emerges. Adam's sin so altered man's nature, transmitted to his posterity, that human will is incapable of redirecting itself from itself as center. For such men, history is simply cyclic. But God's foreknowledge includes not simply man's fall, but God's election of some through grace to a redirected love. For these, history is linear, marked at its center by Jesus Christ, moving toward consummation in eternal life. Thus there are two histories in God's cosmic plan, indicated by two cities. These God permitted in order to show the consequences of pride and to reveal what good can be brought from evil by Grace.

Augustine's primary definition is this: "a people is an assemblage of reasonable beings bound together by a common agreement as to the objects of their love. . . ." History, from beginning to end, is divided by the two "cities" formed by these alternative loves—"the earthly by the love of self, even to the contempt of God; the heavenly by the love of God, even to the contempt of self." Of the first parents, Cain belonged to the city of men and Abel to the city of God. But since all are condemned by God, those in the latter are there only because of God's undeserved election.

Augustine's descriptions of these cities is all the more interesting because he refuses to overstate his case. In the first place, he refuses, for the most part, to equate the human city with historic Rome or the divine city with the visible Church—the churches are "full of those who shall be separated by the winnowing as in the threshing-floor." These are invisible cities, and their members are interspersed in these institutions, to be separated only at the end of history. In the second place, he refrains from painting the human city with totally black strokes—"the things which this city desires cannot justly be said to be evil, for it is itself, in its own kind, better than all other human good. For it desires earthly peace for the sake of enjoying earthly goods, and it makes war in order to attain to this peace." This city is characterized not by its goods but by its supreme love of them.

With meticulous care Augustine traces the history of both cities, carefully exegeting scriptural history as both literal and as allegorical of the abiding presence of the city of God. Throughout, in event, figure, and word, Augustine sees Christ's coming prophesied and prepared for. Since not even the Jews held that they alone belonged to God, Augustine maintains that it cannot be denied that other men and nations prophesied concerning Christ, and thus many of these may belong to the heavenly city.

It was Christ who, after his resurrection, opened the Scriptures to the disciples so that they could understand the eternal foundation of history and God's dual plan. But most especially, it was Christ's death, resurrection, ascension, and sending of the Holy Spirit which were the instruments of God's grace to the elect. Through his Incarnation he became Mediator, partaking of humanity so that in its purification by atonement on the Cross it could be resurrected with him in glory and through faith men could participate in his divinity. Faith begins purification not only of the will, and thus of one's nature, but also of the mind. As Augustine says, impregnated with faith, reason may advance toward the truth. Theology and philosophy belong together because will and reason are inseparable, both in impotence and in restoration.

Throughout history those of the divine city will know suffering at the hands of the human city, yet, being of the elect, they will not fall again. No evil will be permitted ultimately evil results; through suffering God bears witness to himself, and through it the believer is tempered and corrected. Such members (striving for the ideal balance of contemplation and action) obey the laws of the earthly city and are concerned with the necessities which do not undermine faith. To the end, the true Church goes forward "on pilgrimage amid the persecutions of the world and the consolations of God," its life aimed at universal love, its endurance based on the hope of future happiness. The peace of the city of God is "the perfectly ordered and harmonious enjoyment of God, and of one another in God." But in this life such peace is more the "solace of misery," and righteousness consists more in forgiveness than in the perfecting of virtues. The peace of the unbeliever is earthly pleasure, but in the life to come it will be an eternal misery of the will and passions in conflict. Expressed in terms of sin, history began with man's ability to sin or not to sin; it will end for the elect with man's higher freedom, the ability not to be able to sin, for in true freedom sin no longer has delight.

With meticulous detail, often disturbing in its literalness, Augustine outlines the epochs of future history, climaxing with the "new heaven and the new earth." Such an attempt escapes the charge of speculation, Augustine believes, because it has as its point of departure scriptural revelation, interpreted from the perspective of the Christ-event. Throughout these reflections there is a tension which has its roots in Augustine's own life. On the one hand is the rejection of this world in otherworldliness, holding alone to God's unfailing omnipotence and justice, and the eternal duality of heaven and hell. On the other hand, Augustine is world-affirming, straining for a transformational vision of which God's love gives foretaste. Both have their basis expressed in one of Augustine's concluding statements, emerging not only as a statement of faith but as a yearning hope issuing from his own tempestuous life. Speaking of that which is to be, he says that "then there shall be no more of this world, no more of the surgings and restlessness of human life. . . ."—*W. P. J.*

PERTINENT LITERATURE

Deane, Herbert A. *The Political and Social Ideas of St. Augustine.* New York: Columbia University Press, 1963.

Historians of political thought have disagreed sharply concerning Saint Augustine's theory of the state. In general terms, the question is whether Augustine held, with the early Church, that the sole function of the state is to preserve order by restraining and punishing evildoers, or whether, anticipating the Middle Ages, he held that the state is obliged to promote morality and religion. As Augustine said little on this subject, the actual point at issue turns out to be how far Augustine agreed with Cicero's definition of the state.

In expounding the concept *res publica*, Cicero had declared that not every assemblage of men is a commonwealth—only one which is "associated by a common acknowledgement of law and by a community of interests." Augustine replied that to make law and righteousness a criterion was, in effect, to say that Rome had never been a commonwealth, and he offered a new definition according to which the bond uniting men in states is "a common agreement as to the objects of their love."

In discussing these passages, some writers have argued that Augustine did not mean to reject the Ciceronian definition but merely to deny that it could be applied to pagan states. According to this view, Augustine remains in the tradition, stemming from Plato, which holds that the state is part of the Cosmos, being the means nature uses to establish right order in human associations and in the souls of men. All that he meant to dispute was whether any but a Christian state could claim to be guided by this higher law. Other writers, however, have argued that Augustine found the classical theory incompatible with man's fallen condition and, setting it aside, substituted a more realistic account of what states are and what can and cannot be expected of them.

Herbert A. Deane, probably in common with most recent students of Augustine, holds to the latter view. According to Deane, Augustine retained the Platonic ideal but denied that it can be realized or even approximated except in heaven. For this reason, Augustine was free to view politics with a cold eye and to ask in the modern fashion what ends states serve and how far they are successful. According to this interpretation, Augustine has more in common with Niccolò Machiavelli and Thomas Hobbes than he does with Boniface VIII or Richard Hooker.

Deane does not restrict his study to politics nor does he draw only from *The City of God*. The first half of the book lays the foundation for Augustine's political thought in his teaching concerning man's Fall and the effect of the fall on human society. Three orders are distinguished: the natural order, prior to the Fall, in which true justice reigned; the human order, in which selfish pursuit of worldly goods eventuates in the coercive state; and the divine order, realized only in heaven, but of which the redeemed are members even now by faith. Augustine, writing at a time when the Empire was officially Christian, recognized that the number of Christians had not significantly increased and the fact that a few Christians now held important positions in the Empire did not alter the character or operation of government. Indeed, according to Augustine, the chief effect of the conversion of Constantine had been to dilute the membership of the Church.

In Chapter 4 of his book, titled "The State: The Return of Order upon Disorder," Deane takes account of the more traditional "clerical" interpretation of the City of God, citing C. H. McIlwain (*The Growth of Political Theory in the West*) as giving the most plausible version. McIlwain contends that Augustine's quarrel with Cicero amounted to no more than a dispute as to whether a pagan state ought to be called a commonwealth. He says that when Augustine redefined the commonwealth he meant the new definition to apply to pagan states only. "Great states before Christianity were *regna* (realms) but they were not true commonwealths, because there was no recognition in them of what was the one true God. . . . No heathen state can ever quite rise to the height of a true commonwealth."

Deane raises several objections. In the first place, Augustine nowhere makes any distinction between heathen and Christian states; nor does he suggest that pagan states cannot, while Christian states can, exhibit true justice. Moreover, McIlwain does not take sufficient account of Augustine's revised definition, which Deane regards as a major contribution to political theory profoundly based on Augustine's doctrine of man. Most damaging of all, McIlwain overlooks Augustine's clear statement that "true justice has no existence save in that republic whose founder and ruler is Christ," a statement which Deane understands to mean that no earthly state meets Cicero's criterion of a true commonwealth and that only the heavenly Jerusalem does.

According to Deane, Augustine held that the state is an external order designed to achieve the social stability which all men desire in order to pursue their various goals. It depends entirely on force, being a "non-natural remedial institution." Its purpose is not to make men good, nor has it at its disposal any means to mold the thoughts and wills of its subjects. If rulers and citizens alike were truly virtuous and pious men, and were they to hear and obey God's commandments and prefer the good of others to their own, "then would the republic adorn the lands of this life with its own felicity, and mount the pinnacle of life eternal to reign most blessedly." However, as Deane notes, when Augustine speaks in this way he uses the form of a condition contrary to fact. In any case, says Deane, if this condition were to be realized the result would not be a Christian state; rather, the state would "wither away" and the anarchist ideal of a noncoercive order would take its place.

Markus, R. A. *Saeculum: History and Society in the Theology of St. Augustine*. Cambridge: Cambridge University Press, 1970.

The City of God was composed over a period of fourteen years (A. D. 413 to 426). Times were changing; and, according to R. A. Markus, it was part of the greatness of Saint Augustine that his ideas were amenable to change. Markus explains that *The City of God* grew out of two separate projects. The notion of "two cities" appeared in his writings before the sack of Rome, and, in 411, he announced his plan to write a book dealing with that subject. But charges by pagans that Christianity was to blame for the Gothic invasions prompted him instead to begin work on a book dealing with Rome's place in history. As this work progressed the two themes tended to coalesce.

Rome's significance in God's plan of salvation was subject to dispute in the early Church: one party identified the Empire with anti-Christ, whereas the other saw in the *pax Romana* a preparation for the spread of the gospel. The conversion of Constantine and the suppression of pagan cults by Theodosius I lend support to the latter opinion. The collapse of paganism seemed the end of an epoch; and in his early period Augustine was, says Markus, "bewitched by the Theodosian mirage." However, the chaos that followed the death of Theodosius "broke the spell" and led Augustine to develop the view that Rome's destiny was a matter of theological indifference.

According to Markus, the originality of Augustine's mature views concerning Rome lay in the distinction which he worked out between sacred and secular history. Taking it for granted that God's providence extends to all nations, he concluded that what distinguishes sacred history from world history is not any quality attached to events but has to do solely with the interpretation of events—namely with the prophetic insight which links events into a single redemptive pattern. Prophecy included Christ's life on earth and the promise of his return as King, but it was silent as to the intervening years. Therefore, the age of the Church and its relation to gentile powers belongs not to sacred but to profane history.

Augustine's theology of the "two cities" originated in a different context, having to do not with history but with society. During the reign of Theodosius, when he was inclined to see Christ's power evinced in the overthrow of paganism, Augustine had held to the Neoplatonic vision in which the social order occupies a place in nature, having for its goal the liberation of man's spiritual from his bodily elements. But gradually he abandoned this attempt to combine Christianity with the classic ideal of the *polis*. Close study of the Bible taught him to think less in terms of flesh and spirit and more in terms of sin and salvation and to see the Christian as a citizen of the heavenly Zion and as a stranger in the world. This tragic view of existence, reinforced by the troubles of the times, made it easy for Augustine to identify Rome with Babylon as the ultimate embodiment of the perverse and selfish loves which constitute the earthly city. Nevertheless, his attitude toward Rome remained ambiguous; and before he had completed *The City of God* he had found a way of reconciling the Christian's alienation from society with a recognition of the deep obligations which bind the Christian to the temporal order. "The heavenly city uses the earthly peace in the course of its earthly pilgrimage. It cherishes and desires, as far as it may without compromising its faith and devotion, the orderly coherence of man's wills concerning the things which pertain to the mortal nature of man; and this earthly peace it refers to the attainment of heavenly peace."

For Markus the term *saeculum*, which can be translated either as the age or the world, designates Augustine's new perspective. Heaven has receded from the earth. No longer can any people claim to enjoy God's special favor, nor can any social institution claim divine authority. History is the intermixture of two classes—those with worldly and those with otherworldly goals. The state has no particular identity, being merely a collection of individuals, some seeking one thing, some seeking another, but all agreed on the need for civil order. In its restricted area the state is autonomous; but relative autonomy also belongs to other societies, including the Church. In the language of recent theology used by Markus, church and state are irreconcilable eschatologically but not temporally: their ultimate destinations are different but their careers through history are "inextricably intertwined." It follows that the attitudes of the Christian toward the two societies must be governed not by principle but by expediency.

In a chapter entitled *Coge Intrare* ("compel them to come in"), Markus tries to resolve the conflict between Augustine's conception of a secular state and his approval of the use of coercion in behalf of the Church. That he favored Theodosius' use of force to suppress paganism and schism was compatible with his initial belief in the victorious progress of Christ's Kingdom and his Neoplatonic conception of the *polis*; but his advocacy of compulsion after he had revised these opinions raises difficulties. The concept of *saeculum*, in which the Church is seen as engaged in a "historical, perplexed, and interwoven life" with the world, provides Markus with a solution. In the first place, Augustine's new pluralistic view of society tended to dissolve the notion of the state, so that he thought less in terms of corporate action than in terms of action by individual magistrates and bishops whose duty required them to use the best means of upholding morals and religion. In the second place, armed conflict between Catholics and Donatists being one of the facts of life in North Africa, the question for Augustine was not one of principle but of "pastoral strategy." At first he judged the results of coercion to be harmful to the Catholic cause; later he revised his opinion.—*J.F.*

ADDITIONAL RECOMMENDED READING

Baynes, Norman H. "Political Aspects of St. Augustine's De Civitate Dei," in *Byzantine Studies and Other Essays*. London: Athlone Press, 1955, pp. 288-306. A public lecture by an outstanding historian of the period. The state, although founded on injustice, receives relative justification through its role in maintaining the peace.

Brown, P. R. L. "Saint Augustine," in *Trends in Medieval Political Thought*. Edited by Beryl Smalley. Oxford: Basil Blackwell, 1965. In Markus' judgment, a "deeply perceptive study" of political obligation.

Figgis, J. N. *The Political Aspects of St. Augustine's City of God*. London: Longmans, Green, and Company, 1921. A major contribution to the debate concerning Augustine's definition of the state. Includes a chapter on Augustine's view of history.

Löwith, Karl. *Meaning in History*. Chicago: University of Chicago Press, 1949. Chapters on leading philosophers of history from Augustine to Carl Burckhardt. "The interpretation of history is an attempt to understand the meaning of suffering by historical action."

THE CONSOLATION OF PHILOSOPHY

Author: Anicius Manlius Severinus Boethius (c. 480-524)
Type of work: Ethics, metaphysics
First transcribed: 523

PRINCIPAL IDEAS ADVANCED

Boethius is a political prisoner, and he complains to Philosophy, who is a fair lady, that virtue is not rewarded; he questions God's justice.

Philosophy answers that God is the source of all things, and that through study of God's nature, Boethius can rediscover his own true nature.

Man's possessions come through good fortune; anyone who realizes this and who does not become attached to his possessions can lose them with equanimity.

Since nature is always inconstant, man should seek to be master of himself and to bear changes of fortune with a calm mind.

Truth, happiness, and even divinity may be found in man himself; man should exercise his God-given freedom to raise himself in accordance with the vision of the divine nature.

This classic of prison literature bears all of the marks of great Roman philosophical writing. Formulated as a dialogue between the prisoner Boethius and Lady Philosophy, it exhibits the unique Roman quality of combining literary appeal with technical philosophy. Whereas philosophy in Greece was for the most part academic and theoretical, when transplanted to Rome it became a widely followed way of life, as in Stoicism. It is often said that philosophy in Rome was eclectic and unoriginal; what would perhaps be more accurate to say is that the original Roman element was to mold philosophy into forms which could deal effectively with serious and perennial human problems.

Like other philosophical writers of the era, Boethius took full advantage of his knowledge of Plato, Aristotle, the Stoics, and Neoplatonism. Modern philosophers often attempt to break completely with tradition; but Boethius used and blended classical sources as the means to develop his own views. His attempt was not to construct a novel metaphysics, but to apply philosophical views to the solution of pressing problems. Boethius had done philosophical writing before, but on the whole his life had been spent as a man of affairs. For reasons shrouded in political mystery, he was imprisoned and then put to death a few months after completing this work.

The work was widely known in the Middle Ages, and Boethius, in fact, was the source of several of the prominent philosophical questions of that later period. It is still debated, however, whether Boethius was himself a Christian. It seems likely that he was, although his writing contains no specific Christian doctrine. Perhaps, like the early writings of Augustine, his intellectual discussions were strictly philosophical, even though his formal religion was Christianity.

Although *The Consolation of Philosophy* has exerted enormous influence for centuries, it is largely neglected today. Religion is more independent of philosophy, and philosophy itself seems never to have been less concerned with practical affairs than it now is. Probably the *Consolation* is now more often read outside of professional philosophical circles, but whatever its current fashion, its position as a classic of applied philosophy is secure.

Boethius opens with a lament about the sudden reversal of his circumstances, a lot which has reduced him from the role of a consul to that of a prisoner in a dungeon near Milan. As he accuses fortune of being fickle, Philosophy, in the form of a fair lady, appears to him in his cell and attempts to answer his doubts about the justice of the world. She joins him in lamenting his present plight, but tells him it is time to search for healing rather than to complain. She chides him for his lack of courage in his present state, reminding him of Plato's struggle and of Socrates' valiant death. Philosophers, she tells him, have always been at variance with the ways of men and therefore have always been subject to attack. To oppose evil men is the chief aim of all philosophers, a course that cannot help leading them into trouble repeatedly. Therefore, a philosopher must learn to reconcile his life to fate, to conquer his fear of death, and to show himself unyielding to good and bad alike.

Ever since man has been able to speak, he has complained that his just life has not been properly rewarded, either by God or by man. Boethius continues this complaint, that his prison sufferings prove the injustice of the world when they are considered as the reward for the just life he has lived. Wicked men make attacks upon his virtue, and all because he is too honest ever to have engaged in deceit. Why does God allow a wicked man to prevail against innocence? With Job and a chorus of others, Boethius questions God, whose ways are unnatural to him. "If God is, whence come evil things? If he is not, whence came good?" Thus Boethius phrases the age-old question. Why should he be exiled, condemned to death without an opportunity to defend himself, because of his too great zeal for the Senate?

Furthermore, Boethius argues, Philosophy too has been dishonored in this process, for Boethius has never sought perishable riches but has instead "followed after God." Thus, in his misfortune, Philosophy's wisdom is also brought under question. In return for kindness he has received persecutions. Even his reputation has been stained. Honest men are crushed with fear; wicked men oppress good men and prosper by doing so. At this point Philosophy scolds Boethius mildly: she tells him that his mind is so beset by passions that nothing can come close enough to him to bring any healing. Philosophy then asks the basic question on which the argument will rest: Is the universe guided by a rule of reason, or are its events random and guided by chance? If it is the latter, then no explanations for misfortune can be given.

If it is the former, however, then one can question the reason and hope for a reasonable reply.

First, we must ask if there is an aim and end of all things. Is there a goal to which all nature tends? Boethius and his questioner agree that all things have their source in God. Then, if the beginning can be known, why not also the end of all things? But even more important than such cosmic questions, which establish the framework for man's life, is the fact that Boethius seems to have forgotten who he is and what his role as a man can be. He can rediscover his true nature, fortunately, through one spark within him: his knowledge of the hand that guides the universe. Through his knowledge of God and his purpose within the world Boethius can perhaps recover a true knowledge of his own nature.

What needs to be considered first, Philosophy urges, is the way of Fortune. Life cannot stand still; change must be understood. Anyone who complains over lost possessions has mistakenly assumed them to be his private property, rather than the gift of Fortune. To rise to the top is not a guarantee that the next phase may not be to sink to the bottom. Fortune, not your own just deserts, may bring you alternately high and low. These are the rules of the game, and understanding them prevents unnecessary misery. If you are violently attached to your position and possessions, they do not really satisfy you but cause you to desire more. If you are not so attached, then their loss will not disturb you.

Nature constantly changes. Why, then, should man alone wish to be exempt from cyclical flow? One thing alone is certain: nothing which is brought to birth is fixed or constant. Since these are nature's ways, nothing is wretched unless you think it so. On the other hand, if you bear everything which comes with a calm mind, then you will find your lot blessed. Why seek happiness without, when it really lies within? If you are the master of yourself, then you possess all that it is important not to lose, and even fickle Fortune cannot take that from you. Fear alone prevents a man from being happy. Self-mastery excludes fear, and only a life based on inner calmness can ignore the raging passions which always threaten to destroy. In the light of this knowledge, why would anyone embrace as his good anything outside of himself?

No fame or power appears lasting when compared with eternity. Death has no regard for high position, however great, but claims high and low alike. And even ill fortune has its blessings: it distinguishes true friends from doubtful acquaintances. The loss of riches is a gain, since it brings you your true friends, a possession greater than riches. Love rules the universe, and men can be happy if their hearts are ruled by love. Happiness is, after all, man's highest good. And friends, who are one chief source of happiness, depend upon virtue more than upon Fortune's uncontrollable ways. They may argue over means, but they agree in their highest good and happiness.

The man who would gain true power must subdue his own wild thoughts—

so Philosophy consoles Boethius. Since God is our author, no man is degenerate or base except the man who leaves his creator. Since God and the highest good form a union, every happy man is, in his happiness, divine. If it is truth that one searches for, let him only turn upon himself the light of an inward gaze. It is of no use to search elsewhere; truth, happiness, and even divinity may be found within man himself. God governs the universe for the highest good. He who turns his thoughts away from the light above is in danger of losing whatever he has won for himself here below, for he will lose his sense of direction.

Next comes the age-old question: If there exists a good ruler of the world, why do evils exist and, what is worse, seem to go unpunished? Philosophy answers: Power is never lacking to the good, while the wicked are weak. Yet all men, good and bad alike, seek to arrive at the good, although by different means. Bad men seek the same ends that good ones do, but they do it through cupidity. Such is the weakness of wicked men that it is hard to allow that they are men at all. The power of evil is no power at all, especially since nothing evil ever reaches happiness. The wicked man is oppressed by his own passions; all good men become happy by virtue of the very fact that they are good. Therefore, as honesty is itself the reward of the honest, so wickedness is itself the punishment of the wicked. The man who loses his goodness ceases to be a man and turns into a beast.

We should love good men, for it is their due, and show pity for the evil, since to be oppressed by the disease of feeble wickedness is much more worthy of pity than of persecution. Providence is a guide for all, and there is no such thing as chance. Yet all who have reason also have the freedom of desiring and of refusing, although the working of human reason cannot approach the directness of divine foreknowledge. Such foreknowledge does not bring necessity to bear upon things as they come to pass. Man sometimes rises to see all things as God might see them and sometimes sinks down and fails to grasp such connections at all. His freedom is preserved by his lack of vision.

Near the end, having raised the question of a divine vision of all things, Boethius turns to the question of whether there are universals, and it is here that much of the famous medieval controversy takes its start. What is comprehensible to the senses and to the imagination cannot be universal, yet reason holds to be universal what is really an individual matter comprehensible to the senses. It sees from a general point of view what is comprehensible to the senses and to the imagination, yet this is not a knowledge of real universals but only a way reason has of comprehending. Nothing set in time, for instance, can at one moment grasp the whole space of its lifetime. God, of course, sees all things in his eternal present, but man does not. Seen from God's perspective, an event may seem necessary; when examined in its own nature, it seems free and unrestrained.

In this dialogue Philosophy has the last word, and that refers to the theological problem of the difference in perspective between God and man. Consolation comes in trying to raise oneself to see the events of the world as God views them. Dejection, then, is caused by a too limited, a too human perspective; Philosophy's job is to raise man's sights, to give him divine vision. Since Philosophy can accomplish this, she is man's hope of consolation. Any individual's turn of fortune is not understandable in isolation; it must be placed in the total scheme of things, and to do this is to philosophize. Philosophy does not change events or reverse Fortune, but it does provide the understanding with which the events of life may not only be accepted but also enjoyed. When Fortune reverses itself, the first cry is for restoration. Philosophy teaches that man's chief need is not for change but for understanding.

In Boethius' work we have a classic in applied philosophy. According to the usual standards, no real argument or analysis supports the points introduced. In some sense there is not a novel doctrine here; all parts may be traced to preceding classical sources. Yet this work is itself a classic. This is true because of its historical situation, in that it came to be a source for philosophical argument. The *Consolation* raises an interconnected series of important philosophical and theological problems. Its answers are not original, but they are classical and the problems themselves perennial. In this work we see an enduring example of philosophy's application to a serious human need and of the consolation which results.—*F.S.*

PERTINENT LITERATURE

Pieper, Josef. *Scholasticism: Personalities and Problems of Medieval Philosophy.* New York: McGraw-Hill Book Company, 1964.

Josef Pieper contends that, allowing for the fact of historical continuity, there is a point in assigning a beginning to medieval philosophy and dating that beginning at A.D. 529. In that year, a decree of the Christian Emperor Justinian closed the Platonic Academy in Athens, ending its nine-hundred-year history, and, in the same year, the first Benedictine Abbey, Monte Cassino, was founded by St. Benedict.

Granting that the coming of Christianity separates such figures as Thales and Plato on the one hand and Origen and St. Augustine on the other, Pieper still maintains that Augustine and his predecessors found their intellectual home in Hellenistic thought as formed by Neoplatonism, Stoicism, and Epicureanism. He argues that Boethius, a century after Augustine, still lived intellectually within classical philosophy and politically within the Roman empire, although his listeners and readers did not. Boethius, Pieper notes, was the first thinker to turn to those who had come from the North into the ancient world.

Pieper records that Boethius was a student in the Platonic Academy (closed in 529) and enjoyed the advantages of culture present in the court of Theodoric which, for all its opulence, was essentially an armed camp; a decade after Boethius' death a twenty-year war of annihilation began against the kingdom Theodoric had founded. Boethius was the last layman in the history of European philosophy for almost a millenium.

Pieper adds that Boethius' unfulfilled intention was to translate all of Plato and Aristotle. He coined the terms "universal," "subject," "speculation," "define," and "principle." According to Pieper, part of his greatness as a translator consisted in his ability to coordinate just the right Latin term with the Greek term it replaced, as in the case of "principium" for "arche," expressing "origin" and "rule."

Further, Pieper indicates, Boethius saw that preserving for posterity an account of the common foundation which made philosophical diversity possible was more valuable than preserving the diversity itself. A Neoplatonist himself, he wished to preserve both Platonic and Aristotelian perspectives and also to show how much these perspectives have in common. He wrote basic textbooks on astronomy, music, and arithmetic, as well as his theological treatises.

Pieper emphasizes that writing the *Consolation* was not part of Boethius' plans. He was accused of conspiring against Theodoric the Goth, tried, condemned, and executed in Milan in 525. As a prisoner awaiting death, he wrote the *Consolation*. Used to wealth, power, and influence, a Roman consul at the age of thirty, Boethius found himself in a tiny cell awaiting a cruel death. Thus, Pieper says, the writing of the *Consolation* was forced upon him, and it was a far different sort of work from any of his previous efforts.

The *Consolation* can be read as an imitation of a Platonic dialogue or early Aristotelian work, or as an expression of Neoplatonic and Stoic doctrine and perspective. But Pieper maintains that it is in fact an attempt on Boethius' part to ask, and answer, the question of whether he could still hold that the world and his own life had significance or point. "Everyone has within himself something he does not know as long as he has not searched it out; but if he has searched it out—he shudders."

Pieper reminds us that the *Consolation* is a dialogue between Boethius the prisoner and Boethius the philosopher. Lady Philosophy, who enters the cell to discourse with the prisoner, is Boethius himself insofar as he is able to believe that the world, and his own life, retain significance for him, even under his lamentable circumstances. This inner struggle, Pieper contends, is presented without any false resolution. Boethius restricts his answers to those he takes to be available to reason alone, without revelation. And he will not allow himself, particularly in his dire circumstances, to hide any difficulties. Given that the questions discussed are of the sort they are—If there is a God, why is there evil? But if there is not a God, why is there good? Is evil really only a privation, a lack or absence of something good? If God exists and is an omnipotent Providence, can there yet be human freedom?—Pieper suggests that it is no wonder that the book ends with no definitive conclusion. Still, Pieper finds, Boethius does find consolation in his vision of being part of the cosmos that the *Consolation* describes.

It is Pieper's view that the endeavor to explain matters only so far as reason can do so, manifested in the *Consolation*, is present also in Boethius' works on the Trinity. No biblical passages are quoted in these tractates; they are filled with logical analysis. Pieper finds that Boethius is explicit in stating his policy in these works of relying on reason alone, and in the explicitness of his policy lies a major reason for his being regarded as the first of the Scholastics.

The idea, Pieper tells us, is not that revelation is rejected. It is rather that it is appropriate and justified rationally to grasp the content and grounds of what is proffered for belief by authority—a belief which even Bonaventura was to share. The effort to grasp, as fully as is rationally possible, what is accepted on authority is an extremely complex and difficult task, as becomes clear in the steps of such later thinkers as St. Thomas and St. Bonaventura. When they make this effort, Pieper concludes, others follow a practice whose rationale was first made explicit by Boethius.

Gilson, Étienne. *History of Christian Philosophy in the Middle Ages*. New York: Random House, 1955.

In contrast to Josef Pieper, Étienne Gilson begins his study of medieval philosophy with the thought of the Greek Apologists—Christians such as Justin Martyr (d. 163-167) and Iraneus (d. 203)—who wrote reasoned presentations of Christianity which included responses to criticisms of Christianity made by educated pagans. Boethius is thus viewed, by Gilson, not so much as a transition figure between two cultures, as part of a sequence of thinkers which runs from the Greek Fathers to Thomas Aquinas and beyond. Nevertheless, Gilson notes, he did convey an important part of the Greek message to the Latin world, including the definition of "philosophy" as "love of wisdom." Boethius takes wisdom to be the intelligent causeless cause of all that exists. Philosophy is thus conceived as the love of, and quest for, Wisdom or God.

According to Gilson, Boethius accepts three kinds of beings: *intellectibles*, which exist but are immaterial; *intelligibles*, which are fallen (and so embodied) intellectibles such as human souls; and *natures*, which cannot exist apart from matter. Speculative philosophy has three divisions, one each for the study of each kind of being; these are, respectively, theology, psychology, and physiology or physics, although Boethius does not actually name the discipline that studies intelligibles.

Gilson indicates that the highest knowledge, according to Boethius, is knowledge of the intellectibles, and God is the primary intellectible. God is that being than whom no better is conceivable. That there is such a being, Gilson explains, is argued on the basis that, obviously, there are imperfect beings. But the existence of a being which, in a particular manner, is imperfect is caused by a being which is perfect in the manner in question. So there is a being which is perfect in all the ways in which other beings are imperfect. To deny that this being is God is to suppose that God has a cause, which is a contradiction.

Beatitude, Gilson reports Boethius as contending, is a condition made perfect by the union of all that is good. Being perfect, God has perfect beatitude. Given that within a kind of perfection anything has the quality of perfection only insofar as it is caused to have it by the property's Paradigm Exemplar, if we are to have beatitude, Boethius held, God must cause it in us.

For Boethius, Gilson indicates, human beings by nature possess, to some degree, freedom of choice. God's knowledge is perfect; his choice always accords with his knowledge of what is good; perfect freedom is a matter of always choosing what is good; hence God is perfectly free. The more like God's knowledge our knowledge is, and the more our choice accords with such knowledge, the more free we are. (This seems to use "free" in a descriptive sense—one is free with respect to an action one actually, and not merely hypothetically, can perform or refrain from performing, as one chooses—while in a normative sense one is free to the extent that one does the right thing for the right reason.)

Gilson makes clear that Boethius is aware that the objection can be raised that God has perfect foreknowledge and that this is incompatible with human beings possessing freedom of choice. For suppose God knows that I will choose to take tomorrow off. If, come tomorrow, I cannot but take the day off, where is my freedom? And if, come tomorrow, I can decide to work after all, is not God's foreknowledge in danger? For then I can choose to work, and if I do, God will have "foreknown" something false. So God can be wrong. One part of Boethius' response, Gilson reports, is that God is eternal; his consciousness is one to which all events are timelessly present. So he does not literally see what I will do, before I do it. God's consciousness bears no temporal relationship to my choice about what to do tomorrow (or to anything). The objection presupposes otherwise.

Another part of the answer, according to Gilson, is this. If God forces that I shall freely choose, then I shall freely choose, from which it follows that my choice will be free; nor is God's foreseeing what I will do tantamount to his determining, or causing me to do, what I shall do. In this part of his reply, Boethius sets aside the issue raised in the other part concerning God as an eternal being.

Like Plato and Augustine, Boethius identified being with good and nonbeing with evil. Like Augustine, he also held that God alone is good in Himself, or by nature. But then if anything is, insofar as it is at all, good, how will any given item, with respect to goodness, differ from God? Gilson suggests that one answer would be that in God the relation between existence and essence differs from that which obtains in creatures, but this was not Boethius' line. Instead, Gilson remarks, he held that every individual created thing is a collection of accidents or properties which is unique; such an item is a collection of qualities. A human being, for example, is made up, according to Boethius, of soul and body, being identical to neither by itself, but to both together. So with every compound or complex being; it is identical to the sum of its parts. Gilson explains that for Boethius, by contrast, God is not compound or complex. He is simple, having no parts at all. God is a simple being, and a creature is a complex being. So the sort of being that, in God, is identical to His goodness is different from the sort of being that is, in creatures, identical with their goodness.

Gilson adds that in Boethius' view, in each created thing there is something which determines that its parts will be ordered in the way that they are rather than in some other. The soul plays this role in a human being. So a created thing is not an unordered or randomly ordered set of parts.

Boethius, except for one case, Gilson points out, does not quote or appeal to the support of Scripture because it is philosophy which is the speaker. But, Gilson contends, however, that the *Consolation* is the work of a Christian philosopher who followed his own rule, "Conjoin faith and reason, if you can."—*K.E.Y.*

ADDITIONAL RECOMMENDED READING

Copleston, Frederick C. *A History of Medieval Philosophy*. New York: Harper & Row Publishers, 1974. An illuminating discussion of Boethius in part of this one-volume treatment of Medieval philosophy by the author of the excellent multivolume *A History of Philosophy*.

De Wulf, Maurice M. *Scholastic Philosophy*. New York: Dover Publications, 1956. An older work published in French in 1903, translated into English in 1907, and reissued in 1956; one can still learn much from it.

Henry, D. P. *Medieval Logic and Metaphysics*. London: Hutchinson University Library, 1972. A careful discussion of various topics in Medieval logic and ontology.

Knowles, David. *The Evolution of Medieval Thought*. New York: Random House, 1962. A very helpful survey of medieval philosophy from its roots in ancient philosophy to the dissolution of the "medieval synthesis."

Leff, Gordon. *Medieval Thought: St. Augustine to Ockham*. Baltimore: Penguin Books, 1958. Useful account from A.D. 400-1350.

Vignaux, Paul. *Philosophy in the Middle Ages: An Introduction*. Cleveland: World Publishing Company, 1959. Briefer than Knowles or Leff, but very good.

THE PLATFORM SCRIPTURE OF THE SIXTH PATRIARCH

Author: Hui-neng (638-713)
Type of work: (Zen) Buddhist sermon, ethics, metaphysics
First transcribed: c. 677

PRINCIPAL IDEAS ADVANCED

Perfect, Buddha wisdom is in everyone.

Insight into one's original, pure nature is possible only by putting that nature into practice.

To attain insight into one's Buddha nature, one's mind must be free from attachments and error.

The practice of direct mind leads to sudden enlightenment.

Through no-thought—not being distracted by thought while thinking—one's original nature, the True Reality, is thought.

The original wisdom and such meditation are one.

The Platform Scripture of the Sixth Patriarch (*Liu-tsu t'an-ching*) is generally regarded as the basic classic of Ch'an (Zen) Buddhism. The work is reputed to be a record of the teachings of the great Ch'an Master Hui-neng, as expressed in his remarks delivered in the Ta-fan Temple in Shao-chou in or about the year 677, and as recorded by his disciple Fa-hai. The most authentic version of the work is regarded by such scholars as Wing-tsit Chan and Philip B. Yampolsky to be the *Tun-huang* manuscript, found in a cave in Tun-huang, northwest China, in 1900. (Both Chan and Yampolsky have translated the Tun-huang manuscript and have provided copious commentary. See the *Pertinent Literature* section that follows.)

Although the details of the life of Hui-neng are uncertain, and although some commentators have questioned the authorship of the *Platform Scripture*, the prevailing legends, embellished by commentators over the years, tend to agree on the following biographical items: Hui-neng was born in 638 into a humble family, the Lu family, originally in Fan-yang and later, at the time of Hui-neng's birth, in Hsin-chou in southwestern Kwangtung. Hui-neng was a firewood peddlar. In his early twenties he was inspired by a reading of the *Diamond Scripture*, and he traveled to the north to visit the Fifth Patriarch, who was an exponent of the scripture.

Legend has it that Hui-neng was appointed Sixth Patriarch after having served a stint under the Fifth Patriarch as a pounder of rice and having subsequently impressed the Patriarch with a poem requested of all his disciples by the Fifth Patriarch. Whether or not the story is true, it appears clear that Hui-neng did "receive the robe" as Sixth Patriarch in 661, just a few months after arriving in Huang-mei to visit the Fifth Patriarch.

In 676, after several years of preaching in south China, Hui-neng moved to Canton. He had become a Buddhist priest at the age of thirty-nine. The following year (so the story goes) he was invited to lecture in the Ta-fan Temple in Shao-chou. There his remarks were recorded by his disciple Fa-hai (according to the *Platform Scripture*), and the resultant work is, or at least provided the foundation for, the *Platform Scripture of the Sixth Patriarch*.

Hui-neng is honored as the Ch'an Master who initiated the "Southern School" of Ch'an Buddhism in opposition to the Northern School led by Shen-hsiu (c. 605-706). The Northern School maintained that enlightenment would come gradually as a result of practicing formalized procedures of meditation; the Southern School argued that meditation must be free, a matter of allowing the pure Buddha-nature to reveal itself, and that enlightenment would be sudden. According to Chan, although this difference of opinion about the speed of enlightenment was present as a matter of emphasis, the two schools differed more fundamentally in their concepts of mind, the Northern School maintaining that the mind or Buddha-nature, common to all persons, cannot be differentiated and that its activities are functions of the True Reality, while the Southern School argued that the pure mind can function only in quietude or "calmness," and only after having freed itself from the false or erroneous mind with its attachments to individual thoughts. In any case, according to Chan, the Southern School became the most influential force in the development of Zen Buddhism in China from the ninth century.

As translated by Chan, the heading of the *Platform Scripture* is as follows: "The Platform Scripture Preached by the Sixth Patriarch, Hui-neng, in the Ta-fan Temple in Shao-chou, the Very Best Perfection of Great Wisdom Scripture on the Sudden Enlightenment Doctrine of the Southern School of Zen, one book, including the Giving of the Discipline that Frees One from the Attachment to Differentiated Characters for the Propagation of the Law. Gathered and recorded by disciple Fa-hai." As translated by Yampolsky, the heading is: "Southern School Sudden Doctrine, Supreme Mahāyāna Great Perfection of Wisdom: The Platform Sutra preached by the Sixth Patriarch Hui-neng at the Ta-fan Temple in Shao-chou, one roll, recorded by the spreader of the Dharma, the disciple Fa-hai, who at the same time received the Precepts of Formlessness."

The *Platform Scripture* recounts that the Master Hui-neng lectured to more than ten thousand monks, nuns, and followers, all gathered in the lecture hall of the Ta-fan Temple. His topic was the Dharma (law) of the perfection of Wisdom (of the original, pure wisdom of the Buddha-nature). Hui-neng begins with an autobiographical account. The material is interesting, but it has little philosophical or religious import. In Section 12 Hui-neng declares that he was determined or predestined to preach to the officials and disciples gathered there in the temple, and he maintains that the teaching is not original with him: it has been handed down by the sages. Sections 13 through 19 contain the fundamental teachings of Hui-neng. In 13 Hui-neng declares that calm meditation and wisdom are a unity, that such meditation is the substance of wisdom, and that wisdom is the function of meditation.

The Buddhist doctrine, here implicit, is that everyone shares the Buddha-nature (wisdom) and that if one can turn one's mind inward and not be distracted, one can receive enlightenment. Wisdom and meditation are one in that meditation (of the kind advocated by Hui-neng) is regarded as the function or practice of the original nature. Hence, Hui-neng declares that meditation exists in wisdom, and wisdom is within meditation. Neither gives rise to the other, he insists. If the mind and words are both good and the internal and external are one, then wisdom and meditation are one.

Hui-neng next stresses the critical importance of practicing—actively attaining—a straightforward or direct mind. A straightforward mind requires having no attachments and attending to no differentiating characters, thereby realizing that all is one; there is a unity of nature in everything. To achieve such realization in the practice of the straightforward mind is *samādhi* of oneness, a state of calmness in which one knows all dharmas to be the same. But the calm realization of oneness is not, as some people think, a matter of simply sitting without moving and not allowing erroneous thoughts to rise in the mind. To act in this way is to make oneself insentient, and that is not in accordance with the Way, the *tao*, which can work freely only if the mind is free from things. If one attempts, as some people do, to view the mind and keep it inactive, they become radically disturbed and never achieve enlightenment. (Section 14.)

Hui-neng indirectly criticizes the Northern School in his description of the meditation method which, in effect, renders people insensible and inactive; and he continues his criticism in Section 16 when he states that the deluded teachers recommend a gradual course to enlightenment, while the enlightened teachers practice the method of sudden enlightenment. In this passage Hui-neng clearly states that to know one's own mind or to know one's original nature is the same thing, and if people differ in coming to enlightenment it is because some people are stupid and deluded while others know the method of enlightenment.

Hui-neng then remarks that everyone has regarded "no-thought" as his main doctrine. His remark ties in with what he had just been saying about meditation method, for the doctrine to which he alludes is the meditation method he endorsed, a method that came to be identified with the Southern School. Put informally, the statement of method would be put injunctively, "Practice no-thought," and sense would be made of the injunction by presuming the point to be that the mind will be open to its nature, will be able to "think" (intuit) the pure nature common to all within oneself, only if it is not distracted by thoughts *about* things, including the thought about achieving enlightenment by not thinking about anything else. The truth is, one cannot achieve awareness even of the Buddha-nature by thinking *about* it.

Hui-neng speaks of no-thought as the main doctrine (of meditation), of "non-form as the substance" and of "non-abiding as the basis" (to follow Yampolsky's translation). He then adds that "Non-form is to be separated from form even when associated with form. No-thought is not to think even when involved in thought. Non-abiding is the original nature of man." Presumably, as the next passage (of Section 17) implicitly indicates, the original Buddha-nature is absolute, in no way dependent upon or related to or attached to any particular being or characteristic of being; hence, "non-abiding" (non-attachment) is the original nature of man. When involved in the thought consisting in the awareness of original nature (or while succeeding in the practice of freeing the mind), one is not thinking this or that. In that sense, the thinking of the original nature is no-thought. As Chan translates a relevant passage here, "If one single instant of thought is attached to anything, then every thought will be attached. This is bondage. But if in regard to dharmas no thought is attached to anything, that is freedom."

To be separated from forms is not to attend to the characters of things; it then happens, so Hui-neng preaches, that the substance of one's nature is pure. One must not be affected by external objects and one must not turn one's thought to them. But one must, of course, *think*—that is, one must think the pure nature of True Reality. No-thought is thought free from the error of attending to external things and characters and from all attachment. If your pure nature is allowed to function, as it will if there is no-thought, then True Reality becomes the substance of thought.

Hui-neng then speaks of "sitting in meditation" (in Section 18). He contends that this teaching does not call for looking at the mind or at the purity of one's nature. The objects of such viewing are illusions, and to suppose that one is looking at objects or that there are such objects to look at is to be deluded. However, if delusions are avoided, then the original nature is revealed in its purity. Purity has no form, Hui-neng argues, and hence one cannot grasp the form of purity and then pass judgment on others. Deluded people are quick to find fault with others because they (the deluded) presume themselves to know the form of purity. By criticizing others, such persons violate the *tao*, the true Way.

Sitting in meditation, then, is not a matter of looking for forms or characters; sitting in meditation is, rather, to be free and not to allow thoughts to be activated. Hence (Hui-neng concludes in Section 19), true meditation is the achievement of internal calmness and purity. (To "see" the original nature and in purity and freedom to *be* the original nature—to meditate and to be wise—are one and the same. Meditation is the practice of original wisdom; wisdom is the internal subject of meditation.)

The remaining sections of the *Platform Scripture* are concerned with provoking ritualistic attention to the central features of Mahāyāna Buddhism or are taken up with miscellaneous material, most of it probably added by later writers to the sermon core.

Whether or not the ideas represented in the *Platform Scripture* were actually enunciated by Hui-neng and recorded by Fa-hai, they represent the central doctrines of Ch'an Buddhism of the Southern School and are of philosophical and historical interest whatever their origin. In many ways the *Platform Scripture* can be seen as an argument for intuition as the way of enlightenment, in opposition to those who argue for the way of intellect and its distinctive mode, analysis.—*I.P.M.*

PERTINENT LITERATURE

Hui-neng. *The Platform Scripture.* Edited and translated by Wing-tsit Chan. New York: St. John's University Press, 1963.

Wing-tsit Chan's *Platform Scripture* is the first unabridged English translation of the *Tun-huang* manuscript (probably eighth century) discovered in 1900 in Tun-huang, northwest China. In Chan's opinion this manuscript is the most authentic and is to be preferred to the "Ming Canon" (derived from the version edited by Sung-pao in 1291), the Kosho Temple copy (of Hui-hsin's 967 version), and the Daijo Temple copy (dated 1228, with a preface dated 1116), probably also a copy of the Hui-hsin version.

The *Platform Scripture* is described by Chan as the basic Zen classic, the only Chinese work honored as a Buddhist scripture.

The chief feature of Zen Buddhism, Chan writes, is its emphasis on meditation (*dhyana* in Sanskrit, *ch'an* in Chinese, *zen* in Japanese), but it should be noted that the Zen school eventually discarded formal meditation. Zen is a way of life, Chan contends, not merely a state of mind. It is distinctive for its method, and it aims at teaching the acceptance of and insight into life. Thus, it is not accurate, he argues, to treat Zen as a specific philosophy, religion, or ethics.

As Chan summarizes the ideas of Zen, they are the following: the mind is identical with Reality; Reality is one and universal; it is the Void, beyond expression in thought or words, for Reality has no differentiated characteristics; Reality must be known directly and immediately; the mind must operate spontaneously and unconsciously if one is to attain Buddhahood. Thus, Chan writes, "the best approach to Reality is to 'have no thought,' and the best way of being is to 'have no mind.'"

Chan explains that such expressions as "no-thought" and "no-mind" are not to be taken literally because what they are intended to endorse is a method of thinking and a way of mind that is not egocentric and that is not impeded and distracted by the conscious effort to find the Way or to become a Buddha. Hence, the emphasis in Zen Buddhism is not on action but on being; it is not so much what one is to *do* as what one is to *be*.

Since Zen maintains that all persons have the Buddha-nature, the Buddha wisdom, and since Reality is universal, there is no particular way of seeking Buddhahood; there is only the need to *be* one's original, pure self. What is called for, then, is a kind of self-reliance that is nevertheless not an absorption in one's individuality but in the original Buddha-nature that one is.

Chan remarks that the influence of Zen is clear in Chinese art. In landscape painting nature is presented as a whole by way of a simple representation of the essence of Reality; there is no unnecessary color, detail, or shading.

Indian Zen techniques were introduced into China from India in the second century, Chan relates. Early Zen Masters were Tao-an (312-385) and Hui-yüan (334-416). But Zen became a distinctive Chinese school with the emergence of Bodhidharma, who arrived in Canton in the 470's and acquired devoted followers whom he advised to discard all Buddhist scriptures except the *Scripture About the Buddha Entering into Lanka*. This scripture, according to Chan, fosters the idea that the "True State or Nirvāṇa is total Emptiness devoid of any characteristics, duality, or differentiation." Through intuition into our Buddha-nature we achieve emancipation. The method of unattached concentration is comparable to what one would achieve by facing a wall to free the mind. (Chan refers at this point to the legend of Bodhidharma's sitting in meditation for nine years while facing a wall.) By such a method the mind is free from both being and nonbeing.

Bodhidharma is usually called the First Patriarch of the Zen Buddhist school, but he was not the first Chinese Zen Master. After Bodhidharma, several generations of Lanka Masters perpetuated the doctrine, and Hui-neng, author of the *Platform Scripture*, was the Sixth Patriarch, deriving the "robe" from Hung-jen (601-674), the Fifth Patriarch.

Hui-neng's family was poor, and consequently Hui-neng was illiterate, but when he heard a recitation of the *Diamond Scripture* (when he was about twenty-four) he was inspired to visit its principal exponent, the Fifth Patriarch, Hung-jen. Hui-neng so impressed the Patriarch that within a few months he was proclaimed the Sixth Patriarch, and he became a Buddhist priest in 676. In 677 (it is reported) he received an invitation from the prefect of the city of Shao-chou to lecture in the Ta-fan Temple there. Purportedly Hui-neng's disciple Fa-hai recorded the sermon, and the *Platform Scripture* is the result.

Chan offers a summary account of the lecture. Hui-neng is described as having "emphatically declared" that everyone possesses the Buddha-nature, that the "great wisdom" is nothing but this nature, and that putting the original, pure nature into practice would make one equal to the Buddha. Outside activities are useless (reading scriptures, building temples, praying, recitations, and so on); what is needed is to "take refuge in the nature within. . . ." The way to intuit one's nature is through "calmness and wisdom," attained when one frees oneself from thoughts, characters, and all attachments. True meditation is not of the conventional, ritualized sort; it consists of the calmness that is the unattached true and original nature within. Seeing one's own nature is "sudden enlightenment." If one holds to the *Diamond Scripture* (Chan concludes his summary account), one will "attain wisdom . . . see his own nature . . . and become a Buddha in his own physical body. . . ."

Chan's Introduction to the *Platform Scripture* provides an account of the contributions to Zen Buddhism made by Hui-neng's successors, an analysis of the differences between the *Diamond Scripture* and the *Lanka* scripture (the *Diamond Scripture* emphasizing freedom of the mind from attachments, the *Laṅka* emphasizing the nonduality and nondifferentiation of the True State), the differences in teachings of the Southern and Northern Schools, the later developments of Zen, and a survey of the Zen methods, including the devices of the *koan* (problem inviting an enigmatic answer), shouting, and beating.

Chan explains that the "platform" is the raised structure from which ordination is administered. The sermon part of the *Platform Scripture* is genuine; the autobiographical parts and the last sections include modifications and additions.

Hui-neng. *The Platform Sutra of the Sixth Patriarch: The Text of the Tun-huang Manuscript*. Edited and translated by Philip B. Yampolsky. New York: Columbia University Press, 1967.

Philip B. Yampolsky, at the time Lecturer in Japanese at Columbia University, provides an extensive introduction to his translation of the *Platform Sutra* (or *Scripture*). Yampolsky gives an account of the growth of Ch'an Buddhism in the eighth century, including a detailed account of the Lankāvatāra School and of Shen-hui, a disciple of Hui-neng and champion of what came to be called the Southern School of Ch'an Buddhism. The story of eighth century Ch'an Buddhism then focuses on Hui-neng, and Yampolsky offers a detailed and carefully documented biography of the Sixth Patriarch. In "The Making of a Book: *The Platform Sutra*," Yampolsky reviews the history of the Tun-huang manuscript (which he estimates was written between 830 and 860); he traces the developing history of versions of the work; and he offers 820 as the probable date of the *Platform Scripture*. He then discusses the *Platform Scripture* in considerable detail, concluding with a careful analysis of content.

The contents of the Tun-huang text fall into five classes, according to Yampolsky: (1) the autobiographical material, (2) the sermons, (3) arguments against Northern Ch'an (Zen) Buddhism and in defense of the Southern School, (4) sections relating to Fa-hai (the transmitter of the book) and various miscellaneous verses and stories.

The sermons exhibit a striking similarity to passages in the works of Shen-hui, and thus Yampolsky suggests that there is the possibility that the *Platform Scripture* is derived from Shen-hui's works. Yampolsky advises that one regard the sermons of the *Platform Scripture* as representative of middle and late eighth century Ch'an thought, later organized, modified, and enlarged by subsequent Ch'an Masters.

The autobiographical section of the *Platform Scripture* tells of Hui-neng's humble beginnings, of his illiteracy, of his interviews with the Fifth Patriarch, of the Patriarch's expounding the *Diamond Scripture* to Hui-neng, of his being made Sixth Patriarch, and of his departure for the south. Throughout the remainder of the *Platform Scripture* Hui-neng is a "rather disembodied voice represented by the phrase: 'The Master said,'" Yampolsky comments.

The *Platform Scripture* contributes little to one's understanding of how the doctrine was transmitted from teacher to disciple; the teaching methods are left unclear, Yampolsky reports. However, he adds, the sermons played an important role, and by the time Hui-neng delivered his sermons at the Ta-fan Temple in Shao-chou he was "a renowned Ch'an Master, the recognized Sixth Patriarch. . . ."

Most of the central ideas in the *Platform Scripture* are taken from canonical sources, according to Yampolsky, and are presented in comparatively simple form. Other Ch'an scholars later elaborated and commented on the ideas as presented in the *Platform Scripture*.

Yampolsky summarizes the content of the sermon as follows: The identity of *prajñā* (original wisdom) and *dhyāna* (meditation) is said by Hui-neng to be basic in his teachings; neither comes before the other, he argues. The true wisdom is possessed from the beginning by everyone; thus, one does not attain it through meditation. Knowledge of the true nature is enlightenment. Practicing "direct mind" and having no attachments, Hui-neng taught, is the "*samādhi* of oneness," that is, concentration on the oneness of the universe. Sudden enlightenment comes to one who uses the method of direct mind (but, Yampolsky points out, Hui-neng does not suggest that the method is a quick one). Enlightenment is a state of no-thought, achieved by cutting off attachment to any instant of thought and hence attachment to thoughts and to thought itself. (Yampolsky suggests that the references to direct mind, no-thought, the original and pure nature, the Buddha-nature, and all related matters, appear to involve a conception of the Absolute as that which is beyond conception and statement in words.) Hui-neng speaks of "sitting in meditation" (*tso-ch'an*) and explains meditation as an internal seeing of the original nature by not activating thoughts. (Yampolsky points out that Hui-neng rejects the formal meditation practices of other schools of Buddhism and Ch'an, but he does not reject meditation itself.) Then the sermon turns to Mahāyāna Buddhism in general and to the recital of the Precepts. Throughout the sermon, Yampolsky emphasizes, the doctrine is enunciated that holds that the Buddha-nature is in all sentient beings and that to find this nature is "to see one's own original mind." The miscellaneous stories, verses, and other passages with which the *Platform Scripture* closes tend to bear out the principal ideas of the central section of the scripture and to offer points in criticism of other Buddhist schools. —*I.P.M.*

ADDITIONAL RECOMMENDED READING

Conze, Edward, ed. and tr. *Buddhist Wisdom Books: The Diamond Sutra and the Heart Sutra.* London: George Allen & Unwin, 1958. A careful translation of two classic scriptures, with copious explanatory notes. Conze reports that it is said that Hui-neng achieved enlightenment by meditating on the following passage in the *Diamond Scripture*: "Therefore then, Sub-huti, the Bodhisattva, the great being, should produce an unsupported thought, i.e. a thought which is nowhere supported, a thought unsupported by sights, sounds, smells, tastes, touchables or mind-objects."

Fung Yu-lan. *The Spirit of Chinese Philosophy.* Translated by E. R. Hughes. London: Kegan Paul, Trench, Trubner & Company, 1947. The distinguished Chinese philosopher Fung Yu-lan here assumes the role of historian of thought and offers a thorough and clear account of Chinese philosophy, including a chapter on the "Inner-light School (*Ch'an Tsung*) of Buddhism."

Koller, John M. *Oriental Philosophies.* New York: Charles Scribner's Sons, 1970. Koller provides a helpful and explanatory survey of Hindu systems, Buddhist philosophies (including a chapter on Zen Buddhism), and Chinese philosophies.

Wing-tsit Chan, ed. and tr. *A Source Book in Chinese Philosophy.* Princeton, New Jersey: Princeton University Press, 1963. An excellent collection of basic writings; includes illuminating introductory sections and notes. Selections from the *Platform Scripture* are provided, together with selections from *Shen-hui yü-lu* (*Recorded Conversations of Shen-hui*).

CREST JEWEL OF WISDOM

Author: S'añkara (or Shankara, Samkara, Sankaracharya, c. 788-c. 820)
Type of work: Metaphysics
First transcribed: Unknown

PRINCIPAL IDEAS ADVANCED

In this existence, all is illusion (maya).

To achieve liberation the wise man will discriminate between the permanent and the transitory; he will be indifferent to the fruits of action; he will achieve tranquillity of mind, self-control, cessation of action by the mind, forbearance of suffering, faith, and deep concentration on Brahman; and he will yearn to be liberated from the bonds of ignorance and egoism.

Liberation from this existence can be achieved only through direct perception of the oneness of the individual self (ātman) with the universal self (Brahman).

The self is none of the five sheaths of the human being.

To achieve nirvana the disciple must overcome the feeling of "I," follow his guru's teachings, study the scriptures, and come to full awareness of the truth of the mystic formula: "This is Brahman; that thou art."

It would be incorrect to speak about "the philosophy of S'añkara" since he and other great Indian sages never claimed a philosophy of their own but were merely expounders of the great spiritual knowledge bequeathed them by a long lineage of predecessors. They differ according to the emphasis placed upon the various aspects of that knowledge, and their greatness is measured by the degree to which they mastered it. By that measure, S'añkara was perhaps the greatest of the historical Hindu sages, not including, however, Gautama the Buddha.

In the East the belief is common that there is a "soul-redeeming" *truth* which can make of its possessor a divine being, one liberated from the wheel of *samsāra*, that is, from obligatory rebirth. The state of liberation, nirvana, is the supreme aim, the *summum bonum* of all six Hindu schools of philosophy, as well as of the various Buddhist sects. The Western reader must, therefore, constantly keep in mind that there are three basic doctrines of Oriental philosophy:

(1) The doctrine of *rebirth*, meaning the periodic appearance of the same human egos in new physical bodies.

(2) The doctrine of *Karma*, or moral retribution, the regulatory law under which rebirth takes place.

(3) The doctrine of *spiritual evolution* by which a relative perfection is attainable, in principle, by all beings—those of the lower kingdoms of nature included.

We can realize why no Hindu sage bothers to prove or defend these three doctrines, for they are never questioned even by an opponent. This will also explain the universal belief in India of the existence among men of advanced beings who have acquired supernormal powers (*siddhis*) and who are no longer subject to the normal laws of birth and death. Having learned the hidden secrets of nature, mainly by following the Delphic injunction "Man, know thyself!" they discovered that a thorough knowledge and understanding of their own egos enabled them to become masters not only of themselves, that is, of the actions of the outer body and the inner mind, but also of external nature to an extent that the Western reader would be inclined to call miraculous. Yet it is claimed by these sages that their supernormal powers are definitely not *supernatural*, but are exerted within the framework of nature's laws, which therefore, they are able to make use of, whenever the occasion calls for the exercise of their *siddhis*.

Such a sage was S'ankara. Because of the fact that many of his successors adopted the same name, S'ankara, there is a great confusion as to his dates as well as to his writings. Many of the writings of the later S'ankaras have been fathered upon their illustrious predecessor, not always to the benefit of the latter. Although some biographers place him as early as 510 B.C., most scholars are agreed that he was born much later, about the beginning of the ninth century.

S'ankara, by writing his commentary on the *Brahma Sūtras*, in which he stressed non-dualism (*a-dvaita*), became the founder of the Advaita system of the Vedanta school of Hindu philosophy.

S'ankara's writings consist of a number of important commentaries as well as original treatises of various lengths. Of his commentaries, the one on the *Brahma Sūtras* is of the greatest importance for his followers. Also important are the ones on some of the principal *Upanishads* as well as his commentary on the *Bhagavad Gītā*.

Most of S'ankara's original treatises seem to have been written for his disciples' use only. Among these is the very short one, entitled *Ten Stanzas*, consisting of precisely ten quatrains. Somewhat longer is the *Hundred Stanzas* consisting of 101 quatrains. Of his two compendiums of Advaita philosophy, the *Thousand Teachings* consists of a part in prose of 116 numbered paragraphs and a part in verse consisting of 649 couplets arranged in nineteen chapters. The other compendium is the *Crest Jewel of Wisdom* (*Vivekacūdāmaṇi*), which consists of 581 stanzas, most of which are couplets and quatrains with a few triplets interspersed.

The Vedanta viewpoint (*vedāntadarśana*) was firmly established by Bādarāyana in his *Brahma Sūtras*, also called *Vedanta Sūtras*. He is claimed to be identical with Krishna Dvaipayana who is the compiler of the Vedas, to whom also the *Purānas* are attributed, not to speak of the *Mahābharata*. But the Vedas were compiled 3100 B.C., according to Brahman chronology and this is, perhaps, too early a date for the *Brahma Sūtras*.

The *Brahma Sūtras* starts with an inquiry into Brahman, the world soul, then continues with a refutation of erroneous views, after which the means of reaching union with Brahman are discussed. Finally the fourth and last part is dedicated to the nature of liberation from the rounds of rebirth, and discusses the kinds of liberated beings. The sūtras (aphorisms) are extraordinarily terse, often consisting of only one or two words, and generally without any verb. Commentators are needed to explain these riddles. But, as one would expect, commentators are wont to disagree among themselves, and so the Vedanta school split into three main systems, known as the *Advaita*, or Non-Dualistic system; the *Viśistādvaita*, or Qualified non-Dualistic system; and the *Dvaita* or Dualistic system.

Of these, the first system is that of S'aṅkara and his commentary; the second is that of Rāmānuja and his great commentary (*S'rībhāṣya*); the third system is that of Madhva, or Anandatīrtha, and his *Sutrabhāṣya*.

S'aṅkara teaches the unity of the self of man with Brahman, and that their apparent separation is an illusion (*māyā*). Rāmānuja, while admitting that the self of man can unite with Brahman, claims that both are real. His system is theistic and anthropomorphic, based on religious devotion rather than on rules of logic, as is that of S'aṅkara. Madhva, however, teaches that the duality of man's soul and Brahman persists, that both are real and independent of each other. His dualism is unqualified and opposes S'aṅkara's monistic views as well as the views of Rāmānuja.

There have been other commentators on the *Brahma Sūtras*. Perhaps the most recent is Baladeva (eighteenth century), whose extensive commentary, known as *Govinda Bhāṣya*, gives the Vaisnava viewpoint, since he was a follower of S'rī Chaitanya. The *Govinda Bhāṣya* is therefore theistic, like the one by Rāmānuja.

The *Crest Jewel of Wisdom* was written by S'aṅkara to assist the would-be aspirant to spiritual wisdom in his efforts to free himself from the rounds of incessant rebirths. There is a strong similarity between the teachings and methods of S'aṅkara and the Buddha. Both aimed to teach mankind how to conquer pain and suffering, how to reach the acme of manhood, and finally how to obtain the highest spiritual state possible while still living on earth. Both considered conditioned existence as *unreal* and stressed its illusory character (*māyā*). Neither of the two had any use for personal gods (*devas*), knowing themselves superior to the latter. The Buddhists and Advaita Vedantists have been called atheists by their opponents, and Buddha as well as S'aṅkara discarded rituals completely. There is no real difference between the path leading to Buddhahood and the path leading to the state of a *Jivanmukta*. All this makes it more difficult to explain the nearly complete silence of the Buddha on the subject of the Self (*ātman*) and the almost continuous reference to the *ātman* by S'aṅkara. Buddha's silence led many Buddhists as well as non-Buddhists to believe that Buddha denied the existence of the *ātman* and, therefore, of a soul, which, of course, would contradict Buddha's statements upon a number of other subjects.

S'añkara's writings are too metaphysical, even for the average Hindu, to be useful for any but advanced disciples in Hindu mysticism. This he frankly admits at the outset of most of his treatises, and so in the case of the *Crest Jewel of Wisdom* he directs himself to a "wise man" (*vidvān*) who strives for liberation and has renounced his desire for the enjoyment of external objects. He advises the "wise man" to apply to a true and great spiritual teacher for guidance. After some further advice of a general nature he states the qualifications necessary for success in this venture, apart from being learned and of strong intellect: (1) *Discrimination* between things permanent and transitory; (2) *indifference* to enjoyment of the fruits of one's actions in this world and in the next; (3) the six accomplishments:

S'ama (tranquillity), which is a state of mind devoted to its goal;

Dama (self-control), which is the fixing in their own proper sphere of both the organs of perception and of action, after reverting them from their objects;

The height of *uparati* (cessation), which is the spontaneous abstaining from action by the mind;

Titiksā (forbearance), which is patient endurance of all suffering, without retaliation, free from anxiety and complaint;

S'raddhā (faith), which is reflection and meditation on the truth of the words of the Guru and of the sacred texts; and

Samādhana (deep concentration), which is the constant fixing of the discriminating mind (*buddhi*) upon the pure Brahman, and not the indulging of the mind (*citta*);

and (4) *yearning to be liberated* (*mumuksutā*), which is the desire to be liberated by knowing one's own real nature and the bonds made through ignorance, from egoism down to the body.

The necessary qualifications for the Guru, the teacher whom the well-equipped aspirant to liberation or nirvana must now seek, are even more severe. The Guru, through whom freedom from bondage is to be attained, must be spiritually wise, conversant with sacred knowledge, sincere, and not suffering from desires; he must know the nature of Brahman; he must be one who is at rest in the Eternal, like a fire that is tranquil when destitute of fuel, one who is a river of disinterested compassion, a friend of all living creatures.

Having found such a preceptor and having asked him for guidance, the disciple, when found worthy, is then instructed by his Master, who praises him for his desire to rid himself of the bonds of ignorance (*avidyā*). He is told that liberation can only be achieved through the *direct perception* of the oneness of the individual self (*ātman*) with the universal self (Brahman). Neither the Vedas, nor the scriptures (*śastras*), nor the incantation (*mantras*), nor any medicine can help him who is bitten by the snake of ignorance.

It is necessary to know how to discriminate between spirit and non-spirit, between the self and not-self.

In order to show the difference between spirit and non-spirit, the Guru outlines the visible and invisible part of nature, beginning with the grossest of man's constituent vehicles.

The *gross body* is produced from the five subtle elements, whose functions are responsible for the five senses. The Guru warns of the danger of sense enjoyments and of desires pertaining to the body, and he describes the danger in no uncertain terms.

The *internal organ* consists of *manas*, the mental faculties of postulating and doubting; the intellect, having the characteristic of certainty about things; the ego-conforming power, producing the conception "I"; and the mind, having the property of concentration.

The *vital principle* manifests itself, according to its transformations, as one of the five "vital airs."

The *subtle or astral body* is the vehicle of the five faculties, the five sense organs, the five vital airs, the five elements, ignorance, desire, and action. It is also known as the vehicle of characteristics, and is active in dreams.

The *causal body* of the self is the unmanifested condition of the three universal qualities. Its state is that of dreamless sleep. The three universal qualities are purity, action, and darkness. When the purity is unalloyed there will be perception of the self.

The Guru now defines in many ways the Supreme Spirit (*Paramātman*) through the knowledge of which Isolation (*Kaivalya*) or Freedom is obtained.

A description follows of the five sheaths (*kośa*), another way of looking at the constituents of a human being. They are the *annamaya*-sheath, sustained by physical food—that is, the gross body; the *prāṇamaya*-sheath, the vehicle of the vital forces, through which the ego performs all the actions of the gross body; the *manomaya*-sheath, consisting of the organs of sensation and *manas*, the latter mental faculty being the cause of ignorance and consequently the cause of the bondage of conditioned existence, although the same *manas* when pure becomes the cause of liberation; the *vijñānamaya*-sheath, consisting of intellect and the powers of perception, the doer of actions and the cause of the rounds of rebirth, the embodied ego which has no beginning in time and which is the guide of all actions; the *ānandamaya*-sheath, the reflection of absolute bliss, yet not free from the quality of darkness.

The Guru explains that these five sheaths are *not the Self*. The latter is self-illumined and remains after the subtraction of these sheaths. It is the witness of the three states, of the waking, dreaming, and deep sleep state.

The disciple is now given subtler teachings about the Self and the Supreme Spirit. In a number of stanzas is repeated, paraphrasing the *Chāndogya-Upanishad*, the mystic formula: ". . . this is Brahman, that thou art (*tat tvam asi*)."

The subject of the mental impressions which are the seeds in the mind through which *karma* manifests subsequently to any act is now discussed by the Guru, and the disciple is told how to exhaust them. At the same time the disciple must overcome the feeling of "I," the power of egoism, and many stanzas are dedicated to the elaboration of this subject. Other subjects are interwoven in the discussion, such as that of *nirvikalpa samādhi*, a superior type of meditation.

The stanzas become more and more abstruse while the disciple advances in spiritual matters. The characteristics of *jivanmukta*, he who is *liberated while living on earth*, are described, and also the consequences of this achievement, especially in relation to the three kinds of *karma*.

Finally comes the moment when the disciple, through the Guru's teaching, through the evidence of the revealed scriptures, and through his own efforts, realizes the full truth and becomes absorbed in the universal self. He speaks and informs his Master about his spiritual experiences.

He tells about the Absolute (*Parabrahman*) and his spiritual bliss. He is without attachment and without limbs, sexless, and indestructible. He is neither the doer nor the enjoyer, for he is without change and without action. He is now the self-illumined *ātman*. He bows down before his Guru through whose compassion and greatly esteemed favor he has achieved the goal of his existence.

The Guru, greatly pleased, explains the position of the Knower of Brahman in the remaining stanzas. At the end, the disciple salutes his Guru respectfully. Liberated from bondage, with the Guru's permission he goes away.
—*W.B.R.*

PERTINENT LITERATURE

Dasgupta, S. N. *Indian Idealism*. Cambridge: Cambridge University Press, 1969.

Indian Idealism contains elaborate discussion of S'aṅkara's monistic idealism, which finds its succinct expression in the *Crest Jewel of Wisdom*. S. N. Dasgupta traces India's idealistic thought back to the *Upanishads* and to early Buddhism and explains in what sense the Upanishadic and the Buddhist philosophies can be called "idealistic." His account of the Upanishadic idealism contains separate treatment of each of the principal *Upanishads* and prepares the ground for understanding the Vedāntic idealism of S'aṅkara, whom he regards as the most important interpreter of the Upanishadic thought. The book also compares Buddhist idealism with S'aṅkara's.

In sketching the Upanishadic idealism, Dasgupta observes that the transition from the realistic and ritualistic world view of the Vedas to the mystical and idealistic philosophy of the *Upanishads* is quite explicit. In view of the Upanishadic affirmation of the transcendental reality of Being, which is claimed to be beyond thought and perception, Dasgupta wonders whether it is correct to regard such a philosophy as idealistic. Without being able to characterize the Upanishadic idealism in terms of any of the models of Western systems of idealism, Dasgupta concludes that the philosophy of the *Upanishads* may be best described as "mystical idealism." However, he notes that the *Upanishads* do not present to us a philosophy in the technical sense, as a systematic and coordinated unity of thought. Nevertheless, numerous attempts have been made to interpret the *Upanishads*. The earliest attempt at a consistent interpretation of the Upanishadic philosophy is to be found in the *Brahma Sūtras* of Bādarāyaṇa. The earliest available and most well-known commentary on the *Brahma Sūtras* is that of S'aṅkara.

Dasgupta notes that in the *Māṇḍūkya Upanishad* the highest reality, Brahman, is described not even as pure consciousness but as a negation of any attempt to describe it in any way. In comparing this *via negativa* description of the ultimate reality with the nihilistic Buddhist idealism of Nāgārjuna, Dasgupta finds much similarity between the two approaches. He also points out the close similarity between the subjective idealism of the Buddhist philosopher Vasubandhu and the idealism of S'aṅkara. In fact, it is noted that one early interpreter of the Upanishadic idealism, Gaudapāda, who was probably a teacher of S'aṅkara, was profoundly influenced by both Nāgārjuna's and Vasubandhu's philosophies in his interpretation of the *Upanishads*. Nevertheless, Dasgupta points out some important differences between the Vedāntic idealism of S'aṅkara and Buddhist idealism: unlike the subjective idealism and phenomenalism of the Buddhist schools, S'aṅkara's *Vedānta* admits of an independent objective reality, Brahman, and a quasiobjective category, *māyā*, which is said to be the source of the illusory appearance of the empirical world.

Dasgupta claims that S'aṅkara accepts Upanishadic metaphysics, especially its monism, without proof and without question. Such monism believes in the only reality of Brahman the Absolute, which is said to be immutable, indescribable, and the true self (*ātman*) of us all. We are all Brahman, and nothing other than Brahman is real. The manifold reality of the empirical world is claimed to be illusion and is explained away by S'aṅkara as the product of *māyā*. The doctrine of *māyā* helps S'aṅkara in affirming the only reality of Brahman. In this respect he departs from Bādarāyana, the author of the *Brahma Sūtras*, who equally emphasizes the immanence and transcedence of Brahman.

S'aṅkara's philosophy espouses a twofold view of things, one referring to the ultimate reality and the other to the illusory existence of empirical entities. One's mistaken understanding of the empirical world of appearance as real is the root cause of one's desires for and attachments to things, which, in turn, is the seed for misery and loss of freedom. This is one's bondage, according to S'aṅkara, and the knowledge of Brahman is liberation. One's supreme task in this world is to realize one's true self as identical with Brahman.

Deutsch, Eliot. *Advaita Vedānta: A Philosophical Reconstruction.* Honolulu: East-West Center Press, 1969.

In his attempt at a philosophical reconstruction of S'aṅkara's *Vedānta* philosophy, Eliot Deutsch selects those ideas in the *Vedānta* metaphysics, epistemology, and ethics which have central importance in the system and which are philosophically interesting on their own. He lifts such ideas from their historical and cultural settings and examines them from a critical point of view to determine their philosophical worth. The result is a book on S'aṅkara's *Vedānta*, perhaps the only one of its kind, which is readily understandable and appreciated by readers who are philosophically inclined but who may not have familiarity with the scholastic details of the long Vedāntic tradition.

S'aṅkara's *Vedānta* philosophy is known as *Advaita*, meaning nondual, because it purports to show the unreality of all distinctions. Deutsch observes that the usual Upanishadic and Vedāntic characterization of Brahman as existence-bliss-consciousness is inappropriate if it is meant to isolate the nature of Brahman, which is, *ex hypothesi*, limitless. However, he believes that such attribution in positive terms is not really aimed at capturing the "essence" of Brahman, but, from experiential and pragmatic points of view, is geared to direct a seeker of truth toward Brahman and to steer him away from the opposites of these positive attributes. Deutsch notes that it is the *via negativa* approach toward Brahman, first found in the *Māṇḍūkya Upanishad* and later widely used by the Advaitins, which ensures the undifferentiated nature of the highest reality.

For *Advaita Vedānta*, even though the world of appearance is not real, it is not unreal either. From the standpoint of appearance, which is a state of ignorance, there are three fundamental modes of being: reality, which is Brahman; appearance, which accounts for the empirical reality of the world; and unreality, like a logical contradiction. The world is apparently real to those people who are yet to attain the realization that all is Brahman. However, once Brahman-realization is obtained, all distinctions between the levels of reality disappear. Any differentiation belongs to the realm of appearance; in reality, only Brahman exists.

The usual account of creation of the world in the *Advaita* literature—that the world evolved out of Brahman through the latter's creative potency (*māyā*)—is to be taken only as an apparent truth, like the status of the world itself. There is no real modification of Brahman; hence, all change, including creation, is only apparent. Deutsch believes that such an analysis of the relation between Brahman and the world is philosophically valid once it is affirmed that Brahman is the only reality. If one accepts the possibility of a nondual spiritual experience and believes that such experience reveals the really real, then one must accept that the world of our ordinary experience is something less than real.

Consistent with its nondualistic position, S'añkara's *Vedānta* affirms an identity between one's true self (*ātman* the Self) and Brahman. The Self is One and is Brahman, whereas one's phenomenal or empirical self (*jīva*), due to misidentification of itself with things other than the Self, perceives itself to be limited and fragmented. This is one's bondage which is due to ignorance (*avidyā*). Deutsch observes that S'añkara does not so much explain the nature and existence of empirical self as he describes the process whereby one comes to be aware of one's self-existence. S'añkara's analysis, according to Deutsch, basically takes the form of phenomenology of consciousness. S'añkara attempts to show through his analysis how one comes to accept something as true which is in fact an illusory appearance.

The central concern of *Advaita Vedānta* is to establish that reality is one and to guide people to a realization of it. Even though the world is claimed to be an appearance, yet within the phenomenal world the Advaitins are not subjective idealists but realists. A variety of philosophical theories are used, including those of *māyā*, the levels of reality, the hierarchy of knowledge, and *karma* (Deutsch believes that *Karma* is a convenient fiction in the *Advaita* system), which help in interpreting and ordering experiences but which in themselves are no more real than those experiences themselves. The path to Brahman-realization is through Self-knowledge; however, any device which helps in ordering and understanding experience and taking one closer to the path of Self-realization is helpful and is considered good.

Organ, Troy W. *The Self in Indian Philosophy*. The Hague, The Netherlands: Mouton, 1964.

Troy W. Organ introduces his study of self in Indian philosophy with a saying attributed to S'añkara: Man is on a pilgrimage to his own self. The author believes that both the Western and the Indian traditions have been concerned with the nature and existence of the self even though their emphasis and treatments have differed. Western man, in spite of his traditional interest in the self, has been more interested in the outward than in the inward, especially during the last five hundred years. The Indians, on the other hand, have been preoccupied with investigation of man's inner nature, which is the self. This is evident in their perception of philosophy as self-knowledge. Consequently, Organ thinks that it is not too unrealistic if in approaching the philosophy of India one expects to discover a better understanding of the self. However, he cautions that such an approach must be based on solid scholarship and not on superficial interests or blind faith.

Organ's study spans eight different, but often closely related, views of the self in Indian philosophy, including those of the *Upanishads* and S'añkara's

Advaita Vedānta. He observes that the Upanishadic seers were in quest of a reality quite different from the Vedic gods, who were mostly deified symbols of external nature. The Upanishadic search took a transcendental form, from phenomenal reality to the Absolute. Its metaphysical approach affirmed Being as the basis of all becomings; but such Being, from a psychological point of view, was also understood as the inner core of the self. Hence arose the Upanishadic realization that *ātman* the Self is Brahman the Absolute, the knowledge of which was viewed as leading to liberation from the bondage of the phenomenal world.

At the outset of his study of the *Advaita Vedānta* view of the self, Organ comments that he will not try to assess S'ankara's reliability as an interpreter of the *Upanishads*; rather, he examines S'ankara's ideas on their own strengths. Central to S'ankara's philosophy of the self is the idea that since the existence of the self is a presupposition of all experience and reasoning, it is self-proven. It cannot be doubted, because even the very act of doubting proves it. Hence, unlike René Descartes', S'ankara's position implies that it is more natural first to accept self's existence and then to conclude that therefore the self thinks, than the other way around. It is the self's nature which needs to be proved, not its existence.

Against the nonsubstantive "bundle" theory of the self as found in Buddhism, S'ankara argues for an unchanging substantive self which is the basis of a continuous person. He believes that the common experience of memory proves that not everything in a person is transitory. Regarding S'ankara's observation that the self is a subject, Organ comments that, as subject, the self cannot then be an object of knowledge. That is, the self cannot be known through our usual cognitive processes based on a subject-object distinction. Further, the self as a subject can reveal the objects of knowledge, but it cannot create them. This explains, according to Organ, why S'ankara's doctrine of the priority of consciousness is compatible with his realistic belief in an independent world. Organ further observes that the self as subject must have consciousness as its essence, and he notes that S'ankara is well aware of this implication because the latter attempts to prove that consciousness does not lapse even during the deepest sleep.

The difference between the individual self (*jīva*) and the Self (*ātman*) is an illusory one because any difference, in the *Advaita* philosophy, belongs to the realm of appearance. However, even though *jīva* and *ātman* are both spiritual in nature, the latter is mistakenly thought to be the former because people usually take their real selves to be finite and fragmented. Such misidentification is the source of bondage; accordingly, liberation from bondage is attained through self-realization. Because the Self is Brahman, and Brahman is One, the moral implication of the *Advaita* philosophy is that one ought to treat others as oneself.—*D.C.*

ADDITIONAL RECOMMENDED READING

Deutsch, Eliot and J. A. B. van Buitenen, eds. and trs. *A Source Book of Advaita Vedānta*. Honolulu: The University Press of Hawaii, 1971. Contains essays on the philosophical and cultural background of *Advaita Vedānta*, as well as relevant selections, in English translation, from the source materials of all important *Advaita Vedānta* schools, including S'aṅkara's. Each selection is properly introduced.

Isherwood, Christopher and Swami Prabhavananda, eds and trs. *Shankara's Crest-Jewel of Discrimination*. New York: New American Library, 1970. A nontechnical and readable introduction to Sankara's philosophy, with a liberal translation of his *Crest Jewel of Wisdom*.

Murty, K. Satchidananda. *Revelation and Reason in Advaita Vedānta*. New York: Columbia University Press, 1959. A scholarly and faithful exposition of S'aṅkara's *Advaita Vedānta*.

Raju, P. T. *Idealistic Thought of India*. Cambridge, Massachusetts: Harvard University Press, 1953. A study of the historical as well as the logical development of the main schools of India's idealistic metaphysics. Contains a detailed exposition of S'aṅkara's philosophy.

ON THE DIVISION OF NATURE

Author: Johannes Scotus Erigena (c. 810-c. 877)
Type of work: Metaphysics
First transcribed: Ninth century

PRINCIPAL IDEAS ADVANCED
God created man in such a manner that man shares the nature of other animals as well as the celestial nature.

Our minds are ignorant and unwise, but in God the mind finds its discipline; man is an intellectual idea formed eternally in the divine mind, and for man to know he must come to full consciousness and recall the eternal ideas.

The idea by which man knows himself is his substance; consequently, man may be known through intellectual causes or by effects.

Man exists in the divine mind, for man is by his essence divine idea.

Man is by nature omniscient, but he lost the knowledge of himself and of his creator when he sinned; insofar as man can know, it is by the grace of God, who allows man to become aware of essences by acts of understanding in which the idea in man's mind and in God's mind are one.

Johannes Scotus Erigena is often regarded as the first of the real medievals. Boethius and Augustine are his only substantial predecessors, and they are several centuries earlier. Erigena was familiar with Boethius, since he wrote about his life; and he introduced classical Neoplatonism into the formative years of the medieval period through his translations from pseudoDionysius the Areopagite. He was also familiar with the fathers of both the Latin Church and the Greek Church. Yet, more than the fact that he is the first major writer to appear in several centuries, his importance to the Middle Ages lies in his production of one of the first complete metaphysical schemes, his *On the Division of Nature.* The Middle Ages became noted for its systematic, speculative, and constructive effort, and the tone for such effort is set here in Erigena's major work.

His Platonistic tendencies are immediately evident in the use he makes in his writing of the dialogue form. Master and Disciple answer and question each other, although the form is more that of alternating brief essays than it is of Plato's more dramatic dialogue form of rapid reply. Of course, Plato also tends to adopt a more sustained form of speech in his later dialogues, and it is perhaps primarily from the Neoplatonists that Erigena learned his writing style. Another similarity to Neoplatonism (in contrast to Plato) can be seen in the cosmic perspective which Erigena adopts. Plato's metaphysics is more fragmentary; the Neoplatonists tend naturally to deal with problems in the total setting of a cosmic scheme. Such a scheme Johannes Scotus Erigena here outlines. (The analysis which follows is of Book IV, Chapters vii-ix, available in Richard McKeon's *Selections from Medieval Philosophers*.)

Why did God create man, Erigena's Disciple asks, as one of the family of animals instead of in the form of some higher celestial creature? As it is, man needs his terrestrial body and can perceive only with the aid of perceptions received from without. With angels it is not so; no such limitations bind them, and yet man is supposed to have been made in God's image. Man's sin and fall from grace cannot account for his animal nature, since even if he had not sinned he would still be an animal. It is not by sin but by nature that man is an animal. And man's position is even more strange if we consider that he may in a future life be transmuted into a celestial form of being.

To answer his Disciple's question, the Master resorts to the divine will, saying that why God willed this is beyond inquiry, since the causes of the divine will cannot be known. Why God willed it is beyond all understanding.

Yet one can say that the whole of created nature, both visible and invisible, is present in man, and this is a valuable position. What is naturally present in the celestial essences subsists essentially in man. We can say rationally, therefore, that God wished to place man in the genus of animals for the reason that he wished to create every creature in him, and for this to be possible man had to share in all of nature and not only in celestial nature. No irrationality is implied, for everything from God can be understood and anything not from God cannot be understood because it simply is not. Things exist outside the knower, and the knowledge of them is produced in man by them. The ideas of things and the things themselves are of different natures. And things must be granted to be of a more excellent nature than the ideas of them.

To continue, that which understands is better than that which is understood, and, one step more, the idea of intelligible things is older than the intelligible things themselves. The human mind derives its knowledge from things, but the things themselves were originally formed from intelligible ideas (existing in God's mind). Although our human mind is born inexpert and unwise, nevertheless it is able to find in itself its God, its expertness, and its discipline. As in God, so in man there is a kind of trinity: mind, learning, art. Still only the divine mind possesses the true idea of the human mind, since the human mind cannot of itself comprehend itself. To define man truly we must say: Man is an intellectual idea formed eternally in the divine mind.

What results is a Platonic doctrine of recollection, now transferred to the divine mind. What man essentially is, all the knowledge he can possess, is eternally contained as idea in the divine mind. To know, then, is to come to full consciousness, to recall this set of ideas eternally formed. Self-consciousness means increased knowledge of the divine nature. A true knowledge of all things is implanted in human nature, although its presence is concealed until by divine light the soul is turned to God. What else is there, then, except ideas? Accordingly, the very idea by which man knows himself may be considered his substance. Yet, how could it be that we do not always and naturally see man as this divine idea? Because (as Spinoza was to say later) all things in nature may be viewed in two perspectives: either as a creature in the Word of God in which all things have been made, or as an individual considered in himself without reference to his divine origin.

Man has one substance understood in two ways: in one fashion, the human substance is perceived through its creation in intellectual causes; in the other, by its generation in effects. Accordingly, one and the same thing is spoken of as double because of the double observation of it. What difficulties do we encounter in such a theory? In order to know man's essence properly, God's nature must first be understood, for here is the true focus of knowledge. And yet, Erigena holds to the traditional assertion: it is in no way granted to the human mind to know what the essence of God is, although we may know "that it is." The result is that, although man was first rendered intelligible by understanding his essence as an idea in the divine mind, the knowledge of man is, because of this, subjected to all of the traditional difficulties surrounding the knowledge of God.

God is entirely uncircumscribed and is to be understood through no thing because he is infinite. What about man? Here, too, we deny that the human mind is *anything* and affirm only that it *is*. If the human mind were circumscribable, it could not express the image of its creator wholly, which means that because the human mind is so much like the divine it also cannot be grasped directly. The same problems which surround the divine nature now surround the human mind's understanding of its own essence, since this cannot be grasped except as part of the divine mind. Amazingly enough, even infinity is transferred to the human mind: just as the divine essence is infinite, so the human determination is not limited by any certain end. It is understood only to be, but what it *is* is never understood. Infinity, once God's unique possession, man now comes to share, and he immediately becomes subject to its rational difficulties.

Aristotle rejected infinity as an attribute of divine perfection because of its inaccessibility to rational comprehension. Transcendentalists applied unlimitedness to God in spite of the difficulties for knowledge. Now Erigena, by defining man's essence as a divine idea, subjects the understanding of human nature to the same insurmountable difficulties, since God's mind must be understood before man's essence can be found. In God, however, there is no ignorance, except the divine darkness which exceeds all understanding. Since man subsists more truly in his idea than in himself, he must be understood in and through his idea, and this is located in God, who is himself not fully knowable. Yet this cannot be avoided, for when a thing is known better, then it must be judged to exist more truly. Man, then, exists more truly as an idea in the divine mind than he does in himself, which means that God's understanding (and darkness) is involved in the knowledge of the true existence of all things, man included. Geometrical figures do not exist in themselves, for instance, but only in the theoretical structure of the discipline in which they are the figures. So man does not exist in himself truly but exists in the divine plan of which he is a part. If, therefore, geometrical bodies subsist only in their rational ideas, what is there so astonishing about the fact that natural bodies should subsist in that nature (God) in which there is the idea of them? Reality is never ultimately located in the natural world; it is in the divine mind. Intelligible things are actually prior to sensible things in the mind which understands them. The thing understood, furthermore, is preceded by the understanding soul which perceives it. Finally, the divine nature is prior to the human soul, since it provides the locus for both the soul's self-understanding and its ultimate existence.

Why should it be so difficult for man to learn these facts about his nature and his understanding? If man had not sinned, the reply comes, he certainly would not have fallen into so profound an ignorance of himself. In the fall, human nature perished entirely in all men, except in the Redeemer of the world, in whom alone it remained incorruptible. He alone was joined in a unity of substance to the Word of God, in whom all the elect by grace are made sons of God and participants of the divine substance. Before sin each creature had implanted in it a full knowledge of both itself and its creator, so that if human nature had not sinned, it would assuredly be omniscient. Sin alone separates man from God, human from divine nature. First, Erigena made man infinite by linking his self-understanding with God's understanding. Now man becomes omniscient by nature, losing this quality only through the bondage of sin.

At the present time human nature still has this perfect knowledge, both of itself, its creator, and all things (present before sin), but this perfect knowledge is held in possibility alone. In the highest man this knowledge becomes actual again. All things are known in and are created by the Word of God; thus, the created wisdom of man knew all things before they were made. In fact, everything in the human understanding proceeds from and through that very idea of the creative wisdom. All things subsist in the divine understanding causally and in the human understanding effectually. In knowledge and in dignity, but not in time and place, the creation of man precedes those things which were created with it and by it. Yet, in the end, no created intellect can know what a thing is, since the essence of everything is involved in the problem of divine ignorance.

Man's rational processes are so great, in fact, that his understanding would naturally be equal with the angels—if he had not sinned. Man and angel are by nature so alike that they reciprocally understand each other. In fact, any two human understandings can essentially become one, since they can both apprehend ideas, and our essence and our understanding are not two things but one. Man is essentially his understanding. This is incorporeal and, ultimately, is to be seen as an idea in the divine mind. Our one true and supreme essence is the understanding made specific in the contemplation of truth. Here is an antecedent to Descartes' definition of man as a "thinking substance." Here is the final identification which makes man in his real nature so much like God and thus involves the understanding of man in the difficulties of comprehending God. Man is his knowledge; he is his ideas whose locus is in the divine mind.

God created by separating light from darkness; were there no dark element, all would be angelic nature and understanding. As it is, darkness precipitated man into ignorance as a penalty for his pride, and man could neither foresee his fall nor his misery. Were it not for the unshapeliness of darkness, all creatures would cling immutably to their creator, and men would not need to struggle for understanding. As it is, man must first see God, the presence of the idea of man in the divine mind, in order to understand his own nature. But this requires overcoming the ignorance of sin and grasping the divine nature—surely a job for an angel, unless man is first restored by divine grace.

A speculative system of such scope and daring as Erigena has presented here is quite difficult for the modern mind to grasp for many reasons. Such pure speculation, for one thing, is not very prevalent today; and, for another thing, one does not expect to find speculation of such vigor arising as the first philosophy of consequence since Augustine, who wrote nearly four centuries earlier. Here Erigena easily ranges between God and man, comprehending in his theory the whole of creation with the greatest of ease. Modern caution has restrained us from such far-ranging flights of philosophical reasoning. When we think of the Middle Ages, it is not Erigena's ideas that we think of most naturally, and it is true that they were quickly considered unorthodox by his own church. Nevertheless, they exerted a powerful influence (particularly in Platonic circles) in the fruitful centuries ahead and still stand as a monument to independent and original speculative construction.—*F.S.*

Pertinent Literature

Weinberg, J. R. *A Short History of Medieval Philosophy*. Princeton, New Jersey: Princeton University Press, 1964.

J. R. Weinberg offers a brief biographical sketch of Johannes Scotus Erigena, who was born in Ireland around 810. He translated the works of an author who has come to be known as pseudo-Dionysius, who was mistakenly believed to be Dionysius the Areopagite, a traveling companion of St. Paul, but who was in fact an unknown person who, around the beginning of the sixth century, wrote a variety of works in which the incomprehensibility of God was a major theme. Erigena translated the works of pseudo-Dionysius, as well as a commentary on pseudo-Dionysius by Maximus the Confessor, and was strongly influenced by the themes he found there. He also translated

On the Creation of Man by the Cappadocian Gregory of Nyssa, and was influenced by this work and the works of the other Cappadocians, Gregory of Nazianzus and Basil of Caesarea, and, perhaps more significantly, by Saint Augustine. In 851 he wrote *On Predestination*, a refutation of the views of the monk Gottschalk, which was later condemned. His main work, *On the Division of Nature*, was condemned in 1225 by Pope Honorius III.

Isaiah 7:9 (Revised Standard Version) reads, in part: "If you will not believe, surely you shall not be established." (This is part of a message Isaiah was instructed by God to give to King Ahaz.) Weinberg notes that Erigena reads this passage as meaning, "If you had not believed, you would not have understood." So, Weinberg tells us, the message Erigena finds in Isaiah 7:9 is that faith precedes reason; one must believe in order to understand. To the same effect, Erigena suggests, is the story in the *New Testament* of John and Peter running to the empty tomb of Christ. Peter reaches the tomb first; Peter represents faith, while John, who arrives after Peter, represents reason. Finally, in the vision of God which is the fate of all who are saved, reason will replace faith; at least Erigena so reads St. Paul. Thus, Weinberg explains, for Erigena reason and faith do not conflict; they have the same divine source that leads to the same goal.

Weinberg suggests that these examples of biblical interpretation by Erigena are, if no less, then also no more fanciful than the allegorical readings others (for example, Origen) gave to biblical passages in order to harmonize biblical teaching with their particular philosophical or religious perspective. Further, he adds, they illustrate Erigena's theme that philosophy is the enterprise of rationally interpreting Scripture. The Bible is viewed as written basically in figurative language and thus containing allegorical meanings. Thus, Erigena holds, while the Scripture is a source of truth, its truths have to be gained by allegorical interpretation.

Weinberg indicates that if one asks why, according to Erigena, God could not just speak the truth in literal clarity, the answer comes in terms of the doctrine, so favored by pseudo-Dionysius as well as Erigena, that God is utterly incomprehensible, so no literal lanaguage can describe him. (There remains the question as to how, if he is ineffable, *any* language can describe him.)

According to Weinberg, Erigena offers us a system of thought which classifies or divides nature into various classes. The highest division is into those things which are, *versus* those which are not. Obviously, "not" is being used in an unusual, technical sense; something is said not to be if it can be neither an object of perception nor an object of cognition. Erigena, Weinberg continues, operates in a tradition which views the world as comprised of items which are rankable on a scale of perfection-and-privation. God is at the top of the scale, perfect without any lack or privation. Insofar as anything is not identical to God, it lacks something, and so is partly privative; and insofar as anything (in the ordinary, untechnical sense) exists at all, it is not purely privative. Some things are so nearly purely privative, however, that they cannot be perceived or thought, and God is so purely perfect that he cannot be perceived or thought. Both, then, in the unusual and technical sense, "are not." Apparently, Weinberg notes, this distinction, while defined in terms of our comprehension of nature, is intended by Erigena to be both a distinction of reason (involving two distinct ways of conceiving) and a real distinction (some things, independent of our ways of conceiving them, *are*, and others, independent of our ways of conceiving them, *are not*). Weinberg notes that Erigena even goes so far as to say that God is ignorant of himself; having no determinate essence, he cannot know what his determinate essence is. In the technical language Erigena uses, this can be put by saying that since he is not, he cannot know what he is.

A further division of nature that Erigena offers, Weinberg tells us, is fourfold into that which creates but is not created, that which both creates and is created, that which is created but does not create, and that which neither creates nor is created. The first division contains God, considered as the origin of all things. The second division contains the Logos, conceived along Neoplatonic lines as a go-between between God and the material universe, which provides the content of the third division. God again, considered as the final cause or goal of the universe, fills the fourth division. Weinberg explains that, for Erigena, the distinction between the first and fourth divisions is but a distinction of reason, arising from our regarding God now as efficient, now as final, cause, while the second and third divisions are not merely distinctions of reason; things are in themselves different in the ways they are conceived as being different when we make these divisions.

In spite of his claim that God is utterly ineffable, Weinberg reports, Erigena also offers a doctrine intended to make knowledge of God possible by offering a theory of theophanies or divine appearances. By knowing *what* these are, one can know *that* God is. This is, in effect, Erigena's theory of revelation.

Weinberg tells us that Erigena takes over from pseudo-Dionysius the view that there are three sorts of theology: affirmative, negative, and symbolic or superlative. These Weinberg explains as follows. Affirmative theology applies to God terms taken from Scripture, so that he is said to be living, good, and so on. Negative theology is then viewed as correcting affirmative by denying that these predicates describe God, who is approached best by a learned ignorance which ascribes ineffability to him. Erigena's intent, Weinberg indicates, is then to reconcile affirmative and negative theology by saying that God is "Super-living" and "Super-good," by which it is meant that there are living things and good things in the world, and that the world has its origin in God, without saying that God himself is living or good.

Weinberg concludes that the result of obtaining this sort of knowledge of God is viewed as a kind of illumination in which (by appeal to the ancient doctrine that in some sense, in knowledge, the knower becomes one with the object known) the knower is deified. Maximus, Weinberg remarks, put this by saying that in such illumination the knower remains human but seems to consist only of the divine.

Copleston, Frederick, S. J. *A History of Philosophy*. Vol. II. Garden City, New York: Doubleday-Anchor, 1962.

In *On the Division of Nature*, Frederick Copleston contends, Johannes Scotus Erigena offers the first great intellectual system of the Middle Ages, a work probably composed between 862 and 866. It consists, he reports, of five books, written in dialogue form, which attempt to communicate Christian doctrine and the philosophy of Saint Augustine in a way suggested by Neo-platonism and the doctrines of pseudo-Dionysius. Some have thought that Erigena was an orthodox Christian, and this view, Copleston suggests, finds confirmation in his remark that the authority of the Scriptures must be followed in all things. But others have thought that he was something much like a pantheist and that he regarded philosophy as superior to theology; this latter view, Copleston suggests, finds support in his remark that every authority not confirmed by reason is weak, whereas reason itself needs no support by any authority.

According to Copleston, Erigena uses "nature" to mean "all that exist," both God and creation. Nature is divided into "that which is" and "that which is not." Copleston explains that Erigena uses various criteria for making this division. Human nature, estranged from God by sin, "is not," but, reconciled to God by grace, it "is." Abstract objects not susceptible to change and comprehensible by reason but not sensory perception "are"; perceptible material objects, subject to change, "are not." Things accessible to cognition or perception "are"; things not accessible to cognition or perception "are not."

It is not Erigena's intention, Copleston says, to assert that God is the genus of which creatures are species or that God is a whole of which creatures are parts. Nevertheless, his explanation of the egress of creatures from, and their return to, God may have unintended pantheistic implications.

Copleston adds that, for Erigena, nature is also divided into four species: nature which creates but is not created, nature which both creates and is created, nature which is created but does not create, and nature which neither creates nor is created. Further, God creates from nothing, according to Erigena and is not himself created. Copleston emphasizes that this makes God transcendent with respect to the creation, which is not something God spins, spiderlike, from his own substance. Erigena uses language which says that God is made in his creatures, or begins to be in things which begin to be. But what he means, Copleston insists, is that creatures are a theophany, that God has left his stamp on creatures, whose existence and nature bear witness to his activity. Even when Erigena says that when the human intellect becomes actual in thinking, it may be said to be created in its thoughts, and that, analogously, God may be said to be made in the creatures which proceed from him, this must be interpreted, Copleston maintains, in the light of the claim that God is Nature which creates but is not created. Copleston argues that, in endeavoring to offer a system of Christian wisdom which shall include both what can be proved (that God exists) and what can only be revealed (that God is Trinitarian), Erigena, who in any case does not sharply distinguish between theology and philosophy, expresses himself in the only philosophical terminology really available to him, which is Neoplatonic. It is not surprising, then, Copleston suggests, that some of his illustrations are questionable from orthodox theological perspectives.

For Erigena, Copleston notes, knowledge of God can be expressed affirmatively, in which case one ascribes to God "things that are," or negatively, in which one can deny that these things are ascribable to God. Copleston explains that this apparent contradiction is, in Erigena's view, reconciled by the claim that "God is wise" is to be read as "God is the origin of wisdom—the cause of wisdom in wise things," while "God is not wise" is to be read as "God does not Himself possess the property we ascribe to created things when we say that they are wise." The two claims may be expressed in the one sentence: "God is super-wise." Copleston adds that the net effect is that, according to Erigena, we may know that God exists but not what properties he has. Further, for Erigena, Nature as both created and creating is comprised by the Word, or Son, of God, viewed as eternally generated or created—a creation which involves eternally sustaining archetypal ideas in the mind of the Son, which serve as blueprints for creation. Nature which is created but does not create consists of creatures exterior to God, Erigena argues. These participate in God in the sense that they derive their essence from him. Nature which neither creates nor is created is God as final cause.

Copleston notes that, on the one hand, Erigena holds that God created the world from nothing. "Nothing," he explains, does not refer to material, even unformed. On the other hand, Copleston remarks, Erigena wants to combine this doctrine with the Neoplatonic philosophy of emanation. Copleston holds that the variety of interpretations of Erigena derives from some interpreters taking one theme, and other interpreters taking the other, as more basic.

Copleston indicates that interpretation of Erigena is not made less complex by his statement that "nothing" may refer to Nature which creates but is not created, or God. As we saw, he holds that God is ineffable. So "God creates the universe from nothing" is to be read as "God creates the universe from Himself," and this in turn may be understood as saying that divine creation is really a matter of God's spinning the creation from himself. Copleston concludes therefore, that regarding creation which run through Erigena's thought: God freely creating a universe he transcends, and the universe emanating from God along Neoplatonic lines. Probably, in Copleston's view, Erigena intended all his views regarding nature and creation to be acceptable philosophical explanations or accounts of orthodox Christian doctrine, even though it is difficult to reconcile all the explanations with the doctrine.— *K.E.Y.*

ADDITIONAL RECOMMENDED READING

Bett, Henry. *Johannes Scotus Erigena*. Cambridge: Cambridge University Press, 1925. One of the few book-length discussions in English of Erigena's thought.

Copleston, Frederick, S. J. *A History of Philosophy*. Vol. II. London: Burns, Oates, and Washbourne, 1950. The Medieval volume of the best multivolume history of philosophy in English.

—————— . *Medieval Philosophy*. London: Methuen, 1952. A good one-volume survey by the foremost contemporary general historian of philosophy writing in English.

Gilson, Étienne. *History of Christian Philosophy in the Middle Ages*. New York: Random House, 1955. Comprehensive discussion, with copious footnotes, by one of the greatest of the Medievalists.

Hawkins, D. J. B. *A Sketch of Medieval Philosophy*. London: Sheed and Ward, 1947. A brief, very helpful survey, at an introductory level.

Leff, Gordon. *Medieval Thought: St. Augustine to Ockham*. Baltimore: Penguin Books, 1958. A readable and reliable introduction to the thought of the period indicated.

THE BOOK OF SALVATION

Author: Avicenna (ibn-Sina, 980-1037)
Type of work: Metaphysics, philosophy of mind, epistemology
First transcribed: Early eleventh century

PRINCIPAL IDEAS ADVANCED

God is the eternal, unmoved First Mover, who exists necessarily by his own nature and who eternally generates the first created being, a pure intelligence, by a creative act of thought.

The First Intelligence creates the Second Intelligence and also the first celestial sphere and its soul; the Second Intelligence produces the Third Intelligence and the second celestial sphere; the process continues to the Tenth Intelligence, the giver of forms.

Souls are vegetable, animal, and human; the human soul is characterized by the faculties of growth, reproduction, nutrition, motion, perception, and reason.

There are five external senses and five internal senses; the internal senses are common sense, representation, imagination, estimation, and recollection.

Reason has two faculties: the practical and the theoretic; the theoretic faculty may develop to the stage of actual intellect, as activated by the Tenth Intelligence; knowledge then consists of discovering the necessary relations between universals.

In the year 529 Justinian closed the Schools of Athens, but fortunately for the West, Greek learning had been transmitted to the Near East, principally through the institutions of Alexandria and the Christian communities of Syria and Persia. Later, after the advent of Islam, this learning was fostered and developed by various Islamic philosophers and eventually carried across North Africa into Spain, where it flourished in such places as Toledo and Cordova. From the eleventh to the thirteenth centuries it trickled and then flooded into Western Europe to augment the Christians' meager and unbalanced knowledge of Greek philosophy.

Avicenna was, perhaps, the most important Islamic philosopher. Besides being a prolific writer on philosophy and religion, he was a court scholar and physician, an active politician, a civil administrator, and the writer of medical texts which were standard works in Europe through the seventeenth century. Of his approximately one hundred works the two most important are the philosophic encyclopedia, *Kitab al-Shifa* (*The Book of Healing*), the bulk of which was known to late medieval thinkers, and an abridgment of it, *Kitab al-Nadjat* (*The Book of Salvation*). The present essay is based primarily on the section of the *Nadjat* dealing with his philosophy of mind, a section translated by F. Rahman and published under the title *Avicenna's Psychology* (1952).

Before we can discuss Avicenna's philosophy of mind and his epistemology it will be necessary to outline the system within which it is elaborated. Avicenna regarded himself as an Aristotelian, but his Aristotelianism, like that of both his predecessors and successors, was influenced by the pressure of religious considerations and by the fact that the Aristotle transmitted to him had become colored by Stoic and Neoplatonic elements.

The modifications in Aristotle are evident in Avicenna's notion of God, his doctrine of creation, and his cosmology. He describes God not only as an eternal, unchanging, immaterial Unmoved Mover, but also as a being whose existence is necessary because his essence is identical with his being, as the One who is indivisible, as True Perfection, as Pure Benevolence, and as a continuously active agent intellect who, by emanation, creates the cosmos and all that is in it. Since intellect and will are identical in a pure intelligence, God can create simply by thinking. When he contemplates himself he automatically generates the first created being which is, because it stems from him, a pure intelligence.

The first created intelligence, too, can create by contemplation, but since it is a finite intelligence it can contemplate and create in different ways. In contemplating God, it creates the Second Intelligence; in contemplating its own essence and in knowing that it is a contingent being characterized by potentiality, it creates the body of the first celestial sphere; and in contemplating itself and in knowing its existence as necessary in that it flows necessarily from God, it generates the soul of the first celestial sphere.

Since the celestial sphere is attached to a body, its soul is not a pure intelligence and therefore does not create, but it does seek to emulate the perfection of its creator, the First Intelligence. It does so by contemplating the Intelligence and by perfecting its own body. Since the only change simple celestial matter can undergo is a change of position, the soul perfects celestial matter by circular motion. Hence, the First Intelligence is the final cause of both the existence and motion of the first sphere. The Second Intelligence, by contemplating the First Intelligence and by contemplating itself in the twofold manner, produces the Third Intelligence and the body and soul of the second celestial sphere, that containing the stars. In a similar manner, further intelligences and spheres are produced as the creative process works down through the spheres of Saturn, Jupiter, Mars, the sun, Venus, Mercury, and the moon. The Tenth Intelligence does not produce a sphere but it does produce sublunar things by providing souls and forms and by uniting them with suitably disposed complexes of sublunar matter. These complexes of matter come about as the four Aristotelian elements combine and recombine under the influence of the celestial spheres. The Tenth Intelligence is the Agent Intellect or Giver of Forms which looms so large in Avicenna's psychology and which provides a linkage between Aristotle's active intellect and the active intellect of the Scholastics.

Avicenna agrees with Aristotle and disagrees with the theologians in claiming that this creative process is not a temporal process and that it is not creation *ex nihilo* (out of nothing). Creation is not a temporal event, since time is the measure of change and thus presupposes the existence of matter, and it is not a temporal process because a cause must be contemporaneous with its effect. Furthermore, creation is not *ex nihilo* since form can only be imprinted on matter that is already available. Consequently, God, matter, the cosmos, and creation itself are eternal. Things exist because God exists, because he contemplates himself necessarily, and because their existence flows directly or indirectly from this contemplation. Insofar as it explains why things exist, the theory of emanation suggests a nontemporal sequence of active, efficient causes grounded in the supreme efficient cause, but it also suggests a hierarchy of essences following from one another in sequence. When God contemplates his own essence he sees the network of implications that flow from it and thus, unlike Aristotle's God, knows the cosmos in detail.

Avicenna's views influenced much subsequent philosophy. Many, if not all, of the later Christian philosophers appreciated the proof of God's existence from the existence of contingent things, the notion of God as an agent, the step in the direction of a suitable creation theory, the doctrine of intelligences as a foundation for a study of angels, God's knowledge of the world, and the identity of essence and existence in God but their sharp separation in other things. They objected to the eternity of the world, the denial of creation *ex nihilo*, the piecemeal emanation of the created world, the determinism, and the doctrine of the Agent Intellect.

Avicenna's reliance on Aristotle, and in particular on the *De anima*, is evidenced from the beginning of his psychology when he classifies souls as vegetable, animal, and human. The vegetable soul is characterized by the faculties of growth, reproduction, and nutrition; the animal has, in addition, those of motion and perception; and the human being is completed by the faculty of reason. There are really two faculties of motion in the animal soul: a psychic one characterized by desire and anger which incite motion towards objects or away from them, and a physical one that actually moves the body by contracting and relaxing the muscles. There are five external senses, each operative when the form of the sensed object is impressed on the physical sense organ. For instance, when light falls on an object it transmits an image through the transparent medium and this image is impressed on the vitreous humor of the eye where it is apprehended by the psychic faculty of sight.

Avicenna's analysis of the internal sense goes considerably beyond that of Aristotle, who did not distinguish explicitly between internal and external senses, and it anticipates in considerable detail that of the Scholastics. There are five internal senses: fantasy or common sense, representation, imagination, the estimative sense, and the recollective or retentive sense. These are unique faculties, each being associated with a different part of the brain. The common sense receives images transmitted to it by the five external senses, enabling us both to know that they differ from one another and to collate the data received from them. The function of representation or sense memory is to preserve the data received by the common sense. An external sense, such as vision, abstracts the form of a particular object from its matter, but it can do so only in the presence of the object, seeing the form with all the determinations imposed upon it by that matter and seeing it as being present in matter. The form in the representative faculty is still particular but it is not seen as being present in or presented by matter. This further abstraction makes memory possible. Imagination is the faculty that enables us to separate and combine the images preserved by representation.

The estimative faculty detects the intentions of animate things and the effects of inanimate ones, thus enabling us to discover their significance for our welfare. On the first occurrence of such an insight, such as the sheep's recognition that the skulking wolf means it no good, the response is an instinctive one in which the estimative sense operates on the images of common sense or representation to abstract the intention. Later it also seems to work by association, for after sense memory has stored up past correlations of a certain sort of visual data, say, with subsequent pain, the occurrence of such a visual datum will trigger the associated image of pain in the imagination and the estimative sense will then note the evil of that object.

Avicenna and the Scholastics note that intentions are not the objects of any of the five external senses, yet they insist, without explaining how it is possible, that intentions can be grasped only by attending to the images of common sense or representation. These intentions are particulars, but since they are nonsensible, our apprehending them marks a yet higher degree of abstraction for here we are abstracting an immaterial thing from a material thing in which it exists only accidentally. Avicenna also points out that non-cognitive judgment is involved here and that this is the supreme judging faculty in the animal. Furthermore, it is the function of this faculty to guide the two motive faculties. The function of the recollective or retentive faculty is to retain the judgments or insights of the estimative faculty, just as the representative retains the images of sensible things.

The apprehension of particulars occurs only through bodily organs, for a spatial thing can be present only to another spatial thing. This is so even in the case of the faculties of imagination, representation, and estimation, despite the fact that they operate in the physical absence of the object. This point may be shown thus: imagine two squares of exactly the same size, but separated from each other, and then ask yourself how it is possible for there to be two separate squares. Since the difference cannot be accounted for as a difference of form, it must be the consequence of the same form being manifested in two different places. That is, there must be two images impressed on different areas of the middle ventricle of the brain, which is the physical seat of the psychic faculty of imagination. The point is a general one: the determinate features of our imagery can be accounted for only if the form perceived by the faculty is at the same time a form manifested in matter. This line of reasoning, which does not appear in Aristotle, influenced the Scholastics and reappears quite explicitly in Descartes.

Reason is divided into practical and theoretic faculties. With the help of the theoretic faculty the practical faculty elaborates basic moral principles such as "Tyranny is wrong," "Lying is wrong"; it considers purposes, deliberates, initiates behavior, and produces in the faculty of appetite such responses as shame and laughter.

The theoretic faculty can occur in various degrees. It may be dormant; it may develop to the point where it possesses the primary principles of thought, such as "The whole is greater than its part" and "Things equal to a third are equal to one another"; or it may perfect its potentiality by grasping the secondary principles as well, and thus be in a position to think without the further acquisition of any other principles. These are the various degrees of the Potential Intellect. Finally, the intellect may actually think, exercising the capacities it has perfected at the prior stage. It is then called the Actual or Acquired Intellect. As we shall see later, this last stage is not attained unless the Potential Intellect is activated by the Agent Intellect, the Tenth Intelligence.

In order to achieve its end of contemplating pure forms, theoretic reason must complete the process of abstracting forms from matter, a process already initiated by the external and internal senses. That is, it must turn to the imagination, to the images of particular objects, and, through the agency of the Agent Intellect, grasp the forms appearing there free of all the materially imposed determinations they still exhibit. This process of abstraction can be by-passed only by highly gifted individuals, such as the prophets, whose intellects are illuminated directly by the Agent Intellect, the Giver of Forms. Reason recognizes that these pure forms could be manifested in many particular cases, so it regards them as universals; but it also sees that these forms need not have been manifested at all, and therefore that they are, in themselves, neither particular nor universal.

Though he departs from Aristotle in holding that a form is not restricted to its occurrence in matter, Avicenna is not quite a Platonic realist, for he does not admit that a form can exist or subsist by itself. He introduces the famous doctrine of *ante rem*, *in rebus*, and *post rem*, a doctrine accepted later by Aquinas and others as the solution to the problem of universals. The essences are *ante rem* insofar as they are the exemplars in the Giver of Forms, *in rebus* insofar as they are manifested in sensible objects, and *post rem* insofar as they are grasped free of material considerations by the human intellect.

Knowledge involves the discovery of necessary relations between universals, relations noted directly by intuition, which is a kind of illumination, or established indirectly by syllogistic reasoning. While his model seems to be that of a body of knowledge derived by reason alone from universals and self-evident truths, Avicenna does point out that much of our knowledge about the world, though certain, is based partly on experience. Having noted the constant conjunction between things such as man and rationality, and day and being light, and constant disjunctions such as its not being both day and night, we cannot avoid concluding that the noted constancy reveals a necessary conjunction or disjunction. Thus we are forced to acknowledge necessary truths about the world, truths such as "Man is rational," "If it is day, then it is light," and "Either it is day or it is night." But apart from this sort of assistance, and the assistance of the internal senses as providers of data, the intellect does not need the assistance of the body. It does not operate through a physical organ, for it can know itself and is not disrupted by strong stimuli, as the physical organ of sight is disrupted by a dazzling light. Furthermore, as is required by a faculty that apprehends pure forms, it is an immaterial faculty.

In defending his view that the soul is an immaterial substance, Avicenna invokes his famous "man in the void" argument. Suppose, he says, that a man is created in a void and suppose that his feet, hands, and other physical parts are separated from him in such a way that he has no sensation of them. Under these circumstances he would have no experience of an external world and no experience of his body; nevertheless, he would still be conscious of himself. Consequently, the self he is conscious of must be an immaterial thing. Furthermore, since he can think of himself without thinking that he has a body, having a body is not essential to being a self and therefore is excluded from the nature of the self. That is to say, the immaterial self exists in its own right independently of other things and is therefore a substance. If it is associated with a body, the association is accidental. The soul is an entelechy because it governs and guides the body, but it is no more the form of the body than the pilot is the form of the ship.

This soul did not exist prior to the existence of its body, for if there were a number of preexisting souls, they would have to differ from one another; to do so is impossible since they would not differ in form nor would they be individuated by matter. If there were one preexisting soul, it would have to be shared by all men—an absurd idea. Therefore, the individual soul is created when there is a body suitable for it. By binding itself closely to its body the soul is influenced permanently by the peculiar nature of the body and the particular events that befall it. Since the soul is a simple substance it survives the death of the body, carrying over into the hereafter the individuality it has acquired.

In these various respects Avicenna departed from the Aristotelian view of the soul in order to satisfy the requirements of theology. Thus the later Jewish and Christian philosophers welcomed his guidance when they encountered Aristotle. There is also a remarkable coincidence between Avicenna's position and arguments and those of Descartes. The influence of the "man in the void" argument is particularly evident.

To complete the survey of Avicenna's psychology, one must consider the relationship between the human intellect and the Active Intellect. The human intellect does not achieve its highest status, that of apprehending universals and the relations between them, unless it is activated by the Tenth Intelligence, which is the Active Intellect or Giver of Forms. Avicenna describes the Active Intellect as radiating a power which illuminates the potentially intelligible but actually sensible forms of imagination, thereby making them intelligible and thus present to a suitably prepared mind. In this way our potential intellect becomes an actual or acquired intellect. In this process, images are important for two reasons: first, we must abstract the form from an image of the object if we are to grasp the form as the form of an object, and second, we must compare and contrast images in order to raise our intellect to a level where the divine illumination is able to enlighten it. It is to be noted that the Active Intellect, not the human intellect, abstracts the intelligible form from the image in the imagination. Our dependence on the Giver of Forms is evinced further by the fact that since we have no intellectual memory we must re-establish contact with it every time we think. Later, Thomas Aquinas and others objected to Avicenna's Active Intellect and insisted on fragmenting it into individual active intellects occurring as faculties of individual human souls, thus making man himself responsible for the activating of his potential intellect. They also feared, though Avicenna himself did not, that as long as we all shared the same Active Intellect, personal immortality was jeopardized. Also, they introduced intellectual memory and insisted that when intellection occurs the knower and the known become one.

Since the human intellect is able to contact the Giver of Forms more easily on subsequent occasions, it is able to perfect itself, approaching the ideal of constant contemplation of the forms. By thus emulating the Giver of Forms, which contains all intelligible forms, the soul prepares itself to enjoy a higher and more worthy status when it leaves the body. Insofar as it is the emulated intelligence, the Giver of Forms is a final and formal cause as well as an agent, and insofar as it functions in these ways it brings the human soul into the sequence of efficient, formal and final causes that stems from and culminates in God.

Besides influencing later Jewish and Christian philosophers in the various ways already indicated, Avicenna had a great influence on the work of Averroës, the other great Islamic philosopher. Anyone interested in a critical but sympathetic evaluation of Avicenna, should turn to Averroës.—*L.M.*

PERTINENT LITERATURE
Avicenna. *Avicenna's Psychology*. Translated by F. Rahman. London: Oxford University Press, 1952.

In this book F. Rahman presents an English translation of the section of *The Book of Salvation* which corresponds to Aristotle's *On the Soul*. He also provides an introduction and a commentary with notes. The main themes dealt with by Avicenna in this section of *The Book of Salvation* are the definition of the soul, the classification of its faculties, sensation, intellection, prophecy, the relation between body and soul, and the immortality of the soul.

In his Introduction, Rahman provides the historical background required to understand the evolution of some of these key issues and to compare Avicenna's and Aristotle's positions. He first focuses his approach on the relation between soul and body and its analogy to the relation between a sailor or a pilot and his ship alluded to by Aristotle in *On the Soul*, II, 1, 413 a 9. The points of view of Aristotle, Alexander of Aphrodisias, Plotinus, Simplicius, and Philoponus are discussed and explained by referring to their uses of the analogy of the pilot and his ship. The link between the different conceptions of the relation between soul and body and an acceptance or rejection of the immortality of the soul is clearly indicated. Avicenna's position is compared to and contrasted with the positions of his predecessors. Rahman sees Aristotle arguing in favor of a mutual dependence of the body and the soul and thus denying the immortality of the soul. Avicenna, on the contrary, holds that the human soul is incorporeal, substantial, independent from the body, and therefore immortal.

Since the human soul is incorporeal and substantial, it is also self-conscious, as it is shown by the famous argument of "the man in the void." Rahman is thus led to discuss the conception of self-consciousness among some of Avicenna's predecessors: Aristotle, Strato, Alexander of Aphrodisias, Plotinus, Simplicius, and Philoponus. He claims that these philosophers did not really grasp the essential unity and persistence of self-consciousness and therefore did not have a real theory of the Ego; Avicenna somehow builds such a theory and is thus original.

Finally, Rahman offers clarifications of some aspects of Avicenna's theory of intellection: the grades of abstraction, the active and the passive intellect, and the practical intellect.

The detailed notes at the back of the volume provide for each chapter a summary of the chapter and then further clarifications and comments on difficult passages. It is in these notes that one can find some enlightenment on the main issues which are not discussed in the Introduction.

Rahman shows very clearly how Avicenna's psychological and epistemological conceptions in *The Book of Salvation* are, on the one hand, embedded in the Greek tradition of the commentaries on Aristotle's *On the Soul* and, on the other hand, constitute a truly original contribution to the solution of difficult and perennial problems.

Davidson, Herbert A. "Alfarabi and Avicenna on the Active Intellect," in *Medieval and Renaissance Studies*. III (1972), pp. 109-111, 154-178.

Herbert A. Davidson claims that Aristotle's statement on the necessity, on epistemological grounds, of the existence of an active intellect in *On the Soul*, III, 5, is very ambiguous. All subsequent philosophers try to make sense of it and to relate it to Aristotle's metaphysical positions. Focusing his study on the active intellect, Davidson is therefore led to discuss many aspects of Avicenna's epistemology and metaphysics. To do so he makes use not only of *The Book of Healing* and *The Book of Salvation* but also of all the other Arabic philosophical works of Avicenna. He really presents a synthesis of Avicenna's main tenets and an explanation of the basic arguments used to defend them. Davidson's work is therefore much broader in scope and depth than Rahman's, which limited itself to a quick introduction to one section of *The Book of Salvation*.

According to Davidson, Avicenna's active intellect is the cause, with the help of the heavenly bodies, of (1) the matter of the sublunar world and (2) the forms occurring in matter, including the souls of all animated beings and, therefore, the cause of the soul of the human being. Furthermore, but this time only by itself, the active intellect is the cause of the existence and actualization of the potential human intellect. It actualizes this intellect in providing it with the universal concepts or intelligibles. These intelligibles emanate directly from the active intellect into the human one. Therefore, there is no abstraction by the human intellect of the universal concepts from experience or images. Images are useful only to prepare the human intellect for the reception of what emanates from the active intellect. The human mind is therefore basically passive but can reach a high level of development by means of a conjunction with the active intellect, or, more exactly, by the light emanating from the active intellect and transmitting the intelligibles.

The actualization of the human intellect by the active intellect is consistent with Avicenna's contention that the human soul is independent from the body and therefore immortal. The existence of the body is only the occasion of the emanation of the human soul, and the use of images is only the requirement for the preparation of the soul for the reception of the emanation of the intelligibles from the active intellect. Once the human intellect has reached a high level of conjunction with the active intellect and so can reach it at will, preparation by the use of images is no longer necessary. Also, at the level the human intellect is no longer subject to the limitations of discursive thought but reaches the highest stage and becomes endowed with intellectual prophecy, which is an illuminative or intuitive stage.

Davidson shows very clearly how Avicenna's conception of the immortality of the human soul and of prophecy are linked to his epistemological positions and in contrast to the positions of one of his most famous predecessors, al-Farabi, who claims that only people who grasp the right philosophical ideas or their imaginative representation will achieve immortality.

Davidson's presentation is very detailed and carefully documented. It is also critical and indicates how on some points of detail Avicenna's position does not seem to be fully consistent, although Davidson assumes that Avicenna's philosophy is basically a unified and coherent one.

Zedler, Beatrice H. "The Prince of Physicians on the Nature of Man," in *The Modern Schoolman*. LV, no. 2 (January, 1978), pp. 165-177.

Beatrice H. Zedler examines Avicenna's conception of man not only in his philosophical texts, as do F. Rahman and Herbert A. Davidson, but also in the medical ones. For the philosophical approach she bases her presentation exclusively on the Latin version of the sections *On the Soul* and *Metaphysics* of *The Book of Healing*. In what concerns the medical aspect she uses the best-known Latin versions of some of his medical books, such as the *Canon of Medicine*. Her work is therefore based only on medieval Latin translations and some references to a few modern translations.

From the philosophical texts she concludes that for Avicenna, the body, although needed for the individuation of the human soul and for the reception of most intelligibles, is not a part of the essence of man. Avicenna compares the body to an animal that one needs to ride in order to reach some place but which, once one has arrived at this place, is no longer needed and even becomes an encumbrance. In such a conception man is essentially spirit and the body a mere tool which is only temporarily needed.

From the medical texts emerges the picture of man as a being of nature whose physical well-being assures him his full realization. Nothing except a higher level of complexity distinguishes him from other beings of nature. Man seems to be a mere body, reducible to his physical elements.

Zedler claims that such a discrepancy between the medical and the philosophical approaches is not a sign of a lack of unity in Avicenna's thought. A closer reading of both kinds of texts shows that the philosophical texts include statements which imply that man is also a being of nature and that medical texts do not deny that; although man is a being of nature, there is more to be said about other aspects of him. Furthermore, in his *On the Divisions of the Rational Sciences* Avicenna considers both the study of medicine and the study of the soul as divisions of natural philosophy and therefore acknowledges that they are dealing with different aspects of a reality somehow related to matter and nature. He is therefore fully aware of holding two different positions, but, rather than considering them as completely different positions, he sees them as distinct emphases on different aspects of man. Man, on the one hand, is one of the intellectual substances; but he is the lowest one and therefore still in need at some stage of a body. On the other hand, he is a being of nature, a body which should be taken care of since it is needed by the soul—at least for a while—for its own development.

Finally Zedler claims that Avicenna's awareness of his duality of positions as emphases on different aspects of man does not lead him to reconcile that duality and to articulate clearly the relation between soul and body. She concludes that Avicenna simply juxtaposes the two aspects of man and that one has to wait for Thomas Aquinas to find a solution to the tension between a spiritualist and a naturalist approach and thereby reach a truly unified conception of man.—*T.A.D.*

ADDITIONAL RECOMMENDED READING

Afnan, Soheil Muhsin. *Avicenna, His Life and Works*. London: George Allen & Unwin, 1958. The standard general presentation of Avicenna and his various works with an emphasis on the Eastern influences.

Avicenna. *Liber de Anima seu Sextus de Naturalibus*. Edited by S. Van Riet. Louvain-Leiden: E. Peeters and E. J. Brill, 1968-1972. Critical edition of the medieval Latin translation of the section *On the Soul* of *The Book of Healing*, with a very good presentation of Avicenna's psychological doctrine.

_____ . *Liber de Philosophia Prima sive Scientia Divina*. Edited by S. Van Riet. Louvain-Leiden: E. Peeters and E. J. Brill, 1977. Critical edition of the medieval Latin translation of the metaphysical section of *The Book of Healing*, with a very good presentation of Avicenna's conception of metaphysics.

_____ . *La Métaphysique du "Shifā."* Translated by Georges C. Anawati. Paris: Vrin, 1978. French translation from the Arabic of the metaphysical section of *The Book of Healing*, with an introduction showing the influence of this text in both the East and the West.

Goichon, Amélie Marie. *The Philosophy of Avicenna and Its Influence on Medieval Europe*. Translated by M. S. Khan. Delhi: Motilal Banarsidass, 1969. Translation of three lectures given for a broad public by a specialist. Insists on Avicenna's influence on Western Europe.

Morewedge, Parviz. *The "Metaphysica" of Avicenna (ibn Sīnā)*. New York: Columbia University Press, 1973. Translation of the metaphysical section of Avicenna's chief Persian work, which presents a concise outline of his philosophy.

MONOLOGION and PROSLOGION

Author: Saint Anselm of Canterbury (1033-1109)
Type of work: Theology
First transcribed: Monologion, 1076, *Proslogion*, c. 1077-1078

PRINCIPAL IDEAS ADVANCED

Since everything good must have a cause, and since the cause is goodness, and since God is goodness, God exists.

Since whatever exists must have a cause, and since a cause depends upon the power to cause, and since God is that power, God exists.

Since degrees of value or reality depend upon reference to absolute excellence and reality, and since God is absolute excellence and reality, God exists. [From the Monologion.]

Since God is the being than whom no greater can be conceived, and since it is better to exist in fact than merely in the imagination, God must exist in fact. [The ontological argument.]

God is not substance but Essence (the Father) and a set of essences (the Son); as Father he is the efficient cause (the creator) of all that exists; as Son he is the formal cause (the idea).

St. Anselm was an Augustinian who was unaware of Plotinus and who lived just before the great influx of Aristotle's works through the Arabian and Jewish philosophers. His fame rests to a great extent on his belief that faith is prior to reason, a belief he expresses thus in the well-known words of the *Proslogion*: "For I do not seek to understand that I may believe, but I believe in order to understand. For this I also believe—that unless I believed, I should not understand." After we have accepted on faith the revelations given through Scripture and through the Fathers, reason is able to fulfill its secondary role of clarifying meanings and providing proofs. Yet Anselm was an ambivalent figure, for despite his emphasis on the priority of faith, he felt a very strong need to support it with proofs. Indeed, he extended the scope of reason considerably farther than did the Scholastics who followed him, for they would not have thought of trying to prove doctrines like those of the Trinity and the Incarnation. His rationalism led others to characterize him as the first of the Scholastics.

This summary will concentrate on the other element that contributed to Anselm's fame, the ontological argument as developed in the *Proslogion*. But since they are relevant, the three proofs given in his earlier work, the *Monologion*, will be considered first.

According to the first argument, the goodness of things in this world must be caused and must therefore stem from one thing that is good, or from many. But if many causes have their goodness in common, it is by virtue of this goodness that they cause good things; therefore, we must assume a common source. In either case, whether the cause be one or many, we are led to a single, unitary source of goodness. Since it is the source of all goodness, this source is not good because of something else, but is itself Goodness. (Notice that this argument depends upon a realistic doctrine of essences which will allow an essence such as *goodness* to function not only as a form but also as an active First Cause.) God is Goodness itself, not merely something that possesses goodness.

The second argument follows a similar course with respect to existence. Since whatever exists must have a cause and since an infinite regress of causes is impossible, there must either be one ultimate, nonfinite cause or several causes. If there is but one cause, we have encountered God. If there are several, then either they support each other mutually or they exist independently. The former is impossible, for that which is supported cannot be the cause of that which supports it. But if there are several independent ultimate causes, each must exist through itself, and therefore they must share this common power. Now, since it is this common power that is the source of all else, there cannot be several causes, but only one. (This proof also depends upon the above mentioned doctrine of essences.) God is not something that has this supreme power; he *is* this power.

The third proof depends upon the fact that things in the world can be ranked according to their degrees of "dignity," goodness, or reality. For instance, he says, all will admit that a horse represents a higher degree of reality than a piece of wood, for the horse is animate; similarly, a man outranks a horse, for he is rational. However, the sequence of degrees of reality cannot be an infinite one, for there must be some boundary, some limiting value by which all the rest are measured, a value which is real absolutely. If there should be several things that share this degree of reality, it is nevertheless the case that they are equal because of the common excellence they share. This excellence is the absolute reality which is the source of all relative degrees of reality.

Apparently Anselm thought these proofs too complex, for he tells us in the *Proslogion* that he searched a long time for a simpler proof. The result is the well-known ontological argument. When we think of something, Anselm says, and we are really thinking of it and not just uttering the associated verbal symbol, that thing is in our understanding. Of course, we need not understand that it exists, for we may be thinking of something which we believe does not exist, as in the case of the fool who says in his heart that God does not exist, or we may be thinking of something about whose existence we are uncertain. But in any of these cases, if we are thinking of something, if we understand *it*, then *it*, and not something else, is in the understanding. This point applies to our thought of anything, including God. However, in the case of God, we are thinking about a unique thing, for we are thinking about the greatest thing conceivable, the being "than which nothing greater can be conceived." Now if a being exists in the understanding alone, it cannot be the greatest conceivable thing, for a being that exists in reality as well as in the understanding would be greater. Consequently, since God is the greatest being conceivable he must exist in reality as well as in the understanding. Or, to put it another way, if the greatest conceivable being exists in the understanding alone, then it is not the greatest conceivable being—a conclusion which is absurd.

This argument met opposition from the beginning in the person of the monk Gaunilo, who criticized Anselm in his *In Behalf of the Fool*. First, Gaunilo says that because God's nature is essentially mysterious we do not have an idea of him. We may think we do, but we have only the verbal symbol, for when we hear the word "God," what are we to think or imagine? The proof fails, then, for the term "God" does not denote any *conceivable* thing. Second, he says that if the argument were sound, we could prove the existence of other things. By way of example he invites us to think of an island which is blessed with more good features and is therefore better than any actual land with which we are acquainted; then he suggests that we must admit its existence, since if it exists in the mind alone it would not be as good as lands which we know to exist. Third, he says that an idea or concept is only a part of the understanding itself, and that the existing object, if there is one, is something else. From the fact that an idea occurs it does not follow that something quite different in status also occurs. The fact that I am thinking of a being, thinking of it as the greatest conceivable being, and therefore thinking of it as existing necessarily, does not provide the slightest evidence that there actually is such a being, for the thought of a necessarily existing being is one thing and a necessarily existing being is another.

Anselm replies to the first objection by saying that the proof does not require a complete understanding of God, but only that we understand this much: that whatever else he may be, God is such that no greater being than he can be conceived. Even the fool must admit this much before he can refuse to believe. In reply to the second objection he says that God, unlike the blessed isle, is not thought of simply as the greatest thing of a certain type, or even as the greatest thing of all, but as the being than which nothing greater can be conceived. This latter concept can refer to only one thing, and that thing quite obviously is not the blessed isle. Later proponents of the argument, such as Descartes, make the same point by asserting that existence is contained in the essence of only one thing; namely, the greatest conceivable being.

The third objection, which has ever since been a standard one, is more difficult to handle. It seems to pinpoint an obvious defect, yet Anselm and many others were not daunted by it. In his reply to Gaunilo, Anselm hardly seems aware of it, for he simply repeats again, as if the objection had not been raised, that if we understand a thing, then it exists in the understanding.

Since we are likely to feel more at home with Gaunilo's theory of ideas than with Anselm's, it will be necessary to reconstruct Anselm's doctrine in order to see why the objection seemed so unimportant to him. To do so we must explore a little further the nature of the divine being whose existence is supposed to be proved by the argument.

Anselm regarded God as self-caused, but the nature of this causation is quite mysterious. God could not have functioned as his own efficient, material, or instrumental cause, for all these causes must be prior to their effect, and not even God could exist prior to himself. For a similar reason God did not create himself. Yet he does exist through himself and from himself. By way of explication, Anselm presents us with a model, that of light. Light lights another thing by falling on it, but it also lights itself, for it is lucent. Its lucidity must come from itself, though, of course, it does not fall upon itself. Now, he says, in God the relation between *essence, to be, and being (existing)* is like the relation between *the light, to light,* and *lucent.* The implication is that the essence of God, the being he enjoys, and the generating of this being are one and the same thing. Like his master Augustine, Anselm conceived of God as an active essence, an activity which necessarily exists, not simply because it is active, but because its activity is the activity of existing.

In other places, too, Anselm indicates quite clearly that God is not a substance having matter and form. First, he points out that if God were such a substance he would be composite, a state impossible in a being that is the unitary source of all and in a being that has no prior cause. Furthermore, God cannot be a substance possessing such qualities as justness, wisdom, truth, and goodness; for if he were, he would be just, wise, true, and good through another and not through himself. God does not *possess* justness and wisdom; he *is* justice and wisdom. That is, as was indicated in the earlier proofs, God is identical with these essences, and since in him they are one and the same essence, God is an Essence.

We are led to this same conclusion by another route, that of creation. As pure spirit, God creates the matter of the world *ex nihilo*, but he creates it according to a model he had in mind prior to the creation. That is, as Augustine had said earlier, all the essences that are manifested in the world existed in God's thought prior to the creation. Insofar as this network of essences is the model according to which the world is created, it is the formal first cause of the world (Augustine had called the divine ideas "the reasons"), and as first cause it is identical with God. Following Augustine, Anselm says that insofar as God *is* this expression of the world he has an intelligence; he is Wisdom, the Word, the Son. But the important point as far as the ontological argument is concerned is this: God is not thought of as a substance in the ordinary sense, but as an Essence (the Father) and also as a set of essences (the Son) that function respectively as efficient and formal cause of the world. Again, as in the proofs of the *Monologion*, God the Creator is thought of as an acting essence. It is to be noted that we have in God the Father the highest degree of reality an essence can enjoy—that of an eternally acting essence that exists in and through itself.

Anselm's doctrine of creation throws still further light on the ontological argument. It is to be noted that the essences that exist prior to creation are not created, for they are the eternal exemplars. As the Son, they are sustained by God insofar as he is the ground of all, but since they *are* the intellect of God, they are not the products of a mind and they do not depend for their existence on being in a mind. Thus, there are essences which do not enjoy the highest degree of reality, but which do enjoy a degree higher than that which they would if they were mind dependent. As Anselm says, prior to their manifestation in matter, they were not nothing. Since they are consubstantial with God, they are beings in their own right. Anselm leans as far in the direction of a Platonic realism as his theology will allow him.

Anselm was not clear about the manner in which we apprehend general ideas, but he insists that these ideas are the essences we have just discussed. This follows not only from his realistic doctrine of ideas, but also from his theory of truth. When we apprehend a thing truly, we apprehend its nature, but if it exists truly, then it manifests truly the essence God intended it to manifest. Hence, when we think truly we are apprehending one or more of the essences that constitute the intellect of God. (Thus, God is Truth.) This is not to say that we apprehend essences as they exist in God, for there they are exemplars, but what we apprehend does come directly or indirectly, clearly or obscurely, from God. Since the ideas in our understanding *come* into our understanding, their existence does not depend upon our understanding and is not restricted to their occurrence there. This is what Anselm means when he says that the things we understand are in our understanding.

In speaking as if we already knew that these essences constitute the mind of God, it might seem that we beg the question which is to be settled by the ontological argument, but an account of Anselm's doctrine of creation serves to illuminate the way in which he thinks of God and of essences. In both the *Proslogion* and the *Monologion*, Anselm emphasizes the proposition that essences are characters that may be shared in common by many things and that they are ontologically prior to these things. And we may assume that he would agree with Augustine, whom he follows in so many respects, that the eternity and immutability of self-evident truths and of the essences involved in them, and the fact that many minds can share the same ideas, are sufficient evidence that general ideas are not created by mutable and independent minds. At any rate, the argument presupposes that since they are not mind dependent, essences can occur elsewhere than in minds. Thus, we can conceive of an essence enjoying a higher degree of reality, such as existing in the physical world or, perhaps, existing in such a way that it is self-sustaining. That some of the essences we apprehend also enjoy a higher degree of reality cannot be denied, for they are manifested as material objects. The only question, and the interesting one, is whether any essence we can apprehend also enjoys the supreme degree of reality. It would be worth examining the various essences we apprehend to see if there is any case where this is so. Anselm says we are led to a positive answer in the case of one and only one essence, that of the "being than which none greater can be conceived," for in this case alone the essence is such that it necessarily exists.

If we are to do justice to Anselm and understand the strong appeal this argument had for him and many others, we must be clear about the fact that throughout the argument he is talking about an essence. The premises are premises about an essence and the conclusion is a statement about this very same essence. It is not, as Gaunilo insisted, a conclusion about something else. Gaunilo's objection would be valid, as it is in the example of the blessed isle, if Anselm had concluded that an essence has been manifested in matter. But since manifestation in matter is always an accident, this is not something that could be discovered by examining an essence alone. It is crucial to the argument that existence in matter should not be thought of as the highest level of existence and that the being concerned should not be thought of as a composite of form and substance. The argument can move only from essence to Pure Essence, or *Essentia*. That is, it can only reveal to us something more about essence, and this is just what it does when it shows that one of the essences we apprehend is an active self-sustaining essence.

This discussion does not show that Anselm's argument is sound, but perhaps it does show that the whole question centers around two radically different theories about ideas, essences, and objects. Historically, philosophers who have found Anselm's argument acceptable have leaned toward a Platonic or Neoplatonic realism in which the role of essences is emphasized and that of matter minimized. The proof was not accepted by the Aristotelians who dominated the philosophic world for four or five centuries after Anselm, nor by the nominalists and empiricists who have dominated so much of philosophic thought in the last three hundred years; but it is adopted in one form or another by Descartes, Liebniz, Spinoza, and Hegel, who, despite the fact that they diverge radically from one another, are each influenced, directly or indirectly, by Plato, Plotinus, or Augustine.—*L.M.*

PERTINENT LITERATURE

Hopkins, Jasper. *A Companion to the Study of St. Anselm*. Minneapolis: University of Minnesota Press, 1972.

The past few years have witnessed a flurry of Anselmian studies coming from quite different quarters. Among philosophers and logicians there has been a revival of interest in Saint Anselm's ontological proof for the existence of God. Meanwhile, stimulated by the appearance of a new critical edition of Anselm's writings, historians have been busy reconstructing his life and thought. Jasper Hopkins' *A Companion to the Study of St. Anselm* is an informed and critical introduction to both spheres of activity. Of particular interest to students of philosophy are his chapters on Faith and Reason and on the Ontological Argument.

Anselm's formula, "I believe in order that I may understand," is, as Hopkins shows, more complicated than might at first appear. Belief may signify only intellectual assent, but it may also include the conversion of the will. Moreover, understanding, as used by Anselm, is broad enough to include probable as well as necessary reasoning. Hopkins, after tracing the formula through Anselm's writings, concludes that it is meant to affirm both the reasonableness of the Church's teaching and the need for faith in one who is to understand that teaching. This last consideration Hopkins explains along lines similar to those which lead modern-day apologists to define faith as interpretation. One who is committed to the teaching of the Church, says Hopkins, perceives his destiny in a new light and is able to appreciate the meaning of grace and mercy. Thus, when Anselm says that belief leads to experience and experience to understanding, he has in mind not merely understanding that something is, but understanding what it is for something to be of that kind.

This interplay between faith and reason has led some contemporary scholars to inquire more closely into the intentions underlying Anselm's philosophical writings. The first question is whether his method in the two treatises is the same. Whereas the *Proslogion* begins with the profession of believing as the condition of understanding, the *Monologion* simply announces the author's intention to proceed by reason alone without appeal to authority. Some have seen a conflict here and have argued that Anselm's conception of the relation between faith and reason changed from one work to the other. A second question is whether both works envisaged the same public, which is another way of asking whether both were intended to demonstrate the truth of the faith to unbelievers. Karl Barth has maintained that in neither work was Anselm addressing unbelievers, it being Barth's contention that argument neither brings a man to faith nor strengthens the faith that a man has but rather brings to the believer the joy of understanding. A. Stolz, on the other hand, distinguishes between what he sees as the rationalistic method of the *Monologion* and the devotional method of the *Proslogion*, the latter being in his opinion no argument but merely an attempt to understand the implications of the divine name, "He who truly is." Hopkins denies that there is any fundamental change in purpose between the two works and concludes that, although Anselm intended the arguments in the first instance to strengthen the faith of Christians, he also thought that to the degree that they were valid they must convince the honest skeptic.

In his chapter on the ontological argument Hopkins calls attention to the debate among philosophers in our time as to whether there is more than one argument in the *Proslogion*. As stated in the summary above, the proof in *Proslogion* 2 turns on the definition of God as "that than which nothing greater can be conceived." But in *Proslogion* 3, Anselm makes the further claim that this being, conceived of as existing, "cannot be thought not to exist." This latter claim is not introduced in the framework of a proof, but only as a further statement about the greatness of God. However, in his *Reply to Guanilo*, Anselm does argue that if it is conceivable for God to exist, then it is necessary that he exist; and this argument, restated in contemporary terms, has been defended independently by Norman Malcolm and by Charles Hartshorne, who refer to it as Anselm's second proof.

In evaluating the two proofs, Hopkins is mainly concerned with Anselm's use of key words. In the first proof, as Anselm recognized, there is a possibility of confusion arising from his use of the words think (*cogitare*) and understand (*intelligere*); and in *Proslogion* 4, in order to explain how the Fool could say in his heart what he could not think, Anselm distinguished between thinking, which concerns the meaning of words, and understanding, which concerns the essences of things. In the first sense, but not in the second, God can be thought not to exist. The distinction was taken up by Guanilo, who in effect accused Anselm of basing his refutation of the Fool on an equivocation. According to Hopkins, there should have been a further step in the first argument, permitting the Fool to say that he understands the use of the term but denies that there is any essence corresponding to it.

Hopkins' discussion of the second argument centers on Anselm's use of the term "necessity," and on how Anselm's argument differs from Saint Thomas Aquinas' Third Way, which also turns on the difference between possible and necessary being. Both philosophers, he contends, "become entangled in the linguistic web of their respective versions of these modal terms." Nor, in Hopkins' opinion, have Anselm's modern defenders done more than camouflage the proof's flaw behind their modal definitions. For, as in the first proof, so in the second, the Fool can admit the claim construed linguistically while denying that it is valid construed according to fact.

Evans, G. R. *Anselm and Talking About God*. Oxford: Clarendon Press, 1978.

"Talking about God" covers two concerns: the speculative problem, what man can say about God, and the practical problem, how the teacher can best suit theological truths to the minds of his readers. According to G. R. Evans, Saint Anselm answered the former question to his satisfaction in the *Monologion* and the *Proslogion*, his first two works, and had no need to raise it again in subsequent studies; but the practical problem was ever with him, and in Evans' opinion, the care with which he framed his expositions to the understanding of monastic brethren who shared his interests but lacked his technical training helps to explain the perennial appeal of his writings.

The ontological proof for God's existence, although not central to the author's undertaking, does receive special notice, and her treatment of it draws together much of what she has to say concerning the question of what man can say about God.

As Anselm explains, the distinguishing feature of the *Proslogion* is that in this work, unlike the *Monologion* where a chain of arguments was used, only one argument comes into play. Most readers have understood the expression *unum argumentum* as referring to the proof in *Proslogion* 2-4. Evans, however, who approaches the work against the background of her studies in the arithmetic and geometry of the eleventh and twelfth centuries, takes it to mean "a single axiom," and argues that what was original in the *Proslogion* was Anselm's attempt to find "a single, generally accepted notion" that would enable him to deduce by rational necessity not merely God's existence but also, as he is careful to say, God's goodness, and the other divine qualities which, in the earlier work, had been deduced from a number of axioms.

Evans is not disquieted by the fact that Anselm nowhere expressly formulates his new axiom. She thinks that the well-known Augustinian principle according to which God is "that than which nothing greater can be thought" is not the axiom but its first application, and that the axiom proper, which has to bear the weight not merely of Chapters 2-4 but of the whole treatise, can be stated as, "God is 'more than' whatever we can conceive of as a good." Evans suggests the formula, "for whatever a we can imagine, God is $a + x$." Thus, taking for granted the absolute $a + x$-ness of God, Anselm is arguing in *Proslogion* 2 that if it is better to be in reality than in thought alone, God must exist in reality; and, in Chapter 3, that if that the nonexistence of which is unthinkable is greater than that the nonexistence of which is thinkable, then God's nonexistence must be unthinkable. In *Proslogion* 5, Anselm says explicitly that God is "whatever it is better to be than not to be," and he goes on to apply the principle to omnipotence, mercy, and other biblical attributes of God.

Evans does not suppose that in reformulating the proof she has done anything to appease its critics. If the proof merely unfolds implications already present in a single axiom, then obviously the existence of God has been taken for granted from the beginning. But this, she thinks, is entirely as it should be, given the views about language set forth in the *Monologion*, according to which God's existence, his goodness, and his faithfulness are presupposed every time we use language significantly. For Anselm, language is not merely a device for making statements about reality; created by God so that men might know and worship him, it has its own reality on a level with other things.

Human language, according to Anselm, is a repetition of divine speech. Anselm's description of the process by which God created the world parallels the activity of a human craftsman to the point of equating God's thought with a kind of internal speech. God could not have created the world out of nothing had there not existed in him from the first an expression (*locutio*) of all things that were to be. This power of thinking directly of things, in God and in rational creatures, Evans calls primary language.

The parallel between divine and human speech does not remove the gap between Creator and creature. When God speaks, he creates; his words are realities. When man speaks, using the language of *naturalia verba*, or universal ideas, he comes as close to reality as is possible for the created mind; but reality always lies beyond.

Anselm regularly equates thinking and speaking, whether he is talking about God or about man. This need causes no difficulty if we keep in mind Anselm's observations concerning the three ways in which men may be said to speak: we speak in sensible signs, or inwardly by thinking these signs, or by contemplating things directly without their signs. These three constitute a kind of "ladder of language," says Evans, with the natural words (what we would call innate ideas, although Anselm did not have the word "idea"), assumed to be present in every man's mind, being closest to the thoughts of God himself.

All of this, Evans allows, adds up to little more than taking a position on the interdependence of thoughts and things. The axioms which Anselm lays down, largely on the authority of Augustine, are assumptions so fundamental that they can be neither proved nor disproved. But Evans is interested chiefly in understanding Anselm in his historical situation. As prior, he was in the habit of discussing theological questions with his monks. Presumably the monks were in a hurry to get their questions answered, but they were listening to a philosophical genius who was willing to let the answers wait until he was satisfied as to the legitimacy of the questions. The *Monologion* provides a basis for speaking about God. At the same time it leaves room for doubt as to how far ordinary words can be used of the Creator. The most Anselm allows is that "huge abstractions" such as eternity, omnipotence, and truth can be spoken of God. Certain though he is that language is a gift provided to help man draw near God, Anselm denies that we can talk about God as he is.—*J.F.*

ADDITIONAL RECOMMENDED READING

Barnes, Jonathan. *The Ontological Argument*. London: Macmillan and Company, 1972. Restatement of traditional and contemporary formulations and refutations of the argument.

Barth, Karl. *Fides Quaerens Intellectum*. Translated by I. W. Robertson. London: Student Christian Movement, 1960. Views Anselm as a confessing Christian rather than as a philosopher.

Hartshorne, Charles. *The Logic of Perfection*. La Salle, Illinois: Open Court,

1962. Chapter Two presents a symbolic expression of the ontological argument and a defense of the argument as valid.

Henry, Desmond Paul. *The Logic of Saint Anselm*. Oxford: Clarendon Press, 1967. An important contribution to the history of logic; includes an original interpretation of the Ontological Argument.

———————— . *Medieval Logic and Metaphysics*. London: Hutchinson University Library, 1972. An experiment in applying the logic of S. Lesniewski to selected problems of medieval philosophy, including Anselm's proof.

Hick, John and A. C. McGill, eds. *The Many-Faced Argument: Recent Studies on the Ontological Argument for the Existence of God*. New York: Macmillan Publishing Company, 1967. Includes selections from Barth, Stolz, Malcolm, Hartshorne, and others.

McGreal, Ian P. *Analyzing Philosophical Arguments*. San Francisco: Chandler Publishing Company, 1967. McGreal devotes Chapter Seven to a line-by-line semantical and logical critique of Anselm's ontological argument and argues that the argument fallaciously exploits the ambiguity of the expression "understand to exist."

Schufreider, Gregory. *An Introduction to Anselm's Argument*. Philadelphia: Temple University Press, 1978. Summarizes the present state of the Anselmian question and seeks by a renewed study of the text to reach the truth of the matter.

THE GLOSSES ON PORPHYRY

Author: Peter Abelard (1079-1142)
Type of work: Epistemology
First transcribed: Early twelfth century

PRINCIPAL IDEAS ADVANCED

A universal is that which is formed to be predicated of many; since things cannot be predicated of many, only words are universals.

A universal word is imposed on things because of a common likeness conceived by the person imposing the word.

The common likeness of things is a function of the nature of things considered as causes of common conceptions.

Universals signify existent things; namely, discrete individuals; but, in a sense, universals consist in the understanding alone.

Universal words are corporeal with respect to the nature of things, and they are incorporeal with respect to the manner in which they signify.

Universals signify sensible things, but since the intrinsic substance signified is naturally separated from the things signified, universals are, in that sense, insensible.

One of the most colorful and fascinating figures of the Middle Ages was Peter Abelard. Many who know little about the technicalities of medieval logic still know about the life and loves of Abelard. Some mystery and much romance surround the events of his life, and beneath this fascination the fact that Abelard was undoubtedly one of the more skilled philosophers of the era is sometimes forgotten. For one thing, much less of his work has been translated than that of others from the same period who are, consequently, now better known. Furthermore, his particular doctrines have not gained the fame which has come to others. No matter how important *The Glosses on Porphyry* may be in a medieval setting, the idea of practicing philosophy through such commentary is not a currently accepted form. Yet it is true that few more than Porphyry were responsible for the problems which dominated the Middle Ages, so that Abelard's glosses concern crucial issues.

This work belongs to the branch of philosophy which Abelard, following Boethius, called "rational" (the other divisions being the "speculative" and the "moral"). It corresponds most nearly to what we call logic, although it comprehends a slightly wider area of problems than perhaps our formal logic does. Porphyry prepared an introduction for the *Categories* of Aristotle and upon this Abelard comments. In spite of a lack of available Aristotelian material, he was able to construct Aristotle's doctrines with judgment. Abelard's treatment of the problem of the status of universals really ended the argument in its all-absorbing attraction; from then on it was only one among a series of problems. Abelard, it is true, was condemned by his church for his doctrines, since they seemed to lead to paganism.

Definition, division, and classification are the central logical problems to be considered first. Essential definition is the main issue and consequently all of these logical problems basically involve metaphysical issues. For there is no question but that in Porphyry's mind, and Abelard's too, logical division is division according to real structures actually present in nature. How are the creatures of the natural order divided? This question concerns as much the way of things as it does the ways of logical procedure, for in the medieval mind the two are to be worked on until they become the same. The mind adjusts its classifications to the divisions it finds in nature. Logical investigation is ontological inquiry and through it the structure of the world is grasped.

The prominent controversy regarding the status of universals is raised through logical inquiry, since it has metaphysical overtones. We cannot decide about genus and species without deciding whether universals are real. We divide according to genus and species, but we cannot be content to do this as a logical convenience. We must ask: Does such division represent anything real, when it is obvious that every individual thing is singular and not universal, representative of the species but never the species itself? Abelard asks the question: Do universals apply to things or only to words, once we have been forced to a study of universals through the study of genus and species?

Abelard must first define what a universal is. Then, after quoting Aristotle and Porphyry, he refines his own definition: that is universal which is formed to be predicated of many. The question of the ontological status of universals has been raised by a logical question and formulated in logical terms. Abelard begins by supposing that things as well as words are included within this definition.

If things as well as words are called universal, how can the universal definition be applied to things also? As usual, Abelard begins to deal with this question by considering the views of those who have formulated this problem. Many, he says, solve this issue by asserting that in different things there is present a substance essentially the same in spite of the fact that the various things differ in form. Porphyry seems to assent to this solution in arguing that by participation in the species many men are one. Other philosophers are of different opinions, and Abelard begins to formulate his own solution by finding one opinion from among these which seems to him to be closest to the truth, namely, the suggestion that individual things are different from each other not only in their forms, but also in their essences. He concludes that things cannot be universals because they are not predicated of many.

In retrospect, there seems to be no question but that much early medieval interpretation of Aristotle was substantially influenced by Neoplatonic doctrines. Abelard, like many others, was working toward the empirical stress upon the unique individual, which came to be recognized as more accurate

Aristotelian doctrine. In working on the problem of the status of universals, Abelard attempted to reconcile the Platonic suggestion that universals subsist independently of things with the Aristotelian view which stressed the individual as primary and the universal as a function of the status of things, existing only in things.

Some philosophers maintain that the universal is merely a collection of many individual things, but this is too weak a status to assign to universals, in Abelard's view. He saw that, although a collection of men is called a species, when the universal *man* is predicated of each individual, it is not the whole collection of men which is predicated. A universal must be something other than a collection taken as a whole.

As most medievals came to do, obviously Abelard was trying to mediate between what he considered to be two extreme views, to work out a modified position which would give sufficient status to universals without making them in some sense more real than individuals. Being theologically oriented, he could not do away with universals or make them simply a product of language, since they are present in God's understanding and important to his way of knowing. On the other hand, like all those who became interested in Aristotle in the later Middle Ages, Abelard wanted to correct what he felt had been in error in previous ideas concerning universals and to stress the primacy of individuals and their status.

Abelard, however, could not go along with those who called single individuals predicated of many things universals, on the ground that the many things agreed with the individuals in certain respects. Neither a collection taken together, then, nor an individual thing could be called a universal; consequently, Abelard believed that universals belong to words alone. There are universal words and there are particular words. If this is so, what then had to be done was to inquire carefully into the property of universal words. What is the common cause by which the universal word is imposed and what is the conception of the common likeness of things? And more importantly, is the word called common because of a common cause (or respect) in which the things agree, or because of a common conception, or because of both at once? These questions, Abelard found by his examination of other doctrines, form the heart of the issue concerning universals. Dealing with these questions is the only way a solution can be hoped for.

In order to deal with the issues, Abelard argued, we must first be clear about the process of understanding itself. (This is typically Aristotelian.) When we understand the relation between the mind and the objects which it seeks to understand, and how it comes to form that understanding, then we shall learn the status of the universal. In other words, the universal is to be understood primarily as a part of the process of understanding itself. And what Abelard found is that the understanding of universals differs and is to be distinguished from the understanding of particulars.

Here Abelard turned to theology and considered the question of universals as concerning the operation of God's mind. God must have universal conceptions in his mind as a necessary part of his creative function. Man, as a human artist, however, does not need such universal patterns. Universal conceptions exist in God's mind, but not in man's, and this is one measure of their difference. Man does have certain intrinsic forms which do not come to him through the senses, such as rationality and mortality. (Aristotle had also realized that not all knowledge could be formed from the senses and the apprehension of individuals).

What, then, is responsible for the common reference of universal words? Is it due to a common cause of imposition or to a common conception? Abelard came to the conclusion that it is due to both, but he regarded the common cause in accordance with the nature of things as having a greater force. There is, then, a source for universal conception in the things themselves from which the understanding forms its conceptions, although some universals result merely from the formation of common conceptions. The conception of universals is formed by abstraction.

Having come this far, Abelard believed that his analysis had provided the ground necessary to propose a solution to the question about universals and their status, the question which Porphyry had originally raised. Universals signify things truly existent; they are not merely empty opinions. Nevertheless, in a certain sense they exist in the understanding alone. Again, if we divide things into either corporeal or incorporeal and ask where in this division universals belong, the answer must be that they belong to both divisions. Universals in a sense signify corporeal things in that they are imposed according to the nature of things; and yet in another sense they signify incorporeal things, with respect to the manner in which they signify.

Universals are said to subsist in sensible things; that is, they signify an intrinsic substance existing in a thing which is sensible by its exterior form. However, although they signify this substance which subsists actually in the sensible thing, at the same time they demonstrate the same substance as naturally separated from the sensible thing. Some universals are sensible with respect to the nature of things, and the same universal may be nonsensible with respect to the mode of signifying. Universals refer to sensible things, but they refer to them in an incorporeal manner. They signify both sensible things and at the same time that common conception which is ascribed primarily to the divine mind.

Singular words involve no such doubt as to their meaning. As things are discrete in themselves, so they are signified by singular words discretely, and the understanding of them refers to definite things. Universals do not have this easy reference, which is what involves the understanding of them in such difficulty. There is no definite thing, as is the case with singular words, with which they agree. Nevertheless, the multitude of things themselves is the cause of the universality of the nouns which are used to refer to them, because only that which contains many is universal. Yet the thing itself does not have the universality which the thing confers upon the word.

In some sense such a solution as Abelard has proposed—a moderate realism—could be accused of not being definite. What he did was to reject extreme solutions, on the one hand, and, on the other hand, to set the limits of the question and the mode in which the question ought to be asked. Only an extreme position is likely to be clear; any solution which attempts to hold to a moderate view is always in danger of slipping over to one of the extremes and will suffer from appearing to hold both extreme positions at once.

Yet the value in Abelard's analysis is the raising of the problems, the cast given to the question, and the elucidation of the difficulties involved in any solution. The subtle analysis is to some extent illuminating in its own right, and understanding it gives us an appreciation both of Abelard and of the tradition which set his problems for him.—*F.S.*

PERTINENT LITERATURE

Boler, John F. "Abailard and the Problem of Universals," in *The Journal of the History of Philosophy*. I, no. 1 (October, 1963), pp. 37-51.

John F. Boler takes the key to Peter Abelard's theory of universals to lie in the insistence that universals do nothing but signify many things by one *sign*. This notion can be correctly explained only by asking how signs signify, and by avoiding the temptation to treat signs as *things* (nominalism) or universals as things rather than signs (realism). The latter temptation manifests itself not only in Platonic realism, which takes the universal as an entity separate from its instances, but also in more subtle sorts of realism which take the universal to be the collection of entities referred to by a common noun, or, less persuasively, a substance whose members are its accidents. In general, stress on "thing-talk" leads to asking the wrong sorts of questions, and thus getting the wrong sorts of answers. This tendency is equally found in nominalisms which take the universal to be a mere noise—that is, a *thing*.

Abelard's semantic approach, on the other hand, legitimates such questions as "How do proper and common nouns signify differently?" On this approach it is analytically true that there is such a difference; otherwise proper and common nouns would be indistinguishable. The thing-oriented approach, by contrast, might well obscure this vital difference and preclude questions about it—by holding, for example, that common and proper nouns signify the same way (by naming, presumably) but differ by signifying different things.

What differences, then, Boler asks, does Abelard find between common and proper nouns from his semantic point of view? He answers that proper nouns, for Abelard, do two things: (1) pick out a unique thing ("determinare") and (2) baptize that unique thing with a name ("nominare"). Common nouns do only the latter. Thus Abelard concludes that they "nominate confusedly or nondiscretely."

Boler pushes this inquiry by considering further the act which Abelard calls "nominating." This is not, for Abelard, arbitrary. It depends on the fact that a name has been established for an entity. From the trivial fact that the sound (*vox*) used to "establish" that name is arbitrary it cannot be inferred that one may at will use another sound to "nominate" the same entity. This would be to fail to take into account a fact about the first *vox*: that it *has* an established significance. For Abelard, *voces* with this sort of significance are called *sermones* or, in Boler's translation, "terms." A *sermo* is a *vox* taken as establishing an understanding by means of which one can be said to *know* the subject that the *sermo* stands for.

Boler now takes up the subjects of images (likenesses) and abstraction. The mind uses images to bring to mind the entity nominated by a sign when that entity is not present. Images have the advantage of picking out things in a nondiscrete way. Thus a *sermo* is universal just when, although not just because, it generates an image which depicts or pictures more than one thing. Images are thus associated with universals, but are themselves universals. Next, Boler considers briefly the subject of abstraction, a notion which Abelard inherits from Boethius. Abstraction designates the act of considering a shared property of a thing in isolation from its other properties. Thus, in abstracting one gives up mirroring an object precisely as it exists (as it "subsists," in Abelard's terms). This does not lead to falsity, but neither does it lead to further clarity about nondiscrete signification of universals, for this must grasp entities "as they are" or subsist. In this respect the image is more promising; but to follow out the image notion would tend to make Abelard into a Lockean subjectivist empiricist. To follow out the abstraction notion would make him like his thirteenth century conceptualist successors. Boler, however, thinks that Abelard is neither.

To get a better account of Abelard's theory of universals one must closely consider his claim that the common *cause* for the imposition of a universal is the fact that two (or more) entities referred to by a common term "agree in being such and such," as Plato and Socrates agree in "being a man" (*esse hominum*). This "being such-and-so" Abelard calls a *status*. On an analysis of this term (and the related term *dicta*, which stands to a propositional content as a *status* to a concept) rests the success or failure of Abelard's theory. First, the *status* is not an image or an abstract property. These things are psychological and/or mediate and therefore fail to pick up the objective reference in "*esse*." Are they then really things of a quasi-Platonic sort, and does Abelard's theory collapse into a realism from which he unsuccessfully tries to disentangle himself? Abelard believes not. "Not wanting to appear in court" is a *status*, he argues, because it is the "cause" of the imposition of a term such as "being fined for not going to court." It is not, however, a thing, or a constituent of a thing. For it is only as an object of *understanding* that it "exists," whereas things exist, we may presume, in independence of our understanding of them. Moreover, even this understanding cannot be posited apart from the *voces* which import it. Nevertheless, Boler concludes by expressing some doubt that those considerations keep Abelard's semantic approach from riding on the back of talk about universals as things, and they may still presuppose some sort of realism.

Tweedale, Martin M. *Abailard on Universals*. Amsterdam: North-Holland Publishing Company, 1976.

Martin M. Tweedale's thorough study of Peter Abelard's theory of universals develops the line of interpretation taken by John F. Boler (see above). He does this in two ways. He sharpens Boler's suggestion that Abelard distances himself from a theory of universals that rests on the psychology of image-making and abstraction. He then undertakes to defend Abelard's theory as being clearly and persuasively nonrealist in a way that might be of interest to current thinkers.

The upshot of the first point is to show that Abelard is in no way a conceptualist, and so is in no danger of lapsing into the subjectivism that is so closely connected with conceptualism. This undercuts the common tendency in Abelard studies to ascribe to Abelard the view that universals are "figments" of the mind. These views derive from the anachronistic ascription to Abelard of either thirteenth century Aristotelianism or, worse, the seventeenth and eighteenth century Lockean "way of ideas." More positively, this frees Tweedale to assert that Abelard is a nominalist, although with apologies for having to use these conventions. A nominalist holds (1) that universals are nothing but signs and (2) that logic is the study of signs. Because images and abstractions *can* be treated as signs, nominalism has been conflated with conceptualist subjectivism. It should not be, and Abelard can be said to have subscribed to the two nominalist propositions stated above and not at all to conceptualism. Second, although Abelard has in common with the fourteenth century Ockhamist nominalists a belief in (1) and (2), the absence of reductive techniques for sentences with specious subjects in Abelard, and their prominence in Ockhamist thought, in no way undercuts Abelard's nominalism. He has his own ways of dealing with such problems.

To hold that Abelard is, if anything, a nominalist is to commit oneself to taking seriously his attack on various forms of realism. This Tweedale does in a very thorough review of the inheritance Abelard received from Plato, Boethius, and Porphyry, and of Abelard's conception of and refutations of various forms of realism. Tweedale lists two major kinds of realism: "material essence" realism, which speaks of intelligible objects apart from their instantiations; and the more interesting "indifference" realisms, which, according to Tweedale, divide into two or three different positions, depending on how one counts. Tweedale calls these last "the collection theory," "the identity theory," and "the plurality theory." What all of these hold is that the universal just *is* the set of things which are picked out by a common term, either purely extensively ("collection theory") or under certain descriptions ("identity," and in a perhaps different way, "plurality" theories). Abelard's attacks on all of these positions point to the extremely counterintuitive, and sometimes self-contradictory, implications that such positions involve.

Abelard's own approach is the semantic one indicated by Boler. Universals are *voces*, sounds produced by speech, which are "established" to be *vocabula* and *sermones*. *Vocabula* are small units of meaning; *sermones* are complexes of *vocabula* (Tweedale translates *sermo* not as "term" but as "expression"). Tweedale shows that in his earlier commentary on Porphyry, the *Logica Ingredientibus*, Abelard was willing to hold that the identity relation between *voces* and *sermones/vocabula* was such that everything which can be predicated of the latter can be predicated of the former, and thus that *voces* are themselves universals. Later, however, in the *Logica Nostrorum Petitioni Sociorum*, the notion of "establishing" yields a more subtle view, resisting the implication suggested by this treatment that universals are things-*qua*-sounds.

Tweedale devotes the rest of his book to defending Abelard from the imputation that his view might fall back into realism. He recognizes with Boler that the key to this issue lies in the notions of *status* and *dicta*. He begins, however, with an examination not of the former concept, but of the latter, on the basis of an examination of Abelard's *Dialectica*. *Dicta* assert the existence (*esse*) of whatever is stated to be the case in a proposition. They do not, however, signify this, according to Tweedale, by *naming* it, and so do not semantically function as do proper nouns. This is shown by proving that Abelard regards predicate nouns (which tempt us to treat them as common names) as *inseparable* parts of predicate verbs, and the verbs as containing an assertoric copula which carries the existence claim made by the whole predicate. This two-part, rather than three-part, analysis of the proposition removes much that otherwise inclines us to conflate the significance of common and proper nouns. From this point, Abelard can argue that predicates only function when attached to subjects and assert something to be the case about such subjects. In other words, it allows us to speak of the referents of common terms, *status* or types, as *signified* by universals, but to resist treating such objects as named. The effect of this, according to Tweedale, is to make it possible to countenance Abelard's claim that his theory is not a disguised realism.

Tweedale concludes with a helpful comparison between Abelard and Gottlob Frege. If the latter's views were to be revised in the direction pointed to by Abelard, Frege's "thoughts," which are roughly Abelard's "*dicta*," would be the referents of propositions, and not just their "senses" (*Sinn*) in Frege's sense. Frege's "concepts," roughly equivalent to Abelard's "*status*," would allow us to make better sense out of the latter by treating them in a Fregean way as functions unsaturated or unfilled until completed by a Fregean "object" or Abelard's denotative nouns.—*D.J.D.*

ADDITIONAL RECOMMENDED READING

Carré, M. H. *Realists and Nominalists*. London: Oxford University Press, 1946. Abelard as conceptualist.

Fumagalli, Maria Teresa. *The Logic of Abelard*. Dordrect, The Netherlands: D. Reidel, 1970. Good treatment of Abelard's *dicta*.

Sikes, J. G. *Peter Abailard*. Cambridge: Cambridge University Press, 1932. Standard biography; somewhat inadequate on theory.

Tweedale, Martin M. "Abailard and Non-things," in *The Journal of the History of Philosophy*. V, no. 4 (October, 1967), pp. 329-342.

THE INCOHERENCE OF THE INCOHERENCE

Author: Averroës (ibn-Roshd, 1126-1198)
Type of work: Theology, metaphysics
First transcribed: Twelfth century

PRINCIPAL IDEAS ADVANCED

Since any series of causes necessary through another cause must ultimately depend upon a cause necessary in itself (a first cause), God, as the first cause, exists.

God did not create the world in time, either by willing it at the moment of creation or by willing it eternally, for to act in time is to change, and God is changeless because he is perfect.

God, as first cause and unmoved mover, does not act in time, but he produces immaterial intelligences which, because of their imperfection, can change in time.

The being of existent things is inseparable from their essence.

Averroës, the last of the great Islamic philosophers, lived roughly one hundred and fifty years after Avicenna, his philosophic rival, and about three generations after Ghazali (1058-1111) the greatest of Moslem theologians. In his controversy with these two men he concerned himself primarily with the defense and purification of Aristotle, whom he followed as closely as he could. Since he, too, accepted such spurious works as *The Theology of Aristotle*, his interpretation is still permeated by Neoplatonic elements, but to a lesser extent than that of Avicenna. The success of his endeavor is indicated by the fact that he was known to scholastic writers as *the* Commentator and that no less a person than Thomas Aquinas had him constantly at hand as he wrote his *Summa contra Gentiles* (c. 1258-1260) and his various commentaries on Aristotle.

The Incoherence of the Incoherence was written in reply to Ghazali's book, *The Incoherence of the Philosophers*, a book in which Ghazali had attacked the philosophers, and in particular Avicenna, for advocating doctrines that were incompatible with their faith. As the title of his own book suggests, Averroës came to the defense of the philosophers by attacking the incoherence of *The Incoherence*. Adopting a position similar to that of the later medieval thinkers who distinguished between revealed and natural theology, Averroës scrupulously avoided denying any tenet of his faith; nevertheless, he sided firmly with the philosophers. His interpretations of religious doctrines were so far removed from those of the theologians that even though he was studied carefully by Hebrew and Christian philosophers, he was not recognized to any great extent by his Islamic contemporaries. Averroës' book plays a very important role in the long controversy between the philosophers and the theologians, since it is concerned chiefly with the nature and existence of God, and with the relationship between God and the cosmos. Averroës does not spell out his position in detail, for he agrees on the whole with the earlier commentators on Aristotle and with the version of Aristotle he receives from them. In particular, he agrees largely with Avicenna, disagreeing on those points, and they are important points, where he thinks Avicenna departs from Aristotle. (The reader is referred to the article on Avicenna in this book.)

Averroës agrees with Aristotle that there is a First Cause, and he accepts a modified version of Avicenna's proof from contingency. Objects whose existence is contingent rather than necessary must have a cause. If the cause is itself contingent, and if its cause is contingent, and so on, there would be an infinite regress and therefore no cause at all, a conclusion which, it can readily be seen, denies the assumption that contingent objects must have a cause. Hence, any series of contingent objects must be preceded in existence by a necessary cause which is either necessary through another or necessary without a cause—necessary in itself. But if we have a series of causes each of which is necessary through another, once more we have an infinite regress and thus no cause. Hence, any series of causes necessary through another must depend upon a cause necessary in itself—a First Cause.

The nature of this First Cause and of the way in which it causes is illuminated by Averroës' discussion of creation. Averroës agrees with the philosophers against Ghazali that the world was not created in time. The philosophers had argued that if the world was created in time, it was created directly or indirectly by God, since an infinite regress of causes is impossible. If God created it in time, then he acted at a time and therefore underwent a change in time; but unquestionably, this is an impossible state of affairs since God is perfect and changeless. To Ghazali's objection that God did not act in time, but decreed from all eternity that the world should come into being at a certain time, Averroës replies that even if God had so willed from all eternity, he must also have acted at the time of creation in order to implement his decision, for every effect must have a contemporaneous cause. Consequently, the philosopher's objection cannot be avoided. It can be shown similarly that the cosmos is incorruptible; that is, that there is no time at which it will come to an end, for this too would require a change in God. Change occurs only within the world and then only when one thing is changed into another. The world itself is eternal and everlasting.

Ghazali had already attacked Avicenna on this point, asserting that the followers of Aristotle now have a problem on their hands, for they must give some account of how an eternal First Cause produces things that have a beginning in time. The problem is complicated by the fact that Averroës and Avicenna agreed with Aristotle that since the world is eternal, infinite temporal sequences do occur. For instance, there was no time when the celestial sphere began to move and no time when the first man appeared. Why not,

chides Ghazali, agree with the materialists that since there is an infinite sequence of causes, a First Cause is not only superfluous but impossible?

In reply, Averroës asks us to consider the case of the infinite sequence of
past positions of a celestial sphere. Like Avicenna, he says that so far as the
sphere is concerned this sequence is an accidental infinite, for the motion of
the sphere at any given moment does not cause the motion it has at any other
moment. First, if motion did cause motion there would be an infinite regress
of causes and therefore no cause at all. Second, since motion is continuous,
there are in it no discrete units that have a beginning and an end and therefore
no units that could stand in a causal relationship to one another. Finally, since
the cause must be contemporaneous with the effect, the causal relation cannot
span an interval of time, and past motion cannot influence present motion.
In the case of the celestial sphere, the motion it has at any given moment
follows, not from the motion it had at some previous moment, but from its
desire at that moment to emulate the perfection of the associated Intelligence.
Through all eternity this Intelligence has sustained it in motion from moment
to moment by continuously acting as its final cause. Since this Intelligence is
itself a being whose existence is necessary through another, we are led back
to the First Cause, the Unmoved Mover who stands behind the world. The
Mover itself does not operate in time nor does it cause time directly, but it
does produce an Intelligence which, because it is immaterial, is changeless,
but which, because it is imperfect, is able to produce change of position in
the sphere and thus to produce change in time.

Averroës' treatment of the infinite sequence of man begetting man is somewhat different from the preceding argument, for in this case there are discrete
objects which do seem to cause one another successively. But here, too,
Averroës says the sequence is, in itself, an accidental infinite. To be sure, the
sequence does depend upon man, but only in several secondary senses. First,
as he puts it, the third man can come from the second only if the first man
has perished. That is, since the amount of matter in the universe is limited,
human bodies can continue to come into existence only if others perish.
Second, through the phenomena of conception and growth, man is the instrument by which God produces other men. But having functioned in both
cases as a material cause by providing suitable matter, man's role is complete,
for no body can produce a form in another. Directly or indirectly, the First
Mover is the source of the eternal form that, when individuated by matter,
animates that matter. Here again Averroës describes the Mover or one of
the Intelligences as operating eternally as a final cause, again and again drawing forth from complexes of matter the form that is contained in them potentially.

Averroës then considers the question raised by Ghazali as to how it is
possible for the plurality in the world to arise from the Mover, who is simple.
Avicenna had argued that only one thing can emanate from God, but that

this thing, the First Intelligence, is able to generate more than one thing by contemplating both itself and the Mover. Averroës replies, first, that since thought and its object are identical, the Intelligence is really identical with its thought of God and with its thought of itself and, therefore, that these thoughts are identical with each other. Hence, there is no plurality of thought and no plurality of creation. Second, he says that when Avicenna insists that only one thing can come from God, he is thinking of the Supreme Intellect as if it were a finite empirical one, but this concept is a mistake. Since our intellect is limited by matter, any particular mental act can have only one object, but since God is not so limited he can think all things even though his simplicity and changelessness preclude a plurality of acts. If it be replied that to think of all things is to have many thoughts, and that since thinker and thought are identical, God must be plural, Averroës replies that when God thinks all things he does not think them discursively as we do. In our case either we entertain images, a process which unquestionably involves spatial apprehension and thus spatial plurality, or we understand concepts by genus and species, a process which again introduces plurality. In either case, since we apprehend the object of thought by abstracting it from its material context, we apprehend it imperfectly. God, who is perfect, does not apprehend the natures of things in these ways and therefore does not apprehend them as either individual or universal. In some manner which we do not understand, he comprehends that which is plural to us but does not comprehend it as numerically plural. (This is a particular application of the general principle that any property or capacity we attribute to God must be attributed only by analogy.) God, then, is the source of all plurality even though he is simple and changeless.

Averroës accepts the Avicennian cosmology in its general outlines. The First Mover produces a number of pure Intelligences which may produce others and which cause the motions of their respective spheres or, in the case of the Agent Intellect, preside over generation and corruption in the sublunar world. The Mover is the efficient cause of these Intelligences, producing them by means of a power that it emanates, and the final and formal cause insofar as it is the thing they seek to emulate. They in turn are the efficient, final, and formal causes of the motion of the spheres. Averroës agrees with Avicenna that though prime matter is not created, the existence of material things depends upon the Mover in that he is the source of the forms and also the agent, final, and formal cause of the manifestation of any form in matter.

But despite this agreement Averroës disagrees with Avicenna on a number of points. Some, such as the number of Intelligences (over forty), and the nonlinear order of the Intelligences (the Mover may have produced all of the Intelligences of the principle spheres directly) are unimportant, but others are crucial. As we have already indicated, Averroës insists that the Intelligences really are simple in that they do not contemplate themselves in several essentially different ways. It follows that the spheres are not composites of soul and body even though they are animate, and that God is the source of plurality. Consequently, God does not function as Avicenna says he does. Whether by intention or not, Avicenna left the impression that God's role in the creative process was completed when he produced the First Intelligence and that the further creative acts were contributed piecemeal by the various Intelligences acting from their own natures. In locating the source of plurality in God, Averroës is insisting that direct responsibility for the whole creative process rests with God. It is true, he says, that the Intelligences are creative agents, but they are the Mover's subordinates who, out of respect for him, implement his commands throughout the cosmos. Setting aside the theological analogy, we understand a theory such as this to mean that God's essence functions as the efficient, formal, and final cause of the First Intelligence, that this intelligence is an imperfect manifestation of the essence of God, that God as thus reflected functions once more as the efficient, formal, and final cause of an Intelligence or soul inferior to the first one, and so on down through the hierarchy.

Averroës also differs from Avicenna in a respect which anticipates the contrast between Spinoza and Leibniz, for he loosens the Avicenna bonds of necessity. To be sure, in some sense God does what he does necessarily, but this is not logical necessity, for the world he contemplates and thus produces is the best of all possible worlds. Similarly, the various intelligences respond to God, not because it would be contradictory not to, but because they respect him. There is a definite normative element permeating the system. On the general issue of the relation between God and the world Averroës does not differ from Avicenna as greatly as he frequently says he does; nevertheless, his modifications are important and they do result in a weakening of the Neoplatonic elements, a fact that was appreciated by later Aristotelians.

Another historically important feature of Averroës' philosophy is his rejection of Avicenna's sharp distinction between essence and existence. Avicenna had insisted that except in the case of God, existence is an accident that happens to an essence. For Avicenna, existence is a condition that must be satisfied by an essence before it can occur outside a mind, a property that must be added to it. Thus, the existence of a material object does not stem from its essence, but from what happened to its essence. On the other hand, Averroës insists that the very being of an existent thing is its essence, that its being depends upon the essence and not upon what happens to the essence. For him the terms "being" and "existence" are not verb terms, but substantives applied primarily to the object itself and secondarily to the essence that makes it the sort of thing it is. Since the object is a being or existent in virtue of its essence, it is impossible to separate essence and existence save in thought. The essence itself may be regarded as an existent in a secondary sense of that term, but in this case it is impossible to separate essence and existence even in thought.

This difference between the two men is reflected in their views, inasmuch as Avicenna is very much concerned with how things come into existence and Averroes shows himself to be more concerned with the manner in which things change. Thus, in their proofs of the existence of God, Avicenna moves from the contingent existence of things to a necessarily existing ground, whereas Averroës proceeds from the occurrence of motion to an unmoved mover. Again, whereas Avicenna's Giver of Forms is bringing essences into existence by impressing them upon suitably prepared matter, Averroës' Agent Intellect is coaxing out forms nascent in complexes of matter. Averroës insists correctly that Avicenna is moving away from Aristotle and that he himself is truer to their common master. Later, Thomas Aquinas and his followers follow Avicenna in making a sharp distinction between essence and existence, but they acknowledge Averroës' objection by transforming existence from a property into an act of being that is prior in principle to essence. On the other hand, Ockham and the Averroists of the fourteenth, fifteenth, sixteenth, and seventeenth centuries insist that Averroës is right and that Avicenna and Thomas are wrong.

Another historically important feature of Averroës' philosophy is his disagreement with several aspects of Avicenna's psychology. First, and not so important, he believes that Avicenna added a superfluous faculty to the animal soul when he attributed an estimative sense to animals, a sense paralleling the cogitative sense in man. The ancients were correct, he says, in maintaining that imagination can detect intentions as well as sensible forms and that it can make judgments about these intentions. More importantly, Averroës gives a radically different account of the theoretic intellect. He agrees with Avicenna that the individual human intellect is activated only by the Agent Intellect which is external to us and acts on all of us alike, but he disagrees about the nature of the intellect that is activated. According to Avicenna, it is the potential intellect, an immaterial intellect, that can survive the body; but according to Averroës, it is the passive intellect, a corporeal faculty, that cannot survive the body. Averroës does admit an immaterial potential intellect in addition to the corporeal passive intellect; but it is not a personal faculty, for it is simply the Agent Intellect insofar as it individuates itself when it illuminates the passive intellect in order to prepare it for the reception of intelligible forms. Averroës thinks of the immaterial soul as being individuated when it strikes a physical object. Thus, there is no personal immortality, for individuality within the immaterial intellect disappears when the corporeal passive intellect dies. From the point of view of the Christian philosophers of the twelfth and thirteenth centuries, Averroës is correct insofar as he gives the potential and agent intellects a common status, but incorrect insofar as he denies that they are personal faculties. They preferred to modify Avicenna by eliminating the Tenth Intelligence and endowing each human being with an individual agent intellect to accompany the individual potential intellect he already has.—*L.M.*

PERTINENT LITERATURE
Averroës. *Tahafut al-tahafut (The Incoherence of the Incoherence).* Translated by Simon Van den Bergh. London: Luzac, 1969.

Simon Van den Bergh presents a full translation of Averroës' reply to most of Ghazali's arguments in *The Incoherence of the Philosophers.* He also gives the translation of Ghazali's arguments, so that the book is self-contained and one does not need first to read a translation of Ghazali's *The Incoherence of the Philosophers* to be able to understand fully Averroës' answer in *The Incoherence of the Incoherence* to Ghazali's criticisms. For each issue discussed one finds Ghazali's argument or arguments and then Averroës' criticism or criticisms. The main theses and arguments of Averroës' *The Incoherence of the Incoherence* are analyzed in the Introduction, and further clarifications on more particular points and details of argumentation can be found in the notes located in the second volume.

In his Introduction, Van den Bergh first presents the historical background to the controversy in Islam between the theologians and the philosophers. According to the author, the controversy has its roots in the dispute between two main late Greek philosophical streams: (1) the Neoplatonic Aristotelianism which is somehow adopted by the Muslim philosophers and (2) the Skeptic Stoic School used by the theologians.

Van den Bergh claims that Ghazali's criticisms of the philosophers in *The Incoherence of the Philosophers* are of a rather piecemeal kind and do not aim at a systematic destruction of philosophy by an attack on its foundations. Ghazali simply deals one by one with the issues on which philosophers hold positions contrary to the Islamic faith. By the philosophers Ghazali means Aristotle and his best Arabic interpreters, al-Farabi and Avicenna. So Ghazali's attack is not so much an attack on philosophy as such as it is an attack on Neoplatonic Aristotelianism. On each of the twenty disputed issues— sixteen in theology and four in natural philosophy—Ghazali tries to show the inconsistency of the position of the "philosophers." He goes from one issue to another but does not indicate connections between them; nor does he relate them to a general basic approach.

Averroës' reply to Ghazali's *The Incoherence of the Philosophers* follows the same pattern and does not present an articulate and unified defense of his philosophical positions. It is to other works that one should look for a systematic exposition of Averroës' thought.

For most of the disputed issues Van den Bergh gives an interpretation of the basic arguments of both Ghazali and Averroës and a critical evaluation thereof. He also shows the perennial character of the issues in drawing parallels between Ghazali's or Averroës' position and the position of some ancient, modern, or contemporary philosophers.

His main contention—a rather unusual one—is that, although Ghazali and Averroës seem to be in great disagreement, they basically hold the same position but let formulations divide them. Their quarrel was about words not substance. Both, in fact, present a philosophical approach; but their ways of treating philosophy differ. Ghazali, who is, according to Van den Bergh, mainly a theologian and therefore under Stoic influence, looks for a philosophy of the heart which does not so much seek abstract truth as a God of Pity. Averroës, on the other hand, who is a philosopher in the Neoplatonic Aristotelian line, seeks a sort of disembodied truth. So Van den Bergh presents Ghazali as the champion of some sort of existential philosophy and Averroës as the champion of some sort of dry rationalism.

According to Van den Bergh, the dispute between Ghazali and Averroës is not a dispute between theologians and philosophers, or between faith and reason, but a dispute between representatives of two approaches to philosophy.

Averroës. *On the Harmony of Religion and Philosophy*. Translated by George F. Hourani. London: Luzac, 1961.

The Incoherence of the Incoherence is a reply to Ghazali's criticisms of the philosophers. It presents a discussion of some issues on which the philosophers hold positions contrary to the faith. It does not try to articulate a general theory of the relation between philosophy and religion. The texts translated in *On the Harmony of Religion and Philosophy* do so.

The first text, known as *The Decisive Treatise*, according to George F. Hourani is a juridical defense of the study of philosophy. It is a defense of philosophy written by a lawyer for other lawyers in function of the categories of Islamic law. It attempts to demonstrate that the study of philosophy, according to Islamic law, is obligatory.

The first part shows that the Law commands the study of philosophy considered as a demonstrative science. By philosophy Averroës means Aristotelian and therefore Greek philosophy. If sometimes philosophy leads to harm it is purely accidental, just as the taking of a medicine can cause harm by accident. Philosophy will cause harm only to people who are unable to follow demonstrative arguments. Therefore, although the study of philosophy is obligatory for anyone who is qualified, it should be forbidden to those who are not qualified to use demonstrative arguments.

The second part contends that, contrary to appearances, philosophy contains nothing opposed to Islam. If the apparent meaning of the Koran and the Traditions conflicts with the conclusions of philosophy, one must interpret that meaning allegorically. The three main points of contention between Ghazali and the philosophers (God's ignorance of particulars, the assertion of the eternity of the world, and the denial of the bodily resurrection, issues that are discussed in *The Incoherence of the Incoherence*), are dealt with, and the lack of real conflict between faith or religion and philosophy in what concerns them is argued for. Averroës also elaborates some basic principles for the allegorical interpretation of the Scriptures in case of opposition with sound philosophical positions.

The third and final part insists on the fact that such allegorical interpretation should be reserved to the philosophers and hidden from the masses, whom it would confuse. For them the literal meaning is enough, and safer.

The second text translated in this book is the *Appendix* to *The Decisive Treatise*; it again deals with the problem of God's knowledge of the particulars. The third and last text deals with the allegorical interpretation of the bodily resurrection as an expression of the immortality of the soul and provides some more principles of allegorical interpretation of the Scriptures and criteria to determine when the Scriptures require such an intepretation.

In his Introduction to these texts, Hourani offers a historical background and some evaluation of Averroës' position. He first maintains that both in *The Incoherence of the Incoherence* and in *The Decisive Treatise* Averroës presents his true philosophic positions, although he exercises caution in discussing them, and, therefore, is rather involved and sometimes obscure. Hourani also contends that *The Decisive Treatise* shows that Averroës is a believing Muslim and that his text gives an impression of sincerity.

According to Hourani, *The Decisive Treatise* is the only book in Medieval Islam that attempts to give an answer to the problem of the harmony of Sunnite Islam with Greco-Arabic philosophy. Philosophy, on the one hand, is the last resort in case of conflict between the literal meaning of the Scriptures and itself, although its study should be reserved for the intellectual elite. Philosophy thus gives the true meaning of the Scriptures. Ordinary Islam, on the other hand, and therefore literal meaning, should lead the masses because they are unable to understand philosophy. Basically, for Averroës, there is only one truth; and it is philosophy which brings about, when necessary, the true meaning of religion, a meaning beyond the reach of the ordinary man. This of course excludes a "double truth" interpretation of Averroës, as some had proposed.

Tallon, Andrew. "Personal Immortality in Averroës' 'Tahafut al-Tahafut,'" in *The New Scholasticism*. XXXVIII, no. 3 (July, 1964), pp. 341-357.

One of the main contentions of Ghazali in his *The Incoherence of the Philosophers* is that philosophers not only deny the bodily resurrection but furthermore are also unable to explain individual immortality of the soul (pp. 333-363). In *On the Harmony of Religion and Philosophy* Averroës explains that the true meaning of the bodily resurrection is the immortality of the soul. But in what exactly does the immortality of the soul consist for Averroës?

In his commentary on Aristotle's *On the Soul*, Averroës states that there is only one Active Intellect for the whole of mankind, and also only one Passive Intellect. This Passive Intellect is "outside" the human being and thinks through this being by making use of the images produced by man. Only imagination, which is not a part of the intellect, is individual; but it is also mortal.

Since there is some question as to whether Averroës holds the same positions in his Aristotelian commentaries written for philosophers as he does in his defenses of philosophy written for a broader public, such as *The Incoherence of the Incoherence* and *The Decisive Treatise*, Andrew Tallon tries to determine his position on immortality in *The Incoherence of the Incoherence*.

Tallon first maintains that Averroës' text is difficult, obscure, and ambiguous. He then contends that Averroës states that intellect is separate and one for all men, although it is not an aspect of the soul since it is separate from it. The question then becomes: Is soul immortal for Averroës? Tallon indicates a few passages in which Averroës states that the soul as such is immortal, but does man have an immortal individual soul or only a collective one? Here Tallon argues that Averroës' concern is for the species and not for individuals, even though he does not say so.

To understand Averroës' position one needs to consider what his metaphysical conception of individuation implies. It is clear that for Averroës the sole principle of individuation is matter. Soul is by itself immaterial and immortal and so cannot be individuated by matter or bodies; therefore it cannot be individuated at all. Thus, Averroës believes that the soul too is separate. In other passages, however, Averroës describes the soul as *in* the body. What does Averroës mean by that? Tallon suggests that the soul is *in* a body as light is *in* a mirror. As there is one light which can be reflected in many mirrors, there is one soul which is temporarily reflected in diverse bodies. Thus, when Averroës claims that the soul is the form of the body, he is no longer holding a traditional hylomorphic position in which form and matter are interdependent, but asserting the temporary relation of the separate immaterial and immortal soul to many individual bodies.

Tallon concludes that the wording of Averroës' statement, as well as the internal coherence of his metaphysical positions, prevent him from asserting an individual immortality since *the* Soul, although immortal, is not individual.

Yet, according to Tallon, the ambiguities of Averroës' text probably indicate that Averroës the philosopher and Averroës the man are in conflict. As a philosopher Averroës does not see any way to argue in favor of an individual immortality of the soul and therefore claims only the immortality of *the* Soul. Such an immortality is an immortality of the species, not of individuals. On the other hand, as a man and a Muslim, Averroës either believes in personal immortality or wants to do so. The ambiguities are therefore not in Averroës' philosophy but in Averroës the man. Tallon is convinced that Averroës has not realized the true harmony between Averroës the believer and Averroës the philosopher, and between his intellectual integrity and his religious beliefs or desires. Such claims imply that, according to Tallon, Averroës, in what concerns his conception of the soul and of the intellect and their immortality, holds basically the same position in *The Incoherence of the Incoherence* as in his commentaries on Aristotle. In both, he defends what is traditionally known as monopsychism, or the theory that there is only one soul for all mankind and therefore no individual souls and no personal immortality.—*T.A.D.*

ADDITIONAL RECOMMENDED READING

Aquinas, Saint Thomas. *On the Unity of the Intellect Against the Averroists (De Unitate Intellectus contra Averroistas)*. Translated by Beatrice H. Zedler. Milwaukee: Marquette University Press, 1968. Translation of Thomas' attack against some of his adversaries who were defending Averroës' monopsychism. Shows the influence of Averroës on the West and includes a criticism of his epistemology.

Arberry, A. J. *Revelation and Reason in Islam*. London: George Allen & Unwin, 1957. A standard presentation of diverse approaches in Islam to this question.

Averroës. *Destructio Destructionum Philosophiae Algazelis*, in *the Latin version of Calo Calonymos*. Edited by Beatrice H. Zedler. Milwaukee: Marquette University Press, 1961. Transcription of the Venice 1550 Latin edition, with a historical introduction.

Ghazali. *Tahafut al-Falasifah (The Incoherence of the Philosophers)*. Translated by Sabih Ahmad Kamali. Lahore: Pakistan Philosophical Congress, 1963. Complete English translation of *The Incoherence of the Philosophers*, including the Introduction and the arguments not included in Averroës' *The Incoherence of the Incoherence*. Allows an examination of Ghazali's work for its own sake.

Ivry, Alfred L. "Towards a Unified View of Averroës' Philosophy," in *The Philosophical Forum*. IV, no. 1 (Fall, 1972), pp. 87-113. A new and controversial interpretation of Averroës which tries to present a synthetic outlook.

GUIDE FOR THE PERPLEXED

Author: Maimonides (Moses ben Maimon, 1135-1204)
Type of work: Metaphysics, theology
First transcribed: 1190

PRINCIPAL IDEAS ADVANCED

Those who have become perplexed about religious matters as a result of studying philosophy can be helped by realizing that scriptural writings may often be understood in a figurative sense.

It is precisely because of the difficulty of understanding the divine that metaphor becomes useful in religious utterances.

Once the necessity for an indirect approach to religious matters is admitted, faith becomes a way of relating oneself to a Being whose mystery is understood metaphorically.

"From Moses to Moses there was none like Moses" is a famous phrase which indicates something of Maimonides' place of importance in Jewish thought. The First Moses represents the origin of the great Jewish religious tradition and the Jewish Law. The Second Moses stands for, as is now well known, an attempt to reconcile this inherited tradition with the growing Arabian and Western philosophy and culture which were being absorbed in the eleventh century.

Intellectuals of his age were perplexed by the disparity between the Law, which meant so much to them, and the philosophical sophistication they could not resist acquiring. For them Maimonides provided a *Guide*, as well as a new summary of the Law, both of which were so successful that they have now become classics in the religious tradition as well as in secular philosophy. Can Maimonides once again serve as a guide for our time, or does our situation require new prophets? Let us begin by an inquiry into the way in which Maimonides met the need of his own day.

Maimonides addressed his *Guide* to those who had studied philosophy and had acquired knowledge and who "while firm in religious matters are perplexed and bewildered on account of the ambiguous and figurative expressions employed in holy writings." We are not, then, beginning here with philosophic reason and attempting to find a religious view which will fit it. Moses' audience was from the beginning firmly committed to its religious tradition; but, now that philosophy had penetrated religion, the question was never one as to whether religion should be maintained but only how it was to handle its philosophical content. Maimonides wrote for those whose religious roots were deep and who had held to religious practice. "The object of this treatise is to enlighten a religious man who has been trained to believe in the truth of our holy Law, who conscientiously fulfills his moral and religious duties, and at the same time has been successful in his philosophical studies." This is not the description of a hollow man.

It is not difficult to see why such a person was "lost in perplexity and anxiety," caught in tensions he could not easily resolve. His religious training was too deeply ingrained even to consider surrendering it, and yet the new sophistication made philosophy naturally attractive. It is not that such a person had for the first time become an intellectual, since as a Jew he had inherited a long and subtle intellectual tradition; but that formerly reason had worked only within the Law, while afterwards philosophy took this same reason outside the Law and offered it new and alien foundations. This was the general cause for concern, but *Guide for the Perplexed* focuses on the particular problem of trying to explain certain words in Scripture central to the religious tradition whose common interpretation sets them at odds with philosophical refinements. Reason never ceased to accept the Law, but it found it difficult to accept any teaching based on a literal interpretation of the Law.

Furthermore, the perplexity had to be met by finding a way to live with it, since to surrender either the Law or the newly found philosophy was unacceptable. Moses' attempt is never to try to remove the source of the anxiety, as might seem natural, but to try to find a way in which to adapt to it. To surrender religion would mean to break down the context which gave meaning and continuity to Jewish life, but to surrender philosophy would be no service to religion either, since it would leave religion still disturbed by the unanswered philosophical questions. To reject philosophy would not remove the objections with which philosophy perplexes religion. Since there could be no escape from perplexity, it had to be met and accepted as the starting point and the necessary condition.

Maimonides' first step toward meeting this perplexity is the ancient one of suggesting that the offending words in Scripture may also be understood in a figurative sense. While this is the general line of Maimonides' reply, he was quick to see that it would provide only temporary relief from perplexity unless backed up by an explanation as to why it was necessary to use figurative language in the first place. This he began to do by explaining that even in Natural Science some topics are not fully explained, that most difficult problems cannot be thoroughly understood by any one of us, and that, since men differ in degree of intelligence, truth is withheld from the multitude of ordinary men, and, therefore, their objections can be ignored. The necessity for metaphor, it seems, cannot be explained until men are convinced that reason allows only a few to reach great heights, and that even here they must all accept final limitations.

If such is the case, we are forced back to metaphor as the most adequate means available for expressing what we do know. If all obscurity could be removed from the subject, then literal terms could be used without reservation. Since literal description is completely successful only where all tinges of mystery can be removed, the acceptance of metaphorical expression depends upon the existence of some sense of mystery where God is concerned. The purely philosophical mind might have difficulty accepting mystery, even in the case of God, but what must be recognized is that Maimonides wrote for a man overtly religious, for whom the sense of mystery in the divine nature did not seem at all abnormal.

Maimonides was not fooled, it is important to note, into thinking that an allegorical interpretation of religious literature is a full explanation to a philosophical mind. Instead, the intention of this method is to show the philosophical-religious mind the reasons why to ask for a complete exposition in these matters is an exorbitant demand. The difficulty of understanding a literal impossibility arises only for the intelligent, since the ill-informed do not recognize an impossibility when it appears. Yet the intelligent observer who can admit the plausibility of a secret meaning need not reject the difficult religious doctrine at once, since he can treat it allegorically, as well as literally, to see if it may be accepted in this second mode. What is important to see here is that for Maimonides the literal meaning was never to be rejected but was always to be retained along with the more subtle metaphorical treatment.

All of this can serve to relieve philosophical perplexity, but, interestingly enough, it can do so only for one made sensitive to the limitations of human reason through a religious tradition. Without the religious sensitivity no solution can be found. The religiously untrained person simply cannot see the need for metaphorical expression. It takes some acquaintance with God, which only a religious discipline is likely to provide, to convince one of how difficult a matter it is to deal with the divine.

When the mind comprehends one thing it tends to think that it can comprehend everything, but it is just this view of knowledge which must be guarded against if the metaphorical method is to be successful in dealing with man's perplexity. If there are no limitations set for the mind, everything would theoretically be open to literal interpretation. Metaphor can become meaningful when the mind finds that it cannot go everywhere directly. Metaphor is the shortest distance between two points only when the direct path is not open to the human mind.

Here is the paradox: The religious spirit, which feeds on the sense of the final mystery within the divine nature, leads to perplexity when brought into contact with philosophical optimism and its literal, one-level mode of statement. Yet the only hope for the reconciliation without surrender is that a sense of divine mystery might force us to see that a frontal attack is not possible in the case of God. Thus, allegorical interpretation provides a genuine basis of latitude which alone is generous enough to retain both the religious sense of a divine mystery never fully disclosed, together with a philosophical directness whenever possible.

Such an interpretation of mystery and literalness together, which requires metaphorical expression, opens the way for a genuine meaning for faith. "By 'faith' we do not understand merely that which is uttered with the lips, but also that which is apprehended by the soul, the conviction that the object of belief is exactly as it is apprehended." If God is not directly approachable by literal means, faith always concerns something seen only incompletely through the figure of a symbol. Such belief cannot be compelled; but if the necessity for indirect approach is admitted in the case of objects exceeding the limits of direct grasp, metaphor becomes meaningful and faith an appropriate and possible way of relating oneself to such a Being. If all things were open to direct knowledge, a relation of faith could only seem unnecessary and inappropriate.

Metaphor is not a completely successful or controllable means of communication. We can employ only inadequate language where God is concerned, and metaphor is the best method at our disposal, since it allows the mind to get around barriers by subtle and indirect means. "We therefore make the subject clearer, and show to the understanding the way of truth by saying He is one but does not possess the attribute of unity." Here we seem to contradict ordinary expression, but this may indicate only that we are dealing with no ordinary object. By negating part of the phrase in the figurative statement we cause the sensitive mind to pass on to a grasp of God's nature, which could not be given by direct statement. What we learn from this example is that "we cannot describe the Creator by any means except by negative attributes." Metaphor and negative theology, then, are natural companions.

Positive assertions about God allow the imagination to mislead us, whereas proof by negation leads us gradually to more perfect knowledge of God. The mystery involved in the divine nature turns the ordinary situation around, so that we can now be convinced that certain qualities must be negated, whereas we cannot be as sure of positive attributes as we might be in an ordinary instance. The method of negative attributes is necessary "to direct the mind to the truth which we must believe concerning God," but it could be adopted only by one who felt the presence of mystery in the divine nature and realized the inappropriateness of frontal attack.

Our only complete knowledge concerning God, it turns out, "consists in knowing that we are unable truly to comprehend Him." God alone comprehends himself, and one not made aware of these matters too quickly jumps to the conclusion that man can know nothing about God at all. The truth lies somewhere in between, and it requires the energy of religious interest to keep from slipping into either extreme. God may be approached, but only by indirection. The negative method provides the mind with positive apprehensions of the divine nature, but not such that all mystery is removed, since God remains never fully comprehended by any being other than himself.

Thus, Maimonides has provided a context in which perplexity may be stabilized, but it is not a simple solution. He speaks to men whose sense of religious tradition is basic to them, and thus he is able to call upon their religious discipline to hold a flexible position which does not go all the way in either direction. The use of metaphor allows the literal meaning of the ordinary religious language to remain, while making room for the more subtle and refined meaning of the term in philosophical usage. A willingness to grant metaphor as legitimate and applicable depends upon an agreement that knowledge reaches its limits at least in the case of God, and it is almost inconceivable that one should allow this limit to be placed on knowledge philosophically unless he had experienced some feeling of the mystery present at the center of the divine nature. Recognizing the difficulty, we employ the negative method to protect us while we look directly into the light, and the knowledge we achieve will not seem contradictory so long as it is regarded as at least partly metaphor and symbol. If a man's religious sense is strong enough to feel this, he can accept metaphor and control the anxiety which philosophical sophistication has brought to him. This is the guide for the perplexed, but only for one whose perplexity stems from a strong religious tradition and its accompanying sense of the mystery encountered whenever the mind is turned toward God.

Turning to Maimonides' doctrine of nonliteral or metaphorical interpretation, we have to ask with him what it is that allows such duality of meaning without simple equivocation of terms? Maimonides' answer is that this is possible only when one finds himself dealing with a kind of existence not capable of reduction to a single level, and one is not likely to grant this if he has lost all sense of mystery in the divine nature. Philosophy can be counted on to take the mystery out of the natural order, as well it should; but it cannot be asked to provide one with some feeling for the irreducible mystery in the divine nature. The cultivation of the religious life provides the datum upon which philosophy applies itself in order to develop theology; that is, the rational statement of the divine insofar as this is possible. But if theology is not to become pure philosophy, the devotional life must have provided it with some sensitivity regarding the difficulty of handling God on our own terms.

In spite of this rather clear framework and simple objective, the casual modern reader is likely to be struck by the elaborate scholarly nature of much of the *Guide*. The opening pages are entirely given over to an exegesis or analysis of the use of certain Hebrew terms, all of which are central to Jewish religious thought. Interspersed is a discussion of the limits of man's intellect as well as an appraisal of the value of studying metaphysics. Such a diversity gives a correct picture of the blend of religious thought, scholarly study of concepts, and traditional philosophy which makes up the *Guide*. Then follows a more or less standard consideration of the nature of God and of the attributes appropriate to him.

It should be realized that the scope of the *Guide* is as wide as all traditional theology and religious thought. It is by no means simply a piece of philosophical apologetic, as might be thought from its title. Maimonides correctly sees that the only adequate way to provide a guide out of any perplexity is to take up and to discuss all of the major theological issues. To do so successfully is to provide the best, most substantial guide that can be produced. After considering the traditional attributes of God (such as unity, incorporeality), the second Moses begins Part II with a discussion of twenty-six propositions employed by philosophers to prove God's existence.

Next comes the question of creation versus the eternality of the universe, and Maimonides sets forth as best he can the way in which a doctrine of creation *ex nihilo* can be justified philosophically. Prophecy and the prophets then occupy him, as one might almost guess, for the Jewish tradition demands that prophecy be made acceptable. Visions are discussed, but evil and divine providence, as always, are the two central problems in this section. A religious belief in God runs into its greatest philosophical difficulty in trying to reconcile its conception of divinity with the evils and difficulties of the world.

It is easy to see that what Maimonides has provided is actually a comprehensive *summa* of traditional religious belief and philosophical tradition. Out of this meeting a theology is born, although its material setting within the literature of Judaism makes it appear less abstract than most modern questions. The *Guide* is actually a vast compendium of philosophical and religious material, which is then given shape through Maimonides' attempt to draw answers out of this combination. The towering position of influence which he occupies within the Jewish tradition gives some measure of his success.

Philosophy and religion in certain areas treat the same questions, but they do so in quite different ways and in quite different settings. When they are kept apart, as they can be in some ages, no conflict arises. Whenever an age becomes generally sophisticated philosophically, as was true in Maimonides' time and as is also true in our own day, then perplexity is bound to come. To those who can drop neither perspective, some reconciliation of the two bodies of material must be made. Out of the attempt to reconcile philosophy and religion each age arrives at a new theological perspective, which has implications for both technical philosophy and the religious life.—*F.S.*

Pertinent Literature

Strauss, Leo. "Introduction," in Moses Maimonides' *Guide for the Perplexed*. Translated by Shlomo Pines. Chicago: University of Chicago Press, 1963.

Leo Strauss's introductory essay to this new translation by Shlomo Pines from the original Arabic focuses on the structure of the *Guide for the Perplexed* and the hidden teachings which Moses Maimonides intended to communicate only to those who were already initiated into the mysteries of philosophy and of Judaism, as opposed to those who might read his book more superficially.

Strauss's outline of the *Guide* is extremely helpful to the student who is trying to grasp Maimonides' overall plan. In addition, it raises a number of questions which Strauss is at some pains to answer. For example, the first theme of the *Guide* is God's incorporeality, one of the fundamental truths which Maimonides believed was an essential principle of the faith. Maimonides devotes the first forty-nine chapters of the book to this subject, and most of those chapters are analyses of terms employed in Scripture to describe God or his actions—terms which appear to be anthropomorphic, but which Maimonides claims must be interpreted metaphorically when applied to God. Strauss, however, observes that certain terms, such as *hand*, which occur repeatedly in the Bible, are not analyzed by Maimonides at all, while some of the chapters among the forty-nine devoted to this subject appear to be completely out of place, dealing with other subjects entirely. Strauss maintains that these apparent anomolies were deliberately created by Maimonides in order to provoke the initiates to seek for the hidden meanings and messages which he felt were not suitable for the general public. Strauss points out that Maimonides employed certain numerical symbols that were likely to be recognized only by those familiar with the more arcane aspects of ancient and medieval Jewish theology. Thus, the Hebrew word for hand has a numerical equivalent of fourteen—and it is in Chapter XIV that Maimonides interrupts his analyses of seemingly anthropomorphic terms to discuss man, whose principal physical difference from the rest of creation is his possession of a hand, the major organ which one might have supposed Maimonides had neglected to include. Similarly, in Chapter XXVI (the numerical equivalent of God's name), the narrative is interrupted to discuss both the principle that the Torah "speaks in the language of man" and the idea of spatial relations—suggesting, perhaps, that spatial relations in the ordinary sense cannot be applied to God, and also that there is some sense in which God and his Torah are one.

According to Strauss, Maimonides' theory of the divine attributes leads to the conclusion that the ordinary man's conception of God is not only inadequate and misleading but also downright false—for there is no such God. Maimonides is therefore compelled to seek a demonstration, not only of God's unity and his incorporeality, but also of his very being—although in a sense of "being" that (unlike God's other attributes) is not entirely homonymous. Maimonides approaches this problem in three ways: that of the Aristotelian philosopher, that of Kalam (a medieval Islamic school), and by his own method, which is rather complexly but beautifully elucidated by Strauss. Maimonides felt compelled to show that both the Aristotelians and the Kalam were incorrect, for the Aristotelian proof for the existence of God proceeded under the assumption that the world was eternal, while the Kalam's proof depended upon the assumption that the world was created. Maimonides showed, according to Strauss, that the Kalam's proofs for the creation of the world were sophistical and that the Aristotelians merely assumed that the world was eternal without offering any proof for that proposition. After rejecting both approaches as separately considered, Maimonides synthesized them and showed that the synthesis (the unmoved mover of the Aristotelians and the God of providence of the Kalam) led precisely to the doctrine of God to which his own theory of the divine attributes pointed.

Strauss offers many fascinating insights into the *Guide* which the ordinary reader would almost surely miss without such expert instruction. In any event, he more than adequately proves his thesis that the work is not merely a key to a forest, but is itself an enchanted forest containing many mysteries—one that is both a challenge and a delight to the reader willing to plunge into it to seek the treasures that it contains. For the ordinary reader, as well as for those who are well schooled in the mysteries of philosophy and theology, Strauss provides some important tools and offers insights that help to illuminate this important milestone in medieval philosophy.

Husik, Isaac. "Moses Maimonides," in *A History of Mediaeval Jewish Philosophy*. Philadelphia: Jewish Publication Society of America, 1946.

In this chapter of his monumental summary of the principal works of medieval Jewish philosophy, Isaac Husik includes a discussion of the *Guide for the Perplexed* and of Moses Maimonides' other philosophical works as well, including some of his more important letters, the more philosophical chapters of his Code of Jewish Law, and his commentaries on talmudic works.

Husik claims that Maimonides possessed by far the most comprehensive mind in medieval Jewry and that his philosophy was the coping stone of a complete system of Judaism. His great commentaries and legal works won him the admiration of his contemporaries and of all subsequent generations. But the *Guide* divided the Jews of his day into two opposing camps, upsetting the theological equilibrium of Jewish society.

Husik summarizes most of the major doctrines which Maimonides discusses in his great work, placing them in historical context and rendering them in terms readily comprehensible to the modern student. He begins with a discussion of Maimonides' theory on the preparation necessary for a student of philosophy, and especially of metaphysics—an educational theory that has its precursors as far back as Plato. One of the principal problems with which Maimonides had to deal was the conflict, as it was perceived by many of his contemporaries, between science and religion. It was his purpose to reconcile such conflicts and to explain how biblical and talmudic Judaism could be perfectly harmonized with the science and the philosophy of his own day. In order to effect that reconciliation, it was necessary for him to recount the doctrines of some of the chief philosophical movements of his time and to show how they might be harmonized with the doctrines of Judaism, or to expose their errors.

In addition to discussions of Maimonides' proofs for the existence of God, Husik goes into some detail about his theory of the nature of the infinite and the possibility of its existence; his critique of atomism; his explanations of motion; his theory of attributes, particularly the theory of negative attributes; his critique of Aristotle (despite the widespread assumption that Maimonides was a thoroughgoing Aristotelian); his theory of causation; his psychological theories; his views on prophecy; his ethics; his response to the problem of evil; his approach to free will and providence; and his method of explaining and rationalizing the various laws of the Torah.

Husik also discusses Maimonides' considerable influence on Christian scholasticism and Moslem theology. Maimonides' work reached the Christian philosophers and theologians through William of Auvergne and Alexander of Hales and passed through Albertus Magnus to Thomas Aquinas.

According to Husik, Maimonides' impact on Judaism was enormous, although his philosophical work was not received everywhere with general favor. In fact, some of the more extreme anti-Maimunists excommunicated Maimonides and invoked the Inquisition of the Roman Catholic Church to sanction burning the *Guide* in Paris. Nevertheless, despite persecutions that drove them from one country to another, Jewish philosophers pursued their studies and drew inspiration from the book over the following centuries. His works were translated, and learned commentaries were written, not only on the *Guide* and Maimonides' other philosophical (as well as his legal) works, but also on the works of other philosophers, following his philosophical style and approach. In the post-Maimonidean age, Husik concludes, all Jewish philosophical thinking was in the nature of a commentary on Maimonides, whether avowedly so or not.—*B.M.L.*

ADDITIONAL RECOMMENDED READING

Baron, Salo W., ed. *Essays on Maimonides*. New York: Columbia University Press, 1941. An excellent collection of critical essays on various aspects of Maimonides' life and thought.

Cohen, Arthur. *The Teachings of Maimonides*. Prolegomenon by Marvin Fox. New York: Ktav, 1968. Clear, lucid discussions of Maimonides' doctrines.

Epstein, Isadore, ed. *Moses Maimonides, 1135-1204; Anglo-Jewish Papers in Connection with the Eighth Centenary of His Birth*. London: Soncino Press, 1935. Essays by noted scholars on Maimonides' life and thought.

Hartman, David. *Maimonides: Torah and Philosophic Quest*. Philadelphia: Jewish Publication Society of America, 1976. An attempt to reconcile Maimonides' hidden theories with those he openly expounds, and to integrate Maimonides' religious views with his philosophical doctrines.

Wolfson, Harry A. "Maimonides on Negative Attributes," in *Louis Ginzberg Jubilee Volume*. New York: American Academy for Jewish Research, 1945.

One of the greatest historians of philosophy engages in a detailed analysis of one of Maimonides' most important contributions.

ON THE REDUCTION OF THE ARTS TO THEOLOGY

Author: Saint Bonaventura (Giovanni di Fidanza, 1221-1274)
Type of work: Theology
First transcribed: c. 1250

PRINCIPAL IDEAS ADVANCED

Every kind of knowledge, if understood rightly, is knowledge of God; all of the arts reduce to theology.

God created light on the first day of creation as the source of activity in all living things, the link between soul and body.

There are two sorts of light, the created and the spiritual.

The mechanical arts are illuminated by external light, the sun; other knowledge comes from the light of sense perception, the light of philosophical knowledge, and the light of Sacred Scripture.

As seen by man, the four lights whose source is God become six because of distinctions within philosophy between rational philosophy, natural philosophy, and moral philosophy; the six lights correspond to the six days of the creation.

One central problem pervades the philosophical writings of Saint Bonaventura: the reconciliation of the mystical insights of Saint Francis of Assisi with a rational understanding of reality. For his solution Bonaventura turned to the Platonic tendency in medieval philosophy as developed by Saint Augustine, Alexander of Hales, and Robert Grosseteste. Thus, his work stands outside the Aristotelian tradition of his contemporary, Saint Thomas Aquinas. *On the Reduction of the Arts to Theology* was probably written while Saint Bonaventura was teaching at the University of Paris, and it may have been a lecture. We find in it a typical medieval scheme for the classification of knowledge.

Saint Bonaventura is often referred to by the title Doctor Seraphicus. A seraph is a ministering angel to God. Not only did Saint Bonaventura show his devotion to God in the way in which he lived, but in his writing he shows his belief in the complete absorption of every aspect of reality into the infinite goodness of God. The *Reduction* is an example of this conviction. Every kind of knowledge, if understood rightly, is knowledge of God: all of the arts reduce to theology.

The *Reduction* opens with a biblical quotation, one from the first chapter of the epistle of James, "Every good gift and every perfect gift is from above, coming down from the Father of Lights." Light is a symbol of special importance for Saint Bonaventura. In Plato's allegory of the cave, the sun is identified with the good. This symbol came to be identified with God in the writings of the Neoplatonists and of the early Church philosophers. For Saint Bonaventura it is not the sun but light that has a special place in the created universe. Light was made by God on the first day of creation, according to the account in Genesis, while the sun was not created until the fourth day. Light is the source of activity in all created things, the source of their extension and the source of their beauty; it is the link between the soul and the body. There are two sorts of light: the *created*, which we experience as the light of the sun, and the *spiritual* light, with which God acts upon the human soul and which is perfectly reproduced in Jesus Christ, the Son. Because of its association with Christ, light and truth have the same meaning.

Saint Bonaventura distinguishes between types of knowledge by the kinds of light which are responsible for them. The mechanical arts are illuminated by external light, the sun, which reveals their structure as artifacts. They are of seven types; weaving, armor-making, agriculture, hunting, navigation, medicine, and drama. Drama includes what we would now call the fine arts. Armor-making includes all of the implements of war. Cooking is a subdivision of the art of hunting; all sorts of buying and selling are included under navigation. By extending the meaning of terms in this way the seven mechanical arts become inclusive enough to take care of the physical needs of men.

The light of sense perception is the second light. Sense perception is directed toward a material object and is of five sorts corresponding to the five senses. Saint Bonaventura argues in accord with Saint Augustine that there are five senses because there are four elements—fire, air, water, earth—and a fifth substance, aether or light. Fire is apprehended through the sense of smell, air through hearing, water through taste, earth through touch, and light through sight. Since all created things are made up of these elements, the five senses are sufficient for man to perceive the physical universe.

Man apprehends the world by means of the third light, the light of philosophical knowledge. Through it he learns the principles and causes of the things that he perceives. There are three sorts of truth, says Saint Bonaventura, the truth of speech, of things, and of morals; and to these correspond the three types of philosophy, the rational, the natural, and the moral. The truth of speech is learned through grammar, logic, and rhetoric, which apprehend, judge, and persuade. Natural philosophy is divided into physics, which considers change as a natural process; mathematics, which considers quantity abstractly; and metaphysics, which studies being as such and which leads back to God as the first principle. Moral philosophy consists of ethics, economics, and politics, which are concerned with the individual, the family, and the state.

The fourth light illuminates the mind for the understanding of redemptive truth (*veritas salutaris*). It is the light of Sacred Scripture and is the highest truth because it leads beyond reason and human research, coming directly from God through inspiration. Although this truth is one in the literal sense, it is understood spiritually in three ways: the allegorical, by which we learn about God and man; the moral, by which we learn how to live; and the anagogical, by which we learn how to be united with God. These three types of truth are concerned with faith, morals, and the ultimate ends of both.

Thus, says Saint Bonaventura, there are four lights when they are considered in terms of their source, who is God; but when seen by man there are six: the light of Sacred Scripture, of sense perception, of the mechanical arts, of rational philosophy, of natural philosophy, and of moral philosophy. These six illuminations are related to the six days of creation in the order listed. The knowledge of Sacred Scripture corresponds to the creation of light on the first day, and this light permeates the whole of subsequent creation. So, too, all knowledge is contained in, and ends in, knowledge of the Sacred Scripture, going back to God from whom it came. Saint Bonaventura concludes this section of the *Reduction* by saying, "And there the cycle ends; the number six is complete and consequently there is rest."

It is interesting that Saint Bonaventura should mention both the circle and the number six. For him the circle is the perfect figure and six the perfect number. The circle is perfect because it is a closed figure represented by one continuous line. Six is the perfect number because it is equal to the sum of its factors, 1, 2, and 3, which are the first three numbers.

In the second part of the *Reduction*, Saint Bonaventura considers how each kind of knowledge leads to knowledge of the Sacred Scripture. One example from each of the five kinds of knowledge will be sufficient to explain his method.

The lowest kind of knowledge is sense perception; but just as the eye enjoys seeing, so the soul delights in its union with God. Thus there is a parallel between physical and spiritual function.

The purpose of the mechanical arts is to produce artifacts. Their production is a symbol of the generation and the incarnation of God's word. The craftsman produces the object from a pattern or idea in his mind. So God creates the world and man in it to know and love him, and God became flesh to lead us from sin back to himself. In this way the mechanical arts can teach divine wisdom.

Rational philosophy deals with the three aspects of speech: the person speaking, the delivery of the speech, and the effect of the speech on the hearer. In its third aspect the purpose of speech is to express, instruct, and persuade. Speech can express only if it has an inherent likeness to its object, can instruct only if it sheds light, and can persuade only if it has power. But likeness, light, and power describe the relation of the soul to God. Saint Bonaventura quotes Saint Augustine: "He alone is a true teacher who can impress a likeness, shed light, and grant power to the heart of his hearer. He who teaches within hearts has his chair in heaven."

Natural philosophy is concerned chiefly with formal causes in matter, in the soul, and in Divine Wisdom. If we consider causes according to their effects, we find that corruptible matter can become living only by the beneficial light of incorruptible bodies: the sun, the moon, and the stars. "So too the soul can perform no living works unless it receive from the sun, that is, from Christ, the aid of his gratuitous light; unless it seek protection of the moon, that is, of the Virgin Mary, Mother of Christ, and unless it imitate the example of the other saints."

Moral philosophy is concerned primarily with right. *Right* has three meanings. It is a mean between extremes; it is conformance to a rule; and it refers to what is raised upward, that is, upright. In the second sense, he lives rightly who conforms to the rule of God.

"And so it is evident," Saint Bonaventura says in conclusion, "how the manifold Wisdom of God which is clearly revealed in Sacred Scripture, lies hidden in all knowledge and in all nature."—*J.Co.*

PERTINENT LITERATURE

Healy, Emma Thérèse. *Saint Bonaventure's De Reductione Artium ad Theologiam: A Commentary with an Introduction and Translation.* New York: Franciscan Institute, 1955.

Besides offering facing Latin and English texts of Saint Bonaventura's treatise, this book contains the leading commentary on it. The commentary is one of the few scholarly works that are concerned specifically with this treatise, as distinct from other writings of Saint Bonaventura.

Saint Bonaventura was a strong (some said a ruthless) administrator, who headed the Franciscan order in a difficult period. By principle and policy, his speculative work was traditional. He wrote that his aim was not to seek out new opinions, but to go back over the common and approved ones. He held that tradition was a trustworthy guide. These attitudes were of course not unusual in the middle ages, but in the work of Saint Bonaventura they reach an exceptional intensity. His own works became traditional authorities in their turn. (In the case of his works on the life of Saint Francis, this result was encouraged by a decree of the Order—made during his administration—that all previous writings on the subject should be permanently suppressed. Long afterward, however, some of them resurfaced.) Some of Saint Bonaventura's works became widely popular, even influencing the history of painting.

Since Saint Bonaventura venerated tradition, it is not surprising that he mentions an earlier work, the influential *Didascalicon* of the twelfth century writer Hugh of Saint Victor, as the source of several parts of his classification of the branches of knowledge. In addition, Emma Thérèse Healy maintains that the basic idea of the treatise—that of reducing (leading back, retracing) the other branches of knowledge to theology—was taken from another work of the same Hugh, the *Exposition* (Commentary) *on the Celestial Hierarchy.* (The *Celestial Hierarchy* was a leading book about angels, written around the year 500 by someone who pretended to be a man of the first century named

Dionysius the Areopagite.)

Regarding the title *Reduction*, Healy reminds us that "arts" was the name of the basic university degree program, which was normally a prerequisite for the advanced programs in theology, medicine, or law. To lead the arts back to theology was, among other things, to suggest that philosophy (which was beginning to be studied in more and more depth in the arts course) should not set itself up as a specialty in competition with theology, but should remain a subordinate study. A complementary point, not mentioned by Healy, is that by showing that the arts could be led back to theology, Saint Bonaventura may have been working to legitimatize learning, including philosophy, in the eyes of the antiintellectual faction among the friars. The question about Saint Bonaventura's aim in "reducing the arts to theology" is therefore complex.

A further point not mentioned by Healy is that the title itself is based on tradition rather than on the earliest manuscripts. Some scholars think it would be more appropriate to use a different title, such as "The Six Illuminations of the Human Understanding." The initial plan of the treatise recognizes *four* kinds of light, but later one of them is subdivided, making six lights in all. Six is supposed to be an important number; and it is supposed to go together with another important number, seven. In this case, the six lights of the human understanding lead to a seventh, which is the immediate apprehension of God that transcends all human understanding (even human understanding as illuminated by the "superior light" of revelation).

After discussing the four (or six) lights, Healy concludes not only that Saint Bonaventura has illustrated his claim that the arts are to be reduced to theology but also that he has *proved* it.

Hinwood, Bonaventure. "The Principles Underlying Saint Bonaventure's Division of Human Knowledge," in *S. Bonaventura 1274-1974*. Vol. III. Grottaferrata, Italy: Collegio S. Bonaventura, 1974, pp. 471-504.

This article is especially useful for understanding the treatise *Reduction*, although it is not confined to that work.

Bonaventure Hinwood says that Saint Bonaventura distinguishes two ways in which knowledge can be the starting point for a person's return to God. One way is to start with what one knows about the things God has created, and move toward knowing God. This is the route of the *Journey of the Mind to God* (see below). The other way is to start with what one knows about knowledge itself. From the classification of knowledge into its various branches, one can move to the principles behind that classification. From those principles one sees that theology is the leading form of study, and that the others derive their significance, and even their assurance of accuracy, from their relation to it.

The final aim of our studies, as of all our activities, is to return to God.

Because original sin has impaired our ability to learn about God through our natural powers, we must relay on revelation; therefore, we must study the Scriptures. To understand the Scriptures, we must rely on the inspired interpretations given by the Church Fathers. These, in turn, are explained by the systematic theologians. The systematic theologians make use, in their works, of bits of secular learning, including bits of philosophy. Therefore, we must study secular subjects, including philosophy, in order to understand the theologians; the theologians, in order to understand the Fathers; and the Fathers, in order to understand the Bible. This is what makes the study of secular subjects, including philosophy, worthwhile. Any so-called "knowledge" which does not contribute to our return to God is meaningless.

What is more, because human nature is corrupt, the seeker of knowledge (even knowledge of secular things) will fall into error unless elevated and steadied by God's grace. A prerequisite for receiving this grace is moral self-discipline and the desire to find God. So the search for knowledge of even secular things must take place in the context of the search for God.

The help that we need comes from Christ, through whom all created things are created, and in whom are the exemplars (creative likenesses) of all created things. Every creature is, not just by some outward mark, but in its inmost nature, a likeness (close or remote) of the triune creator. Therefore, if anyone tries to study a created thing without considering its relation to God, that person will miss what makes the created thing intelligible.

The division of knowledge into its various branches is used by Saint Bonaventura to provide the details of his position. These details do not always work in the same way. For example, in at least the first few sections of the treatise *Reduction*, the "exterior light" (by which we manipulate objects to promote our own well-being) is placed *below* the "inferior light" (by which we learn about the world through the senses). This helps the argument, because it places human artifice below God's creation. Elsewhere in his writings, however, Saint Bonaventura treats the topic differently, and the "exterior light" in particular is sometimes difficult to fit into the account. Hinwood, drawing on several works of Saint Bonaventura, finds that he must place the exterior light *above* the inferior light, as imagination is placed above sense. This also helps the argument, because of a parallel which Saint Bonaventura wishes to draw between these two lights on the one hand, and the upper and lower "portions" of reason (the next highest faculty) on the other. Therefore, Hinwood's explanatory chart of the various lights and faculties differs from Emma Thérèse Healy's (in the work discussed above) in the order of the two lowest lights. It seems that what matters to Saint Bonaventura is not in which order they appear, but that they do come in order and can be made to fit into an account which puts knowledge of God at the top.

Gilson, Étienne. *The Philosophy of St. Bonaventure*. Translated by I. Trethowan and F. J. Sheed. London: Sheed & Ward, 1938.

This book gives an overall interpretation of Saint Bonaventura's intellectual system, drawn from his writings in general. Although there is no separate section on the short treatise *Reduction*, the book is important for the student of this treatise. It argues that the parts of Saint Bonaventura's system can only be understood in relation to the whole, and it interprets the whole as a singleminded reduction of all other inquiries to theology. Indeed, from the account given in this book, one could conclude that Saint Bonaventura was not a philosopher at all, as distinct from a theologian. If philosophy is based on pure reason, then, according to this book, there is no philosophy of Saint Bonaventura.

The author, Étienne Gilson (1884-1978), was a leading authority on medieval Christian philosophy. Many of his books and essays are standard reference works. Reversing the view of Ibn Rushd (Averroës) that there is one true philosophy and many faiths that imitate it, Gilson held that there is one true Catholic faith, and many philosophies that interpret it. The Christian philosophy of Saint Augustine is different, as philosophy, from the Christian philosophy of Saint Thomas Aquinas, even though their faith was the same. Accordingly, we might expect to find a "philosophy of Saint Bonaventura" as well.

However, it turns out, according to Gilson, that in Saint Bonaventura's system philosophy is not an autonomous discipline, but a heteronomous one (or, as the English translator has it, a "contingent" one). That is, it does not rely only on its own method (the use of reason), but has to be guided by something external to it (faith). The light of reason is in principle infallible; however, we are not able to use this infallible light in an infallible way unless we are assisted by faith. All philosophical inquiry which is not directed toward finding God, or is so directed but is not assisted by faith, will inevitably fall into error. Although reason has absolute cognitive certitude, the certitude of faith is stronger, because it is founded not just on the cognition of the intellect but on the unbreakable adherence of the will.

According to Gilson, Saint Bonaventura's philosophy exists only as scattered fragments embedded in his theology. He has a tightly constructed intellectual system, but one can enter into that system only by an act of faith, not by the use of reason alone. Although Saint Bonaventura (unlike Saint Francis and some other Franciscans) was an intellectual, his use of the intellect was not motivated by curiosity. He held that curiosity was vicious. Instead, Gilson suggests, Saint Bonaventura used the discipline of the mind as a replacement for the discipline (that is, mortification) of the body, which Saint Francis practiced and Saint Bonaventura did not. The motive in each case is to prepare the soul for its return to God.

Unlike his contemporary Saint Thomas, Saint Bonaventura was not, in

Gilson's view, an Aristotelian. Although he used Aristotelian language, he rejected and condemned Aristotle's philosophical system. Many of Saint Bonaventura's contemporaries thought that Aristotle, even though he was a pre-Christian author, succeeded very well in those philosophical and scientific inquiries which do not require revelation. Accordingly, they gave to Aristotle some of the same extravagant deference which as Christians they gave to their own authorities. (Some even gave it to Aristotle and *not* to Christian authorities; this was particularly exasperating to Saint Bonaventura.) Gilson says that Saint Bonaventura held, by contrast, that Aristotle had gone wrong from the beginning. By trying to understand physical objects apart from God, Aristotle missed the key to understanding them: that they all depend on exemplars in the mind of God. By denying exemplarism, he wrecked his system. Placing the mystic vision at the center of his system, Saint Bonaventura was the thinker who carried the Augustinian tradition to its logical conclusion.—*J.C.*

ADDITIONAL RECOMMENDED READING

Bettoni, Efrem. *Saint Bonaventure*. Translated by Angelus Gambatese. Notre Dame, Indiana: University of Notre Dame Press, 1964. Despite its erudition, this little book must be used with caution.

Bougerol, Jacques Guy. *Introduction to the Works of Bonaventure*. Translated by José de Vinck. Paterson, New Jersey: St. Anthony Guild Press, 1964. The concluding section, "The Unity of Knowledge," is a summary of the treatise *Reduction*.

Copleston, Frederick. *A History of Philosophy*. Vol. II. Westminster, Maryland: The Newman Press, 1950. A textbook-style survey.

McInerny, Ralph M. "Saint Bonaventure," in *A History of Western Philosophy*. Notre Dame, Indiana: University of Notre Dame Press, 1970, pp. 255-286. An intelligent, original treatment. Highly recommended.

Quinn, John Francis. *The Historical Constitution of St. Bonaventure's Philosophy*. Toronto: Pontifical Institute of Mediaeval Studies, 1973, pp. 744-752. Detailed and painstaking, with an outline of the treatise *Reduction*.

Weisheipl, J. A. "Classification of the Sciences in Medieval Thought," in *Mediaeval Studies*. XXVII (1965), pp. 54-90. Not on Saint Bonaventura, but on his predecessors and contemporaries; extremely useful for understanding what Saint Bonaventura wrote.

JOURNEY OF THE MIND TO GOD

Author: Saint Bonaventura (Giovanni di Fidanza, 1221-1274)
Type of work: Theology, epistemology
First transcribed: 1259

PRINCIPAL IDEAS ADVANCED

The six stages of the soul's powers correspond to the six stages of the ascension unto God.

God is reflected in the traces in the sensible world.

Then, in considering the powers of the self, through self-love, self-knowledge, and memory, the mind comes closer to God.

Memory, intelligence, and will are recognized as reflecting God's trinitarian nature.

By disciplined contemplation we are led even closer to the divine.

In recognizing the necessity of God's being for our understanding, the mind's work is done.

The final stage is the mind's abandonment of intellectual powers in the mystical knowledge of God.

Both the size and the title of Saint Bonaventura's most famous little work (*Itinerarium Mentis ad Deum*) belie its contents. From its size, the innocent reader might take it to be a meditation on some single point; from its title one might easily come to think of it as vague and mystical. Actually the opposite of both of these common impressions is the case. The *Itinerarium* belongs in the company of the *Summa Theologica* of Thomas Aquinas, although its brevity indicates the quite different temper of its author. Bonaventura, the "Seraphic Doctor," does not use the elaborate compendium method. Yet in brief compass we see unfurled in this work a view of nature, man, and God no less comprehensive than that contained in a many-volumed work.

As to its "mystical" qualities, what must first be grasped is that this work does in fact reflect classical mysticism but that Bonaventura's presentation of this viewpoint is both detailed and highly technical. To sketch completely the structure which Bonaventura outlines would require a quite detailed study. It is rational in every detail—right up to the point at which reason finds its own end and realizes its own boundaries. Reason will be left behind and ecstatic vision will become the goal, but this does not transpire until the very peak of possible human understanding has been reached. Only when reason has done its utmost at description and explanation can a way be seen to transcend reason. In this brief work what we find is an elaborate, intricate, and technical view, rational to its core, but aimed from the beginning at finding reason's limiting point in order thereby to leave it behind.

What is perhaps hardest for the modern mind to grasp is that Bonaventura both begins and ends with God. The modern prejudice which must be overcome here is the same one which plagues Anselm's famous "ontological argument." The contemporary philosopher is addicted to the primacy of a theory of knowledge. Before any question is asked the modern reader must inquire whether, methodologically considered, the quest is justifiable and the object knowable. Bonaventura and a host of others, on the other hand, pose the ultimate question of God at the outset just as if it were answerable. Only through the technical process of attempting to construct the answer can the success or the failure of the endeavor be discovered. The process of the attempt itself is the source of our correction. The limits of the question are recognizable, not at the beginning, but only at the end of the argument.

Not unlike the Greek invocation of the muses in the face of a difficult task, Bonaventura in the Prologue calls upon God to enlighten him in his quest. His use of the term "Father of Light" for God, and his stress upon illumination place Bonaventura well within the Augustinian and Neoplatonic tradition. God is to be immediately addressed at the outset of all serious consideration, since he is cast in the role of a first principle and as such is central to any knowing process.

For all of this, the work still has a devotional element woven into it as one thread of its fabric. Francis of Assisi, the founder of Bonaventura's order, is mentioned reverentially at the outset, and Bonaventura himself claims to have undergone a vision like that experienced by Francis. However, coupled with this theme must be the awareness that Bonaventura served as a highly successful administrator, in fact as Minister General of his order. This obvious organizational skill, which daily must have called for the solution of dozens of practical problems, is balanced against the visionary quality of his writing.

Six stages of ascension to God are described in this little work. Their delineation is purely technical and rational, but Bonaventura at the same time considers prayer one means of becoming enlightened about them. To modern minds so used to splitting spirituality and rationality completely apart, such duality in Bonaventura's thought is hard to grasp. To do so, however, is also to come close to understanding the special feature of the *Itinerarium*. For all natural objects have a double side: they are at once parts of a structured natural order discoverable by reason, and at the same time, when properly viewed, may come to be seen as traces of God himself. Such divine traces are uncoverable in many places, but we begin with those which are corporeal and outside of us (as contrasted to those spiritual and interior).

Man's mind has three principal aspects, one of which is animal or sensual, another of which makes it capable of introspection, and a third in virtue of which it is able to look above itself and to grasp levels of existence higher than its own natural order. And since all natural objects have a divine side, the six stages of the soul's powers correspond to the six stages of the ascension unto God. To describe the levels of ascent to God is to delineate the soul's powers; to set forth the soul's capacities is to outline the levels through which God is to be approached.

Theology itself has three modes: symbolic, literal, and mystical. The symbolic gives proper interpretation to sensible things; the literal corresponds to an intelligible level, and the mystic transcends the level of rationality. All three are properly theology. But none of these is to be undertaken without preparation, since rectitude of the will and the clarity of unimpeded vision are necessary. Then the sensible world may be taken up for consideration, and it will be transformed upon reflection into a veritable Jacob's ladder, the sense world being as it is so full of the traces of God.

We proceed by transposing natural qualities into a divine setting. Weight, number, and measure provide a basis for grasping the power, wisdom, and immense goodness of the Creator. One inquires after the origin, course, and terminus of the natural order, and then a grasp of the various levels of natural organisms can be acquired. From this one moves to consider God as a counterpart of these levels and of this order, as spiritual, incorruptible, and immutable. The natural order is a plenitude, full of every level and variety of kind. Such munificence is a source of natural illumination for the mind in its search for the proper road to God.

God is reflected in his traces in the sensible world, and he is known not only through them but also in them. The reader would move too quickly if he thought Bonaventura considered the natural order only to pass beyond it so quickly. Like others before him in his tradition, in this work Bonaventura sees the natural world as being both good and beautiful, so that to an eye sensitive to such structure God can actually be seen without taking our eyes away from the world of the senses even for a moment. The five senses are like doors. Through apprehending motion we are led to the cognition of spiritual movers, as a progress from effect to cause.

Our senses lead us to apprehension, then to delight in the natural order, and finally to judgment, which operates by abstraction and renders the sensible objects intelligible. Then, following Augustine's *On Music*, Bonaventura regards number as the outstanding examplar of God to be found in the physical world. All Platonists have been fascinated with the intelligible and yet non-sensible properties of number, especially its relation to the qualities of rhythm and proportion. The invisible things of God come to be seen, being grasped in and through the changing, sensible world. Like a sign, the sensible order leads the discerning mind to the intelligible; and, seeing this, we are led to turn from an outward vision and to consider the mind itself.

Grasping how divine things may be seen as reflected in the order of nature leads us to turn inward to consider ourselves, and here divine images appear most clearly. For the natural psychical phenomena are self-love, self-knowledge, and memory. Here Bonaventura follows Augustine's classical model and finds in these a representation of the divine Trinity. Particularly in memory the soul is most like an image of God, for God lives with all objects eternally present to him, and the soul imitates this power in the grasp of its own power of memory. Nor can we understand the being of any particular object until we come to understand Being-in-itself. Memory, intelligence, and will form in us a second reflection of God's trinitarian nature, so that when the mind considers itself, it rises through itself as through a mirror to the contemplation of the divine Trinity.

Having brought the mind so close to God in structure, Bonaventura turns to inquire why not all men see God clearly in themselves. And his answer is that most men lie so buried in the world of the senses that they are unable to regard themselves as in God's image. Here, for the first time, specifically Christian doctrine enters, since Bonaventura sees in Christ a mediator who accomplishes this needed purification and illumination. Spiritual hearing and vision must be recovered.

After the conversion of the mind to a new direction comes the disciplining of the self, and here Bernard of Clairveaux' famous "steps" are outlined to bring the soul to vision through humility and the inculcation of strict habits of thought. We must learn contemplation, and this requires a strict order in the soul. The acquired habits of the rationally ordered soul yield powers capable of leading us to the divine.

Thus, we have learned to contemplate God *outside* us in his traces in the natural and sensible order, *inside* the self through the trinitarian structure of the soul's powers, and then finally *above* the mind as the contemplative powers are strengthened by discipline. We may fix on Being-itself, rejecting, as all Neoplatonism does, any positive status for non-being. Here a little dialectical exercise on being and non-being convinces us that being is actually what first enters the intellect and that this is the Being of pure actuality. Thus, analysis indicates the immediate orientation of all intellection toward Being-itself and therefore toward God. Since this orientation is at the foundation of every intellective act, it only remains for the mind to become aware of just how necessary its orientation toward God is for our understanding in every instance. For intellect to operate, the being of the divine being must be ever present as a referent and standard.

Only because we are accustomed to the lesser beings of the sensible world do we fail to recognize the mind's natural orientation and nearness to God. As the eye seems to see nothing when it sees pure light, so we seem to see sensible images and lesser beings and do not recognize the highest Being. The darkness which seems to surround Being-itself, in comparison with the ease of grasping lower objects, can now be disclosed as the fullest illumination of the mind. The purest being, necessary for every grasp of impure beings, appears only by contrast to be empty of content.

At the height we reach the traditional Platonic and Neoplatonic name for

God, the Good. The fecundity of the Good is given as a rational necessity for the multiplicity of a Trinity within God, as more adequately expressing the fullness of the Good than could any less multiple first principle. Yet Bonaventura is quick to add that such rational arguments do not make the Trinity comprehensible; since it is incomprehensible, it is not fully understandable.

Having arrived at the end of the sixth step, our mind's work is done (like God's work in the days of creation), and it rests. The mind, having traversed the whole of the sensible order, then the intelligible realm, has finally understood itself and disciplined itself to raise itself to consider God himself. But the end of this gigantic and rigorous activity is rest. The mind has reached the place at which it has done all it can do; nothing more is within its power and so it must rest. Rationally it has exhausted itself and has reached its limit. Reason, illumination, devotion, and discipline have brought the mind to the pinnacle of its powers and transformed it in the process of the journey, although at the end it sees that the final vision was never far away. At the outset the goal was near but not seen. It was present from the beginning (Being-itself), but our powers were not then sufficient to grasp it directly.

What remains? By looking at sensible things the mind passed beyond them and then turned to consider itself. Now it passes not only beyond sensible things, by way of a rational dialectic, but beyond even itself. In this final passage, if the rational discipline has been perfected, all intellectual operation should at this point be abandoned. All our affection should be transferred from ourselves to God. The final step is most certainly mystical, but mysticism enters only at this final point and not before. No one can know this final phase who has not experienced it; and, even to the mind undergoing the experience, it seems like moving into death and darkness to leave rational structure behind. But the soul, having set out to find God, is now at the terminus of its itinerary and willingly surrenders what it could not have surrendered before (the guidance of its rational powers) and passes over into what appears to be (as contrasted with structured reason) darkness.

How shall a modern mind appraise such a scheme and its importance to the history of, and the present developments within, philosophy? The immediate concentration upon God, the mixture of philosophy with religious discipline, as well as the view of all mundane things as immediately reflecting God—all of these are nearly the opposite of the modern approach. In some basic sense modern philosophers, as well as most Protestant theologians, are fundamentally rationalists, and to them Bonaventura's ultimate mysticism seems strange. Consequently, the *Itinerarium* has an important function to fulfill as an example of a possible and different approach.

Historically its significance cannot be overestimated. In any form of the religious life, Neoplatonism has always been extremely influential, and what we must not overlook here is that Bonaventura represents a philosophical and a theological view which has for centuries been closely associated with devout practice. Since philosophy's divorce from theology in the modern period, philosophy has been largely academic. In the *Itinerarium* we have an example of how a philosophical view can be intimately associated with, and even be determinative for, a way of life.

Out of a religious desire to see God this philosophical view arises as a disciplined guide. Such desire actually causes us to seek for and to see aspects of the natural order which might otherwise have remained unnoticed. A more abstract intellect may derive its philosophical problems internally simply from philosophical discussion. Bonaventura finds his questions through the attempt to guide the soul toward God. Neither approach to philosophy or theology excludes the other, but a secular and a rationalistic age has trouble recognizing the legitimacy of a philosophy generated from such a practical (and in this case religious) goal.

Perhaps the most interesting comparison is to remember that Bonaventura was a contemporary of Thomas Aquinas. The two considered together offer a fascinating contrast. Both represent the use which was made of philosophy in the Middle Ages. Thomas has had wide circulation in non-Catholic and even in nonreligious circles. Bonaventura is still widely read within religious orders and in theological circles which do not receive as much public notice.

Bonaventura's little work could be considered purely as a devotional classic if it were not for its elaborate technical structure and his use of "Being" as God's primary name. Nothing indicates the presence of an abstract metaphysician more than his preference for the traditional name "Being" as opposed to more personal names for God. God is discussed in his role as a metaphysical first principle and not as an object of worship. In fact, except for the trinitarian reference, little specifically Christian or biblical doctrine is discussed. It is only by contrast to modern anti-metaphysical interests that this work seems "religious." Actually by comparison it is both technical and abstract.

In considering Being and Non-Being, Bonaventura adopts the traditional Neoplatonic role of giving Non-Being status only as a privation of Being, not as anything independent of or opposed to it. In fact, upon analysis it appears that nothing within the natural order can be known unless Being itself has first entered the intellect. In this way God is involved in even the simplest act of cognition, as a prerequisite for any apprehension. For a particular being to be known, Being itself must be present to the intellect, a fact that may not be recognized until after the analysis of Being and Non-Being has been carried out.

Bonaventura stresses the traditional Neoplatonic attribute of God, his unity. He possesses no diversity, and it is primarily this central characteristic of unity which places God above intellection and forces reason ultimately to transcend itself. Although God is close to and visible through the natural order, in himself his nature is quite different, reflecting none of the multiplicity of nature's variety. Because of such a basic dissimilarity any man who would have the vision of God must finally leave himself behind, insofar as he is a rational creature dealing with multiple objects.

Being which is absolutely one is seen also to be the Good, but the different ontological level involved here forces the apprehending mind to pass beyond the multiple sensible world and also beyond itself as a discursive mind. It is not so much Bonaventura's view of the order of nature which dictates this as it is his view of the Divine nature. Just as Bonaventura begins with God, so any criticism of his whole scheme must start by attempting to set forth and to defend a different view of the divine nature.

In order to see the point of Bonaventura's theory of knowledge and his theory of the orders of nature, each must be seen in its relation to his view of the divine nature, coupled with his ethical and religious goal of seeing God. In order to criticize the Seraphic Doctor's theories, what we must do is to begin with a theory of the Divine nature too. As that is altered, so also are the theory of knowledge, and the view of nature and of human psychology.—*F.S.*

PERTINENT LITERATURE

Mathias, Thomas R. "Bonaventurian Ways to God Through Reason," Part I, in *Franciscan Studies*. N. S. XXXVI (1976), pp. 192-232; Part II, in *Franciscan Studies*. N. S. XXXVII (1977), pp. 153-206.

This two-part article gives a comprehensive review of Saint Bonaventura's writings on the use of reason to find God. It draws not only on the *Itinerarium* but also on seven other works. Particular reliance is placed on an unpublished notebook (Assisi manuscript 186) which may have belonged to Bonaventura. Thomas R. Mathias defends the authenticity of this notebook as a work of Bonaventura's. Then, in his main discussion (which is mostly in Part II of the article), he arranges material from all eight works in the order followed by the *Itinerarium*, constructing a single well-organized story.

Mathias considers that Bonaventura provides rational proofs of God's existence, not just meditations on what we already know about God's essence. In this he differs from Étienne Gilson, who held that Bonaventura's mystical approach placed knowledge of God's essence first. According to Gilson, Bonaventura's approach was incommensurable with the rational proofs of God's existence offered by Saint Thomas Aquinas. According to Mathias, all five of Aquinas' ways of proving God's existence fit perfectly into Bonaventura's First Way.

Mathias notices that each of Bonaventura's three stages on the road to God is itself a separate way of proving the existence of God by reason. There are, then, three different Bonaventurian ways to God through reason, not just one. They are:

The First Way (empirical and cosmological), which starts from the perception of external things (physical objects);

The Second Way (anthropological and psychological), which starts by looking within, at one's own soul;

The Third Way (epistemological and metaphysical), which starts by looking above, toward the First Principle.

Each of the three ways provides a number of alternative proofs. All the proofs that use the same way have important structural features in common, and any one proof would suffice to show that there is a God. For example, physical objects have many different properties, any one of which, perhaps, could be used as the starting point for a proof of the existence of God by the First Way. For details of the three ways, the student should consult the article.

Mathias' work shows considerable intellectual power. It is not merely comprehensive; it is also unified. At the same time, it must be said that Mathias' disdain for nonreligious philosophical achievement rivals that of Bonaventura himself. Among the authors whose influence Mathias expects Bonaventura's philosophy to combat are Friedrich Nietzsche, Auguste Comte, Karl Marx, Bertrand Russell, Martin Heidegger, and Jean-Paul Sartre. Also like Bonaventura, Mathias can be discreet. For example, he says that Bonaventura became the head of the Franciscan order when the previous head, Blessed John of Parma, declined reelection because of a controversy among the friars. One must turn to other sources (for example, Ignatius Brady, writing in the *New Catholic Encyclopedia* under "Bonaventure") to learn that the pope had insisted that Blessed John of Parma resign because of the position which he took in that controversy.

Perhaps Mathias is also discreet when he denies that Bonaventura ever embraced ontologism. "Ontologism," in this context, is the doctrine that the human mind can in this life achieve an immediate apprehension of God and know God as he is. According to Mathias, Bonaventura held the more orthodox view that in this life our knowledge of God is always indirect. Some parts of the language of the *Itinerarium* are troublesome in this regard, but the other works, and notably the notebook, are relied on by Mathias as evidence for a nonontologistic interpretation.

Steenberghen, Fernand van. *Aristotle in the West.* Translated by Leonard Johnston. Louvain: E. Nauwelaerts, 1955, pp. 147-162.

The chief philosophical controversy about Saint Bonaventura has been that involving Étienne Gilson, Fernand van Steenberghen, and Patrice Robert. Gilson's main work on Bonaventura is discussed above, in the section on the treatise *On the Reduction of the Arts to Theology*. Robert's two-part article is discussed below. Steenberghen's conclusions about Bonaventura appeared first as part of the background information included in a massive work about Bonaventura's important younger contemporary, Siger of Brabant. Later, the background material and a brief account of Siger were made into a separate book. *Aristotle in the West* is a revised English-language version of this general survey of thirteenth century European philosophy.

Gilson had said that Bonaventura's philosophy was Augustinian, by contrast with that of Saint Thomas Aquinas, which was Aristotelian. Steenberghen replied that both men were Aristotelians in philosophy. (Aristotle's *Physics*, *Metaphysics*, and *Ethics* first became available to students in Western Europe around the beginning of the thirteenth century, and their impact dominated the philosophical inquires of the period.) Of course Bonaventura was not a *pure* Aristotelian in philosophy, but then neither was Saint Thomas. Both were influenced also by the various Neoplatonic writings—including, but not limited to, the philosophical works of Saint Augustine—which continued to be available in the thirteenth century as in previous eras. According to Steenberghen, then, Bonaventura was a Neoplatonic Aristotelian in philosophy. In theology, on the other hand, he was mostly an Augustinian.

Gilson and others objected that although Bonaventura may have adopted an Aristotelian position on this or that individual point and used many Aristotelian words and phrases, the "spirit" of his system was Augustinian. Steenberghen replied that the features of Bonaventura's thought which these critics offered as evidence of an Augustinian spirit—for example, the superiority of revelation to reason, and of Christian doctrine to philosophy—were not specifically Augustinian, but simply Christian. These features, he added, were found in the works of Aquinas as much as in those of Bonaventura and Augustine.

Steenberghen went on to say that in his speculative works, Bonaventura always wrote as a theologian, and never as a philosopher. He knew the difference between philosophy and theology (a point that Gilson came close to denying), and his work in philosophy was not negligible; but he only did philosophy when it could be of service to something he wished to say in theology. (The work of Bonaventura conforms to the medieval maxim: "Theology is the queen of the sciences; philosophy is the handmaiden of theology.") He did not think out philosophical issues for their own sakes; the unity of his work is not philosophical but theological; he did not go into philosophical problems deeply (as Aquinas did) before using the results to help his theology; he juxtaposed clashing philosophical theories (for example, the Neoplatonic doctrine of illumination and the Aristotelian doctrine of abstraction), without giving enough attention to the rational coherence of the result. Still, it is not true, as Gilson said, that if we mean by "philosophy" something accessible to unaided reason, there is *no* philosophy of Bonaventura.

Steenberghen rejects Gilson's assertion that Bonaventura condemned Aristotle's system from the start. In his main early work (the *Commentary on the Sentences*), according to Steenberghen, Bonaventura had a respectful attitude toward Aristotle. He always tried to interpret Aristotle in a way which made his views compatible with the faith, and corrected them only when the conflict was clear. His knowledge of Aristotle was extensive, but not deep. It was in his late works (for example, the various *Collations*) that Bonaventura expressed hostility to Aristotle. This was because at that time some students and teachers were following Aristotle in ways which seemed detrimental to their own orthodoxy as Christians. Bonaventura was naturally upset.

Robert, Patrice. "Le Problème de la Philosophie Bonaventurienne," Part I, "Aristotélisme Néoplatonisant ou Augustinisme?," in *Laval Théologique et Philosophique*. VI, no. 1 (1950), pp. 145-163; Part II, "Discipline Autonome ou Hétéronome?," in *Laval Théologique et Philosophique*. VII, no. 1 (1951), pp. 9-58.

Étienne Gilson is an expert on medieval Christian philosophy in general; Fernand van Steenberghen is an expert on thirteenth century philosophy and especially on the "radical Aristotelian," Siger of Brabant; but Patrice Robert is an expert on Saint Bonaventura. He knows the text and has at his command even the enormous *Commentary on the Sentences*.

Robert says that Bonaventura knew the difference between philosophy and theology; for example, he remarked that philosophers cannot tell us how to obtain the remission of sins. When he treated philosophical questions—for example, whether the matter of which the angels are composed is the same as the matter of which corporeal things are composed—he wrote as a philosopher, not as a theologian.

Gilson's view was that Bonaventura recognized the distinction between philosophy and theology, but considered it illegitimate to distinguish them in practice. If philosophy is not guided by theology, it will fall into error; so philosophical problems must be investigated not by the method of philosophy (relying on reason), but by the method of theology (relying on revelation). Philosophy is, then, in Gilson's words, a "heteronomous" discipline (ruled by another), not an "autonomous" one (self-governing). Robert rejects this interpretation of Bonaventura as incoherent and not supported by the text.

The source of Gilson's error, according to Robert, was his assumption that if our goal is to find God, then the object of our philosophical inquiry must also be God. In that case, philosophy and theology have the same object, and the methods of philosophy are inadequate to reach the conclusions of theology.

Contrary to Gilson, Robert maintains that for Bonaventura, philosophy contributes to our goal of finding God by investigating its proper objects; namely, nature and the soul. Philosophy requires the help of theology not because its methods are unreliable within its subject matter but because its results are incomplete, and because it can be an occasion for the sin of pride. In its own sphere, philosophy is autonomous.

Robert agrees with Steenberghen that Bonaventura never pursued philosophical questions *for their own sake*; he only pursued them when it was helpful for understanding the things of faith. It does not follow, however, according to Robert, that he failed to pursue philosophical questions *sufficiently*. Bonaventura was a theologian, and the unity of his system was theological, not philosophical. This does not mean, however, according to Robert, that the unity of the philosophical *part* of his system was theological, or that it had no unity. Bonaventura's philosophy was not a foolish eclecticism. There is material in the work of Bonaventura for a genuine philosophical synthesis.

Robert also agrees with Steenberghen that Bonaventura's knowledge of Aristotle was wide but not deep. The reason that he did not bother to become an expert on Aristotle was not that he despised philosophy, but that he thought Augustine's philosophy was better. Contrary to Steenberghen, Bonaventura was an Augustinian in philosophy as well as in theology.

Steenberghen's mistake, according to Robert, was to suppose that a philosophy could not be Augustinian at the core if it made extensive use of Aristotelian terminology. With a stroke of his pen, Steenberghen eliminated a whole philosophical school—the medieval Augustinian school, of which Bonaventura would have been the leading representative. In consequence, Steenberghen had to represent the conflict between the two philosophical schools as a conflict between the philosophical and the theological "spirit," or even between the Faculty of Arts and the Faculty of Theology in the University of Paris.—*J.C.*

ADDITIONAL RECOMMENDED READING

Bonaventura. *Itinerarium Mentis in Deum*. Translated by Philotheus Boehner. New York: Franciscan Institute, 1956. Facing Latin and English.

_____ . *The Souls Journey into God, The Tree of Life, The Life of St. Francis*. Translated by Ewert Cousins. New York: Paulist Press, 1978. A good translation with a helpful introduction. The typography takes some getting used to.

McGinn, Bernard. "Ascension and Introversion in the *Itinerarium Mentis in Deum*," in *S. Bonaventura 1274-1974*. Vol. III. Grottaferrata, Italy: Collegio S. Bonaventura, 1974, pp. 535-552. An analysis of the stages in the ascent, with a comparison to the views of an earlier writer, Richard of St. Victor.

Robert, Patrice. "St. Bonaventure, Defender of Christian Wisdom," in *Franciscan Studies*. N. S. III, no. 2 (1943), pp. 159-179. A biographical sketch by the author of the important article discussed above.

Roch, Robert J. "The Philosophy of St. Bonaventure: A Controversy," in *Franciscan Studies*. N. S. XIX, nos. 3-4 (1959), pp. 209-226. An account of the Gilson-Steenberghen-Robert controversy, unfavorable to Steenberghen.

Steenberghen, Fernand van. "Saint Bonaventure or Augustinian Aristotelianism," in *The Philosophical Movement in the Thirteenth Century*. Edinburgh: Nelson, 1955. Gives Steenberghen's account of the controversy.

SUMMA CONTRA GENTILES

Author: Saint Thomas Aquinas (c. 1225-1274)
Type of work: Theology, metaphysics
First transcribed: c. 1258-1260

PRINCIPAL IDEAS ADVANCED

The wise man is one who deals with the first beginning and the last end of the universe; truth is the final end, and the divine nature must first of all be considered if one is to understand first and last things.

No truth of faith is contrary to principles known by reason.

God understands not temporally but eternally; he understands all things at once by understanding their intelligible counterparts, but he knows individuals as well as universals.

God's will is free, having no cause but his own wisdom; he does not of necessity love things other than himself.

In God there is active power, but no potentiality; he is essentially infinite, and his knowledge and understanding are infinite.

Since man is a rational creature, his final happiness lies in the contemplation of God; but this end cannot be achieved in this life.

The *Summa contra Gentiles* is less widely known and much less widely read than Thomas Aquinas's later, longer, and more famous *Summa Theologica* (written from 1265 until Aquinas's death). In some sense this is strange, since the *Summa contra Gentiles* is simpler in its structure, and in that sense more readable and less involved. Perhaps the *Summa Theologica* has gained its fame through its more widespread use in church dogmatics, since it is that *Summa* which contains most of the detailed argument on doctrinal issues. By comparison, the *Contra Gentiles* is more philosophical, as its author intended and as its title implies. As such it is likely to be of more interest to the non-Catholic reader. It is true that it is an earlier work, but not so much so as to make any radical difference in Thomas's ideas, and a comparison of the basic doctrines does not reveal any wide discrepancy.

It is interesting that whereas the *Summa Theologica* begins with an apologetic approach, explaining the relation of philosophy to theology and arguing for the existence of God, the *Contra Gentiles* begins immediately with God as he is in himself. As a work directed to the non-Christian, one might have expected the reverse. Yet in style the *Contra Gentiles* is less doctrinal and does not base its arguments on a prior acceptance of Scripture as authoritative, as the *Theologica* does. The *Contra Gentiles* is more directly metaphysical, defining the "wise man" as one who deals with the first beginning and the last end of the universe. Truth is conceived of as the final end of the whole universe, and the treatise begins directly with a consideration of the divine nature as that which must be delineated if we are to explain first and last things.

Thomas Aquinas agrees with classical philosophy in holding that the chief aim of man is to achieve wisdom. In his case, however, this consists specifically in a knowledge of God. Since the Bible must be accepted as authoritative in order to be convincing, it cannot be used to prove any question about God's nature. With Jews, of course, a Christian may use the Old Testament as a basis for argument, and even a heretic may recognize the New Testament as valid evidence; he simply does not agree with the orthodox interpretation. For those who are neither heretics nor Jews, all argument must be based solely on natural reason. And then the first thing to establish is what mode of proof is possible where God is concerned. Some things true of God are beyond the scope of human reason, as, for example, that God is three in one. Other things, such as the unity and existence of God, are demonstrable under the light of natural reason. Yet human reason cannot go on further to grasp God's substance directly. Under the conditions of our present natural life, the knowledge which our understanding can obtain commences with sense data.

To discover anything true about God is exceedingly difficult, and for such arduous work not many have either the time or the natural capabilities. Some men devote themselves to business affairs and never study theology seriously. Furthermore, first of all one must master philosophy, so that a study of the divine nature requires a lot of preparation. Thus, in one sense, it is a study better suited to man's old age, when some naturally disturbing influences have subsided. As difficult as theology is and as restricted and as demanding as it is, faith was provided so that not everyone need find out about God for himself. It was necessary, Thomas argues, for the real truth about divine things to be presented to men with a fixed certainty by way of faith.

Reason and faith must agree, however, and Thomas begins by asserting that it is impossible for the truth of faith to be contrary to principles known by natural reason. No opinion or belief, Thomas is sure, is sent to man from God as an item of faith which is contrary to natural knowledge. For one thing, although as human beings our knowledge begins with sense objects, these retain in themselves some trace of the imitation of God. Here is Bonaventura's doctrine of the natural world seen as a sense world but also as one containing traces within itself of its supernatural origin as a creation of God. Thomas also affirms the use of the negative method, another traditional doctrine. We may have some sort of knowledge of the divine nature by knowing "what it is not."

The famous proofs for God's existence also appear in the *Contra Gentiles*, but they are in briefer form than in the other *Summa* and seem less fully developed. One might have expected this work, directed at pagans as it is and not dependent upon Scripture for its arguments, to make more use of the "proofs." Instead, the proofs receive less stress, and Thomas moves directly into a discussion of the divine attributes. He discusses in sequence God's eternality, his freedom from potentiality, his lack of composition, and his incorporeality. All of these are rather directly stated as if they needed little expansion.

It does not take much vision to see the *Contra Gentiles* as the framework upon which the *Summa Theologica* was finally built. The arguments need expanding, and more biblical material is included, but the structure is very much the same. In the *Contra Gentiles* very few authors are quoted, and the argument is simply advanced in a straightforward way. Later, in the *Summa Theologica*, Thomas attempted to blend a number of important views together and to reach a more detailed conclusion. In the earlier work, however, he seems satisfied to provide the outline of the important questions and the basic structure of each argument. Little of great significance is changed in the later *Summa*, but the arguments receive a great many refinements, and the reasoning is made both more subtle and more complex in order to deal with the multiplicity of views presented there.

Aquinas considers God's understanding at length and describes its difference from man's. God does not understand temporally but eternally. He does not understand by knowing an object directly but by knowing its intelligible counterpart in his own understanding. God's understanding does contain a multitude of objects, but he understands all things at once and together. Propositional truth is also present in the divine understanding, and God also knows individuals, not merely universals. Nonexistent things are known by God, even though they never will become actual, and he knows individual events, contingent upon man's action, as they will happen. In order to do this God must know the motions of the human will as well as his own will, and through these he understands evil as well as good.

Aquinas agrees to the traditional self-sufficiency of God's nature: God does not of *necessity* love things other than himself. Things outside of God need him in a way in which he does not depend on them. God's will is free, subject to no external conditions, and has no cause other than his own wisdom. His goodness is the reason why he wills all things, and in that sense it is possible to assign a reason for the choice of God's will. Will, understanding, and goodness exist in God, but not passion, since that would indicate imperfection. There is love in God but not such that he suffers from it or is subject to anything else because of it. God cannot, it is true, will evil, but such a limitation is no imperfection. God hates nothing, although his attributes are such that it is proper to describe him as "living."

In contrast to this extended and direct discussion of God's nature, philosophy considers man and the natural order as these things are in themselves. Philosophy makes no necessary reference to God, but the Christian faith considers natural beings, not in themselves, but inasmuch as they represent the majesty of God. Furthermore, Christians focus specifically on that in man which is directly involved in his relation to God's will. The other qualities of man are not as important in the Christian's view. The philosopher takes his stand on the immediate and natural causes of things; but the Christian argues from God as first cause, indicating what things are revealed and what we can learn about the divine nature. Philosophically we begin with creatures and then may be led to a knowledge of God; faith studies creatures only in their relation to God and so studies God first and creatures after that.

Turning then directly to God, Aquinas asserts that God's power and his action are not distinct. They are not two things, and this view actually results in a stronger doctrine of necessary predestination here than Thomas was to adopt in the *Summa Theologica*. God does not create the natural world out of anything preexistent, and therefore he does not create merely by moving material. The act of creation means bringing a thing into being without any preexistent material, not even potentiality. Nor is creation a successive movement. Creation takes place in an instant. A thing is at once in the act of being created and is created. Such a drastic form of creation is an action proper to God alone, and he creates directly with no intermediaries. God's power extends to every possible thing, except to those which involve a contradiction.

In God there is an active power, but no potentiality. Whatever would necessarily involve potentiality, those things are impossible to God. Nor could God make one and the same thing to be and not to be, since that would involve a contradiction. He cannot make a thing which lacks any of its essential constituents. And his will cannot be changeable; he cannot cause what once was willed not to be fulfilled. On the other hand, God's knowledge or understanding is bounded by no limits in its view. This means that God is essentially infinite, although all other things are limited. The infinite reach of God's understanding means that his knowledge extends even to things that neither are, nor shall be, nor have been.

God needs nothing and depends on nothing other than himself; every other being is in his neighbor's debt on God's account. In all these matters, God is not a debtor to any creature, but a debtor to the fulfillment of his own plan. There is no absolute necessity for the being of any creature. The creature begins to exist in time exactly when God from eternity arranged that it should begin to exist. God brought into being creation and time simultaneously. Thus, questions which concern a "before creation" are improperly asked. There is no account to be given of why he produced a creature *now*, and not before, but only why the creature has not always been. Having thus been always willed, a new thing that has not always been may be produced by God without any change in him. But if time has not always been, we may mark a nonexistence of time prior to its being.

Multiplicity and variety characterize creation, to the end that the perfect likeness of God can be found in creatures and in each according to his measure.

Taken all together, they are very good, because the order of the universe is the finest and noblest creation. Of course, in created intelligences, both potentiality and actuality are present in a way in which they are not in God. The potential intellect in man does not subsist apart from matter, but is intimately dependent on the body's functions. In each man it is individual, just as his body is individual. There is no common potential intellect which is the same for all men. Despite the individuality of the human intellect and its close association with the passive intellect, particularly with the functioning of the body, the human soul does not perish with the body but is capable of independent existence. However, this does not mean that the human soul is of the same substance as God, since they differ quite markedly in basic nature. The human soul is neither an eternally existing thing nor is it transmitted by generation, but it is brought into being by a creative act of God himself.

Aquinas's description of the divine nature is metaphysical; his doctrine of the creation of the natural order can stand on its own logical ground. It fits into Christian doctrine, it is true, but Aquinas does not expect it logically to depend upon this, nor does he consciously derive his two doctrines from specifically or exclusively Christian materials.

Two objectives of the vast scheme remain: to consider the end of man and the created world in relation to God, and to consider finally what God can be said to have revealed. Using a quotation from the Psalms, Aquinas begins his discussion of the last end of man with the assertion that God will not abandon his creation once constituted. Every creature acts to attain some end, so that the natural world in this sense seems constantly directed toward the attainment of some goal. Furthermore, the goal desired is always some good; evil is a thing aside from the attention of an agent. In fact, the very cause of evil is something which in itself is good; and even when evil appears it never cancels out completely the good upon which it is based.

Since the end of everything is always some good, the ordained end of all things is actually the source of all good: God. God is the end of all things in the sense that all rational creatures desire to be like God, to understand him. Happiness in any ultimate sense does not consist, for man, in bodily pleasures. He knows, as a rational creature, that all final happiness lies in the contemplation of God. But this happiness is not based on a general knowledge of God, or upon the knowledge of God's existence which is to be had by demonstration. Our problem is that we cannot in this life see God as he essentially is, which means that the final happiness of man cannot be attained in this life. Nor can any created substance of its own natural power arrive at a point where he can see God as he essentially is. To achieve his aim in life, a created intelligence needs an influx of divine light enabling his intellect to be lifted up to see God.

Yet even in seeing God, no created intelligence could comprehend the divine substance or see all things that can be seen in God. Nevertheless, this is not an exclusive affair; every intelligence of every grade can, by being lifted up, partake of the vision of God. Those who do see God will see him forever, and in that final happiness every desire of man will be fulfilled. Since God is the cause of the activity in all active agents, God is everywhere and in all things. The progress toward man's final goal, then, is within the scope of divine providence. The providence of God watches immediately over all individual things. This does not deny a freedom of the will, since the action of divine providence is not direct but operates by means of secondary causes. However, the motion of the human will is caused by God and subject to his providence.

From this point Thomas moves on to consider specifically the utility of prayer, the question of fate, miracles (which God alone can work), and the purposes for the giving of a divine law for human conduct. The divine government of man here on this earth is like paternal government, since man's acts are punished or rewarded by God. Of course, not all punishments or rewards are equal. There is a distinction between venial and mortal sin, the latter being material in determining final reward or punishment. Since man cannot attain happiness for himself, he needs divine assistance, or grace. The presence in us of grace causes us to love God and produces faith. Such grace is given gratuitously. Man can, it is true, easily do good from time to time, but he needs the assistance of grace in order to persevere in good action. Man may be delivered from sin, but only by grace.

All these things man needs to know, if he is to understand his final goal and the possibility for achieving it. Yet the human mind cannot of itself arrive at the direct vision of the divine substance. God cannot, Thomas has established, abandon his creation; therefore revelation is necessary in order to show man the way. God himself is prevented by his nature from descending to man, but here we reach over into the heart of Christian doctrine. For the Son of God, as a coequal member of the Trinity, is at the same time God and capable of descending to man to make the necessary revelation to man's knowledge of his final end and the means thereto. Thomas began by addressing rational arguments to non-Christians, but the discourse is brought to the place where the Christian doctrine of revelation through Christ is considered to be necessary for the completion of creation's plan.

Thomas, having laid the rational ground work for considering the nature of Jesus, turns to consider various theories of Christology and their adequacy. Revelation through an agent of God himself is necessary to the fulfillment of this rational plan, and now everything depends upon describing Jesus' nature so that we see him as fulfilling this role successfully. No one needs to be converted to Christianity by this means, but at least its rational basis can be examined. Thomas rejects Arian and Sabellian views as heretical, as orthodox Christians have done, and goes on to discuss each person of the Trinity and to work out a theory of their functions and relationships. Next, a theory of the incarnation is developed. The human nature assumed by the Word (Christ) must be perfect in soul and body in every respect and from the instant of conception.

The need for sacraments and the doctrine of original sin are discussed. Since Thomas concludes with a discussion of the office of the minister and the resurrection of the body, one might almost forget that the *Contra Gentiles* was written for non-Christians. But its non-Christian basis still remains: it aims to present Christian doctrine on the basis of arguments and materials which do not themselves depend for their validity on the prior acceptance of authority. Thomas Aquinas had no intention of avoiding specifically Christian doctrines, but what he meant to do, and did, was to present them in the form of rational discourse, moving on from a theory of God and the nature of man to show the consistency of Christian doctrine with such a rationally developed view. Taking in as it does nearly every major metaphysical, theological, and ethical question, this work is truly a vast *summa*, written to present Christian doctrine upon the basis of rationally structured argument.—*F.S.*

PERTINENT LITERATURE

Aquinas, Saint Thomas. *On the Truth of the Catholic Faith* [*Summa Contra Gentiles*]. Garden City, New York: Doubleday & Company, 1955-1957.

Four distinguished Catholic scholars (A. C. Pegis, J. F. Anderson, V. J. Bourke, and C. J. O'Neil), having severally translated the four books of the *Summa Contra Gentiles*, each wrote an introduction to the part which he translated. Taken together with the General Introduction, they provide the most authoritative analysis of the work available to the English reader. The following summary is limited to the General Introduction, in which Pegis undertakes to resolve two problems which the *Summa Contra Gentiles* has posed for modern historians: the occasion of the work and its internal organization.

The first problem arises from an old tradition according to which Saint Thomas Aquinas wrote the *Summa Contra Gentiles* for use by missionaries laboring among Spanish Jews and Moslems. Many scholars dismiss this tradition as a pious legend and explain the author's preoccupation with Islamic philosophy by pointing out that, unlike the *Summa Theologica*, which was written for students, the *Summa Contra Gentiles* was composed for mature scholars who, like Thomas himself, had to meet the challenge posed in European universities by the recent acquisition of Aristotelian works through the medium of Arabic and Jewish translations and commentaries. Pegis, however, upholds the traditional account, adding that his own study has led him to conclude that Thomas' work was written with non-Christian readers in mind.

The second problem, that of the outline, reflects the difficulty that many philosophers find in considering the *Summa Contra Gentiles* as a unified treatise with a single purpose. The common impression is that in the first three books Thomas takes the standpoint of philosophy and in the final book he shifts to the standpoint of faith. According to Pegis, however, a close study of the rubrics by which the four books are joined makes it clear that the work is a whole. The point of view throughout is that of the wise man who, certain that man's blessedness lies in finding the truth, is unwilling to reject either the light of reason or that of revelation. "In its plan and procedure, therefore, the *SCG* is the work of a Christian believer expounding what he believes about God by means of demonstration where the truths in question allow it and by means of an appeal to Scripture where the truths in question surpass reason."

According to Pegis, one of the central themes of Thomas' work is the attitude of the Christian toward philosophy, in particular toward the philosophy of Aristotle. Thomas, who at the time he was composing the *Summa Contra Gentiles* was also writing commentaries on Aristotle's philosophical works, could frame an independent judgment on the merits of the latter and at the same time could see the Aristotelian question as part of the larger question: How competent is man's reason to deal with matters of human destiny?

Aristotle had, in fact, taught many things which were contrary to Scripture, such as the eternity of the world and the mortality of the soul. Must the followers of Aristotle accept his teaching *in toto*, as his Arabian commentator Averröes (1126-1198) had maintained? Or could one adopt his approach to knowledge without giving up the tenets of the Church? Thomas gave "a creative and even revolutionary" answer, venturing that reason was given to man so that he might rise to participate in the divine life, and that it does not merely serve as a preamble to revelation but is completely "at home in revelation as in a transcending truth that answers to its deepest needs." In this way, he came to terms with Aristotle. Philosophers may err and require correction from Scripture; still, within its own dominion, philosophy can be without error.

All of this, says Pegis, is borne out in the plan and organization of the *Summa Contra Gentiles*. The autonomy of philosophy is preserved, but in due subordination to theology. In a word, the subject matter throughout is revealed truth. But in expounding what is really one truth, Thomas observed the twofold character of this same truth: namely, that some truths about God are and some are not accessible to reason. Sound method led Thomas to treat the two separately. When he dealt with truths accessible to reason, as in Parts One to Three, Thomas proceeded "by way of demonstrative arguments with a view to convincing his adversaries"; but when he dealt with truths which surpass man's natural capacities, as in Part Four, he relied on Scripture, using only "likely arguments" for the edification of believers but without any pretense of refuting unbelievers. Thomas gave arguments to show that doctrines of both kinds are rightly proposed to men by revelation for their belief; at the same time he maintained that it is the responsibility of Christian teachers to supplement the light of revelation wherever possible by the light of reason.

As confirmation of his interpretation, Pegis cites an eighteenth century Dominican, Bernard de Rubeis, who raised the question of why the book was entitled *On the Truth of the Catholic Faith*, if, as appears to be the case, most of the doctrines there discussed (such as the existence and unity of God, God's attributes, his power and providence) are "open to our natural light." But, Rubeis continues, Thomas anticipated this difficulty and answered it in his doctrine of the twofold character of revealed truth, showing that of the integral body of Christian doctrine that which reason can attain to and that which surpasses reason are alike "proposed for belief by supernatural revelation."

This conclusion, says Pegis, still holds. The inclusive title is fully justified by a study of the work's plan and organization.

Copleston, Frederick C. *Aquinas*. Harmondsworth, England: Penguin Books, 1955.

Mortimer Adler, during his Thomist period, delivered a lecture entitled *Saint Thomas and the Gentiles* in which he urged Catholic philosophers to look beyond the circle of believers and make the case for perennial philosophy against contemporary positivists, relativists, materialists, and idealists, citing as his warrant the fact that Saint Thomas Aquinas composed his *Summa Contra Gentiles* before starting work on his *Summa Theologica*.

Frederick C. Copleston has undertaken just such an assignment. The chapters on Saint Thomas in his highly respected *History of Philosophy* deal with questions of the kind that Catholic students might ask. By contrast, his contribution to the Penguin series attempts to answer objections against Thomas' philosophy arising from the standpoint of analytic philosophy. This is particularly so in the long introductory chapter, which attempts to show that there is philosophical truth as distinct from the truth of empirical science. But it is hardly less so of the expository chapters that follow (on Metaphysics, God and Creation, Body and Soul, Morality and Society), each of which is framed to take account of the contemporary viewpoint.

Copleston points out that, in taking its stand on sense experience and rejecting all forms of innatism, Thomism has much in common with the British tradition. The sensible world for Aquinas is the only immediate object of human knowledge, and whatever knowledge we have of our own minds or of God derives from reflection on our experience of the material world. As Aristotelians use the term, experience includes what Copleston calls first reflection, an awareness (for example) of myself implicit in every act of external perception, but also an awareness of such facts as that whatever changes passes from potentiality to actuality and that whatever comes into existence must have a cause. A person may give these truths no further thought, but if he attends to them by a second act of reflection, he is on his way to common sense, and, perhaps, to metaphysics. Thomas claims no privileged information for the philosopher: "His [the philosopher's] insight into the intelligible structure of the world presented in experience is the result of reflection on data of experience and of insight into those data which are in principle data of experience for everyone, whether he is a philosopher or not." Thus, William James was not far from the truth when he called scholasticism "common sense's college-trained younger sister."

One of the misunderstandings that Copleston is most concerned to remove is the common impression that Thomism is a deductive system. As an Aristotelian, Thomas took it for granted that systematic knowledge rests on truths that are self-evident; but he did not hold that new information can be deduced from such principles in a quasimathematical manner. Reminding us that, for Thomas, there are no innate ideas or principles, he shows that even such principles as the whole is greater than the part, and that the good ought to be chosen and the evil rejected, represent insights into the real world which play an important role in our thinking, whether or not most people ever reflect on them. For example, while it is true that animals pursue good and shun evil just as man does, it is nevertheless essential to a human act that man form concepts of tendencies which for animals remain on the level of instinct.

The principle of efficient causation ("everything which begins to exist begins to exist through the agency of an already existing thing") is self-evident but in a way that differs from the principles just mentioned, inasmuch as it is not logically necessary that there should be anything which has begun to exist. This truth arises out of experience. We observe things coming into being and we observe causal agency, not in the sense that causality is the object of vision, but in the sense that perception involves the cooperation of sense and intellect. Moreover, the experience of concrete instances of causal efficacy yields insight into the truth that a thing which begins to exist must do so through the agency of another thing which already exists.

Causal dependence is an aspect of the structure of finite beings which, when attended to, discloses "the relation of dependence of things which come into being and pass away on something other than themselves which does not come into being or pass away, and cannot do so." Other aspects of the empirical world, such as motion, disclose the same relation; and it is the function of the so-called proofs to make this dependence explicit. According to Copleston, it is misleading to start with the traditional idea of God and to suppose that the proofs are meant to answer the question: Does God exist? Rather, for Thomas, they answer the question: What are things considered simply as beings? As the mind is led to see things as dependent on something beyond our sensible experience, a second question arises: What sort of being is this something? "His proofs of God's existence constitute a prolongation of the reflection on things as things. He is prepared to say that all cognitive agents know God implicitly in everything they know."

Copleston warns that, in spite of the simplified form of the arguments (particularly as they are presented for "novices" in the *Summa Theologica*), Thomas did not regard a metaphysical approach to God's existence as an easy matter. In particular he warns against supposing that the proofs rest on logical necessity. To affirm that some things come into being and to deny that there is an eternal and necessary being involves one in a contradiction, but the contradiction is not formal or verbal but ontological, and can be made apparent only by means of metaphysical analysis. And for this purpose Copleston regards the third proof (from contingency to necessity) as fundamental; for, he says, all the arguments turn on this existential aspect of metaphysics, which Thomas brought to the fore, and may be said to treat of dependence in some form or other.—*J.F.*

ADDITIONAL RECOMMENDED READING

Adler, Mortimer. *Saint Thomas and the Gentiles*. Milwaukee: Marquette University Press, 1938. An address exhorting modern Thomists to talk less among themselves and, following the example of their master, to meet the challenge of modern opponents of the perennial philosophy.

Bryar, William. *St. Thomas and the Existence of God: Three Interpretations*. Chicago: Henry Regnery Company, 1951. A study of the argument from motion in the two *Summas*.

Chenu, M. D. *Toward Understanding Saint Thomas*. Chicago: Henry Regnery Company, 1964. An authoritative introduction to the writings of Aquinas.

Salamucha, Jan. "The Proof *Ex Motu* for the Existence of God: Logical Analysis of St. Thomas' Arguments," in *Aquinas: A Collection of Essays*. Edited by Anthony Kenny. Garden City, New York: Doubleday & Company, 1969. A Polish logician interprets and criticizes the proof from the *Summa Contra Gentiles*.

SUMMA THEOLOGICA

Author: Saint Thomas Aquinas (c.1225-1274)
Type of work: Metaphysics, theology
First transcribed: c. 1265-1274

PRINCIPAL IDEAS ADVANCED

Man requires more than philosophy in his search for truth; certain truths are beyond human reason and are available only because of divine revelation; theology, which depends on revealed knowledge, supplements natural knowledge.

The existence of God can be proved in five ways: by reference to motion (and the necessity of a first mover), by reference to efficient causes (and the necessity of a first cause), by reference to possibility and necessity, by reference to the gradations of perfection in the world, and by reference to the order and harmony of nature (which suggests an ordering being who gives purpose to the created world).

God alone is the being whose nature is such that by reference to him one can account for the fact of motion, efficient cause, necessity, perfection, and order.

God's principal attributes are simplicity (for he is noncorporeal and without genus), actuality, perfection, goodness, infinitude, immutability, unity, and immanence; but the created intellect can know God only by God's grace and only through apprehension, not comprehension.

It is a difficult task to comment on Thomas's *Summa Theologica* briefly; it has meant and can mean many things to many people. Partly this is due to its length; it runs to many volumes. And partly it is due to the scope of the questions considered; they range from abstract and technical philosophy to minute points of Christian dogmatics. The situation is further complicated because of Thomas's style. Such works were common in his day, and his is only one of many which were written in this general form. The work consists entirely of questions, each in the form of an article in which the views Thomas considers important are summarized and then answered. Objections to the topic question are listed, often including specific quotations, and then an equal number of replies are given, based on a middle section ("I answer that") which usually contains Thomas's own position; but this, in turn, is sometimes based on some crucial quotation from a philosopher or theologian.

Out of this complexity and quantity many have attempted to derive Thomistic "systems," and both the commentators and the group of modern Thomists form a complex question in themselves. Thomas was considered to be near heresy in his own day, and his views were unpopular in some quarters. From the position of being not an especially favored teacher in a very fruitful and exciting era, he has come to be regarded as perhaps the greatest figure in the

Catholic philosophy and theology of the day. His stature is due as much to the dogmatization and expansion of his thought which took place (for example, by Cardinal Cajetan and John of St. Thomas) as it is to the position Thomas had in his own day. Without this further development his writing might have been important, but perhaps it would be simply one among a number of significant medieval works. The Encyclical Letter of Pope Leo XIII, "On the Restoration of Christian Philosophy," published in 1879, started the Thomistic revival. The modern developments in philosophy had gone against the Church of Rome, and Thomas Aquinas was selected as the center for a revival and a concentration upon Christian philosophy. Since that time Thomas has been widely studied, so much so that it is sometimes hard to distinguish Thomas's own work from that of those who followed him.

Part I contains 119 questions, including treatises on creation, on the angels, on man, and on the divine government. The first part of Part II consists of 114 questions, including treatises on habits and law, and in general it covers ethical matters as against the metaphysical and epistemological concentration in Part I. The second part of Part II is made up of 189 questions, and Part III contains ninety. These cover laws, the ethical virtues, and questions of doctrine and Christology. Taken as a whole, it is hard to imagine a more comprehensive study, although it is important to remember that Thomas wrote a second *Summa*, "against the Gentiles," which was intended as a technical work of apologetics for those who could not accept the premises of Christian theology. The works overlap a great deal, but a comparative study cannot be made here. The *Summa Theologica*, then, has as its unspoken premise the acceptance of certain basic Christian propositions, whereas the *Contra Gentiles* attempts to argue without any such assumptions.

The influence of any single philosopher or theologian on Thomas's thought is difficult to establish, and probably too much has been made of Thomas's use of Aristotle. It is true that Aristotle is quoted in the *Summa Theologica* more than any other pagan author and that Thomas refers to him on occasion as "the philosopher." The availability of Aristotle's writings in fairly accurate translation in Thomas's day had a decided influence upon him and upon others of his era. Plato's works as a whole were still unrecovered, so that Aristotle is one of the few outside the Christian tradition who is quoted. Particularly in psychology and epistemology Thomas seems to have followed at least an Aristotelian tradition, if not Aristotle himself. But the authors Thomas quotes with favor cover a wide range, including frequent citations of the Neoplatonic pseudo-Dionysius and Augustine. Moreover, in a theologically oriented *summa*, the Bible and church tradition must play a major role, so that to sort out and label any strain as dominant is extremely difficult in view of the peculiar nature of a *summa*. There are positions which can clearly be recognized as Thomas's own, but the real perplexity of understanding Thomas is to grasp the variety of sources blended there and to hold them altogether for simultaneous consideration and questioning as Thomas himself did.

The first question, consisting of ten articles, is Thomas's famous definition of the nature and the extent of sacred doctrine or theology, and it opens by asking whether man requires anything more than philosophy. Thomas's contention that the Scriptures are inspired by God and are not a part of philosophy indicates the usefulness of knowledge other than philosophy. Scriptural knowledge is necessary for man's salvation, for Scripture offers the promise of salvation and pure philosophic knowledge does not. Philosophy is built up by human reason; certain truths necessary for man's salvation, but which exceed human reason, have been made known by God through divine revelation. Such knowledge is not agreed to be reason; it is by nature accepted only on faith.

Now the question arises: Can such revealed knowledge be considered as a science (a body of systematic knowledge) along with philosophy? Of course, such a sacred science treats of God primarily and does not give equal consideration to creatures. This means that it is actually a speculative undertaking and is only secondarily a practical concern. Yet it is the most noble science, because of the importance of the questions it considers, and in that sense all other forms of scientific knowledge are theology's handmaidens. Wisdom is knowledge of divine things, and in that sense theology has chief claim to the title of "wisdom." Its principles are immediately revealed by God, and within such a science all things are treated under the aspect of God.

Naturally there can be no argument on these terms with one who denies that at least some of theology's truths are obtained through divine revelation, for such a person would not admit the very premises of theology conceived of in this fashion. That is the sense in which this *summa* is a *summa* of theology intended for Christians. Since its arguments, at least in some instances, involve a claim to revealed knowledge, the *Summa* may be unconvincing to the non-Christian. Thus, the reception of grace, sufficient to become a Christian, is necessary to understand the arguments. In the Christian conception, the reception of grace enables the receiver to accept the truth of revelation. But Thomas's famous doctrine here is that such reception of grace does not destroy nature (natural knowledge) but perfects or completes it. Nothing is countermanded in philosophy's own domain; grace simply adds to it what of itself could not be known.

As compared with other classical theologians Thomas believed in a fairly straightforward approach to questions about God. However, Thomas did admit the necessity of the familiar "negative method," since where God is concerned what he is *not* is clearer to us than what he is. The proposition "God exists" is not self-evident to us, although it may be in itself. The contradictory of the proposition "God is" can be conceived.

In this case Thomas seems to oppose Anselm's ontological argument, although the opposition is not quite as straightforward as it seems. Thomas denies that we can know God's essence directly, even though such vision would reveal that God's essence and existence are identical and thus support Anselm's contention. But the ontological argument, he reasons, is built upon a kind of direct access to the divine which human reason does not have.

The existence of God, then, needs to be demonstrated from those of his effects which are known to us. Thomas readily admits that some will prefer to account for all natural phenomena by referring everything to one principle, which is nature herself. In opposition he asserts that God's existence can be proved in five ways: (1) the argument from motion, (2) the argument from the nature of efficient cause, (3) the argument from possibility and necessity, (4) the argument from the gradations of perfection to be found in things, and finally (5) the argument from the order of the world. Without attempting an analysis of these arguments individually, several things can be noted about them as a group. First, all are based on the principle that reason needs a final stopping point in any chain of explanation. Second, such a point of final rest cannot be itself within the series to be accounted for, but it must be outside it and different in kind. Third, in each case it is a principle which we arrive at, not God himself, but these principles (for example, a first efficient cause) are shown to be essential parts of the nature of God. God's existence is agreed to by showing reason's need for one of his attributes in the attempt to explain natural phenomena.

It is probably true that Thomas's five proofs have been given a disproportionate amount of attention, for following them Thomas goes into elaborate detail in a discussion of the divine nature and its primary attributes. Simplicity, goodness, infinity, and perfection are taken up, and then the other chief attributes are discussed before Thomas passes on to the analysis of the three persons of the trinitarian conception of God. Taken together, these passages form one of the most elaborate and complete discussions of God's nature by a major theologian, and it is here that much of the disagreement about Thomas's philosophy centers, rather than in the more formal and brief five proofs.

In spite of Thomas's use of Aristotelian terms, he indicates his affinity with the Neoplatonic tradition by placing the consideration of "simplicity" first. This is the divine attribute most highly prized and most stressed by Neoplatonists, and Thomas concurs in their emphasis. God's simplicity is first protected by denying absolutely that he is a body in any sense, since what is corporeal is by nature subject to division and contains potentiality, the opposite of God's required simplicity and full actuality. Nor is God within any genus, nor is he a subject as other individuals are. The first cause rules all things without commingling with them.

God's primary perfection is his actuality, since Thomas accepts the doctrine that a thing is perfect in proportion to its state of actuality. All created perfections preexist in God also, since he is the source of all things. As such a source of the multitude of things in this world, things diverse and in themselves opposed to each other preexist in God as one, without injury to his simplicity. This is no simple kind of simplicity which Thomas ascribes to his God as a perfection. God is also called good, although goodness is defined primarily in terms of full actuality, as both perfection and simplicity were. Everything is good insofar as it has being, and, since God is being in a supremely actual sense, he is supremely good. An object can be spoken of as evil only insofar as it lacks being. Since God lacks being in no way, there is in that sense absolutely no evil in his nature but only good.

When Thomas comes to infinity he is up against a particularly difficult divine attribute. By his time infinity had become a traditional perfection to be ascribed to God, but Aristotle had gone to great lengths to deny even the possibility of an actual infinite. Without discussing Aristotle's reasons here, it can be noted that Thomas makes one of his most significant alterations at this point in the Aristotelian concepts which he does use. Aristotle had considered the question of an actual infinite in the category of quantity. Thomas agrees with him: there can be no quantitative infinite and the idea is an imperfection. Form had meant primarily limitation for Aristotle, but here Thomas departs. The notion of form, he asserts, is not incompatible with infinity, although the forms of natural things are finite. In admitting the concept of the form of the infinite, Thomas departs from Aristotelian conceptions quite markedly and makes a place for a now traditional divine perfection. Nothing besides God, however, can be infinite.

Turning to the question of the immanence of God in the natural world, Thomas makes God present to all things as being the source of their being, power, and operation. But as such, God is not in the world. For one thing, God is altogether immutable, whereas every natural thing changes. He must be, since he is pure act and only what contains potentiality moves to acquire something. It follows that in God there is no succession, no time, but only simultaneous presence. God's unity further guarantees us that only one such God could exist. Of course a God of such a nature may not be knowable to a particular intellect, on account of the excess of such an intelligible object over the finite intellect; but, as fully actual, God is in himself fully knowable. The blessed see the essence of God by grace; for others it is more difficult. However, a proportion is possible between God and man, and in this way the created intellect can know God proportionally. This is not full knowledge, but it established the possibility for a knowledge relationship between God and man.

The created intellect, however, cannot fully grasp the essence of God, unless God by grace unites himself to the created intellect, as an object made intelligible to it. It is necessary in the case of God only that, for a full grasp, the natural power of understanding should be aided by divine grace. Those who possess the more charity will see God the more perfectly, and will be the more beatified. Here is Thomas's statement of the famous goal of the beatific vision. Even here God is only apprehended and never comprehended, since only an infinite being could possess the infinite mode necessary for comprehension, and none is infinite except God. God alone can comprehend himself, yet for the mind to attain an understanding of God in some degree is still asserted to be a great beatitude. God cannot be seen in his essence by a mere human being, except he be separated from this mortal life. Thomas here follows the famous Exodus XXXIII:20 passage: "Man shall not see Me, and live."

For Thomas faith is a kind of knowledge, since we gain a more perfect knowledge of God himself by grace than by natural reason. Such a concept of faith has had wide implications. That God is a trinity, for instance, cannot be known except by faith, and in general making faith a mode of knowledge has opened to Christianity the claim to a more perfect comprehension than non-Christians possess.

Names can be applied to God positively on Thomas's theory, but negative names simply signify his distance from creatures, and all names fall short of a full representation of him. Not all names are applied to God in a metaphorical sense, although some are (for example, God is a lion), but there are some names which are applied to God in a literal sense (for example, good, being). In reality God is one, and yet he is necessarily multiple in idea, because our intellect represents him in a manifold manner, conceiving of many symbols to represent him. However, univocal predication is impossible, and sometimes terms are even used equivocally. Others are predicated of God in an analogous sense, according to a proportion existing between God and nature.

In the first thirteen questions Thomas considers God as man approaches him. He then considers the world as it is viewed from the standpoint of the divine nature. Even the attributes of perfection which Thomas discussed, although they truly characterize God's nature, are not separate when viewed from the divine perspective. Now we ask how God understands both himself and the world, and the first thing which must be established is that there actually is knowledge in God. This might seem obvious, but the Neoplatonic tradition denies knowing to its highest principle as implying separation and need. Thomas admits a mode of knowing into the divine nature but he denies that God knows as creatures do. God understands everything through himself alone, without dependence on external objects; his intellect and its object are altogether the same and no potentiality is present. God's knowledge is not discursive but simultaneous and fully actual eternally. This is true because of God's role as the creator of the natural world; God's knowledge is the cause of things being as they are. God knows even some things which never were, nor are, nor will be, but it is in his knowledge not that they be but that they be merely possible.

God knows future contingent things, the works of men being subject to free will. These things are not certain to us, because of their dependence upon proximate, contingent causes, but they are certain to God alone, whose understanding is eternal and above time. There is a will as a part of God's nature, but it is moved by itself alone. The will of man is sometimes moved by things external to him. God wills his own goodness necessarily, even as we will our own happiness necessarily. Yet his willing things apart from himself is not necessary. Supposing that he wills it, however, then he is unable not to will it, since his will cannot change. Things other than God are thus "necessary by supposition." God knows necessarily whatever he knows, but does not will necessarily whatever he wills. And the will of God is always reasonable in what it wills. Yet the will of God is entirely unchangeable, Thomas asserts, since the substance of God and his knowledge are entirely unchangeable. As to evil, God neither wills evil to be done, nor wills it not to be done, but he wills to permit evil to be done; this is good because it is the basis of man's freedom. We must say, however, that all things are subject to divine providence, not only in general, but even in their own individual selves. It necessarily follows that everything which happens from the exercise of free will must be subject to divine providence. Both necessity and contingency fall under the foresight of God.

It should not be overlooked that Thomas devotes considerable time to a consideration of the nature and function of angels. Part of his reason for doing so, of course, is undoubtedly their constant presence in the biblical record. Part of his interest comes from the necessity of having intermediary beings between God and man. Having assigned to God a nature so different from man's nature, beings who stand somewhere in between are now easy to conceive. When Thomas comes to describe the nature of man, he follows much of the traditional Aristotelian psychology, which he finds more amenable to Christianity than certain Platonistic theories. Angels are not corporeal; man is composed of a spiritual and a corporeal substance. The soul has no matter, but it is necessarily joined to matter as its instrument. The intellectual principle is the form of man and in that sense determines the body's form. Since Thomas claims that the intellect in each man is uniquely individual, he argues against some Arabian views of the universality of intellect. In addition to a twofold intellect (active and passive), man has appetites and a will.

The will is not always moved by necessity, but in Thomas's views it is subject to the intellect. When he turns to the question of free will, Thomas's problem is to allow sufficient causal power to man's will without denying God's providence and foreknowledge. His solution to this problem is complicated, but essentially it involves God's moving man not directly and by force but indirectly and without doing violence to man's nature.

To obtain knowledge the soul derives intelligible species from the sensible forms which come to it, and it has neither innate knowledge nor does it know any forms existing independently from sensible things. The principle of knowledge is in the senses. Our intellect can know the singular in material things directly and primarily. After that intelligible species are derived by abstraction. Yet the intellectual soul cannot know itself directly, but only through its operations. Nor in this present life can our intellect know immaterial substances directly. That is a knowledge reserved for angels, but it means that we cannot understand immaterial substances perfectly now (through natural means). We know only material substances, and they cannot represent immaterial substances perfectly.

The soul of man is not eternal; it was created. It is produced immediately by God, not by any lesser beings (as is suggested in Plato's *Timaeus*, for instance). Soul and body are produced simultaneously, since they belong together as one organism. Man was made in God's image, but this in no way implies that there must be equality between creator and created. And some natures may be more like God than others, according to their disposition and the direction of their activities. All men are directed to some end. According as their end is worthy of blame or praise, so are their deeds worthy of blame or praise. There is, however, one last fixed end for all men; and man must, of necessity, desire all that he desires for the sake of that last end. Man's happiness ultimately does not consist either in wealth, fame, or honor, or even in power. Thomas never doubts that the end desired is to be happy, but he does deny that the end can consist of goods of the body. No created good can be man's last end. Final and perfect happiness can consist in nothing else than the vision of the Divine Essence, although momentary happiness probably does depend on some physical thing.

Now, it is possible for man to see God, and therefore it is possible for man to attain his ultimate happiness. Of course, there are diverse degrees of happiness, and it is not present equally in all men. A certain participation in such happiness can be had in this life, although true and perfect happiness cannot. Once attained, such happiness cannot be lost since its nature is eternal, but man cannot attain it by his own natural powers, although every man desires it.

Next Thomas considers the mechanics of human action, voluntary and involuntary movement, individual circumstances, the movement of the will, intention and choice. His discussion forms an addition to his psychology and a more complete discussion of the ethical situation of man. When he comes to good and evil in human action, Thomas easily acknowledges that some actions of man are evil, although they are good or evil according to circumstance. As far as man's interior act of will is concerned, good and evil are essential differences in the act of will. The goodness of the will essentially depends on its being subject to reason and to natural law. The will can be evil when it abides by an erring reason. The goodness of the will depends upon its conformity to the divine will.

In his more detailed psychology, Thomas discusses the nature and origin of the soul's passions, joy, sadness, hope, fear, and then love and hate. Pleasure, pain or sorrow, hope, despair, and fear all are analyzed in a way that anticipates Spinoza's famous discussion of the emotions. When Thomas comes to virtue, his opinion is largely based on Aristotle's. There are intellectual virtues and moral virtues, and to these he adds the theological virtues of faith, hope, and charity. Moral virtue is in a man by nature, although God infuses the theological virtues into man. For salvation, of course, there is need for a gift of the Holy Ghost.

Thomas continues with a discussion of sin, its kinds and causes. Such discussion has been extremely important both to church doctrine and in church practice. Not all sins are equal; therefore, sins must be handled in various ways. The carnal sins, for instance, are of less guilt but of more shame than spiritual sins. Mortal and venial sins are distinguished, but the will and the reason are always involved in the causes of sin. "Original sin" as a concept is of course extremely important to Christian doctrine, and Thomas discusses this in detail.

The treatise on law is one of the more famous parts of the *Summa Theologica*, for it is here that Thomas develops his theory of natural law. First, of course, there is the eternal law of which natural law is the first reflection and human (actual legal) law is a second reflection. The eternal law is one and it is unchanging; natural law is something common to all nations and cannot be entirely blotted out from men's hearts. Human law is derived from this common natural law, but human law is framed to meet the majority of instances and must take into account many things, as to persons, as to matters, and as to times.

A brief survey such as this cannot do justice even to the variety of topics considered in the *Summa Theologica*, nor can it give any detailed description of the complex material presented or of the views Thomas distills from them. The impression which the *Summa Theologica* gives is that of an encyclopedia to be read and studied as a kind of source book for material on a desired issue. In fact, the only way for any reader to hope to understand Thomas and his *Summa Theologica* is to become engrossed and involved in it for himself— undoubtedly what Thomas intended.—*F.S.*

PERTINENT LITERATURE

Gilson, Étienne. *The Christian Philosophy of St. Thomas Aquinas*. Translated by L. I. Shook from the fifth edition of *Le Thomisme*. New York: Random House, 1956.

As Professor of the History of Medieval Philosophy at the University of Paris, Étienne Gilson was largely responsible for bringing the philosophy of St. Thomas Aquinas to the attention of secular scholars. Meanwhile, by calling his fellow Catholics back from the schematized doctrines found in their hand-books to the life and teaching of the thirteenth century master, he helped raise official Thomism to a new plane. Medieval philosophy was not taught at the Sorbonne when Gilson was a student, and his acquaintance with Aquinas' writings began when he undertook to explore for his dissertation the influence of medieval thought on the philosophy of René Descartes. A series of lectures published in 1914 under the title *Le Thomisme*, the first of the five editions through which the present book has passed, is noteworthy, says its author, only as a monument to his ignorance. But ignorance of medieval philosophy was widespread: one of his reviewers denied that Aquinas had a philosophy distinct in any way from the scholastic synthesis which he shared with his contemporaries.

The words "Christian philosophy" in the English title highlight the author's conviction that one can understand Thomas' philosophy only if one approaches it through the faith of the Church. Earlier representatives of the Thomist revival, eager to prove to their secular counterparts that Catholics can philosophize like anyone else, argued that Thomas' philosophy, which they closely identified with that of Aristotle, was completely independent of his theology. As a historian, Gilson challenged this interpretation, maintaining that, not indeed in his commentaries but in his *Summas*, Thomas philosophized as a theologian, taking up into Christian doctrine such philosophical truths as could be used to amplify and explain what God had revealed through the Church.

The present work is a detailed exposition of Thomas' philosophy against the full background of Greek, Christian, and Arabian thought. But special attention is always given by Gilson to points at which Thomas went beyond his predecessors. This appears in each of the three parts into which Gilson divides his book: God, Nature, and Morality.

Gilson plunges the reader at once into what he considers Thomas' greatest contribution to philosophy: his revolutionary conception of being. Aristotle had, indeed, pointed the way when, in his analysis of substance, he affirmed that matter owes its existence to form and that form exists only in conjunction with matter. Aristotle, however, had failed to answer the question of how existence can arise from what does not exist. Had he pursued his analysis he must have arrived at existence as "the ultimate term to which the analysis of the real can attain." Thomas, in insisting that forms, by which matter is actuated, are themselves actuated by existence exposed the inadequacy of earlier essential ontologies and for the first time presented an existential ontology.

Much of Gilson's book is devoted to showing the consequences of this metaphysical innovation. One result is that God is no longer defined as Perfect Being or as Pure Act but as "the act of being that He is." "Like whatever exists, God is by His own act-of-being; but in His case alone, we have to say that *what* His being is is nothing else than that by which He exists, namely the pure act of existence." A further result is that the existence of God cannot be proved, in the strict sense, and that the five ways are not to be understood as a demonstration but rather as "a search beyond existences which are not self-sufficient, for an existence which is self-sufficient and which, because it is so, can be the first cause of all others."

A chapter entitled "Creation" serves Gilson as a transition from the doctrine of God to the doctrine of Nature. The notion that everything in the world depends on God both for its nature and its existence was foreign to the Greeks; and one of Thomas' major achievements was his doctrine of concurrent causes, by which he combined the Christian doctrine of dependence with the Greek assumption of a self-sustaining cosmos. God causes everything; but he does so in a manner that preserves the potentiality and actuality proper to each thing. In this way the creature's autonomy is secured and the groundwork is laid for a doctrine of natural law.

Thomas' moral philosophy, based on his philosophy of nature, is not to be confused with what is commonly called Christian ethics, for in the *Summa* Thomas treats the theological virtues (faith, hope, and love) separately from the moral virtues (prudence, fortitude, temperance, and justice). The law for every creature is a function of that creature's nature. Lower creatures obey it unconsciously; human beings, endowed with reason, have to "find out what they are so that they may act accordingly." As a moral philosopher, Thomas gave full scope to all types of human fulfillment, showing princes, merchants, scholars, artists—persons of every type—"at grips with the problem of doing well whatever they have to do, and above all with the problem of problems, not to ruin the only life it is theirs to live." Much of his practical philosophy parallels that of Aristotle. Still, there are differences, as when, in considering justice, Thomas internalizes and personalizes what for the Greeks remained primarily a civic virtue.

In his concluding chapter, "The Spirit of Thomism," Gilson opposes Thomas' existentialism to that of Søren Kierkegaard and Martin Heidegger, but finds in it affinities to that of Blaise Pascal as preserving the ineffability of the individual against the tendency of reason to stop at the level of abstract essence. Viewed in this way, his philosophy is not limited by what the human mind knew about the world in the thirteenth century; no more, by what it knows in the twentieth. "It invites us to look beyond present day science toward that primitive energy from which both knowing subject and object known arise."

O'Connor, D. J. *Aquinas and Natural Law*. London: Macmillan and Company, 1968.

In this college paperback, D. J. O'Connor has abstracted St. Thomas

Aquinas' views on ethics from the rest of his philosophy and undertaken to interpret and criticize them in the light of contemporary philosophical assumptions. The longest chapter is given over to the problem of natural law, but others provide enough background material to make the book a suitable introduction to Aquinas' thought, which, as the author points out, has proved of interest to many contemporary philosophers who do not share his religious beliefs. In a time when, as O'Connor writes, "fashionable and influential moral philosophers have abandoned objectivist theories of morals," Aquinas' views offer a special challenge to the critical philosopher.

O'Connor does not linger over the problem of faith and reason. The only way that one could support the claim that certain truths are divinely revealed would be by producing historical evidence, such as miracles. Although Thomas says that miracles "nourish faith by way of external persuasion," he falls back at last on grace, which, he says, is the "chief and proper cause of faith," moving a person to assent inwardly. This prompts in O'Connor the usual question as to how one is to judge between the claims of rival faiths. Felt conviction, he says, is not a sufficient criterion.

We shall find that O'Connor raises the same objection to the theory of natural law that he brings against religious belief. All objectivist theories of morality, he says, rest on moral intuition, which is merely a private feeling, allowing of no independent test. There are, according to O'Connor, two kinds of moral intuitionism. The modern kind likens moral awareness to sensory awareness and implies that moral qualities are "objective and directly knowable features of experience." The analogy breaks down, however, because there is no "acceptable and public test for resolving disagreements" about moral qualities, as there is about, say, whether a thing is yellow or merely appears so. The older kind of intuition, which underlies the theory of natural law, O'Connor finds more difficult to refute since it does not imply that moral judgments are self-evidently true but that there are self-evident moral principles, and that particular judgments are derived from these by syllogistic arguments. This kind of intuitionism raises all the questions which have traditionally divided empiricists from rationalists and nominalists from realists.

O'Connor argues that if one is to maintain that moral judgments can be proved to be correct, he must present us, first, with a list, of the principles which he holds to be self-evident, and second, with a set of rules by means of which he proposes to deduce secondary moral truths from the former. As to the first, O'Connor points out the ambiguities involved in calling any proposition self-evident, and shows that the ones which Thomas offers as examples ("good is to be pursued and evil is to be avoided"; "one should do evil to no man") are tautologies, true in virtue of the meaning of their terms. As to the second, O'Connor credits Thomas with recognizing the problem, as when he distinguishes between the logical deduction of conclusions and the practical application of principles: for example, one concludes that one must not kill from the principle that one should do harm to no man; but one applies the principle that the evildoer should be punished by determining a suitable penalty. As O'Connor understands him, Thomas held that only the method of logical deduction preserves the force of natural law. On this ground we may ask how Thomas was able to leap from the principle that one should do harm to no man to the conclusion that one should not kill—this being the very claim which a defender of euthanasia or suicide would reject. "And in general, no conclusions can be obtained, by derivation, from the master principle, 'Good is to be done and evil avoided,' without the help of other more disputable propositions."

Thus, despite its strong *prima facie* appeal to common sense, Thomism cannot stand up to modern criticism. "The rise of natural science, mathematics, and formal logic" has made clear to us both the limits of rational argument and the kind of evidence we can appropriately use as material for reasoning. Thomas, O'Connor states, "had the bad luck to be born too early." Underlying his theory of law is the claim that morality must be based on metaphysics; more precisely, that knowledge of man's duties must be derived from knowledge of man's nature. The notion that there are natures or essences to be grasped by intellectual intuition, however, is unacceptable to modern man.

The Humean objection to any reasoning which attempts to derive moral conclusions from factual premises applies to the theory of natural law. O'Connor allows that Thomas is in a better position than most philosophers to meet this criticism because he has grounded his account of moral dispositions in a description of human nature. We do, in fact, tend to apprehend as good those things to which our nature inclines us; but once more, says O'Connor, the principle is useless unless we are shown in detail which inclinations entail which duties.

The relation between natural law and positive law is not discussed by O'Connor, except in the conclusion, where he mentions a kind of minimal natural law, developed by H. L. A. Hart in *The Concept of Law*, according to which certain facts about human nature (man's vulnerability, his need for society, his limited power and foresight) make necessary certain rules for living. However, says O'Connor, although Hart has made natural law uncontroversial, he has done so by extracting from it "the mainspring of morality." No reasons are contained in it why anyone should act in a particular way.—*J.F.*

ADDITIONAL RECOMMENDED READING

Aquinas, Thomas. *Basic Writings of St. Thomas Aquinas*. Edited by Anton C. Pegis. New York: Random House, 1945. Contains an introduction and annotations by Anton C. Pegis.
Copleston, F. C. *Aquinas*. Harmondsworth, England: Penguin Books, 1955.

A general introduction with a good chapter on morality and society.

Gilson, Étienne. *Being and Some Philosophers*. Toronto: Pontifical Institute of Medieval Studies, 1949. A study of essential and existential ontologies.

Kenny, Anthony, ed. *Aquinas: A Collection of Critical Essays*. Garden City, New York: Anchor Books, 1969. Papers by contemporary analytic philosophers sympathetic with Thomism. The last two papers deal with Aquinas' moral philosophy.

A TRACT CONCERNING THE FIRST PRINCIPLE

Author: John Duns Scotus (c. 1265-1308)
Type of work: Theology
First transcribed: c. 1300

PRINCIPAL IDEAS ADVANCED

God, the First Principle, is the most perfect Being, that which causes but is not itself caused, that which is independent and on which everything else is dependent.

The First Principle is possible since an infinite series of causes is impossible; such an uncaused being must be necessary in itself.

There is but one First Principle, for multiple first principles are not necessary.

The First Principle is simple, infinite, wise, indefinable, intelligent, and endowed with will.

God created the natural order by a free act of will.

With so little of Duns Scotus' writing translated into English, we are fortunate indeed that *A Tract Concerning the First Principle* has been made available. Scholars admit that Scotus' Latin is difficult. Sometimes it is said that he represents scholastic subtlety at its height (implication: at its most obscure). However, such an estimate represents more a lack of sympathy with the mode of Scotus' thought than it does any extraordinary obscurity. It is true that Duns Scotus is aptly called the "subtle doctor," but the technical philosophy of any age is couched in specialized terms. Scotus belongs with the host of those before him whose central concern is metaphysics; and, like his profound compatriots, his writing reflects the difficulties inherent in such interests.

Scotus wrote in conscious opposition to Thomas Aquinas, as Ockham did after him. Both of these later men felt that there were certain deficiencies in Thomas' position, especially as it related to Christian doctrine. Both were somewhat more avowedly philosophical than Thomas, and both preferred to separate more radically philosophy and theology as disciplines, although Ockham is the real innovator here. The appearance of Aristotle in translation was new in Thomas' day; and both of these later writers actually seem closer to Aristotelianism than does Thomas, since the Aristotelian corpus had had more time to be appraised, with erroneous impressions corrected and Platonic glosses removed.

The study of Thomas Aquinas received papal encouragement in Leo XIII's encyclical of 1879. The result has been a widespread concentration upon Thomas, together with a much more general acquaintanceship with his work in non-Catholic philosophical circles. The philosophical and theological descendants of Scotus are equally vigorous today but less numerous, although many signs point to an increasing revival of interest in his thought. A critical edition of his work is under way and some additional English translation ought to follow. When this is done, we may find Scotus to be a much more modern thinker than has been generally recognized, rather than the last and most ponderous of the Scholastics. If traditional metaphysical and theological interest is due to be revived in our own day, Scotus may very well prove to be the modern starting point for such a revival.

Even a brief glimpse of the *Tract* will tell us that it is not in any sense a devotional work, even though its subject is God. Nor are any practical or religious goals specifically in view. "God" is mentioned only occasionally. Instead, Duns Scotus prefers an abstract title, the "First Principle." This piece of writing is a technical consideration of metaphysical structure and attributes, and it deals directly with the central speculative questions that surround the divine nature. Theory of knowledge and arguments for God's existence are present, but they are a side issue and a by-product of this straightforward metaphysical analysis of the First Principle of all things.

Systematically speaking, Scotus does not consider man and nature first but rather God. In the solution to questions about the natural order, Scotus holds to the classical belief that an analysis of the divine nature is central in determining the outcome of all such discussion. But this treatise is not long. To discuss man and the world and historical events would require a system and volumes of books. In something like seventy-five pages, on the other hand, an entire theory of the central characteristics of God is outlined. From there Scotus could go on to use his theory both as a fixed point of reference and as a fulcrum in the discussion of the wider range of philosophical and theological issues.

Despite this unapologetic approach to a direct discussion of the First Principle, there is a decidedly nondogmatic flavor to Duns Scotus' writing. His own opinion is clear and is elaborated technically, but one never gets the impression that he considers his to be the only possible theory or to be binding upon the reader. Here is an exploration simply offered for discussion.

Since no consideration of God can begin from an observed fact, it must receive its focus from some suggested theory, and it is in this spirit that Scotus seems to write. To be sure, the scholastically elaborate form in which the discussion is couched gives the modern reader some initial difficulty in extracting a straightforward statement. But Scotus, like many classical metaphysicians, seems to rely more upon the presence of a single significant statement than on structural simplicity of style or upon the modern directness of the essay form.

Although Scotus' *Tract* has fewer religious overtones than, say, Anselm's *Proslogion*, he still begins with the traditional prayer for divine assistance in his task. Then he turns to Moses and the Old Testament and opens with a brief consideration of the famous "I am Who am" passage (Exodus III:14).

But this leads him immediately to a consideration of "being" as the primary name for God, which shifts the discussion on to a metaphysical plane from which it seldom returns. Now comes the traditional "division of orders," a discussion of the various meanings for and divisions of "being."

Eminence versus dependence is the first and traditional division. Whatever is perfect and more noble in its essence is prior, according to Scotus. That which causes but is itself uncaused is first, and everything of a more dependent nature is posterior. The prior is whatever is able to exist without the posterior, whereas the posterior cannot exist without the prior. And this division is accurate even if the prior produces the posterior orders necessarily. After this first and essential division of being, the posterior orders may then be subdivided.

Duns Scotus goes on to quote Augustine with approval: there is not anything at all which brings itself into being. Nothing which we know from its nature to be an effect can be its own cause. A circle is impossible in casual relations. And some aspects are ruled out as being incidental. Only certain crucial relations and orders are to be considered, not all data (as some nineteenth century views attempt to encompass). The goal of such a delimited investigation is an understanding of the first cause in causing, although in addition to this, myriad efficient causes are needed to account for the majority of temporal events. An efficient cause acts for the love of some end; a first cause produces from itself without ulterior motive. No causation, therefore, is perfect other than that which comes from a first cause itself uncaused; lesser causes necessarily have some imperfections connected with them. Of course, in any individual case an analysis may find all levels and modes of causation to be in operation.

Scotus departs from Aristotle in making "matter" prior according to independence, whereas Aristotle completely subordinates matter to form. However, Scotus reasserts with Aristotle the priority of form according to eminence, because it is more perfect. Turning then to Plotinus and to the Neoplatonic tradition, he affirms the traditional preference for unity: plurality is never to be posited without necessity. Actually, this is the classical form of what was to become known as "Ockham's razor." Order is due to simplicity. It is really the preference for simplicity which dictates that the fewest possible principles should be introduced, and this is one of the strongest arguments for positing only a single first principle.

Then Scotus offers his version of the traditional "proofs" for God's existence, phrasing it as being a demonstration "that some one nature is simply first." But Scotus prefers to couch his argument in terms of "possibles," rather than to argue from the nature of the actual natural world. If his reasoning holds for all possible states, he argues, then it would hold for whatever set of states happens to be actual, whereas an argument based on actualities need not hold necessarily for possible states. With Scotus, and later with Ockham, an increasing stress is laid upon simply considering the order of possible entities as something prior to (and thus nearer to God than) the actual order of nature.

Scotus follows the traditional view that an ascent through an infinite series of prior levels or causes is impossible. All he concludes here is, not the assumed existence of a God, but merely that it is possible that some single causal principle should be simply first. As a preliminary step, and as the limit of philosophical argument, God is proved simply to be possible, and then only in the form that "an efficient causality simply first is possible." Metaphysics explores possible arguments; it does not support dogmatic conclusions.

Furthermore, Scotus never attempts to prove that such a cause which is simply first is necessarily itself uncaused. He simply goes on to argue that this is possible, since it is not affected by anything else and yet it affects other things independently. A first cause in the possible order is then shown to be required to bring some set of possibles into actual existence. From this point on, such a being can be examined as to its nature, although it is merely a being whose possible existence (although perhaps it has now become probable) has been established. Scotus reasons: such an uncaused being must be necessary in itself, since it depends upon no prior causes. Of itself, it is impossible for such a first cause not to be. Such is Scotus' line of contingent reasoning.

Considering such a principle, it becomes evident that there could be only one being of such a nature, since the kind of necessity which belongs to a being that owes its existence to no outside cause cannot be shared. Since there cannot be multiple beings all of whom derive the necessity of their existence from themselves, the unique perfection of such a single and preeminent nature is insured. Arguing like a mathematician for the elegance of simplicity, Scotus turns from the internal consideration of such a first principle to argue that, moreover, there is nothing about the multiple entities in the world which requires more than a single first principle for their explanation. And since multiple first principles are not necessary, it would be foolish to posit more than the single first cause which the explanation requires.

A multitude cannot be from itself; a first cause is required to explain such existence. A unitary and unique being requires no previous cause; it can explain multiple beings without itself requiring explanation. Explanation ends when simplicity is reached. In the essential orders an ascent is made toward unity and fewness. So, there is a stop in one cause. Such a first efficient cause is actual because it contains every possible actuality. No possible entities can be conceived of as being outside its nature. Thus it is perfect, as containing every possible goodness within itself.

Nothing shares perfectly unless it shares, not of necessity, but from the liberality of its nature. Such a consideration of what perfection means leads Duns Scotus on to consider the divine will. If such a first principle must share its being with other beings, due to its natural liberality, then "will" must have an important place in such a nature as essential to its perfection. Along with this necessary endowment of will, Scotus describes his God as being simple, infinite, and wise. Such essential simplicity excludes all possible composition in the divine nature. It is not a being made up of parts as other beings are. None of its perfections are really distinct from the others, although our language and the process of analysis force us to consider each perfection as if it were in some way separate and distinct.

Scotus repeats the phrase common in medieval theology: the First Nature does not fall under a genus. The First Principle is unique and not subject to description according to any ordinary classifications. Normal discussion proceeds by classifying but this principle alone fails to fit the pattern for normal relations or to fall under any of the standard categories. Opinion among metaphysicians is divided as to just how radical this difference is, as to just how inadequate our normal language might be. Scotus falls among those who feel that common terms may be used to describe God if they are properly qualified to fit the special situation.

It seems perfectly acceptable to Duns Scotus to say that the First Efficient is intelligent and endowed with will, although such assertions require special argument to support them and special qualifications to accept them. For instance, most intelligence looks to some end outside itself, but Scotus' First Efficient is made unique by being said not to love any end different from itself. Thus the traditional categories are used to describe such a First Principle, but they are qualified in a way that makes their application nevertheless unique. However, it is when Scotus turns to the question of contingency that he becomes his most radical and the most subject to innovations.

The First Cause causes contingently, Scotus asserts; consequently, it causes freely. The classical tradition had been united in making the creation of lesser orders in nature necessary and in viewing necessity often as the very hallmark of the perfection characteristic of a First Principle. Christian theologians in considering God and his creative activity had modified this somewhat, although necessity still seemed to be preferred. Scotus for the first time raises contingency to a central place in the divine nature and designates the creation of the natural order as a free act.

What is most important here is that Scotus sees that, if any freedom of action is to be preserved for man, some freedom of action must first be found to be possible in God. For if the First moves necessarily, every other cause is moved necessarily and everything is caused necessarily. The locus of the problem of freedom is not in human nature; it really revolves around an issue concerning God's initial action. If God's creative act is necessary, if he has no freedom of movement in originating the natural order, then it is hardly likely that men could move contingently or freely when even God cannot.

Now Scotus turns to the question of human will. If there is to be freedom in man's causal activity, then he must act contingently. If such contingent action is to be possible, God must first of all have been open to such possibilities in his initial creative act. But nothing, says Scotus, is a principle of contingent operation except will. And this is the source of Scotus' famed "voluntarism." Anything other than an action which is contingent upon the will is a necessary action, so that the possibility of allowing for contingency depends upon upholding a doctrine that gives a primary place to the will, both in men and in God. Contingency means that the act is dependent upon the will's direction. Any view which wishes to preserve at least some human actions as being free must begin with the divine nature and preserve will as an independent power within that nature. Will can give rise to contingent actions and opens a freedom to man, through the similarity discovered between the activity of man's will and God's.

Then Scotus carries the argument for contingency and the primacy of will one step further. There is something evil among us, and this, he feels, argues for the First Efficient's causing through contingency. If contingency (and thus the operation of will) is not present in his action, then every evil factor in nature becomes a necessity, and he becomes directly responsible for every evil act. A perfect First Principle, he argues, that operated necessarily would create a world lacking no perfection. Due to the presence of evil, our world is by no means such a perfect place. As a lesser world, our order must have been selected freely as something below the optimum possible. Reversing Leibniz, Duns Scotus argues from the fact that we do not live in the best of all possible worlds to prove that we can account for this deficiency only through contingent causation on the part of the First Efficient Cause. Necessity did not force him to create the best possible world; the operation of will allowed the contingent choice of a natural order containing some evil.

The First Principle wills nothing outside his nature of necessity; consequently neither does he cause any effect necessarily. There could be no contingency in any second cause in causing unless there were contingency in the First Principle in willing. The presence of evil demands that God be free either to will or not to will this less perfect order into existence. Thus his freedom in willing also allows us a similar freedom in willing and opens the way for contingent causation by men (second causes). Every effect in nature is contingent, because it depends upon the efficiency of the First Principle, whose efficiency is contingent.

Will becomes identical with the First Nature although no act of his understanding can be an accident for him. Thus, God's understanding of all things is necessary, but the action of his will in causing is not. Necessary cognition of everything whatsoever is a part of the divine nature, which means that God understands everything continually. Thus God must understand everything he wills, and this removes the possibility of a blind action by the divine will. With men, no such necessary understanding exists, so that with them ignorant action is always possible. God is unique in this respect.

No act or intellection in the First Principle is an accident. Men, on the other hand, come by a great deal of their information accidentally; the human act of will often depends either on accidental or incomplete information; with the divine will such is never the case. God's understanding is always perfect, whereas man's is not. Both, however, may cause contingently through an act of will. God's contingent volition is necessarily based on knowledge; man's is not.

Every intelligible concept was understood distinctly and of necessity by the First Principle prior to its existence within the natural order, and also prior to the natural order itself. Every possible state God now knows and always knew. The actual state of affairs in the natural order is subject to contingent volition, first by God and then by men. From this eternal understanding of every intelligible concept Scotus goes on to argue for the necessity of God's being infinite. The possible intelligible concepts are infinite and God must actually understand them all eternally and simultaneously. An intellect capable of such comprehension must itself be infinite and in turn must reside in a nature also actually infinite. God's infinity is claimed as a consequence of the infinity of possible objects of understanding and of his necessary grasp of them all. An intellect which is applicable to an infinity of objects must itself be altogether unlimited.

In a way which would seem strange to Plotinus, Duns Scotus ties simplicity and infinity together. If a being is infinite, then Scotus argues that its various aspects are not formally distinct. Since simplicity must be predicated of God as a primary perfection, Duns Scotus concludes that God must be infinite. Only an infinite principle seems to be free of the distinctions within its nature which cause disruptive multiplicity. A finite entity is subject to division whereas one characterized by infinity holds all of its attributes together in an essential unity. Scotus' argument at this point is both interesting and unusual.

If such arguments appear subject to many objections, it must be remembered that what is most characteristic of Scotus' *Tract* is a certain tentativeness about his reasoning. The spirit which seems to pervade it is that of a speculative intellect testing interesting forms of argument. Scotus is serious about his topic, but the reader nowhere gets the feeling that he expects it necessarily to compel anyone else. His reasoning is more suggestive than logically foolproof. Not every sentence is equally essential to the reasoning, but during the course of it all Scotus obviously thinks that some important things have been discovered and announced. It is hoped that the reader will similarly share his moments of insight.

How can we understand the infinite? Scotus answers that it is through the finite, for the infinite can be defined only through the use of the finite. The meaning of the infinite is grasped negatively, as that which exceeds any given finite limit. Since finiteness itself does not belong essentially to the meaning of being, the natural intellect can easily come to see that "being" may be classified as either finite or infinite. This means that the human intellect apprehends being in general as neither finite nor infinite and then goes on to see whether the particular being it is dealing with is or is not actually finite (subject to limits) or whether it is to be understood negatively as exceeding all finite limits. Such a doctrine allows a much more direct and natural understanding of the divine nature than is usual among theologians.

What is infinite can also be a being, although other beings are finite. The natural intellect finds nothing repugnant or difficult about understanding the concept of an infinite being. On the contrary, "infinite being" seems to be the most perfectly intelligible concept. This is the beginning of the newfound ease of the modern metaphysician in dealing with the infinite, which is an almost complete reversal of the classical fear of the infinite as being an unintelligible object. Traditionally, the human intellect seemed specifically adapted to finite objects; now, as Scotus begins the modern era, infinity becomes the hallmark of perfect intelligibility and is easily grasped.

The argument for the intelligibility of infinity for the human understanding again comes from the will. When we examine our human will, what we see as most characteristic about it is that it is never satisfied by any finite object. It is always restless, always seeking something greater than any finite end. After understanding this, our intellect can then pass on to understand what infinity means: a lack of any specifiable limit or end. In comprehending the phenomenon of will, our intellect grasps what infinity connotes, and recognizes the ease with which it grasps the concept of infinity. The stress upon will makes infinity an easy and a natural concept.

God has the power to actualize all possible states simultaneously, but he does not choose to do so. Some states mutually exclude one another at any given moment, and other possibilities his will does not choose to actualize. If all possible states existed simultaneously, our world would be absolutely unlimited. Scotus believes the natural order to be finite, its limits representing the original self-restraint of the divine will in creating.

Thus Scotus' First Principle comes to have some of the attributes (will, contingent choice, freedom) which we usually associate with human activity; although in other respects (power, unlimited knowledge, infinity) it belongs to no natural genus. Here is a view which, in certain respects, makes the First Principle very much like man and in other respects distinguishes it radically. Yet more important than this is the overall modernity of Scotus' thought. "Freedom" and "will" predominate in these considerations, and a tentative quality pervades the argument as a whole. The metaphysical framework of most medieval theology is basically classical. Duns Scotus represents, not so much the decline of medieval theology as the beginning of a modern metaphysical spirit, much of which remains as yet essentially unexplored.—*F.S.*

PERTINENT LITERATURE
Wolter, Allan B., ed. and tr. "Introduction," in John Duns Scotus' *A Treatise on God as First Principle*. Chicago: Forum Books, 1966.

Allan B. Wolter reports that John Duns Scotus' *Tract* is referred to as Scotus, by several of his immediate disciples and auditors and cross-referenced in other works recognized as his; four manuscripts of the work go back to the early fourteenth century; so, he concludes, the work is by Scotus. Further, he maintains, comparison with the doctrine of other works by Scotus confirms what the external evidence tells us: in fact, the substance of the doctrine of the *Tract* is taken from Scotus' *Ordinatio*. This doctrine concerns the existence and unicity of an Infinite Being.

Wolter indicates that Scotus seems to have sketched the outlines of the *Tract* and then to have left it to assistants to fill in the outline from indicated passages from the *Ordinatio*—in three portions of which about half of the *Tract* can be found verbatim. Given various textual comparisons, he continues, it seems that the *Tract* is late among Scotus' works—perhaps the latest. The *Tract*, Wolter declares, is perhaps the most thorough attempt by a Schoolman to prove that God exists while staying (very nearly) within the theory of demonstration that Aristotle expressed in his *Posterior Analytics*.

Wolter notes that Scotus accepts Aristotle's definition of demonstration: "a syllogism productive of scientific knowledge." Such knowledge must be certain (not mere opinion), necessary (not contingent), and inferred from evident necessary truths. That scientific knowledge must be necessary (that the sentence expressing such knowledge must express a necessary truth), Wolter adds, causes trouble for a Christian theologian or philosopher. If one accepts at least some forms of determinism (for example, Avicenna's) one can claim that there is a First or Uncaused Cause which Itself has necessary existence and by which everything else that exists is necessarily (proximately, or else ultimately) caused. Wolter explains that the necessary role of empirical data in discovering causal connections will be due to a lack of knowledge of the necessary relations between members of a causal chain which begins with the First Cause. (Correspondingly, belief in one's freedom of choice will be due to one's ignorance of the causes of one's choices.)

Wolter reminds us of Avicenna's remark that those who deny that there are any evident necessary truths should be burned until they grant that there is an evident necessary truth to the effect that not burning is distinct from burning. Analogously, Scotus says, those who hold that whatever occurs occurs necessarily, should be tormented until they grant that their being tormented is not a necessary occurrence. Thus, Wolter continues, Scotus takes it to be evident that what occurs might not have occurred, and so occurs contingently, and that the choices of agents need not have been made as they were made, and are made freely. Wolter adds that, according to Scotus, any actual event or choice, then, is contingent; it could have failed to exist. Hence the sentence which says it is actual, although it will express a truth, will not express a necessary truth. So for Scotus it cannot appear in a demonstration. Must, then, anyone who thinks that there are contingent occurrences swear off offering demonstrations?

According to Wolter, Scotus thinks not. It is a necessary and evident truth that if it is true that *A* occurred, then it is possible that *A* occur, no matter what *A* may be—the eruption of a volcano, or God creating the world, or whatever. Wolter explains that the rules of demonstrations allowed the move from, say, (1) *Scotus exists*, something known independently of any demonstration and which is not to be a premise in the demonstration one is about to construct, to (2) *It is possible that Scotus exists*, which may be a premise in the demonstration one is about to construct. The inference is "immediate" (does not require a syllogism or a chain of reasoning) and the result—namely, (2)—is a necessary truth. Nor does the truth of (2) depend on the truth of (1); even if Scotus never existed, it is possible that he would. And what makes (2) *It is possible that Scotus exists* true (or the absence of which would render it false) is different from what makes *Scotus exists* true (or absence of which will render it false). Scotus' interest in his own particular arguments for God's existence, according to Wolter, is in what makes it true that it is possible that Scotus exists.

Wolter says that one task of metaphysics, in Scotus' view, is to show that God is the being on whom all others depend without himself depending on anything. He notes that a crucial premise in his argument for this conclusion depends on the claim that a certain sort of infinite regress is impossible. Scotus distinguishes between an essentially ordered causal series and a causal series that is not so ordered. An essentially ordered causal series is one in which a set of elements coexist in order to produce and conserve an effect. Wolter offers the sequence grandparent-parent-child as an example of a series that is not essentially ordered; and he adds that the Neoplatonic sequence of beings, each lower on the chain of being than its cause, starting with a Deity and ending with the material universe, if it existed, would be an example of an essentially ordered series. Wolter emphasizes Scotus' claim that it is in essentially ordered series that an infinite regress is impossible.

Weinberg, Julius R. *A Short History of Medieval Philosophy*. Princeton, New Jersey: Princeton University Press, 1964.

Julius R. Weinberg reports that, working in the tradition of St. Anselm and St. Bonaventure, John Duns Scotus believes that he can prove conclusions about what actually exists from premises about what is possible. Scotus believes, Weinberg adds, that he does not need to deny that all concepts are obtained from sensory experience, even though any sensory experience may give rise to mistaken beliefs; for one can discover the truth of statements which depend on the connections between concepts, however one may have come to possess them.

Weinberg reminds us that the Medievals regarded such terms as "being," "one," "good," "true," and so on, as transcendental; they are not restricted in their proper application to things that fall under one of Aristotle's categories. (The categories are: substance, quantity, quality, relation, place, date, posture, possession, action, and passivity.) He adds that *being* is one such term, and so, for Scotus, is any other term which applies to being indifferently, whether being is finite or infinite.

Scotus accepts, Weinberg tells us, four classes of transcendentals: those commonly applicable to God and creature (for example, *wisdom*), those he regarded as convertible with *being* (for example, *one*), those which express important disjunctive attributes of being (*finite or infinite, substance or accident, necessary or contingent*), and those expressing perfections, some of which are attributable only to God (*omnipotence, omniscience*), while others may be attributed to God and some creatures (*wisdom, knowledge, freedom*).

According to Weinberg, Scotus argues that we have a concept of being which applies to whatever is; for we can be in doubt that whether whatever is, is either finite or infinite, and so we must have a concept of being which does not include its being finite or its being infinite (and so on for the other transcendentals other than *being*). For Scotus, the concept of being applies to anything the assumption of whose existence is not a contradiction. Further, he holds that it is being, not God, which is the object of metaphysical inquiry. Were God the object of metaphysics, Weinberg explains, then the only proof of God's existence, according to Scotus, would be the one (like Aristotle's) which begins with the observation of motion and ends with God as an unmoved Mover. Since for Scotus a science does not prove, but begins with, its principles, one can begin with *being* and argue to God's existence, provided only that it is being and not God that is the object of metaphysics.

For Scotus, Weinberg notes, some things differ from one another really and numerically; one flower differs really and numerically from another in that it involves no contradiction that either exists without the other. Other things differ only rationally; when one considers a thing in diverse ways, each of which fits the thing being considered, although it is not logically impossible that one way might have fit and the other not, there is a rational distinction among the ways of considering, but not a corresponding multiplicity to that which is being considered. Besides *real* distinction and *rational* distinction, Weinberg indicates, Scotus discusses *formal* distinction. If one can think of something in one way without also thinking of it in another, although it is logically impossible that the thing be the one way and not the other (and conversely), then, Weinberg notes, for Scotus there is but a formal distinction between the item's being one way and its being the other. One can consider the *closed-three-sidedness* of a Euclidean triangle, or its *closed-three-angled-ness*, without considering the other; so these are formally distinct. But the triangle cannot be one without being also the other; so this distinction is not more than formal.

Weinberg adds that in Scotus' view, in the world there are individuals which belong to the same species. Two horses, for example, are both equine. For Scotus, each differs from the other, not by virtue of containing different matter, but by having an individual nature in addition to the equine nature that they share. Further, Weinberg indicates, Scotus holds that the essence of a thing and the existence of a thing are formally (and not really) distinct, even though it is logically possible that the thing not exist. The existence of a horse, he holds, is not really different from its essence. A particular horse cannot exist without being equine, or be equine without existing; its essence and its existence are hence only formally distinct. But, as Weinberg says, reporting Scotus' views, it does not follow from this that the horse exists with logical necessity—that its nonexistence would involve a contradiction.

According to Weinberg, Scotus teaches that we can know with certainty that something (for example, ourselves) has being and is contingent, or might not have existed. Hence, he contends, something is effectible, or capable of being caused. So, he reasons, something is effectible by itself, or by nothing, or by another thing. But it is logically impossible that anything be caused by itself, or by nothing at all. From the foregoing, it follows that something must be caused by another. Hence something is effective, or capable of causing, for if something *is* caused by another, it must *be possible that* it be caused by another, and so it must be possible that another be capable of causing it.

Now, according to Scotus, either this being is effective without being effectible, in which case there is an actual uneffectible being, and thus its being possible for there to be such a being, or else it is both effective and effectible. If the latter, since there cannot be an infinite regress of beings which are effective only by virtue of being affected by something else, some other being must actually be effective without being effectible, and hence it is possible that there be something which is effective without being effectible—something which is *capable of causing* without *being capable of being caused*.

If something is capable of causing but is not capable of being caused, then it can be said to exist by virtue of itself, or as uncaused. And it is a necessary truth that if something *does* not exist by virtue of itself, it *cannot* exist by virtue of itself, or as uncaused. Thus we can argue: (1) If nothing exists uncaused, nothing can exist uncaused. (2) Something can exist uncaused. Hence: (3) Something does exist uncaused. Weinberg explains that Scotus' intent is to have proved (2) by the sort of argument just discussed, and to rely on (1) being an evident necessary truth. (3), he adds, follows validly from (1) and (2).

Scotus, Weinberg notes, is also concerned with the nature of God. He reasons, Weinberg tells us, that God, as uncaused, must be simple or non-composite. But theology ascribes omnipotence, omniscience, and omnibe-nevolence to God, and these seem to be different attributes. Scotus' explanation of how a noncomposite Deity can have such attributes, Weinberg informs us, is that the attributes are not really distinct, or distinct by a distinction of reason, but are only formally distinct in the sense explained above.—*K.E.Y.*

ADDITIONAL RECOMMENDED READING

Bettoni, Efrem, O. F. M. *Duns Scotus: The Basic Principles of His Philosophy*. Edited and translated by B. Bonansea. Washington, D.C.: Catholic University of America Press, 1961. An introduction to Scotus' thought from the perspective of the Catholic philosophy and faith.

Gilson, Étienne. *The Spirit of Medieval Philosophy*. London: Sheed and Ward, 1936. Gilson's Gifford lectures; an illuminating commentary.

Grajewski, M. J., O. F. M. *The Formal Distinction of Duns Scotus*. Washington, D.C.: Catholic University of America Press, 1944. A clear discussion of an important technical theme in Scotus.

Micklem, N. *Reason and Revelation: A Question from Duns Scotus*. Edinburgh: Nelson, 1953. A discussion of the relation of Scotus' thought to a perennial problem.

Ross, James F. *Philosophical Theology*. Indianapolis: Bobbs-Merrill, 1969. A recent attempt to restate a natural theology using a contemporary terminology and method.

Wolter, Allan B., O. F. M. *The Transcendentals and Their Function in the Metaphysics of Duns Scotus*. Washington, D.C.: Catholic University of America Press, 1946. A discussion of Scotus' thought concerning *being*, *good*, *true*, and *one*.

WILLIAM OF OCKHAM: SELECTIONS

Author: William of Ockham (c. 1280-c. 1350)
Type of work: Logic, epistemology
First transcribed: Early fourteenth century (Selections from his writings)

PRINCIPAL IDEAS ADVANCED

All abstractive cognitions (knowledge derived from experience, made possible by reflection upon experience) depend upon prior intuitive cognitions (sense experience of things).

Our knowledge of the existing world is contingent upon God's will, for he can affect our intuitive cognitions whatever the facts may be.

Predication occurs only if the predicate term of a sentence refers to the object referred to by the subject term, and if the predicate term refers to the object not by naming it, but by referring to some feature of it.

Universals are not single properties common to many things, but signs which have application to a number of things.

An explanation involving fewer assumptions than an alternative explanation is preferable to the alternative. [Ockham's "razor."]

William of Ockham was born at Ockham, Surrey, became a Franciscan, attended Oxford, and taught there for several years until he was summoned to the papal court at Avignon to answer charges of heresy arising from his writings and teaching. He was not formally condemned, but during his stay in France he became embroiled in a controversy that split his order into bitter factions, a controversy over the ideal of poverty espoused by its founder, St. Francis. After strenuously opposing both the Pope and the majority of his order on this issue, he and several others found it expedient to flee to the court of the Emperor of Germany, who had just installed an anti-Pope and who was glad to accept their assistance in his battle with the Pope. Excommunicated by the Pope and his own order, Ockham lived in Munich until his death. In his last years he was trying to reconcile himself with his order, but apparently he died before he was successful. Ockham wrote a great deal, but very little of it is available to the reader of English. Such a reader is limited to several books of selections: *Ockham: Philosophical Writings*, by P. Boehner; *Ockham: Studies and Selections*, by S. C. Tornay; *Selections from Medieval Philosophers*, by R. McKeon; and T. B. Birch's translation of *De sacremento altaris*.

Ockham is known for his famous "razor," for his logic, and for his nominalistic and empirical viewpoint. Living in the fourteenth century, he was the dominant figure in the movement away from Albertus Magnus, Thomas Aquinas, and John Duns Scotus, the great system builders of the thirteenth century. He was the inspirer of an empirically and nominalistically inclined movement that contended with the Thomistic, Albertist, Scotist, and Averroistic schools of the next several centuries. Although he has been called the Hume of the Middle Ages, Ockham was not a skeptic. Negatively, he undermined and rejected most of the metaphysics and a good deal of the natural theology of his contemporaries, but positively, he was a theologian who accepted the traditional Christian dogmas on faith and who preferred to accept them on faith alone rather than to argue for them on dubious philosophic grounds.

His basic inclination toward empiricism is revealed in the distinction between intuitive and abstractive cognitions. When we are looking at Socrates, he says, we can see that he is white. In this case we are aware of the existence of Socrates, of the occurrence of the quality, and of the fact that this individual, Socrates, is white. That is, the senses enable us to know with certainty a contingent fact about the world. This is an instance of what Ockham calls *intuitive cognition*. But we can think of Socrates when he is not present, and of white when we are not seeing it, and we can think of Socrates as being white. In this case we are cognizing the same things, Socrates and white, and we are entertaining the same proposition, but we do not know that Socrates still exists or that the proposition is true. This is an instance of what Ockham calls *abstractive cognition*, abstractive not because the terms are abstract, but because we have abstracted from existence.

The terms of the intuitive cognition are sensed and are particular, while the terms of the abstractive cognition are not sensed and are common. In intuitive cognition the cognition is caused in us by action of the object on our sensory and intellectual faculties, a process that culminates naturally, without any initiative on our part, in the knowledge that Socrates is white. No judgment, at least no explicit one, is involved here, for we simply see that Socrates is white. On the other hand, in abstractive cognition the cognition is not caused by the object, for either the object is absent or, if present, it is not sufficiently close to produce a clear sensation. Under such circumstances we scrutinize the data given by memory or sensation and, perhaps, go on deliberately to judge or refrain from judging that something is the case.

In abstractive cognition an apparently simple idea, such as the concept "Socrates," must be understood as a complex of common terms, for neither Socrates nor any other individual is operating on us to produce the cognition of him. In such a cognition we are entertaining such common terms as "intelligent," "snubnosed," "white," and "Athenian" which, when taken together, constitute a complex abstractive term limiting our attention to the one desired individual.

By contrast, in intuitive cognition we apprehend Socrates in a different manner, for in this case the object itself is producing in us a simple noncomplex idea of itself. Indeed, we obtain the terms appearing in abstractive cognitions only by attending to and separating in thought the various features of the sensation. Thus, Ockham concludes, all abstractive cognitions depend upon prior intuitive ones, and intuitive cognition must be the source of all our knowledge about the world. Furthermore, Ockham says that we intuit or sense nothing but individual things, and these are either sensible substances such as Socrates, or sensible properties such as the sensed whiteness of Socrates. Even relations are regarded as properties of groups of individuals.

When we add to all these considerations Ockham's famous "razor"—"What can be explained by the assumption of fewer things is vainly explained by the assumption of more things"—his nominalistic and empiricistic views follow immediately, for now we have an epistemology that not only makes us start with the senses but also prevents us from going very far beyond them. The senses reveal to us a multitude of sensible individuals and provide us with a great deal of information about them and about their temporal and spatial settings, but they do not reveal any necessary connections, causal or otherwise—and the razor prevents us from assuming any. This epistemology obviously limits the scope of metaphysics but does not quite eliminate it, for the metaphysician can still tell us a little about God. Given the terms "being," "cause," and "first," all of which are derived from experience, and assuming that they are univocal terms, as Ockham does, we can form the complex idea of a being who is a first cause. Furthermore, given intellectually self-evident principles such as "Every thing has a cause," we can demonstrate the existence of a first cause that exists necessarily and which, as the most perfect existent, has intellect and will. However, we cannot prove that there is only one such God or that there might not have been a greater God, and we cannot demonstrate that he has the various features required by Christian dogma.

The sort of world suggested by Ockham's epistemology is also required by his theology. Like Scotus before him and Descartes after him, Ockham emphasizes God's will rather than his intellect. God can do nothing that is contradictory, but this fact does not limit his will, for his ideas are not of his essence and are not exemplars between which he must choose. They are his creatures and the world is whatever he has cared to make it. Consequently, the world does not exist necessarily, and within this world nothing follows necessarily from anything else and nothing requires the existence of anything else. This radical contingency stems from God's complete power over the circumstances in which things shall or shall not come into existence. God ordinarily uses instruments to produce in us the experiences we have, but he could, if he wished, dispense with them and operate on us directly. For instance, Ockham says, it would require a miracle but God could make us see a star even where there actually is no star. That is, we could have exactly the same cognition that is normally caused in us by the star even if there were no star or any other physical cause. Since the seeing of the star is one distinct event and the star itself is another, it is not impossible that either should exist independently of the other.

The possibility of cognition without a corresponding fact reveals a limitation of intuitive cognition, for even though such a cognition makes us certain that something is the case, we could nevertheless be mistaken. Ockham skirts around the threat of skepticism by remarking that although an error of this sort can occur if God interferes with the natural order, miracles are rare. Consequently, the probability of error is insignificantly low. Yet, he acknowledges, it is still the case that our knowledge of the existing world is contingent upon God's will.

There is a remarkable agreement between Descartes and Ockham concerning the contingency of our knowledge. Because Descartes held a more extreme doctrine about the power of God, he took skepticism more seriously, but, of course, he believed he could escape by using reason. On the other hand, Ockham regarded the risk of empiricism as slight and claimed that it is better to exercise a little faith than to accept the grave risks of rationalism.

In his writings, Ockham, who was probably the best of medieval logicians, commences his discussion of logic by considering the nature of terms. First, he distinguishes between written, spoken, and conceptual terms. The latter are mental contents that function as private signs of things. Since these mental signs are not deliberately produced by us, but come about naturally through the operation of the object on us, they are called *natural signs*. Since spoken signs, on the other hand, are sounds which have been conventionally attached to particular mental signs, they are *conventional signs*. They denote the same object as the associated concept, thus enabling us to communicate what would otherwise be private. Written signs have a similar relation to spoken signs. Ordinarily, when Ockham speaks of terms he has in mind such terms as "man," "animal," "whiteness," and "white," which signify or denote things and which can function as the subject or predicate of a proposition. These terms, which he calls *categorematic* terms, are to be contrasted with *snycategorematic* terms such as "every," "insofar as," and "some," which do not denote anything when they stand by themselves. He also distinguishes between concrete terms such as "white" and abstract terms such as "whiteness," and between discrete terms such as "Socrates" and common terms such as "man."

A more important distinction is that between absolute terms and connotative terms. An *absolute term* is one that denotes directly, whereas a *connotative term* is one that denotes one thing only by connoting another. "Socrates," "man," and "whiteness" are absolute terms for they are used to point to, respectively, a specific individual, any one of a number of similar individuals, or to a property. A connotative term such as "white" is not used as a label, for there is no such thing as white. When it is used in a proposition such as "Socrates is white," it denotes the same object as does the subject term, but it does so by connoting a property of the object; namely, whiteness. The distinction can be formulated in another way. At least some absolute terms, such as "man," have real definitions in which each term, such as "rational" and "animal," can denote the same objects as the defined term. Connotative terms have only nominal definitions, for the definition will require a term in the oblique case that cannot denote the same object as does the defined term. Thus "white" may be defined as "that which has the property whiteness," but "whiteness" does not denote the white thing. In certain definitions connotative terms may occur, but these can always be defined in turn until we reach definitions that contain absolute terms only. That is, language is grounded in terms that denote only, and cognition is basically a matter of being aware of objects and features of objects by intuitive cognition.

This distinction also brings us back to Ockham's epistemology by indicating the way in which a proposition is related to the world. Since there are only particulars in the world, each term of a true proposition, such as "Socrates is white," can refer only to one or more individuals. Such a proposition does not assert that two different things are identical, nor that the subject and predicate are one and the same thing, nor that something inheres in or is part of the subject. In our example, "white" is not another name for Socrates, it is not the name of another individual, and it is not the name of the property *whiteness*; but it must denote something. It can only denote Socrates, but not, of course, as "Socrates" does. That is, it denotes him indirectly by connoting his whiteness. Predication occurs only if (1) the predicate term denotes the very same object as the subject term, and (2) the predicate term denotes the object not by naming it but by connoting some feature of it.

In the above discussion we have mentioned abstract terms such as "whiteness" that are absolute and that denote properties rather than substances. Lest it seem that Ockham was a realist after all, we must turn to his discussion of universals. He denies emphatically that there are universals of either Platonic or Aristotelian varieties, for both doctrines require that something simple be common to many things. This state of affairs, he says, is impossible unless that simple something be plural, a condition which itself is impossible. Furthermore, he says, the problem should be turned around, for since the world is composed of particulars only, the problem is not the way in which some universal thing becomes particularized, but our reason for attributing universality to anything in the first place. The only thing to which we can attribute it is a sign, and even here only by virtue of its function as a sign, for as a mere existent it is as particular as anything else. Thus a universal is a sign or concept that has application to a number of things.

The nature of this universal concept, or common term, can be understood better by considering what it is and how it is produced. First, as a result of intuitive cognition there occurs in sensation, and then in memory, sensations or images that function as natural signs of the individual objects that cause them. Now, through the medium of these images the intellect notices the similarity of the objects so signified and notes that there could be still other entities similar to them. In noting these similarities it produces naturally another entity that resembles the particulars in such a manner that it might very well be used as an exemplar for the construction of similar things. Ockham is not clear about the nature of this new entity, but he says that it is produced by ignoring the differences between the similar particulars. The new sign, or universal, is an indeterminate image that could represent any of the determinate particulars that fall under it. But whatever it is, since it is a natural rather than a conventional sign, this resemblance has come into being as a sign that denotes indifferently any of the particulars it resembles. Ockham says this entity is a fiction only, for since it is not a particular sign produced in us by a particular object, it has no literal counterpart in the world. In Ockham's terms, if we say "Man is a universal," and insist that we are saying something is common to many things, then in this proposition the concept "man" refers to itself (it has "simple *supposition*") and not to men (it does not have "personal *supposition*"), and the concept "universal" is of the second intention (it refers to a mental sign) rather than of the first intention (it does not refer to something other than a sign). That is, the universal "man" is only a concept that can be applied to many things; in the world there are only men.

It is to be noted that Ockham is not a nominalist of the Berkeleian-Humean sort, for his general ideas are not particulars standing for other particulars. Perhaps it would be more accurate to say that he holds to a kind of conceptualism. It is to be noted also that later in his life he applied his razor to his own doctrine to eliminate the fictitious entity we have just described, for he then argued that since the act that produces the generalized picture must be able to generalize without the assistance of such a picture, such pictures must be superfluous. In the end, then, universals turn out to be acts of the intellect; the other features of his earlier doctrine are retained.

Finally, it is to be noted that though they have different grammatical functions, concrete substantives and their abstract counterparts (such as "man" and "manness") denote exactly the same things (men). Nonsubstantive qualitative terms such as "white" denote indifferently individuals such as Socrates and this piece of paper; and their abstract counterparts, such as "whiteness," denote indifferently similar features of individuals, such as a certain sensible feature of Socrates and a similar sensible feature of this piece of paper. In these ways all common terms, whether they be concrete or abstract, denote particulars and particulars only.

Ockham discusses terms in greater detail than this summary statement suggests, and he goes on to discuss propositions and arguments. He was concerned primarily with formal syllogistic reasoning, but he did make a number of observations which impinge on the areas we know in symbolic logic as the propositional calculus and modal logic. Among other things he discussed the truth conditions of conjunctive and disjunctive propositions, reduced "neither-nor" to "and" and "not," discussed valid arguments of the form "p and q, therefore p," "p, therefore p or q," and "p or q, not p, therefore q," pointed out the related fallacies, and stated Augustus De Morgan's laws explicitly. At the end of his treatment of inference he discussed some very general nonformal rules of inference. Assuming in appropriate cases that we are speaking about a valid argument, they are as follows: (1) if the antecedent is true the conclusion cannot be false; (2) the premises may be true and the conclusion false; (3) the contradictory of the conclusion implies the contradictory of the premise or conjunction of premises; (4) whatever is implied by the conclusion is implied by the premises; (5) whatever implies the premises implies the conclusion; (6) whatever is consistent with the premises is consistent with the conclusion; (7) whatever is inconsistent with the conclusion is inconsistent with the premises; (8) a contingent proposition cannot follow from a necessary one; (9) a contingent proposition cannot imply a contradiction; (10) any proposition follows from a contradiction; and (11) a necessary proposition follows from any proposition. He illustrated the last two with these examples: "You (a man) are a donkey, therefore you are God," and assuming God is necessarily triune, "You are white, therefore God is triune." Ockham concluded his discussion by saying that since these rules are not formal they should be used sparingly.—*L.M.*

PERTINENT LITERATURE

Weinberg, Julius R. *Ockham, Descartes, and Hume: Self-knowledge, Substance, and Causality.* Madison: University of Wisconsin Press, 1977.

Representative realism posits ideas which interpose between our consciousness and its objects of awareness, insofar as these objects are physical. Julius R. Weinberg notes that many experiences were appealed to in order to show the necessity of positing ideas; in particular Peter Aureoli (d. 1322) listed several, and William of Ockham responded to the arguments based on appeal to them.

In a long summary statement, Weinberg informs us that the experiences appealed to were these: (1) When a person is riding in a boat on a river, the river and trees sometimes appear to be moved; (2) when an ignited stick is rapidly moved in a circular manner, a circle appears to the observer; (3) a half-submerged stick appears to be broken; (4) if we press against one eye while looking at a candle, there appear to be two candles; (5) there appear to be a multitude of colors on the neck of a pigeon; (6) virtual images produced by concave and convex mirrors sometimes appear to be behind the mirror and sometimes to be between the mirror and the observer; (7) a person who stares at the sun and then looks away sees spots which soon vanish; (8) if one looks at something red or something latticed and then reads a book, one then sees the letters on the pages as red, or as latticed. That there are such experiences, Weinberg points out, may be taken as common ground by opponents in the dispute over whether there are "ideas" in the sense not of "thoughts," but of intracognitive items which are intermediaries between perceiving minds and perceiving objects. The question, he adds, concerns how one accounts for, analyzes, and explains the experiences in question. Weinberg reports that Aureoli, arguing for positing ideas, claims that: (1) the trees and bark do not move, and the eyes do not perceive themselves, although they perceive something that moves but is not the trees or bark; (2) the circle is not in the stick, the air, or the eyes; it must be something (since it is seen) but is not in physical space; (3), and also (5), are cases of "seeing" things which must be something or other (we see the bentness, and the colors) but are not properties of the physical objects (the stick, the pigeon's neck) that we see; (4) we "see" two candles where there is only one, so the second candle must be in "intentional" being—it must be an idea; (6) the mirror images are not physical objects in physical space, but we experience them, so they must be "intentional" or "apparent" beings; regarding (7) and (8), physical objects do not appear and then vanish as do the spots and lattices, and we do "see" them.

The gist of the argument, then, is clear enough from Weinberg's exposition. We "see" things which are not actual physical objects or properties or states of physical objects. These things are not in physical space. But we can refer to them, describe them, and specify conditions under which others will see things just like those that we see. So there are such things—things which exist and are nonphysical and have "intentional" or "apparent" being. (That they are intermediaries between us and physical objects is another, apparently very natural, step; but it will not be a plausible step unless the argument for positing intentional beings, as developed so far, is successful.)

According to Weinberg, Ockham denies that such experiences as these do justify one in claiming that there are intentional or apparent intermediaries between perceiving minds and perceived physical objects. His account of Ockham includes the following reasoning: everyone agrees that perceptual judgments, sometimes mistaken ones, are made. Consider, then, the first experience. The trees are seen successively on the bank as one moves along in the boat. They are not seen to move, since they do not. There is nothing the motion of which is observed. Trees on a bank, observed under the described conditions, can make one mistakenly judge that the trees are moving. Perceiving stationary trees under the described conditions elicits a response in the sensory organisms much like that elicited by actually moving trees. Thus one may be caused to judge, falsely, that the trees on the bank are traveling. The circle of fire case is treated analogously, as are the straight stick looking bent and the one candle appearing as two, and so on through the others, except that Ockham held the colors actually to be on the neck of the pigeon.

It comes down to this: when there is only one candle and there appear to be two because we press one eye, pressing the eye stimulates it (or the sensory mechanism as a whole) in much the way that it would be stimulated by two candles. Under these circumstances, one may, although one need not, judge that two candles are present. And similarly for other cases of its appearing that something is there which is not, or its appearing that some fact has a property which it lacks.

The main objection, then, that Weinberg finds Ockham offering to the positing of ideas as intermediaries between perceiving minds and perceived objects is that one need not posit them in order to describe, analyze, and explain the experiences which allegedly involve them. Both parties to the dispute, Weinberg notes, admit that perceptual judgments are made, sometimes erroneously. He adds that the judgments—in the experiences cited, erroneous ones—explain (in the context of sensory organs being stimulated by external objects) what needs explanation. To posit, in addition, intentional or apparent intermediaries, Weinberg reports Ockham as contending, posits entities beyond what is necessary to explain what calls for explanation. Hence, Weinberg explains, they may be shaved from our theory by "Ockham's razor."

Moody, Ernest A. "Empiricism and Metaphysics in Medieval Philosophy," in *The Philosophical Review*. LXVII, no. 2 (April, 1958), pp. 145-163.

Ernest A. Moody recounts that the late thirteenth and early fourteenth centuries witnessed a decline of metaphysics and a rise of empiricism. He reports that historians of the period tend to speak of this period as a time of intellectual disintegration, and the assumption behind this evaluation is that the rationale of medieval philosophy is the provision of a metaphysical jus-tification for Christianity. After all, most major thinkers were professional theologians. Thus, he suggests, when an empiricist criterion of knowledge is developed on which one cannot develop the sort of connections between knowledge and faith present in the metaphysical systems of the earlier Middle Ages, the analysis is that an intellectual breakdown has occurred. The major figure of the rise of empiricism, and so of the "breakdown," Moody reminds us, was William of Ockham.

In fact, however, the empiricists, according to Moody, were themselves participants in theological teaching and debate, and their empiricism was itself theologically motivated. Moody says that the philosophy of René Descartes and John Locke in the seventeenth century was in fact radically different from that of the Greeks; and the influence of Christianity and the work of medieval theologians in between were significant in bringing about this change. But why this influence brought about fourteenth century empiricism, he says, requires explanation. He holds that this explanation should conform to the fact that in theology, logic, mathematics, physics, and political theory, there was great activity in the fourteenth century.

Moody suggests that four terms require definition before providing the explanation: (1) *theology* is "the systematization and elaboration of the beliefs constitutive of religious faith"; (2) *philosophy* is "a type of inquiry which seeks to develop a body of general statements whose claim to acceptance is based on no other ground than the kind of evidence that is open to public corroboration by all men through their natural cognitive powers"; (3) *metaphysics* will include "any theory concerning the existent as such"; and (4) "empiricism" is "a theory of method in the aquisition and evaluation of knowledge."

With these definitions in mind, and particularly since some of the scholastics did criticize metaphysics, Moody maintains that it is appropriate to ask whether it was uniformly the aim of scholasticism to develop a metaphysical support for theological positions. Christianity, he says, offered doctrines concerning a supersensory realm based on the authority of revelation, not as one philosophy among many philosophies all of which appealed to the same data. The dominant philosophy, he reports, was Neoplatonism, to which the Church was hostile on the whole, and which played little role in even Saint Augustine's Christian scheme of education. From the sixth through the twelfth century, Moody tells us, the Western Church had no rivals against which to defend its doctrines, and what occurred within it in terms of speculative thinking was theological in nature. Philosophy reentered in the twelfth century by way of the Arabs, with pagan philosophers translated into Latin. The Church did not welcome the reentry. The concern of theologians with philosophy, Moody indicates, was limited to viewing it as partly a threat to the faith and partly a source of ideas and arguments adaptable to theological uses. One line of defense against philosophy was to set up an impossible divide between the two, with philosophy and theology having each its own purposes, methods, evidences, and intellectual terrain. Another was a critique of the nature and scope of human knowledge intended to show that theological claims could be neither established nor refuted by philosophical arguments. (These, of course, are not incompatible tactics.)

Moody emphasizes that Ockham did not invent empiricism; what he did was to provide a technique of logical analysis which allowed him to state empiricism with a new force and clarity. Hitherto, psychological description was the empiricist method; Ockham replaces psychological description with logical analysis.

One doctrine Ockham propounded, Moody remarks, was that necessary truths are formal, and existential truths are contingent. If a statement expresses a necessary truth, then it is a statement of what can be the case, not of what is the case; its truth does not entail the existence of any actual item. If a statement is existential, entailing the existence of some actual item, then it is logically contingent; it can be denied without the denier involving himself in any contradictions.

Another of Ockham's doctrines, according to Moody, was that we cannot properly construct inferences whose premises are confirmed by experience and whose conclusions do not concern anything that can be experienced. We cannot, for example, infer from the observed order of nature the existence of an unobserved and unobservable Author of natural order. Nor can we infer from the existence of an observable item—a star or a tree—the existence of an unobserved and unobservable Uncaused Cause of that item. Moody notes that, for Ockham, one cannot even infer the existence of our own souls. Hence, Moody declares, Ockham rejects metaphysics insofar as this involves accepting a realm of unobserved and unobservable beings on the basis of inference from the observable properties of observable items (plus some principles which provide the rails of inference).

Further, Moody indicates that Ockham offered a powerful critique of the doctrine that our knowledge of external objects is mediated by internal objects, called "ideas," which the external objects cause in us. George Berkeley and David Hume, four centuries later, were to offer very similar arguments. The doctrine that such ideas are needed is called "representative realism"; it contends that the existence of objects independent of minds are represented to us by acquaintance with mind-dependent "ideas." The gist of Ockham's critique, Moody tells us, is that unless we can know some external object independent of its being represented to us by an internal object, we have no way of knowing that there are any external objects to be represented.

Further, Moody informs us, Ockham held that any knowledge we gain of causal relations—of what is caused by what—must be gained by observation. No statement expressing a causal relationship expresses a necessary truth, and from no one thing does the existence of anything else follow. A thing or event of one sort is said to be the cause of a thing or event of another sort when we have experienced the first accompanied by the second, but have never experienced the second unchaperoned by the first.

No necessary existential truths; no inference from the observed to the unobserved and unobservable; no necessary causal propositions; no necessary connections between things or events: this, Moody suggests, amounts to a rejection of natural theology.

According to Moody, Ockham's empiricist perspective was partly motivated by the sort of critique already mentioned. It was also in part motivated by more theological considerations of the following sort. If the natural order is created by God in a free act of creation—an act he need not have performed, but performed graciously—then the existence of the natural order must be both logically and causally contingent. Its nonexistence would involve no contradiction; its existence will depend on God's activity; it will not be an emanation which inevitably overflows from God's nature. These ideas, Moody adds, were denied by varieties of theological necessitarianism.

Moody concludes that, for Ockham, religion was a matter of faith. He interpreted theology as a matter of developing syntax for a semantic system for which no empirical interpretation is available. So, Moody tells us, Ockham found nothing inconsistent in his being both a believing theologian and an empiricist, and he offered as the theological sanction for empiricism the consideration that it avoids theological necessitarianism and allows for the free creation of the world by God.—*K.E.Y.*

ADDITIONAL RECOMMENDED READING

Boehner, Philotheus. *Collected Articles on Ockham*. St. Bonaventure, New York: Franciscan Institute, 1970. A useful collection of essays by a leading Ockham scholar.

Copleston, Frederick C. *A History of Medieval Philosophy*. New York: Harper & Row Publishers, 1972. A one-volume survey by the foremost contemporary general historian of philosophy writing in English.

Gilson, Étienne. *History of Christian Philosophy in the Middle Ages*. New York: Random House, 1955. A comprehensive discussion, with copious footnotes, by one of the greatest medievalists.

Henry, D. P. *Medieval Logic and Metaphysics*. London: Hutchinson University Library, 1972. A valuable selective discussion, with references to Ockham, especially concerning the topic of formal distinction.

Moody, Ernest A. *The Logic of William of Ockham*. London: Sheed and Ward, 1935. A careful treatment of Ockham's logic and its intellectual context by a distinguished scholar.

_____ ."Ockham, Buridan, and Nicholas of Autrecourt," in *Franciscan Studies*. VII (June, 1947), pp. 113-146. An astute comparison of Ockham with two other medieval thinkers, especially concerning the Parisian Statutes of 1339 and 1340.

OF LEARNED IGNORANCE

Author: Nicholas of Cusa (Nicolaus Cryfts or Krypffs, c. 1401-1464)
Type of work: Metaphysics, theology
First transcribed: 1440

PRINCIPAL IDEAS ADVANCED

God is the absolute maximum and also the absolute minimum; he is in all things, and all things are in him.

If man makes his own ignorance the object of his desire for knowledge, he can acquire a learned ignorance; although God cannot be comprehended, some knowledge of him can be acquired by reflection on our limitations.

The absolute maximum (God) is absolute unity, for unity is the minimum (and God is the absolute minimum); God, as a unity excluding degrees of more or less, is infinite unity.

The visible world is a reflection of the invisible; man mirrors the eternal and the infinite by his conjectures.

God is best studied through the use of mathematical symbols.

In the Providence of God contradictories are reconciled.

The world is the absolute effect of the absolute maximum; it is a relative unity.

Jesus is the maximum at once absolute and restricted; he is both God and man brought to perfection.

Nicholas of Cusa (Nicolas Cusanus) was both a man of action and a man of speculation. He spent his years as a churchman in the cause of reform and ecclesiastical diplomacy; he was a Cardinal and Bishop of Brixen. As a metaphysical theologian he synthesized the ideas of such predecessors as Johannes Scotus Erigena, Eckhart, and pseudo-Dionysius the Areopagite. His work had a considerable influence on Giordano Bruno, particularly on the latter's *Dialogues Concerning Cause, Principle, and One* (1584). *Of Learned Ignorance*, Nicholas' most important treatise, is particularly interesting as an attempt to reconcile the Neoplatonic ideas prevalent in the Middle Ages with the growing confidence in empirical inquiry and the use of the intellect. The reconciliation is only partly successful from the logical point of view, and it involves an appeal to the revelatory power of mystical intuition. But for those who sought to understand the possibility of unifying an infinite God and an apparently finite universe, and who were disturbed by their learned ignorance, the efforts of Nicholas of Cusa were a godsend.

The work is divided into three books and is unified by a concern with the *maximum*, the greatest. The first book is a study of the "absolute maximum," or God, the being who is greatest in the sense that he is one and all, all things are in God, and God is in all things. Nicholas describes this study as one "above reason," and as one that "cannot be conducted on the lines of human comprehension. . . ."

The second book is concerned with the maximum effect of the absolute maximum. The maximum effect is the universe, a plurality which is, nevertheless, a relative unity.

The third book is devoted to the maximum which is both relative and absolute, the perfect realization of the finite plurality of the universe; this maximum is Jesus.

Nicholas begins his work by explaining that men have a natural desire for knowledge but are frustrated in their desire to know by the enduring fact of their own ignorance. Men strive to understand what is not understandable—for example, the infinite as infinite, which is beyond comparison. The only solution, then, is for men to seek to know their own ignorance, even as Socrates advised; if a man makes his own ignorance the object of his desire for knowledge, he can acquire a learned ignorance. The suggestion is that from reflecting on his limitations man can, in knowledge, surmount his own ignorance, at least to some extent.

Finite intellects proceed by comparisons, according to Nicholas; and it is on that account that the Pythagoreans came close to the truth in saying that it is by numbers that all things are understood. But if the effort is to understand the absolute infinite, the means of comparison will not work, for the absolute infinite is beyond comparison. To realize that the quiddity of things, the absolute "whatness" of them, is beyond our intellects—and that, in regard to the truth about ultimate being, we must be ignorant—is to draw closer to truth.

But if we cannot comprehend the absolute maximum (which is God), then what is the point of working out the implications of the conception of the absolute maximum? Nicholas argues that although we cannot comprehend the absolute maximum, nevertheless we can have some knowledge about it; we can know, for example, that the precise nature of the absolute maximum is beyond our powers of understanding. But there is more than that which we can know.

We can also know that the absolute maximum is also the absolute minimum. Nicholas proves this point in an engaging and simple argument: "By definition the minimum is that which cannot be less than it is; and since that is also true of the maximum, it is evident that the minimum is identified with the maximum." There is another good reason for supposing that the maximum and the minimum are synonymous: since the absolute maximum is actually all that it can be, it is both as great as it can be and as small as it can be; and since it is the absolute, it can be absolutely minimum as well as absolutely maximum, and since it can be, it is. Furthermore, the maximum considered in itself, not as the maximum of a certain matter or quantity, is the infinite;

but, then, so is the minimum; since both the maximum and the minimum are the infinite, they are one.

The maximum is absolute unity, for unity is the smallest number, or the minimum, God is a unity which "excludes degrees of 'more' or 'less,'" and is, consequently, an infinite unity.

Nicholas introduces his version of the cosmological argument: finite beings are effects which could not have produced themselves; therefore, there must be an absolute maximum, not itself dependent on causes, without which nothing else could exist.

The conception of the Trinity is introduced by an elaboration of the Pythagorean idea that unity is a trinity. Diversity involves unity (two, for example, is two ones); inequality depends upon equality (and, therefore, upon unity); connection depends upon unity, for division is a duality or involves duality. Diversity, inequality, and division, then, necessarily involve unity, equality, and connection; and the latter three are all unities, but unity is one. Unity is a trinity, since unity means nondivision, distinction, and connection.

According to Nicholas of Cusa, the visible world is a reflection of the invisible. By the use of conjectural images man can, at least to some extent, mirror the eternal and infinite. The images most helpful to man are mathematical images, for, as Pythagoras pointed out, "the key to all truth [is] to be found in numbers. . . ."

The symbols which Nicholas found most useful in suggesting the nature of the absolute maximum are the line, the triangle, and the circle. An infinite line, according to Nicholas, would be at once a straight line, a triangle, a circle, and a sphere. He argues, for example, that as the circumference of a circle increases, the line becomes less curved; and he concludes that the circumference of the absolutely greatest possible circle would be absolutely straight, the smallest possible curve. (Although logically there is an essential difference between a curve, however slight, and a straight line, Nicholas' figure, considered as a metaphor, achieves the purpose of suggesting that entities disparate in character are nevertheless such that, when taken to infinity, they are indistinguishable.)

A finite line can be used to form a triangle, he argues, by keeping one end fixed and moving the line to one side. (Actually, the figure so formed is not a triangle, but a segment of a circle, a pie-shaped segment.) If one continues the movement of the line (so that it functions as an infinite number of radii), the figure formed is a circle. Half a circle, if turned in three dimensions on its axis, forms a sphere.

An infinite triangle would have three infinitely long sides; infinitely extended, the triangle would finally be indistinguishable from a line. Such a triangle would have three lines in one and in that respect would resemble the infinite absolute maximum (God). (Apparently Nicholas conceived of a triangle's sides as increasing and its base angles, say, as becoming more acute, the apex as becoming more and more obtuse, until finally there would be no triangle distinguishable from a straight line. But he need not have conceived of it this way. He could have conceived of a triangle expanding while its angles remain constant. Part of Nicholas' argument, however, depends upon the assumption that there cannot be more than one infinite. To maintain this point involves a peculiar use of the term "infinite.")

Having demonstrated to his satisfaction that an infinite line is a triangle, a circle, and a sphere, Nicholas develops the image to suggest by analogy the relationship of the absolute maximum to all things: the infinite line is to lines what the absolute maximum is to things. The analogy is developed at great length, but the most important features are these: an infinite line is not divisible; it is immutable and eternal; and, oddly, it shares its essential features with finite lines—for finite lines, for example, cannot be divided into anything other than lines and are, in that sense, indivisible. Just as the essence of an infinite line is the essence of all finite lines, so the essence of the absolute maximum is the essence of everything. This point is developed by reference to beings who have only a participation in being; since the essence of such beings is the essence of the absolute maximum, once the feature of participation is eliminated, the distinction between beings who participate in being and the being in which they participate disappears.

Again, by mathematical analogy, Nicholas argues that there could not be four or more divine persons; there must be a trinity. A four-sided figure is not the smallest, simplest measure of things, as is the triangle.

A circle, having neither beginning nor end, being perfect, possessing unity, and so forth, is an ideal figure of the divine.

Nicholas thus comes to one of his characteristic contentions: "In the Providence of God contradictories are reconciled." God's Providence includes all that shall be together with all that shall not be. He has foreknowledge of everything, for he foresees opposites. The absolute maximum is in all being, and all beings are in him.

By the analogy of the infinite sphere Nicholas argues that God is the "one infinitely simple, essential explanation of the entire universe." He is the final cause of everything, the determiner both of existence and of end.

All names attributed to the infinite absolute maximum are anthropomorphic; none is adequate as a name, for God is beyond distinctions. Only the four-letter word "ioth-he-vau-he," one which is unspeakable, is a proper name for God.

Since God is ineffable, negative propositions are truer than affirmative ones. It is better to count on learned ignorance, as enlightened by God, than to count on positive knowledge. Nicholas proceeds, in the second book, to demonstrations of the absolute effect of the absolute maximum; the unity and infinity of the universe are shown to be a consequence of that infinitude of matter which arises from its incapacity to be greater than it is. Since God is not jealous, and since the essence of every created thing is his essence, and since he is essentially perfect, every thing is, in its way, perfect. The universe (and everything in it) is a principle and a maximum, but in a restricted sense; the absolute maximum brings the universe into existence by emanation (a timeless outpouring of its essential nature).

Thus, everything is in everything, as Anaxagoras said. Since God is in all things by medium of the universe, "all is in all, and each in each." Of course, the universe is in each thing only in a contracted or restricted manner; in fact, the universe is contracted, in each thing, to whatever the thing is. The unity of the universe, which comes from the absolute unity of God, is a unity in plurality; the unity of the universe, then, is not an absolute, but a relative, unity.

The universe is also a trinity as well as a unity, but just as it is a relative unity, so it is a relative or contracted trinity. The unity of the universe is a trinity in the sense that contraction involves a limitable object, a limiting principle, and a connection—or potency, act, and the nexus.

There are four modes of being: the absolute necessity, or God; the mode of being of things according to natural necessity or order; the mode of being of individuals; and the mode of being of that which is possible.

The Soul of the World is a universal form which contains all forms, but it has only a contracted existence; forms are actual only in the Word of God. However, it is possible to use the term "Soul" in such a way that the Soul and God are one. Every possibility is contained in the Absolute Possibility, God; every form (or act) in the Absolute Form, the Son of God; and every connecting harmony in the Absolute Connection of the Holy Spirit. The Father is potency; the Son, act; and the Holy Ghost, connecting movement. Thus, God, who is unity as well as trinity, is the efficient, formal, and final cause of all things; and the movements of the earth and stars are attributable to him, who is the center and circumference. In reflecting on the world and on the wonder of its arrangement, one cannot hope to understand God's reasons; but in the wonder of him and in our learned ignorance we find intimations of his light.

Jesus Christ is "the maximum at once absolute and restricted," and to the defense and clarification of this description Nicholas devotes the third book. Human nature is peculiarly suited to provide God with the possibility of a maximum which reconciles the infinite and the finite by being at once absolute and contracted. As sensible and intellectual, human nature is a microcosm, a world in miniature. Unlike other things which, raised to perfection, could easily become greater because of the inferiority of their natures, man is such that, if perfected, he reveals the nature of all things as perfected. By joining the nature of humanity to the divine nature God made possible the union of the absolute maximum and the nature of all things. In Jesus, God is both God and man.

The remainder of Nicholas' work is a defense, in terms of his mystical metaphysics, of familiar dogmas: that Christ was conceived of the Holy Ghost and born of the Virgin Mary, that he was resurrected after the Crucifixion, that he ascended into heaven, that he is the judge of the living and the dead, that he redeemed all mankind. In this account Jesus is God utilizing the nature of humanity and bringing it to perfection; Jesus is man made perfect in the image and essence of God. Because of Jesus the Church comes into being, the fullest possible realization of the unity of the many "with the preservation of the personal reality of each, without confusion of natures or degrees." And by Jesus the union of the subjects and the Church is resolved into the divine unity. Thus, for Nicholas of Cusa, as for Bruno of Nola, God is the cause, the principle, and the One.—*I.P.M.*

PERTINENT LITERATURE

Randall, John Herman, Jr. *The Career of Philosophy from the Middle Ages to the Enlightenment*. Vol. I. New York: Columbia University Press, 1962.

Nicholas of Cusa was born Nicholas Krebs c. 1401, and died, a Bishop and a Cardinal, in 1464. An eclectic scholar, he was aware of the various currents of thought present in Germany and Italy and was himself a speculative thinker. Learned in Greek and Hebrew, aware of the latest developments in Ockhamite physics and mathematics, he was, John Herman Randall, Jr., suggests, the father of German Humanism. He used his learning to attempt to solve various theological problems which arose in the mystical Neoplatonic Tradition concerning the relationship between God and the world. Randall informs us that he transposed the Platonic tradition into German Transcendentalism and developed the notions of the relativity of human knowledge and the homogeneity of the physical universe.

Randall compares Nicholas' practical activities with his theoretical ones. His first work was *De Concordantia Catholica* (1433); he wished to unite councils and the Papacy, and the Eastern and the Western Church. He also wished to bring together humanism and a mystic version of supernaturalism; and he developed a perspective in which he endeavored to find a place for various things he regarded as opposites, each being justified in its own context and each being woven into a unity with its opposite at a higher level. Examples of such opposites are mystical theology and natural science, faith and reason, and mathematics and Aristotelian metaphysics. Randall informs us that he groped for, but never realized, a system in which his aims would be accomplished, although he sketched it at the outset of his career. In 1440, he wrote *De Docta Ignorantia* and *De Conjectaris*, which sketched his basic problem— the relation, as he saw it, between Absolute and Relative, or God and the World—and suggests some of his solutions. Randall finds the thought of Nicholas "exceedingly subtle and never overclear" and can discern no "neat pattern" in it. While he continues the tradition of negative theology, his theology is, Randall believes, but the "thread on which his many interests are strung."

Going behind Christian Platonists to pagan Platonists, Nicholas seeks a vision of things which in some way goes beyond that provided by sensory observation or rational reflection. Randall reminds us that Christian tradition had developed a conception according to which the world is comprised of a graded hierarchy of levels which one can progressively come to understand. The Greek Platonists, he continues, instead present a picture of one "supra-intelligible" world, different sorts of reality being but various images thereof. Thus knowlege involved, in this view, not so much a progression from one level to another as a penetration to an overarching vision. This notion proves the underlying motif of Nicholas' work, according to Randall.

Randall reports that Nicholas begins not with metaphysics and levels of reality but with theory knowledge. Knowledge, Nicholas contends, requires comparison—he views knowledge as a sort of measurement. Measurement, in turn, requires a homogeneity or proportion between the items measured. But between the Absolute and the Relative, which he views as a proper way of referring to God and the World, Nicholas holds that there is no homogeneity or proportion—no common unit of measurement. Hence, Randall explains, he concludes that there is no knowledge of the Absolute, or of God. Logic—which then meant Aristotelian logic—applies, for Nicholas, only to the relative, to the World.

By reason, then, one can come only to a doctrine of "learned ignorance." Randall quotes Nicholas to the effect that (1) knowledge requires measurement and comparison; (2) we can find no objects so similar that there cannot be another "in between" them—no two experienced objects are ever perfectly alike; and (3) truth has no degrees. If one adds some such claim as that (4) we can know something to be true only if we can discover perfectly similar objects, then one will have a perspective which claims that knowledge even of the relative is impossible. However, Randall indicates, Nicholas posits an *intellectus*, a *Nous*, which is freed from the law of noncontradiction and is able to gain insight into the alleged "coincidence of contraries in the Infinite." This, Randall continues, is for Nicholas the beginning of the ascent into mystical theology. Randall sees in this doctrine a reaffirmation of the Platonic theme that one can have a vision which can be expressed only in terms of "conjecture."

Still, Randall insists, Nicholas rejects blind faith; Nicholas holds that mathematics, a science which assumes the law of noncontradiction, alone can give conjectural knowledge of the Absolute. His favorite example was that of a polygon whose sides, ever increased in number, would approach ever nearer to a circle without reaching it. He takes this, Randall writes, as an illustration of opposites uniting in the Absolute.

Randall reports that Nicholas was the first to take the idea of an infinite universe seriously and to draw various consequences from the notion—for example, that the universe has no fixed center, that there are no perfect motions in the celestial region, and that motion is relative. This challenged the received Ptolemaic and Aristotelian conceptions of the world, although Nicholas was a philosopher of nature, not a scientist.

Nicholas also applied his basic motif to religion, Randall continues, holding that every creed, expressing the doctrinal content of a religious tradition, was itself a "conjecture"; only so can the absolute be cognized by human beings. Thus, Nicholas holds that to some degree each religion is true, and none is adequate to express the nature of the Absolute.

Nicholas of Cusa, or Nicholas Cusanus, Randall concludes, was a mystic theologian and Platonic metaphysician. He stated a restricted version of Platonism which allows no knowledge of the nonrelative, and in Germany he is viewed as the first modern philosopher.

Gilson, Étienne. *History of Christian Philosophy in the Middle Ages*, Part Eleven. New York: Random House, 1955.

Étienne Gilson informs us that Nicholas of Cusa studied law at Padua and theology at Cologne. He served as an archdeacon at Liège, was an active member of the council of Basel (1437), was renewed as a pontifical legate in 1448, and was given the bishopric of Brixen (1450). He continually held one or another official office in the Church until his death on August 11, 1464.

Gilson finds Nicholas' work to be a blending of theology and philosophy, a synthesis adapted to the needs of his day. Aristotelian dialectics, Gilson says, was the standard tool for philosophical reflection; Nicholas appealed instead to the thought of Plotinus. The dominating concept in Nicholas' thought is that of infinity, which Gilson explains as being understood in the sense of a "fullness of positive being." Gilson interprets this along Anselmian lines—God is viewed as that being than whom no greater can be conceived, and Gilson discerns a similar theme in the thought of Boethius, Henry of Ghent, and John Duns Scotus. Gilson contends that this notion of infinity is completely non-Greek.

In his *Of Learned Ignorance*, Gilson reports, Nicholas contends that inquiry consists in relating some notions to others. This, in turn, requires that the notions used be proportional to, or commensurate with, one another. (Presumably, in this fashion, one also understands something of the relationships that hold between the things the notions represent.) Nicholas holds, however, that the infinite is not proportional to or commensurate with anything.

Nicholas, Gilson notes, reasoned along these lines: the infinite is an absolute maximum—nothing can be added to it or subtracted from it. Therefore, it is a unity. Given the view, held by Nicholas, among others, that whatever is a unity is a being, it follows that the infinite is a being or entity. If it is an entity, it is all-encompassing or all-inclusive (presumably on the grounds that, were there something "outside" it, it would not be infinite after all). But then it has no contrary. What has no contrary is a minimum. So the infinite is both a maximum and a minimum. This reasoning, such as it is, forms, according to Gilson, the basis of Nicholas' contention that opposites coincide in the infinite.

As Gilson notes, this suggestion that opposites may somehow coincide or coexist in the infinite runs counter to a view accepted by Thomas Aquinas, Duns Scotus, William of Ockham, Nicholas of Autrecourt, Siger of Brabant, and many others: namely, the principle of noncontradiction. Instead, Gilson remarks, Nicholas appeals to such philosophers as Hermes Trismegistus, Asclepius, and Denis the Aeropagite to reject what they regarded simply as part of Aristotelian dialectic. Admitting that it would take something like conversion, some sort of miracle, for one deliberately to reject the principle that of two logically contradictory propositions, P and not-P, one must be true and the other false (or, of two states of affairs, A and not-A, it must be the case that one obtains and the other does not). Nicholas thought some such event to be required before one could obtain a vision of an infinite in which opposites coincided, an infinite which he took to be ultimate reality.

Thus, Gilson explains, Nicholas' goal is to drown all conceptual distinctions in the unity of mystical intuition. Among Nicholas' critics, Gilson tells us, was John Wenck, who claimed that Nicholas failed to distinguish between Creator and creature—that Nicholas embraced pantheism. Gilson defends Nicholas against this criticism on the ground that, for Nicholas, the finite participates in, but is not identical to, the infinite, though the finite depends for its existence on the infinite. Perhaps more basic, there is also, Gilson notes, the view in Nicholas that once one has the alleged vision of God, such questions as "How are God and human beings related?" would become (to the visionary, anyway) nonsensical; the sort of "knowledge" one would need to have to answer them, according to Nicholas, is ineffable: "Nothing can be said about it."

Nicholas offers, then, Gilson explains, a doctrine of "learned ignorance." Nicholas reasons that where no proportion exists between A and B—where A and B are incommensurable—one cannot reason from A to B. There is, he thinks, no proportion between finite and infinite. Nor are any two finite beings perfectly similar. From this, Nicholas infers that knowledge of even finite items is imprecise. The quiddity, or essence, of things, he claims, is inaccessible to us. Gilson notes, however, that Nicholas does not derive a total skepticism from these claims; instead, he falls back on analogies from mathematics (God is to the universe as an infinite line is to finite lines) and the teachings of Denis the Aeropagite.

Gilson finds in Nicholas a rejection of the Aristotelian view of the world and a return to the perspective of the School of Chartres. His *Learned Unknowing* contains many references to Thierry of Chartres, Gilbert of Porrée, Clarenbaud of Arras, and John of Salisbury, and to their sources, Chalcidius, Macrobius, Asclepius, and Hermes Trismegistus. Since the Platonism of these figures agreed with that of Denis, Gilson suggests, Nicholas thought it correct and endeavored to substitute it for the dominant Aristotelianism.—*K.E.Y.*

ADDITIONAL RECOMMENDED READING

Copleston, Frederick. *A History of Philosophy*. Vol. II. New York: Image Books, 1962. (Originally published by Newman Press, 1950.) Introductory, comprehensive discussion of medieval philosophy.

Hopkins, Jasper. *A Concise Introduction to the Philosophy of Nicholas of Cusa*. Minneapolis: University of Minnesota Press, 1978. A splendid introduction to, and analysis of, Nicholas' thought.

Hyman, Arthur and James J. Walsh, eds. *Philosophy in the Middle Ages*. Indianapolis: Hackett Publishing Company, 1973. An excellent anthology of medieval philosophy.

Nicholas of Cusa. *Nicholas of Cusa on God as Not-Other: A Translation and an Appraisal of "De Li Non Aliud"*. Translated by Jasper Hopkins. Minneapolis: University of Minnesota Press, 1979. A good translation and helpful account of Nicholas of Cusa's views concerning God.

Vignaux, Paul. *Philosophy in the Middle Ages: An Introduction*. New York: Meridian Books, 1959. A very good introduction to medieval thought, with a brief discussion of Nicholas' views.

UTOPIA

Author: Sir Thomas More (1478-1535)
Type of work: Political philosophy
First published: 1516

PRINCIPAL IDEAS ADVANCED

Philosophers ought not to advise princes, for rulers are not interested in advice, but would much prefer to have others assent to their fixed policies.

An economic system which allows private property drives the poor from the land and thereby creates thieves whom the existing laws require to be hanged: such a system and policy is neither just nor expedient.

In opposition to the former ideas which are defended by Raphael Hythloday, a world traveler, Thomas More (as a character in the conversation) argues that a nonspeculative, prudential philosopher might be useful in politics, but Hythloday is skeptical.

More objects to Raphael Hythloday's call for the abolition of money and private property by arguing that unless men have the profit motive, they will not work.

Hythloday describes Utopia, a carefully organized state in which the citizens engage in scientific farming according to assignments from magistrates and then return to the cities; they work a six-hour day and spend their leisure moments reading, attending lectures, and conversing on academic subjects.

In Utopia gold has no worth, marriages are regulated, work is cooperative, and pleasure in accordance with virtue is the aim of life.

Unlike men who treat human beliefs and institutions as if their simple persistence were evidence of their truth and unalterability, there are writers who judge the actual in terms of the possible, the real in terms of an ideal. Such men usually object passionately to the evils of existing customs and habits. Many consume their energies in important practical efforts to achieve social and political reforms. But only a few possess the knowledge, sustained moral dedication, and literary ability to produce books which—however radical and even sometimes absurd some of their views about organized social life may appear—confront their readers with ideal maps of the political countryside against which to measure actually existing states. The great ancient classic which fashioned such a mirror toward which men might direct their vision is Plato's *Republic*, a book inexhaustible in imaginative suggestions and incomparable for the range of subject matter treated. An important modern work reflecting the influence of Plato's thought, written during the turbulence of sixteenth century English political strife, is Thomas More's *Utopia*.

The English word "utopia" derives its meaning from a Greek term which can be translated "nowhere." To this day, a scheme called "utopian" suggests the idea of nonexistence. Thomas More invented the term and applied it to a mythical community, and then used his account of this community as a means of criticizing certain European social and political practices which he considered unreasonable.

More's own life lends interest to the contents of his famous book, for More served Henry VIII, the strongwilled English king, in a number of important political capacities. In 1535 he died on the block for resistance to the monarch's policies in a power struggle between the English nation and the Roman papacy. In spite of his humanistic leanings, More stood firm in refusing to recognize Henry's claim to the title which in fact made him head of the Church in England. As an adviser to the monarch, More became a tragic figure caught between opposing institutional pressures which played a unique role in shaping modern English history.

In form, More's *Utopia* is quite simple. Two separate books comprise its contents. Book II (which contains an elaborate description of the Utopians) was written first, in 1515, a year before the completion of Book I (which discusses several general political questions, including whether philosophers ought to advise princes). The latter portion of the *Utopia* introduces the primary figures in the work, who include More himself, presented as having heard the ensuing account of social affairs while serving his monarch on state business in Antwerp (Belgium); a gentleman named Peter Giles; who is said to have introduced More to the leading participant in the written work; and a stranger named Raphael Hythloday, a world traveler widely acquainted with political matters, who shows impatience with several customs then little questioned in European social and political life. Raphael Hythloday is a spokesman for what must have been More's own critical opinions about contemporary practices.

The early discussion centers on whether philosophers ought to advise rulers—a question provoked by Giles's and More's suggestion that Raphael's extensive knowledge could be put to such use. Raphael shows little interest in attempting to advise rulers. At the same time, he argues that the social arrangements of the Utopians (whom he discovered somewhere below the equator) would serve well as a basis for "correcting the errors of our own cities and kingdoms." He is nonetheless convinced that to serve a king in an advisory capacity would make him miserable. "Now I live as I will," Raphael argues—illustrating the tension existing between private and public demands on a person—"and I believe very few courtiers can say that." Raphael insists that princes do not want advice from philosophers, that what they seek is agreement with their fixed policies of waging constant, aggressive warfare. Princes ignore sound advice and refuse to tolerate any posture except that of absolute agreement among their counselors. "They are generally more set on acquiring new kingdoms rightly or wrongly, than on governing well those that they already have." Raphael illustrates his viewpoint by recounting an episode which had occurred at a dinner given by a famous Cardinal. At this affair Raphael became entangled in a discussion when another person present praised some judicial practices which Raphael thought foolish.

What astounds a twentieth century reader is the modernity of the reported discussion. What Raphael advocates during the discussion is something like a reformist as opposed to a retributionist theory of punishment for wrong-doing. He also seeks a general theory which will explain why so many individuals (Englishmen, in this case) risk the death penalty by stealing. Raphael Hythloday wants to understand the causes of thieving. Here he presents a crude yet clear economic thesis, arguing that the land enclosures in sixteenth century England create economic conditions which increase the compulsion to steal. The existing practice of hanging culprits who steal deals only with the symptoms and not with the causes of that unfortunate practice. Unable to gain a fair hearing for their economic situation, the poor are finally driven from the land. "They would willingly work," Raphael insists, "but can find no one who will hire them." Glaring social extremes tend to develop, such as abject poverty existing side by side with extreme luxury. Raphael presents a bald and bold environmentalist theory about the origins of criminal activities. His views condemn the legal and judicial customs of the day. The economic situation inevitably produces the thieves whom the existing laws then require to be hanged. This policy is neither just nor rationally expedient.

Raphael then proceeds to sketch a wiser policy respecting theft and its legal treatment. Citing the Roman practice of employing thieves to work quarries, he mentions the procedures of the mythical Polyerites (meaning "much nonsense") who require apprehended thieves to make full restitution. Thieves convicted of their crimes must work at public services, under state supervision, thus producing some social benefit. They are dressed in a common uniform and distributed in different regions of the country to prevent possible formation of rebellious political groups. Each year some are pardoned. This picture of penal procedures suggests the practices of a number of twentieth century states as opposed to the generally cruel systems prevalent in More's century.

Having heard Raphael's account, the Cardinal admits that such procedures might well be tried. By this admission he introduces a note of experimentalism into the discussion. The Cardinal concludes that if, on trying such means, the thieves were not reformed, one could then still see them hanged.

Thomas More is described as wanting to hear even more from the interesting stranger, Raphael Hythloday. He reminds Raphael that Plato thought that political wisdom could never prevail until philosophers became kings, or kings became philosophers. Raphael replies to this argument by setting up imagined cases in which a philosopher attempts to advise an actually existing ruler— say, the French king, in one instance. Raphael attempts to show that if he asserts that the king, as shepherd of his people, ought to care more for the welfare of the sheep than for himself (an obvious borrowing from Plato), he will be ignored by the royal council. His conclusion is that the philosopher should never give advice when he knows it will fall on deaf ears. Raphael also refers to the practices of mythical peoples like the Achorians (a word which means "no place") and the Macarians (meaning "blessed"), the latter of whom permit their king to possess only a thousand pounds in his treasury at any time. The point of these cases is that Raphael wants to convince the participants in the discussion that "there is no place for philosophy in the councils of princes."

To this somewhat cynical position Thomas More makes a significant counterargument. More admits that speculative philosophy is unhelpful to practical princes. But he argues that there exists another kind of philosophy. This practically useful philosophy "is more urbane" and "takes its proper cue and fits itself to the drama being played, acting its part aptly and well." Thus, More reveals himself as a believer in nonspeculative, prudential philosophizing able to adjust to changing circumstances. For this reason he cautions Raphael: "Don't give up the ship in a storm, because you cannot control the winds." The prudentially oriented philosopher must seek to guide policy-formation in an indirect manner. Raphael's response includes the argument that the prudential philosopher must "rave along with them" (meaning the ruling council). He insists that even Christ's teachings run counter to many existing customs, even in England. Even Plato, Raphael reminds his listeners, advised outstanding men to refuse to meddle in politics.

Raphael returns to his economic thesis—that the chief cause of evil customs is the existence of private property. Only among the Utopians has he found a social system making virtue the primary goal of living. Other nations seeking to create sane institutional arrangements undermine their own efforts by maintaining private property and a money economy. Their laws hopelessly try to protect for the individual what, by the nature of private property, must always stand under threat. Raphael advocates the total abolition of money and privately held property.

To this view More objects, although he shows interest in a fuller description of the Utopians while insisting that absolute equality of possessions means that many will cease working. Men need the incentive of the hope of gain, according to More. From a policy enforcing equal possessions in cases when all men experience extreme want, only warfare and constant factionalism can ensue. Men require authority over themselves based on some distinction in abilities and worth. To More's objections Peter Giles adds his own view that other men are not better governed than the English. His reason for so thinking is that the abilities of English and European rulers are equal to those of other persons. European governmental practices also rest on long historical experience. Raphael replies that the Utopians also possess a long history—that their peculiar success in managing their affairs results from their willingness to learn. His associates in the discussion ask Raphael to provide more information about the Utopians.

In Book II three aspects of Utopian civilization receive consideration under a number of separate headings. There is, first, a description of the island where Utopia exists as well as of the number, distribution, and geographical arrangements of its cities. Next are described the social and political institutions of Utopia. Finally, Raphael discusses the ideas and moral norms by which the Utopians live.

Each city in Utopia is divided in a manner to require several magistrates. From the body of the magistrates, three representatives are chosen to meet in the capital city once a year. Individual cities contain households fixed in number and built on a planned model, thirty households requiring one magistrate in a given district. Agricultural pursuits aiming at economic self-sufficiency require existence of country households containing forty men and women each. These households receive their members on a rotational basis from the cities. Each Utopian must take a turn at farming and related forms of labor, thus spreading the burden of physical work; but individuals particularly fond of country life and work may remain longer than the otherwise stipulated two-year period. Something very much like scientific farming operates in Utopia.

A wall surrounds each city. Its inhabitants work only six hours each day (an astounding suggestion in More's time). The remainder of a citizens time is devoted to private pursuits. These pursuits indicate that Utopia is a society composed of professorial humanists or transcendentalist moral philosophers who enjoy academic talk. The citizens are well read. They also attend a wide variety of public lectures. Raphael claims the Utopians undertake these surprising intellectual pastimes on a voluntary basis. The six hour day in Utopia produces no idlers or maladjusted persons. Apparently, though a Christian, More could picture a human society in which evil does not exist. His Utopia fails to discuss the problems associated with possible misuses of leisure time.

Living in a balanced, well-planned society, the Utopians wear casual, common dress (indicating that More's humanism reflects also some puritanical dislike of color and variety). Gambling, drinking, and related activities do not occur. Good teaching leads Utopians to ignore the usual allure of gold and precious stones. Gold is used for children's ornamentation and, in the adult world, for the making of chamber pots. The Utopians thus learn that gold has no intrinsic worth. Indeed, as Raphael points out, most of the genuinely valuable elements in nature, like air and water, exist in plentiful quantities. In Utopia marriages are also regulated. Children and parents dine in common halls (suggesting some of the practices of organized camplife). The Utopians live moderately, each doing his share of work—including cooperative building and repair of roads.

Social habits in Utopia remind one of aspects of Plato's ideal state, which also emphasized communal domestic life. The general picture reveals a society which trains men so as to minimize cupidity, channeling strenuous energies to productive community ends. Yet each Utopian retains a large share of time for private pursuits. More's ideal society combines a moderate Puritanism with a humanistic stress on learning and moral development. Nowhere in More's *Utopia* is there a discussion concerning the realism or lack of realism of the humanistic social image presented.

More then considers the Utopians' moral philosophy, their marriage customs, the unique love of learning displayed by the citizens, their bondmen (who seem to do a large amount of bothersome menial labor), care of the sick, legal procedures and punishments, warfare, foreign relations, and religion. The Utopians seek knowledge without requiring irate schoolmasters or crass materialistic inducements. They are an admirably tolerant people, as consideration of a few of their beliefs will indicate.

Happiness (defined as pleasure in accordance with virtue) stands as the Utopian moral ideal. This shows the influence of Epicurean and Aristotelian ethical notions on More's humanism. In fact, the Utopians possess books given to them by Raphael on a return voyage he made to their island— philosophical works by Plato and Aristotle; literary productions by Aristophanes, Homer, Sophocles, and Euripides; historical narratives by Herodotus and Thucydides. The Utopians are a rather philosophical people able to make fairly sophisticated ethical judgments based on reason. As More describes them, the Utopians "discriminate several kinds of true pleasure, some belonging to the mind, others to the body. Those of the mind are knowledge and the delight which comes from contemplation of the truth; also the pleasant recollection of a well-spent life and the assured hope of future well-being."

Bodily pleasures are classified in accordance with the way they produce some immediate sense effect or turn the senses inward (as in the case of the enjoyment produced by hearing music). The Utopians debate aesthetic issues and seek to find delight in "sound, sight and smell." They guard and nourish the mental and physical capacities.

Utopia does enforce some rigid sexual rules. Marriage occurs only when a male reaches twenty-two years and a female, eighteen. Premarital sexual experience leads to severe punishment. Indeed, in the Utopian scheme, those who are caught in illicit affairs forfeit the right to marry for a lifetime unless pardoned by a prince. A few divorces are permitted, but only on the authorization of the senate.

More's account of the religious beliefs of the Utopians provides an interesting instance of tolerance. Different religious systems exist in Utopia, including Christianity—the latter a rather recent missionary introduction meeting with favorable reception. Dogmatic fights over doctrines and creeds are outlawed. Respect for views other than one's own prevails and is defended by the laws. Priests must be elected and are kept relatively few in number.

All Utopians must accept belief in an afterlife as well as the view that God punishes in accordance with one's conduct in this life. No one may challenge these beliefs in public. The common element shared by all religions in Utopia affirms a providential order which reasoning about nature can discover. Some priests are celibate while others marry. The different religious worshipers call the object of their devotions Mithra. They pray for guidance in moral endeavors and ask for an easy death. Nowhere does More explain how Christianity manages to exist side by side with so diversified a group of religious systems. Reason rather than revelation seems adequate to determine religious beliefs and practices.

Raphael Hythloday (as More's spokesman) ends his account of Utopia with a criticism of man's essential weakness: pride. Only human pride keeps the world from adopting the sensible laws and customs of the Utopians. Reason shows that class distinctions, property rights, and human anxiety exist only in societies which fail to curb pride. More writes that Raphael's picture of society fails fully to satisfy him, yet he concludes: "I must confess there are many things in the Utopian Commonwealth that I wish rather than expect to see followed among our citizens.—*W.T.D.*

PERTINENT LITERATURE

Ames, Russell. *Citizen Thomas More and His Utopia*. Princeton, New Jersey: Princeton University Press, 1949.

At the outset of his study of Sir Thomas More, Russell Ames says that he is concerned partly with assessing More's place in the middle class in England in the early sixteenth century; he also analyzes the character of the middle class at the time. He tells us that he is not the inventor of this socioeconomic method of investigation. The important Marxist thinker Karl Kautsky had advanced such a thesis in his *Thomas More and His Utopia* of 1890. Those who have followed this economic road to interpretation have, Ames declares, treated More and his book as if they could be studied abstracted from the business life and politics of the time. Thus, Ames slowly and carefully builds up his case that More was one of the leading spokesmen for the middle class in England at that time. He also patiently shows, in great detail, how More was involved in many middle-class pursuits. The actual More is frequently compared with his spokesman, Raphael Hythloday. Kautsky had sought to portray More as the first Marxian socialist, far ahead of his time. Ames argues that the available information indicates that More was forward-looking about some things and backward about others, but was nevertheless advancing an ideal that was based on the humane treatment of people and the sharing of wealth through slow democratic procedures.

To provide the background to make his interpretation plausible, Ames explores first what late feudalism was like in England and on the Continent.

He points out that the processes that were to lead to a capitalist economy were coming to a climax in England around 1515, a year before More's *Utopia* was written. More was involved in various aspects of the developing new European economy. In spite of his satirizing the actions of the merchants and wealth accumulators in *Utopia*, he himself went on fulfilling his role as a leader and protector of the City. More's relations with the city government and his connections with merchants grew during the period of the writing of *Utopia*. His relations with Henry VIII are more mysterious. Before *Utopia* appeared More had been offered posts by the King which he declined. He did, however, perform special duties for the King. In *Utopia* one of the crucial questions discussed at the outset is whether or not an honest, thoughtful person can be a royal adviser. Raphael Hythloday insists that the answer is no. Ames reveals all the efforts that Henry VIII made to get More to accept a post at the Court. Having in mind all of the political posts that More had held before he finally accepted Henry VIII's, Ames argues that there was no significant change of heart on More's side; he continued to function as the spokesman of the middle class.

The book carefully provides background material on such topics as the possibility that *Utopia* might be censored. The actual Utopian society is contrasted with Switzerland and the cities of the Hanseatic League. The character of the reforms proposed in *Utopia* are analyzed in terms of what Desiderius Erasmus and his friends were proposing at the time. More is also seen in terms of other radical reformers such as Girolamo Savonarola. In More's tale the reform of the clergy has already taken place. Prior to Martin Luther's revolution, More could be regarded as a religious reformer.

The book is packed with data, the background material often helping to elucidate More's text. More expressed the idea of developing a new economic order; and he introduced some democratic concepts in *Utopia*. Ames concludes by contending that "The humane democracy of the first book of Utopia gives us the obvious meaning of the work as a whole." The reader, however, may not be so convinced that news about London is enough to explain the power of More's ideas.

Hexter, Jack. *More's Utopia: The Biography of an Idea*. Princeton, New Jersey: Princeton University Press, 1952.

In restricting himself to the course of Sir Thomas More's idea in *Utopia*, Jack Hexter contends that all that he has to explain is what happened in More's intellectual life from the time More had the idea for the book until it was published. In so restricting his subject, Hexter is able to deal basically with what happened to More sometime between the summer of 1515 and the fall of 1516, when the work was published. (The date of the birth of the idea of *Utopia* cannot be established.) Hexter discusses only material in this short time frame except for one item—More's decision to accept service for the King in 1518, although he had had his hero, Raphael Hythloday, explain why honest men cannot work for a king.

Hexter begins by examining the idea of *Utopia*, contending that the book was written in two stages; the first, which is now Book II, was written when More was in the Netherlands with a group of humanists, including Desiderius Erasmus, who took care of the publishing details. He tells us that Book I was written after More returned to England. Hexter, however, in a careful analysis of the text, contends that a curious paragraph in Book I makes little sense where it is. It seems to deal with material relating to the Utopians while such material does not appear until the end of Book I and in Book II. (This odd paragraph is on pages 100-101 of More's *Utopia* in the edition of J. H. Lupton; page 42 in the Everyman edition; and page 41 of the Clarendon edition of *Utopia* edited by J. C. Collins.)

The curious paragraph is used by Hexter to reconstruct the text both in terms of when it was written and in terms of what More was trying to express. Hexter states that the curious paragraph is introductory to what More wrote in Holland. Even though this does not yield a literary text in which the paragraph naturally flows into Book II, it makes for a logically developing text—stressing first the question of whether a good and wise man can and should work for a ruler, and then whether the Utopian society is better than the actual one we are living in. Hexter's reconstruction makes it clear that the latter question is the one that grew out of More's discussions with Erasmus and others. In analyzing the Communist element in *Utopia*, Hexter tries to show that even though some, like Karl Kautsky, can see Marxism emerging from Utopia, it is the case that almost all that More said could have been lifted from the economic views of the time, or from feudal and religious views that were still being taken seriously. Hexter therefore contends that More's views about property are neither "novel nor remarkable."

Hexter claims that the views set forth by Hythloday in Book I on whether a good man should serve as a royal counselor were added in England in 1516, probably during or after Erasmus' visit to London that year. During his visit Erasmus stayed with the Mores. When More sent the finished manuscript with its dialogue on royal service to Erasmus to have it published in Holland, he classified it as "our Utopia." Hexter suggests that both the utopian element and the discussion about working for the King were written after lengthy discussions with Erasmus.

The problem remains: Why did More set down many good reasons for the intellectual to avoid public service, and then two years after the publication of *Utopia*, accept high office under Henry VIII, who finally had him killed? Hexter analyzes what More said and did before becoming a civil servant and constructs a possible scenario culminating in More's letter to Erasmus in 1518. Erasmus was thunderstruck. Hexter insists that More's rejection of any government post in 1516 and his acceptance in 1518 are both based on rational considerations.

Hexter's well-written book is now accepted as a minor classic by those interested in More and his time.

Surtz, Edward L. *The Praise of Wisdom: A Commentary on the Religious and Moral Problems and Backgrounds of St. Thomas More's "Utopia."* Chicago: Loyola University Press, 1957.

Edward L. Surtz's book, in contrast to many others, from Karl Kautsky's to Russell Ames's and Jack Hexter's, does not try to show how radical and modern Sir Thomas More was. Instead, Surtz turns away from secular interpretations and seeks to explain More's view in terms of Catholic theology, philosophy, and doctrine. The very title indicates the direction the author takes in casting More in a more traditional role than that indicated by seeing him as a close collaborator with the author of *The Praise of Folly*.

Surtz carefully examines the many forms of religious belief and practice that are discussed in More's work. He shows that far more attention is given to religious matters than is noticed by the casual reader. Exploring such themes as toleration and heresy, death, euthanasia and suicide, miracles, asceticism, celibacy, the role of bishops and priests, religious devotion, confession, sacrifice, the family, divorce, adultery, fornication, slavery, and war, Surtz outlines the status of More's (and Hythloday's) beliefs. Considering that More was writing soon before Martin Luther's public and direct challenge to the Church, Surtz shows that More was never really unorthodox. His deviant views were for the most part the same as those of some of the leading Church authorities. Then what is the point? More uses *Utopia* as a mirror in which people can look at themselves. When they do this and see that Utopia is a better place to live in than Europe, why does this not lead to a preference for the Utopian religion and a rejection of Christianity?

Surtz argues that More's book *Utopia* is in praise of wisdom. The Utopians are more rational than the Europeans. The wisdom they have is not that of Christian revelation, but rather that of the Greek and Roman thinkers. Using this rational base, the Utopians have constructed a basis for morality. What is lacking is knowledge of the Christian revelation. Surtz declares that "the Utopians have advanced in religion and morality as far as it is possible for rational creatures, unassisted by supernatural grace, to go." This may not seem to be the case when one reads *Utopia* as a critique of the human world of the time. When one reads *Utopia*, especially if one reads it as if it were written with Desiderius Erasmus looking over More's shoulder, one also might question some of the claims about religion. However, the reader should not forget that More, a secular merchant and politician, was elevated to sainthood. He died because he would not allow secular factors to enter into religious commitments. When he had to choose between the King's commands and those of the Church, he chose the latter and was beheaded by Henry VIII. More contended that Europeans should pick and choose among pagan views and customs. They should gather in the good elements and discard the bad. Some of the good features of religious practice would, if adopted by Europeans, lead to various forms of religious renovation (the kind of reformation that More and Erasmus were fighting for). If the Utopians, using only their natural reason, are able to raise natural religion to a high plane, how much more might they not accomplish if, with the aid of revelation and grace, they helped to reform the Christian world. Surtz sees More as a constructive reformer at least from the time that he wrote *Utopia*. Surtz's volume has a long bibliography of the literature about More.—*R.H.F.*

ADDITIONAL RECOMMENDED READING

Brémond, Henri. *Sir Thomas More. The Blessed Thomas More.* London: R. & T. Waterhouse, 1904. A useful biography.

Campbell, William E. *More's Utopia and His Social Teaching.* London: Eyre & Spothiswoode, 1930. Provides the kind of background information one needs to understand *Utopia*.

Chambers, Raymond W. *Thomas More.* London: J. Cape, 1938. A reliable and informative modern biography.

Kautsky, Karl. *Thomas More and His Utopia.* New York: Russell and Russell, 1959. One of the more penetrating studies of *Utopia*.

THE PRINCE

Author: Niccolò Machiavelli (1469-1527)
Type of work: Political philosophy
First published: 1532

PRINCIPAL IDEAS ADVANCED

In order to win and retain power a man is fortunate if he is born to power, for a man who rises to power by conquest or treachery makes enemies who must be eliminated.

If a prince must be cruel—and sometimes he must to retain power—he should be cruel quickly, and he should cause great injuries, for small injuries do not keep a man from revenge.

A prince should be concerned for the people he governs only to the extent that such concern strengthens his hold on the state.

Although a prince can sometimes afford to be virtuous, flattery, deceit, and even murder are often necessary if the prince is to maintain himself in power.

Great political thinkers often write about specific historical situations and yet succeed in making recommendations which apply to times other than their own. Niccolò Machiavelli must be numbered among such thinkers. An Italian patriot deeply involved in the diverse political maneuvers of sixteenth century Italy, he addresses advice to Lorenzo de' Medici which, first written in 1513 and later published as *The Prince* five years after his death, marks him as one of the most controversial, enduring, and realistic political theorists of the modern world.

In this short book Machiavelli undertakes to treat politics scientifically, judging men by an estimate of how in fact they do behave as political animals rather than by ideal standards concerned with how they ought to act. The hardheadedly consistent refusal of the author to submit political behavior to moral tests has earned the named "Machiavellian" for amoral instances of power relations among nation states and other organized groups. The power divisions of Machiavelli's Italy are now seen to have been prophetic of the massive national rivalries which followed in the Western world. The problems encountered by Renaissance princes endured long after the princes themselves fell before more powerful enemies. Machiavelli understood how success is always a minimal condition of political greatness. In *The Prince* he presents a manual of advice on the winning and retention of power in a world containing extensive political factionalism and lust for dominion.

Critics who are clearly aware of the amoral aspects of Machiavelli's political recommendations sometimes attempt to gain him a sympathetic hearing in unfriendly quarters. They do so by placing *The Prince* in its limited historical setting and relating its contents to certain biographical facts about the author. They tell us how Machiavelli longed for one ultimate goal—the eventual political unification of Italy as an independent state under one secular ruler, strong enough to rebuff the growing might of powerful neighbors like Spain and France. The armies and policies of these neighboring countries had already seriously influenced internal affairs even in Machiavelli's beloved Florence. Critics often suggest that Machiavelli's subordination of religion to the temporal aims of princes followed from his hatred of the political machinations of the Roman Catholic Church, which, by maintaining a series of temporal states, helped to keep Italy divided. The Church situation also invited foreign intrigues and corrupted the spiritual life of the Italians. In this context, another peculiarity of *The Prince* deserves mention. It is its total unconcern for forms of government other than monarchical ones. This might suggest that Machiavelli favored the monarchical form over the republican form. But such a view would be false. In the *Discourses on the First Ten Books of Titus Livius*, Machiavelli openly expressed preference for republics whenever the special conditions for their existence could be obtained. He tells us, in *The Prince*, that he has discussed republics elsewhere.

Such historical insights help to gain for *The Prince* a more understanding reading by those who reject its sharp separation of politics from morals. Yet the fact is clear that—whatever the author's motives—*The Prince* does ignore all moral ends of organized life and rather emphasizes the need to maintain sovereignty at all costs. Coldly, calculatingly, Machiavelli tries to show princes the means they must use in seeking power as an end-in-itself. He does not discuss moral rules. Discouraging to unsympathetic critics is the extent to which actual political life often seems to fit Machiavelli's somewhat cynical model.

Machiavelli classifies possible governments as either republics or monarchies. In *The Prince* he confines his analytic attention to the latter. Any monarch with a legitimate inheritance of power and traditions is most favored. The reason is that, unlike newly risen rulers, he need offend the people less. Established rulers reap the benefits from forgotten past abuses which led to the established system. Men who rise to power by virtue of conquest or favorable circumstances must confront incipient rebellions. They must also make more promises than the established ruler, thus falling under various obligations. Machiavelli believed newly created rulers must perform their cruelties quickly and ruthlessly. They must never extend cruelties over a long period of time.

Machiavelli insists that if a prince must cause injuries, he should cause great injuries, for small injuries do not keep a man from revenge. In any case, what the prince does must fit the circumstances and the nature of his particular dominion. Not all princes should attempt to use the same methods. All princes must act, however. For example, they should never postpone war simply to avoid it. In political conflicts, time is neutral regarding the participants; it produces "indifferently either good or evil."

Newly created monarchs often find themselves involved with members of a mixed state. Extreme difficulties confront a ruler in such situations. Mixed monarchies usually require rule over possessions whose citizens either share the monarch's language or they do not. A common language and nationality help to make ruling easier for the monarch, especially if his subjects' experience of freedom has been a limited one. There are two general ways in which to treat subjects who lack the monarch's nationality and language. One is that the monarch can take residence among the subjects. To do so permits a ready response to contingent problems and allows the subjects to identify themselves with the person of the ruler. The other is for the ruler to establish select colonies at key positions in the subjects' territory. Such colonies cost little. Their injured parties are also often scattered, thus proving easier to handle. If he maintains such colonies, the monarch should use diplomatic maneuvers aimed at weakening the stronger neighbors and protecting the less powerful ones. Machiavelli uses historical examples here, as he does elsewhere in *The Prince*. For example, he admires the manner in which the Romans anticipated contingencies in governing their colonies and acted promptly, if sometimes brutally, to meet them. On the other hand, Machiavelli asserts that Louis XII of France made basic blunders in a similar situation.

There will be times when the ruler must govern subjects accustomed to living under laws of their own. Machiavelli coldly suggests three methods of ruling these. First, the ruler can totally despoil them, as the Romans did to certain rebellious cities. Second, he can make his residence among the subjects, hoping to keep down future rebellions. If he chooses neither of these alternatives, the ruler must permit the subjects to live under laws of their own. In this event he must exact tribute from them. If possible, he should also put control of the laws in the hands of a few citizens upon whose loyalty he can count. It is dangerous to ignore the activities of men accustomed to living in freedom if they are part of one's sovereign state. The reason is that "in republics there is greater life, greater hatred, and more desire for revenge; they do not and cannot cast aside the memory of their ancient liberty, so that the surest way is either to lay them waste or reside in them."

Machiavelli shows great interest in how men acquire their rule over possessions. Methods of ruling must be made adaptable to differences in manner of acquisition. For example, a ruler may obtain his power as a result of someone else's abilities; or he may win power by his own abilities. Machiavelli judges the "do it yourself" method as the surest. There is no substitute for princely merit. Also, the prince should command his own military forces without depending too heavily on aid from allied troops. The wise prince will imitate great personal models, since life is primarily a matter of imitative behavior. The prudential prince must show careful regard to the right circumstances for seizing power. Once in power, he can use force if he possesses soldiers loyal to himself. Machiavelli warns princes to beware the flattery of their subjects. Especially should they show suspicion of the flattery of their ministers, who are supposed to advise them. Machiavelli's model of the state seems to be the Renaissance city-state—small in population and territorial extent. As an example of a ruler who arises by virtue of talent, he mentions Francesco Sforza, of Milan. Cesare Borgia is used to illustrate the nature of successful ruling by a prince whose power initially results from conditions created by others.

In all, there are four ways in which a prince can attain to political power. These ways are: by one's own abilities; by the use of fortunate circumstances (wealth or political inheritance); by wicked conduct and outright crime; and by the choice of one's fellow citizens. Machiavelli does not condemn the ruler who succeeds by using criminal techniques. Thus, Agathocles the ancient Sicilian used such methods in rising from a military rank to kill off the rich men and senators of Syracuse. Yet Agathocles used such excessive cruelty that Machiavelli warns scholars not "to include him among men of real excellence." Instances of power criminally seized and successfully held lead Machiavelli to suggest that cruelty is intrinsically neither good nor bad. Cruelty must be said to have been used well "when all cruel deeds are committed at once in order to make sure of the state and thereafter discontinued to make way for the consideration of the welfare of the subjects."

Nonetheless Machiavelli never asserts that cruelty is the best means of attaining to power. His judgment here as elsewhere is a hypothetical one: if the situation is one requiring cruelty for the realization of power, then the prince must do what is necessary. Thus, although Machiavelli prefers methods which do not involve cruelty, he refuses to condemn the Prince who uses cruelty.

The conditional nature of Machiavelli's recommendations about seizing power becomes evident when he discusses the case of the prince who rises by the consent of his fellow citizens. This makes the most promising situation for a prince. But it rarely happens. Thus, this case cannot serve as a universal model. Chosen in such a manner, a prince need not fear that men will dare to oppose or to disobey him. "The worst a prince can fear from the people is that they will desert him." On the other hand, if his power stems from the nobility, the prince must fear both their possible desertion and their possible rebellion. In order to prepare for a rebellion the people obviously require trained leaders. Thus, a prudent ruler supported by the people must attempt to retain their favor. A prince initially supported by the nobles can win over the people by making himself their protector. If he succeeds, he may end up stronger than the prince originally chosen by the people; for the people will appreciate the benefactor who guards them against internal oppression. Machiavelli is never so cynical as to argue that a wise prince can endlessly ignore the needs of his own people. Yet he justifies a concern for the people solely in terms of its value toward guaranteeing a continuing rule. Realistically, Machiavelli insists that the prince must lead an army. This is true even of churchmen who manage ecclesiastical states. Force or the threat of force serves as the basis of the state. Times of peace should never be permitted to divert the ruler's mind "from the study of warfare." In peaceful times the prudent ruler estimates future events. By thought and preparation he gets ready to meet such events.

A morbid sense of the contingency of human events runs through the book. Any ruler must show concern for changes of fortune and circumstance. The prince should show caution in delegating any of his own powers. Machiavelli hardly ever discusses economic or ideological problems. Normally, the prince of whom he writes is a single man bent on political self-preservation and the quest for methods by which to coerce his enemies into submission or inaction. The picture is one of a ruler feverishly studying the histories and actions of great men to be ready for the possible day when relatively stable conditions may alter for the worse. The reader concludes that, in Machiavelli's view, stability in politics is extremely rare. Yet Machiavelli understands that no prince can stand completely alone. Some powers must be delegated. Some men must be favored over others. How the prince treats his friends and subjects will always influence future political events. The prince should work to create a character able to make sudden adjustments in terms of his own self-interest. The most successful ruler must "be prudent enough to escape the infamy of such views as would result in the loss of his state." He must never cultivate those private virtues which, in a public man, can prove politically suicidal. He should develop vices if these will help to perpetuate his rule.

Generosity is a value in a prince only if it produces some benefit and no harm. A wise ruler will tax his subjects without becoming miserly. Yet he should prefer the name "miser" to a reputation for generosity which may prevent him from raising monies needed to maintain security. Generosity can more easily lead to the subjects' hatred and contempt than can miserliness. The prince can even show mercy if it is not interpreted as mere permissiveness. The cursedly cruel Borgia proved more merciful than the Florentine rulers who lost the city to foreigners. As long as he keeps his subjects loyal and united the ruler may sometimes act strenuously against them. Especially is this necessary in newly created monarchies. Machiavelli's advice goes something like: try to be both loved and feared, but choose being feared if there is no other alternative. The subjects obey a prince who can punish them.

In maintaining order the prince has some rule-of-thumb rules to follow. He should keep his word unless deceit is specifically called for. He should use admired private virtues if they do not interfere with the play of political power. A conception of human nature operates here. Machiavelli thinks the plain man is capable of some loyalty to a ruler. But such a man is easily led. "Men are so simple," Machiavelli writes, "and so ready to follow the needs of the moment that the deceiver will always find someone to deceive." A prince must know how and when to mingle the fox's cunning (the ability to avoid traps) with the lion's strength (capacity to fight the wolves). He should often conceal his real motives. Internally, he must avoid conspiracies. Externally, he should keep enemies fearful of attacking. Against conspirators the prince always has an advantage. Conspirators cannot work in isolation; thus they fear the existing laws and the threat of detection. Only when the population shows some open hostility need the prince genuinely fear conspirators.

Machiavelli realizes that men seldom get to choose the circumstances most favorable to their political hopes. They must settle for what is possible rather than for the ideal. Princes must avoid the lures of utopian political constructions—"for how we live is so different from how we ought to live that he who studies what ought to be done rather than what is done will learn the way to his downfall rather than to his preservation." Machiavelli regards men as weak, fickle, and subject to changing loyalties. These psychological traits are the bedrock on which a wise prince must build his policies.

Nonetheless the author of *The Prince* understands that success in politics, however rationally pursued, is beyond the complete control of any man. The Renaissance worry about "Chance" and "Fortune" haunts the final pages of Machiavelli's book. Large-order events in the world often seem to drive men onward much like "the fury of the flood." Yet not all events happen fortuitously. Men are half free to shape their political lives within the broader forces of the universe. That prince rules best, therefore, whose character and conduct "fit the times." It will be better for the ruler to be bold rather than cautious. Fortune is like a female—"well disposed to young men, for they are less circumspect and more violent and more bold to command her." Thus Machiavelli argues for a partial freedom of will and action within a world largely made up of determined forces.

The Prince stands as a classic example of realistic advice to rulers seeking unity and preservation of states. Its picture of human nature is somewhat cynical, viewing man as vacillating and in need of strong political direction. Yet the work is not modern in one sense; namely, it fails to discuss ideological aspects of large-scale political organization. Machiavelli's prince is one who must learn from experience. His conclusion is that ruling is more like an art than like a science. What is somewhat modern is the realistic emphasis on tailoring political advice to the realization of national ends whose moral value is not judged. *The Prince* is therefore a fascinating if sometimes shocking justification of the view that moral rules are not binding in the activities of political rulers.—*W.T.D.*

PERTINENT LITERATURE
Cassirer, Ernst. *The Myth of the State.* New Haven, Connecticut: Yale University Press, 1946.

Written against the background of modern totalitarianism, this book was an attempt to explain the recrudescence of myth in modern times. The significance of Niccolò Machiavelli, according to Ernst Cassirer, was that he helped to demythologize politics, preparing the way for the rational understanding of the state which guided Western thought until it was challenged by the romantic reaction in favor of political myth.

Cassirer has no patience with modern scholars who obscure the significance of Machiavelli's thought by representing him as writing only for his generation and saying pretty much what others had said before. Machiavelli believed that what he was saying was new and that it was true for all time to come. Moreover, readers as discerning as Cardinal Richelieu, Catherine de Médicis, and Charles Talleyrand were of the same opinion. Galileo was to say of his own *Dialogues* that they "set forth a very new science dealing with a very ancient subject." Cassirer believes that Machiavelli could have made the same boast respecting *The Prince*. As the one laid the foundations for modern physics, so the other paved the way for political science.

Clearly, Machiavelli was not simply pandering to men's penchant for evildoing: already there were books which extolled the role of tyrants. What excited Machiavelli and his readers was the conception of politics divorced from medieval notions of divine right and natural law. Political changes were then taking place which adroit rulers such as Cesare Borgia had learned to accommodate. Machiavelli was the first thinker to understand the changes and to explain that they entailed a reversal of the relation between might and right. Appearance of right remained one of the constituents of power, but the substance was gone; a strong ruler, at least briefly, could do without even the appearance of right. *The Prince* shocked many readers simply by telling things the way they were. But according to Cassirer, besides describing facts, the book offered its readers a whole new theory and art of politics.

Medieval social theory no less than medieval cosmology took for granted a natural hierarchy of being. The boldness of Machiavelli lay in the fact that a hundred years before Galileo he destroyed the cornerstone of this tradition, denying the theocratic principle and asserting the independence and sovereignty of the temporal power. Frederick II had long before this achieved complete secularization of the state: Christians, Jews, and Saracens shared in his administration. No theory, however, had accompanied that development. Machiavelli was the first to define the state without reference to theological ideas, going so far as to treat religion simply as a tool in the hands of political architects. In Cassirer's words, the secular state henceforth existed not only *de facto* but also *de jure*.

It was one thing, of course, to declare the state independent of religious authority; but it was another thing to view the state as fully autonomous. Here, according to Cassirer, lay the danger of Machiavelli's position. A state has roots in the organic needs of human existence. Machiavelli, in his zeal to free it from religious and metaphysical ties, cut it loose from the economic, moral, and cultural life of the people as well. Politics was treated much like a game of chess. It made no difference to Machiavelli who the players were or who won. Fascinated by the game, he rallied the prospective prince, reminding him that the strategy included fraud and treachery, and urging him to play with no thought but to win. Unfortunately, says Cassirer, he forgot that politics is played not with pieces of ivory but with human beings.

There is, Cassirer recognizes, a real question as to how a man of Machiavelli's nobility of character could openly counsel princes to commit criminal acts. The conventional answer is that in the author's eyes these acts were justified because they served the common good. But this answer, in Cassirer's opinion, blurs the distinction which Machiavelli insisted upon between the viewpoint of the prince and that of the private person. When someone said that Napoleon's execution of the Duke of Enghien was a crime, Talleyrand is supposed to have remarked that it was worse than a crime: it was a mistake. This, says Cassirer, well expresses Machiavelli's view. Machiavelli insisted that if a person is unwilling to perform criminal acts when necessary he had better leave politics alone. He makes this clear in what he has to say about being beastly to beasts: his reference to Chiron, the Centaur, as the first preceptor of princes shows how radically his view of the art of government differs from that of Plato, who made Socrates the preceptors, and who equated the art of ruling with the highest wisdom. Plato and his followers saw the state as founded on law. Discarding this ideal, Machiavelli started from the fact that actual politics has always been full of crime and concluded that if such things are to be done they should be done well. This meant that the arts of practical control, even when criminal from the conventional point of view, should be included in the art of governing, and taught as such.

Cassirer doubts whether Machiavelli realized the full implications of his teachings and draws a distinction between his teachings and Machiavellism as we know it today. Politics in Italy was small in scale compared with what it came to be under the great monarchs and more recently under the great dictators, and techniques of political crime were in their infancy. Moreover, there remained in Europe strong moral and intellectual forces which worked to keep governments within the bounds of law. Then, in the nineteenth century, romantic philosophers, reacting against the Enlightenment, launched their attack against theories of natural law. In this way, the last barrier to the triumph of Machiavellism was removed.

Meinecke, Friedrich. *Machiavellism: The Doctrine of Raison d'État and Its*

Place in Modern History. Translated by Douglas Scott. New Haven, Connecticut: Yale University Press, 1957.

As Friedrich Meinecke uses it, the term "reason of state" designates the particular course of action which an official must take in order to preserve the health and strength of the state on a given occasion. Because the state is an independent organism pursuing its own ends, reason of state presupposes an understanding of the state and its environment. Thus, what began as statecraft led on to a theory of the state and its place in nature. Like man, the state is amphibious, living partly in the realm of nature, partly in the realm of mind. Machiavelli, the first to grapple profoundly with this polarity of the physical and the spiritual in man, was, so far as modern history is concerned, the discoverer of reason of state.

What gave Niccolò Machiavelli's work its historical power was the fact that he fully explored both the bright and the dark aspects of political life. Machiavelli understood the uses of power, but he despised senseless greed for power and insisted that it be subordinated to the common well-being. Although he is usually thought of as a realist, that side of his work cannot, in Meinecke's opinion, be rightly estimated without recognition of his fundamental idealism.

Central to this idealism was his concept of virtue (*virtù*) drawn from pagan antiquity where there was no conflict between politics and ethics because everyone regarded participation in civic life as his main good. The originator of reason of state, says Meinecke, had to be heathen; and this was eminently possible during the Italian Renaissance, with its romantic attitude toward the past. Virtue, as Machiavelli elaborated it, was a dynamic force which raised man's native impulses to the level of a code of values for rulers and citizens. No great civic achievements, he maintained, are possible without virtuous citizens, men and women capable of great labors and sacrifices for the common good; but in addition to the virtuous citizens, there must be leaders with special virtues—men capable of founding and ruling states. Machiavelli's argument with himself concerning republics and monarchies was resolved in the light of these considerations. His judgment with respect to Italy in his day seems to have been that because citizens lacked the proper virtues, republics were doomed. He held, however, that by means of their special virtue, princes create virtue in their subjects. Indeed, the development of virtue was the one completely self-evident purpose of any state, whether republic or monarchy.

Virtue so conceived exists only in tension with necessity; and it is what Machiavelli had to say about causal determination that makes him appear to us to be a realist. Human beings are not wicked; they are sluggish and will never do anything unless they are driven to it, either by hunger and poverty or by the lash of a taskmaster. The only break in the causal order is the creative power of the great man who is able to change the sluggard into a citizen. Thereafter, physical necessity is absorbed by the necessity of the state; and if rulers are to follow the real truth of things, they must "learn how not to be good" when this necessity constrains.

Necessity is the intelligible feature of circumstance. But for heads of state there are unknown and unpredictable features to be reckoned with as well. These are known as fate or fortune. Hence, the great leader must be a gambler. Fortune overcomes where men have not much virtue, and this explains the instability of most states. As we are told in the *Discourses*, however, "sooner or later there will come a man who so loves antiquity that he will regulate fortune." Fortune is malicious; so must virtue be. When it is a question of winning, unclean methods are allowed.

Meinecke is aware of the sinister aspects of reason of state. Granted that there are occasions when the common good makes immoral measures necessary, there is a temptation for rulers to employ this principle to justify immoral acts which, although expedient, are not necessary. That the sanctity of moral law is not permanently impaired when law is made to yield to supraempirical necessity was the judgment of scholastic thinkers; but when truth and justice are treated simply as elements in the empirical situation, to be weighed against material advantages, then the gates are opened to forces of active evil which traditional morality had opposed. Meinecke finds here the source of a new dualism which plagues modern civilization. By declaring their independence from any transcendent law, secular states have achieved a degree of rational organization inconceivable to the Middle Ages. At the same time, the indispensable foundation for this achievement remains the fidelity of the mass of mankind to values regarded as absolute.

Meinecke finds further fault with Machiavelli because of his failure to demand of rulers a certain moral restraint. It was vicious to tell princes that they need not possess loyalty and sincerity although they must appear to have these qualities. Meinecke would have liked to find in Machiavelli some recognition of the fact that a truly great leader does not ride rough-shod over his fellows but knows how, when occasion demands, to take on himself some of the suffering, even to the point of accepting personal disgrace if that is the only means of saving the people. Apparently the ability to think in terms of inner conflicts and tragic sacrifices was beyond Machiavelli.—*J.F.*

ADDITIONAL RECOMMENDED READING

Berlin, Isaiah. "The Question of Machiavelli," in *The New York Review of Books*. Special Supplement, XVII, no. 7 (November 4, 1971), pp. 20-32. Argues that Machiavelli shocks his readers mainly because he makes it clear that mankind has to choose its values.

Butterfield, Herbert. *The Statecraft of Machiavelli*. London: G. Bell and Sons, 1955. Stresses Machiavelli's use of history in political analysis.

Jensen, De Lamar, ed. *Machiavelli: Cynic, Patriot, or Political Scientist?* Boston: D. C. Heath and Company, 1960. A useful selection of contemporary writings about Machiavelli.

Maritain, Jacques. "The End of Machiavellianism," in *The Review of Politics*. IV, no. 1 (January, 1942), pp. 1-32. According to Maritain, politics is not an art in the technical sense as Machiavelli takes it to be, but a branch of ethics.

APOLOGY FOR RAIMOND SEBOND

Author: Michel Eyquem de Montaigne (1533-1592)
Type of work: Skeptical criticism of theology
First published: 1580

Principal Ideas Advanced

True religion must be based on faith; but, given faith, reasons can be used to strengthen faith.

Rationality is a form of animal behavior; in many respects animals excel men, and in comparison to animals, men seem to be vain, stupid, and immoral.

The Greek skeptics, the Pyrrhonists, were sensible in doubting everything, contesting all claims, and living according to nature and custom.

Scientists, philosophers, and all others who seek knowledge—including those who seek knowledge of probabilities—fail in their efforts.

We depend on sense experience for our knowledge of the world, but we do not know whether five senses are adequate, nor can we determine how accurately the senses represent the real world.

This essay, the longest of all of Montaigne's writings, sets forth the reasons for the great French humanist's belief in skepticism. It is the work which was most influential in reviving and popularizing the Greek skeptical theory Pyrrhonism, during the Renaissance and in the seventeenth century. Montaigne's followers based their arguments upon this essay, and many important philosophers, including René Descartes, Pierre Gassendi, Blaise Pascal, and Nicolas Malebranche studied it and used some of Montaigne's ideas in developing their own philosophies. The essay is also one of the first writings which discuss philosophical issues in a modern language. It had a tremendous vogue in the seventeenth century. Late in the century it was put on the Index of prohibited books. It has remained one of the major classics of French literature and thought, and is one of the richest examples of Renaissance humanism and skepticism.

The essay was apparently begun in 1575, when Montaigne was studying the recently translated (into Latin) writings of the Greek skeptic, Sextus Empiricus, a third century writer. These works so impressed Montaigne that they caused him to doubt all of his previous views and led him to go through his own personal skeptical crisis. During the period of this crisis, he sought to show that the knowledge which men claimed to have gained through the use of their senses and their reasoning capacities was all open to doubt.

The *Apology for Raimond Sebond* purports to be a defense of the views of the fifteenth century rationalist theologian from Spain, Raimond Sebond. At the outset, Montaigne tells us that he had published a translation of Sebond's *Natural Theology* (which appeared in 1569) shortly after his father's death because of his father's wish that he do so. His father had received the work much earlier from a French theologian who reported that he had been saved from Lutheranism by studying Sebond's rational arguments in favor of Christianity. After Montaigne's edition of Sebond appeared, he found that many of the readers (especially, he tells us, the ladies) required assistance in comprehending and accepting Sebond's message. Objections had been raised against Sebond's audacious contention that all of the articles of the Christian faith can be proved by natural reason. Because of the difficulties that readers were having with the work, and because of the objections, Montaigne reports that he undertook the task of writing an "apology"—a defense. Because of the character of the *Apology*, scholars have debated and are still debating the question of Montaigne's real intent in publishing this essay. Was it to defend Sebond (which seems quite unlikely in view of the contents of the essay)? Was it to offer a different defense of Christianity through skepticism— or was it to employ skeptical thought to undermine all beliefs, including those of Christianity? The essay can be, and has been, read in both the latter two ways, and it has greatly influenced the fideists (those who base their religious beliefs on faith alone) and those who are skeptical of all religious beliefs.

The *Apology* is written in Montaigne's inimitable rambling style. It presents a series of waves of doubt, with occasional pauses to reflect on these. The various skeptical themes are interwoven with the recurring note that faith and revelation are the only unquestionable sources of any truth.

Montaigne begins his serious discussion by considering two kinds of objections that have been raised against Sebond's views, one that Christianity should be based on faith and not on reason, and the other that Sebond's reasoning is not sound. In discussing the first point, Montaigne develops his fideistic theme, and in discussing the second, his skepticism. He alleges to defend Sebond by contending first that Christianity is founded solely on faith, and then that, since all reasoning is unsound, Sebond should not be singled out for blame on this score.

Early in the essay, Montaigne excuses Sebond's theological rationalism by stating that there is nothing wrong with using reason to defend the faith, as long as we realize that faith does not depend upon reasons, and that our rational capacities are unable to attain supernatural and divine wisdom. As far as Montaigne can see, true religion must be based on faith given to us by the grace of God. Our purely human capacities are too weak to support divine knowledge. When we rely on human faculties to find and accept the true religion, we end up by accepting religions because of custom, habit, or geographical location. If, however, we have the real light of faith, then reasons like those Sebond offers can be employed as aids to our faith, although not as proofs of it.

To "defend" Sebond on the second charge—that his arguments are too weak—Montaigne begins a general attack on all human reasoning by arguing that no one can attain certainty by rational means. The first level of skepticism offered purports to show that man's capacities are unimpressive when compared with those of animals. Man, egotistically, believes that he, and he alone, can comprehend the world, which was created and which operates for his benefit. But he cannot tell that this is the case. And when he compares his capacities with those of animals, he finds that he possesses no faculties or capacities that beasts lack; in fact, the beasts excel man in many respects. Montaigne introduces various examples from the writings of Sextus Empiricus to show that rationality is just a form of animal behavior. Montaigne insists that even religion is not a unique human possession, for even elephants seem to pray. When man's behavior is carefully contrasted with that of animals, man is seen as rather vain, stupid, and immoral. With all of our alleged superior faculties, we are not able to live as well or as happily as the animals. The illustrative material presented by Montaigne is supposed to have the cumulative effect of making us doubt our superior wisdom and knowledge. We think we know the truth, but our knowing is only a form of animal behavior, and it does not enable us to achieve even as much as the rest of the animals can and do. Hence, Montaigne insists, our disease is our belief that we can know something. And this is why our religion recommends a state of ignorance to us as most proper for belief and obedience.

Montaigne continues this attack on our intellectual pretensions by comparing the wisdom of the educated European of his day with the ignorance of the "noble savages," the recently discovered inhabitants of Brazil. The latter are portrayed as living a far superior life, because "they pass their lives in an admirable simplicity and ignorance, without any learning, laws, kings, or any religion whatsoever."

Christianity, according to Montaigne, teaches us to acquire a similar ignorance in order that we may believe by faith alone. Whatever truths we know are gained not by our own abilities, but by God's grace. Even our religion is not acquired through our reasoning and comprehension. Instead, we receive it only by God's revelation to us. Our ignorance is an asset in this regard, in that our own inability to know anything leads us to be willing to submit ourselves to God's will, and to accept what teachings he gives us. To show that Christianity is based on an awareness of our ignorance, rather than on any knowledge we might have, Montaigne quotes one of his favorite texts from the Bible, the attack on rational knowledge that appears at the beginning of St. Paul's first letter to the Corinthians.

Next, Montaigne presents a more philosophical basis for his complete skepticism in the form of a description and defense of the ancient Greek skeptical view, Pyrrhonism, as well as an explanation of the value of this theory for religion. The Pyrrhonists doubt and suspend judgment concerning any and all propositions whatsoever, even the claim that all is in doubt. They contest every assertion that is made. If they are successful, they exhibit their opponents' ignorance. If they are unsuccessful, they show their own ignorance. While they are doubting everything, the Pyrrhonists live according to nature and custom. Montaigne tells us that this attitude is both the finest of human achievements and that which is most compatible with religion. The Pyrrhonists show man naked and empty, a blank tablet, ready to receive any message that God wishes to write on it. The Pyrrhonists expose man as he really is, in his total ignorance. This exposé should make man humble and obedient, ready to receive divine truth.

The ancient Pyrrhonists not only reached the summit of human wisdom in seeing that all is in doubt, but also, Montaigne and his disciples insisted, provided the best defense of Catholicism against the Protestant Reformation. The complete skeptic would have no positive views and, consequently, no incorrect ones. He would accept only the laws and customs of his community. Hence, in sixteenth century France he would accept Catholicism. Further, by being in doubt about everything, the Pyrrhonist would be in the perfect state to receive the revelation of the true religion. Thus, if God so willed, Montaigne tells us, the skeptic will be a Catholic by both custom and tradition, and by faith also.

Montaigne next compares the achievements of the ancient Pyrrhonists with the failings of the more dogmatic philosophers. The latter have quarreled over every possible question without coming to any definite conclusion. In the end, the dogmatic philosophers have had to admit their failure to attain any indubitable knowledge in any field whatsoever. A survey of the attempts of philosophers throughout history to achieve any true knowledge only leads one to the conclusion that "philosophy is only sophisticated poetry." All that philosophers ever offer us are theories that they have invented, not truths about the world. Some of these theories become accepted at various times, and are regarded as authoritative and unquestionable. But there is no more evidence that these theories are true than that they are false. The only true principles that men possess, Montaigne insists, are those that God has revealed to us. All other alleged truths are nothing but dreams and smoke.

The debacle of human intellectual undertakings is so complete that even the Pyrrhonist is unable to survive unscathed. If the Pyrrhonist declares, after looking at the sad history of man's intellectual achievements, that all is in doubt, then he has asserted something positive and is no longer in doubt about everything. The Pyrrhonist, Montaigne says, cannot state his doubts without contradicting himself. The fault lies with our language, which is basically assertive. Only a negative language would allow for a genuine statement of the Pyrrhonian view.

After making all these points, and digressing in many different directions, Montaigne, toward the end of the essay, finally states the evidence offered by the Pyrrhonists to show that all is in doubt. We do not seem able to gain any knowledge either from our experience or from our reasonings. We appear to be unable to tell what it is that we experience, and whether we actually experience the things we think we experience. We cannot, for example, ascertain the true nature of heat or of any other experienced quality. Similarly, we cannot tell what our rational faculty is, or even where it is. The experts disagree about everything, and when we look at their various opinions, we are led to realize how uncertain they *all* are. From these considerations, we come to the conclusion once more that our only genuine understanding comes from God, and not from any of our information or faculties.

Some philosophers, after seeing how everybody disagrees about everything, have come to the conclusion that nothing can be known, either about ourselves or anything else, but that some opinions are more probable than others. This view, developed by the Academic skeptics in antiquity, Montaigne maintains, is more unsatisfactory than the complete doubt of the Pyrrhonists. If we could reach any agreement about probabilities, then we should be able to come to agreements concerning the probable characters of particular things. But, as a matter of fact, our judgments change constantly with our various bodily and emotional states; we do not find one view more probable than another, except at specific times and under specific conditions. As our views change, we find that we disagree with what we formerly thought was probable and with what others think is probable. Thus, we cannot take probabilities as guides to truth, but can only fall back on the Pyrrhonian view that everything can be doubted, and on the truths that God gives us.

When we examine the scientific achievements of mankind, we find these as dubious as anything else, since in every science the experts disagree, and what is accepted as true at one time is rejected as false at another. For example, Montaigne points out, earlier astronomers said that the heavens moved around the earth, and now a new astronomer, Nicolaus Copernicus, says that the earth moves. Perhaps centuries from now another astronomer will disprove all of them. Prior to Aristotle, other theories seemed acceptable. Why should we now accept Aristotle's as the last word? Even in a science as apparently certain as geometry, there are difficulties which render it dubious. Paradoxes, like those developed by Zeno of Elea in the fifth century B.C., indicate that geometry is not completely certain. The recent discoveries in the New World indicate that the accepted beliefs about human nature are not so certain. (Montaigne was perhaps the first to realize the extent to which the information about the cultures in America indicated that the beliefs of Europeans about human nature were relative to their own experience and civilization.) Similarly, information about ancient Greece and Rome, as well as about the various cultures in Europe itself, shows that views about law, religion, social customs, and the like change all the time, and that what has been accepted as true in one culture has been rejected by another.

From here, Montaigne moves on to the theoretical basis of the Pyrrhonian position, the critique of sense knowledge, "the greatest foundation and proof of our ignorance." All of our knowledge appears to come from sense information, but there are certain basic difficulties with regard to this information which cast it in doubt. First of all, we do not know whether we possess all the necessary senses for obtaining true knowledge. We have five senses, but it may require ten to see nature correctly. Our sense information may be as far removed from the truth as a blind man's view of colors. Second, even if we possess all the needed senses, there is the possibility that they may be deceptive. The occurrence of illusions gives us some grounds for distrusting our senses. Further, our sense experience seems to vary according to our emotional state. Besides the many reasons that Sextus Empiricus offered for distrusting our senses, there is also the problem that we cannot tell whether our sense experience is part of a dream or a genuine reflection of what the world is like. When we consider all the Pyrrhonian arguments about sense knowledge, we realize that we can know only how things appear to us, and not how they are in themselves.

Besides, Montaigne argues, for all that we know, the senses may distort what we perceive, in the same way that certain kinds of lenses do. The qualities we perceive may be imposed upon objects rather than actually being in them. What we experience differs with our condition, our location, and so on. Unless we possess some standard by which to judge when we have the right experience, we have no way of distinguishing true information about the world from false information. But this raises the classical skeptical problem of the criterion—how do we tell what standard is the true one? To answer this question we need another standard. If we try to use our reason to decide, we will need further reasons to justify the ones we have employed, and so on to infinity.

Hence, if our senses are the sources of all of our ideas, we can be sure of nothing. We have no completely certain standard to use to judge when or if our ideas or sense impressions correspond to the real objects outside of us. We are forever in the position of the man who tries to determine whether a picture of Socrates is a good likeness, when he has never seen Socrates.

These successive waves of skepticism leave one finally with the realization that trying to know reality is like trying to clutch water. It cannot be done. Until God decides to enlighten us, all of our supposed knowledge will remain uncertain. It is only through the grace of God, Montaigne concludes, that we can ever achieve any contact with reality.

Montaigne's *Apology* introduces, in its unsystematic way, many of the traditional arguments of the Greek skeptics. Throughout the essay, Montaigne couples the argument for complete skepticism with an appeal to faith as the way out of doubt. For some of his readers, his important message is that human beings cannot be certain of anything, including the truths asserted by traditional religions. For other readers, both his doubts and his fideistic solution were equally important. For them, Montaigne showed that human beings by their own devices could not find any certain knowledge; they could find it only through faith.

The *Apology for Raimond Sebond* is one of the works which was most important in setting the stage for the beginning of modern philosophy, for it provided a series of doubts about all previous theories. The new philosophers of the seventeenth century had either to find a way of answering the many skeptical arguments of Montaigne, or to accept his skeptical conclusion. In the *Apology*, Montaigne provided the starting point for "the quest for certainty," as well as a skeptical resolution of the problems he considered. —*R.H.P.*

PERTINENT LITERATURE

Brush, Craig B. *Montaigne and Bayle: Variations on the Theme of Skepticism*. The Hague, The Netherlands: Martinus Nijhoff, 1966.

Craig B. Brush's thoughtful study examines the skeptical views of Michel Eyquem de Montaigne and Pierre Bayle in order to delineate the similarities and the differences in their views. The study is very carefully documented. Brush first describes the skeptical tradition prior to Montaigne. Starting with a discussion of ancient Greece, Brush goes on to describe the Renaissance revival of skepticism, much in the manner that it appears in R. H. Popkin's *History of Scepticism from Erasmus to Spinoza*. Brush presents the story up to the point of describing the amazing coincidence that Montaigne and his cousin, Francisco Sanches, published their skeptical works in 1580-1581. Even more coincidentally, the cousins, who may never have met, both wrote the most skeptical part of their work in 1575-1576.

Brush next turns to evaluating Montaigne's skepticism, first in Montaigne's early essays, and then in a very careful detailed analysis of the *Apology for Raimond Sebond*. After describing Sebond's *Natural Theology*, Brush turns to a consideration of Montaigne's defense of that work.

Montaigne seemed to be embarrassed that he had translated Sebond's work at his father's request, and felt that he could not really defend its rationalism. Yet he did republish his translation after writing the *Apology*. Brush argues that Montaigne had genuine respect for Sebond. But the best way that Montaigne could find to defend him was to counterattack against Sebond's opponents by developing a broader and broader skepticism and by contrasting human knowledge and divinely inspired faith. Brush sets forth a careful summary of the content of the *Apology*, showing when the Pyrrhonian material from Sextus Empiricus was appropriated by Montaigne. The use of total skepticism as a road to faith is spelled out.

Brush rejects those who held that Montaigne's attacks on a rational basis for faith were intentionally dishonest. There is no evidence of malice, *and* Montaigne stated what in its day was the Christian fideist view, held to by some notable Churchmen. The Church of Rome examined the *Essais* in 1581 and found nothing to object to in the *Apology*; and Montaigne's skepticism was used by Catholics to oppose Protestantism.

In summing up the meaning of the *Apology*, Brush contends that it was basically a defense of Montaigne's religion, showing the path from dubious human religions to real faith. The fact that Montaigne said so little about the actual content of Christianity has, of course, made many critics dubious of this interpretation. They also question whether Montaigne left Christian doctrines apart from his skeptical attack. Brush replies that if Montaigne's religious views were based on faith, then they would be impervious to his skeptical doubts: one could have real faith only if all dubious dogmatic reasons for belief had been eradicated by skeptical arguments.

In analyzing the final portion of the *Apology*, Brush indicates that Montaigne was much more concerned than Sextus with the turmoil around him. He was living through ghastly religious wars. Skepticism, if applied to the political and social scene, might lead to a much-needed toleration of opposing views.

When Brush turns to comparing Bayle with Montaigne, he sees the former as pedantic and argumentative. The two skeptics both professed a religious fideism, but Brush states that Montaigne's was more complete than Bayle's. The fact that Montaigne was a Catholic and Bayle a Protestant may account for some of the difference. Also, he contends, Montaigne, his skepticism notwithstanding, had an optimistic art of living, while Bayle was almost thoroughly pessimistic. However, Brush concludes, both thinkers despised the assurance and cruelty of dogmatic arrogance. "They were skeptics, and as such, respecters of men."

Hallie, Philip P. *The Scar of Montaigne: An Essay in Personal Philosophy.* Middletown, Connecticut: Wesleyan University Press, 1966.

Philip P. Hallie's excellent study traces Michel Eyquem de Montaigne's development of a personal philosophy of extreme skepticism. Hallie begins with the political and cultural conditions of the time, especially the religious wars, the humanistic revival, and the new geographical discoveries. Living in a world in which such radical changes were taking place, Montaigne was a moderate in the face of the political and religious dogmatic fanaticisms that were undermining the stability of France. His moderate views then led him to adopt a form of skepticism. Hallie, who contends that skepticism was a large and integral part of what he called Montaigne's personal philosophy, goes on to present the Pyrrhonian skepticism that Montaigne found in the works of Sextus Empiricus. (Hallie had earlier made a translation of selections from Sextus, published under the title *Scepticism, Man and God*, 1964.)

To show what type of skeptic Montaigne was, Hallie naturally examines the *Apology for Raimond Sebond* in detail. From the outset of his study, Hallie underscores the fundamental point that Sextus, Montaigne's main source, was speaking as the leader of a philosophical school. Montaigne, on the other hand, was speaking for himself, perhaps following Sextus' dictum that each person should announce his own impressions at the moment of stating them. Hallie sees the *Apology* as the root of a personal philosophy. The work grew out of events in the bitter religious controversies of the time. It purports to be a defense of an unskeptical theologian, Raimond Sebond. The defense, of course, is to show that everybody's reason, including Sebond's and Montaigne's, is too weak to reach absolute conclusions about matters of philosophy, theology, and science. We may be able practically to find sufficient answers to live by, but we cannot find any overall system of truth by using only our faculties of reason and the senses. So the opponent of Sebond (or of anyone else) is unable to justify his objections. Only if we go beyond our natural faculties and seek assistance through faith and grace can we find any certain answers. Hallie insists that, for Montaigne, the full-blown skepticism of the *Apology* was itself an artifact, a human creation that is useful for curing sick, dogmatic souls by exhibiting the world to us in its many different aspects.

Going on to survey the other essays, Hallie traces how Montaigne moved from general doubts to seeking within oneself some kind of acceptable or functional reactions to experiences. Montaigne had said at the outset of the essays that he was painting himself. He was not, like Sextus, fighting for a philosophical position. His essays, even including the *Apology*, are personal statements. His philosophy, Hallie declares, is a personal one in that it is the portrait of the mind of Montaigne; it portrays the human mind as a means for aiding in finding health and life, rather than objective truth; and it is addressed to people who might wish to know this particular author. Skepticism is a way of gaining relief from personal and public troubles. Personal philosophy deals with what Montaigne or anyone else needs, in his particular circumstances, to live as he would like. (Hallie's appendix on Montaignian and Cartesian doubt brings this out very well.)

The second half of Hallie's book deals with two aspects of Montaigne's adoption of skepticism as a personal philosophy. The first treats the role of language in the troubles of the world. Hallie ably discusses what was involved in Montaigne's day in the humanistic studies of language, as well as the significance of modern linguistic diagnoses such as those of Ludwig Wittgenstein. We are shown how Montaigne's style was vital in the statement of his views. The last part of the book deals with the fruits of personal philosophy. Montaigne had a scar—namely, his inability to take the lead in public causes; but his personal philosophy, born out of Pyrrhonian skepticism, made it possible for him to live. It is up to each reader, Hallie concludes, to respond to the public and private Montaigne in terms of his or her own personal philosophy.

Frame, Donald M. *Montaigne: A Biography*. New York: Harcourt Brace & World, 1965.

Donald M. Frame's biography of Michel Eyquem de Montaigne interprets Montaigne's ideas in terms of their place in Montaigne's life and in terms of the social and cultural context in which they appeared. In the light of such an interpretation, Frame portrays the *Apology for Raimond Sebond* as of central importance for the author. The *Apology* is seen as liberating Montaigne completely from any dogmatic philosophy. It is, according to Frame, "Montaigne's declaration of complete intellectual independence," a work which allowed the author to look within himself for wisdom and guidance.

The early part of the book deals in great detail with Montaigne's background, his training, and his early political and intellectual career. Frame details Montaigne's half Jewish, half Catholic background, influenced by his numerous relatives who became Protestants, including his mother. Frame sees the family background, together with the cosmopolitan atmosphere in Bordeaux, as the root of Montaigne's great tolerance and humanism. The school Montaigne attended, the College of Guyenne, was staffed by dissidents from as far away as Scotland and Portugal. Some have seen it as a hotbed of Renaissance skepticism.

Montaigne's role in the political-religious affairs of Bordeaux seems to have left him skeptical about both the political and the religious resolutions of man's problems. Montaigne retired at thirty-eight and began writing his *Essais*. Frame explores the themes in the early essays that led to the complete skepticism of the *Apology*. Then Frame presents a very detailed summary of the lengthy essay. After the summary, he commences his evaluation by asking in what sense this extremely skeptical essay can be an apology for Raimond Sebond, who was a rational theologian. Is the apology actually an attack on Sebond's religion, Christianity, by showing that it cannot be supported by rational means?

Frame, by analyzing the probable order of the composition of the various parts of the *Apology*, indicates that by the time Montaigne read Sextus Empiricus and became so involved with skeptical views, he had pretty much set Sebond's ideas aside. In 1576 Montaigne was apparently most forcefully struck by Pyrrhonian skeptical ideas. The arguments of the Pyrrhonists were used in parts of the *Apology* to attack all sorts of dogmatic claims. However, Frame points out, the conclusion of the *Apology* is not an affirmation or advocacy of Pyrrhonism, but a repudiation of Stoicism. Frame points to passages in the *Apology* indicating that after 1576 Montaigne was no longer so skeptical. Montaigne admitted that although we cannot have perfect knowledge, there is much value in the imperfect kind we are able to attain.

From this limited skepticism, Montaigne went on in the *Apology* to discredit various moral theories. In terms of their presumption they seek unattainable human goals. Therefore, the best human philosophy is that of Pyrrhonian skepticism, because it prepares the human mind for Christian faith and revelation. Montaigne definitely made this assertion, as did his followers for the next century. The question of Montaigne's sincerity is not directly dealt with. Frame, in analyzing the essays after the *Apology*, sought to show how Montaigne patiently found moderate and tolerant truths within himself that he could apply to the grim political and religious situation around him. His personal truths blended with a Christian morality. These together made Montaigne in both theory and practice the enemy of dogmatism.—*R.H.P.*

ADDITIONAL RECOMMENDED READING

Boase, Alan M. *The Fortunes of Montaigne: A History of the Essays in France, 1580-1669*. New York: Octagon Books, 1970. A history of Montaigne's influence in France during most of the seventeenth century.

Frame, Donald M. *Montaigne's Discovery of Man: The Humanization of a Humanist*. New York: Columbia University Press, 1955. An intellectual biography showing how Montaigne's views developed.

Lanson, Gustave. *Les Essais de Montaigne; étude et analyse*. Paris: Mellottée, 1958. The standard French commentary on Montaigne.

Popkin, Richard H. *The History of Scepticism from Erasmus to Spinoza*. Berkeley: University of California Press, 1979. Treats of the skeptical background, and places Montaigne in the ongoing history of skepticism.

DIALOGUES CONCERNING CAUSE, PRINCIPLE, AND ONE

Author: Giordano Bruno (c. 1548-1600)
Type of work: Metaphysics, theology
First published: 1584

PRINCIPAL IDEAS ADVANCED

Knowledge of the first cause and principle of the universe can be acquired only with difficulty through the study of remote effects.

God is the first principle of all things in that, as world soul pervading all nature, his nature is the nature of all things.

God is the first cause of all things since all things have being as the result of the informing action of the world soul.

There is but one substance; but one may distinguish form, the power to make, from matter, the power to be made.

Matter is passive potency in that it can be more than it is; but it is also act in that it contains the forms which, given the efficient cause, it unfolds.

The universe is one, infinite, immobile; all multiplicity is in appearance only.

Bruno's *Dialogues Concerning Cause, Principle, and One* is the work of one of the most brilliant and courageous philosophers of the Italian Renaissance. He was a man of faith with an independent and creative mind. His views did not win favor with the Dominicans with whom he had allied himself, and he was forced to leave the Order. He moved from place to place, provoking criticism wherever he settled. In France and England he produced some of his most famous works, but he finally had to move on. He spent some time in Germany and Switzerland. When he went to Venice in 1591 he became a victim of the Inquisition. He was tried, imprisoned in Rome, and finally burned at the stake because of his refusal to retract.

His philosophy of the universe is in the grand tradition of metaphysics and theology in that it describes an infinite universe which is God, and it attempts to explain how a world which presents a bewildering number of aspects to those viewing it from various perspectives can nevertheless be regarded as a unity. Perpetuating Neoplatonic ideas, and showing the influence of Plotinus, Bruno used his philosophic and poetic resources to build an image of a universe made perfect by the light of God which affects the existence and nature of everything. God is the principle, the cause, and the unity of the infinite universe.

Like Leibniz, whom he influenced, Bruno used the idea of the *monad*, unity of body and soul, and a manifestation of divine energy. The *Cause, Principle, and One*, an earlier work than the *De Minimo* in which the monad conception is developed, prepares the way for the new idea by describing

God as the World Soul pervading all being.

The first dialogue of the work introduces Filoteo, a philosopher who serves as the figure of Bruno. It presents a good-humored defense of philosophy, but not without suggesting the difficulties which come to one who has the courage of his convictions. The conversation is with two friends, Heliotropio and Armesso. Bruno, in an "Introductory Epistle," describes the first dialogue as "an apology, or something else I know not what, concerning the five dialogues of 'Le cena de le ceneri,'" one of his satirical dialogues.

With the second dialogue the proper body of the work begins. The interlocutors are Alexander Dixon, described as having proposed the subject matter to Theophilus, who is Filoteo (or Teofilo), or Bruno; Gervasius, not a philosopher, a person who "neither stinks nor smells" and who "makes jokes of the things that Polyhymnius says"; and Polyhymnius, a "sacrilegious pedant . . . one of the most rigid censors of philosophers. . . ."

Theophilus (the lover of God) explains to the others that it is only with the greatest difficulty that the first cause and principle is known; the divine substance, because of its infinitude and distance from its effects, can be known only through traces, the remote effects of its action. To call God first principle and first cause is to say the same thing from different points of view; God is first principle "inasmuch as all things are after him . . . either according to their nature, or according to their duration, or according to their worthiness." God is first cause "inasmuch as all things are distinct from him as the effect from the efficient. . . ." Theophilus explains that the term "principle" is more general than the term "cause": a point is the principle of a line, but not its cause. Principle has to do with the nature of a thing, cause with its production.

God is then described as "universal physical efficient cause" and as "universal intellect." In response to a question from Dixon, Theophilus explains what he means by "universal intellect." The intellect is the most real and proper faculty of the world soul; it illumines the universe and is the mover of all things; it is the "world architect"; it is what the Magi regarded as the seed sower, what Orpheus called the eye of the world, what Empedocles regarded as the distinguisher, what Plotinus called the father and progenitor, the "proximate dispenser of forms," and what Theophilus himself calls "the inner artificer."

Dixon wonders what the formal cause (the idea, the plan) of the universe is, if God, or the universal intellect, is the efficient cause (what brings things to existence); he ventures the answer that the formal cause is the "ideal concept" in the divine intellect. Theophilus agrees, and he supplements Dixon's remark that the final cause (the purpose) of the universe is the perfection of it by saying that the final cause, as well as the efficient cause, is universal in the universe.

A problem disturbs Dixon: he wonders how the same subject can be both the principle and the cause of natural things.

Theophilus answers that although the soul informs the entire universe and is an intrinsic and formal part of it—the principle of the universe—nevertheless, considered as governor and efficient cause, it is not a part.

Theophilus then comes forth with an idea that startles Dixon; it is the claim that the forms of natural objects are souls and that all things are animated. Although Dixon is willing to concede that the universe is animated, he has not considered that Theophilus would regard every part as animated, and he protests, "It is common sense that not all things are alive." Theophilus is insistent; everything has a vital principle. This claim is too much for Polyhymnius: "Then my shoes, my slippers, my boots, my spurs, my ring and my gloves will be animate?" Gervasius assures him that they are because they have within them "an animal such as you." Theophilus finally reassures them by saying that tables as tables, glass as glass, and so forth, are not animate, but as composites of matter and form they are all affected by spiritual substance and in that sense are animated by spirit. But not everything having soul is called animate. There is an intrinsic, formal, eternal principle in all things; it is the One in all things, the world soul in every part, the soul of all parts. Although distinctions can be made between forms, all forms are finally unified in one substantial ground. But the world soul is not present corporeally; it does not stretch out to cover the universe; rather, it is present in its entirety in every part as the formal principle of every part.

When the discussion is resumed (in the third dialogue), Theophilus mentions philosophers who have taken matter as primary and as the only reality. Confessing that he himself once held this view, he adds that he has come to the opinion that there are two forms of substance in the world: form and matter, active potency and passive potency, the power to make and the power to be made. Neither matter nor form can be dissolved or annihilated, although changes of form are common. There is, then, the one soul and formal principle that is the cause and principle of all things; there are the forms supplied by that principle; and there is one matter, the "receptacle of forms."

Matter is regarded as a potency and as a substratum. Potency is either active or passive. Passive potency is common to all matter; it is the capacity to be other than in actuality it is. Only the One is all that it can be, for it contains all being; consequently it contains all that which is passively potent as well as all other being. But death, corruption, vices, and defects, according to Theophilus, are neither act (actively potent) nor passively potent. God is both absolute act and absolute potency, and he cannot be apprehended by the intellect except in a negative way.

After some jesting between Polyhymnius and Gervasius—the theme being that matter is like woman, stubborn, inconstant, never satisfied with its present form, and so forth—Theophilus resumes (in the fourth dialogue) his discussion of matter, arguing that matter is the substratum of all beings, both corporeal and intelligible. He quotes Plotinus' remark that "if this sensible world is the imitation of the intelligible world, the composition of this is the imitation of the composition of that." Other reasons are offered in support of the thesis that there is only one matter. Matter in itself has no determinate dimensions and is indivisible; it is only in virtue of form that what is capable of receiving dimension actually acquires it. But matter, even when deprived of form, is not pure potency; matter as deprived of form is not like darkness deprived of light, but like "the pregnant . . . without its progeny, which she sends forth and obtains from herself. . . ." Matter is that which unfolds "out of its own bosom" that which it has enfolded; it contains within itself all the forms which it is capable of taking on; it is not a pure nothing, but a subject. Form could not arise to inform the matter which enfolds it were matter pure potency.

The fifth dialogue begins with the words of Theophilus: "The universe is, then, one, infinite, immobile." The multiplicity in the universe, the change, the diversity—all this is in appearance and relative to the senses; properly considered, every part of the universe is, in its mode of being, the One. Despite the existence of particular things, everything is one in substance, being, form, and matter; and there is but one cause and principle of all things. Properly speaking, there are no distinctions if one considers the substance of things; for there is but one substance, the infinite, the world soul, the divine intellect. To Polyhymnius, who hears but does not understand and begs for an example, Theophilus explains how a unity can account for apparent multiplicity; he uses an example from arithmetic: a decade is a unity, but is embracing; a hundred is more embracing, although still a unity; a thousand is even more embracing. But the one is the highest good, the highest beatitude, perfection; it is "the unity which embraces all."

Theophilus, having faithfully served as the apologist of the philosophy of the Nolan (Bruno of Nola), closes with words of praise: "Praised be the Gods, and extolled by all the living be the infinite, the simplest, the most unified, the highest, and the most absolute cause, principle, and the one."—*I.P.M.*

PERTINENT LITERATURE

Singer, Dorothea. *Giordano Bruno: His Life and Thought*. New York: Henry Schuman, 1950.

Dorothea Singer regards Giordano Bruno as an intrepid spirit who, by following unflinchingly the implications of his vision of infinity, shattered the medieval world view and set forth the elements of the faith of modern man. No progress could be made by tinkering with the orbits of the traditional system as long as the assumptions of Aristotelian physics remained unchallenged. Bruno not merely rejected the traditional view of a static earth surrounded by concentric spheres; he also raised the discussion to a new level when he rejected *ad hoc* principles designed to explain appearances and set forth the rational order which must govern the universe as a whole. "Universal relativity" is an expression which Singer uses to sum up Bruno's new vision of nature as a "vast interrelationship." His vision of infinity was far more than a denial that the world is bounded: it was the recognition that, with infinitely numerous worlds moving in relation to one another, all talk of direction, position, and weight must be relative.

Dialogues Concerning Cause, Principle, and One is the second of three Italian dialogues written by Bruno while he lived in England in the suite of the French ambassador. The first, *The Ash Wednesday Supper* (*La cena de le ceneri*) praised the Copernican theory of the heavens, which was still highly controversial. In so doing Bruno anticipated Johann Kepler and Galileo Galilei, but, says Singer, to Bruno alone the Copernican theory gave rise to the "marvelous intuition" that each star is a sun, the center of its own world. This dialogue contained some scurrilous comments on Oxford scholars for which Bruno felt obliged to apologize in *Dialogues Concerning Cause, Principle, and One*. This second dialogue developed Bruno's cosmological views in opposition to the prevailing Aristotelian philosophy. The third, *On the Infinite Universe and Worlds*, which Singer has translated, further expounds the doctrine of the second dialogue, setting forth, as Bruno says, "the birth of the ideas inseminated" in that work. Here the views of Lucretius and of Nicholas of Cusa are given particular attention; but so are those found in Job, in the Orphic theologians, and in the Jewish Cabala.

Bruno was neither a scientist nor a mathematician. No one, says Singer, was as devoid of experimental understanding as was Bruno; and, although he was fond of Pythagorean numerical and geometrical speculations, he regarded attempts to interpret the world in mathematical equations as misguided. Thus, his interest in Copernicus' theory and in Tycho Brahe's observations was polemic rather than scientific—they provided evidence that the Aristotelian world view was mistaken.

More importantly for the development of Bruno's thought than the new astronomy was the speculation of the pre-Socratic philosophers, familiar to him through his reading of Aristotle, and the Epicurean philosophy of Lucretius, whose poem, rediscovered in 1417, had been digested by Nicholas of Cusa and others before Bruno's time. Here, as Singer points out, Bruno found not only the conception of numberless worlds each inhabited like our own— one of Nicholas' favorite conceits—but also the groundwork for what Singer calls Bruno's "cosmic metabolism": that is, his theory that the multiplicity of phenomena which make up the worlds are to be explained as temporary groupings of "minima" which are constantly in motion, "leaving and returning to their own natural body and place."

The suggestion that things have a natural place shows that Bruno was not, properly speaking, a disciple of Epicurus; nor were Bruno's minima discrete atoms, all alike except for quantitative differences. On the contrary, according to Bruno, minima are endowed with life and thought, and are both discrete and continuous. This view is in line with his principle that "the potentiality of all parts is in the whole and in each of the parts." Here, according to Singer, Bruno presupposed Nicholas of Cusa's principle of the identity of opposites, for which he found support in the pre-Socratics, notably in "the divine Parmenides," but also in Plato's *Timaeus* and in the writings of various Neoplatonists.

Not all who have studied Bruno find his eclecticism palatable. Singer mentions, for example, the complaint that Bruno oscillated between theism and pantheism. But she contends that the principle of the identity of contraries brings everything together, arguing that theism and pantheism are reconciled in Bruno's single infinite continuum, in which each part is both discrete and continuous, each obeying its own intrinsic law, yet all who fused into a whole by one universal spirit. The atomism of Lucretius, according to Singer, served Bruno merely as a "symbol of the spiritual universe," there being no question that for Bruno the universe is alive, both as a whole and in its least parts. The human soul, he says, is not confined to its body, and if certain impediments are removed, it is suddenly present to distant bodies. Furthermore, he explains in a Latin work on magic, just as a pain in one's finger is felt in other members of the body so the human soul can be diffused throughout nature.

Those who have called Bruno a forerunner of the scientific age have, Singer believes, read into him something that is not there. She acknowledges, moreover, that he was not an entirely admirable man, that he lacked social tact and worldly wisdom, that he wasted much of his time on mnemonics, and that he was credulous of "natural magic." Yet she speaks of his "mystic exaltation in the apprehension of an infinite universe, a Unity informed by an immanent Mind," the awful majesty of which, she says, sustained him during the eight years of imprisonment that led to his death.

Yates, Frances A. *Giordano Bruno and the Hermetic Tradition.* London: Routledge & Kegan Paul, 1964.

Frances A. Yates is a historian of the Renaissance who, as she studied Giordano Bruno in connection with the court of Henry III of France and with the circle of Philip Sidney in England, suspected that something was missing in the portrait which represented him as the most advanced philosopher of the Renaissance until it struck her that he was not an advanced philosopher who dabbled in magic, but rather an advanced magician who dabbled in philosophy. Historical studies in Renaissance magic had made good progress, but no one as yet had perceived that Bruno belonged in that tradition. The magic in question was high-minded and extremely literate, not to be confused with medieval magic, which Renaissance magicians such as Pico della Mirandola and Tommaso Campanella called "modern magic," in contrast to the ancient magic of the Egyptians and Chaldeans which they found in the writings of Hermes Trismegistus and in the Cabala.

The first half of Yates's book is a history of Renaissance magic, which began in 1460 when Cosimo de Medici came into possession of a copy of the pseudo-Hermetic writings and asked Marsillio Ficino to put aside his translating of Plato and to translate this work instead. Ficino, who was both a priest and a physician, became absorbed in the subject, and in his later writings championed what came to be known as natural magic—an art which used plants, metals, and talismans to draw spiritual forces from the planets and from beyond. Others went further, abandoned Christianity, undertook to promote what they took to be Egyptian philosophy and religion, and, going beyond natural magic, cultivated the "deep magic" which gave to its adepts supernatural powers. Incidentally, Yates makes the point that, in contrast to the humanists, such as Petrarch and Deseridius Erasmus, the philosophical circle which flourished in Medicean Florence had no historical sense. They believed the Hermetic writings not merely to be older than the writings of Plato but older than the time of Moses; they did not suspect otherwise until the humanist Isaac Casaubon proved in 1614 that the writings date from the second and third centuries of the Christian era.

In the second half of her book, Yates redraws the portrait of Bruno. By the time he left the Dominican monastery in Italy and crossed the Alps, he had given up his belief that Christ is the world's savior and embraced the belief that salvation is in the hands of divine magi—men who, by means of the Egyptian arts, have it in their power to bridge the heavenly spheres and bring God down. It was as a universal reformer that he preached his philosophy in France, in England, and in Germany; and when he returned to Italy, it was in the belief that he could interest the Pope in his system.

He visited Paris, where he lectured on mnemonics. King Henry, a son of Catherine de Medici, suspected that Bruno's mnemonics was really magic. And so it was, says Yates, being a method of acquiring a magically powerful personality by imprinting on the mind images from the zodiac and the planets. Henry took kindly to Bruno, who also preached the need for harmony between Catholics and Protestants, and gave him diplomatic protection when he wanted to go to England.

In London Bruno became part of the scene, so that Yates thinks we may even find his portrait in the Berowne of *Love's Labor Lost*. Of primary interest, however, is his appearance at Oxford where he lectured in Copernicus. This fact is usually taken as an indication of his interest in science; but Yates reminds us how uncertain the borders between science and magic were at the time, and argues that Bruno interpreted the Copernican diagram as a hieroglyph of divine mysteries. In the *Ash Wednesday Supper*, Bruno reviles the Oxford humanists for their obtuseness; and, until recently, his account of the event was the only one known to historians. But in 1960, R. McNulty discovered a passage in a book published in 1604 which tells the Oxford side of the story. One of those present thought that the lecture sounded familiar and went to his study to consult a copy of Ficino's book where he found the lecture almost verbatim. When he showed his discovery to the dean of his college, the latter proposed to let the visitor give a second and third lecture before exposing him.

Although one needs to read the whole of Yates's book in order to form a judgment, Chapter 13, "The Hermetic Philosophy," deals most directly with Bruno's system. Readers accustomed to considering Bruno as the initiator of the modern outlook are reminded that he completely transformed the Lucretian world view, giving it life and taking it as a revelation of the infinite divinity which the magus undertakes to reflect within himself. For the rest, we are shown that many of Bruno's supposedly advanced notions, such as the perpetual dissolution and renewal of worlds and their parts, are Hermetic commonplaces. For example, Hermes says: "Know child, that all that is in the world, without exception, is in movement, either diminishing or increasing." This was brought forward by Bruno as an argument against those who held that the earth does not move.

Nineteenth century liberals, says Yates, went into ecstasies over the passage in which Bruno spoke of man's mind suffocating in the narrow prison of "blind and popular philosophy" and in which he presented himself as one who had broken down the divisions between the spheres and, by the light of sense and reason, had thrown open the doors of truth. If they had studied the Hermetic tradition, however, they would have recognized that in this passage Bruno was describing the ascent made possible to him by virtue of his having experienced the gnostic trance and come into possession of divine power. Thus, says Yates, when he rejected humanism and mathematics and abandoned Christianity, Bruno was turning his back on the future and moving toward "a darker, more medieval necromancy."—*J.F.*

ADDITIONAL RECOMMENDED READING

Greenberg, Sidney. *The Infinite in Giordano Bruno*. New York: King's Crown Press, 1950. A concise exposition of Bruno's world view followed by a translation of this central work.

Horowitz, I. L. *The Renaissance Philosophy of Girodano Bruno*. New York: Coleman-Ross Company, 1952. Bruno is seen as blazing the path for the new scientific and rationalist tradition in philosophy. A systematic exposition.

Kristeller, Paul O. *Eight Philosophers of the Italian Renaissance*. Stanford, California: Stanford University Press, 1964. Chapter 8, on Bruno, contains a résumé of *Dialogues Concerning Cause, Principle, and One*. The author is a leading Renaissance scholar.

Michel, Paul Henri. *The Cosmology of Giordano Bruno*. Translated by R. E. W. Maddison. Ithaca, New York: Cornell University Press, 1973.

Detailed account, written in 1962, of Bruno's place in the history of science.

Trevor-Roper, Hugh. "The Last Magician," in *New Statesman*. LXVII, no. 1734 (June 5, 1964), pp. 879-880. Review-article on Yates's book by a well-known contemporary historian.

Yates, Frances A. "Bruno, Giordano," in *The Encyclopedia of Philosophy*. Edited by Paul Edwards. Vol. I. New York: Macmillan Publishing Company, 1967, pp. 405-408. A summary of Yates's book on Bruno.

THE ADVANCEMENT OF LEARNING

Author: Francis Bacon (1561-1626)
Type of work: Epistemology, philosophy of science
First published: 1605

PRINCIPAL IDEAS ADVANCED

Scholars should free themselves from bondage to the past; Europeans should cease being awed by the accomplishments of Greece and Rome.

Practical investigation should be emphasized, and scholars should cease wasting their time with vain speculations.

Modern history should be studied with as much enthusiasm as ancient, and there is a need for new sciences: a science to study races in relation to climate, geography, and natural resources; a science of education, a history of mechanics, and sciences having to do with business and diplomacy.

Scientific invention is encouraged by attention to negative instances and to exceptions to rules; calendars of doubts and problems should be kept, and nature should be studied inductively, not deductively.

Human learning has three main parts corresponding to the three capacities of the human understanding: history, based on memory; poesy, based on the imagination; and philosophy, based on reason.

In this, his first major philosophical work, Francis Bacon was directly concerned to influence King James I and the Court in favor of a new concept of learning. The reign of the Tudors (1485-1603) had seen great changes in the Church, in government, and in the economy of England, but not in the universities. Fired with the same spirit of adventure which had motivated the explorations of Sir Francis Drake and Sir Walter Raleigh, Bacon undertook in this work to make "as it were a small globe of the intellectual world, as truly and faithfully as I could discover; with a note and description of those parts which seem to me not constantly occupate, or not well converted by the labor of man."

Because Bacon believed that the enterprise of exploring and conquering new realms of knowledge would have more appeal to the men who directed the nation's affairs than to sequestered scholars, he wrote the book in English. When his belief proved mistaken, he published a revised edition in Latin to make it uniform with his other philosophical writings, and gave it the name *De Augmentis Scientiarum* (1623). Bacon's effort was wasted on the court of King James, but by the middle of the century independent scholars had made his book the banner of a major crusade; they hailed its author as "the secretary of nature" and the "architect" of the new learning. The Royal Society of London for Improving Natural Knowledge, founded in 1660, is an example of his influence.

In our eyes, it is a fault of *The Advancement of Learning* that it contains so much shameless flattery of King James. Besides beginning each of the two parts of his book with a dedication to the king, Bacon especially praised James's notorious tract called "The True Law of Free Monarchies" (1603) as being "a work richly compounded of divinity, morality, and policy, with great aspersion of all other arts; and being in mine opinion one of the most sound and healthful writings that I have read." But as if the only true flattery were imitation, Bacon seems deliberately to have composed the first book of *The Advancement of Learning* in the pedantic fashion that his monarch esteemed, citing Adam and Moses, Alexander and Caesar and a host of others to prove the excellency and worthwhileness of learning and knowledge. What saves the first book from utter tedium is the sharp criticism which now and again he let fall upon divines, politicians, and scholars for bringing learning into stagnation.

Bacon had two main faults to find with the learning of his day. The first had to do with its bondage to the past. In this respect, he considered Renaissance humanists and Protestant theologians worse offenders than the schoolmen, because they gave far too much attention to the ancient languages, to style and phrase, to the correction and annotation of texts. In his opinion, it was time for scholars to wake up to the age in which they were living. No longer need Europeans feel overawed at the achievements of Greece and Rome. What we call antiquity was in fact the youth of the world. "These times are the ancient times, when the world is ancient, and not those which we account ancient by a computation backward from ourselves."

The second main fault was in mistaking the goal or purpose of knowledge. Too great precedence had, he thought, been given to intellectual activity and not enough to practical investigations. Bacon pleaded for scholars to lay aside "vain speculations" and to turn to "the contemplation of nature and the observation of experience." Contemplation, he said, should ever be conjoined with action and should be pursued not out of mere intellectual curiosity or for the honor or gain of the scholar, but for its utility to civil society.

It is instructive to note how closely Bacon's strictures on the learning of his times agreed with those of his younger contemporary, Descartes, in his *Discourse on Method* (1637). A modern parallel is found in John Dewey's *The Quest for Certainty* (1929).

In the second and more substantial part of the book, Bacon turned his attention from the scholars to the matter of their scholarship. His purpose was to point out areas of study that had not received sufficient attention, and in passing to note those that had not been neglected. Among the latter he placed mathematics and physics, grammar and eloquence, ancient and ecclesiastical history. This was not to say that he considered them in a satisfactory condition. "I am not now," he noted, "in hand with censures, but with omissions." Of physics, for example, which he did not report as deficient, he nevertheless noted: "In what truth or perfection [its branches] are handled, I make not now any judgment; but they are parts of knowledge not deserted by the labor of man."

Bacon's originality appears in the number of new sciences which he envisaged a place for, and the gaps he saw in the old ones. For example, he urged that modern history should be studied with the same zeal as ancient, and he called for a new science that would study human races in connection with climate, geography, and natural resources. There was need for a science of education and for books on practical morals which would deal with ways of improving the mind and cultivating virtue. A history of mechanics and inventions was needed to parallel the history of thought. And handbooks were needed in the fields of business and diplomacy, comparable in "form of writing" to Machiavelli's works on government. Theology might seem to be over-cultivated, but Bacon suggested two new areas—one dealing with the limits of human reason in speculating about divine things, the other defining the latitude which ought to be allowed for theological differences. Medicine, Bacon thought, was in a particularly deficient way, being "a science which hath been more professed than labored, and yet more labored than advanced; the labor having been in my judgment, rather in a circle than in progression." He complained that Hippocrates' method of keeping case histories of his patients had fallen into disuse. He argued for the reinstitution of vivisection, particularly of beasts, in order that anatomy might again go forward. And he wished that physicians would give more attention to searching out specific medicines and less to compounding confections for ready sale.

As would be expected, Bacon gave special attention to the arts of reasoning, anticipating many of the themes of his famous *Novum Organum* (1620). He argued that invention has been far too much the sport of chance rather than the child of intelligence. "Hitherto men are rather beholden to a wild goat for surgery, or to a nightingale for music, or to the ibis for some part of physic, or to the pot-lid that flew open for artillery, or generally to chance or anything else than to logic for the invention of arts and sciences."

Bacon recommended several new angles of approach. He pointed out the importance to invention of the negative instance and the exception to the rule; consequently, he strongly recommended keeping calendars of doubts and problems and popular errors, together with a history of the wonders and monstrosities of nature. He mentioned the need of putting nature to torture in order to make her answer our questions. He criticized the adequacy of syllogistic reasoning for the investigation of nature, and he urged a more particular induction. Also, he pointed to characteristic fallacies which he was later to call the "idols" of the mind.

Perhaps more important than any of these details is the new principle of "the classification of the sciences" which Bacon employed in this work, several features of which deserve notice. In the first place, he drew a sharp division between human learning and divine, the obvious purpose of which was to set human reason free from the authority of revelation. In the second place, he divided human learning into three main parts, paralleling the "three parts of man's understanding": *memory* he saw as the basis for all kinds of history—natural, civil, ecclesiastical; *imagination*, as the basis for poesy—narrative, representative, and allusive; and *reason*, as the basis for philosophy—divine, natural, and human.

Bacon's emphasis upon the divisions within philosophy has been influential in empirical circles to this day. He deprecated the generalized kind of thinking which schoolmen called "philosophy" and parceled out its matter to special sciences. It was, he thought, rather a depradation of other sciences than anything solid and substantive itself. In its place, he proposed a new discipline under the name of "first philosophy," which would be a receptacle for axioms and rules which are valid for several parts of knowledge. Such a science, were it cultivated, would prove a fruitful fountain from which all might draw.

Of special interest is the account he gave of the relation between physics and metaphysics. Both, in his view, are branches of natural science, the former dealing with material and efficient causes, the latter with formal and final causes. Physics, in his estimation, stands above natural history in that it is explanatory and not merely descriptive; but it is below metaphysics, in that it sees causes in their particularity. For example, if the cause of whiteness in snow or froth is inquired, physics will explain that it is due to the subtle intermixture of air and water. Metaphysics must explain it in terms of the "form of whiteness" and show why this particular intermixture of elements is united with this universal character. Bacon said he was not surprised that little progress had been made in metaphysics understood in this way, because men had not paid enough attention to particulars. But he also let escape the doubt that much could ever be accomplished in this direction. Natural philosophy, he said, is like a pyramid, with natural history as the base, physics as the middle, and metaphysics as the vertical point. But "as for the vertical point, the summary law of nature, we know not whether man's inquiry can attain to it."

It is not difficult to see that behind the new division of the sciences lay Bacon's complete rejection of the medieval synthesis of Aristotle and St. Augustine. Without repudiating theology, he sealed it off, restricting "divine knowledge" to faith, manners, liturgy, and church government. As for Aristotelianism, while Bacon preserved much of its terminology, he rejected its fundamental tenets and turned to Democritus, the materialistic atomist, for his model of the world. (Compare in this respect his younger friend, Thomas Hobbes.)

The new system of classification also points up the anthropocentric ("humanistic" in the twentieth century sense of the word) character of Bacon's thinking. Bacon did not accept Copernicus' theory of the heavens, but the kind of "Copernican revolution" which Kant claimed to have brought about was incipient in Bacon's decision to abandon the traditional division of the sciences based on nature, and to reorganize knowledge according to the faculties of the mind. For example, Bacon brought botany and the rise and fall of civilizations together as branches of a single kind of inquiry: one is "natural history," the other "civil history"; what they have in common is the fact that they are both founded in man's memory and observation, rather than in imagination or reason.

Bacon made no secret of his conviction that all knowledge has for its end the use and benefit of man. This attitude is evident from what has appeared already in what has been said about the necessity of combining contemplation with action and in the deficiency he reported in respect to mechanical and practical knowledge. He was the champion of the kind of learning we associate with polytechnic colleges, business schools, and research institutes. His bias is underscored by the disproportion in the amount of space which he devotes to "human" philosophy (fifteen chapters) as against "natural" philosophy (two chapters). "Know thyself," he said, following the ancient oracle; for the knowledge of man is the "end and term" of human learning, notwithstanding the fact that it is but a portion of "the continent of nature."

Bacon thought of himself as standing on the threshold of a new age. Among its harbingers he mentioned the vivacity of the "wits" of that time, the improved knowledge of the past, the invention of printing, worldwide navigation, the increase of leisure, and political stability. He spoke of the period as constituting a third great age in the history of the world, which he hoped would far exceed in glory and achievement the days of Greece and Rome. Of his own writings, he said that men could say of them what they wished, as long as they observed and weighed them. He suggested that it was comparable to the "noise or sound which musicians make while they are tuning their instruments: which is nothing pleasant to hear, but yet is a cause why the music is sweeter afterwards."—*J.F.*

Pertinent Literature

Anderson, F. H. *The Philosophy of Francis Bacon*. Chicago: University of Chicago Press, 1948.

In this book F. H. Anderson interprets and assesses the full scope of Francis Bacon's philosophic writings, thereby giving the reader interested in *The Advancement of Learning* and *De Augmentis Scientiarum* a sense of the place and importance of these works in the Baconian canon.

Anderson identifies four themes or projects which he thinks constitute the Baconian program. First, Bacon aimed at replacing the prevailing Platonic and Aristotelian traditions with a philosophy which found its roots in Democritus and which would thus be naturalistic and materialistic. Second, he

attempted to formulate a new methodology to replace the inadequate syllogistic method of Aristotle. Third, he wished to encourage the development
of a natural history and to establish a new kind of institution to carry out this
work. Fourth, in order to give his own work full prominence, Bacon undertook
a refutation of the methods and principles of scholastic thought. Anderson
argues that all four of these projects are present in *The Advancement of
Learning* and in *De Augmentis Scientiarum* although they are emphasized in
varying degrees.

In Bacon's project to revive materialism, a prominent place is given to a
reorganization of knowledge. A major component of this reorganization is
the drawing of a sharp division between revealed theology and philosophy
proper. Anderson argues that this division is fundamental to Bacon's program
and not, as some commentators have felt, merely a device to placate ecclesiastical authorities. Anderson comments, however, that Bacon's separation of
theology from philosophy, and his inclusion of physics and mechanics within
the bounds of metaphysics, views expressed in *The Advancement of Learning*,
account in large measure for Bacon's failure to secure support for his philosophic work. Nevertheless, says Anderson, the aim of the reorganization is
to foster a knowledge which will "culminate in the summary law of nature."

Anderson notes that in the earlier *The Advancement of Learning* Bacon
has not fully developed his account of fallacies known as the *Idols*. Here only
three are mentioned and they are unnamed. (What later was called the *Idols
of the Theater* is not included.) In the later *De Augmentis Scientiarum* all are
fully developed and labeled.

Although, as we have noted, Bacon sought a philosophy which was naturalistic and mechanistic, Anderson comments that in terms of methodology
Bacon showed definite Platonic tendencies. For example, in dealing with the
distinction between modes of knowledge, reason and sense, and the distinction
between objects of knowledge universal and particular, Bacon speaks of pre-
knowledge in the *The Advancement of Learning* and of prenotion in *De
Augmentis Scientiarum* in ways that are similar to Plato's use of the Doctrine
of Reminiscence. Anderson regards the idea of the "cutting off of infinity of
inquiry" as the basic principle of Bacon's methodology.

In his overall assessment of the importance of Bacon's philosophy, Anderson believes that Bacon's impact on the course of knowledge "can hardly
be overestimated." He argues that *The Advancement of Learning* became
part of a major crusade. Bacon's work was intended to separate firmly scholastic philosophy from experimental philosophy. Anderson believes that Bacon's attack was inordinately successful; he thinks that, although it is a
question whether Bacon's theory of nature is original, Bacon's refusal to
accept or be bound by any ontological doctrine opened a path which led from
John Locke to David Hume and modern views of a "universalized natural
science." The result is, says Anderson, that metaphysics in the traditional

sense "all but disappears from British and European philosophy."

Farrington, Benjamin. *Francis Bacon, Philosopher of Industrial Science.* New York: Henry Schuman, 1949.

This book outlines both Francis Bacon's life and his philosophic writings. Central to Benjamin Farrington's understanding and assessment of Bacon is the idea that science and its pursuit should aim at the improvement of the material conditions of human life. To achieve this, says Farrington, Bacon tried to systematize and organize both the development and application of knowledge of the natural world.

Many commentators on Bacon, Farrington believes, have concentrated too heavily on the *Novum Organum* and have thus arrived at unfair conclusions assessing Bacon's importance. Although Farrington acknowledges that the *Organum* is Bacon's most important work, he points out that it is only a part of a much larger project, *The Great Instauration*, and that it is only by appreciating the full scope of Bacon's vision and work that a fair assessment of his contributions can be made.

According to Farrington, *The Advancement of Learning* resulted from a compromise Bacon effected between his efforts to gain an appointment in public life and thus secure his position, and his inclination to press ahead with his great project. Thus the first book attempts to legitimize the pursuit of knowledge by kings and statesmen and the second prepares the way for his project by criticizing existing knowledge and its methods and suggesting ways of improvement. Farrington illustrates the work of the second book in a passage dealing with Bacon's attitude toward Scholasticism.

The second book of *The Advancement of Learning* was supplemented, revised, and rewritten in Latin as *De Augmentis Scientiarum*. It is Bacon's criticisms of scientific forms and methods of knowledge which constitute for Farrington the most important aspect of the *De Augmentis Scientiarum*. He further maintains that these criticisms did not stem from long study and reading, but rather from Bacon's personal experiences.

The stated purpose of *De Augmentis Scientiarum* is to survey and report on the totality of human knowledge, and, says Farrington, it demonstrates that Bacon's vision was not limited to an improvement of the material standard of living, for it contains suggestions for the improvement of man's cultural life as well. In this connection, Farrington points to Bacon's proposal for a History of Learning, in appreciation of the role of poetry and literature.

Farrington suggests that the most important portion of *De Augmentis Scientiarum* for an understanding of Bacon's philosophy of nature is in Book III; and Farrington argues that the correct interpretation of Bacon's work requires that we recognize that although Bacon used traditional vocabulary, he had different meanings in mind. For example, he makes use of the term "Forms" while repudiating Platonic philosophy. Bacon also makes metaphysics a part of Natural Philosophy rather than a subject which transcends science.

Farrington concludes his treatment of *De Augmentis Scientiarum* by considering "an ethical passage" which, he believes, "is all important for understanding man." In this passage, Bacon considers the good of the individual and the good of the social whole and argues for the latter on several grounds; first, on the level of the inorganic, Bacon argues for the dominance of the collective over the individual; second, he refers to classical and Christian sources and then, says Farrington, characteristically uses his results to condemn Aristotle.

It was Bacon's faithfulness to the conception of public duty as taking priority over private good which resulted in the *De Augmentis Scientiarum*'s being the last book Bacon was to write. During the two and a half years before his death, Bacon's only academic work was on his *Natural and Experimental History*, a mere collection of secondary material.

Nichol, John. *Francis Bacon, His Life and Philosophy*. Vol. II. London: W. Blackwood & Sons, 1901.

In this book John Nichol takes the view that although there is disagreement about the philosophic value of Francis Bacon's work, there is no room for dispute about the aims and purposes of that work, which Nichol understands to be the exploration of nature in order to give mankind mastery over it. He thinks, however, that Bacon is frequently undervalued because he is not understood in his proper historical context; there is little appreciation of the full Baconian program (not completed by Bacon himself) and the treatment of Bacon as a bare empiricist. Properly understood, Bacon should be viewed both as a critic and as a creator.

According to Nichol, Bacon regarded *The Advancement of Learning* as a provisional sketch of his larger work. This sketch was composed and published in English in order to attract support for his program. Nichol sees two guiding principles at work in Bacon's program; on the one hand, Bacon's philosophy was intended to improve and correct existing thought, and on the other hand Bacon wished to stimulate invention. Both of these principles were to serve the larger goal of improving human life.

Nichol treats *The Advancement of Learning* and *De Augmentis Scientiarum* together, seeing the two as "merged." His analysis follows the nine Books of *De Augmentis Scientiarum*, searching out questions they raise which are of greatest interest. It is in the second Book, Nichol says, that Bacon begins the core of his work. Here Bacon offers a classification of the sciences based upon psychological categories. One psychological category, memory, is the foundation of history, both natural and civil. Natural history must treat nature in three contexts: free in its workings (that is, natural processes themselves);

free in errors (that is, nature which gives rise to uncritical beliefs, myths, folk-knowledge, and superstition); and bound in the arts (that is, principles of nature captured in human technology). Commenting on the second of these three contexts, Nichol argues that Bacon had really one thing in mind: namely, that "in most widely spread beliefs there is an element of truth exaggerated."

Nichol believes the third Book is of special interest because it illuminates certain parts of the *Organum*. Although Bacon repeatedly stresses his rejection of Aristotelianism, Nichol notes that much in this book, as in the former, is concerned with a classification of knowledge. Here he likens the organizational structure of knowledge to a tree, the trunk of which is a universal science, "Philosophia Prima." Nichol gives special attention to a passage in this book dealing with astronomy. In this passage Bacon urges astronomers to look for the physical causes of what they observe instead of merely constructing systems on the basis of mathematical calculations.

The fourth and sixth Books Nichol dismisses as being outside Bacon's main concerns. (The fourth Book looks at Man from a physiological point of view, while the sixth is "given to collateral subjects.") The fifth Book is devoted to logic, which is approached more directly in the *Organum*.

In the seventh Book, Bacon discusses ethics. Nichol believes that Bacon's theory of ethics is as "superficial as his psychology." This view is due in large part to Bacon's distinctly unmetaphysical turn of mind. The eighth and ninth Books turn to civil knowledge—that is, civil ethics and politics. Nichol again notes the lack of system (that is, metaphysical foundation) of Bacon's view; but he finds a "wealth of practical wisdom." Discussing "The Knowledge of Advancement of Life," Nichol notes that Bacon's views have been subject to severe criticism. Although Bacon counsels that full truthfulness may not always be in one's own interest, Nichol nevertheless suggests that Bacon is speaking only of the "morality of consequences" and that he is aware of a higher moral standard.

Finally, with respect to practical politics, Nichol sees in Bacon both Platonic and Aristotelian tendencies, inclinations which are always subject to the guiding rule that one should in politics have a range of priorities so that if one end is not achieved, then another may be. Nothing, Bacon remarks, is "more impolitic than to be entirely bent on one action."—*D.N.M.*

ADDITIONAL RECOMMENDED READING

Broad, C. D. *The Philosophy of Francis Bacon*. Cambridge: Cambridge University Press, 1926. An evaluation of Bacon's contribution to inductive logic.

Eiseley, Loren. *The Man Who Saw Through Time*. New York: Charles Scribner's Sons, 1973. A general account of Bacon's work and his impact.

Farrington, Benjamin. *The Philosophy of Francis Bacon*. Chicago: University of Chicago Press, 1964. An assessment of the evolution of Bacon's thought from 1603 to 1609.

Luxembourg, L. K. *Francis Bacon and Denis Diderot: Philosophers of Science*. New York: Humanities Press, 1967. An examination of Bacon's influence in France and a comparison of the work of Bacon and Diderot.

NOVUM ORGANUM

Author: Francis Bacon (1561-1626)
Type of work: Philosophy of science
First published: 1620

PRINCIPAL IDEAS ADVANCED

To acquire knowledge about the world one must interpret the particulars given in sense experience.

Various false ideas and methods have handicapped man in his attempt to study nature impartially; they are the Idols of the Tribe (conventional beliefs which satisfy the emotions), the Idols of the Cave (erroneous conceptions resulting from individual predilections), the Idols of the Market Place (confused ideas resulting from the nonsensical or loose use of language), and the Idols of the Theatre (various systems of philosophy or other dogmatic, improperly founded assertions).

The discovery, investigation, and explanation of Forms (the properties of substances) by controlled observation and experimentation, utilizing tables of instances by reference to which inductive generalizations can be made, is the philosophical foundation of all knowledge.

This important work in scientific methodology was part of a larger work, *The Great Instauration*, which was proposed in six parts (the *Novum Organum* to be the second) but never completed. Even this work itself is partial, as is indicated by the fact that the author listed in Aphorism XXI of Book II a number of topics which he proposed to discuss, but never did, either here or in his other works. The content of the book clearly indicates that he considered it to be a correction of, or a supplement to, Aristotle's logical writings, the *Organon*. A large portion of Bacon's text is devoted to a demonstration of the futility, if not the error, of trying to understand nature by the deductive method. We cannot learn about the world, he insists, by arguing, however skillfully, about abstract principles. On the contrary, we must *interpret* nature by deriving "axioms from the senses and particulars, rising by a gradual and unbroken ascent, so that the method arrives at the most general axioms last of all. This is the true way, but as yet untried." It was a new "inductive logic" whose rules Bacon proposed to disclose.

The work is divided into two Books, the first concerned mainly with setting down the principles of the inductive method and the second with the method for collecting facts. Book I is further divided into two parts, of which the first is designed to purge the mind of the wrong methods (Aphorisms I-CXV), while the second is planned to correct false conceptions of the method which Bacon is proposing (Aphorisms CXVI-CXX).

He begins by showing that the relation of man to nature is such that man can know the world only by being its servant and its interpreter. In man knowledge and power meet, for man can control nature only if he understands it; "nature to be commanded must be obeyed." Man can modify nature only by putting natural bodies together or by separating them. Moreover, his control over nature has been very much limited because man has chosen to spend his time in "specious meditations, speculations and glosses," which are well designed to systematize the knowledge which he already has but poorly designed for the discovery of new ideas. The syllogism, for example, serves only to give stability to the errors of tradition; it deals with such unsound notions as substance, quality, action, passion, and essence, rather than with those which have been abstracted from things by the proper inductive methods.

Bacon writes that there are three methods commonly employed for understanding nature. He describes these metaphorically in Aphorism XCV as those of the ant, the spider, and the bee. The ant is an experimenter, but he only collects and uses. The spider is not an experimenter, but he makes cobwebs out of his own inner substance. The bee takes the middle course; he gathers material from the flowers but transforms and digests this by powers of his own. Natural philosophy is exemplified neither by the ant nor by the spider; it does not gather material from natural history and from mechanical experiments and store it away in memory, nor does it rely solely on the powers of the mind. It alters and digests the particulars which are given in experience and then lays them up in memory.

In further clarification of his method Bacon suggests that there is an important distinction between the *Anticipation of Nature* and the *Interpretation of Nature*. *Anticipations* are collected from very few instances; they are sweeping generalizations which appeal to the imagination and thus produce immediate assent. Indeed, if all men went mad in the same manner they might very well agree on all anticipations. But *Interpretations* are obtained from widely dispersed data; they cannot produce consent since they usually disagree with accepted ideas. *Anticipations* are designed to be easily believed; *Interpretations* are designed to master things.

One of the contributions to scientific methodology for which Bacon has become most famous is his doctrine of the *Idols*. These are false notions and false methods which have taken possession of our minds, have become deeply rooted in them, and strongly resist our efforts to study nature impartially. Bacon believes that we can guard against these only if we are aware of what they are and how they mislead thinking. He calls them the *Idols of the Tribe*, the *Idols of the Cave*, the *Idols of the Market Place*, and the *Idols of the Theatre*. The first have their foundation in human nature itself, the second in the individual man, the third in the vagueness and ambiguity of language, and the fourth in the dogmas of philosphy and the wrong rules of demonstration.

The *Idols of the Tribe* are exemplified in the following: the beliefs that all celestial bodies move in perfect circles, because we are predisposed to find more order and regularity in the world than we actually find; superstitions, which are accepted because we are reluctant to abandon agreeable opinions even when negative instances arise; unwillingness to conceive of limits to the world, or of uncaused causes, and the resulting eternal search for principles which are ever more and more general; the swaying of our beliefs by emotions rather than by reason; the deceptions which arise because of the dullness and incompetency of the sense organs; and our proneness to prefer abstractions to the concrete realities of experience.

The *Idols of the Cave* are due to the mental and bodily peculiarities of the individual. Men become attached to certain beliefs of which they are the authors and on which they have spent much effort. Some men see resemblances and overlook difference; others reverse these; both err by excess. Some men worship the past and abhor novelty; others reverse these; truth, however, is to be found in the mean between these extremes. Similar examples are to be found in the respective overemphasis on particles as against structure, both of which distort reality.

The *Idols of the Market Place* are the most troublesome of all. They are of two kinds: words which are names of things that do not exist (Fortune, Prime Mover, Element of Fire), and words which are names of things that exist but which are vague and confused in their meanings. The latter can be exemplified by the word *humid*, which may apply in its many meanings to flame, air, dust, and glass.

The *Idols of the Theatre* are subdivided into those of Systems of Philosophy and those of False Arguments. Among the former are the *Sophistical* (exemplified by Aristotle, who corrupted philosophy by his logic and his theory of the categories), the *Empirical* (exemplified by the alchemists and all those who leap to generalizations on the basis of a few, "dark" experiments), and the *Superstitious* (exemplified by those who employ their philosophies to prove their theologies). The False Argument idols are found when men improperly extract the forms of objects from the objects themselves, and when, in a spirit of caution, they withhold judgment even though a truth has been well demonstrated, or dogmatically assert a conclusion without sufficient grounds. The only true demonstration is experience, not by means of careless experiments, or experiments in play, or experiments performed repeatedly with only slight variations until one wearies in the process, but by planned and controlled experiments whose motive is true understanding rather than an "overhasty and unreasonable eagerness to practice."

Bacon shows that if we examine the traditional natural philosophy we can easily see why it has not met with success. In the first place, it was largely disputational—a feature which is most adverse to the acquisition of truth. It was primarily dialectical, described by Dionysius as "the talk of idle old men to ignorant youth." Much of it was argued by itinerant scholars, who put their wisdom up for sale and were primarily concerned with defending their own schools of thought. In addition, these men had the disadvantage of there being no historical knowledge, other than myths, on which they could base their conclusions, and they had very limited geographical knowledge. Furthermore, such experimental knowledge as existed was largely a kind of "natural magic" which had almost no utility, philosophy not having realized, apparently, that it, like religion, must show itself in works. Indeed, it proved sterile, not only of mechanical progress but also of theoretical development; it thrived under its founders, remained stagnant for a few years, then declined and disappeared. As a result, many of its advocates not only apologized for the limited character of their knowledge by complaining of the subtlety and obscurity of nature, and of the weakness of the human intellect, but also argued defensively that nature was completely beyond the reach of man and essentially unknowable. To claim that the soundness of Aristotle's philosophy has been demonstrated by its long survival is fallacious, Bacon argues; it has survived not because of the consensus of the judgments of free minds (the only real test of truth), but only because of the blind worship of authority. "If the multitude assent and applaud, men ought immediately to examine themselves as to what blunder or thought they have committed."

Why, then, has science not progressed more rapidly in the long period of its history? Bacon argues that several reasons may be advanced. In terms of the total history of the race, of course, the few centuries which have elapsed since the Greeks is not a long period; we should therefore not be too hasty in disparaging the meager results of man's attempt to understand the world. The poverty of results in natural philosophy can be explained by the great concentration of effort on study in the other areas of thought—religion, morals, and public affairs. Furthermore, the sciences have failed to progress because the natural philosophy on which they must be based for sound support has not been forthcoming; astronomy, optics, music, and the mechanical arts lack profundity and merely glide over the surface of things. In addition, the sciences have remained stagnant because their goal has not been clearly formulated, and the method for attaining this goal has not been stressed; men have tended to rely mainly on their wits, on an inadequate logic, and on simple experiment (which is like a broom without a band). "The true method of experience first lights the candle, and then by means of the candle shows the way; commencing as it does with experience duly ordered and digested, not bungling or erratic, and from it educing axioms, and from established axioms again new experiments; even as it was not without order and method that the divine word operated on the created mass."

Any tendency to praise the accomplishments of the mechanical arts, the liberal arts, and alchemy should be tempered by the recognition of how ignorant we still are in these areas; we know much, but there is so much that we do not know. Much of which poses as knowledge, Bacon insists, has been set forth with such ambition and parade that one easily comes to feel that it is more nearly complete and perfect than it really is; its subdivisions seem to embrace all fields, but many of these fields prove to be empty and devoid of content. Even worse, much of what is practiced in the arts is pure charlatanism, claiming without grounds to prolong life, alleviate pain, bring down celestial influences, divine the future, improve intellectual qualities, transmute substances, and much more. The main defects of such arts are to be found in their combination of littleness of spirit with arrogance and superiority; they aspire to very little, but claim to accomplish very much; they engage in trifling and puerile tasks, but claim to solve all problems.

On the positive side, Bacon believes that there are strong grounds for hope. Knowledge is so obviously good that it bears the marks of Divine Providence on its surface. All that is required is that men should realize that we need a new science, a new structure built on a new approach to experience. The old science is inadequate. "Nothing duly investigated, nothing verified, nothing counted, weighed, or measured, is to be found in natural history: and what in observation is loose and vague, is in information deceptive and treacherous." Accidental experiments must be replaced by controlled experiments— "of light" rather than "of fruit," which are designed simply for the discovery of causes and axioms. Data should be arranged in *Tables of Discovery* (which Bacon discusses in Book II), and from these we should ascend to axioms educed from these particulars by a certain rule, and then descend again to new particulars. In this activity the understanding, prone to fly off into speculation, should be hung with weights rather than provided with wings. The induction which is based on simple enumeration of accidentally gathered data is a childish thing; it should be replaced by one which examines the axioms derived in this way to see whether they are applicable to new particulars not included in the original enumeration, and whether they should be extended to wider areas or modified and restricted to what the new experience discloses.

The second section of Book I is devoted to a correction of the misconceptions of the Baconian method. Bacon assures the reader that he is not trying to set up a new sect in philosophy and not trying to propose a new theory of the universe. He is not even willing to promise any new specific scientific discoveries which may occur as a result of the introduction of the new method. He grants that his method probably contains errors of detail, though he believes these to be minor in character. Among the results which he is able to show, some will be claimed by others to be trivial, some to be even mean and filthy, and some to be too subtle to be readily comprehended. In reply to these charges Bacon repeats the statement of the poor woman who, having asked for a grant from a haughty prince and been rejected on the grounds that such an act would be beneath his dignity, replied, "Then leave off being king." If Bacon is criticized on the grounds that his method is presumptive, since he claims with one blow to have set aside all previous sciences and all earlier authors, his reply will be that with better tools one can do better things; thus, he is not comparing his capacities with those of his predecessors, but his skill at drawing a perfect circle by means of a compass with that of his predecessors who would draw a less perfect one without this instrument. And to the charge that in urging caution and suspension of judgment he is really denying the capacity of the mind to comprehend truth, he can answer that he is not *slighting* the understanding but *providing for* true understanding, not taking away authority from the senses but supplying them with aids.

Book II is concerned with the method for collecting facts. In order to explain this method Bacon first shows what he means by *Forms*. Every body may be regarded as a collection of "simple natures." Gold, for example, is yellow, malleable, heavy, nonvolatile, noncombustible. These constitute the Form of gold, for in gold these properties meet. Anyone who knows what these properties are, and is capable of transforming a body which does not possess these properties into one which does, can create gold. The Form of gold can therefore also be called the "law" of gold, for it is a description of the nature of this substance and of the various ways in which it may be created or generated. While it is true that in the world itself there exist only bodies, not empty Forms, nevertheless the discovery, investigation, and explanation of Forms is the philosophical foundation of all knowledge and all operations on objects. There is in the world a limited number of "simple natures," or Forms, and every body can be understood as a compound of such natures.

"The Form of a thing is the thing itself, and the thing differs from the Form no other wise than as the apparent differs from the real, or the external, or the thing in reference to man from the thing in reference to the universe." In view of this fact we must set up procedures which will enable us to distinguish the true Form from the apparent Form. These procedures are employed in the setting up of *Tables and Arrangements of Instances*. These are obtained by the collection of particulars discovered in nature. "We are not to imagine or suppose, but to discover, what nature does or may be made to do." But since nature is so various and diffuse it tends to distract and confuse us as it presents itself. Consequently the particulars must be arranged and organized in order that understanding may be able to deal with them. In this way it is able to use induction and to educe axioms from experience. There are three kinds of such tables. *Tables of Essence and Presence* consist of collections of all known instances of a given nature, exhibiting themselves in unlike substances. As an example, Bacon gives a long list of instances of heat—in the sun, in meteors, in flame, in boiling liquids. A second kind of collection is a *Table of Deviation, or of Absence in Proximity*. These instances are cases where heat is absent; for example, in moonlight, light from the stars, air on mountain tops, and so on. Finally, there are *Tables of Degrees* or *Tables of Comparisons*. These involve noting the increase or decrease of heat in the same substance, or its varying amount in different subjects. For example, different substances produce different intensities of heat when burned; substances once hot, such as lime, ashes, and soot, retain their former heat for some time; dead flesh, in contrast to living flesh, becomes cold. These three *Tables* are devices by which we assure ourselves that where the nature is present the Form will be present, where the nature is absent the Form will be absent, and where the nature varies quantitatively the Form will vary quantitatively. On data thus arranged we go to work by the inductive process. If we proceed simply on the basis of affirmative cases, as we are naturally inclined to do, the results will be fancies, guesses, and ill-defined notions, and the axioms must be corrected every day. God and the angels may have the capacity to extract Forms solely from affirmative cases; but man must proceed by affirmation, negation, and variation. What we obtain by this process, however, is only the *Commencement of Interpretation* or the *First Vintage*. Bacon presumably means by this what present-day scientists would call a "hypothesis"; that is, a tentative interpretation which we employ as a guide to the selection of further instances (such as *Prerogative Instances*, which he discusses in great detail). On the basis of the hypothesis we then proceed either to collect the instances by controlled observation or to produce them by experimentation.—*A.C.B.*

Pertinent Literature

Anderson, Fulton H. *Francis Bacon: His Career and His Thought*. Los Angeles: University of Southern California Press, 1962.

This volume is the most complete biography and overall interpretation of Francis Bacon's achievements presently available. Fulton H. Anderson tries to show that, in spite of many detractors, Bacon was actually an original systematic thinker. He was, according to Anderson, a political thinker actively seeking to work out definite and consistent philosophical views, and he was not, as he has been accused of being, a self-seeking opportunist.

The first two-thirds of Anderson's volume deals with Bacon's political career, defending his actions from unfair interpretations. Anderson tries to show that Bacon's political actions during the reigns of Elizabeth and James I were based on his theory of royal prerogative and on his view that sovereigns are to be obeyed because they are God's agents. Anderson believes that even in the most notorious events in Bacon's political career, the Essex affair and the struggle with Coke and the Howards, Bacon behaved virtuously or, at least, was philosophically justified. Even the events that led to Bacon's political fall, his taking of bribes, are interpreted here not as indicating dishonesty, but as the outgrowth of a philosophical defense of royalism.

After dealing with Bacon as the "philosophical" politician, Anderson devotes the last third of the book to Bacon's philosophy. Starting with Bacon's early dissatisfactions with what he studied at Cambridge, Anderson follows his career up to the revolutionary proposals in the *Novum Organum*. He shows how Bacon kept working on his scientific writings all through his political career and how he kept seeking political support for educational reforms that would give man dominion over nature. Anderson contends that Bacon's view was a rich, coherent, original system of thought involving both a pluralistic philosophy and a metaphysical naturalism. The latter was materialistic in character, influenced by Democritus, but was also based on inductive procedures that Bacon developed in much detail, and not on philosophical speculation.

Anderson contends that the bulk of Bacon's philosophical contribution is original. To make this case, Anderson carefully delineates the new advances Bacon made over the various ancient philosophers he had studied. Bacon's views are also considered in relation to many of the Renaissance naturalistic theoreticians of the time—thinkers whose theories were being taken very seriously in the late sixteenth and early seventeenth centuries, thinkers such as Paracelsus, William Gilbert, Girolamo Cardano, Giordano Bruno, Bernardino Telesio, and Tommaso Campanella. As Anderson presents the case, Bacon seems most impressive and original when compared to them. Bacon's naturalism, and the means he proposed for studying nature, have turned out to be more fruitful and more intellectually revolutionary than the views of contemporaries who presented inspired, strange, wild speculations about the nature of the universe and how to control it.

Frances Bacon, seen against this background, appears (at least in Anderson's rendition) to be a somber, careful thinker, employing inductive products to unravel the universe. Rejecting speculations and inspired interpretations, Bacon sought knowledge by a most deliberate and monumental inspection of the Kingdom of Nature, through gaining all of the facts and then making careful inductions. Only through this procedure, Bacon thought, would one discover the springs and principles of nature and be able to realize the dream of Dr. Faustus that knowledge is power.

Jardine, Lisa. *Francis Bacon: Discovery and the Art of Discourse*. Cambridge: Cambridge University Press, 1974.

Lisa Jardine accepts at face value Francis Bacon's claim that his *Novum Organum* is a logic, in which the author claimed to be making great innovations over his predecessors and contemporaries. By a very careful examination of the logic texts available in the sixteenth century, Jardine shows that Bacon was neither as completely original as Fulton H. Anderson has claimed, nor as thoroughly involved with his contemporaries as Paolo Rossi has declared him to be. By very detailed historical scholarship, Jardine attempts to establish Bacon's place in intellectual history. She maintains that she is offering a consistent rather than a revolutionary reading of Bacon's works. By reconstructing the intellectual background against which Bacon set forth the particular methodological questions in which he was interested, we are able, Jardine believes, to appreciate the originality and ingenuity of the solutions he offered. She also contends that seeing Bacon in this manner restrains us from reading back into his work concerns that in fact only later became important in the development of method in science and philosophy.

First the dialectic handbooks in use in sixteenth century schools are examined, with special attention to what is now called "methodus," a newly introduced term transliterated from the Greek. The Aristotelian and Ramist books circulated widely. Among textbook reformers the subject of dialectical methods received much attention, as in Rudolf Agricola's *De Inventione Dialectica* of 1515, which is based more on Cicero and Quintilian than on Aristotle. Agricola heavily emphasized invention. The Reformer Philipp Melanchthon followed out Agricola's approach. Jardine details the various kinds of approaches throughout the century, devoting considerable time and space to Peter Ramus and his followers, as well as to such late Italian commentators as Giacomo Zabarella. The background material is used to show that there was a dispute in Cambridge in the late sixteenth century between Everard Digby and William Temple concerning the nature and use of dialectical method. The dispute, Jardine asserts, provides some significant clues for understanding Bacon's polemical response to the discussion of dialectic. Bacon rarely cited what he was reading, and few of his books have survived. He did attack what he saw as the artificiality of some of the elements of the dialectical tradition, and he saw his own inductive method of discovery as a natural method by which people operate. Bacon proposed to establish progressive stages of certainty in the sciences by means of taking advantage of the inherent human capacities of the natural faculties. Bypassing human tendencies to err, or the Idols, Bacon sought to develop the basis for what he called "true and legitimate induction," "the very key of interpretation." Jardine carefully shows how Bacon's theory of knowledge can be seen, and perhaps be better understood, in the light of sixteenth century discussions about method.

Much of the book consists in applying the interpretation of Bacon's proposed method for understanding nature to the actual scientific procedure. In so doing, Jardine illuminates the novelty in Bacon's program. Besides clarifying Bacon's contribution to the development of natural science (and making clearer what he did not accomplish), Jardine also examines the use of Bacon's methods in ethics and civics. One must always remember that Bacon was a major political figure who wrote a great deal about moral matters. The limited possibilities of inductive moral and political sciences are discussed by Jardine, and the reasons for these limitations are examined. The role of the parable in Bacon's examination of what people can understand is dealt with in a worthwhile chapter. Other applications of Bacon's method, his kinds of examples, and his ultimate view of rhetoric are also considered. The book closes with an important chapter on Bacon's method in the *Essays* showing that what he was doing there can be seen as part of his overall method of discovery and discourse.

Rossi, Paolo. *Francis Bacon: From Magic to Science.* London: Routledge & Kegan Paul, 1968.

Paolo Rossi's study of Francis Bacon stresses that Bacon's scientific theory must be understood in its historical and social context. Even more, Rossi insists that Bacon's theory is more than the theme of one book of the *Novum Organum*: his theory is the sum of a life's work, starting when he was a rebellious college student wanting to reform all knowledge, and ending when he was a retired Lord Chancellor trying to show mankind how to deal with the inordinate varieties of nature and the basic limitations of human nature. Rossi traces many fascinating themes through the whole *corpus* of Bacon's writings, not merely through the few works that have become famous as classic accounts of the scientific method.

As the subtitle indicates, this study begins by placing Bacon's early works among those of the Renaissance magicians. Then it is shown why Bacon rejected the magicians for their esoteric doctrines, their elitism, and their failure to see that the progress of human knowledge requires joint undertakings. Certain elements of the magicians' beliefs remained with Bacon, however, and in his last work, *Sylva silvarum*, he borrowed from those he had so vehemently attacked.

Rossi deals extensively with Bacon's treatment of mythology. Bacon's attitude towards the significance of classical mythology changed from seeing it as primitive and useless to regarding it as meaningful parable. Bacon came to see mythology as an important way in which philosophical proposals were diffused. Bacon, however, regarded Greek philosophy, with the possible exception of Democritus' theory, as inadequate. (Some of Bacon's views about mythology were adopted by Giovanni Battista Vico.)

The reform that Bacon felt was needed in the intellectual world had to be built on more than the classical fable. It was in the logic, rhetoric, and methodology of his time that Bacon found the materials for his revolutionary proposal. It was not that Bacon discovered the inductive method, but that he saw how it could be adopted. From the rhetoricians, especially Peter Ramus, Bacon saw the value of method. In his new scientific logic, Bacon incorporated some of the typical concepts of traditional rhetoric. He substituted the collection of natural data, however, for the use of empty rhetorical devices. He used his tables, or instruments of classification, as ways of organizing reality, as ways by which memory could assist in the intellectual understanding of nature.

Bacon rejected deduction and the deductive science of mathematics and failed to appreciate what Galileo or Copernicus had accomplished. Instead, he saw his own method as a "thread" that could guide mankind through the "chaotic forest" and "complex labyrinth" of nature.

Bacon, Rossi points out, was challenging an implicit connection between deductive methods and a tendency to accept classical traditions and theories (such as Aristotle's) blindly. Bacon's real contribution, Rossi believes, lies not simply in being the spokesman for induction, "but in his courageous rejection of pre-established limitations to scientific enquiring." Bacon designed a logic as a human instrument to enable man to dominate a resisting, recalcitrant nature. He saw abstract theoretical methods as inadequate in natural research and as a result appealed to experimental data and used elaborate tables of data in his attempt to understand nature.

Rossi's book is most helpful in placing Bacon's contribution in a broader context than that provided by simply examining his proposals in the *Novum Organum*. By tracing Bacon's views through all his writings, and by seeing him in relation to the magicians, alchemists, mythologists, rhetoricians, logicians, and deductive scientists of his time, Rossi makes Bacon's contributions much clearer.—*R.H.P.*

ADDITIONAL RECOMMENDED READING

Anderson, Fulton H. *The Philosophy of Francis Bacon*. Chicago: University of Chicago Press, 1948. A careful and thorough examination of Bacon's new logic of inquiry.

Broad, C. D. *The Philosophy of Francis Bacon*. Cambridge: Cambridge University Press, 1926. An interesting, although brief, critical account.

Farrington, Benjamin. *Francis Bacon: Pioneer of Planned Science*. London: Weidenfeld and Nicolson, 1963. The author of *Francis Bacon: Philosopher of Industrial Science* (New York: H. Schuman, 1949) continues his account of Bacon's contribution to the modern temper in science.

Rossi, Paolo. *Francis Bacon: From Magic to Science*. Translated from the Italian by Sacha Rabinovitch. Chicago: University of Chicago Press, 1968. Emphasizes Bacon's logic, rhetoric, and method.

DISCOURSE ON METHOD

Author: René Descartes (1596-1650)
Type of work: Philosophy of philosophy, metaphysics
First published: 1637

PRINCIPAL IDEAS ADVANCED

The proper method for philosophy is as follows: Never accept any idea as true which is not clearly and distinctly beyond doubt; divide each complex question into simple, basic questions; proceed from the simple to the complex; review all steps in reasoning.

If this method is put into practice, there seems to be no proposition that cannot be doubted except the following: I think, therefore I am. (Cogito, ergo sum.)

As thinking substance, I have the idea of God; and since the idea of a perfect being could not have been derived from my own experience or being, God must exist as the source of my idea.

Furthermore, imperfect and dependent beings could not exist unless there were a perfect being, God, who made their existence possible; in addition, God by his very nature exists, for if he did not exist of necessity, he would not be perfect.

Since God exists, he provides the ground for our knowledge about the external world provided that we are careful to accept as true only those ideas which are clearly and distinctly beyond doubt once the reliability of the senses and of the reason can be seen to be derived from God.

In 1633, the year of Galileo's recantation, Descartes was just finishing his first major scientific treatise, *The World*. Because he made use in it of the Copernican theory, prudence dictated that the work be withheld from publication. But a strong sense of the importance of his discoveries prevailed upon him to issue three token essays as samples of what he was doing, and to compose a kind of prospectus of his work to date for publication under the same cover. This latter is the *Discourse on Method*. Besides explaining the author's method and reviewing his labors, it summarizes his metaphysical reasoning and sketches the plan of the larger, unpublished volume.

Strangely, perhaps, for one whose declared intention was to set all human knowledge on impersonal foundations, the *Discourse on Method* is a highly personal communication. It begins with a biographical reminiscence.

Familiar with books from childhood, the young Descartes had entered the new Jesuit College of La Flèche with high expectation; but he early fell victim to the skepticism which attended the passing of the Renaissance. The study of ancient tongues, of classic treatises on morals and philosophy, and of jurisprudence and medicine were excellent for ornamenting the person and preparing him for a life of riches and honor, but he decided that they yielded nothing that could be called knowledge. The only good to come from the revival of learning, so far as truth is concerned, was the rediscovery of mathematics, which, however, he was inclined to take without the Pythagorean mystifications which so delighted Kepler. The thing that pleased him in mathematics was the certitude and evidence which accompanied its demonstrations; and he was surprised to find that no higher science had been erected on such solid foundations. By contrast, philosophy, on which so much had been based, could exhibit no single claim that was not in dispute.

The young graduate had no further incentive toward books or toward the past. On the hunch that practical men might be wiser than scholars, in that they cannot entertain follies with impunity, he resolved to see the world and talk with men of every rank and occupation. He soon found, however, that practical men disagree as much as do philosophers; and, as for the experience of traveling in foreign lands, nothing so quickly undermines one's confidence in the judgment of one's fellow men.

Then came the turning point in Descartes' life. While he was still in his early twenties, he made the discovery—for which he is celebrated in the history of mathematics—that it is possible to bring geometry and algebra together into a single science by plotting equations along rectangular axes. This startling discovery encouraged him to look into his own mind for still more fundamental truths. "I resolved at length to make myself an object of study, and to employ all the powers of my mind in choosing the paths I ought to follow." The time was the winter of 1619-1620; the place was Germany, where he was serving in the army. He was barely twenty-three when these new prospects opened before him. For another nine years he was content to travel, assuming the role of spectator rather than actor in the affairs of the world. But he was not wasting his time. Part of his program consisted in systematic doubt; by painstaking reflection upon every matter that could be a source of error, he deliberately attempted to destroy beliefs which were not certainly true.

At the end of this period, he retired to Holland. He was then ready to undertake the recovery of truth. The first step was to replace the old metaphysics with one founded on his newly formed principles. This task he accomplished in his book *Meditations on First Philosophy*, written in 1628-1629 (but not published until 1641). When this was out of the way, he was free to set about the main enterprise, which was to lay bare the secret laws which govern the world of matter. In the eight succeeding years his progress was astonishing. But the innumerable experiments which kept suggesting themselves required many hands. His motive in presenting the summary of his ideas in the *Discourse* was to recruit workers.

There is evidence independent of the *Discourse on Method* that the first powerful conviction which lifted Descartes out of skepticism and set his feet upon the rock of certitude was the discovery of certain rules for the direction of the mind. In the *Discourse* he associates this phase of his development with the winter in Germany when he was twenty-three. It antedates his enterprise of systematic doubt and, indeed, is presupposed by it, the doubt being but the first step toward carrying through the rules.

The brilliant young mathematician was led to conclude that just as the most difficult demonstrations in geometry can be arrived at easily by a long chain of simple steps, so "all things, to the knowledge of which man is competent, are mutually connected in the same way, and . . . there is nothing so far removed from us as to be beyond our reach, or so hidden that we cannot discover it, provided only we abstain from accepting the false for the true, and always preserve in our thoughts the order necessary for the deduction of one truth from another." These were intoxicating thoughts. What he had discovered, he believed, was a key that would open for mankind all the doors to knowledge. For it was no new power of insight or of reasoning that was needed—every man, essentially, has as much insight and reason as any other. The failure of previous inquirers stemmed from no natural deficiency, but from clumsiness and inexperience. Chiefly, man had been seduced by the powerful claims of his senses and imagination, so that the sober witness of reason had been obscured. What men needed was a set of rules which would help them to keep faithfully to truths which, once the debris had been removed, would shine upon the mind with a natural light.

Descartes was, therefore, a bold exponent of what is known as the deductive or *a priori* method. Still, his approach must not be confused with the scholasticism which, in Bacon's words, "flies from the senses and particulars to the most general axioms, and from these principles, the truth of which it takes for settled and immoveable, proceeds to judgment and to the discovery of middle axioms." The fault of the Aristotelian syllogism, Descartes said, was that, although it helps us to reason persuasively about things we already think we know, it is of no help in investigating the unknown. Thus, Descartes' method was more radically *a priori* than Aristotle's, which drew its premises from induction. Turning his back on traditional logic, and taking his cue from geometry, he envisaged a chain of linear inferences which would progress from an initial truth so simple and obvious as to be self-evident, to a second which would be seen at once to be included in the first, and thence to a third, and so forth. In practice, the problem would always be to find the simple truth to which the chain could be anchored; afterward, all that would be necessary would be to preserve the true order. Each particular truth along the way would be entirely obvious to anyone who understood what was being affirmed—just as in arithmetic, a child who understands a sum fathoms everything that is within reach of the greatest genius who contemplates the same set of figures.

For convenience, Descartes summed up his principles in four rules, abridged as follows:

(a) Never accept any idea as true which is not so clearly and distinctly true as to be beyond all possibility of being doubted.

(b) Divide each complex question into simple ones.

(c) Order one's thoughts from the simplest to the most complex.

(d) Review the series of inferences to make sure there are no breaks or false links in the chain.

If these rules were rigorously followed, an obscure matter, such as the function of the lungs in the body, would be rendered perfectly intelligible. Such, at least, was the promise that inspired the youthful Descartes and launched him on his great career.

The biographical narrative and the exposition of method make up the first half of the *Discourse*. Part IV is an abridged version of the *Meditations on First Principles*, a work composed in Holland at the end of the nine-year period during which Descartes had sought to uproot all erroneous and unfounded opinions from his mind. Sensing Descartes' preeminently scientific interests, one may be surprised to find that he plunged into a metaphysical work. But, as he explained, to have ventured at once into the difficulties of the sciences would have been contrary to right order, since he regarded all such particular truths as dependent on principles borrowed from philosophy.

The investigation of these First Principles was "so metaphysical and uncommon" that the author questioned whether his readers would find it acceptable. It is, in fact, the only part of the *Discourse* which makes serious demands upon the intelligence. Yet, because the *Meditations* had not been published in 1637, he felt obliged to include a précis of that work. The chief advantage to us, who can read the *Meditations*, of having the argument reviewed in the *Discourse* is that we can see it in its proper perspective—on the one hand, as the first serious attempt to make use of the method of doubt, and, on the other, as being not an end in itself but the foundation for physics and physiology. Lacking this perspective, we might suppose that his preoccupation with God and the soul stemmed from a religious interest. His scholastic-styled proofs suggest to the twentieth century reader that he is laboring to shore up traditional beliefs. Quite the contrary! If we reflect that when Descartes speaks of soul he means "thinking" (and ideally "reasoning," for all the rest of the conscious life is illusion), and that when he speaks of God he means the "ordered necessity" against which all apparent "contingency" is rendered intelligible, it will appear that, far from seeking to preserve the Christian view of the world, he is substituting for it an uncompromising formulation of the presuppositions of modern (seventeenth and eighteenth century) science. Just how far his philosophical work strengthened the cause of science and speeded its development is impossible to say, but it seems likely that his metaphysics was more useful than his method.

The method required that Descartes discover a truth so simple and self-evident that it could not be further reduced and yet would verify itself. Yet every belief he considered seemed to him to be a possible error. He supposed that even his strongest convictions might have been planted in him by a malevolent and deceiving god. But finally it struck him that even though his beliefs were mistaken, even though he could not go beyond the activity of doubting, the doubting itself existed; thinking existed; and if thinking, then he, as thinking substance, also existed. He expressed his conclusion in the triumphant words, *"Cogito, ergo sum"*: "I think, therefore I am."

When he sought to discover the ground of his certainty, he found nothing that guaranteed the truth of the proposition, "I think, therefore I am" other than his seeing "very clearly that in order to think it is necessary to exist." He thus took as a general rule for further philosophical investigations the principle "that all the things which we very clearly and distinctly conceive are true. . . ." At the same time, he admitted the difficulty of deciding which of the objects of thought were being conceived "clearly and distinctly."

Descartes then realized that he, as one who doubted, was not perfect— and yet he had the idea of perfection and of a perfect being. He found nothing in his own experience to account for his having arrived at the idea of perfection; and he finally concluded that the idea must have been placed in him by a being possessing all the perfections he conceived; namely, by God himself. Descartes was thus led to a renewed conviction in God's existence.

Other arguments in support of the belief in God's existence were quickly generated. All imperfect bodies and intelligences show by their imperfection their dependency on the perfect, on God; hence, God exists. Furthermore, the idea of a perfect being entails the idea of the existence of such a being; for if a being otherwise perfect did not exist, he would lack an essential perfection. (This ontological argument, reminiscent of St. Anselm's more famous version, was regarded by Descartes as having the same rigorous character as a geometric proof.) Finally, Descartes decided that no belief whatsoever could be accepted as a "metaphysical certitude" except by presupposing the existence of God. Even the principle of clarity—that clear and distinct ideas are true—depended for its certainty upon God's perfection and existence.

It has seemed to many critics of Descartes that to prove the certainty of a principle by reference to a God whose existence is proved by the use of that very same principle is certainly a circular procedure. But Descartes probably would have argued that clear and distinct ideas are certainly true whether we know the ground of our certainty that such is the case. He presumed that by his arguments he revealed the ground of all certainty: God, the perfect being, the independent support of all dependent beings and of all truths endorsed by reason.

Having reassured himself and his readers of the reliability of reason and of the method he had outlined, Descartes then proceeded to summarize the conclusions of his unpublished treatise. According to his account, the treatise was a comprehensive work containing "all that . . . I thought I knew of the nature of material objects." Beginning with light, it touched upon the sun and the stars, on the heavens, the planets, the comets, and the earth, upon terrestrial bodies, and finally, upon man considered as organized matter. Out of caution, the author adopted the device of speaking about an imaginary world rather than about one created as described in the Bible. Suppose that there be matter "without form and void" in some imaginary space; if it is governed by the laws which God's perfection has established and fixed in our minds, it must work itself out of its initial chaos and arrange itself in a manner like our heavens and our earth. Tides, air currents, mountains and seas, summer and winter, minerals and vegetables are all accounted for in terms of fixed laws of nature. One has to turn to the original work to find the laws stated. Perhaps the most significant point Descartes communicates in his summary of *The World* is the important principle that the nature of anything is more easily conceived when understood in terms of its origin than when viewed simply in its completed state.

The greater part of the summary is given to human physiology. Continuing his hypothetical mode of argument, he asks us to think of God as forming the body of a man exactly like ours, but without a rational soul. This being granted, Descartes undertook to show how, according to the same laws as obtain everywhere else in nature, all the internal and external motions of the body must take place exactly as we observe them to, with the exception of intelligent speech and certain inventive actions. The circulation of the blood is taken as an example. Its motion through the body, as Descartes explains it, is the result of the presence in the heart of one of those fires-without-light (the kind present in processes of fermentation). The heat purifies the blood, and the resulting expansion and contraction drives it through the cavities of the heart. Hot blood warms the stomach, enabling digestion to take place. The lungs serve as condensers which cool the blood before returning it to the left ventricle. This cooling releases the animal spirits which are the "most agitated" part of the blood. These go to the brain because the arteries leading in that direction are nearly straight, and "according to the rules of Mechanics, which are the same with those of Nature . . . the weaker and less agitated parts must necessarily be driven aside by the stronger which alone in this way reach" their destination.

Surely this one example is sufficient to make clear the character of Descartes' scientific work. Nothing seems so dated as the scientific theories of yesteryear, but this fact should not obscure for us the original quality of Descartes' purely mechanistic account of vital phenomena. While he continued to hold that man's mind is perfectly adjusted to the body (our feelings and appetites are evidence of this), he was careful to stress their complete mutual independence. And as for animals other than man, they are simply very cunningly contrived machines without any kind of mind or soul.

The modern reader who has followed Descartes' account of nature to this point is impatient to ask whether observation and experimentation have no place in scientific work. Could Descartes' armchair method discover the circulation of the blood? The answer, obviously, is that it could not. (He learned it from the physician William Harvey.) Like everyone else, Descartes had to combine experiences and inference in order to obtain knowledge of the existing world. But Descartes' view of the relation between these two ways of knowing is peculiar. He thought that it is a mistake to begin with experiment. Our ordinary observation provides adequate material to arrive at the laws of nature, provided only that we reflect on it, for the germs of the most general truths exist naturally in our minds. Thus, he found no special observation necessary to account for the gross aspects of the universe—the motions of the heavenly bodies, the properties of the elements which make up the earth. But when he came to particular problems, the situation altered. There are so many ways God might have worked that it is impossible for us to infer which is the case. We know in general the laws by which a clock measures time, but we have to look behind the face of a particular clock to see what combinations of wheels and weights or springs the mechanic has employed. Similarly, in the case of the motion of the blood: once we have observed the arrangement of the heart with our eyes and felt the temperature of the blood with our fingers, we are in a position to understand the method which God has employed, and we can then demonstrate by the laws of physics why the motion must take place as it does.

Experimentation became increasingly important to Descartes the further he progressed in scientific studies. But we must not suppose that his youthful preference for demonstrative knowledge was laid aside. His program for future studies, as he hinted at the close of the *Discourse*, was to devote himself exclusively "to acquire some knowledge of Nature which shall be of such a kind as to enable us therefrom to deduce rules of Medicine of greater certainty than those at present in use. . . ."—*J.F.*

PERTINENT LITERATURE

Koyré, Alexandre. "Introduction," in René Descartes' *Philosophical Writings*. Translated and edited by E. Anscombe and P. T. Geach. Edinburgh: Nelson, 1954.

One of the clearest and most concise introductions to René Descartes' thought is provided by Alexandre Koyré, for he outlines the social and intellectual context within which Descartes was writing, identifies the main themes of Descartes' work, and then connects his work to that context; and this is all accomplished in the space of thirty-seven pages.

The social and intellectual turmoil which constituted the Renaissance and

Reformation had left the intellectuals of Europe in a deeply pessimistic and skeptical state. The arguments which had been advanced in criticism of the former orthodoxies had been powerful enough to undercut them, but little or nothing had been established to replace them. This culminated, Koyré contends, in the skepticism of Michel de Montaigne, who believed that we can have knowledge of neither ourselves nor our world.

In the seventeenth century there were three main varieties of reaction to this skeptical crisis—namely, faith, experience, and reason, as articulated in turn by Pierre Charron, Francis Bacon, and Descartes. Charron proclaimed the vanity of human inquiry as grounds for embracing faith and obedience to the traditional forms of religious authority; while Bacon and Descartes rejected skepticism in favor of a New Science, which for Bacon could be constructed out of pure experience, while for Descartes it would arise from pure reason.

Koyré argues that Descartes' intellectual horizons were dominated by Montaigne's skepticism, but that Descartes criticized Montaigne for being too timid—that is, for being insufficiently skeptical. Montaigne had reluctantly succumbed to skepticism, while Descartes proposed to adopt freely the strongest possible skeptical critique of his beliefs; in other words, he intended to turn skeptical doubt against itself in the hope thereby of attaining some complete certainty. Descartes proposed, and believed that he could perform, a completely clean sweep to provide a totally new beginning. As Koyré recognizes, this is anything but a modest enterprise, but then Descartes was willing to doubt possibly anything except his own abilities.

Descartes tried to treat his mind and his beliefs like a basket of apples, some of which are rotten. He proposed to examine them all, one by one, and not to return any to the basket until all have been removed and inspected, and to return to the basket only those which have been certified as sound. This negative phase culminated in the attainment of the *cogito*, the certainty of his own existence, from which he proceeded to develop a positive set of beliefs about the world.

Descartes claimed that his scientific method is a generalization of the ideal type of mathematical method, which starts from a pure intellectual intuition and then proceeds by way of strict deductively valid steps to demonstrably true conclusions. Descartes intended to create an integrated structure of knowledge analogous to the structure of a tree. Logic and mathematics provide the root, philosophy the trunk, and the branches and fruit correspond to the scientific knowledge for which Descartes was searching.

Descartes believed that the seeds and soil for this tree are innate within each of us as God-given ideas, and that we could establish *a priori* that God created a material world which functions in a strictly mechanical fashion and in accordance with precise mathematical laws of nature. We can gain certain knowledge of these laws and, as Koyré emphasizes, knowledge of these laws of nature were sought in order to provide us with control over the material world so that we can exercise our freedom in arranging it in accordance with our own needs and wishes. Although we may be able to establish *a priori* that God created the material world as a mechanical system, we cannot establish *a priori* the particular organization of the material world. Which of the many possible sets of laws actually governs this world needs to be established, at least partly, by reference to empirical considerations.

Koyré notes that the God whose existence Descartes proclaims is in many ways unlike the God of the Old and New Testaments, for in Descartes there is no reference to prayer, grace, salvation, or sin. Descartes' God, rather, is like an engineer or clockmaker; yet Koyré maintains that Descartes was a sincere Christian and that his conception of the Deity could be assimilated within Christian theology. After all, Descartes did argue that an atheist could have no possible grounds for epistemological certainty and would always be prey to absolute epistemological skepticism.

For Koyré, the major weakness or anomaly in Cartesianism is the account of the dual nature of human beings. Descartes defined mind and matter as essentially independent of each other, and therefore in principle unable to interact. Yet when Descartes tried to characterize a human life he felt obliged to do so in terms of a unity of mind and body. For Descartes this idea was both indispensable and irredeemably unclear and indistinct, and therefore essentially mysterious.

Roth, Leon, *Descartes' Discourse on Method*. Oxford: Clarendon Press, 1937.

Most philosophers who write about René Descartes examine several of his works in one study; but in 1937, to commemorate the three hundredth anniversary of the publication of Descartes' *Discourse on Method*, Leon Roth published a book specifically on the *Discourse*, the main points of which were published in the article in *Mind* (January, 1937). Roth explores the role which Descartes intended for the *Discourse*, and he explains that it was intended merely as a brief introduction to a set of scientific texts.

Roth insists that Descartes' main concerns were scientific rather than philosophical, and that the arguments concerning the *cogito*, and the existence of God, were intended to be incidental hypotheses on the way to his main goal, the establishment and articulation of his New Science. For Roth, the *Discourse* is the primary work by Descartes, and all his other works should be interpreted by reference to it; and furthermore Roth maintains that the *Discourse* constituted a major break in the history of thought, and that it was the primary document in the creation of a science of nature. Roth argues that Descartes' innovation was his refusal to follow Aristotle in basing his metaphysics on physics. Aristotle's argument for the existence of God depended essentially on the reality of physical motion, from which he argued to the existence of a First Mover. By contrast, Descartes intended to base his physics on a metaphysics which is both prior and absolutely certain.

Roth places great emphasis on the practical character of Descartes' ultimate interests. He wanted scientific knowledge of the material world because he wanted to provide people with the means to control, manipulate, and dominate the material world. As Roth says, Descartes came to doubt that he could conclusively establish the immortality of the soul, but he never lost his abiding concern to extend mortal embodied life. He was at least as much concerned with conquering the death of the body as with confirming the eternality of the soul.

Roth devotes considerable space to a detailed comparison of Descartes' *Discourse* with Francis Bacon's *Novum Organon*. Both sought knowledge which would yield practical and profitable power over nature. Both sought a unique method of inquiry which could be applied in a systematic and mechanical fashion and which would be applicable in all domains. One major difference, however, was that Bacon expected a steady accumulation of knowledge while Descartes sought and expected rapid and complete results.

One of the major novelties in Descartes' *Discourse* was the emphasis he placed on, and the account he provided of, the role of mathematics in our knowledge of nature. For Descartes, mathematics is not just one useful tool; it is fundamental and indispensable. The material world, according to Descartes, is essentially that subject matter which can always and only be described and represented mathematically, by algebra, geometry, and arithmetic. Nevertheless, Roth also recognizes that Descartes could not, and did not try to, establish a complete science *a priori*. He recognizes that empirically obtained facts are also indispensable, although Roth does not provide an account of how this empirical input might be incorporated.

The great irony of Descartes' *Discourse* is that it was intended merely as an introduction to several scientific essays on method. By Descartes' own standards the *Discourse* would be judged a total failure. Descartes' essays were rejected as unsatisfactory and muddled. His physics was rapidly superseded by that of Sir Isaac Newton, and only because of this the *Discourse* survived to become highly influential in philosophy, but only when separated from Cartesian physics. As Roth says: "The failure of Cartesianism lay in its *connecting* the *Discourse* with the *Essays*. The history of its *triumph* is the history of their dissociation." Only by abandoning Descartes' science has his philosphy gained its profound influence.

Garber, Daniel. "Science and Certainty in Descartes," in *Descartes: Critical and Interpretive Essays*. Edited by Michael Hooker. Baltimore: Johns Hopkins University Press, 1978, pp. 114-151.

Daniel Garber's essay is one of the most interesting and controversial of recent contributions to Cartesian scholarship. Many commentators, including both Alexandre Koyré and Leon Roth, have pointed out that René Descartes came to recognize the necessity of an empirical input into his science. Garber undertakes to show how Descartes thought that this could and should be done, and why he thought he could introduce empirical information into his science without diminishing the certainty of that science. Garber claims, and attempts to prove, that Descartes' distrust of experience has been both overemphasized and misunderstood. Garber argues, despite some evidence to the contrary, that Descartes' science is not entirely *a priori*, and that it does depend on an indispensable empirical input, and that this science is no less certain for that.

Garber argues that Descartes defined certainty in terms of intuition and deduction. A belief is certain if, and only if, it *could* have been (not necessarily that it was) reached by a process of deduction from intuition—where the notion of deduction is interpreted more rigorously, but more liberally, than in terms of the classical syllogism. In the *Discourse*, Descartes provided an alternative definition of certainty in terms of clarity and distinctness, but Garber argues that these definitions are equivalent and that the account in terms of clarity and distinctness is the more fundamental. (It is interesting to note in passing that Garber maintains that Descartes did not believe that his method of scientific inquiry was the only way to reach the desired goal, merely that he claimed for his method that it was the most reliable and effective method. On this point, however, Garber's views are at variance with most other commentators, including Koyré and Roth.)

Garber carefully considers the suggestion that Descartes' account of the contribution of empirical information to the scientific method can be accommodated within the model envisaged in Karl Popper's hypothetico-deductive procedure. He argues that although Descartes did write in a hypothetical form in certain contexts, Descartes makes it explicitly clear that he did so only because it served to abbreviate his account, not because he thought it a suitable means for either the discovery or the validation of scientific knowledge. The conclusions of a hypothetico-deductive method are always, and inevitably, provisional and uncertain, whereas Garber is trying to show that Descartes' science was intended to be both certain and partially empirical.

Garber's argument is essentially that Descartes believed that we can establish *a priori* the existence and essence of the material world, but that we cannot establish *a priori* the particular characteristics of *this* material world. God could have created many possible material worlds in accordance with a variety of possible laws, and so empirical considerations are indispensable in passing from the variety of possible worlds to a determination of the *actual* character of *this* world. That is to say, experience is required when we descend from general principles to particulars, selecting the actual from the many possibles. In relation to some particular phenomenon, several possible explanations could be offered that would be consistent with the basic assumptions of Cartesian materialism. Descartes' method, then, consists in enumerating all the possible explanations and then introducing crucial experiments to eliminate all but one, correct, explanation. In other words, the results of crucial experiments could serve to exclude all the possible, but unactualized, explanations. According to this view, empirical facts are not the starting points for deductive arguments; rather, they serve to eliminate unwanted and unneeded deductive chains. In this way, Descartes' science starts from intuition, proceeds by deduction, and still depends on an essential empirical input, and yet yields results which are as certain as any thesis which is demonstrated deductively from certain premises. Garber provides as an example of the use of this intuitive, deductive, enumerative, and eliminative method the account, to be found in the *Meteorology*, which Descartes provided of the structure of water. Whether Garber's account of Descartes' methodology is correct cannot be settled here, but what is clear is that he provides a fascinating and important suggestion which deserves careful attention.—*E.M.*

ADDITIONAL RECOMMENDED READING

Doney, Willis, ed. *Descartes: A Collection of Critical Essays*. Garden City, New York: Doubleday & Company, 1967. An impressive collection of contemporary scholarship, with a useful bibliography.

Kenny, Anthony. *Descartes: A Study of His Philosophy*. New York: Random House, 1968. A straightforward and useful introduction to Descartes' philosophy.

Rée, Jonathan. *Descartes*. London: Allen Lane, 1974. An excellent discussion of Cartesianism as a whole, and of the relation between Descartes' science and philosophy in particular.

Williams, Bernard. *Descartes: The Project of Pure Enquiry*. Harmondsworth, England: Penguin Books, 1978. A detailed analytic dissection of the fine structure of Descartes' philosophical argument.

Objective reality, -
truth of ideas

MEDITATIONS ON FIRST PHILOSOPHY

Author: René Descartes (1596-1650)
Type of work: Metaphysics, epistemology
First published: 1641

PRINCIPAL IDEAS ADVANCED

Perhaps everything we believe is false.

There seems to be no way of avoiding the skeptical consequences of systematic doubt.

But if one is doubting, one exists.

This is the starting point for a philosophy based on certainty.

But if one exists, one is a thinker, a mind; and since one conceives of a God whose conception is beyond one's powers, there must be such a being.

But if God exists, then we can count on our sense experience and our reason, provided we are careful to believe only what is clearly and distinctly true.

The complete title of this work, *Meditations on the First Philosophy in Which the Existence of God and the Distinction Between Mind and Body Are Demonstrated*, prepares the reader for an essay in metaphysics. And we shall not accuse Descartes of mislabeling his product. But in order to understand Descartes' interest in these questions, and therefore the fuller import of the work, one must be prepared to find that he is actually reading an essay in epistemology, or the theory of knowledge. Is there such a thing as knowledge? If so, what distinguishes it from opinion? How is error to be explained? Such questions as these seem to have been uppermost in the author's mind. But in order to answer them, to validate knowledge, to lay hold on the necessity which to Descartes (quite in the Platonic tradition) was the mark of truth, it was necessary to raise the fundamental questions of Being.

In choosing to set down his thoughts as meditations, Descartes shows the greatest consideration for his reader. He represents himself as seated before a fire in a cozy Dutch dwelling, wrapped in his dressing gown, freed from worldly care, and devoting himself to a task which he had for some time looked forward to—a kind of mental housecleaning. On six successive days he pursues his meditation, taking us with him step by step. He pursues the task of clearing his mind of all error.

From *Discourse on Method* we learn that the work was actually composed in circumstances much like those here alleged. In 1628 Descartes was in his thirties and living in Holland, to which he had withdrawn from the more active life for the special purpose of carrying on his philosophical and scientific investigations. The *Meditations* was circulated in manuscript, and when it was published (1641) it included a lengthy appendix composed of objections by leading philosophers—including Thomas Hobbes and Pierre Gassendi—together with Descartes' replies.

The "First Meditation" is, in a way, distinct from the rest. It describes Descartes' effort, which in fact engaged him for many years, to accustom himself not to think of the world in the imagery of the senses or according to the notions of common sense and the traditions of the schools.

Can it be, Descartes wonders, that all beliefs which he had formerly held are false? Perhaps not: but if he is to achieve his goal of building up a body of incontrovertible truth, he must exercise the same rigor toward beliefs that are merely uncertain as toward those which are demonstrably untrue. That is to say, he must make *doubt* his tool. Instead of allowing it to hang over him, forever threatening, he must grasp it firmly and lay about until he has expunged from his mind every pretended certainty.

The first to go are those beliefs that depend on our senses—notably our belief in the existence of our own bodies and of everything that appears to our sight and touch. Our habitual judgment protests. What can be more certain, Descartes asks himself, than that I am seated by the fire holding this paper in my hand? But, he writes, when we reflect that our dreams are sometimes attended with equal confidence, we are forced to conclude that there is no infallible mark by which we can know true perceptions from false.

Of course, what one doubts is, in this case, only that one's ideas *represent* something beyond themselves. Descartes is one of the first philosophers to use the word "idea" in the modern sense. He means by it "whatever the mind directly perceives." But he distinguishes between the idea taken only as a mode of thought, and the idea as a representation of reality. Even in dreams we cannot deny the former of these. What we challenge is the "truth" of the ideas—Descartes calls it "objective reality"—and of judgments based on them. And his question is, whether there is anything in our sense-images that testifies unmistakably to the truth of what they represent. Obviously not, in those that we ourselves initiate in dreams and fantasies. But no more, in those that come from without, through the senses—else how could we make mistakes as to sounds and sights?

There is, he says, another class of ideas which we seem neither to originate ourselves, nor to receive from without, but to be born with—those, for example, which make up the sciences of mathematics. Two and three are five even in dreams: for this sum does not require material counters to make it true. Yet, the ideas of numbers profess to be something besides modes of thought. They do have "objective reality." Moreover, we have been mistaken about mathematical matters. No more than sense-images are they self-authenticating. Our habitual trust in them is not unlike that which we place in our senses, and has the same foundation, namely, that we are creatures of a benevolent deity who would not deceive us. Suppose that this is not the case, and that mathematics is merely a fancy of my mind. Or, worse, suppose it is an illusion deliberately imposed upon us by a malicious demon who has access to the workings of our minds. This is not unthinkable.

These are the thoughts with which the "First Meditation" leaves us. Instead of supposing that the good providence of God sustains his thinking, Descartes resolves to hold fast to the hypothesis that he is constantly being deceived by an evil spirit, so that all his ordinary beliefs are false. In this manner, while he seems to make no progress in the knowledge of truth, he at least habituates himself to suspend judgment concerning things that he does not certainly know. But this is not easy. Descartes pleads with his readers (in the replies to his objectors) not merely to give the exercise such time as is required for reading the meditation through but to take "months, or at least weeks" before going on further. How loath one is to break old habits of thinking he suggests in the figure of a slave who, when sleeping, dreads the day, and conspires to weave the sounds of gathering dawn into his dreams rather than to embrace the light and labors which it brings.

The daylight enterprise that lies before him in the "Second Meditation" is to discover, if possible, some foundation of certainty which doubt is powerless to assault. He has doubted the reality of the world presented to him through his senses. Shall he affirm that some God (or devil) must exist to put these ideas into his mind? That hardly seems necessary, for perhaps he has produced them himself. One thing, however, seems now to loom up in Descartes' mind: "I myself, am 1 not something?" Suppose all my ideas are hallucinations, whether self-induced or planted in me by some God or devil: in this, at least, I cannot be deceived: "I am, I exist, is necessarily true each time that I pronounce it, or that I mentally conceive it."

Here, then, for the first time, we have encountered a self-validating judgment. It is the unique instance in which man immediately encounters the existence which is represented to him by an idea: I have an idea of "myself." Like other ideas, this one claims to have objective reality. But unlike other ideas, this one's claim is open to inspection—by me. Both the idea and the existence which it represents are present each time I think them. In a simple act of "mental vision" (to use Descartes' expression) I know that I exist. As Locke will say, I know my own existence intuitively.

With this certitude to serve as a cornerstone, Descartes proceeds to raise his palace of Truth. Let man explore the structure of his own inner consciousness, and he will find the clue to universal Being. For instance, we can ask the question, "What am I?" And the answer lies at hand. "I am a thing that thinks." For was it not in the act of thinking (taken broadly to include all conscious activities) that I found the reality of the idea of myself? Contrast with this the traditional view that man is a body indwelt by a subtle essence— a very fine grade of matter—known as spirit. What confusion surrounds the whole conception! There is nothing certain, or even intelligible, about it. In fact, we have only to press ahead with our methodical doubt to discover that most of the ideas which we habitually associate with matter are illusory. Take a piece of wax fresh from the comb: we think of it in terms of color, taste, odor, texture. But none of these is essential to the wax. Place it near the fire, and all the qualities which engross the imagination are altered. All that remains unchanged, so that we can call it essential to the wax, is "something extended, flexible, movable"—properties that are knowable to the intellect and not to the senses. In any case, whether I have a body, it is not as body that I know myself when I behold myself as existing. The realm of being which I discover there has nothing about it of extension, plasticity, mobility. I am a thinking being, Descartes concludes, a mind, a soul, an understanding, a reason: and if the meaning of these terms was formerly unknown to me it is no more.

These are very important results of the second day's meditation, especially when we remember that the forward progress was all made along the path of doubt, for it was the act of doubting that gave Descartes both the certainty that he existed and that his nature was mind. But we have not yet exhausted the implications of his consciousness of doubt. Does not doubt carry with it, and actually presuppose, the idea of certainty, just as error carries with it the idea of truth? Descartes finds in his mind the idea of a perfect being by comparison with which he is aware of his imperfections, a self-sufficient being by which he knows that he is dependent. Following this lead, he proceeds in his "Third Meditation" to demonstrate the existence of God.

His argument takes two forms. First, he asks directly concerning the *idea* of a perfect being, whence it could have come into his mind: From some other creature? From himself? Or must there exist a perfect being to originate the idea? His answer is obscured for the modern reader by the late-medieval philosophical framework in which it is expressed. The idea of God contains more "objective reality" than any other idea (including my idea of myself). But a more perfect idea cannot be generated by a less perfect being. Therefore, the idea of God in his mind must have been placed there by God himself.

The second form of the argument proceeds from the contingent quality of his own existence, made up as it is of fleeting instants, no one of which is able either to conserve itself or to engender its successor. Much in the argument reminds one of the traditional Aristotelian proof; but there is this difference, which makes it clear that the new argument is only another version of the first—it is not merely the existence of a contingent being that has to be explained, or of a thinking being, but of "a being which thinks and which has some idea of God." Thus, the principle that there must be at least as much reality in the cause as in the effect precludes the possibility that any being less perfect than God could have created Descartes—or any man.

The argument here abbreviated is of scarcely more than historical interest. And the same is true of the further argument (from the "Fifth Meditation") that, since existence is a perfection, the idea of a Perfect Being entails the

exisTence =perfectioi

existence of that Being. But we would not be just to Descartes if we did not point out that behind the framework of traditional theistic proof lies a claim which rationalistic philosophers have found valid even in our own time. "I see that in some way I have in me the notion of the infinite earlier than the finite—to wit, the notion of God before that of myself. For how would it be possible that I should know that I doubt and desire, that is to say, that something is lacking to me, and that I am not quite perfect, unless I had within me some idea of a Being more perfect than myself, in comparison with which I should recognize the deficiencies of my nature?" Here, in effect, is a new kind of reasoning. The scholastics were committed to demonstrate the existence of God by syllogisms; and, whether through expediency or inadvertency, Descartes makes a show of doing the same. But in Descartes a new, quasimathematical way of reasoning was pushing the syllogism to one side, as the quotation (which could be matched with several others) makes clear. His true ground for affirming the existence of God was not that it *follows from* but that it is *implicit in* his consciousness of himself.

Pascal's famous memorial which insists that the God of the philosophers is not the God of faith is a useful reminder to the general reader. There is no need, however, to suppose that Descartes needed it. The certainty of God's existence is a great triumph—but for scientific, rather than for religious, reasons. It is the *sine qua non* of all further knowledge, since "the certainty of all other things depends on it so absolutely that without this knowledge it is impossible ever to know anything perfectly." We saw earlier that such obvious mathematical truths as two plus three equals five are not self-validating, because they bear no evidence of the competency of our thought. An atheist cannot be sure; hence his knowledge cannot be called science, Descartes tells us in replying to his objectors: doubt may never rise to trouble him; but if it does, he has no way of removing it. But the doubt is removed when a person recognizes that his mind owes its constitution and working to the creativity of God, and that God is no deceiver.

For the rest, the *Meditations* is chiefly devoted to determining just how far man can trust the faculties which the beneficent Deity has implanted in him.

First, one must distinguish between impulses which incline us to belief (such as "the heat which I feel is produced by the fire") and insights into necessary truths (such as "a cause must be as great or greater than its effect.)" Both are natural, and owing to the good offices of our Creator. But the former can be doubted, even after we have discovered the truth about God; the latter, which Descartes speaks of as "the light of nature," cannot be doubted at all. They are the principles of reason in our minds by which we arrive at knowledge. We have no other means of distinguishing between true and false.

Second, one must consider the causes of error. It is axiomatic that God can never deceive us and that if we make proper use of the abilities he has given us we can never go wrong. Yet obviously, he has chosen to make us fallible. How does this happen? From the fact that our intellects are finite, together with the fact that our wills (as free) are infinite. One can see why both these things must be and how, as a consequent, man does not easily stay within the narrow realm of truth. The crux of the matter is that, for Descartes, judgment involves the will (in the form of "assent" or "dissent"). It is within our power to withhold judgment when convincing evidence is wanting, and to give it only when the light of reason demands. Indeed, as Thomas Huxley and William Kingdon Clifford were to say again in the nineteenth century, Descartes held that we have a duty to bring judgment under this rule. Failure to do so involves not merely error but sin.

Third, we come to a nest of problems having to do with our knowledge of the external world. We have mentioned the famous passage in which Descartes examines a piece of wax in order to find what constitutes the essence of matter. He observed that the sensible qualities which we most readily believe to be in matter are not part of the nature of wax, as are such attributes as extension, figure, and mobility, which are not properly sensible but intelligible. Comparing the two ways of thinking about things in nature, Descartes concludes (following the lead of Galileo) that by the senses we have only the most confused notions of matter—they arise from the influence upon the mind of the body to which it is united rather than from the mind's apprehension by its own light of the necessary attributes of being. It is by the latter that we obtain true knowledge of nature, which henceforth is seen to possess only those qualities which can be described in mathematical terms. In other words, the physical world has to be envisaged as a vast, complicated machine—but not (let us remind ourselves) the way our senses view machines, rather the way they are viewed on the drawing board and in the mind of the engineer.

So far reason leads us, Descartes says. If we are correct in supposing that there is a material world, its nature must be as classic mechanics conceives it. But it does not follow that a material world actually exists. It is conceivable that each time I receive and recognize the idea of a body, God himself impresses it upon my mind. Nothing in the idea of matter is inconsistent with its nonexistence. All that I can discover which inclines me to assent to its existence is an instinctive impulse such as attaches to all our sense perceptions: and this, of course, is no reason.

Descartes' only recourse is to appeal to the good faith of God. Thus, he writes that if God were the cause of our ideas of matter, he would undoubtedly have given us the means of knowing that this is the case, for he is no deceiver. In granting us free wills, he has, indeed, opened the door to falsity and error: but he has not permitted any error without placing within our reach the means of avoiding it, or, at least, correcting it once it has been made. The claims of our sense-images, which reason disproves, is an example. But no analysis disproves the natural inclination which we have to believe that corporeal objects do exist. Hence, we are justified in affirming, along with the existence of finite mind (one's own) and infinite Being, the actuality of the material world. (Apparently, for Descartes, the existence of other minds is never more than an inference.)

The upshot of the *Meditations* is, then, to replace the commonsense picture of nature with one that is amenable to rational investigation. The new cosmology which was being shaped by men such as Kepler, Galileo, William Gilbert, and others rested upon fundamental assumptions which were not clear to the investigators themselves. It was the task of Descartes to give these principles their classic formulation.—*J. F.*

PERTINENT LITERATURE

Rée, Jonathan. *Descartes*. London: Allen Lane, 1974.

Contemporary English-speaking philosophers will readily allow that modern philosophy (as distinct from ancient and medieval philosophy) began with René Descartes. Further, since the *Meditations* is clearly Descartes' central philosophical work, these same Anglo-American philosophers will regard and study that work as the source of the modern philosophical tradition.

It is certainly not wrong to see Descartes as the first modern philosopher, nor is it wrong to think of the *Meditations* as the founding work in the present philosophical tradition. But it is shortsighted to see both Descartes and the *Meditations* in only that way. All such philosophers know that Descartes did not think of himself as solely a philosopher; they know that he was also a scientist and a mathematician. His work covered what we today would regard as a wide and disparate range of disciplines. Moreover, Descartes certainly did not think of his work as scattered over unconnected fields of investigation. That is, he saw his philosophical ideas and scientific investigations as thoroughly interconnected.

Descartes' own image for this interconnectedness was that of knowledge as a tree: metaphysics or first philosophy (the full title of Descartes' work is *Meditations on First Philosophy*) is the root of the tree of knowledge; physics or second philosophy is the trunk; and the other special studies are branches of various sizes of one and the same tree.

One of the interesting and important features of Jonathan Rée's book on Descartes is that he attempts to see Descartes' philosophical work, especially the *Meditations*, in its connections with Descartes' scientific ideas and interests. In fact, there is no other work on Descartes in English which is an equally serious attempt to treat the science and the metaphysics as a unit.

In fact, Rée goes even farther. He tends to regard Descartes as primarily a scientist, as someone whose main aim and interest was to give an account of the behavior of physical phenomena. Hence he tends to describe Descartes' views on the various philosophical issues discussed in the *Meditations* as though those views were determined by the needs of his scientific program.

Now that is certainly a significant thesis about how to understand and examine the philosophical parts of Descartes' writings. But there is reason for thinking that Rée has carried his ambition of uniting Descartes' philosophical and scientific works too far. In Descartes' own image of the tree, it is philosophy (that is, metaphysics) which stands at the root of knowledge, determining how the upper parts of the tree develop. Rée's version of the story tends to invert the relationship. Of course, it might be shown that in fact Descartes' physical conceptions did shape his metaphysics contrary to his own metaphor of their relationship; but that does need to be argued.

There are at least two other innovations in Rée's book when it is compared with most other philosophical writings in English on Descartes. Not only is the context of understanding broadened to include Descartes' scientific activities but also it is broadened to include some social and economic developments. Most especially, when Rée turns to write of Descartes' account of the self, he attempts to show how the Cartesian conception of the self was connected with the rise of a capitalist economic system in Europe. There clearly is some such connection, but most writings in English on Descartes tend to ignore such matters completely. Second, Rée finishes the book by saying something of the history of Descartes' reputation. He reminds us that we tend to forget what Descartes was celebrated for in the seventeenth century and what seems close to the truth: that Descartes founded a wholly new world view.

Kenny, Anthony. *Descartes: A Study of His Philosophy.* New York: Random House, 1968.

The *Meditations* has undoubtedly played a significant role in a variety of historical, cultural, and intellectual developments and consequently ought to be studied in light of those developments. For example, it is true that René Descartes was a great scientist, and so the *Meditations* must be examined in relation to his scientific activities and views. Nevertheless, the work is a piece of philosophy, a piece of metaphysics and epistemology, and was intended by Descartes as a reasoned account of the fundamental nature of reality and our knowledge of it. Consequently, at some point in one's study of the work it is necessary that it be subjected to philosophical scrutiny, its claims and arguments closely examined for their truth and adequacy.

In the English-speaking world the training of many philosophers has involved a heavy and early investigation of the *Meditations*. One of the results of that practice has been the production of a number of very good critical examinations of Descartes' main philosophical work. One of those is Anthony Kenny's book. It is a clear and patient exposition of Descartes' claims and arguments and, along with that, an intelligent critical examination of those claims and arguments.

There is nothing strikingly innovative in the organization of Kenny's book—
he follows that standard procedure of taking up themes and topics in the
order in which they arise in the *Meditations*. The interest comes from how
Kenny handles the exposition and criticism of those topics.

As is well known, the *Meditations* opens with a process of doubt which
does not, however, lead to a skeptical conclusion, since Descartes comes to
the fact of his own thought (consciousness) and holds that accordingly his
own existence is beyond doubt. He expressed that "first truth" in the famous
phrase *cogito, ergo sum*. One of the problems that arises for anyone attempting a critical examination of Descartes' arguments is what the status of that
phrase is. The word *ergo* ("therefore") signals that there is an inference from
"I think" to "I am"; and there is other textual evidence for that view. On the
other hand, the majority of scholars in interpreting the *Meditations* have held
that the *cogito* is not an inference but is rather an intuition, something immediately apprehended as true. There is also textual evidence for this view.

One of the excellences of Kenny's book is that he very patiently works
through the various ways of interpreting the phrase as an intuition and shows
that none of them will stand up. He then reverses the matter and shows that
the inference interpretation does, contrary to most opinion, meet the text.
The result of this is that we learn that the *cogito* is not literally the *first* truth
Descartes comes across but is only the first truth which asserts that something
exists.

Descartes' first proof of the existence of God is what traditionally has been
called a cosmological proof: that is, it proceeds from the existence of something, in this case the idea of God which Descartes has, to the necessity of
there being a divine cause of that thing. Descartes argues that he could not
have the idea of a God unless there is a God to give it to him. One of the
criticisms of that argument, made by some of Descartes' contemporaries, is
that, strictly speaking, we have no idea of God; that is, we have no idea of
a supremely perfect being. Descartes has an argument to show that we do
have that idea. It goes from the fact of his doubting through the idea that
doubt is an imperfection to the claim that he therefore has an idea of a
contrasting being, one without imperfections.

That argument, when fully written out, has seemed to many to be persuasive. Kenny, however, quite clearly demolishes the Cartesian argument. He
shows (see Chapter 6) by a parallel argument that we could similarly "prove"
that we have a coherent idea of a being who has every conceivable shape.
Consequently *that* particular way of proving that we have an idea of God will
not work.

Balz, A. G. A. *Descartes and the Modern Mind*. New Haven, Connecticut:
Yale University Press, 1952.

The student of the *Meditations* must know not only how its argument proceeds step by step but also the broader context in which the work was undertaken. This context includes René Descartes' other, more scientific, aims and writings. No doubt it also includes the fact of a rising new economic and social system. But there is still more to the context in which the *Meditations* must be seen. It is in that regard that A. G. A. Balz's book *Descartes and the Modern Mind* should be read.

The standard way of organizing the outlines of the history of Western civilization is in terms of the Ancient World, The Medieval World, and the Modern Period. (There is presently an argument as to whether we have moved into a Post-Modern phase.) On the whole, writers will say that the first of the modern centuries was the seventeenth century. Balz accepts that general scheme and adds to it his own theses: namely, that the broadest features of the modern mind were first exemplified by Descartes, and that our ways of thinking owe more to Descartes than to anyone else. Descartes, that is, was the first modern man and did more than any other to produce our general intellectual outlook.

It is easy for historians to get carried away by their efforts to mark out the new elements in Descartes (or anyone else, for that matter) and forget the carry-over from the past. Balz does not make that mistake. While he does insist on the role of Descartes in ushering in a new style of life and mind, he is fully aware that, and is concerned to show how, Descartes' ways of thinking still bore strong signs of the medieval period. Balz argues that this backward-looking element is especially strong in Descartes' view of the nature of faith and in his account of the relation of faith and reason. Descartes, although on a voyage of reason, was not able, as were many philosophers who came after him and who drew upon his work, simply to throw off faith; he still had to find some way of accommodating both.

There is one other reason for reading Balz in connection with the *Meditations*. The form of the book will not be strange to one who has read through the type of books usually written in English about Descartes (for examples, Jonathan Rée and Anthony Kenny). All of the writers, Balz included, work their way through the *Meditations*, meditation-by-meditation, step-by-step; but otherwise Balz's style and outlook are greatly different from what one will find in those other works. The reason is that although Balz writes in English, he is writing from the French perspective on Descartes. (See how few English books are cited in Balz's bibliography.) And the French manner of writing and thinking about Descartes is considerably different from that in the English-speaking tradition. After all, Descartes is a culture hero to the French. Anyone who wants to understand the *Meditations* must see how it looks through the eyes of a quite different intellectual tradition from the one in which we are immersed.—*M.R.*

ADDITIONAL RECOMMENDED READING

Buchdahl, Gerd. *Metaphysics and the Philosophy of Science.* Oxford: Basil Blackwell, 1969. See Chapter III for a discussion of the relations of Descartes' method, metaphysics, and science.

Ring, Merrill. "Descartes' Intentions," in *Canadian Journal of Philosophy.* III, no. 1 (September, 1973), pp. 27-49.

Ryle, Gilbert. *The Concept of Mind.* London: Hutchinson's University Library, 1949. The classic statement of opposition to Descartes' views on mind and body.

Wilson, Margaret D. *Descartes.* London: Routledge & Kegan Paul, 1978. A recent critical scrutiny of the arguments in the *Meditations*.

LEVIATHAN

Author: Thomas Hobbes (1588-1679)
Type of work: Political philosophy
First published: 1651

PRINCIPAL IDEAS ADVANCED

A man is a group of material particles in motion.

The state—the great Leviathan—is an artificial man in which sovereignty is the soul, officers the joints, rewards and punishments the nerves, wealth its strength, safety its business, counselors its memory, equity and law its reason and will, peace its health, sedition its sickness, and civil war its death.

Reasoning is the manipulation of names; truth is the correct ordering of names.

Desire is motion toward an object, and aversion is motion away; the good and bad are understood by reference to desire and aversion.

In a state of nature there is a war of every man against every man; to secure peace men make contracts establishing a sovereign power who is not subject to civil law since by his will he creates law.

Of the three forms of sovereignty, monarchy, aristocracy, and democracy, monarchy is the most effective in securing peace.

The *Leviathan*, (*Leviathan, or the Matter, Form, and Power of a Commonwealth, Ecclesiastical and Civil*) is primarily a treatise on the philosophy of politics. It also contains important discussions, some brief, some extended, on metaphysics, epistemology, psychology, language, ethics, and religion. Hobbes develops his views from a metaphysics of materialism and a mechanical analogy in which everything is a particle or set of particles moving in accordance with laws. Though he was at one time secretary to Francis Bacon, English philosopher and essayist, his inspiration came from Galileo Galilei, Italian mathematician and physicist. Hobbes was unusual in being an early empiricist who recognized the importance of mathematics.

In the *Leviathan* the realism of Niccolò Machiavelli, Florentine man of affairs and political writer, the emphasis on sovereignty of Jean Bodin, French legalist and politician, and the attempt of Hugo Grotius, Dutch jurist, to modernize the conception of natural law by relating it to mathematics and the new science are combined and developed with great originality, clarity, and flair for pungent statement to constitute one of the masterpieces of political philosophy.

Hobbes divides all knowledge into two classes, Natural Philosophy and Civil Philosophy. The former is the basis for the latter and consists in turn of two parts, First Philosophy, comprising laws of particles in general such as inertia, causation, and identity; and Physics, which deals with the qualities of particles. These particles, singly or in combination, may be permanent or transient, celestial or terrestrial, with or without sense, with or without speech. A man is a group of particles that is permanent, terrestrial, sensible, and loquacious. Physics contains not only optics and music, which are the sciences of vision and hearing in general, but also ethics, which is the science of the passions of men, poetry, rhetoric, logic, and equity. The four last are respectively the study of man's use of speech in elevated expression, in persuading, reasoning, and contracting. Civil Philosophy deals with the rights and duties of the sovereign or of subjects.

Hobbes makes extensive use of the mechanical model in constructing his system. Life is motion. Therefore, machines have artificial life. The heart is a spring, the nerves are strings, the joints are wheels giving motion to the whole body. The commonwealth is an artificial man in which sovereignty is the soul, officers are the joints, rewards and punishments are the nerves, wealth is its strength, and safety is its business; counselors are its memory, equity and law are reason and will, peace is its health, sedition is its sickness, and civil war is its death. The covenants by which it comes into being are the counterpart of the fiat of creation.

It is apparent that the model is highly oversimplified. This is, in fact, the basis for much of the force it carries. Hobbes does not hesitate to ignore the model if ill-suited to his purpose, as it is in many cases where he has to deal with the details of psychology, religion, and social and political relations.

The simplest motion in human bodies is sensation, caused by the impact of some particle upon a sense organ. When sensations are slowed by the interference of others they become imagination or memory. Imagination in sleep is dreaming. Imagination raised by words is understanding and is common to man and beast.

Ideas ("phantasms" for Hobbes) proceed in accordance with laws of association or of self-interest, as in calculating the means to a desired end. Anything we imagine or think is finite. Any apparent conception of something infinite is only an awareness of an inability to imagine a bound. The name of God, for example, is used that we may honor him, not that we may conceive of him.

Hobbes considered speech the most noble of all inventions. It distinguishes man from beast. It consists in the motion of names and their connections. It is a necessary condition of society, contract, commonwealth, and peace. It is essential to acquiring art, to counseling and instructing, and to expressing purpose. It is correspondingly abused in ambiguity, metaphor, and deception.

When a man manipulates names in accordance with the laws of truth, definition, and thought he is reasoning. Truth is the correct ordering of names; for example, connecting by affirmation two names that signify the same thing. Error in general statements is self-contradiction. Definition is stating what names signify. Inconsistent names, such as "incorporeal substance," signify nothing and are mere sounds. The laws of thought are the laws of mathematics, exemplified best in geometry, generalized to apply to all names. Reasoning is carried on properly when we begin with definition and move from one consequence to the next. Reasoning is therefore a kind of calculating with names. According to Hobbes everything named is particular but a general name can be imposed on a number of things that are similar. He anticipated fundamental distinctions of Hume, Scotch philosopher and skeptic, and later empiricists in maintaining that conclusions reached by reasoning are always conditional.

Hobbes extended the mechanical model in his discussion of the passions by holding that endeavor begins in the motions of imagination. Desire, which is the same as love, is motion toward an object which is therefore called "good." Aversion, which is the same as hate, is motion away from an object which is therefore called "bad." Other passions are definable in terms of these two. Fear is aversion with the belief that the object will hurt; courage is aversion with the hope of avoiding hurt. Anger is sudden courage. Religion, a particularly important passion, is publicly allowed fear of invisible powers. When the fear is not publicly allowed, it is superstition. The whole sum of desires and aversions and their modifications carried on until the thing in question is either done or considered impossible is deliberation. In deliberation, the last appetite or aversion immediately preceding action is will. In searching for truth the last opinion is judgment.

Since desires are endless, happiness is not a static condition but a process of satisfying desires. All motivation is egoistic. Man's basic desire is for power which, like all other desires, ends only in death.

Hobbes completes the foundations for the development of his political theory with an analysis of religion. It is invented by men because of their belief in spirits, their ignorance of causes, and their devotion to what they fear. This explains why the first legislators among the gentiles always claimed that their precepts came from God or some other spirit, and how priests have been able to use religion for selfish purposes. Religion dissolves when its founders or leaders are thought to lack wisdom, sincerity, or love.

Hobbes develops his political theory proper in terms of the time-honored concepts of equality, the state of nature, natural law, natural rights, contract, sovereignty, and justice. In his hands, however, they receive treatment that is very different from his predecessors, the Greeks, St. Thomas Aquinas, Jean Bodin, and Hugo Grotius, as well as from his successors, John Locke, English philosopher, and his followers in the liberal tradition. Machiavelli's views on egoism and the need for absolute power in the sovereign anticipated Hobbes, but were not worked out in detail as a general political philosophy.

In their natural state, according to Hobbes, men are approximately equal in strength, mental capacity, and experience, and everyone has an equal right to everything. If they were without government the conflict arising from their desires, their distrust, and ambition would lead to a state of war of every man against every man. In it there would be no property, no justice or injustice, and life would be "solitary, poor, nasty, brutish and short." Fortunately, both passion—in the form of fear of death, desire for a long and reasonably pleasant life, and hope of achieving it—and reason—in the form of knowledge of the articles of peace in the form of the laws of nature—combine to provide a basis for the establishment of civil society and escape from universal strife.

The first law of nature is to seek the peace and follow it. The second, a necessary means to the first, is *"that a man be willing, when others are so too, as farre-forth as for Peace and defence of himself he shall think it necessary, to lay down this* [natural] *right to all things; and be contented with so much liberty against other men as he would allow other men against himselfe."* This is to be done by making contracts with others. A necessary condition for the operation of the second law of nature is that men perform their contracts, which is the third law of nature. For contracts to be valid it is necessary, in turn, that a sovereign power be established who will make it more painful to commit injustice, which is the breaking of a contract, than to live justly, which is the keeping of contracts. Contracts without the sword, Hobbes reminds us, are only words which guarantee no security. The first three laws of nature, then, combined with the nature of man as a complex set of particles moving in accordance with various sets of laws—not only strictly mechanical laws, but also what might be called egoistic and hedonistic laws—are the source of society, sovereignty, and justice.

Further laws of nature, subordinate to the first three, or special cases, though not specified as such by Hobbes, require the practice of fidelity, gratitude, courtesy, forbearance, fairness, justice, equity, the recognition of natural equality, and the avoidance of contumely, pride, and arrogance. The whole doctrine of natural law, called by Hobbes a "deduction," can be summarized in the general law: do not unto another what you would not want him to do to you. Hobbes considers these laws of nature "eternal and immutable," because breaking them can never preserve the peace. The science of laws is true moral philosophy. He concludes this discussion of natural law with a remark whose significance has usually been ignored, but which must be appreciated if Parts III and IV of the *Leviathan* are to be understood. These "laws," so far, are not properly named; they are only theorems, binding to be sure, *in foro interno*, that is, to a desire they should be effective; but not *in foro externo*, that is, to putting them into practice. If, however, it can be shown that they are delivered in the word of God, who by right commands in all things, then they are properly called laws and are in fact binding.

In working out the details of the second and third laws of nature Hobbes maintains that to achieve peace, contentment, and security it is necessary that men agree with one another to confer their power upon a man or group of men of whose acts each man, even a member of a dissenting minority, will regard himself the original author. "This is the Generation of that great LEVIATHAN or rather (to speak more reverently) of that *Mortal God,* to which we owe under the *Immortal God* our peace and Defence." We may consequently define a commonwealth as "*One Person, of whose Acts a great multitude, by mutuall Covenants one with another, have made themselves every one the Author, to the end he may use the strength and means of them all, as he shall think expedient, for their Peace and Common Defence.*" This person is sovereign. All others are subjects.

The covenant generating the sovereign is not between the sovereign and the subjects, but only between subjects that they will obey whatever ruling power the majority may establish. The covenant may be explicit, actually written, or it may be implicit, for example, by remaining in a conquered country. The covenant is an agreement to refrain from interfering with the sovereign's exercise of his right to everything. The concept of consent is not present, at least not in the sense it carried later with Locke. Making the covenant is the one political act of subjects. Their proper role is to obey as long as the sovereign is able to protect them, unless he should order them to kill, wound, or maim themselves or to answer questions about a crime they may have committed. Even these are not restrictions of the sovereignty of the ruler, but only liberties that subjects retain under the laws of nature. Politically and legally, in Hobbes's system, there is and can be no legal limitation on sovereignty. There is no right of rebellion, for example, since the sovereign is not bound by any contract, not having made one. Subjects have only the legal rights granted them by the sovereign. The sovereign is the only legislator; he is not subject to civil law and his will—not long usage—gives authority to law.

More specifically, the sovereign must have the power to censor all expression of opinion, to allocate private property, to determine what is good or evil, lawful or unlawful, to judge all cases, to make war or peace, to choose the officers of the commonwealth, to administer rewards and punishment, to decide all moral or religious questions, and to prescribe how God is to be worshiped.

There are, says Hobbes, only three forms which sovereignty may take, monarchy, aristocracy, and democracy. Other apparent forms merely reflect attitudes. For example, if someone dislikes monarchy, then he calls it tyranny. Although his arguments would support any absolutism, Hobbes shows a strong preference for monarchy in claiming that it is the best means of effecting peace. The interests of the monarch and his subjects are the same. What is good for the monarch is good for the people. He is rich, glorious, or secure if they are, and not if they are not. He will have fewer favorites than an assembly. He can receive better advice in private than any assembly. There will be no argument and disagreement in making decisions and they will stand more firm. Divisive factionalism and the consequent danger of civil war will not arise. Hobbes admits that monarchy has some problems about succession but says they can be met by following the will of the sovereign, custom, or lineage.

Hobbes maintains that a commonwealth established by acquisition in acts of force or violence differs from one established by institution, peaceably and with something approaching explicit covenant, only in having its sovereignty based uoon fear of the sovereign rather than upon mutual fear of the subjects.

No matter how established or what its form, however, there are certain causes of dissolution which Hobbes warns must be avoided: insufficient power in the sovereign to maintain peace, permitting subjects to judge what is good or evil, considering violation of individual conscience a sin, considering supernatural inspiration superior to reason, considering the sovereign subject to civil law, permitting subjects absolute property rights, dividing sovereign power, regarding tyrannicide as lawful, permitting the reading of democratic books, believing there are two kingdoms, spiritual and civil.

The all-important task of showing that there are not two different kingdoms and at the same time showing that the theorems of the first two Parts of the *Leviathan* are in fact laws and as such binding obligations, are Hobbes's main points in discussing the nature of a Christian commonwealth. The essential mark of a Christian is obedience to God's law. God's authority as lawgiver derives from his power. His laws, which are the natural laws, are promulgated by natural reason, revelation, and prophecy. In the first two Parts of the *Leviathan* knowledge of natural laws and their implications have been found out by reason. Laws are, therefore, only conditional theorems. To be shown to be unconditional laws they must be shown to be the will of God. In fact, Hobbes argues, using extensive quotation and acute, though one-sided, analysis of terms in Scripture and in common speech, all theorems of reasoning about the conduct of men seeking happiness in peace are to be found in Scripture. He concludes that there is no difference between natural law known by reason and revealed or prophetic law. What is law, therefore, depends upon what is Scripture.

Scripture, Hobbes argues, again with extensive quotation, analysis, and interpretation, is what is accepted as Scripture in a commonwealth and is nothing apart from its interpretation. If it is interpreted by conscience, we have competition and a return to the state of nature with its war made fiercer by religious conviction and self-righteousness. All the same arguments for commonwealth apply in particular, therefore, more strongly to the generation of a Christian commonwealth. This is a civil society of Christian subjects under a Christian sovereign. There is no question of opposition between church and state because there is no distinction between them. There are not two laws, ecclesiastical and civil—only civil. There is no universal church since there is no power on earth to which all commonwealths are subject. Consequently, obedience to civil law is necessary for man's admission into heaven. Even if a sovereign is not Christian, it is still an obligation and law for a Christian to obey him, since those who do not obey break the laws of God.

When these truths are obfuscated by misinterpretation of Scripture, demonology, or vain philosophy then, says Hobbes, a kingdom of darkness arises. He applies, in some detail, the test of asking, "Who benefits?" to a number of doctrines in each category and concludes that the Presbyterian and Roman clergy, particularly the Popes, are the authors of this darkness, for they gain temporal power from its existence. Hobbes adds that the errors from which the darkness arises are to be avoided, in general, by a careful reading of the *Leviathan*. Some of the darkness arising from vain philosophy, for example, can be remedied by more careful attention to Hobbes's doctrines of language. These will show that the function of the copula can be replaced by the juxtaposition and ordering of words, thus removing the darkness that arises from the reification of "esse" in its counterparts "entity" and "essence." These words, says Hobbes, are not names of anything, only signs by which we make known what we consider to be consequences of a name. Infinitives and participles similarly are not names of anything. When men understand these and other facts about language they can no longer be deluded by mistaken interpretations of Scripture, demonology, or vain philosophy. In this instance they will no longer be deluded by the doctrine of separated essence and consequently will not be frightened into disobeying their sovereign.

There are flaws in Hobbes's philosophy. He is often crude in his vigor, achieving a logical solution of a problem by omitting recalcitrant details. His errors, however, are usually due to oversimplification, not to being muddleheaded, superstitious, or unclear. No matter how wrong, he is never unintelligible. Moreover, he could not in his own day, and cannot now, be ignored. Puritans and Cavaliers could both condemn him but both Cromwell and Charles II could draw on his doctrines. Abraham Lincoln appealed to his doctrines of covenant and unity of the sovereign power to justify the use of force in dealing with secession.

His philosophy, in its outline, development, method, and logic, very strongly affected the later developments of political and ethical thought. It is doubtful that anyone has stated so strongly the case for political authority or more strongly supported the thesis that unity, not consent, is the basis of government, and conformity to the sovereign will is its strength. His influence is clearly apparent in the doctrines of sovereignty and civil law formulated by John Austin, English writer on jurisprudence. His methods of argument about the nature of law prepared the way for Jeremy Bentham, English ethical and social philosopher, and the movement for scientific legislation based on pleasure, pain, and self-interest. In moral philosophy it is not too much to say that the subsequent history of ethics would not have been the same without Hobbes. Reactions by Richard Cumberland, British moralist and quasirationalist, and the Cambridge Platonists on the one hand, and by Lord Shaftesbury, English essayist, and Francis Hutcheson, British moralist and empiricist, on the other, developed into the eighteenth century opposition between reason and sentiment which is reflected in many of the problems occupying moral philosophers in the twentieth century.—*B.P.*

PERTINENT LITERATURE

Oakeshott, Michael. "Introduction to *Leviathan*," in *Hobbes on Civil Association*. Berkeley: University of California Press, 1975.

Published initially in 1946 with his critical edition of the text of *Leviathan*, Michael Oakeshott's "Introduction" challenged the popular picture of Thomas Hobbes as a materialist and atheist and stimulated new interest in the subject. In Oakeshott's view, Hobbes, far from being a dogmatic materialist, was essentially a skeptic who developed his mechanistic system because causal connection seemed to him the only principle by means of which man can arrive at knowledge. Where the causal principle cannot be applied—for example, to the origin of the world—reason is silent, and man is left to faith. In this view, the second half of *Leviathan*, treating of the Christian Commonwealth and the Kingdom of Darkness, is integral to Hobbes's ethical and political thought.

That the body politic falls within the compass of reason follows from the fact that, as a human construction, it can be traced to man's nature as its cause. Oakeshott follows Hobbes's argument in some detail, but focuses particularly on "the predicament of man" which arises out of the unavoidable conflict between human nature, which is solitary, and the human condition, which is social. Language and reason, by expanding man's fears and hopes, cause the predicament; but they also reveal the nature of the conflict and suggest the means by which it can be resolved.

Having articulated Hobbes's argument, Oakeshott takes up several historical and critical questions, two of which have general interest. In a section entitled "Individualism and Absolutism," Oakeshott locates Hobbes firmly in the nominalist camp, noting that unlike nineteenth century individualists, whose libertarianism was based on a belief in the unique value of each human being, Hobbes held simply to the assumption that only individual substances are real. In society individuals may unite for one purpose or another and may agree for one person to act in place of another; but such arrangements do not alter the individual's point of view, nor is the association they form a new entity. Thus, according to Oakeshott, the authority of Hobbes's sovereign, although absolute as opposed to the individual's claims of right, is not absolute in the vicious sense of denying legitimacy to private views and aspirations.

Of particular interest to philosophers is the section entitled "The Theory of Obligation." Here Oakeshott dismisses as an oversimplification the attempt to interpret Hobbes's theory in terms of self-interest. Holding closely to Hobbes's statement that there is "no obligation on any man, which ariseth not from some act of his own," Oakeshott defines obligation as an external constraint imposed by a man on himself, directly or indirectly. Restraints imposed contrary to a man's will do not oblige him; nor do internal constraints, whether dictated by fear or by reason, oblige him in the sense given by Hobbes to the term. For this reason, Hobbes would not allow that the law of nature imposes obligations apart from sanctions, either political or divine.

Warrender, Howard. *The Political Philosophy of Hobbes: His Theory of Obligation*. Oxford: Clarendon Press, 1957.

As the subtitle indicates, this book is not concerned with Thomas Hobbes's philosophy as a whole but is an attempt to discover "the logical structure of his argument in one of its central aspects, namely, his theory of obligation." The burden of Hobbes's philosophy, says Howard Warrender, is that citizens *ought* to obey the law, adding that if the argument is worth anything, it must be consistent with itself.

There have been those who would question whether obligation is central to Hobbes's philosophy. Impressed with his mechanistic account of the origin of both man's thoughts and his passions, they have overlooked his numerous references to moral concerns or have reduced these to psychological terms as one must do when he reads Jeremy Bentham. Many scholars reject this interpretation, however, holding that alongside his psychological account of man's motivation Hobbes gives a more or less traditional account of his duties and rights. Some have even ventured that Hobbes's moral theory is close to that of Immanuel Kant. In between these two classes are those who, like Michael Oakeshott, allow obligation a limited place in Hobbes's world view, notably when a person binds himself to perform certain acts by a promise or a covenant.

In Warrender's view, Hobbes's entire moral and political system rests on natural law, understood not as something that man invents but as something that he discovers. Without denying the originality of Hobbes's interpretation of this law, he questions whether his understanding of it is as revolutionary as has often been supposed. As Hobbes interprets it, natural law is simply the sum of those conditions under which it is possible for men to form societies. Those individuals who do not have sufficient rational capacity to understand this law are not bound by it, and their social behavior must be determined by external controls. But unless there were, besides these incompetents, a sizable number of people with the capacity for understanding natural law and recognizing the obligation that it imposes, political society could never have come into being, nor could it function.

Hobbes answers the question how far natural law binds man in a prepolitical condition by pointing out that actual obligations vary according to circumstances. To make Hobbes's teaching clear, Warrender distinguishes between the grounds, the conditions, and the instruments of obligation. As he interprets Hobbes, questions of security are conditions of obligation, and the covenant functions instrumentally to determine these conditions. Neither of these is the ground of obligation, which is the law of nature itself, known to reasonable beings.

Hobbes invites confusion, Warrender admits, when he says that natural law discoverable by each individual through reason remains a mere theorem until it becomes the command of the sovereign. If this statement be taken as strictly true, says Warrender, it puts Hobbes in the position of having to say that the law of nature which dictates keeping of covenants does not have the force of law until the sovereign, whose authority rests on the covenant, commands it. The argument is circular, and Hobbes's entire theory of sovereignty and of the obligation of subjects is left without foundation in reason. But other passages in Hobbes, notably those in which he holds that natural law is recognizably instituted by God for the government of creatures who are both rational and passionate, make it possible for Warrender to represent Hobbes's whole system as resting on a prior law of nature.

In working out his interpretation, Warrender finds it helpful to keep distinct what the individual is obliged to do and what he cannot be obliged to do. This is, roughly, the distinction between duties and rights, but Warrender gives it a new turn by suggesting that what one is obliged to do is prescribed by law, whereas what one cannot be obliged to do is determined by analysis of the concept of obligaton. It is often pointed out that some rights are such that one person's right follows from other person's duties. Rights of this kind follow directly from some law. But other rights are merely exemptions from obligation. These rights, which Hobbes calls liberties, are implicit in the validating conditions under which obligations are known to hold, among which is the condition that the individual must have a sufficient motive to perform the action prescribed by the obligation—a condition which precludes a person's ever being obliged to act contrary to what he regards as his best interest, whether that be understood in a temporal sense as the preservation of one's life or in an eternal sense as the salvation of one's soul.

Gauthier, David P. *The Logic of Leviathan: The Moral and Political Theory of Thomas Hobbes*. Oxford: Clarendon Press, 1969.

Acknowledging that it was Howard Warrender's book which aroused his interest in Thomas Hobbes, David P. Gauthier carries the analysis of Hobbes's argument to a new level of precision. Warrender is correct, according to this author, in maintaining that Hobbes's moral theory follows its own necessity, which is different from the causal necessity that governs his psychology. Nevertheless, Gauthier regards as hopelessly wrong-headed the attempt to show that Hobbes kept the two separate in working out his theory of the state.

What is required, and what Gauthier undertakes in this rewarding study, is an analysis which will show how far Hobbes's moral theory can be made to stand on its own foundation, and at what points it depends on the theory of human nature which he has taken such care to elaborate. His procedure is to work out two sets of definitions for ethical terms, one which he calls *formal*, the other *material*. For example, the formal definition of good, in Hobbes, is "an object of desire," whereas the material definition is "an object enhancing vital motion." After an initial chapter on Hobbes's doctrine of Man, the book is given over to the analysis first of his moral then of his political concepts, with a final chapter given to God and Divine Law. Obligation and authorization are taken as the basic concepts respectively of Hobbes's moral and political theories.

The formal definition of obligation, constructed by Gauthier from several passages in the *Leviathan*, turns on the negation involved in laying down one's right: "A has an obligation not to do X" means "A has laid down his right to do X." What strikes Gauthier as noteworthy is that by means of this definition Hobbes is able to explain how obligations emerge immediately in a situation where no prior obligation existed. "Covenants oblige necessarily," says Gauthier. Obligation is a human creation, and there is no need to look for some prior law of nature or divine command requiring that agreements be kept.

Material definitions, in Gauthier's account, flesh out the formal definitions by making clear what, in view of his nature and condition, man ought to do. Thus, a law of nature defined formally as "a precept laying down the requirements of reason" is defined materially as "a precept laying down what is required for preservation." Similarly, the material definition of obligation includes a prudential element, intimating that not all right can be given up and dictating that covenants must be combined with security.

With these definitions of obligation in hand, Gauthier is able to illuminate the problem which has preoccupied Hobbesian studies in recent times; namely, whether morality for Hobbes reduces to prudence. No one doubts that considerations of interest are the motives which lead Hobbesian man to assume obligations, although it would be wrong to infer from this that prudence enters the definition of "ought" even for Hobbes. What needs to be cleared up, however, is whether Hobbes thinks that there are other motives besides self-interest for fulfilling obligations which one has assumed. As Hobbes does not show that there are other motives, Gauthier concludes that his moral system is one of universal prudence.

In treating Hobbes's political philosophy, Gauthier proceeds in the same manner, giving both formal and material definitions for such terms as actor, author, sovereign, and subject. What is of interest here is that the central notion, authorization, admits only of a formal definition, "that procedure by which one man gives the use of his right to another man," and that there is nothing in this definition which prevents authorization from being limited. It is only when the means of the sovereign to uphold covenants become a consideration that authorization is understood as a kind of blank check.— *J.F.*

ADDITIONAL RECOMMENDED READING

Brown, Keith C., ed. *Hobbes Studies*. Cambridge, Massachusetts: Harvard University Press, 1965. Papers by contemporary scholars with various points of view.

Hood, F. C. *The Divine Politics of Thomas Hobbes*. Oxford: Clarendon Press, 1964. Interprets the *Leviathan* as a specifically Christian philosophy of the state.

Peters, Richard. *Hobbes*. Baltimore: Penguin Books, 1956. A readable introduction to the man and his work.

Strauss, Leo. *The Political Philosophy of Hobbes*. Translated by Elsa M. Sinclair. Chicago: University of Chicago Press, 1952. Traces the development of Hobbes's thought.

Watkins, J. W. N. *Hobbes's System of Ideas*. London: Hutchinson University Library, 1965. A study of the political significance of Hobbes's philosophical ideas.

DE CORPORE

Author: Thomas Hobbes (1588-1679)
Type of work: Philosophy of philosophy, metaphysics
First published: 1655 (Part I of *Elementa philosophiae*)

PRINCIPAL IDEAS ADVANCED
The subject matter of philosophy is bodies in motion.
Philosophy is the knowledge of effects acquired by ratiocination from the knowledge of causes, and of causes from the knowledge of effects.
Ratiocination is a kind of computation, the adding and subtracting of notions.
Our knowledge is derived from our definitions and theorems or from our sense experience.
Bodies have no dependence upon thought.

Philosophy, to Hobbes, is simply science. "Philosophy" is defined as *"such knowledge of effects or appearances, as we acquire by true ratiocination from the knowledge we have first of their causes or generation: And again, of such causes or generations as may be from knowing first their effects."* Since God has no cause, and what is known by revelation is not acquired by ratiocination, theology is excluded from philosophy by definition. All that is left to be the subject matter of philosophy is "every body of which we can conceive any generation, and which we may, by any consideration thereof, compare with other bodies, or which is capable of composition and resolution; that is to say, every body of whose generation or properties we can have any knowledge." There are two kinds of bodies, "one whereof being the work of nature, is called a *natural body*, the other is called a *commonwealth*, and is made by the wills and agreement of men." The study of the former is natural philosophy, that of the latter civil philosophy. But ethics, "which treats of men's dispositions and manners," is prerequisite to civil philosophy. There are in consequence three main divisions of philosophy. The *Elements of Philosophy*, which Hobbes projected as the most comprehensive and systematic of his works, was in three volumes corresponding to this division: Part I, *On Body*; Part II, *On Man*; and Part III, *On the Citizen*. Part III was written first, and Part II last.

"The end of knowledge is power," Hobbes declares, following Bacon. The usefulness of natural philosophy lies ultimately in its technological applications, "but the utility of moral and civil philosophy is to be estimated, not so much by the commodities we have by knowing these sciences, as by the calamities we receive from not knowing them." The chief of these is war, of which civil war, the worst kind, comes from the "not knowing of civil duties."

Because Hobbes conceived of *De corpore* not as a self-contained work but as the first division of a comprehensive treatise, he begins with a discussion of philosophy in general.

According to Hobbes, philosophy is ratiocination about causes and effects, and by *ratiocination* Hobbes meant *computation*; that is, adding and subtracting of notions. Magnitudes, bodies, motions, times, proportions, and degrees of quality are computables in an obvious sense, since they can be represented numerically. Hobbes extends the idea of computation to conceptions, speech, and names: for example, "man" is the sum of "body, animated, rational. . . ." It must be emphasized that it is only the *notion* that is thus a sum; a particular man is also a sum, but of arms, legs, and so forth. In modern parlance, "body," "animated," and "rational" are determinables (Hobbes calls them *universals*), while "this body," "this animated thing," (which Hobbes calls *particulars*) are determinates. Only determinates exist; the universe consists of particular bodies.

Hobbes proceeds to develop these conceptions into what is in effect a short textbook of semantics and formal logic. These chapters contain little that is distinctively Hobbesian. He concludes with an important section on scientific method. For Hobbes, method *"is the shortest way of finding out effects by their known causes, or of causes by their known effects."* There are two kinds of methods, corresponding to the fundamental operations of addition and subtraction. One is compositive, or synthetical. By this method one is able to proceed from first principles (which are definitions) to a knowledge of some complex thing. Geometry is entirely synthetical, and so is syllogistic reasoning. The other method is resolutive, or analytical. Here we attain understanding of a thing by resolving the notion into its constituent universals the causes of which are plain, embodied in first principles.

Hobbes's descriptions of these two methods are obscure, and his examples do not help much. But his conceptions of scientific method can be paraphrased in this way: science is a body of organized knowledge, for which geometry provides both the model and the starting point. In geometry we begin with axioms, which according to Hobbes are definitions. We then deduce the consequences of these definitions; that is, we "add" them, in Hobbes's broad sense of addition. Now geometry is, for Hobbes, the most abstract science of *motion*; he always thinks of a line, for instance, as the path of a moving point, not as a given (static) extension. Hence, geometry is closely related to the science of mechanics, though the latter science requires some additional principles—definitions—of force, of quantity of matter, and of other concepts not part of traditional geometry. As there is nothing in the world but matter in motion, if we know the laws of motion, science is then *complete* as far as its theoretical principles are concerned. The sciences of man and his behavior ("ethics") and society ("politics") are in theory only further applications of mechanics to particular groups of bodies. Ideally, science from geometry to politics, if completed, would be *presented* in a deductive system, in which the progress from definitions to conclusions would be "synthetical."

Hobbes was well aware, though, that the discoveries which advance science are not (for the most part) made in this way. The crucial points come in the adoption of "definitions." Since everything is to be deducible from the definitions, and science must give causal explanations, *the definitions must include causes*. So the central question of scientific method becomes one of securing adequate definitions. *These* definitions cannot, of course, be merely arbitrary; we are not at liberty to define force, or quantity of matter, in any way we like. Wherever the concept we are dealing with is complex, we must *analyze* it *correctly*. The way to tell whether a proposed analysis is correct is to deduce (by means of the "synthetical method") the consequences of our tentative definition. These deductions yield certain *theorems* which ought to be descriptions of what happens in certain circumstances. By *observation* we find out whether what, according to our definitions, ought to happen does happen. If so, well and good; if not, we must try again.

Thus Hobbes's "definitions" turn out to be what are now called *hypotheses*, and this method, which Hobbes calls the "combined synthetical and analytical," is in fact the hypothetico-deductive method of science. Hobbes was the first philosopher to grasp the essentials of this very important conception.

So much for ideally complete science. It is not much help in practical affairs. We cannot in practice deduce the principles of psychology and sociology from the laws of motion. Nor does Hobbes recommend that we wait until the science of motion is completed before we begin the social sciences. The impasse is to be broken by an application of the "analytical method" to produce principles (axioms) of human behavior. (Further treatment of these subjects is to be found in Hobbes's political writings.)

Finding causes is the crux of all science. A cause is "the sum or aggregate of all such accidents [characteristics], both in the agents and the patient, as concur to the producing of the effect propounded; all which existing together, it cannot be understood but that the effect existeth with them; or that it can possibly exist if any one of them be absent." In other words, the cause of anything is the necessary and sufficient condition of its production. According to Hobbes, "in the searching out of causes, there is need partly of the analytical, and partly of the synthetical method; of the analytical, to conceive how circumstances conduce severally to the production of effects; and of the synthetical, for the adding together and compounding of what they can effect singly by themselves." In the subsequent discussion it becomes clear that Hobbes grasps the notions later formulated by Mill as the canons of agreement and difference; but his philosophy is superior to Mill's (as well as to Bacon's) in that in emphasizing the "need of the analytical method" he is in effect recognizing the indispensability, for scientific *discovery*, of fruitful "working hypotheses."

Hobbes regarded certain concepts in philosophy as basic, simple, and unanalyzable. We cannot therefore give causal definitions of them. However, clarity about them is essential and is to be achieved by stating definitions which *explicate* them for "by speech as short as may be, we raise in the mind of the hearer perfect and clear ideas or conceptions of the things named." Such are place, time, body, accident, motion, power.

Hobbes asks the reader to suppose all things annihilated, save one philosopher. What would be left for him to "ratiocinate" about? His memories, Hobbes tells us. He could think about those just as if nothing had happened. Indeed, this is what is actually done here and now: "For when we calculate the magnitude and motions of heaven or earth, we do not ascend into heaven that we may divide it into parts, or measure the motions thereof, but we do it sitting still in our closets or in the dark." The memory of just one thing as having existed outside the mind would yield the philosopher the conception of space; hence "space" is defined as "*the phantasm of a thing existing without the mind simply.*" Likewise *time* is "*the phantasm of before and after in motion.*" (What Hobbes had in mind in calling space and time "phantasms" is not entirely clear, except that he wanted to deny that they were either bodies or accidents of bodies. Perhaps he meant that our concept of space is an idea concerning "where there could be a body." Hobbes held that in fact there is no vacuum, though he denied that vacuum is inconceivable.) Hobbes's definition of spatial and temporal infinity is very good; he writes that "*infinite in power* is that space or time, in which a greater number of the said paces or hours may be assigned, than any number that can be given." He argues, correctly, that to say that space is infinite does not commit one to the view that there must exist two places separated by an infinite distance; it entails only the idea that however great a distance separates two places, there are other places more distant still. (Kant never grasped this point.)

Suppose now that one additional thing were created. Under these circumstances, there would be one thing *independent of the philosopher's mind.* Hence "*a body is that which, having no dependence upon our thought, is coincident or coextended with some part of space.*" It is important to take this definition strictly and not read into it more than Hobbes intended. If the body in question were (say) a tomato, all that would be "out there" would be an independent something occupying a certain region of space. (How a "phantasm" can be occupied by something independent of the mind is not explained.) Such characteristics as the redness, juiciness, and taste of the tomato are not parts or constituents of the body but *accidents*, an accident being "that faculty of any body, by which it works in us a conception of itself," or "the manner of our conception of body." Redness is not in blood as blood is in a bloody cloth.

"Bodies are things, and not generated; accidents are generated, and not things." Any accident of a body can be destroyed, without the body's being destroyed. The essence or form is only the accident in virtue of which a name is given to a certain kind of body.

All mutation is motion. (Though Hobbes may be right about this, his proof of the proposition is fallacious.) Since every motion has a cause which determines it to be the motion it is, everything is determined, and "contingency" is only a subjective notion, signifying our ignorance. Everything that is possible will, at sometime or other, come to pass. (Hobbes errs here in company with St. Thomas Aquinas.) All causation is efficient causation. So-called "formal causes" or essences are only causes of our knowledge, while "final causes," which occur only in beings endowed with sense and will, are likewise really efficient causes.

Hobbes has an astute section on the "principle of individuation," which is the criterion of the identity of anything. He shows that neither matter, nor form, nor aggregate of accidents will do as a *general* criterion of identity. The solution is pragmatic: "We must consider by what name anything is called, when we inquire concerning the *identity* of it. . . . That man will be always the same, whose actions and thoughts proceed all from the same beginning of motion, namely, that which was in his generation; and that will be the same river which flows from one and the same fountain, whether the same water or other water, or something else than water, flow from thence." (Hume's philosophy would have been very different if he had taken this section to heart.)

In Part III, concerning the proportions of motions, Hobbes endeavors to work out, in some detail, the principles of the science of mechanics, as he had learned it from Galileo. The discussion is marred by the notorious "squaring of the circle," which led to the long and unseemly controversy with John Wallis, Professor of Mathematics at Oxford. Mainly on this account, scholars have paid little attention to this part of Hobbes's work. This is unfortunate, for the discussion contains statements (more or less) of all three of Newton's laws of motion, as well as anticipations of the differential and integral calculus.

In Part IV, "Physics, or the Phenomena of Nature," Hobbes writes, "I now enter upon the other part; which is the finding out by the appearances or effects of nature, which we know by sense, some ways and means by which they may be, I do not say they are, generated." The first chapter of this part, "Of Sense and Animal Motion," is the only one of philosophical interest. In it Hobbes presents his theory of perception.

"Of all the phenomena or appearances which are near us, the most admirable is apparition itself. . . ; namely, that some natural bodies have in themselves the patterns almost of all things, and others of none at all." We are to find out the causes "of those ideas and phantasms which are perpetually generated within us whilst we make use of our senses." Now, since all change is motion of bodies, it follows that "sense, in the sentient, can be nothing else but motion in some of the internal parts of the sentient; and the parts so moved are parts of the organs of sense." When we look at an object, what happens is that motion from its surface is communicated through the medium to the eye. The pressure thereon is communicated through the humors and retina to the optic nerve and the brain. Everywhere in the line of propagation the actions produce reactions, opposite in direction; the last of these reactions in the brain is the phantasm. Since this reaction is an "endeavour" *out*ward, the object *appears* to us to be outside us, not inside (where the physical occurrence that *is* the perception *really* occurs). Hearing is similarly explained, while the three nondistance senses are easily accommodated to this type of theory. (But Hobbes, strangely, considers and rejects explanation of odors by "effluvia.")

Hobbes defines "sense" as "*a phantasm, made by the reaction and endeavour outwards in the organ of sense, caused by an endeavour inwards from the object, remaining for some time more or less.*" By the "remaining for some time" phrase Hobbes attempted to counter the objection that according to his mechanical theory even stones should have sensations, since they react to pressure. They have no memories, and sensation without memory would be in effect no sensation at all! Imagination is "decaying sense." The train of ideas in the mind is not random, but governed by laws of association. (These principles, which are the foundations of associationist psychology, were developed further in *Leviathan* in 1651.) Appetite and aversion are the first endeavors of animal motion. Deliberation is an oscillation between appetite and aversion; the last appetite in deliberation is the "will," which is subject to laws. "And therefore such a liberty as is free from necessity, is not to be found in the will either of men or beasts. But if by liberty we understand the faculty or power, not of willing, but of doing what they will, then certainly that liberty is to be allowed to both."

The book dies out, rather than concludes, in a miscellany of attempts at explaining various interesting natural phenomena. Such was not Hobbes's forte. His strong points were intelligent receptiveness to the new scientific thought of his day and the ability, unhampered by prejudice or sentimentality, to grasp the broad philosophical implications of it. He has received due recognition as the author of the first scientific social philosophy. That he was also, and preeminently, the first thinker to break completely with the Middle Ages in pure philosophy and philosophy of science, has hitherto not been adequately acknowledged.—*W.I.M.*

PERTINENT LITERATURE

Peters, Richard. *Hobbes*. Baltimore: Penguin Books, 1956.

In the course of this excellent book on Thomas Hobbes's life and work, Richard Peters makes numerous references to *De Corpore*, showing how Hobbes's speculations on physical matters relate to other parts of his philosophical system.

In Chapter III, "Nature and Mind," Peters examines *De Corpore* in greater detail. It was Hobbes's last word on the philosophy of nature, he says, but was nevertheless a strange book, abstract and lacking in observational confirmation (by contrast with Galileo's works, for example), and also remarkable for its failure to treat problems that are now regarded as especially philosophical. Hobbes, Peters concludes, was not so much interested in instructing engineers about the scientific facts of motion, heat, or velocity, as he was in being the "metaphysician" of the new scientific movement that was developing at that time. He was determined to apply the newly discovered laws of motion and the methods of science to man, a part of the mechanical system of nature. His predecessors, from Aristotle to Francis Bacon and René Descartes, had imagined that there were "final causes," that is, purposes or goals, toward which human activities—at least those that are voluntary—were directed. According to Hobbes, however, even voluntary human behavior is to be explained strictly as a form of mechanical motion subject to the same laws that govern all other forms of motion.

Hobbes concluded that everything, including sensation and even the visions one sees in dreams and fantasy, is produced by (or perhaps consists of) mechanical movements. As Hobbes put it in his prose biography, it occurred to him by chance that "if bodies and all their parts were to be at rest, or were always to be moved by the same motion, our discrimination of all things would be removed, and [consequently] all sensation with it; and therefore the cause of all things must be sought in the variety of motion." Thus, geometry and the theory of mechanics should be sufficient to account for such psychological phenomena as sensation and imagination, and no doubt for volition and reasoning as well.

Yet Hobbes had a strong streak of "rustic wonder," which was communicated through his homespun style and in the vigor and homeliness of his metaphors and similes. He was entranced by the fact that men could measure the heavens and let their imaginations roam over continents and into the hidden recesses of the future—even beyond the span of their own lives. He was struck by the marvel of imagery, by the amazing fact that although all the knowledge we possess is derived from sense, we are nevertheless able to ponder their origins and to let our imaginations wander so freely.

Hobbes took it for granted throughout *De Corpore* that motion can be caused only by a body that is contiguous and is itself moved. Action at a distance was summarily rejected. He accepted the first principle of inertia: that a body at rest will always remain at rest unless some other body which is itself in motion displaces it. He proved this in a rather interesting way, by asserting that from within itself there can be no reason for the movement of a body at rest. This of course is a *petitio principii*: assuming the very point at issue. He also argues that if a body at rest in empty space initiated its own movements, it would be moved alike in all directions at once, which (he says) is impossible. His arguments for Galileo's other principles of inertia—for example, the principle that a body in motion would continue to move in the same direction at the same velocity unless some other body intervened to change it—were "proved" in much the same way.

By contrast with the Aristotelian theory that things naturally move toward their natural ends or final causes (for example, that acorns naturally grow into oak trees and that caterpillars naturally transform themselves into butterflies out of an internal force that impels them to do so), Hobbes concluded that only things that have sense and a will have a "final" cause, and that even this was no more than an efficient cause—that is, the same sort of cause that produces motion in a billiard ball upon its being struck by another billiard ball. It has been said that the few lines in which Hobbes wrote these seemingly innocuous statements must have struck his Aristotelian contemporaries like a bludgeon. When final causes were given up, a whole world perished. In place of final causes, Hobbes concluded that there are only bodies composed of particles which are moved by other bodies and other particles. The phantasms which inspired artists to the height of their creative powers, the sensations of magnificent sunsets and glorious battle scenes, the images of Greek gods and goddesses and of centaurs and mermaids were all nothing more than motions produced by other motions.

A "conatus" or "endeavor" Hobbes defined as a motion made in an infinitesimally small space and an infinitesimally small time—a point of space and an instant of time. In short, it was an infinitely small motion. Weight was the aggregate of all such endeavors—that is, the combined tiny motions of the countless tiny particles of the object being weighed upon the pan of the scale in which it was being weighed—the tipping of the scale resulting from the combined onslaught of all those individually imperceptible motions upon the particles of which it was composed. This also explained the phenomena of pressure and resistance. Light and sound were motions propagated in media by the particles of the objects that are perceived to be bright or to be producing sound.

This notion of "endeavor" was extended by Hobbes to still other phenomena, including the phantasms with which we began. Particles in motion produce sensations and phantasms, and also animal motions. Motions from the sense organs proceed to the heart through the vessels of the body and there affect the motion of the blood. When a given sense motion helps the vital motion, we experience pleasure; and when it hinders it, we experience pain. Those motions which produce pleasure also produce animal motions which endeavor to maintain that sensation. Such motions are generally called appetites. The reverse—those motions which result from painful sensations—are called aversions. Hence, there is no significant difference between the motion of a man and that of a projectile: both are ultimately attributable to the mechanical movements of the minute particles of which they are composed. Even habits are explained by Hobbes as motions which are made easier by constant repetition, similar to the bending of a bow. Since the distinction between men and inanimate objects is essentially one of degree only, it should not be surprising to find that Hobbes considers the differences between men and animals to be much less radical than many of his predecessors had supposed them to be. Descartes, for example, thought that animals were mere automata, scarcely different at all from machines or mechanical robots, while men were self-actuating beings capable of rationality and will. Hobbes, however, concluded that the chief difference between men and animals consists of the fact that men desire to know the causes of things and to attach names to things. But animals and men alike possess will and appetite, and animals deliberate just as men do about the course of their actions. Their motions toward or away from objects are initiated not only by immediate sense perceptions but also by images or conceptions which arise in their heads.

Again, unlike most of his predecessors, Hobbes did not believe that space was an existing thing, but that it was merely a phantasm, the appearance of externality. It is an abstraction from our experience of bodies. Time too is a phantasm—of before and after in motion.

Peters argues that Hobbes's use of the notion of "endeavor" was a good example of his tendency to tear terms out of their technical contexts in order to use them to bridge gaps in his conceptual scheme. The same was true of his "dubious" transition from physiology to psychology, in which he jumped from one sense of "motion" to another. Similarly, Peters criticized Hobbes for having failed to relate the subjective frameworks of private experience to the complicated constructs of physical science in his accounts of space and time. In general, Peters argues, Hobbes did not successfully bridge the gap between what appears to sense and what is rationally reconstructed.

Peters suggests that Hobbes may not have been able to avoid taking for granted the basic assumptions of the new science of his day—a science which he understood only imperfectly. He takes Hobbes to task for having assumed that the real world is composed only of bodies in motion, that the secondary qualities (such as color, sound, and flavor) were subjective appearances of the really existing primary qualities (size, shape, and motion), and that causation can take place only between objects that are contiguous and in motion relative to one another.

Moreover, Peters questions Hobbes's tendency to extend scientific concepts into spheres where their applicability is "dubious or trivial." He concedes, for example, that there is a sense in which work is moving bodies from one place to another, and love a motion of the heart, lips, and sexual organs; but he asks whether such descriptions are particularly illuminating. They might have been, Peters adds, if they had led to important and novel deductive consequences, but Hobbes never drew any such consequences from them. Instead, Peters charges Hobbes with merely having redescribed in a rather "bizarre terminology" what we already know and of having offered descriptions of things and events which seem absurd because the mechanical concepts in which they are couched are inappropriate to them.

Peter excuses Hobbes for these failings on the ground that he was living at the dawn of a new world view when the specialized distinctions between science and philosophy that are so common today had not yet been drawn. He admires the "robust versatility" that Hobbes brought to his speculations in such a wide variety of fields, ranging from logic to optics, physiology, psychology, ethics, politics, and jurisprudence. He concludes that Hobbes's very failure to see what later generations would call "philosophical problems" is in some ways the most refreshing thing about him.

Child, Arthur. "Making and Knowing in Hobbes, Vico, and Dewey," in *University of California Publications in Philosophy*. XVI, no. 13 (1953), pp. 271-310.

Arthur Child opens his discussion with a passage from Thomas Hobbes's exchange with the Oxford mathematicians in which he states that the distinction between demonstrable and indemonstrable sciences turns on the fact that the former are our own constructions and the latter not. We understand geometry because with our words and definitions we make it. The same is true of civic philosophy. The case is otherwise with physics, "because of natural bodies we know not the construction, but seek it from its effects." The claim which Hobbes summarized in this passage had been worked out in the opening chapters of *De Corpore*.

Child conceives it as his task to discover precisely in what sense Hobbes supposed that geometry and civil philosophy can be demonstrated and why he supposed that natural philosophy cannot. In a different context Giovanni Battista Vico was to argue that we can understand civil society better than we can understand nature because its principles lie within our own minds. More recently, John Dewey has warned that progress in both physics and social science depends on our recognizing that "we know what we intentionally construct."

In Hobbes's scheme, a distinction is made between everyday knowledge gathered through the senses and retained in memory and what he calls philosophy, science, or ratiocination—knowledge consisting of the truths of propositions and the inferences drawn from them. In Hobbes's view there was no science of nature prior to Galileo and no civil philosophy prior to his own *De Cive* (1642). The only science known to former ages was geometry. But all three sciences employ the same methods, using words to generate or construct truths and adding or subtracting truths in order to increase knowledge. As Child points out, Hobbes uses terms (such as "operation," "production," "causation," "generation," and "construction") which assimilate thinking to the causal process, and this not in a metaphorical but in a literal sense inasmuch as reasoning is a bodily motion and so are the names, the images, and the sensations from which it derives. For Hobbes, says Child, the definitions or premises of any demonstration are efficient causes of the conclusion.

The operations of the geometer are the easiest to understand in this light. There is, first, the external motion by which he constructs his lines and circles; in addition, there are interior motions consisting of the propositions and inferences by means of which he demonstrates his theorems. Here the connection between making and knowing is fairly clear: by drawing, the geometer makes the object which he knows; by adding and dividing, subtracting, and multiplying propositions, he makes the truth by which the object is known.

Physics differs from geometry in that its object is not man-made. Its principles, we are told in *De Corpore*, "are not such as we ourselves make and pronounce in general terms, as definitions; but such as being placed in the things themselves by the Author of Nature, are by us observed in them." Having defined ratiocination as knowledge of effects from knowledge of causes and vice versa, Hobbes does not hesitate to classify physics with geometry as a science, even though the observed connections do not necessarily correspond to the "internal and invisible motions" by which the Author of Nature produces effects. Thus, the physicist can never demonstrate that what appear to us as causes *are* true causes, but only that they *may be*. Physics is demonstrable only in a weak sense, the knowledge which it gives being only conditional or hypothetical.

The science of politics or civic philosophy lies closer to geometry than to physics. Hobbes declares that political philosophy is "demonstrable because we make the commonwealth ourselves." But Child finds it misleading when Hobbes passes immediately from the lines and figures of geometry to the constitutions of states; for, as he points out, when we are thinking about states the "we who make" is not the same as the "we who know." Hobbes contended that states are human constructions and that their originative causes are passions and thoughts lying in the people. He further maintained that, since these causes are identical in all, anyone can discover them by looking within. Still it is his opinion that only the rare person whose grasp of scientific method enables him to frame true principles and construct correct theorems can raise that common knowledge to the level of a science.

Hobbes's constructionism is paralleled in Vico's writings. For example, Vico says, ". . . at first men made things by a certain human sense, without noting them; afterwards, and late enough, applied reflection thereto; and, reasoning on the effects, therein contemplated the causes." In our time, Vico's application of this principle to the interpretation of historical texts (hermeneutics) has received new attention. In Dewey's writings—although the parallels are less striking—the steady insistence that man in knowing interacts with his environment leads Child to say that for Dewey, too, "knowing makes or produces or constructs or generates the objects of knowledge."

Child's concern, however, goes beyond finding similarities between Hobbes and his successors. By examining passages from the latter, he uncovers ambiguities contained in the broad claim that, in Vico's words, "the mind cannot but make the truths that it knows." It is understood today, for example, that in some sense the physical scientist makes the truths that he knows. Still, one must be careful not to confuse that kind of making with the existential transformations with which Dewey is concerned when he argues that social science must play a role in creating the society which it studies.—*J.F.*

ADDITIONAL RECOMMENDED READING

Brandt, Frithiof. *Thomas Hobbes' Mechanical Conception of Nature*. Copenhagen: Levin and Munksgaard, 1928. An excellent and very thorough critique of the theories contained in *De Corpore* and in other portions of Hobbes's writings.

Burtt, Edwin Arthur. *The Metaphysical Foundations of Modern Physical Science: A Historical and Critical Essay*. London: Routledge & Kegan Paul, 1932. A classic in its field; includes an excellent chapter dealing with the relations between Hobbes and his contemporaries and the reactions his theories provoked.

Laird, John. *Hobbes*. London: Ernest Benn, 1934. A very good overall treatment of Hobbes's philosophy.

Reik, Miriam M. *The Golden Lands of Thomas Hobbes*. Detroit: Wayne State University Press, 1977. The humanistic setting in which Hobbes worked is particularly well evoked in this well-written volume, and recent as well as contemporary critiques of Hobbes's theories are thoroughly discussed.

SYNTAGMA PHILOSOPHICUM

Author: Pierre Gassendi (1592-1655)
Type of work: Logic, epistemology, philosophy of nature, ethics
First published: 1658

PRINCIPAL IDEAS ADVANCED

Between skepticism and dogmatism there is a third possibility: constructive skepticism, the theory that although certain knowledge of nature is not possible, a useful but limited type of knowledge is within our grasp.

By cautious evaluation of our sense experience we can reach conclusions which can be tested by future experience.

Epicurus was correct in maintaining that the universe is composed of atoms moving in empty space; atoms are solid, with figure, weight, and extension; changes in nature are the result of collisions of the downward coursing atoms.

The primary cause of atomic motion is God; he is the great designer of the universe.

Unlike the animal soul, which is wholly corporeal, the human soul is only partly corporeal or material; the rational part of the soul is immaterial, derived from God, and immortal.

Our ideas are not innate, but come either from the senses or from intellectual activity.

Pierre Gassendi was one of the foremost philosophers and scientists of the early seventeenth century. He was the most important rival and critic of René Descartes, and he had a crucial role in the revival of the ideas of the ancient Greek skeptics and atomists. Gassendi began his intellectual career as a skeptic, a staunch follower of Sextus Empiricus, a Greek writer of the third century, and of the French essayist Michel de Montaigne. Gradually he mitigated his skepticism in the face of the scientific revolution of the time, in which he played a major role, and he adopted more and more of a materialistic explanation of the world based on the ancient theory of Epicurus. Though a prominent Catholic priest of his day, Gassendi developed one of the first completely mechanistic and materialistic theories of modern times.

The *Syntagma philosophicum*, the most complete exposition of his mature views, was published only after his death. The work is enormous, containing sixteen hundred folio pages, printed in double columns. It is divided into three general sections, the first dealing with logic and theory of knowledge, the second with the natural world, and the third with ethics. Because of his skepticism, Gassendi did not regard metaphysics as a serious subject and so he omitted it entirely from his book.

At the outset, Gassendi seeks to establish a way to knowledge that is between the doubts of the skeptics and the complete assurances of the dogmatists. Neither the view that we can know nothing nor the view that we can know everything is tenable. The skeptics admit that we can know how nature appears to us. But they deny that we can know more than this. The dogmatists, on the other hand, claim that we can know the real natures of things which are not apparent to us. This, Gassendi contends, is exaggerating the power of the human mind. However, between skepticism and dogmatism there is a third possibility, which has been called "constructive or mitigated skepticism," an acceptance of the thesis that although in a fundamental sense we cannot gain certain knowledge of the nature of reality, we can nevertheless gain a type of knowledge which we need have no reason to doubt, and which will suffice to enable us to understand the world.

This limited knowledge is obtained first by accepting what is obvious to us, our sense experience, plus certain obvious conclusions from it, such as that things exist. Signs found in sense experience enable us to know about other matters not immediately obvious to the senses. The ancient Greek skeptics had admitted that, on the basis of the constant conjunctions found in experience, we could judge that certain things temporarily not apparent to us were the case, such as when we see smoke, we can judge that there is a fire. In addition, we are also able to judge, by means of our reasoning ability, that particular sense experiences indicate that the world has certain features, even though we are never able to perceive these features. Thus, we can judge from the appearance of sweat on the skin that it has pores. Long before the invention of the telescope, Democritus was able to judge from the white color of the Milky Way that it is composed of an innumerable quantity of stars. This type of reasoning, which leads us to knowledge about the world, is based upon a careful and cautious evaluation of our sense information by our reason, plus inferences, made from this information, based on careful reasoning and on certain general principles that we have learned from experience. The conclusions we reach in this way about the nature of the world are beyond doubt, and are ultimately evaluated in terms of future information gained from experience (as in the case of the Milky Way) and by the usefulness of these conclusions in explaining the course of our experience. We do not discover the absolute truth in this way, but only a faint shadow of it. This faint shadow will turn out to be the most satisfactory scientific explanation that can be given of experience in terms of the hypothesis (confirmed by experience and reasoning) that the world is composed of atoms in motion.

In terms of this theory of knowledge, Gassendi examines various logical systems, ancient and modern, in order to state the best method for attaining limited knowledge. Many of the classical devices, Gassendi finds, are practically useless. The philosophies of Francis Bacon and Descartes have serious defects, Gassendi claims. Our senses can err, and we cannot, no matter what we do, attain real knowledge of the inner nature of things. But a logical method that is based upon sense information carefully analyzed and upon general, unquestionable principles gained from experience and careful reasoning, constantly checked and verified, can serve as the instrument for attaining what truth is possible.

According to Gassendi, what we can know about the world consists of a modified form of the atomism of Epicurus, modified in terms of the science of the time and the religious principles Gassendi maintained that he accepted. (Whether Gassendi was a sincere Christian has been, and still is, debated among scholars.) After surveying and criticizing the view of various philosophers about the nature of the world, Gassendi offers as the most probable theory (but not as the necessarily true one) the view that the actual components of the universe are indivisible atoms, moving in empty space. Appealing to the recent findings of scientists such as Evangelista Torricelli and Blaise Pascal, Gassendi insists that the essential feature of atoms is solidity. In addition, they have the properties of extension, figure, and weight. The atoms vary in shape and size. They are conceived of as having the kinds of configurations found in ordinary experience, like those of wagon wheels and houses, rather than mathematically describable sizes and shapes. (Gassendi had a distrust of those who maintained that nature was to be described in mathematical terms, since he felt that they were probably advocating some type of Platonic metaphysical theory about the nature of reality.)

God has created the atoms and given them an impulse to move downward. They move at different rates of speed, and for this reason they collide with one another. The collisions change the courses of the atoms, causing still further collisions, and so on. The various changes that take place in the world, both on the apparent and on the nonapparent level, can be accounted for by the movements of the atoms, their collisions, and their combinations. Thus, the real world is conceived as a mechanism made up of small moving parts, the atoms. The qualities and movements of the atoms suffice to account for changes in the real world and the way in which the world appears to us. The qualities that we perceive, the colors, sounds, tastes, smells, and so on (the so-called "secondary qualities") are not actually properties of real objects. Instead, they are the ways we perceive various atomic movements when they affect our sense organs.

Gassendi begins to modify his Epicurean theory when he discusses the cause of the movement of the atoms. He accepts the Scholastic thesis that the primary cause of motion is God. The evidence that God exists is the almost universal natural belief in a deity, and the conclusion drawn from observing the order in the universe, namely, that there must be an Orderer or Designer of the world. The fact that there are some atheists is dismissed by Gassendi as similar to the existence of blind people. The fact that a few people lack the normal, natural human faculties and beliefs is no reason to doubt the reliability of the faculties and beliefs of the rest of mankind. Both the senses and our reasoning ability give us an adequate basis for accepting the view that there is a God.

Our conception of God is that of an omniscient and omnipotent Being who is all-wise and all-good. He is the author and providential guide and cause of everything that exists and everything that happens in the world. Gassendi specifically rejects Epicurus' view that everything can be explained and accounted for solely in terms of the atoms and their motions. Where, he asks, do the atoms come from, and what makes them move? Further, if the world were produced only by "the fortuitous concourse of atoms," why is it that the atoms never, by themselves, make a house, or a temple, or a book? Each of these seems to require a designer to organize the atoms in a specific way, and so does the universe in general.

If God is the primary cause of motion, the secondary cause is the atoms themselves through their collisions. God, having created the atoms and implanted in them their downward motions, allows them to move one another through contact. The laws of atomic movements will provide the bases for scientific explanations of all natural occurrences, whether on the atomic level or on that of human sense experience.

Turning from physical events to mental ones, Gassendi attempts to give an atomic explanation of the nature of the soul. First, he exhibits his vast erudition by examining the opinions of many different ancient philosophers on the subject. Then he offers the theory which seemed most probable to him; namely, that the animal soul is a material object. Though we cannot see the soul, reason convinces us that it must exist. The various processes that occur in living beings, such as nutrition, sensation, and movement, could not take place were there not a soul. But what is the soul like? It is a very tenuous material substance existing in the body. It is like a very subtle fire, giving life to corporeal things somewhat as fire warms objects.

The human soul, however, is more complex than the animal soul, being composed of two parts. The first is the irrational soul, which is material and is like the soul of any other living thing. It accounts for the vegetative and sensitive processes that go on in man. This part of the human soul comes to us from our parents. In addition to this, we possess another feature of our souls, the rational element which, Gassendi insists, contrary to Epicurus' view, is not corporeal and is not derived from other human beings, but only from God. The rational part of our soul, which is responsible for our higher intellectual activities, is also immortal. Epicurus had argued for the mortality of the soul, but Gassendi strongly insists that only the animal soul is mortal. As evidence for his belief in the immortality of the rational soul, Gassendi contends that the fact that it is immaterial suffices to show that it is immortal. Further, the universal agreement of mankind on this point is offered as another proof, as well as the view that the divine and just government of the world would seem to require human immortality in order for a proper system of rewards and punishments to function.

In his discussion of human psychology Gassendi presents a theory to explain how the various mental processes take place. This section culminates with an examination of the sources of all of our knowledge, which, to some extent, anticipates the views that appear in John Locke's *An Essay Concerning Human Understanding* (1690).

The faculties of sensation and imagination are common to man and animals. (Gassendi even asserts that sensation occurs to some extent in plants and minerals.) Sensation occurs by means of a physical process involving material particles affecting a sense organ and causing a sensation, which is a physical event in the brain. The faculty of the imagination, which includes the memory as well, operates on traces or remains of the physical sense impressions. These traces are conceived of as waves in the brain which are actuated by other motions in the body and then cause further movements in the brain, giving rise to sensations or feelings similar to the original sensation which caused the wave. (Much of the account offered by Gassendi is close to that presented by his contemporary, the materialistic philosopher Thomas Hobbes.)

The imagination has three functions: apprehension, judgment, and reasoning. We can apprehend, as a result of the wave motions, the exact experiences and sensations that have occurred. Because of movements inside and also outside us, the various waves can be agitated at later times, so that we can now be aware of what we experienced yesterday. Also, different features of different experiences can be apprehended at the same time, giving rise to apprehensions of objects that have never, as such, been experienced. Thus, for example, our apprehension of a centaur results from our previous sense experience of a horse and a man, plus the simultaneous activation of part of the remaining wave that came from each of them. Judging and reasoning, which Gassendi insists takes place in both men and beasts, involves comparing apprehensions and associating them together according to their relations in actual experience. The faculties of judgment and reasoning put various apprehensions into an ordered sequence based on the experienced sequences of sensations, plus the natural instinct which makes us expect certain consequences to follow from what we have experienced.

Up to this point, the detailed psychological theory that Gassendi presents is much like that later developed by the British Empiricists from John Locke to John Stuart Mill. But Gassendi also insists that there is another mental faculty that exists in men, but not in other animals, that of intelligence or understanding, which belongs to our rational souls. By means of intelligence we are able to know things that cannot be experienced in sensation, such as God, space, and time. By this faculty we are also able to know the abstract essences of things, which transcend the powers of the imagination. Thus, for example, the imagination can know what "man" is, in terms of the sensations received. But, the essence of man, what it is that makes him what he is, can be known only by the intelligence. Lastly, this highest mental faculty is capable

of self-consciousness. It can reflect on its operations and those of the imagination, and make us aware that we see, we think, and so on.

In terms of this theory of the nature of the soul, Gassendi next offers his
opinion about the origin of our ideas. He repudiates completely the theory
of Descartes and of Herbert of Cherbury that we possess innate ideas. Instead,
Gassendi insists on the principle accepted by Aristotle and Epicurus, that
there is nothing in the understanding which was not first in the senses. At the
outset, the mind is a *tabula rasa*, a blank tablet. All of the particular ideas
that the mind ever knows, such as that of the sun, either come directly from
sense experience or result from combinations of elements furnished by the
senses. General or abstract ideas are formed by the intelligence from the
collection of sense materials. In this case, the sense information is necessary,
but not sufficient to account for general ideas, such as that of "man." The
intelligence goes beyond the actual sense-data in forming a unique idea from
all the particular sensations. With regard to ideas of incorporeal things, which
cannot be known by the senses, sense experience and the imagination furnish
the occasion for the understanding to gain this knowledge. Because of certain
experiences the understanding thinks, reflects, and abstracts and arrives at
ideas, such as that of God. The senses provide some of the basic materials
for these ideas and provide the context in which the understanding reasons
in order to reach a conception of an incorporeal being.

Thus, all of our ideas either come from the senses or result from intellectual
activities which are either caused or occasioned by sense information. However, in the cases of abstract ideas and ideas of incorporeal things, the actual
content does not derive from any particular sense experiences. General principles, such as "The whole is greater than the part," are formed by induction
from various particular experiences. When all of our experiences exhibit the
same characteristics, we reach a general conclusion, which then becomes the
basis of all further reasoning.

The last part of the *Syntagma* deals with ethics. Gassendi's theory is only
a slightly modified version of Epicurus' hedonism. Gassendi holds that every
pleasure, considered in itself, is a good and that all things that are considered
good have value only in terms of the pleasure they produce. A completely
pleasurable life is one without pains and troubles. Ultimately, for Gassendi,
such a life can be achieved only by God. We can mitigate the pains in our
lives as much as possible and thus attain a relatively good life.

Gassendi's philosophical system was one of the dominant theories of its
time. It represented a cautious and careful attempt to explain the world in
keeping both with the results of the new science and with the official views
of the Catholic Church. Gassendi adapted various features of the philosophy
of Epicurus to the state of knowledge of his day, and he modified certain
portions of Epicurus' theory that were not in keeping with the Christian
religion. The result was a semiskeptical, semiempirical theory which portrayed

the world in terms of an atomic structure. Gassendi's philosophy remained important throughout the seventeenth century and was the chief modern alternative to Descartes'. It began to lose its appeal and importance after the development of the scientific theories of Sir Isaac Newton. Many of the basic elements of later English philosophy appear in Gassendi's views, and he probably had great influence on such thinkers as Hobbes and Locke.—*R.H.P.*

PERTINENT LITERATURE

Popkin, Richard H. *The History of Scepticism from Erasmus to Spinoza.* Berkeley: University of California Press, 1979.

Chapter V in Richard H. Popkin's study of skepticism deals with the group of so-called learned libertines in the mid-seventeenth century. Pierre Gassendi was usually portrayed as a member of the group, along with his friends Gabriel Naudé, Guy Patin, François de La Mothe Le Vayer, and Isaac La Peyrère. They were all seen as skeptics about various claims to knowledge made by philosophers and scientists, but also as freethinkers casting doubt on accepted religious belief.

Gassendi's place in the development of philosophical skepticism is portrayed in the light of the various kinds of skepticism that were being set forth at the time. Gassendi had an early admiration for the writings of Sextus Empiricus. He employed some of the traditional Pyrrhonian arguments in order to attack various dogmatic theories of his time, such as Aristotelianism and different forms of alchemy and astrology. Although Gassendi had called himself a disciple of Sextus Empiricus, he had no desire to pursue Pyrrhonism until it became destructive of all kinds of knowledge. Skepticism became the means for developing a constructive kind of epistemology that, as Gassendi said, was the *via media* between skepticism and dogmatism.

In Chapter VII Popkin examines the mitigated or constructive skepticism of Gassendi and his very close friend, Father Marin Mersenne. Both of them agreed that the arguments of the skeptics cannot be answered. Mersenne held that they can be ignored, since in practice we can proceed in mathematics and the sciences even though we have no ultimate certainty. Gassendi offered a somewhat similar resolution of the skeptical crisis of the time. Without ending either in complete doubt or unjustified certainty, we can find an acceptable intermediary view. Gassendi's atomism and his theory of knowledge as presented in the *Syntagma* represent this outlook. In spite of all of the skeptical arguments, it is obvious that some things exist, and that there is some knowledge of them. When we examine what we actually seem to know, we can discover the criteria that are employed. Using these we can build up a system of knowledge in a hypothetical sense. Such a system is Gassendi's atomism. He was not claiming that it could be shown to be true, but he did contend that, as hypothesis, it provided the best known way of accounting for our experience and for predicting future experiences. Mersenne and Gassendi gave, according to Popkin, the first full-scale formulations of what we would now call the modern scientific outlook.

Gassendi has often been charged with applying his skeptical arguments and attitudes to religious belief. Although he was a priest all his life, he has been charged with holding to the various heretical views of his libertine friends, and even, perhaps, of having been a secret atheist. In French scholarship, especially in the middle of this century, there has been a sharp debate about whether Gassendi was really a believer or a doubter concerning basic Christian views. A key part of the evidence for characterizing him as a doubter consists in pointing out his notorious friends. Popkin shows that these friends contended, whether sincerely or not, that they accepted orthodox Christianity on faith. Gassendi also made a fideistic appeal the basis for his religious claims. In this he was in a tradition going back to Michel Eyquem de Montaigne. However, both a believer and a doubter could make this fideistic appeal. The question then becomes, Who is sincere? Popkin contends that in the case of Gassendi, in terms of what we know about his life and about how his clerical and secular friends regarded it, it would strain the limits of credulity to maintain that he was totally insincere. He was probably like many of his contemporaries, critical or skeptical of a good deal of popular religion.

Two chapters in Popkin's book (V and VII) contain the most extended discussion of Gassendi's views available in English. Selections from many of his texts appear in *The Selected Works of Pierre Gassendi*, translated and edited by Craig Brush, Johnson Reprint Corporation, New York, 1972.

Brett, G. S. *The Philosophy of Gassendi.* London: Macmillan and Company, 1908.

G. S. Brett's work is the only book-length study of Pierre Gassendi's thought in English. It is based only on the 1658 editions of Gassendi's works and on P.-Félix Thomas' *La Philosophie de Gassendi* of 1889. However, Brett contended that he was offering a much broader view of the subject, showing that Gassendi did more than just patch up Epicurus' theory. He also "tried to write the results, not only of philosophy in the narrower sense, but of all previous and contemporary thought into one whole, as consistent as he thought it could be." Hence, Gassendi is portrayed as an important systematic thinker.

Brett begins with a survey of the ancient atomism of Democritus, Epicurus, and Lucretius. There follows a brief biography. After that, a fairly systematic outline of Gassendi's views, especially as they appear in the *Syntagma*, is given. The bulk of the book consists of this summary, which is carefully done (and which includes an English translation of some of Gassendi's important propositions). Also, illustrations explaining Gassendi's meaning are presented.

In the material on logic (which includes theory of knowledge) Brett does not connect Gassendi's views on signs, on criteria of knowledge, and on reliability of knowledge with the thoroughgoing skepticism he had developed in his earlier writings on these subjects. As a result Gassendi's epistemology is given a more positive emphasis than some critics think it deserves when seen as part of his "constructive skepticism."

Next, Brett surveys Gassendi's physics. Using the term in Aristotle's sense, that of the study of nature, Gassendi first deals with the physical world and the nature of time and space, together with the nature of causality. Then astronomy and astrology are considered. After that, Gassendi treats botanical nature, biological nature, and psychological nature. Brett summarizes Gassendi's scientific views carefully. A great deal of attention is given to Gassendi's views on how the human psyche operates, and indeed on the essential nature of the psyche. Brett relates Gassendi's position to Catholic orthodoxy in the seventeenth century. He also considers Gassendi's views in the light of developments in psychology around 1900. William James, W. K. Clifford, and other psychologists are mentioned in connection with Gassendi's theories.

The remainder of the summary of Gassendi's thought covers his critique of astrology and alchemy, and his ethics. In the last section, Part IV, entitled "General Review," Brett offers his evaluation of Gassendi's philosophy. Brett does not seem to realize how influential Gassendi has been in his time, and sees him as drowned out by René Descartes. This picture is drawn from the histories of philosophy of Brett's day. And so, he writes, "History has done justice to Descartes, but hardly to Gassendi." In trying to compensate for this neglect, Brett contrasts Gassendi's views on various matters with those of later philosophers, from G. W. Leibniz and Benedictus de Spinoza to Immanuel Kant, Rudolf Hermann Lotze, and Herbert Spencer.

Since Brett was apparently unaware of both the traditions of materialistic atomism from Gassendi's time to the era of modern physics, and the skeptical traditions from Michel Eyquem de Montaigne to Gassendi to Pierre Bayle and David Hume, he failed to see where Gassendi's influence was strongest. He also failed to perceive the relationship of Gassendi's empiricism with that of John Locke. (Locke's name does not even appear in the index of the volume.) There are, however, many things in the study that are worthwhile.

Block, Olivier R. *La Philosophie de Gassendi*. The Hague, The Netherlands: Martinus Nijhoff, 1971.

This large volume is the most important recent examination of Pierre Gassendi's thought. Olivier R. Bloch's study is based on the work of earlier French scholars such as Alexandre Koyré and Bernard Rochot, who sought to show the importance of Gassendi's scientific and philosophical ideas.

Bloch considers the entire corpus of Gassendi's writings and attempts to find some fundamental threads and themes throughout his works. The *Syntagma* was the largest undertaking of Gassendi; it appeared only posthumously in 1658. Bloch also examines the available manuscript material. Some of this indicates changes of mind and doubts on Gassendi's part.

Basing his survey on a thorough knowledge of Gassendi's writings, Bloch first accepts the view of some earlier commentators that Gassendi's philosophy does not really constitute an intellectual system. Constructing a system out of the elements of the *Syntagma* fails to make sense of Gassendi's contribution. Rejecting the possiblity of finding a system does not mean that there is not any principle of unity in Gassendi's philosophy. Therefore, Bloch maintains, one should look for the constant elements and the basic ambiguities in Gassendi's thought. One must consider "le cas Gassendi," namely, was Gassendi sincere or duplicitous in presenting his views? Gassendi was a Catholic priest, and yet he seemed to endorse completely skeptical views about knowledge and completely materialistic views about science. He was the major figure in reviving Epicurean atomism, and he was a close friend of the leading libertines of his day. Could he also have been a sincere and believing Christian?

Bloch finds a fairly constant skeptical view throughout Gassendi's works regarding epistemology. However, Bloch claims, contrary to Richard H. Popkin and Tullio Gregory (*Scetticismo ed Empirismo Studio su Gassendi*), this was itself ambiguous. Bloch shows it is difficult to define Gassendi's skepticism. Throughout his intellectual life, Gassendi never definitely chose between probabilism, relativism, phenomenalism, and other skeptical tendencies. However, the central feature of his skeptical view Bloch finds in Gassendi's nominalism. It incorporates much of Gassendi's skeptical attitude toward dogmatic theories with a demand that explanation be given in terms of something concrete.

The second part of Bloch's book connects Gassendi's nominalism with his materialism and explicates his scientific philosophy. His atomism and how it was used to explain the material features of the world led to an overall materialistic point of view. But Gassendi did not try to build this into a traditional metaphysical theory. If he had, this might have led to conflict with his Catholicism. Gassendi the man, Bloch asserts, was no doubt a believer, but was his skeptical and Epicurean philosophy Christian? He opposed mysticism and had more scientific than religious zeal. Gassendi separated religion and philosophy and science so that there could be no conflicts. This position Bloch sees as like the double-truth theory. Gassendi's philosophy and science could have a positive secular value without denying the religious sincerity of his faith. Moreover, his metaphysical views were not intended to imply any theological ones. Gassendi moved from leaving ultimate conceptions of the world to religion, to trying as best he could to make his philosophical and scientific views compatible both with natural religion and with reason enlightened by faith.

Bloch's massive work shows why Gassendi was one of the dominant intellects of the seventeenth century, rivaling René Descartes, Thomas Hobbes, and Benedictus de Spinoza. An extensive bibliography is included.—*R.H.P.*

ADDITIONAL RECOMMENDED READING

Centre International de Synthèse. *Pierre Gassendi, 1592-1655, sa vie et son oeuvre*. Paris: Editions Albin Michel, 1955. Contains articles by Alexandre Koyré, Bernard Rochot, and many other scholars; on Gassendi as a scientist and hilosopher.

Gregory, Tullio. *Scetticismo ed empirismo: studio su Gassendi*. Bari: Editori Laterza, 1961. An excellent examination of two aspects of Gassendi's thought: his skepticism and his empiricism.

Pintard, René. *Le libertinage érudit dans la première moitié du xvii⁰ siècle*. Paris: Boivin, 1943. A major study of the *libertin* thinkers in the first half of the seventeenth century.

Rochot, Bernard. *Les Travaux de Gassendi sur Épicure et sur atomisme*. Paris: J. Vrin, 1944. A pioneering work on the development of Gassendi's atomism.

Spink, J. S. *French Free-Thought from Gassendi to Voltaire*. London: Athlone Press, 1960. A somewhat controversial survey of *avant-garde* thinkers in France, 1650-1750.

PENSÉES

Author: Blaise Pascal (1623-1662)
Type of work: Theology
First published: 1670

PRINCIPAL IDEAS ADVANCED

There are two essential religious truths: there is a God, and there is a corruption of nature which makes men unworthy of him.

Reason is of little use in showing either the existence or the nature of God, but it does reveal man's finiteness and his separation from God.

It is a reasonable wager to stake everything on God's existence, for God either exists or he does not; if God is, then the man who believes in him wins everything, while if God is not, the man who believes in him suffers only a finite loss.

In knowing that he is miserable, man achieves greatness.

Since man's will is subject to his passions, it is important for men to obey custom simply because it is custom, and to obey the law in order to avoid sedition and rebellion.

Pascal's reflections on religion make up a large body of notes, written between 1654 and his death in 1662, intended to form a never-finished work to bear the title, *Apologie de la Religion Catholique.* Composed at different times after a moving mystical experience, the contents of the *Pensées* appeared in print posthumously. These reflections reveal Pascal as belonging to the group of fervently Christian writers who reject the usual claims of natural theology in order the more sharply to separate faith from reason.

Pascal's thought expresses the influence of the Jansenists, a seventeenth century Catholic order indebted to the theological views of John Calvin, one of the Protestant reformers. A group in conflict with the Jesuits, the Jansenists lived at Port Royal, near Paris, where they taught several central beliefs: man's total sinfulness, salvation through God's predestination, grace as sole means to salvation, and the need of the faithful to hold to a Christian belief which can never be proved by reason.

Though never an official member of the Jansenist community, Pascal visited them frequently (his sister belonged) and wrote in their defense in a bitter controversy with the Jesuits. Pascal was a brilliant mathematician as well as a religious writer, aware of the significant mathematical developments of his day. Living an austerely self-disciplined life, he gave away his wealth in an effort to exclude all pleasure and vanity from his practices.

The *Pensées* express numerous reflections concerning a few central themes. The Christian religion as known by Pascal teaches men two essential truths: "that there is a God, to whom men may attain, and that there is a corruption of nature which renders them unworthy of him." Pascal insists that if men deny either of these truths, they must fall into atheism, end up with the philosophers' god so popular among deistic thinkers of his time, or find themselves reduced to a complete pessimism. The Christian God worshiped by Pascal does not require a philosopher's proof of existence, and he writes, "It is a wonderful thing that no canonical author has ever made use of nature in order to prove God." Pascal argues that man's miserable state does not justify total pessimism for the reason that the God worshiped by Christians, as by Abraham, Isaac, and Jacob, is one of love and consolation.

Pascal claims that God becomes available to men only through the mediation of Jesus Christ. Although Pascal makes clear that man is a "thinking reed," man's thinking capacity can nevertheless function religiously only to make clear his absolute finiteness, his total separation from God's actual infinity. In writing about faith, Pascal stresses the utter uselessness of reason for religious purposes. "Faith is a gift of God," he insists. "Believe not that we said it is a gift of reason." Yet reason is never to be disparaged, since it performs its own important functions and provides the key to whatever dignity man may achieve.

Nevertheless, Pascal sometimes does come close to a kind of reasoning about God—as in his famous wager argument for belief in God's existence (although this argument was intended primarily for skeptics who deny the importance of religious belief). In another place Pascal treats the relation of man's miserable condition to his finitude in such a way that he gives something resembling an argument for the necessity of God's existence. This latter argument rests on the awareness that the "I" of Pascal is really a thought. Had Pascal's mother died before his birth, the "I" of Pascal would never have existed. The conclusion is that Pascal is clearly not a necessary being. Pascal sees also that he is neither eternal nor infinite. He asserts that "I see plainly that there is in nature one being who is necessary, eternal, and infinite." This approximation to one of the classical demonstrations of God's existence indicates that Pascal was more concerned to argue that proofs cannot induce one to accept the Christian faith than to claim that proofs are unqualifiedly impossible of formulation. Such proofs, even if possible, turn out to be religiously useless and unimportant.

Pascal contends that men know *that* there is a God without knowing *what* God is. (In this claim he is inconsistent; he also asserts in one place that man can never *know* God's existence.) He insists that men also can know there is an infinite while remaining ignorant of its nature. Numbers cannot be brought to an end. This means simply that men can never mention a number which is the last one. So number must be infinite. Similarly, aware of the infinite's existence and unable to know its nature, men fail to know God's nature and existence because God lacks extension and limits. Men have absolutely no correspondence with the God which Christians worship in faith.

The Christians who refuse to give reasons for their faith are essentially right, according to Pascal. They present their God as a "foolishness" to a world which often complains because the Christians cannot prove this God's existence. Some critics reasonably criticize Christians for holding beliefs which are beyond proof. Pascal attempts to reply to these critics by arguing that it is reasonable to believe. This he does primarily by producing his famous wager argument.

The stakes are clear, in Pascal's view. "God is, or He is not." The agnostic can argue that, since reason is unable to decide the issue, one need make no choice either way. Pascal insists that this will not do—that men must wager. They must choose. "It is not optional; you are committed to it." Pascal claims that men own two things as stakes in such a wager: their reason and their will (blessedness). They have two things to lose: the true and the good. Man's nature involves also two things to avoid: error and misery. Now, according to Pascal, since reason is unable to make the decision, the issue must turn on man's blessedness. How is this to be decided? The answer is that if man wagers on God's existence, he stands to win everything, losing nothing. Thus, to wager for God's existence means either the possibility of finite loss (if God does not exist) or infinite gain (if God does exist). Man's wager stakes a possibility of finite loss against one of infinite gain; namely, happiness. Man can therefore make only one wager—that God does exist.

What Pascal set out to prove was not that God exists, but that men *ought to believe* in God's existence. Once made, however, the wager does not necessarily bring one to the Christian God, as Pascal was clearly aware. Yet the wager is a fruitful beginning. The doubter who makes the wager can still use the possible way of "seeing through the game" associated with the reading and study of Scripture. He can also seek to control his passions. In this present life the man who wagers will be better off for having made the wager. Such a man will be driven to associate with others who have already been cured of their malady. Like them, he must act as if he believed. According to Pascal, no harm can come to such a man, for he will be "faithful, honest, humble, grateful, benevolent, a sincere and true friend."

To read Pascal as if he sought to debase the functions of human reason would be to read him wrongly. Because reason is incapable of knowing what God is does not alter the fact that man's greatness is tied to reason. Pascal insists that thought is not derived from body. Thought is its own kind of entity. Reason alone permits man to know the misery which marks his condition, but this very knowledge accounts for his dignity: "To be miserable is to know one's self to be so, but to know one's self to be miserable is to be great." Only man can possess this kind of knowledge which is denied to the other elements in nature. What makes Christianity the solely adequate religion, in Pascal's view, is that Christianity teaches the otherwise peculiar doctrine that man's misery and his greatness are inseparable. Men need to come to terms with their miserable condition, though they cannot fundamentally alter it. This gives both men and religion something important to accomplish. The central religious problem is to learn to control the human will rather than to pile up theological knowledge by reasoning. To cure pride, lust, and egocentered aggressiveness remains the fundamental task of the Christian religion.

Concern about human willfulness occurs in numerous passages in the *Pensées*. Unlike the reasoning powers, the will operates according to man's perspective. Man finds himself in bondage to his passions. For this reason, custom is a most important necessity of any possible social existence. Against Montaigne, Pascal argued that men should obey custom simply because it is custom and not because it is reasonable. Men should also obey law as law in order to avoid sedition and rebellion. Pascal insists that classical philosophers such as Plato and Aristotle wrote about politics with many reservations. "If they wrote of politics, it was as if to regulate a hospital for madmen." Pascal could not believe that such men thought reasoning about politics the most serious business of life.

Though he understood the limited possibilities of reasoning, Pascal never degraded reason. Reasoning allows men to encircle the universe in certain ways, but "instinct" and "the heart" are essential allies. "How few demonstrated things there are!" Pascal laments in one place. Men are as much automata as minds. No one should ridicule custom in view of this fact. Agreeing with a philosopher such as David Hume, Pascal says it is custom which permits men to believe that tomorrow will dawn and that men must die. Custom influences men to act, while reason directs only the mind. Habit, including religious practice, remains a routine needed in every day and age. "We have to acquire an easier credence,—that of habit,—which without violence, art, or argument, makes us believe things and inclines all our powers to this belief, so that our mind falls into it naturally." Pascal claims that life would be easier for men if reason were unnecessary; but since nature has not so arranged matters, men need to supplement intuited first principles with limited demonstrations.

Pascal makes a distinction between knowledge and judgment. For example, geometry is a matter of the mind, while subtlety is a function of intuition. Men must judge things either literally or spiritually. Honoring reason, men should accept its limits, knowing what it can and cannot accomplish. Although there is criticism of the Pyrrhonists (skeptics) for some of their beliefs, Pascal shows that he was favorably disposed to a partial skepticism concerning the powers of reason. Men can at most achieve a "learned ignorance." Different from the natural ignorance of all men at birth, a learned ignorance is gained by a few "lofty souls who, having traversed all human knowledge, find that they know nothing. . . . This is a self-aware ignorance. Between these two kinds of ignorance dwell the great numbers of the intelligent who "disturb the world and judge wrongly of everything." Genuine philosophers are those who learn how to laugh at philosophy.

The imagination and human sickness are two important elements which shape man's constant susceptibility to deception. The wisest men can hope only to modify, never to eradicate these two sources of illusion. Man tends naturally towards wrong judgment. He finds it difficult, if not impossible, to escape the binding conditions of his own vanity. His actions are motivated by self-love. What makes the Christian view of Incarnation important is the radical cure it suggests for man's pridefulness. Men must hate religion as long as it teaches what it must—that the misery of man is objective and absolutely ineradicable except by God's grace. This side of Pascal's thought shows a relation to the long tradition in Western thought concerned with the numerous psychological and cultural obstacles in the way of genuine discovery of self-knowledge. These obstacles are, for Pascal, as much connected with the human will as with the mind. It is as if men want, in some deep and buried way, to judge things wrongly.

Pascal mentions atheism and deism as the greatest competitors of a genuine Christian faith. He understands how atheism may be a mark of a strong intellect, though only up to a point. The atheist has blind spots when he comes, say, to the notion of immortality. Pascal asks why the atheist should deny dogmatically the possibility that a man might rise from the dead. He wants to know which is the more remarkable—that a living being should appear at all, or that a once-living being should be reborn. By custom the atheist accepts the fact that there are living beings and then seems astounded by the religious notion of rebirth. Here the atheist puzzles Pascal. On the other hand, the deist seeks to know God without revelation, meaning without the mediation of Jesus Christ. The deist thus misunderstands Christianity, ending with the philosopher's God of proofs and first principles rather than with the God of redemption. Pascal clearly aligns himself with those who assert that the Christian faith cannot fully be translated into philosophical terms.

Affirmation of the original sin of all men is a necessity for Pascal. The evidence for this affirmation is that all men are born disposed to seek their own interests, a disposition which runs counter to the necessary conditions of order. Wars and revolutions arise from the individual's pursuit of self-interest even when his reason tells him that he should attend to the needs of a commonwealth. Men should usually seek the general as opposed to the particular interests of a community, but most often they do not. Facts like these Pascal takes as indicative of some basic flaw in human willing. The glory of the Christian religion stems from its insistence on man's inherent sinfulness. "No religion but ours has taught that man is born in sin," Pascal writes; "no sect of philosophers has affirmed it, therefore none has spoken the truth." This dark doctrine, so stressed by Pascal and borrowed from contemporary

Calvinism, helped to bring him into disrepute among the Jesuits, who thought he emphasized it disproportionately. Yet he was quite aware of the nonrational nature of this doctrine and made no effort to prove it.

What makes Pascal's *Pensées* an enduring work is the classical manner in which one aspect of the Christian tradition in theology receives forceful and passionate presentation. Its confessional and personal nature also makes it a work which can help individuals who, like Pascal, find themselves caught up in a struggle to make sense of Christian faith once they have abandoned belief that natural proofs of God's existence are possible. One-sided in emphasis, Pascal's work tries to show that Christian faith is reasonable on its own terms even though not susceptible of rational proofs divorced from reasons of the heart. No matter how extremely emphasized, Pascal's views about the depravity of the will help to counterbalance the more optimistic humanistic conceptions of human perfectibility.

Through the *Pensées* runs a sense of the fragility of human life—a constant reminder of something most men know when they think about it but which they often wish to forget. A sense of the contingency of life, of uncertainty about its duration, pervades Pascal's writings. A mystical sense that there is more to finite existence than meets the finite eye drives Pascal to fall back on intuition and feeling when reason proves unable to establish the kinds of certainty many religious persons hope to find.

Pascal's portrait of man's misery involves a kind of metaphysical sickness. Reasoning man is caught between the finite and an infinite whose nature he can never hope to fathom. He owns a will to self-deception, marked by an endless pursuit of means by which to divert attention from this very fact. On the other hand, a critic may well say that Pascal is too much a puritanical thinker—unwilling or unable to point out the genuinely redeeming features of natural processes. The Pascalian picture of man illustrates the more somber side of puritan thought and feeling. "Imagine a number of men in chains, and all condemned to death, of whom every day some are butchered in sight of the others, those remaining seeing their own fate in that of their fellows, regarding each other with grief and despair while awaiting their turn; this is a picture of the condition of man."

Obviously, some of Pascal's thoughts reflect events of his own biography. He shunned pleasure and picked up the radically austere notions of the Jansenists. Nevertheless, his version of Christian faith remains a recurring theme in the long, unresolved competition between those who argue for a natural theology and those others who insist that revelation is not to be explained in philosophical terms. Pascal's *Pensées* is the expression of a troubled man who seemed to need this specific version of Christian faith to find life itself a meaningful affair. Man's very misery made sense out of the Christian promise, according to Pascal. Unlike many other writers, Pascal attempted to live according to his beliefs. Many men in the twentieth century, including those who would disagree with Pascal, are finding that to live according to one's beliefs is no small achievement.—*W.T.D.*

PERTINENT LITERATURE
Broome, J. H. *Pascal*. London: E. Arnold, 1965.

The two central chapters (VI and VII) of J. H. Broome's work on the life and thought of Blaise Pascal are concerned specifically with the *Pensées*. We are presented with a detailed and solid interpretation of the lasting significance of Pascal's most famous work. Broome's main concern is to capture the spirit of Pascal's religious enterprise and to communicate it to the reader in whatever way he can. Such an enterprise implies that some of the textual problems long associated with the *Pensées* must be overlooked in the conviction that even if an authoritative and complete version of the work had been passed down to us, the central issues involving the structure and spirit of Pascal's religious thought would to some extent have remained beneath the surface, necessitating the kind of interpretative approach Broome sees himself carrying out here.

Broome begins his analysis by suggesting that we think of the *Pensées* as a record of a rescue operation, a literary attempt to save not persons or groups of persons but humanity in general, threatened through original sin with the loss of the hope for redemption. Thus, the *Pensées* is to be seen primarily as the work of a devoted and ingenious thinker trying desperately to capture the attention of an audience assailed by contemporary freethinking and somehow at least to point them in the direction of possible salvation. Broome argues that the major division of the *Pensées* into the nontheological first part in which Pascal presents a series of arguments in dialectical form (including the celebrated Wager argument) and the second traditional part in which most of the arguments are based on Scripture (and in which Pascal's fundamentalism is strongest), arises naturally from an intention first to break down the defenses of the skeptic and then to strike home with the evidence and arguments from Scripture. While Broome acknowledges that this picture of Pascal's plan in the *Pensées* tends to oversimplify and even formalize it, the picture is in the long run most satisfactory, expressing as it does the *charitable* spirit of the whole enterprise, an enterprise Broome understands to be a product of the intellectual structure of the work on the one hand, and of the work as a dynamic but practical undertaking in charity (a work of the heart) on the other. Broome also considers it to be Pascal's own view that the structures are not incompatible and that the stronger the intellectual structure is the stronger and more efficient the work of charity will be.

Ultimately, however, Broome concludes that Pascal's fragments fail to convince many people who are not already convinced; although Broome asserts that what really matters with respect to the reader's reaction to the *Pensées* is that there be *some* response, since Pascal himself recognized that even a hostile reaction is better than no reaction at all. Furthermore, Broome is at pains to point out that although Pascal seems at times to hold out little hope for the majority of mankind, the contemporary impression of him as a philosopher of *angoisse* (thanks in part to his being treated as a forerunner of existentialism) must be resisted. The *Pensées* is not a philosophy of despair without any consolation whatsoever, for the wretchedness of man's natural state can be contained and transcended by a recognition of the order of the heart (love, charity), the third and supernatural order. To reach the point in our spiritual lives where it becomes possible to recognize this third order (the first two orders being mind and body) and to accept grace is, for most, a lifelong task. Man must first recognize that he is sick and must be cured. The *Pensées* is rife with this sort of tragic imagery—man is a prisoner of his own selfishness; he is balanced precariously between infinity and nothingness; man is walking a plank over a precipice—in short, man is in a predicament. Broome emphasizes Pascal's sense of man's disorientation and lack of perspective and sees it as providing the *Pensées* with the urgency to get on with the business of salvation.

Accepting that man is indeed in Pascal's predicament (and Broome never questions this premise), how *practically* is man to extricate himself and initiate the push toward salvation? At this point Broome introduces the analogy of a bridging operation to explain what in effect is Pascal's theory of the Three Orders. Broome postulates two structures of evidence used by Pascal in the *Pensées*: evidence from nature and evidence from Scripture. The two independent structures support each other by a counterpoise effect, thus producing at the center and out of instability a fragile yet provisional stability. It is not a bridge that can be walked on, for only the center is stable; the only way to proceed is upwards from the center.

To clarify the analogy: man is in a natural state of wretchedness; this is his predicament. The proper use of reason and instinct—human ingenuity—can take man only so far along the road to possible salvation, but the completion of the rescue depends in the end not on anything we can do through the use of reason and instinct. Only the operation of grace in human lives can save man from himself, from his own nature; and such grace in turn appears to be only partially the result of our own efforts (through prayer, for example), although Broome is quick to state that Pascal was himself unclear on the point. The operation of grace is the province of the third and supernatural order, the order Pascal adds to the traditional two orders of mind (reason) and body (instinct).

There are obvious problems with an analogy of this sort, and Broome does raise some of them. On what in real life is the bridge structure of the analogy based? The answer, according to Broome, is that the structure is indeed a structure in the void, and for Pascal this corresponds with the Spirit of God, his love and his grace. It is as if Pascal were suggesting that this is how man experiences the void.

Once man's ingenuity has taken him as far as he can go (as in the Wager argument where Pascal constructs an argument to show that our self-interest must impel us to wager for God's existence since we have almost everything to gain and only our wretchedness to lose), he is, so to speak, left hanging in the void, for whatever belief he can summon forth is based only on intellectual assent (rather than its coming from the heart). The rescue (and the bridge) can be completed only by turning toward God through Christ, and this is possible only by appeal to the Scriptures and by constant prayer. Indeed, Broome suggests that Pascal, in the second part of the *Pensées*, comes to treat prayer as the one way in which a certain relationship with God can be built up. We can thus approach a relationship, or possible contact with, God; but of this there can be no guarantee. For Pascal, such a possibility (which is supernatural) must ultimately depend on the intuitions of the heart for those who endure the struggle to the end.

Krailsheimer, A. J. *Pascal*. Past Masters Series. Oxford: Oxford University Press, 1980.

The central thesis of A. J. Krailsheimer's study of Blaise Pascal is that the apparently radically different phases of Pascal's life actually form a coherent whole and, most important, that the *Pensées* could only have been produced by someone who had lived just such a life. In brief, Pascal's unusual life and the *Pensées* are essentially and intimately connected. Krailsheimer argues that Pascal's early work in science, mathematics, and technology is crucially important for a full understanding and proper appreciation of the *Pensées* because it is in the early work that Pascal developed the patterns of thought and the intellectual habits which were to inform much of his later work in religion. Easily the most significant and influential of these early developments is the tripartite theory of knowledge—Pascal's continual recognition of the three ways to truth and knowledge (mind, body, and heart), so radically opposed to René Descartes' dualism of mind and matter. It is this conception of knowledge and truth which eventually links up with the famous Three Orders of the *Pensées*.

For Krailsheimer the concept of the Three Orders is central to the *Pensées* and to an understanding of the interdependence of Pascal's work on mathematics, science, morality, and religion. In rejecting the dualism of mind and body (whether it be Descartes', Michel de Montaigne's, or Plato's) Krailsheimer argues that Pascal was rejecting the supremacy of either the body (impulse) or the mind (reason) in man's nature, and was at the same time recognizing the need for a third order which would allow human beings to overcome the inadequacies of their existence imposed by a slavish submission to the first two orders. The third order, variously described by Pascal in the *Pensées* as the order of the heart or the order of charity, is the order through which we can be moved by the grace of God acting through Christ. Through grace the heart can be turned or inclined upward to charity and the life of the spirit (recognizing Christ as the savior) or downward to the life of the flesh. In this way, the heart can affect (and ultimately ground) the operations of the mind so that the mind can be put to its proper use, which it would not do of its own accord because it is by nature corrupt. Here we come up against an important aspect of Krailsheimer's view of the *Pensées*. Krailsheimer wishes to maintain that although the *Pensées* represents a rejection of the claims of rationalism with respect to man's ends, it would be a serious error to see this as a wholesale rejection of reason (as has been done). Pascal does not reject reason itself so much as its misuse; indeed, intended as they were for the freethinkers of the seventeenth century, the *Pensées* would have to make an appeal to reason and to satisfy its basic requirements if Pascal were to entertain any hope that these fragments would win over his carefully selected audience. Thus in the *Pensées*, Krailsheimer declares, Pascal employs his own form of dialectical argument to exemplify his theory of the Three Orders, which is designed not to rest on any particular conclusion (for the dialectic never stops at any stage) but to persuade gradually by a continuous appeal to the problems of real life. The *Pensées*, it must be remembered, was meant to communicate not a set of doctrines but a way of life that could possibly lead to God. Each of the orders must be used as it was meant to be used, leading to the emergence of a clear hierarchy of excellence wherein faith is experienced as the outcome of God turning our hearts rather than persuading our minds. It follows, according to Krailsheimer, that all rational arguments for the existence of God are totally irrelevant to true Christianity, founded as it is on faith and divine grace. Reason can (and indeed must) strive to explain natural phenomena; but faith and the "heart" belong to the third and most important order, the supernatural. Thus the importance of the proper use of the Three Orders.

Krailsheimer is adamant that the *Pensées* does not form a linear argument. The dialectic is the dominant form of argument: two contradictory positions are stated—usually two contradictory truths about man. Pascal then proceeds to show that the contradiction can be resolved only by a third position which contains and yet transcends the other two. Despite the dialectic, however, the *Pensées* does presuppose that one accept a fundamental premise about the nature of man: that man without God is wretched. The problem here, as Krailsheimer is quick to point out, is that one could just as easily construct a case which would show no less convincingly that happiness is the natural state of man. In any case, Pascal's argument for the wretchedness of man's natural state rests on his conception of man as a creature constituted by two opposing powers or orders, reason and instinct. Whether the one or the other is thought to be man's natural state, it is impossible for man to escape his wretchedness.

The only solution lies in the awareness of a third order, an order outside both reason and instinct. The paradox that man reveals a mixture of skepticism and dogmatism, of reason and instinct, is shown to be the dualism of grace and corruption, of greatness and wretchedness. Man, once knowing happiness, fell into (original) sin so that he is now in the hopeless and agonizing position of continuously striving to retrieve the lost state of grace. If man had never known it, he would have no need to search for it. The only possible solution, the only means of transcending this dualism, is to listen to God and accept his grace; thus the third order transcends the first two. The refusal to submit and accept grace (humility) results in natural selfishness, with each man left to himself.

Krailsheimer presents a lively and comprehensive commentary on the three central themes of the *Pensées*: the theory of orders, with the supernatural order overcoming the natural orders of mind and body; the need for individual men to see themselves as part of a historical process, the most important aspect of which is the fall from grace into original sin; and the crippling effect of the failure to overcome one's natural limitations and selfishness. Inevitably, however (and Krailsheimer does not shy away from this difficulty), the weakest element in the scheme of the *Pensées* is the historical evidence advanced for the truth of Christianity. Pascal thought it absolutely crucial that there be a first Adam. Pascal was, in effect, a fundamentalist, and this attitude does indeed show itself rather disturbingly throughout the *Pensées*. Nevertheless, Pascal's conversion to fundamentalism in no way altered his acquired scientific approach, his respect for facts, and his intellectual openness.

Pascal's third order, the order of faith, charity, and ultimately of divine love, was, according to Krailsheimer, meant to be understood as the only possible escape from wretchedness. By acknowledging his wretchedness, man becomes humble and thus acquires true pride; above all, by freeing himself of his own inadequacy, he submits to the love of God, looking upward instead of inward.—*J.P.D.*

ADDITIONAL RECOMMENDED READING

Adam, Antoine. *Grandeur and Illusion*. London: Weidenfeld and Nicolson, 1972. A translation of the very good *Histoire de la littérature française au XVIIe siècle*, II, Paris: Del Duca, 1962. The English version is much abbreviated but nevertheless supplies an excellent picture of the literary, philosophical, and social background of the age.

Mesnard, Jean. *Les Pensées de Pascal*. Paris: Societé d'edition d'enseignement Supérieur, 1976. An admirable analysis of text and background.

—————— . *Pascal, His Life and Works*. New York: Philosophical Library, 1952. A solid general book.

Miel, Jean. *Pascal and Theology*. Baltimore: Johns Hopkins University Press, 1969. This book is very useful on specific technical issues.

ETHICS

Author: Benedictus de Spinoza (1632-1677)
Type of work: Ethics, theology
First published: 1677

PRINCIPAL IDEAS ADVANCED

Whatever is the cause of itself exists necessarily.

Only substance is self-caused, free, and infinite; and God is the only substance.

God exists necessarily, and is possessed of infinite attributes.

But only two of God's infinite attributes are known to us: thought and extension.

Since thought and extension are features of the same substance, whatever happens to body happens also to mind as another phase of the same event.

A false idea is an idea improperly related to God; by achieving adequate ideas we become adequate causes of the body's modifications: this is human freedom, freedom from the human bondage to the passions.

The highest virtue of the mind is to know God.

Spinoza's *Ethics* is a truly amazing work. In a field which is subject to great differences of opinion, it has always been recognized as a classic by people of most diverse interests. While other philosophers come and go in popularity, Spinoza maintains a stable place, always attracting the interest of serious students. He did not write a great deal, and of his works, few receive much attention except the *Ethics*. It stands as a single work exacting a place of influence usually reserved for a more extensive collection of philosophical writings.

The figure of Spinoza has often attracted as much attention as his work, and he stands, along with Socrates, as one of the few genuine heroes in a field not much given to hero worship. A Jew, ostracized by his own people and excluded from his homeland, he insisted on following his own ideas despite their heretical tendencies. Moreover, the *Ethics* remained unpublished in Spinoza's lifetime. Upon this single posthumous work his great reputation and reservoir of influence depend. Hegel and many of the later romantics acknowledge Spinoza as the modern thinker whose thought suggests the direction for their later developments.

Widespread interest in Spinoza remains even today, despite his central theological orientation and the recent unfashionability of such an approach. Many men who find traditional religious beliefs unacceptable discover in Spinoza a rational and a naturalistic form of religion. His views on God, man, and the human emotions have widespread popular influence. Although Spinoza is sometimes called "the philosophers' philosopher" because of the abstract and technical nature of the *Ethics*, it is still true that few philosophers' general views are more widely known than are his among the nonphilosophical public. It is true that his views are often oversimplified, but it is also true that they are circulated extensively.

A great deal of argument has been generated by the style or form in which Spinoza chose to write the *Ethics*. The Continental Rationalists (Descartes, Leibniz, and Spinoza) were all much impressed by the exciting developments in mathematics, and all of them reflect something of the geometric temper in their writings. Spinoza elected to write the *Ethics* as a geometrical system—definitions, axioms, propositions, and all. Some argue that this form is essential to Spinoza's doctrines; others feel that the *Ethics* can just as easily be read in essay style. All seem agreed that the work does not really have the full deductive rigor of geometry; yet the form indicates Spinoza's desire to be clear and simple in his expression, to be straightforward in his assertions, and to connect the various parts of his thought systematically. All this he achieves with the barest minimum of explanation and with little external reference.

Fortunately we do not need to understand fully Spinoza's own attitude toward this geometrical method of philosophizing, or to appraise its success, in order to grasp the central features of Spinoza's thought. It is true that the geometrical method represents an attempted revolution in philosophical thought. In his unfinished *On the Improvement of the Understanding*, Spinoza agreed with the other modern revolutionaries of his era in stressing methodology and the need for a thorough reexamination of traditional philosophical and theological methods. His break with the scholastic method of the *Summas* is complete. Spinoza firmly believed that the human intellect can be carefully examined and improved and thereby made able to produce a more rigorous and more complete understanding of things—all this through its own strengthened power.

Properly corrected, reason is self-sufficient, its own guide and its own judge. And this is, for Spinoza, as true in ethical affairs as in speculative matters. He does not belong in the class of dogmaticians; there is no indication that he believed his own views to be either complete or final. What is evident is his trust in the human intellect to work out an acceptable and a comprehensive schema. Spinoza depended heavily on previous theological views, but his modern temperament transformed them by placing them in a new humanistic perspective.

The five parts of the *Ethics* take up in order God, the nature and origin of the mind, then the emotions, and finally the twin questions of human bondage and human freedom. In beginning with a consideration of the divine nature, and then developing all other theories in this light, Spinoza was influenced by medieval theology. Theory of knowledge and attention to human powers of knowing received a more prominent place with Spinoza, but systematically speaking a theory of the divine nature is still first. Spinoza called his first principle sometimes God, sometimes substance. Aristotle had defined "substance" as that capable of independent existence. Spinoza interpreted this with absolute rigor and asserted that only God, a substance of infinite attributes, could fulfill this definition exactly.

The *Ethics* opens with the traditional distinction between that which requires no external cause to account for its existence (cause of itself) and that which owes its existence (causally) to another being. That which is the cause of itself exists necessarily and needs nothing other than itself to be conceived. This Spinoza calls substance. On the other hand, what is finite is what is capable of being limited by another thing of its own kind, whereas substance is absolutely infinite, in that it possesses infinite attributes.

Spinoza defines an "attribute" as that which the mind sees as constituting the essence of substance. A "mode" is some modification of substance. "Freedom" means to exist from the necessity of one's own nature alone (only substance as cause of itself fulfills this requirement) and to be set in action by oneself alone. Only substance, or God, is perfectly free, dependent on nothing else for its existence or action; it is absolutely infinite and thus one of a kind.

From here Spinoza turns to a classical definition of knowledge: we can say we know something only when we understand it through its causes. After this he begins his famous proof that there could be only one substance which would be absolutely infinite and thus be its own cause. These "proofs" are simply a modern version of the traditional arguments for God's existence, although in the *Ethics* they take a novel form. The burden of Spinoza's point is that either nothing exists or else a substance absolutely infinite exists. Something does exist, and the presence of such an absolutely infinite substance precludes the existence of more than one such, and it includes everything else as part of itself.

Since God, or substance, consists of infinite attributes, each one of which expresses eternal and infinite essence, God necessarily exists and excludes the existence of anything else not a part of it. Spinoza goes on to argue that such a substance cannot be divided, nor can the existence of a second such substance even be conceived. From this Spinoza turns to the statement of perhaps his most famous doctrine: whatever is, is in God, and nothing can either be or be conceived without God. Popularly this belief is called "pantheism," but such a doctrine (that the world taken as a whole is God) is too simple to express Spinoza's view. It is not enough to say that the natural order as a whole is God, for what really is true is that Spinoza takes all of the usual transcendental qualities of a traditional God and, combining them with the natural order, calls the sum of these God or substance absolutely infinite.

Spinoza's famous doctrine of the infinite attributes of God is easy proof against a simple label of pantheism. In addition to God's infinity in each kind (in thought and extension), Spinoza posits an infinity of attributes as belonging to God, only two of which (thought and extension) are known directly in our natural world. Thus God, as Spinoza conceives him, is infinitely larger than our natural order, since the world we are familiar with actually represents only a very small part of his vast nature. This is a speculative doctrine, as intriguing as it is baffling.

Since everything must be conceived through, and has its existence in, God, the knowledge of any natural event requires a reference to the divine nature. It is for this reason that Spinoza begins the *Ethics* with a discussion of God's nature, since the understanding of everything else, including man's ethical life, depends upon this. Nothing can be understood in isolation, and all adequate understanding involves locating the particular events and their immediate causes within the larger scheme of a substance absolutely infinite. God in traditional theology was used to explain the natural world as a whole; now every phenomenon is to be seen as a part of him and is to be explained on a part-whole analogy. What it is true to say about the divine nature, then, is also in some sense true of every part of the natural world.

Nothing remains unrealized in such a divine nature. Infinite numbers of things in infinite ways will all become real in the course of time, and time is without beginning or end. Rejecting medieval theories of creation, Spinoza returned to a more classical view of the world as eternal. The natural order is equal in duration with God. One side of his nature is timeless, but the side which includes the natural order is temporal. Time applies to God, but only to one aspect. And there are no alternatives to any natural fact, since infinite possibilities will all be realized eventually. God's existence is necessary and so is his production of the natural order as a part of his nature.

Although this production of the natural order is necessary and its pattern without alternative, nothing outside God's own nature compels him to act, and in that sense God's activity is free. Yet God is absolutely the only genuinely free agent; in nature there is nothing contingent, but everything is determined necessarily in whole or in part by factors and causes outside its own nature. "Will" had been stressed as a causal agent by Duns Scotus; again Spinoza reverts to a more classical doctrine and denies that will can be a free cause. Will, he says, is nothing other than reason's tendency to recognize and to accept a true idea. Things could have been produced, by God or by man, in no other manner and in no other order than they are and were.

In the Appendix to Book I, which contains the discussion of God's nature as it includes the world as a part, Spinoza goes on to elaborate his famous refutation of teleology. Christian doctrine necessarily depicts God as acting to achieve certain ends, or otherwise the drama of sin, atonement, and salvation would be difficult to present. God acts to accomplish his purpose, according to the orthodox conception. All of this Spinoza denied. According to the *Ethics*, thought is only one of God's infinite attributes, so that although he is a personal being in some sense, he is so only in part. Will has been denied and thought is not dominant; such a being cannot be said to act purposefully to attain an end unachievable without his conscious action. What happens in nature is simply the necessary outpouring of the divine, absolutely infinite substance, to which there is no alternative conceivable. Although Spinoza's first principle is different, he is very close to the traditional Neo-platonic theories of the necessary (although good) emanation of the world from God.

In Book II, Spinoza begins to trace the nature and the origin of the mind, one of the infinite things which necessarily follow from the nature of God. Although the mind is only one attribute among an infinite number, Spinoza readily admits that it concerns us most and is vitally important for ethical conduct. First he must distinguish between an idea (a concept of the mind) and an adequate idea (one which has all the internal signs of a true idea). Such a distinction is extremely important, since from it will come the whole of the later ethical theory.

For more traditional thought, God alone was considered perfect and all the natural order somehow less perfect (as is implied by a doctrine of original sin). Spinoza takes a radical position here and actually equates reality with perfection. This departure is perfectly understandable. Nothing in nature has an alternative or can be different from what it is, and all things are a part of God and follow necessarily from his nature. God could not be complete without the whole natural order. Thus, it is logical that each part of God (each aspect of the natural order) should be just as perfect as it is real.

Then Spinoza turns to another radical idea: God is extended, or material things are a part of his nature. Christian views had had to make God responsible for the creation of the physical world, but none had made God himself material even in part. Within Spinoza's view, the material world is no longer somehow less perfect, and so it can be made a part of God without lessening his perfection.

And every material thing has an idea paralleling it, although ideas affect only other ideas and physical things affect only things physical. The attribute of extension is reflected fully in the attribute of thought, although the two are only parallel and do not intersect each other. Substance thinking and substance extended are one and the same substance, now comprehended under this attribute, now under that. Nothing can happen in the body which is not perceived by the mind, and the essence of man consists of certain modifications of the attributes of God. We perceive all things through God, although some perceptions may be confused.

How is such confusion as does arise to be corrected? All ideas, insofar as they are related to God, are true. Thus, correct understanding means to take the idea and to place it in its proper locus within the divine nature, rather than to treat it as an independent phenomenon. No idea in itself is false; it is simply improperly related to other ideas if it is confused. For instance, men are sometimes deceived in thinking themselves to be free, but this simply reflects their ignorance of the total causal chain within the divine nature of which their actions are a part. When actions are viewed in isolation, such confusion is possible, although no idea in itself is false.

It is the nature of reason to perceive things under a certain form of eternity and to consider them as necessary. Temporal viewpoints and a belief in contingency simply reflect an unimproved reason, unable to assume its natural viewpoint. For the human mind is actually able to possess an adequate knowledge of the eternal and infinite essence of God. In many previous theological views, the human mind was thought incapable of comprehending God. For Spinoza the human mind is to be seen as a part of the divine intellect, and as such it has within its own nature the possibility for grasping the whole of the divine mind, although to do so requires a great deal of effort.

When Book III begins to discuss the emotions, we begin what ordinarily we would call the ethical part of the work proper. Even here, however, Spinoza's approach is not standard; he claims that no one before has determined both the nature and the strength of the emotions or has treated the vices and follies of men in a geometrical method. And the emotions (hatred, anger, envy) follow from the same necessity as do all other things in nature. Aristotle and others thought that conduct was not amenable to scientific knowledge, but Spinoza's natural necessity, plus the connection of every event with the divine nature, subjects the emotions to the same laws as those which govern all natural phenomena.

Spinoza says that we act when we are the adequate cause of anything; we suffer when we are the cause only partially. An emotion is a modification of the body's power to act. The emotion is an action and the body's power is increased when we are the adequate cause of the modification; the emotion is passive and the body's power of acting is decreased when we are only partially the cause. Our mind acts when it has adequate ideas; it suffers necessarily when it has inadequate ideas.

The law of existence, Spinoza tells us, is that everything should do its utmost to persevere in its own mode of being. This striving is the very essence of every living thing. We feel "joy" when we are able to pass to a higher state of being; we feel "sorrow" when through passivity and suffering we pass to a lower state. Joy, sorrow, and desire are the primary emotions. Love attaches to the things which give us joy (an active and a higher existence); hatred attaches to what gives us sorrow (a passive and a lowered existence). Naturally we endeavor to support those things which cause joy, and just as naturally we tend to destroy whatever we imagine causes us sorrow. Love can overcome hatred and thus increase our joy, and Spinoza recommends that we attempt to return love for hate for that reason. On the other hand, Spinoza feels that the traditional Christian virtue of humility produces impotence and sorrow and is to be avoided for that reason.

Spinoza is often thought of as an unrestrained optimist concerning the powers of human reason, but his treatment of human bondage in Book IV should correct any such impression. In one of the longest books in the *Ethics*, Spinoza outlines in detail the inevitable causes which bind men to the blindness of their emotions and work against any attempted liberation. Good and evil are defined here as, respectively, what is useful to us and what hinders us from possessing something good. Appetite is what causes us to do anything, and virtue and power are defined as being the same thing. Here we have a classical definition of a naturalistic ethical theory.

If our only virtue is whatever power we possess naturally, and if good means only what is useful to us, what on earth could bind men? Spinoza says that there is no individual thing in nature not surpassed in strength and power by some other thing, which means that our power is always threatened and our current well-being always subject to loss. Other things are stronger than we are and continually challenge our powers, which places us in bondage to the passive emotions (sorrow) which necessarily accompany any such threat. The force which we have at our disposal is limited and is infinitely surpassed by the power of external causes. We suffer insofar as we find ourselves to be merely a part of nature surpassed in power and thus threatened by the other parts.

An emotion can be restrained or removed only by an opposed and stronger emotion. Thus our ability to withstand the pressures around us, to prevent sorrow, depends upon our natural power to oppose the emotions surrounding us with an equal vigor. Such a task never ceases and any victory is constantly in danger of being reversed in a weak or lax moment. Yet the highest virtue of the mind is said to be to know God. Why? Simply because such knowledge renders our ideas more adequate; and, as our ideas become more adequate, our power of action is increased. Men disagree as far as their ideas are disturbed by emotions; when guided by reason they tend to understand and thus to agree.

In Book V Spinoza turns finally to an appraisal of the powers of the intellect which make it free, since freedom comes only through the possibility of increased understanding. The primary fact upon which he bases his hope for human freedom is that an emotion which is a passion, and thus destructive of our power, ceases to be a passion as soon as we form a clear idea of it. Thus, we cannot prevent the constant challenge to our power to continue our existence, but we can come to understand all the causes which play upon us. To the extent to which we understand the causes impinging on us, just to that extent we can successfully oppose any threat to our freedom or our power.

There is nothing of which we cannot, theoretically speaking, form an adequate idea, including of course God himself. The way toward increasing freedom is open and is identical with an increased understanding. Such striving toward an increase of our understanding has for its object all or part of God. This is the highest effort of the mind and its highest virtue, since it is the source of the individual's increased power of existence. Such understanding is rarely achieved and is exceedingly difficult, but its unobstructed possibility is a challenge to men and is the source of such freedom as man may have.— *F.S.*

PERTINENT LITERATURE

Wolfson, Harry Austryn. *The Philosophy of Spinoza: Unfolding the Latent Processes of His Reasoning*. Cambridge, Massachusetts: Harvard University Press, 1934.

In this enormously erudite work, written with clarity and good humor, Harry Austryn Wolfson set out to answer three questions about Benedictus de Spinoza's chief work, the *Ethics*: what he said, how he came to say it, and why he said it that way. Spinoza's use of the geometrical method of exposition, though intended to aid clarity as well as rigor, in fact by its terseness often led to baffling obscurity. Moreover, Spinoza is unique among the great philosophers of the European tradition in having been importantly influenced by the Talmud and medieval and renaissance Jewish writers who in their turn incorporate teachings of the Islamic philosophers; and so back to the Neoplatonists and Aristotle. Thus Wolfson's historicocritical method, whereby Spinoza's doctrines are exhibited as developments in these series, demands a rare combination of scholarly abilities. His aim is no less than the reconstruction of the scholasticorabbinical treatise which, he maintains, would express the actual manner in which Spinoza did his thinking.

The first volume in its entirety is devoted to proposition-by-proposition discussion of *Ethics*, Part I, "Of God." Beginning with consideration of the definitions of *substance* as what is in itself and conceived through itself, and of *mode* as in and conceived through another, Wolfson interprets "conceived through" as referring to the relation of genus to species. He consequently holds that substance for Spinoza is related to modes as genus is to species. Substance or God, as highest genus, is not conceivable at all. The attributes of thought and extension, which the intellect perceives as if constituting God's essence, are held to be subjective: inventions of the mind, not discoveries. Although he does not mention Immanuel Kant in this connection, Wolfson's interpretation seems to make Spinoza an anticipator of the doctrine of space and time as forms of intuition.

The second volume is a commentary, briefer but still very full, on Parts II-V of the *Ethics*. In his concluding chapter, "What is New in Spinoza?," Wolfson summarizes the results of his study in the contention that Spinoza's originality consisted not in advancing new philosophical principles but in relentlessly drawing the logical conclusions of premises accepted by his prede-

cessors. In particular he is credited with four "acts of daring": 1. Attributing
extension to God. 2. Denying design and purpose in God. 3. Denying the
separability of body and soul in man. 4. Denying freedom of the will. These
theses eliminate all the traditional dualities from philosophy: mind/body,
God/creation, teleology/mechanism, and freedom/necessity. What results is
a philosophy of nature as an infinite unified organic whole. God-Nature-
Substance manifests itself to our limited intellects in two types of action:
thought and motion, each of which is subsumable under necessary laws. This
conception is of course most acceptable to the scientific spirit. It is, however,
one that theologians can hardly accept, even if logically implied by their
principles. On this view God, while conscious, lacks personality—he does
not, for example, reward and punish. Spinoza's theology, then, is essentially
a return to Aristotle's, which Wolfson characterizes as that of God as "an
eternal paralytic." Wolfson maintains that Spinoza failed to realize the extent
to which his thought was a breaking away from traditional theology, believing—naïvely in Wolfson's estimation—that the dictates of reason would provide effective guides to conduct, and that the indestructibility of mind-stuff
would afford the same kind of emotional reassurance in the face of death that
was purveyed by the traditional doctrine of immortality.

Curley, E. M. *Spinoza's Metaphysics: An Essay in Interpretation*. Cambridge, Massachusetts: Harvard University Press, 1969.

This elegant study looks at Benedictus de Spinoza "through lenses ground
by Russell, Moore, and Wittgenstein," presenting an original and provocative
interpretation.

E. M. Curley begins by rejecting two conceptions of the substance/mode
relation. He contends that the view of Pierre Bayle and H. H. Joachim,
according to which substance is ontologically that in which attributes and
modes inhere and logically the designatum of the subject in propositions
whose predicates refer to attributes and modes, should not be attributed to
Spinoza, who neither speaks of "subjects" nor distinguishes substance from
attributes. Spinoza was in fact the first to break with the tradition, going back
to Aristotle, that conflated the different distinctions substance/mode and sub-
ject/predicate. The Harry Austryn Wolfson interpretation, that substance is
highest genus, of which the modes are species, is attacked with seven arguments, of which the most telling point out conflicts with the text. Wolfson's
account has the consequence, drawn explicitly by its author, that substance-
God is indefinable and unknowable. Spinoza specifically inveighed against
this view, however, and even purported to prove that the human mind has
an adequate idea of God's essence. Curley draws the moral that the historical
approach can be overdone.

Turning to his positive account, Curley takes as the basis of his interpretation Spinoza's repeated assertion that substance is the cause of the modes, and his assimilation or at least analogy of cause-effect to ground-consequent. The author sets up a "model metaphysic" having these features: A set of propositions completely describing the world of extended objects is assumed to exist. Some of the propositions will describe singular facts (not things), some accidental generalizations ("All the bodies in this room weigh less than 150 pounds"), some nomological generalizations (laws of nature). Nomologicals are necessary truths and thus support counterfactual inferences. They are not reducible to truth functions of singulars. Every singular proposition follows from a nomological plus another singular. The nomologicals can be organized into a deductive system. General nomological facts correspond to the nomological propositions.

This model, which amounts to an ideal of unified science, is applied to Spinoza's system by equating the basic (most general) nomological facts to the attribute of extension; the derivative nomological facts to the infinite modes; and the singular facts to the finite modes. Thus the finite modes (facts) can be deduced from axioms and theorems (expressing the nature of God) plus singular propositions (other finite modes, that is, God insofar as modified by finite modifications). Spinoza's determinism thus consists in affirming that everything that happens can in principle be explained by laws of nature plus a specification of antecedent conditions.

Is the model an exact fit? Curley discusses whether it captures Spinoza's conception of necessity. In the model, nomologicals are absolutely necessary, but singulars are necessary only relative to their singular causes. From this it follows that there is more than one possible world—contrary, so it seems, to Spinoza's view. Curley suggests, however, that Spinoza meant only that there could not be another world *besides* the existent one. He concludes, nevertheless, that Spinoza was wrong if he supposed that there is in principle an answer to the question "Why does the world containing just these facts exist, rather than some other consistent set of facts?" There must be at least one brute fact, after all.

On the question of the divine attributes, Curley considers and rejects the view that the identity of thought and extension can be translated into the current theory of mind-body identity, for the reason that watches (for example) do not have thoughts (and Spinoza, so Curley insists, was aware of the fact). Curley's view is that the attribute of extension is the set of facts; ideas (the attribute of thought) are true propositions describing the facts. He holds, furthermore, with most commentators, that consciousness is not ideas but ideas of ideas. These conscious ideas, he suggests, express propositional attitudes: for example, if p is an idea, then the idea of the idea might be of the form "A knows that p."

Curley tries to explain the Spinozistic doctrine of immortality, but in the end confesses to finding it "completely unintelligible." In a postscript he indulges in historical criticism to the extent of explaining Spinoza's philosophy as principally a reaction against René Descartes: in particular, Spinoza insisted that the world is thoroughly intelligible, contrary to the Cartesian account which rests its nature ultimately on the inscrutable will of God.

Hampshire, Stuart. "A Kind of Materialism," in *Proceedings and Addresses of the American Philosophical Association*. XLIII (1970), pp. 5-23.

In this short paper, his Presidential Address to the American Philosophical Association, Stuart Hampshire takes up the problem of how a consistent materialist can hold both that his thoughts and sentiments are embedded in a physical, determined order, and also strive, and exhort others to strive, to alter those thoughts and sentiments for the better. He attributes his answer to Benedictus de Spinoza "rather freely interpreted."

The starting assumption of the consistent and self-conscious materialist is that human acquisition of knowledge must be studied like any other capacity of a living organism: by looking at the observable, therefore physical, mechanisms involved. These will be complex, perhaps of types not yet recognized in physics. At the same time, the materialist keeps himself in focus both as observer and observed. He thinks of people as intricate instruments reacting to environment, but also as internally determined to explore the world in light of their stored knowledge. If knowledge is determined by interests and purposes, however, and the latter also by the former, how can he get out of the circle? By considering the reflexive forms of thought: he knows that even in elementary perceptual situations he must make allowances for his own physical situation. Thus he can distinguish the real from the apparent order of things, whether in ordinary perception or at the highest level of scientific inquiry.

Let us think of all thought, not just perception, as entailing the reflective use of a physical mechanism. All thought thus becomes a kind of perception, although abstract thought is relatively independent of the immediate environment. Knowing brain physiology would enable the philosopher to make corrections analogous to those in perception. We already do this with the more obvious emotions.

The crass materialist tries to eliminate reference to thoughts and feelings in favor of physiological descriptions. The self-conscious materialist, however, replies that while physical knowledge can be put to use in correcting thought, it cannot substitute for what it corrects, any more than the listener can substitute acoustical theory for listening. True, one can make the substitution when merely observing someone else, but not in one's own case. If, for example, the philosopher knows the physiology of anger and becomes angry at someone, he will evaluate his angry thoughts in light of his belief about the physical causes, distinguishing the case where the anger is a mere physical reaction from that in which it is a standard mode of perception of the offending object.

Science has shown us how to correct our perceptions—for example, of the size of the sun. Indeed, the scientific man sees the sun differently from the way the child or savage sees it. Analogously, in the psychology of the sentiments another Copernican revolution is needed. We presently do not think of passions as psychophysical phenomena issuing from complicated causes. Interpretation in light of physiology would correct these self-centered perceptions. The self-conscious materialist would grow more detached. This does not mean that the first impression would vanish; but it would be understood and corrected if correction were needed.

The self-conscious materialist will regard other people as organisms whose sentiments are alterable by changes in their physical states, and also by arguments convincing them that their thoughts about the causes of those states are erroneous. In the materialist's own case, the two methods of correction collapse into one.

Thinking about the causes of one's psychophysical states changes those states. If I think of my fear as causally independent of the feared object, I bracket my fear of that object. Even if the fear does not vanish, it at least is altered, becoming more complicated.

The materialist, however, does not regard the relation between the sentiment and the physical state as a causal one. It is much closer. Knowing that such is the case, the self-conscious materialist knows that his limited power to change his psychophysical states depends on his power to bring more systematic knowledge of their causes to bear. Such power must itself be embodied in an internal physical structure. It is therefore not pointless or inconsistent for the materialist to urge men to recognize their powers of reflection, to be active, not passive. This is the sense and point of Spinoza's so-called double aspect theory of personality, and the thought behind *Ethics*, Book II, Proposition 22: "The human mind not only perceives the affections of the body, but also the ideas of these affections."—*W.I.M.*

ADDITIONAL RECOMMENDED READING

Allison, Henry E. *Benedict De Spinoza*. Boston: Twayne, 1975. Intended for the general reader and student.

Bidney, David. *The Psychology and Ethics of Spinoza*. New Haven, Connecticut: Yale University Press, 1940. The most thorough study of *Ethics*, Parts III-V.

Freeman, Eugene and Maurice Mandelbaum, eds. *Spinoza: Essays in Interpretation*. La Salle, Illinois: Open Court, 1974. Contains a good bibliography of works on Spinoza published 1960-1972.

Hampshire, Stuart. *Spinoza*. Harmondsworth, England: Penguin Books, 1951. A general introduction by a leading Spinoza scholar.

Harris, Errol. *Salvation from Despair: A Reappraisal of Spinoza's Philosophy*. The Hague, The Netherlands: Martinus Nijhoff, 1973. An interpretation emphasizing the ethical and religious significance of Spinoza's philosophy.

Joachim, Harold H. *A Study of the Ethics of Spinoza*. Oxford: Clarendon Press, 1901. A meticulous study, the standard commentary before Wolfson's, and still very worth reading.

Kashap, S. Paul, ed. *Studies in Spinoza*. Berkeley: University of California Press, 1972. The first collection of essays on Spinoza, including a number of classical studies.

McKeon, Richard. *The Philosophy of Spinoza*. New York: Longmans Green, 1928. A lucid study emphasizing the close connection of science and ethics, in Spinoza and in general.

Mark, Thomas C. *Spinoza's Theory of Truth*. New York: Columbia University Press, 1972. The author proposes a view according to which Spinoza held neither a correspondence nor a coherence but an "ontological" theory of truth—"truth as being."

Pollock, Sir Frederick. *Spinoza: His Life and Philosophy*. London: C. K. Paul, 1880. A valuable general survey.

Shahan, Robert W. and J. I. Biro, eds. *Spinoza: New Perspectives*. Norman: University of Oklahoma Press, 1978. A collection of essays.

Van Der Bend, J. G., ed. *Spinoza on Knowing, Being and Freedom*. Assen, The Netherlands: Van Gorcum, 1974. A collection of papers read at a Spinoza symposium held in the Netherlands.

DIALOGUES ON METAPHYSICS AND ON RELIGION

Author: Nicolas de Malebranche (1638-1715)
Type of work: Metaphysics, theology
First published: 1688

PRINCIPAL IDEAS ADVANCED

Human beings exist as thinking beings; they are not material bodies.

The only world we know is an intelligible world, the world of our ideas; but since the ideas have an eternal, infinite, necessary character that is independent of our conception, they must be features of an intelligible extension.

Intelligible extension has its locus in God, but it should not be identified with God.

We understand certain truths only because God illuminates the ideas.

When an event involving the body occurs, an event involving the soul occurs as a result of God's action; in this manner human beings have feelings. [*Occasionalism.*]

The universe contains three types of beings: God, mind, and body; of the three, God alone is an active agent in the universe.

Father Nicolas de Malebranche was the chief Cartesian philosopher of the late seventeenth century. He was a member of the Augustinian religious order of the Oratory in Paris, where he originally devoted himself to the studies of ecclesiastical history, biblical criticism, and Hebrew. At the age of twenty-six he came across a work by René Descartes and was so impressed by its method and the theory it contained that he devoted the next several years to studying Cartesian philosophy and mathematics. The first fruits of these studies appeared in 1674-1675 in his famous work *The Search After Truth* (*De la recherche de la vérité*), in which he developed his modified version of Cartesian philosophy. The work was immediately successful and was translated into several languages, including English. It was studied and discussed by major thinkers everywhere and soon led to a series of polemical controversies between Malebranche and his opponents. His *Dialogues on Metaphysics and on Religion* presents a more literary and definitive version of his theory, as well as answers to many of his critics. It has remained the most popular expression of Malebranche's theory of knowledge and his metaphysics.

Malebranche's views were tremendously influential in their own day. For a period, he was the most important metaphysician in Europe, providing the theory that was debated everywhere. Among the thinkers who were greatly influenced by Malebranche's views were the Irish philosopher George Berkeley and the Scottish skeptic David Hume. Though his works were severely criticized by the Jesuits, and some of his writings were placed on the Index,

Malebranche had, and continues to have, an enormous influence among French philosophers.

The *Dialogues* is written more in the style of St. Augustine than of Plato. It presents a statement of Malebranche's theories rather than a discussion of philosophical issues. In it two spokesmen for Malebranche expound his views to a student, Aristes, and correct the latter's misunderstandings.

The first dialogue begins with Theodore instructing Aristes in the method of finding philosophical truth. Understanding should be gained through reason. Hence, for the time being, faith is not taken as a source of knowledge. The sensuous or material world should be ignored, so that the senses and the imagination will not interfere with the pursuit of rational knowledge. With this much in mind, the analysis of what rational truths we can possess is begun.

Since nothing, or non-being, can have no qualities, I, who think, must exist. (I have at least the quality of thinking; hence, I cannot be nothing, or nonexistent.) But what am I? I am not a body, because a body is only a piece of extension. When I examine my idea of a body, the only properties that I find belonging to it are extensional ones, relations of distance. Thought is not a property or type of extension, since thoughts cannot be defined in terms of distances, and since they can be conceived without reference to any properties of extension. Hence, our conception of ourselves is totally different from our conception of bodies. (Malebranche offers these considerations as evidence that we are not material bodies.)

When we examine our ideas, we find that what we are directly acquainted with is an intelligible world, and not a material one. We know ideas, and not physical things. Even if all material objects disappeared, our ideas might remain the same. Since everything that we can know is an idea, it is only the intelligible world that directly concerns us. When we inspect this intelligible world of our ideas, we find that it has an eternal, immutable, and necessary structure that is not in any way dependent on our thinking about it. Truths, such as 3 times 3 equals 9, are always true and they must be true. I do not decide or will that they be true; instead, I am forced to recognize and accept their truth. Further, the truths of the intelligible world are infinite, in that they apply to an infinite number of objects. Hence, these necessary and unchangeable truths must apply not just to the limited, finite number of things in my mind, but to what Malebranche calls "intelligible extension"—the entire rational world of concepts.

All of this is intended to show that the world of intelligible extension, the realm of true ideas, cannot be a feature of my mind. Intelligible extension has a structure unlike that of myself, in that it is eternal, infinite, immutable, and necessary. Hence, though I am aware of certain aspects of intelligible extension, it must be located elsewhere, in something that possesses the actual characteristics of the intelligible world; namely, God.

The second dialogue deals with the nature and existence of God. Malebranche emphatically denies that intelligible extension is God. Such a view would be similar to that held by Benedictus de Spinoza. Instead, Malebranche contends that the recognition of intelligible extension makes us realize *that* God is, since he alone can be the locus of intelligible extension. But this does not tell us *what* God is. In fact, we know of God only in relation to what he makes us know, or by what he illuminates for us. Anytime that we have any knowledge, we know that God exists, but we never know his nature.

To clarify this point, Malebranche argues that God is unlimited Perfection or Being or Infinite Reality. No idea of mine can represent such a Being, since all of my ideas are determinate. In this lifetime, we cannot attain a clear idea of what God is. We can only see that he is, and how he is related to everything that we know. We realize that the proposition "There is a God" is obviously true, and that God's essence includes his existence, but we cannot understand what his nature really is.

According to Malebranche, "We see all things in God," but we do not actually see him. The ideas we have that constitute knowledge do not properly belong to our own minds, but rather to intelligible extension. Because of the characteristics of intelligible extension, it must be located in God. Hence, whenever we know something, we are seeing a truth in God, and seeing it because he illumines it for us. In this respect, Malebranche's theory of knowledge differs sharply from Descartes'. According to the latter, we establish truths about reality from the clear and distinct ideas in our own minds. Descartes contended that since God gave us these ideas, and since he is no deceiver, whatever is clear and distinct about our ideas must be true of the real universe as well. Critics have noted that Descartes never succeeded in building a bridge from his ideas of reality. Malebranche removes the need for bridge building by insisting that the ideas are not located in *man's* mind, but are in God's Mind. A truth is a direct observation of intelligible extension in God, and we see what is God's Mind because he illuminates the ideas and enables us to see them. Thus, Malebranche's theory is a type of direct Platonic realism. The only truths are truths about the world of ideas, and these are known not by inference from the contents of our minds, but by direct vision of the Divine Mind.

In the third, fourth, and fifth dialogues, Malebranche discusses the relation of ideas to sense information. Ideas are intelligible. This means that they can be defined, so that we can understand why they have the characteristics they do. In terms of this conception of "ideas," the only ideas we have are divine ones. We do not have an idea of ourselves because we do not know our own natures completely, and we cannot make ourselves know ourselves. We do not have ideas of our sense experiences, which Malebranche calls "feelings," since we cannot give clear definitions of them.

In a famous passage, Aristes and Theodore appropriately illustrate this point by discussing music. When one tries to make intelligible the real reason why we hear the sounds we do, the explanation is in terms of the mathematical relationships of vibrating strings, and not in terms of experienced qualities. The mathematical relationships can be defined in terms of the ideas involved in intelligible extension. But the sounds cannot be defined, only "felt." Also, we can discover no intelligible connection between the vibrations and the felt sounds. (Does a certain sound experience *have* to be the result of vibrations of a certain frequency?)

What we can understand relates only to the realm of ideas, the realm of intelligible extension. Sense qualities are not features of our mathematical ideas, for, as far as we know, they are only feelings in us. There is nothing in the mathematical relationships that we can understand about moving bodies that explains the occurrence of these feelings. The ideas that we have of bodies allow us to understand them in terms of the principles of mathematical physics without reference to our feelings.

Then, what accounts for our having feelings, and experiencing them in some orderly relation to physical events? In giving his answer, Malebranche presents his theory of "occasionalism." Bodies cannot cause feelings, since bodies are only extended objects moving. We cannot be the cause of our feelings, since we have no control of them. God, then, must be the cause, giving us a certain set of feelings whenever certain physical events occur. There must be laws of the conjunction of the soul and the body by which God operates on both substances, so that when an event happens to one, a corresponding event happens to the other. Each of these events is the "occasion" but not the cause of the other's occurrence. There is no necessary connection between a physical event and a mental event. God, acting according to general laws he has laid down, causes two independent sets of events, the physical ones and the feelings and ideas. The mind and the body have no contact with each other. But God wills incessantly and produces a sequence of physical events that are correlated with a conjoined series of mental events. By means of the system God employs, we ascertain, through discovering the general laws God provides, what is necessary for our self-preservation. Our feelings alert us to our bodily needs, so that we seek food when we have the feeling of hunger, and so on.

The sense "feelings" that God gives us serve not only as warning signs for the care and maintenance of our bodies (which we would otherwise know nothing about, since our knowledge is only about ideas), but also as the occasions for our becoming aware of truths about ideas. The diagrams employed in mathematics, which are only sensations, cannot teach us since they do not contain the pure ideas. But, they can function as cues, attracting our attention to the truths we can learn from reason. Learning actually consists of our being made aware of some fact about the intelligible world, and of being made aware of this fact by God, who alone has the power to make us think and know.

The sixth and seventh dialogues bring out the crucial characteristics of Malebranche's metaphysical theory, showing why God is the sole causal agent in the universe. The universe contains three types of beings: God, whose existence can be demonstrated from his definition; mind, which can be directly apprehended through its mental processes, though it cannot be clearly known; and bodies, whose existence is known only by Revelation. The last point startles Aristes, and so Theodore examines the evidence available for the existence of bodies.

We do not know bodies by ideas, since our ideas are of intelligible extension, and not of physical extension. We do not feel bodies, since our feelings are only modifications of our own souls, caused by God in consequence of his general laws. In terms of what we know and feel, it is quite possible that bodies do not exist at all. Our knowledge and our experience could be exactly the same, since God directly causes all, whether bodies exist or do not exist. In fact, Malebranche goes on to argue, we cannot show that bodies must exist, but we can show that God need not create bodies. If God is infinitely perfect, there is no reason why he has to create anything. It is compatible with God's nature either that he has created a physical world or that he has not. If it could be shown that he had to create a physical world, then God would not be perfect (and, as Malebranche interprets this term, self-sufficient). He would require something other than himself; namely, what he had to create. Since, by definition, God is dependent on nothing, if he created a physical world, he did it arbitrarily and not necessarily. What Malebranche, in effect, claims is that no necessary conclusion about the nature of created things follows from the concept of an all-perfect, omnipotent deity.

If all of this is accepted, then is there any reason to believe that bodies do, in fact, exist? First, there are some proofs which are convincing but not conclusive. The constancy of our experience, along with our natural inclination to attribute our experiences to bodies, persuades us that there are bodies. But this persuasion could be erroneous, since we know that we could have the experiences we do, together with an inclination to believe certain things about these experiences, without there being any bodies—God could produce all such effects in us. The decisive evidence, according to Malebranche, is given by faith, in the statements that appear in the beginning of the book of Genesis, where we are told that God created heaven and earth. (Bishop Berkeley later disputed whether the text in question says anything about whether God created a physical world, or whether it refers only to a world of ideas.)

In the seventh dialogue, the climax of this metaphysical view is reached. A third character, Theotimus, is introduced, who is a spokesman for Malebranche's theological views. Theodore and Theotimus together defend the theory that God alone is an efficacious agent in the universe. It had already been shown that unaided minds have no power, but receive only those ideas and feelings that God wills to give them. Now it is argued that bodies are also powerless, since their sole defining properties are extensional, that is, relations of distance. Bodies exist only because of God's will, and their particular location at any moment must also be due to God. If all this is the case, then obviously bodies cannot be the cause of their own motions, or of the motions of each other. Only God can be. The same point can be brought out from God's side. If he is omnipotent, then nothing besides God can have any power to act. If it did, then there would be something God could not do, namely, control the actions of a particular object. God's omnipotence implies, according to Malebranche, that God is the only possible active agent in the entire universe. This point is made in the striking assertion that not all the angels and demons acting together can move a bit of straw unless God so wills.

Then, what makes the world operate? In general, God's will. In particular, the world proceeds according to general laws that God provides. Malebranche insists that God wills according to the principle of economy that the smallest set of fixed laws should be employed. God can change everything at any moment, since he is the only active agent. But, because he wills in keeping with his principle of economy, effects continue to occur in lawful sequences, which we can learn through the study of nature. The world as we know it, since it is the effect of God's will, can only be described, never explained. We never know any reason *why* events happen, beyond the general formula that God so wills them. There is no necessary connection between events. Hence, the created world must be known descriptively, not logically.

The remainder of the *Dialogues* deals with Malebranche's theology, in which the author tries to show that his version of Cartesian philosophy is in accord with Christian doctrine and in which he attempts to answer some of the theological objections that had been raised.

To an extent, Malebranche's theory represented the culmination of the grand tradition of seventeenth century metaphysical inquiry. Starting with Descartes, the "new philosophers" had tried to explain why the world discovered by modern science must have the characteristics it does. Malebranche, by consistently following out some of the main themes of Descartes, reduced the hope of reaching a rational explanation of the world to nothing, leaving only theology, instead of philosophy, as the source of knowledge about the world. Berkeley and Hume then followed out some of Malebranche's insights, after which Hume reduced the theological vision of Malebranche to a complete skepticism.—*R.H.P.*

PERTINENT LITERATURE

Gilson, Étienne and Thomas Langan. *Modern Philosophy: Descartes to Kant*. New York: Random House, 1963.

According to Étienne Gilson and Thomas Langan, Nicolas de Malebranche was a follower of René Descartes who wished to use Cartesianism as a means of justifying and explaining traditional Catholic doctrine. He accepted the legitimacy of Cartesian doubt whereby one suspends judgment concerning every claim that it is even possible to doubt. What we know, or are acquainted with, are, for Malebranche, our own representations or mental states, not physical objects.

Gilson and Langan report Malebranche's view that some of the representations, those which are objects of perception and imagination, are not clear and distinct. They are not expressible quantitatively. These are sentiments, according to Malebranche, and in this sense to perceive color or heat is to have a sentiment. To perceive extension is to have an *idea*. Ideas do, and sentiments do not, provide reliable guides to the qualities possessed by external objects.

Malebranche contends that we ascribe colors and other secondary qualities (secondary qualities are qualities perceived by, or proper to, only one sense) to external objects because our perception of them is passive; they appear unbidden in our perceptual field. But, Malebranche notes, while this explains our tendency to ascribe them to objects, it is not a reason or justification for our doing so. Gilson and Langan explain that Malebranche views the importance of sentiments as practical, not for providing knowledge of the nature of external objects "but only for the conservation of our body."

By contrast, the idea of extension, capable of quantitative and mathematical expression, is a reliable guide to the qualities possessed by external objects. (The class of primary qualities—qualities accessible to more than one sense—and the class of qualities that are quantitative or capable of being mathematically expressed, is coextensive.) Still, Malebranche says, this does not mean that we perceive external, physical objects in the sense that our perceptual experiences are caused by them.

Gilson and Langan add that relevant to his rejection of both the view that we simply directly perceive physical objects, and the view that we perceive something caused by them, is Malebranche's doctrine that we "see all things in God." They note that he does not claim, as Descartes had done, that because we have a natural inescapable tendency to believe that there are physical objects, and, since God is the author of our natures he is a deceiver if this belief is false, that there must be external objects. Nor, indeed, they add, have we, in Malebranche's view, a clear and distinct idea of God, since his essence is beyond our ken. His view is that whatever ideas we do have are caused by God, and that the existence of God is evident to us not in spite of, but even because of, the fact that we have no idea of him. Nor, they continue, for Malebranche, have we a clear and distinct idea of our own self or soul, which he claims that we confusedly feel but do not lucidly cognize. Malebranche holds that our clear and distinct ideas cluster about the idea of an intelligible, mathematically expressible, extended material world.

Gilson and Langan explain that in his *Recherche de la vérité* Malebranche considers four explanations of the fact that we are able to have abstract ideas and discern universal, general truths. One is the doctrine of abstraction; in our sensory experience, we notice common characteristics of which we form concepts, and we notice recurrent events, from which we formulate generalizations. Another is the doctrine that we are created with all ideas latent within us, which are then elicited by experience as our lives unfold. Still another is that our self or soul is sufficiently perfect, and our concept of it sufficiently excellent, that from our self-concept we can deduce the other concepts we have. Yet another is the doctrine that ideas whose possession yields knowledge of universal truths are produced by the mind on its own.

Gilson and Langan indicate that Malebranche claims that abstraction from sensory experience cannot yield abstract concepts or evident, general, universal truths. The idea of God creating us with a massive stock of ideas or a massive idea-potential possesses little by way of simplicity or elegance. According to Malebranche, they say, we have no such excellent self-concept as Descartes ascribes to us. Nor has the mind the power to produce ideas from nothing. So while everyone, for example, knows, or easily can be brought to know, elementary mathematical and logical truths, none of these alternatives explains how.

As explanation of such knowledge, Gilson and Langan note, Malebranche proffers the Augustinian notion that everyone is illumined by a single rational mind. Each rational creature is particular. But basic rational insights and capacities are universally shared. Malebranche reasons, they continue, that sentiments are particular and idiosyncratic. Any idea is particular, but its content is universal and nonidiosyncratic. There is a divine, rational cause of our ideas and our common knowledge of evident truths.

This brings us to Malebranche's parallelism. Descartes was an interactionist. He held that mental events can and do cause physical events, and that physical events can and do cause mental events. Malebranche disagreed, holding that minds and bodies, being of different kinds, could not have causal concourse. But they seem to do so. Worry seems to cause ulcers; and bumping one's shins seems to cause pain. What happens, Malebranche contends, is that, on the occasion of one's bumping one's shins, God causes one to feel pain; and, given the occasions of frequent worrying, God causes an ulcer.

Further, for Malebranche, a body is an extended thing, and as such has no activity or causal capacity in its nature. He holds, Gilson and Langan explain, that no physical event can cause any other physical event. (Nor can any mental event cause any other mental events.) Each event, he says, is caused by God. His reasoning, they explain, is that to cause an event is to make it the case that a substance comes to have a modification; this is an act of creation, and only God can create. So only God is a cause. This gives us, Gilson and Langan conclude, Malebranche's occasionalism. Since God creates in accord with laws he has ordained, there is order in the creation. Malebranche does not think that his occasionalism entails determinism, for he holds that while God determines what inclinations a person has, he does not determine whether a person consents to his or her inclinations, and it is in the capacity to give or withhold such consent that freedom lies. In order to hold this view, Malebranche must and does deny that giving or withholding consent is a modification of the soul.

Radner, Daisie. *Malebranche*. Assen, The Netherlands: Van Gorcum, 1978.

A seventeenth century philosopher, Daisie Radner notes, could react to René Descartes' philosophy in a variety of ways. According to Radner, Antoine Arnauld became a disciple; Thomas Hobbes rejected it and produced an alternative; Benedictus de Spinoza tried to solve its problems by dropping some of its basic tenets; and Nicolas de Malebranche retained the essentials without accepting all of the details.

Radner reminds us that Descartes' ontology, or doctrine of what there is, was one of substance and mode; for Descartes, anything that exists is either a substance or a mode of a substance. A substance is something that subsists by itself (or with the concourse of God alone). A mode, or modification, is a property or state of some substance—"substance itself in a certain manner." Radner reports that Malebranche accepts this ontology, and notes that the definition of "mode" leads to certain principles: (1) that a mode cannot exist save as it is a mode of some substance, (2) a mode can belong to only one substance, (3) a mode cannot be conceived without also conceiving the substance whose it is, (4) a mode cannot be located other than where its substance is, (5) a mode cannot go from one substance to another, (6) a thing can bring about a mode only if it can bring about a substance, and (7) a mode cannot have greater extent than its substance.

Radner tells us that Descartes had remarked that a property or quality could not be a property or quality of nothing; a mode or modification cannot be nothing's mode or modification. This, she says, is the background for (1). Nor, Malebranche contends, can a mode be the mode of some substance other than the one to which it initially belongs. Even if two modes are identical in quality, they are numerically different. Radner's account of Malebranche's meaning can be put as follows: If Jane and Sally simultaneously see the same red dragon against the same black background, and their visual fields have exactly the same content, there is Jane's seeing the dragon, and also Sally's. Although both see the same dragon, there is a modal complexity which we might characterize as *seeing the dragon (Jane)* and *seeing the dragon (Sally)*. This is the context for (2).

Malbranche claims, Radner indicates, that a substance, but not a mode, can be "conceived by itself." She explains that, for Malebranche, the idea of *A necessarily involves* that of *B* if *A*'s definition includes reference to *B*. For Malebranche, the idea of a substance does not necessarily involve the idea of some particular mode, but the idea of a mode does necessarily involve the idea of some particular substance. This, she suggests, is part of the context of reasoning behind (3). That behind (4), Radner tells us, is simply that, since a mode is only a modification of a substance in some manner, obviously a manner in which a substance is characterized or modified will be located where the substance is. For material substances, "location" will be "location in space." Pain and color are modifications of minds, or immaterial substances, and will be states of consciousness of (and so "located in," in that sense) a mind, although they have no location in space.

Radner informs us that Henry More queried Descartes as to how motion, "which cannot exist outside of its subject," can pass from one substance to another, and Descartes granted that, in his view, a motion, being a mode of some particular body, cannot be transferred from one body to another. (A crucial consideration here, as elsewhere in reasoning regarding modes, is that reference to exactly one substance is involved in defining, and so in stating, the identity conditions of any particular mode.) The view, she explains, is that if *A* is moving in a particular direction at a particular speed and bumps into *B* with the result that *A* stops moving and *B* now moves in that same direction at the same, or a somewhat reduced, speed, *A*'s motion does not become *B*'s motion. That, at least in Malebranche's view, would involve a contradiction. Hence he proposes (5).

Radner adds that Descartes declared, and Malebranche agreed, that if a substance is created by a creator, then it is also kept in existence by that creator. She explains that, for Malebranche, contingency of existence is a matter of perpetual dependence, and conservation of a substance—maintaining it in existence—is a matter of continuous creation. Now a mode or modification, for Malebranche, is but a substance being in a certain state or having a certain property; it is a substance existing in one fashion rather than another; and a substance must always exist in some manner or another if it exists at all. So, Radner continues, for Malebranche creating a mode involves creating a substance, and therefore one can create a mode only if one can create a substance. In Malebranche's view, creating a change in a previously existing substance is a matter of bringing about a mode of that substance which it did not previously have; it is one way of conserving that substance. Since conserving a substance is continuously creating it, Radner explains, one cannot conserve a substance without creating it. So, she continues, Malebranche contends that one cannot change or bring about a new mode in a substance without conserving or creating that substance at the moment at which one brings about the new mode. This explains the background of (6).

Finally, Radner notes Malebranche's view that a mode cannot "surpass" its substance. *A* has more extent than *B* in regard to *C*, or surpasses *B* with regard to *C*, only if *A* is unlimited with regard to *C* and *B* is not; or, if both are limited with regard to *C*, *B* is more limited than *A*. She notes, however, that "since the modifications of beings are only those very beings determined in such and such a way," it follows that it will be impossible for the mode of a substance to have greater extent in some respect than its substance. This, she says, gives the conceptual setting in Malebranche's philosophy for (7). A consequence of (7), for Malebranche, is that we have no idea of God. (This, in turn, leads him to argue that since we know what the word "God" means, we must have a direct acquaintance with that Being.)—*K.E.Y.*

ADDITIONAL RECOMMENDED READING

Church, Ralph W. *A Study in the Philosophy of Malebranche*. Port Washington, New York: Kennikat Press, 1970. An older standard reference work on Malebranche's thought.

Connell, Desmond. *The Vision in God: Malebranche's Scholastic Sources*. Louvain: Éditions Nauwelaerts, 1967. An investigation into Malebranche's medieval predescessors and sources.

Locke, John. "An Examination of P. Malebranche's Opinion of Seeing All Things in God," in *Philosophical Works of John Locke*. Edited by J. A. St. John. London: H. G. Bohn, 1854. A discussion of one of Malebranche's central doctrines by the famous British philosopher and author of *An Essay Concerning Human Understanding*.

Lovejoy, A. O. "'Representative Ideas' in Malebranche and Arnauld," in *Mind*. XXXII, no. 128 (October, 1923), pp. 449-461. A discussion of an important theme in Malebranche's philosophy, by the author of *The Great Chain of Being*.

Rome, Beatrice K. *The Philosophy of Malebranche*. Chicago: Henry Regnery Company, 1963. A recent solid study.

Watson, Richard A. *The Downfall of Cartesianism, 1673-1712: A Study of Epistemological Issues in Late 17th Century Cartesianism*. The Hague, The Netherlands: Martinus Nijhoff, 1966. An investigation of Malebranche's views in their historical and philosophical context.

AN ESSAY CONCERNING HUMAN UNDERSTANDING

Author: John Locke (1632-1704)
Type of work: Epistemology
First published: 1690

PRINCIPAL IDEAS ADVANCED

At birth the mind is a blank tablet; no one is born with innate ideas.
All of our ideas come from experience, either from sensation or by reflection.
All simple, uncompounded ideas come from experience; and the mind, by combining simple ideas, forms new complex ideas.
The qualities of objects are either primary or secondary: primary qualities— solidity, extension, figure, mobility, and number—are inseparable from objects; but secondary qualities—such as colors and odors—are in the observer.
The substance of objects is a something—we know not what—which we have to assume as the support of an object's qualities.

Locke's *An Essay Concerning Human Understanding* is the first major presentation of the empirical theory of knowledge that was to play such an important role in British philosophy. The author had studied at Oxford, and later he became a medical doctor. Although he did not practice much, he was greatly interested in the developments current in medical and physical science, and there is some evidence that he first began to formulate his theory of knowledge in terms of considerations arising from medical researches of the day. Locke was a member of the Royal Society of England where he came into contact with many of the important experimental scientists, such as Robert Boyle and Sir Isaac Newton. A discussion with some of his friends seems to have been the immediate occasion of the writing of *An Essay Concerning Human Understanding*, in which Locke attempted to work out a theory of knowledge in keeping with the developing scientific findings and outlook. The completed version of the work dates from the period when Locke, along with his patron, the Earl of Shaftesbury, was a political refugee in Holland. After the Glorious Revolution of 1688, Locke returned to England, and was quickly recognized as the leading spokesman for the democratic system of government that was emerging in his homeland. The *Essay*, first published in the same year as Locke's famous work in political philosophy, *Two Treatises of Government*, quickly established the author as the foremost spokesman for the new empirical philosophical point of view that was to dominate English philosophy from then on.

The question to which Locke addressed himself in his essay is that of inquiring into "the original, certainty, and extent of human knowledge, together with the grounds and degrees of belief, opinion, and assent." By using what he called "this historical, plain method," Locke hoped to discover where our ideas and our knowledge come from, what we are capable of knowing about, how certain our knowledge actually is, and when we may be justified in holding opinions based on our ideas. The value of such an undertaking, Locke asserted, is that one would thus know the powers and the limits of the human understanding, so that "the busy mind of man" would then restrict itself to considering only those questions with which it was actually capable of dealing and would "sit down in a quiet ignorance of those things" which were beyond the reach of its capacities.

Before commencing his investigations, Locke pointed out that human beings do, in fact, have adequate knowledge to enable them to function in the condition in which they find themselves. Therefore, even if the result of seeking the origin, nature, and extent of our knowledge leads us to the conclusion that we are unable to obtain complete certitude on various matters, this should not be grounds for despair, for skepticism, or for intellectual idleness. Too much time, Locke insisted, has been wasted by men in bemoaning their intellectual situation, or in disputing in areas in which satisfactory conclusions are impossible. Instead, he said, we should find out our abilities and our limitations, and then operate within them.

The first book of the *Essay* deals with one theory about the origin of our ideas, the thesis that our knowledge is based upon certain innate principles, which are supposed to be "stamped upon the mind of man." Locke severely criticized this theory, especially in the form in which it had been presented by thinkers such as Herbert of Cherbury (1583-1648). Adherents of this theory of innate ideas had maintained that the universal agreement of mankind regarding certain principles showed that these must be innate. Locke argued in opposition that the fact of universal agreement would be insufficient evidence as to the source of the principles in question. He also argued that, in fact, there actually are no principles that are universally agreed to, since children and idiots do not seem to know or believe the principles that are usually cited as examples of innate ideas. The way in which children acquire knowledge about the principles in question, through the learning process, further indicates that they are not born with innate ideas.

After having criticized the innate idea theory, Locke turned next to the positive side of his investigation. We do have ideas (an idea being defined as whatever is the object of the understanding when a man thinks); this is beyond any possible doubt. Then, if the ideas are not innate, where do they come from?

The second book of the *Essay* begins the development of a hypothesis about the origins of human knowledge; namely, the empirical theory. Let us suppose, Locke said, that the mind initially is just a blank tablet (a *tabula rasa*). Where, then, does it obtain its ideas? From experience, Locke proclaimed. Experience comprises two sources of ideas, sensation and reflection.

We receive many, if not most, of our ideas when our sense organs are affected by external objects. We receive other ideas by reflection when we perceive the operations of our minds on the ideas which we have already received. Sensation provides us with ideas of qualities, such as the ideas of yellow, heat, and so on. Reflection provides us with ideas such as those of thinking, willing, doubting, and so on. These two sources, Locke insisted, give us all of the ideas that we possess. If anyone has any doubts about this, let him simply inspect his own ideas and see if he has any which have not come to him either by sensation or reflection. The development of children also provides a further confirmation of this empirical theory of the origin of human knowledge. As the child receives more ideas from sensation, and reflects on them, his knowledge gradually increases.

Having thus answered the question concerning the origin of our ideas, Locke proceeded to investigate the nature of the ideas that we possess. All of our ideas are either simple or complex. A simple idea is one that is un-compounded, that contains nothing but one uniform appearance, and that cannot be distinguished into different ideas. An example of a simple idea would be the smell of a rose. A complex idea, in contrast, is one that is composed of two or more simples, such as a yellow and fragrant idea. The simples, Locke insisted, can neither be created nor destroyed by the mind. The mind has the power to repeat, compare, and unite the simples, thereby creating new complex ideas. But, the mind cannot invent simple ideas that it has not experienced. The simples, in the Lockian theory of knowledge, are the building blocks from which all of our complex and compounded ideas can be constructed and accounted for.

Many of the simple ideas are conveyed by one sense, such as the ideas of colors, sounds, tastes, smells, and touches. One crucial case that Locke argued for is the idea of solidity, which he claimed we receive by touch. This idea is that of a basic quality of bodies. It is not the same as the space that bodies occupy, nor is it the same as the subjective experience of hardness that we receive when we feel objects. Instead, for Locke, solidity is akin to the fundamental physical notion of "mass" in Newtonian physics. It is that which makes up bodies. To anyone who doubts that he is actually acquainted with such an idea, Locke suggested that he place a physical object, such as a ball, between his hands, and then try to join them. Such an experience, presumably, will give one a complete and adequate knowledge of solidity or, at least, as complete and adequate an idea as we are capable of obtaining of any simple idea. The importance of this idea in Locke's theory wil be seen shortly with regard to his theory of primary and secondary qualities.

Some of our ideas are conveyed by two or more senses. Locke included in this group the ideas of space or extension, figure, rest, and motion, which, he said, we receive by means of both sight and touch. Other ideas come from reflection. And still others are the result of both reflection and sensation.

Included in this later group are the ideas of pleasure and pain, and the idea of power (which we gain from reflecting on our experience of our own ability to move parts of ourselves at will).

If these are the types of ideas that we possess, classified according to their sources, can we distinguish those ideas which resemble actual features, or qualities of objects, and those which do not? The qualities of objects are divided by Locke into two categories, the primary and the secondary ones. The primary ones are those that are inseparable from bodies no matter what state the object may be in. This group includes solidity, extension, figure, mobility, and number. In contrast, the secondary qualities "are nothing in the objects themselves, but the powers to produce various sensations in us by their primary qualities," as, for example, the power of an object, through the motion of its solid, extended parts, to produce sounds, tastes, and odors in us when we are affected by it. Thus, on Locke's theory, objects possess primary qualities, the basic ingredients of Newtonian physics, and they possess secondary ones, which are actually the powers of the primary qualities to cause us to perceive features, such as colors, odors, and so on, which are not "in" the objects themselves. In terms of this distinction, we can say that our ideas of primary qualities resemble the characteristics of existing objects outside us, whereas our ideas of secondary qualities do not. The primary qualities of things are really in them, whereas the secondary qualities, as perceived sensations, are only in the observer. If there were no observers, only the primary qualities and their powers would exist. Hence, the rich, colorful, tasteful, noisy, odorous world of our experience is only the way *we* are affected by objects, not the way objects actually are. The distinction between our ideas of primary and secondary qualities led Locke to argue that some of our ideas give us genuine information about reality, while others do not.

In the remainder of the second book of the *Essay*, Locke surveyed the various other kinds of ideas that we possess, those gained by reflection, those that are complexes, and so on. The most important, in terms of his theory, and in terms of later philosophy, is the complex idea of substance. The idea of substance originates from the fact that in our experience a great many simple ideas constantly occur together. We then presume them to belong to one thing, since we cannot imagine how these simple ideas can subsist by themselves. Therefore, we accustom ourselves to suppose that there must be some *substratum* in which the ideas subsist, and we call this substratum a substance. When we ask ourselves what idea we actually have of a substance, we find that our idea is only that of a *something* which the constantly conjoined ideas belong to. When we try to find out what this something is, we discover that we do not know, except that we suppose it must be a something which can support or contain the qualities which could produce the collection of simple ideas in us. If we attempt to find out something more definite about the nature of substance, we discover that we cannot. What do color and weight belong to? If we answer, to the extended solid parts, then to what do these belong? It is like, Locke suggested, the case of the Indian philosopher who said that the world is supported by a great elephant. When asked what supported the elephant, he replied that it rested on a great tortoise. And, when asked what the tortoise rested on, he conceded and said, "I know not what." This, Locke asserted, is all that can finally be said of the nature of substance. It is something—we know not what—which we suppose is the support of the qualities which we perceive or which we are affected by.

Each constantly conjoined group of qualities we assume belongs to some particular substance, which we name "horse," "gold," "man," and so on. We possess no clear idea of substance, either in the case of physical things or of spiritual things. But, we find that we cannot believe that either the physical qualities or the mental ones which we always experience together can exist without belonging to something. And so, although we have no definite ideas, we assume that there must be both bodies and spirits underlying and supporting the qualities that give rise to our ideas. Our inability to obtain clear ideas of substances, however, forever prevents us from gaining genuine knowledge about the real nature of things.

At the end of the second book of the *Essay*, Locke evaluated what he had discovered about the nature of our ideas. This evaluation commences the examination of the problem of the extent and certitude of our knowledge, which is developed at length in the fourth book. Our ideas are real, Locke contended, when they have a foundation in nature and when they conform with the real character of things. In this sense, all simple ideas are real, since they must be the result of genuine events and things (since the mind cannot create them, but receives them from experience). But not all real ideas are necessarily adequate representations of what does in fact exist. Ideas of primary qualities are both real and adequate. Ideas of secondary qualities are real, but only partially represent what is outside us. They represent powers that exist, but not corresponding features to the ones that we perceive. The ideas of substances that we have are very inadequate, since we are never sure that we are aware of all the qualities that are joined together in one substance, nor are we sure of why they are so joined. Hence, some of our ideas tell us what is really outside us whereas other ideas, caused by what is outside us, or by our reflection on our ideas, do not adequately represent "real" objects. Later philosophers, such as George Berkeley and David Hume, were to argue that once Locke had admitted that some of our ideas were neither representative of reality nor adequate to portray reality, he could not then be certain that *any* of our ideas actually correspond to real features of the world. Hence, they contended that Locke, in trying to build from an empirical theory of knowledge to genuine knowledge of reality, had actually laid the groundwork for a skeptical denial of the contention that man can know anything beyond the ideas in his own mind. Locke's theory rested on maintaining that our ideas of primary qualities resemble genuine characteristics of reality. But, the opponents argued, primary qualities are really no different from secondary qualities, as we know them, and hence we have no assurance from the ideas themselves that some are real and adequate and others are not.

The third book of the *Essay* appears to deal with some unrelated topics, those concerning the nature of words and language. This book, which has begun to evoke more interest in recent years because of the present-day concern with linguistic philosophy, covers problems normally dealt with in anthropology, psychology, linguistics, and philosophy.

Two points that are raised are of central importance to Locke's main theme of the nature and extent of our knowledge, and played a role in the later history of empirical philosophy. One of these is Locke's theory concerning the meaning and referent of general terms, such as "man," "triangle," and so on. All things that exist, Locke asserted, are particular, but by abstracting from our ideas of things, by separating from them particular details or features, we finally form a general idea. In this way we arrive at the general abstract ideas that we reason about. Berkeley and Hume both challenged Locke on this point and insisted that we do not, in fact, possess any abstract general ideas. Hence, they insisted that an empirical account of our ideas of so-called general terms must be developed from the particular ideas that we have.

One of the general terms that Locke claimed gained some meaning from the abstracting process is that of "substance." But, when he analyzed what we might mean by the term, Locke distinguished between what he called "the nominal essence" and "the real essence" of a substance. The nominal essence is that abstract general idea of a substance formed by abstracting the basic group of features that constantly occur together. The real essence, in contrast, is the nature of the object which accounts for its having the properties that it does. The nominal essence describes what properties a substance has, whereas the real essence explains why it has these properties. Unfortunately, Locke pointed out, we can never know the real essence of anything, since our information, which we abstract from, deals only with the qualities that we experience, and never with the ultimate causes which account for the occurrence of these properties. Thus, our knowledge of things is sure to be sharply curtailed because of the fact that we will never discover the reasons why things have the characteristics that they do.

The fourth and last book of the *Essay* deals with knowledge in general, with the scope of knowledge, and with the question as to how certain we can be of such knowledge. Our knowledge deals only with ideas, since these are the only items that the mind is directly acquainted with. What constitutes knowledge, according to Locke, is the perception of the agreement or disagreement of two ideas. Ideas may agree or disagree in four ways. They may possibly be identical or diverse. They may be related in some respect. They may agree in coexisting in the same subject or substance. And, fourthly, they may agree or disagree in having a real existence outside the mind. All of our knowledge, Locke insisted, falls under these headings. We know either that some ideas are the same or different, or that they are related, or that they always coexist, or that they really exist independently of our minds.

If these are the kinds of items that we can know about, how can we gain such knowledge? One source of our knowledge is intuition, the direct and immediate perception of the agreement or disagreement of any two ideas. The mind "sees" that black is not white and that a circle is not a triangle. Also, "this kind of knowledge is the clearest and most certain that human frailty is capable of." Anyone who demands more certainty than that gained by intuition "demands he knows not what, and shows only that he has a mind to be a sceptic, without being able to be so." All certain knowledge depends upon intuition as its source and guarantee.

We acquire knowledge not only by directly inspecting ideas, but also through demonstrations. According to Locke, when we know by demonstration, we do not see *immediately* that two ideas agree or disagree, but we see *immediately*, by means of connecting two ideas with others until we are able to connect them with each other. This process is actually a series of intuitions, and each step in a demonstration is therefore certain. However, since the steps occur successively in the mind, error is possible if we forget the previous steps, or if we assume that one has occurred which actually has not. Intuition and demonstration are the only two sources of certain knowledge.

However, there is another source of knowledge that has a degree of certitude assuring us of truths about particular experiences. This kind of knowledge goes beyond bare probability but does not reach genuine certainty. It is called "sensitive knowledge," which is the assurance that we have on the occurrence of specific experiences, that certain external objects actually exist which cause or produce these experiences. We cannot reasonably believe, Locke insisted, that all of our experiences are imaginary or are just part of a dream. Hence, we have sensitive knowledge, a degree of assurance that something real is going on outside us.

In terms of these kinds of knowledge, types of sources, and degrees of certainty, it is now possible to outline the extent of human knowledge and to evaluate what we can actually know about the real world. We can gain knowledge only to the extent that we can discover agreements or disagreements among our ideas. Since we can neither intuit nor demonstrate all the relations that ideas can have with one another, our knowledge is not even as extensive as our ideas. In almost all cases, we can determine with certainty whether our ideas are identical or different from one another. We can tell if our ideas are related to others only when we can discover sufficient intermediary ideas. In fields such as mathematics, we keep expanding our knowledge as more connections between ideas are intuited or demonstrated. The areas in which we seem to be most limited in gaining knowledge are those dealing with the coexistence and real existence of ideas. Since we can never know the real essence of any substance, we can never know why any two ideas must necessarily coexist. We never discover why particular secondary qualities occur when a specific arrangement of primary qualities exists. We are aware of the fact that certain ideas occur over and over again in combination, but we do not know why they do this. With regard to real existence, we are, Locke maintained, intuitively certain of our own existence and demonstratively certain that God exists. We are only sensitively certain that anything else exists, which means that we have serious assurance that objects other than ourselves and God exist only when we have experiences which we feel must be caused by something outside us. Our assurance in these cases is limited to the actual moment when we are having these experiences. Once an experience is over, we have no certitude at all that the object which caused the experience still continues to exist. All that we can know about an object when we know that it exists is that at such times it actually possesses the primary qualities that we perceive, together with the power to produce the other effects that we experience.

This assessment of the extent of our knowledge indicates, according to Locke, that we can never know enough to develop a genuine, certain science of bodies or of spirits, since our information about their existence and their natures is so extremely limited. Since we can, however, obtain sufficient knowledge and probable information to satisfy our needs in this world, we should not despair or become skeptical just because investigation has revealed how limited our knowledge actually is and how uncertain it is in many areas.

Locke's *Essay* represents the first major modern presentation of the empirical theory of knowledge. In developing an account of human knowledge in terms of how it is derived from experience, what its nature is, and how limited it is, Locke provided the basic pattern of future empirical philosophy. In attempting to justify some basis for maintaining that we can have some knowledge of some aspects of reality, Locke raised many of the problems that have remained current in philosophical discussions up to the present time. Empiricists after Locke, such as Berkeley and Hume, showed that if one consistently followed out the thesis that all of our knowledge comes from experience, one could not be certain that substances exist or that anything exists beyond the ideas directly perceived. Locke's *Essay* is the source of many of the methods, ideas, and problems that have prevailed in philosophy, especially in British and American epistemology, ever since its first publication.—*R.H.P.*

PERTINENT LITERATURE

Gibson, James. *Locke's Theory of Knowledge and Its Historical Relations*. Cambridge: Cambridge University Press, 1917.

James Gibson's book is one of the most important commentaries on John Locke's *An Essay Concerning Human Understanding*, and the work also includes a helpful group of discussions of Locke's relations with various seventeenth century thinkers, and an examination of Locke's influence on Immanuel Kant. The first seven chapters present a detailed commentary and interpretation of the *Essay*.

Gibson begins by attacking the view that the *Essay* simply dealt with a theory of the genesis of ideas, in which the mind was completely passive, an interpretation that makes Locke the founder of empiricism. However, this interpretation does not entirely represent either Locke's aim or the theory he developed. After all, Locke was seeking complete certainty about something real. The knowledge he sought was of certain and universal propositions. What Gibson sees as original in Locke's starting point was that he put the investigation of the nature of knowledge prior to the investigation of reality. Nevertheless, from the outset Locke insisted that the mind and the rest of reality exist. However, since these two kinds of substances can have no direct relation with each other, ideas are needed to mediate between the two.

Gibson then carefully examines Locke's polemic against innate ideas. (Although Gibson contends that it was principally directed against the Scholastic philosophers, more recent research, especially that of John Yolton, has shown that there were several philosophers contemporary with Locke who advocated the view.) Gibson then carefully fits the various elements of Locke's theory of ideas into his interpretative framework. One of the most interesting chapters is that dealing with the ideas of substance, causality, and identity. Gibson shows how Locke moved from claiming that we suppose some substratum to our ideas, to the much stronger claim he made in his answer to Bishop Edward Stillingfleet that we cannot conceive how ideas could subsist alone. Gibson points out that the basic problem for Locke is neither that we appear to have to believe that there are substances holding our ideas together, nor that these substances are known either by sensation or reflection. The real problem is that although Locke's theory admits of ideas that are not data of immediate experience (namely, relations), it is genuinely difficult to reconcile this with what he says concerning the idea of substance. He could never justify the claim that there is complete knowledge about the supposed substance.

Difficulties such as those involved in accounting for what we can know about substances pervade Locke's account of our very limited knowledge of real existences. Gibson claimed that Locke never realized the difficulty of bringing knowledge of real existences into line with his general theory of knowledge. The former would transcend any ideas we might possess, whereas the latter would deal only with the perception of the agreement or disagreement of ideas that we have. As Gibson outlined Locke's gradual admission of how little we can actually know (based on Locke's standards), he concluded that Locke had shown us what perfect knowledge would be like. Then, unfortunately, according to Gibson, Locke pointed out not only that perfect knowledge is unattainable by human beings, but also, even worse, that we are not able even to conceive of the conditions under which it would be possible.

The second half of Gibson's book is a very interesting series of historical chapters dealing with Locke's relations with various seventeenth century intellectual movements. Gibson starts with the Scholastics, then discusses René Descartes and the Cartesians, then the English philosophers of Locke's day, such as Robert Boyle, Henry More, Sir Isaac Newton, Thomas Hobbes, and Joseph Glanvill. Then he presents two chapters on G. W. Leibniz, mostly on his lengthy critique of Locke's *Essay*. Finally, the work ends with a chapter on the ideas of Locke and Kant. Much of the historical material would have to be reconsidered in the light of more recent historical scholarship on almost all of these topics. Most important, one would have to reexamine the material in the light of the wealth of data in the Locke papers. The new edition of all of the writings of Locke, now under way, should enable one to reevaluate Locke in the context of his time.

Aaron, Richard I. *John Locke*. Oxford: Clarendon Press, 1971.

Richard I. Aaron's work on John Locke, originally published in 1937, has been substantially changed in this edition by taking into account a great deal of new information about Locke that has become available since the discovery of the Lovelace papers in 1935. Aaron's work is both a most important study of Locke's intellectual development and an excellent commentary on and interpretation of Locke's *An Essay Concerning Human Understanding*, as well as his other philosophical writings.

In Appendix I Aaron explains how he discovered the existence of the Lovelace papers. These consisted of thousands of letters Locke had received, together with a great many of Locke's manuscripts, some of which had never been published, and others which showed different versions of Locke's views. The papers were given to the Bodleian Library at Oxford and presently are being used in the publication of a new and much more complete edition of the works of Locke.

Aaron, using some of this material, is able to give a much improved picture of how Locke developed his ideas and how he went about composing the *Essay*. Three drafts exist, two written in 1671 and a third in 1685, which show that the *Essay* began after a discussion with some friends in 1671. The two drafts of that year both break down over the problem of the extent of human knowledge. The major content of Books III and IV are not in these early drafts. Locke did a great deal of work during 1675-1679 during his French visits and went back to the manuscript in the mid-1680's. The work was substantially finished in 1686, although Locke kept making changes until it was published in 1690.

Aaron stresses that Locke considered that what he was doing was preliminary to philosophy rather than setting forth a philosophical system; he also felt that the practical aspect was all-important. Aaron goes on to present a commentary on the work. Since some of the basic problems emerge, such as those connected with Locke's theory of perception, Aaron suggests that Locke held to difficult and seemingly contradictory views not because he was overfond of them, but because he felt that they were inevitable.

Locke's empiricism, Aaron contends, has often been misunderstood and portrayed as a copy theory—a theory that all mental experience can be broken down into identifiable sensory units. Rather, Aaron maintains, Locke held that thought content is based on sense experience in that sensory and reflective experience is essential if we are to have any knowledge at all. Aaron contends that since Locke tried to use this view as a means of explaining what we know about modes, substances, and relations, his treatment was far from adequate.

The ultimate outcome of Locke's analysis, Book IV of the *Essay*, is not part of the original draft of 1671. Aaron tries to trace the stages by which Locke came to his epistemological conclusion as a way of avoiding some of the skeptical pitfalls: We can intuit some information; we can know that an idea is itself; we can know some necessary relations between ideas, as in mathematics. We can, however, find no necessary relations between our ideas and an external world, and therefore no science, in Aristotle's or René Descartes' sense, is possible.

Aaron follows Locke's struggle to secure what Locke called "sensitive" knowledge and what Aaron labels "existential" knowledge, and he shows that Locke could not make his whole theory of knowledge consistent. The more practical theory that Locke closed with, regarding probabilities and the causes of errors, allows for the practical achievement of his undertaking. Much ignorance and mistaken views, according to Locke, can be eliminated; and although one may not possess knowledge of many things, one may still know enough to live happily and successfully. Aaron then goes on to deal with Locke's moral, political, and religious views.

Aaron's commentary presents significant analyses of the course of Locke's theory. In this edition Aaron has added several important notes and appendices based on both the newly examined manuscript material and some recent interpretations of specific sections of Locke (such as Appendix III on "Locke and Modern Theories of Number"). The volume is virtually indispensable for studying Locke's philosophy.

Yolton, John W. *John Locke and the Way of Ideas*. Oxford: Clarendon Press, 1956.

This very important study attempts to place John Locke's philosophy in the intellectual world of the England of his day. John W. Yolton shows that Locke's concerns, starting with the analysis of innate ideas, grew out of discussions then taking place in England. He then follows the impact of Locke's views on English thinkers (and also on several Continental ones) at the end of the seventeenth and the beginning of the eighteenth centuries. Using some of the manuscript materials of Locke in the Lovelace Collection at Oxford, Yolton is able to show Locke's reactions to some of his contemporary critics.

Yolton first surveys the nature and scope of the early reactions to Locke's *An Essay Concerning Human Understanding*, showing how they involved concerns about Locke offering views that would lead to either religious or epistemological skepticism. From the first reactions onward, those who discussed Locke's view were often highly critical. (Locke's theory was first presented in 1688 in a French summary and was criticized immediately because of Locke's denial of innate ideas.)

Yolton then examines the controversy that had been going on in England concerning whether there are innate ideas. He shows that the usual view of the history books, that Locke was criticizing René Descarte's theory, is doubtful. Yolton believes that it is more likely that Locke was dealing with the then-current version of the innate ideas theory. When Locke's view appeared in Book I of the *Essay*, Locke was widely attacked by many philosophers and theologians, mainly because of the possible criticisms of basic theological notions that could result from his denial of innate ideas. Yolton points out that few writers of the time could evaluate Locke's epistemological views without considering their effect on religion.

In tracing the reaction of Locke's contemporaries to the *Essay*, Yolton next examines those criticisms contending that Locke's epistemology leads to a skepticism about the possibility of gaining knowledge. Step by step, critics such as Henry Lee, John Seargent, John Norris, and others sought to show how Locke's positive theory of knowledge, from his theory of ideas to his classification of kinds of knowledge, all lead to skepticism. Locke did not attempt to answer his critics, except for his controversy with Bishop Edward Stillingfleet, who, like the other critics, deplored the religious skepticism that seemed sure to follow acceptance of Locke's epistemological doctrines.

Yolton then examines the opponents who raised the religious issue, dealing with everyone from Stillingfleet to the eccentric critic, William Carroll, who was convinced that Locke was a Spinozist. Those who claimed that Locke's views led to religious skepticism argued that Locke's doctrine of substance, as well as his view on the limitations of human knowledge, had serious consequences for religious beliefs. Furthermore, as vindication of the views of the orthodox opponents of Locke, some portions of his epistemology were taken over by Deist thinkers. Many Christian writers sought to show that there were Lockean elements in the latest publications of the Deists. Yolton also shows that some orthodox thinkers, including Bishop George Berkeley, adapted some of Locke's views as ways of defending Christianity.

In examining the reception of Locke's philosophy, and especially the criticism of it, Yolton follows the arguments of the subject down to the middle of the eighteenth century. By then Locke's views and the attacks on them had become part of the basic features of philosophical discussions. Also, Yolton insists, Locke's views had become part of the radical and revolutionary Deist views. The Deists, using some of the epistemological doctrines of the *Essay*, altered the presuppositions thought to be necessary for religion. Locke himself was not a Deist, though he seems to have been sympathetic with some of their beliefs. The epistemological problems raised by Locke led to an important shift in the religious, moral, and logical attitudes in the eighteenth century.—*R.H.P.*

ADDITIONAL RECOMMENDED READING

Cranston, Maurice. *John Locke: A Biography*. New York: Macmillan Publishing Company, 1957. Best biography available, based on much manuscript material.

O'Connor, Daniel John. *John Locke*. New York: Dover Publications, 1967. A good overall presentation of Locke's thought.

Yolton, John W. *Locke and the Compass of Human Understanding: A Selective Commentary on the "Essay"*. London: Cambridge University Press, 1970. A careful discussion of Locke's theory of knowledge by one of the most important scholars of Locke's ideas.

_____ , ed. *John Locke: Problems and Perspectives: A Collection of New Essays*. Cambridge: Cambridge University Press, 1969. A fine collection of essays on various aspects of Locke's thought by leading contemporary scholars.

OF CIVIL GOVERNMENT: THE SECOND TREATISE

Author: John Locke (1632-1704)
Type of work: Political philosophy
First published: 1690

PRINCIPAL IDEAS ADVANCED

In the state of nature all men are free and equal; no man is by nature sovereign over other men.

The law of nature governs the state of nature; reason reveals the law of nature, which is derived from God.

In a state of nature no one ought to harm another in his life, health, liberty, or possessions—and if anyone does harm another, the one he harms has the right to punish him.

By his labor a man acquires as his property the products of his labor.

In order to remedy the inconveniences resulting from a state of nature in which every man is judge of his own acts, men enter into a contract, thereby creating a civil society empowered to judge men and to defend the natural rights of men.

If a government violates the social contract by endangering the security and rights of the citizens, it rebels against the people, and the people have the right to dissolve the government.

The "glorious revolution" of 1688 saw the expulsion of James II from the throne of England and the triumph of Whig principles of government. James had been accused of abandoning the throne and thus violating the original contract between himself and his people. Two years later, Locke's *Of Civil Government: The Second Treatise* came out and was looked upon by many as a tract which justified in philosophical terms those historical events. The first *Treatise* had been an argument against the view that kings derive their right to rule from divine command, a view held by the Stuarts, especially James I, and defended with no little skill by Sir Robert Filmer in his *Patriarcha* (1680). From a philosophical point of view it is of little consequence whether Locke intended his defense of the revolution to apply only to the events in the England of his day or to all men at any time; certainly we can study his principles for what they are and make up our own minds as to the generality of their scope.

After rejecting Filmer's thesis, Locke looked for a new basis of government and a new source of political power. He recognized that the state must have the power to regulate and preserve property; that to do so it must also have the right to punish, from the death penalty to all lesser ones. In order to carry out the laws passed, the force of the community must be available to the government, and it must also be ready to serve in the community's defense from foreign injury. Political power by which the government performs these functions ought to be used only for the public good and not for private gain or advantage. Locke then set out to establish a basis for this power, a basis which he considered moral and just.

He turned to a concept used by political theorists since the time of the Stoics in ancient Greece: natural law with its concomitants, the state of nature and the state of war. The state of nature has been objected to as a concept by many because history does not indicate to us such a state existed. In this treatise Locke tries to answer this sort of objection by pointing to "primitive" societies known in his day, the nations of Indians living in the New World. But this is not a strong argument and was not really needed by Locke. The concept of the state of nature can be used as a device to set off and point up the difference between a civil state in which laws are enacted by the government and a contrasting state in which either these laws are absent in principle or another set of laws prevails. In this way the basis of civil enactments and the position of the individual within society may be better understood. This applies also to the other concepts mentioned, the state of war and natural law. At any rate, Locke holds that in the state of nature each man may order his own life as he sees fit, free from any restrictions that other men might impose; in this sense he and all others are equal. They are equal in a more profound sense from which, as it were, their right to act as independent agents comes; that is, as children of God. By use of his reason, man can discover God's commands by which he should order his life in the state of nature. These commands we call the "laws of nature." Thus, although one is free to act as he pleases in the state of nature, he is still obligated to act according to God's commands. This insures that his actions, although free, will not be licentious. The basic restriction that God's laws place upon an individual is that he treat others as he himself would like to be treated. Since men are equal and independent, they should not harm one another regarding their "life, health, liberty, or possessions. . . ."

Man's glory as well as his downfall has been free will, whereby he may choose to do or not to do what he ought to do. To preserve himself from those who choose to harm him, one has the right to punish transgressors of the law. Reparation and restraint are the two reasons that justify punishment when an individual by his acts has shown that he has agreed to live by a law other than that which common reason and equity dictate; that is, he has chosen to violate God's orders. The right to punish is thus a natural right by which men in the state of nature may preserve themselves and mankind from the transgressions of the lawless. This right is the basis for the right of governments to punish lawbreakers within the state; thus Locke provides a ground for one aspect of political power which he had noted earlier.

When an individual indicates through a series of acts which are apparently premeditated that he has designs on another's life or property, then he places himself in a state of war, a state of enmity and destruction, toward his intended victim. In the state of nature men ought to live according to reason and, hence, according to God's commands. Each man must be the judge of his own actions for on earth he has no common superior with authority to judge between him and another when a question of aggression arises, and when relief is sought. His conscience must be his guide as to whether he and another are in a state of war.

In The Declaration of Independence, the American colonists proclaimed that men had natural rights granted them by their Creator, that governments were instituted by men with their consent to protect these rights. Locke, as pointed out, held these rights to be life, liberty, and property, whereas the Declaration proclaims them to be life, liberty, and the pursuit of happiness. It is interesting that Jefferson pondered whether to use "property" or "pursuit of happiness" and in an early draft actually had the former set down. Much of Locke's discussion in this treatise influenced the statesmen and leaders of the Colonies during the period of the American Revolution.

Locke seems to use various senses of "property" in his discussions. Speaking quite generally, one might say that whatever was properly one's own (this might mean whatever God had endowed an individual with or whatever the legislature of the commonwealth had declared as legal possession) no one else had a claim to. In spelling out this idea, Locke starts first with one's own body, which is God-given and which no one has a claim upon; a man has a right to be secure in his person. Included in this idea, of course, is the fact that life itself is a gift to which no one else has a claim, as well as the freedom to move about without restriction. There is next the more common use of "property," which is often rendered "estate" and which refers to the proper possessions which one gains in working the earth that God has given man to use for the advantage of his life and its convenience. Since working for one's own advantage and convenience involves the pursuit of happiness, it can be seen in what way the terms "property" and "pursuit of happiness" are interchangeable. This more common use of "property" is, nonetheless, related to the first use in Locke's theory. What is properly a man's own may be extended when, with regard to the common property that God has blessed men with for their use, a man mixes his labor with it and makes it his own. Divine command prescribes, however, that he take no more than he needs, for to take more than one's share may lead to the waste of God's gift and result in want for others. Locke believed that there was more than enough land in the world for men but that it should be used judiciously; he does complicate matters, however, by stating that disproportionate and unequal possessions may be acquired within a government through the consent of the governed. Locke's embryonic economic theory may be looked upon as an early statement of the classical or labor theory of value. This is especially so if we remember that aside from the "natural" or God-given articles of value that man has, he creates objects of value by means of his own labor; more succinctly, labor creates value. This view was held by such influential thinkers in economic history as Adam Smith, David Ricardo, and Karl Marx. Before we leave this aspect of Locke's theory we should note that he has again provided a ground for the use of political power to regulate, preserve, and protect property in all its aspects by establishing its place in the state of nature prior to the institution of the commonwealth.

Locke has shown that although men ought to live according to divine commands, some do not and thus they turn the state of nature into one of war. Since there is no common superior on earth to whom one can turn for restitution, men are often left helpless. It is obvious that not every injury imagined is a wrong, that two individuals in conscience may disagree, that those instances of obvious wrongs are not always rectifiable when men have only their own judgments and strength to depend upon. A disinterested judge supported by more power than a single person has alone may provide people with a remedy for the insecurity that exists in the state of nature. In the most general sense of "property," a commonwealth may provide the solution to its preservation and security by making public the laws by which men ought to live, by establishing a government by which differences may be settled through the office of known and impartial judges who are authorized to do so, and by instituting a police force to execute the law, a protection absent in the state of nature. Men give up their rights to judge for themselves and to execute the laws of nature to the commonwealth, which in turn is obligated to use the power which it has gained for the ends which led to the transference of these rights. In giving up their rights, men consent to form a body politic under one government and, in so doing, obligate themselves to every member of that society to submit to the determinations of the majority. Note that everyone who enters into the society from the state of nature must consent to do so; hence, consent is unanimous and anyone who does not consent is not a member of the body politic. On the other hand, once the body politic is formed, its members are thenceforth subject to the vote of the majority.

In discussing consent and the general question, "Who has consented and what are its significant signs?" Locke uses the traditional distinction between tacit and express consent. Although he is somewhat ambiguous at times, his position is apparently as follows. There are two great classes or categories of individuals within society, those who are members and those who are residents but not members. (A convenient and similar distinction would be those who are citizens and those who are aliens.) Both these two groups receive benefits from the government and hence are obligated to obey it. By their presence they enjoy the peace and security that goes with a government of law and order, and it is morally and politically justifiable that that government expect of them that they obey its laws. Those who are merely residents may quit the body politic when they please; their tacit consent lasts only as long as their presence in the state. Members, however, by their express consent create and perpetuate the society. They are not free to be or not be members at their whim, else the body politic would be no different from the state of nature or war from which its members emerged, and anarchy would prevail. Citizens usually have the protection of their government at home and abroad, and often, at least in the government Locke preferred, a voice in the affairs of their nation. Locke points out, however, that the people who form the commonwealth by their unanimous consent may also delegate their power to a few or to one (oligarchy or monarchy); but in any case it is their government.

There are certain aspects of government which Locke believed must be maintained to insure that it functions for the public good. (1) The legislative, which is the supreme governmental power, must not use its power arbitrarily over the lives and fortunes of the people. The law of nature still prevails in the governments of men. (2) Nor should power be exercised without deliberation. Extempore acts would place the people in as great jeopardy as they were in the state of nature. (3) The supreme power cannot take from a man his property without his consent. This applies also to taxation. (4) The legislative power cannot be transferred to any one else, but must remain in the hands of that group to which it was delegated by the people. In so acting, the legislature insures the people that political power will be used for the public good.

Locke believed that the interests of the people would be protected more fully in a government in which the three basic powers, legislative, executive, and federative, were separate and distinct in their functions. The legislature need meet only periodically, but the executive should be in session, as it were, continually, whereas the management of the security of the commonwealth from foreign injury would reside in the body politic as a whole. Strictly speaking, the federative power —treaty-making and so forth—need not be distinguished from the legislative. It is interesting that the three branches of government in the United States include the judiciary rather than the federative, which is shared by the executive and legislative branches of government. This shows that Montesquieu as well as Locke influenced the Philadelphia convention.

Government, which is made up of these three basic powers, of which the legislative is supreme, must not usurp the end for which it was established. The community, even after it has delegated its power, does not give up its right of self-preservation, and in this sense it retains forever the ultimate power of sovereignty. This power cannot be used by the community which is under obligation to obey the acts of the government unless that government is dissolved. It must be pointed out that the community is for Locke an important political concept. The exercise of its power after the dissolution of government is as a public body and does not involve a general return to the state of nature or war by its members. But in what way is a government dissolved?

When a government exercises power beyond right, when public power is used for private gain, then tyranny prevails. Such acts set the stage for the dissolution of government. It should be pointed out that in forming a community and in delegating power to a government, the people, especially in the latter case, enter into an agreement or, analogously, into a social contract with their government to provide them with security, preservation, and those conveniences that they desire, in exchange for the transference of their rights and the honor, respect, and obligation which they render to the government. The violation of their part of the contract leads government to declare them (as individuals) outlaws, to use its police force to subdue them, and its courts to set punishment for them.

In discussing dissolution in general, Locke points out that it can apply to societies and communities as well as to governments. It is seldom that a community is dissolved. If it does happen, it is usually the result of a foreign invasion which is followed by the utter destruction of the society. Governments, on the other hand, are dissolved from within. Either the executive abandons his office (as was done by James II) and the laws cannot be carried out, or the legislative power is affected in various ways which indicate a violation of trust. If, for example, the property of the subjects is invaded, or if power is used arbitrarily, then government is dissolved. Obviously, it falls upon the community to judge when this power is being abused. Generally, Locke holds, the people are slow to act; it takes not merely one or two but a long series of abuses to lead them to revolution. In fact, he points out that the term "rebellion" indicates a return to a state of war and a denial of the principles of civil society. But when this happens in the dissolution of government, it is the government that has rebelled and not the community; it is the community that stands for law and order and puts down the rebellion. Thus Locke rather cleverly concludes his treatise, not with a justification of the right of rebellion but, rather, with the right of the people to put down unlawful government, unlawful in that it violates the trust and the law of nature, leading to tyranny, rebellion, and dissolution.—*T.W.*

PERTINENT LITERATURE

Strauss, Leo. "Modern Natural Right," in *Natural Right and History*. Chicago: University of Chicago Press, 1952.

In one of the classics of modern historical analysis of political philosophy, Leo Strauss concludes that John Locke did not recognize any law of nature in the proper sense of the term—a conclusion which he himself concedes stands in shocking contrast to what is generally thought to be Locke's doctrine, especially as that doctrine is expounded in the *Second Treatise*. According to most of Locke's critics, Locke is full of illogical flaws and inconsistencies.

These inconsistences are of such an obvious nature that Strauss believes that it is inconceivable that a man of Locke's stature and sobriety could possibly have overlooked them.

Although Locke seems to reject Thomas Hobbes's theory of natural law in favor of a more traditional view of the law of nature, there are certain flaws in his exposition of his views on that subject. Locke says, for example, that the law of nature or the moral law is capable of being developed into a science which would proceed from self-evident propositions to a body of ethics that would incorporate all the duties of life, a code that would contain, for example, the natural penal law. But Locke never seriously attempted to elaborate that code.

Locke also says that the natural law has been given by God, is known to have been given by God, and has as its sanctions divine rewards and punishments in the next life—sanctions which are of infinite weight and duration. Yet he says that immortality cannot be proven by rational demonstration. One can know of it only through revelation. Moreover, we can know of the sanctions for the law of nature only through revelation. It would follow, then, that we cannot come to know the law of nature through reason unassisted by revelation. Elsewhere, Locke attempted to demonstrate that the New Testament contains the entire law of nature and that it is revealed there in perfect clarity and plainness. One would have thought, therefore, that Locke would have written a commentary on the New Testament rather than a treatise on government.

Strauss's explanation for this is Locke's personal caution—his pragmatic refusal to do anything that would jeopardize his safety or his ability to propound his beliefs. Locke was prepared to be cautious in his writings if unqualified frankness would render his entire noble enterprise incapable of execution or if more direct and clear expression of his views would endanger the public peace or expose him to persecution. Thus, even if Locke had believed that unassisted reason was man's only "star and compass" and was all that was necessary for leading man to perfect happiness; even if he rejected revelation as superfluous or doubtful; he might nevertheless have written as he did, claiming to accept New Testament teachings as true. And even if he personally believed those teachings to be true, he was undoubtedly concerned to make his teachings as independent of Scripture as possible.

A further problem arises out of the fact that Locke enumerates certain particular laws as being laws of nature, but fails to show how they might be derived from the text of the New Testament, where, according to his teaching, they ought to be found. For example, according to Locke, one of the laws of God and nature is a requirement that the government not raise taxes on property without the consent of the people or their deputies—but nowhere does he even attempt to show where this might be found in Scripture. Similarly, in regard to marriage, Locke says that according to natural law the purpose of conjugal society is procreation and education. From this, it merely follows that men and women be tied to a longer conjunction than other creatures. But he does not tell us how firm the conjugal bonds should be. Nor does a firmer bond between men and women than between male and female animals of other species require a prohibition against incest. Indeed, Locke mentions nothing at all about incest, but agrees with Hobbes that civil society is the sole judge of which "transgressions" deserve punishment and which do not. And as for the biblical command that one honor one's parents, Locke makes it conditional: in the *Second Treatise*, he states that mere biological parenthood is not sufficient to entitle one to be honored by one's children; rather, that claim derives from the "care, cost, and kindness" which the parent has shown to the child. So, Strauss points out, the categorical imperative, "Honor thy father and thy mother," is transformed into a hypothetical imperative: "Honor thy father and thy mother if they have deserved it of you."

Needless to say, all of these and more are not identical with the teachings of Scripture. Locke calls these teachings the "partial law of nature." Since the law of nature is supposed to be set out in the New Testament *in toto*, it would seem to follow that the "partial law of nature" is not actually a part of the law of nature at all. And unlike the law of nature properly so called, it would not have to be known to have been given by God. Indeed, it would not require belief in God at all. Thus, the partial law of nature might be known even to non-Christians, such as the Chinese. According to Locke, all that is necessary for a nation to be civilized is that it know the partial law of nature. Hence, it is possible for the Chinese to be civilized, as Locke concedes them to be.

Thus Strauss arrives at the puzzling conclusion that Locke did not recognize the law of nature properly so called. Strauss explains the paradox by suggesting that in the *Second Treatise* Locke did not present his philosophical doctrines on politics, but what he calls Locke's "civil" presentation of his political doctrine. Locke writes not as a philosopher but as an Englishman, and therefore, writing for a popular audience, he appealed to popularly accepted traditions.

Nevertheless, Strauss maintains that Locke actually deviated from traditional natural law teaching in the *Second Treatise* and followed Hobbes to a greater extent than is ordinarily realized. Locke recognized the state of nature—so much so, in fact, that he said that "all men are naturally in" the state of nature. Moreover, he affirms that every man has the right to be "executioner" of the law of nature—that is, that each man has the right to impose sanctions upon those who violate the laws of nature. No law worthy of the name can exist in the absence of sanctions. Conscience is not identical with God's will, according to Locke, and therefore conscience cannot suffice as a sanction for acts violative of the law of nature. Besides, conscience is nothing more than private opinion. Meaningful sanctions in this world, at least, must be enforced by men. If the law of nature is to be effective at all in the state of nature, then it must be enforced by private persons—private since there is not yet a civil society. The natural law is given by God, but it need not be known that God has given it, for human beings must enforce it. If human beings are to enforce it, they must know it. Indeed, no law can be a law unless it is known. Hence, the law of nature must be knowable in the state of nature.

The state of nature, however, far from being the golden age which some might imagine it to be, is perfectly dreadful, just as Hobbes said it would be. Peace exists only in civil society. The state of nature, by contrast, is "full of fears and continual dangers," and those who live in it are "needy and wretched." If men only knew the laws of nature, they would live by them; but the laws of nature are not implanted in men's minds, and most men do not have the leisure to work out the proofs for the laws of nature if they live in that awful state. Although the law of nature is at least theoretically knowable in the state of nature, then, in actual fact, the continual dangers and penury of the state of nature make it impossible for the law of nature to be discovered. Since an unpromulgated law is not law at all, the law of nature is not, in the end, a law at all in the proper sense of the term.

According to Strauss, Locke holds a rather peculiar theory of hedonism. (It is surprising that Locke should be characterized as a hedonist at all.) Good and evil he defines as pleasure and pain. But the greatest happiness consists not in enjoying the greatest or the most intense or even the highest pleasures, but in "having those which produce the greatest pleasures." These words appear in a chapter entitled "Power." Locke's thesis is that the greatest happiness consists in the greatest power, power consisting of a man's possessing the means to obtain some "future apparent good." Like Hobbes, Locke rejected the notion of a *summum bonum*. Pleasure and pain, he maintained, differ from one person to another, and even from one time to another in a given individual's life. We cling to life not because of the natural sweetness of living but because of the terrors of death. The ultimate goal of desire is not the good life, but escape from pain. The only way to stave off pain is to suffer pain—the pain of work, the work of striving to ward off even worse pain. There are no pure pleasures. Therefore, the good life is quite compatible with the coercive society of a civil state. The relief of pain through painful labor culminates not in having great pleasures but in "having those things which produce the greatest pleasures." And so, Strauss concludes, "Life is the joyless quest for joy."

Locke, John. *Two Treatises of Government.* Edited by Peter Laslett. Cambridge: Cambridge University Press, 1963.

Peter Laslett's critical edition and annotated text of the *Two Treatises of Government* is introduced by an essay which sets the work in its historical context and offers a fresh interpretation of John Locke's social and political theory. This Introduction conveys the excitement with which a historian greets a new find—in this case, Locke's own corrected copy of the *Two Treatises of Government* and the consequent recovery of his personal library. Taken with Locke's private papers, these are important because, as Laslett tries to show, they upset three conventional assumptions about Locke's political writings. First, the *Two Treatises of Government* was not written in 1689 with a view to justifying the "Glorious Revolution;" second, it was not written with a view to rectifying the teachings of Thomas Hobbes; and third, it was not intended to be read as a philosophical work.

That Locke was a political refugee in Holland when James II was forced to abdicate is well known, but the extent to which he was implicated in the revolt against the Stuarts has not been fully understood. According to Laslett, it was as a confidant and aide to the Whig leader, Anthony Ashley Cooper, Lord Shaftesbury, in the late 1670's and early 1680's when the revolt was brewing, that Locke turned his mind to the problem of political obligation; and in Laslett's opinion only flight saved Locke from the fate of Algernon Sidney, who was executed for having written a book of similar import to that of the *Two Treatises of Government*.

Laslett argues that the *Second Treatise of Government* was begun in 1679 and completed the next year. In 1680, Sir Robert Filmer's *Patriarchia* appeared, and Locke began the phrase-by-phrase refutation of that work which was to become the First Treatise of the two-part work. Two copies of the manuscript were left behind when Locke took flight in 1683, but only part of one manuscript remained when he returned in 1689. Fortunately, all that was missing was the latter part of Locke's lengthy refutation of Filmer.

Hobbes and Filmer were both defenders of absolutism, but according to Laslett it is almost always Filmer's form of absolutism that Locke is concerned to refute. Hobbes at this time had no following, but Filmer was enjoying a great vogue not only among the royalists but also among others who, on religious grounds, held to the principle of passive obedience. Filmer had argued that God sets kings over men just as he sets father over children. This, of course, is what Locke denies when he argues, in the *Second Treatise*, that in the natural state no adult has authority over another. The argument in this treatise is empirical and rational: experience shows that the superiority of fathers is only temporary, and reason shows why this must be so. But because religious authority carried weight with so many people, Locke found it wise even in the *Second Treatise* to undergird his conclusions by quoting the highly respected churchman, Richard Hooker. Certainly it was the religious dimension of the controversy which led Locke to write the lengthy *First Treatise* in which he supported the conclusions of the *Second Treatise* by appealing to divine revelation.

That Locke was influenced by Hobbes need not be denied. Although he had probably read the *Leviathan* when he was young, he seems to have had no recent contact with any of Hobbes's works when he wrote the *Two Treatises of Government*. Hobbes's influence, Laslett suggests, was like the gravitational influence exercised by a large body at some distance. On the whole, the influence was positive. English defenders of liberty have usually viewed the state in terms of its constitutional history. Locke learned from Hobbes to think of it in abstract terms, with the result that his response to what was an immediate political situation reads as if it were a statement of universal truth. This, says Laslett, makes the book unique and accounts for its wide influence.

The *Two Treatises of Government* and *An Essay Concerning Human Understanding* both appeared in 1690. The former, however, did not bear Locke's name; nor was Locke willing publicly to acknowledge his authorship until shortly before his death. Part of the reason for such secrecy, Laslett suggests, could have been that James II's return remained a possibility; but more significantly, he believes, is the fact that the doctrine of the *Two Treatises of Government* was difficult to reconcile with the theory of knowledge advanced in *An Essay Concerning Human Understanding*. The doctrine, for example, that the mind is a blank table on which experience alone can write leaves little room for the doctrine that reason teaches a Law of Nature to all who will consult it.

In Laslett's opinion, Locke could have explained that the object of *An Essay Concerning Human Understanding* was to limit our claims to theoretical knowledge in order better to determine "those things which concern our conduct," and the *Two Treatises of Government* fitted into this program by showing how people ought to behave. In any case, says Laslett, Locke's philosophy was not meant to be a system, as Hobbes's was, but an attitude— the conviction that the universe, including human relations, is to be found out by experience and understood according to reason.

The thirty pages which Laslett devotes to expounding Locke's political theories are noteworthy as an attempt to avoid reading back into Locke the views of subsequent thinkers. Laslett emphasizes what he calls Locke's doctrine of natural political virtue, according to which individual persons, whether in formal or in informal groups, tend to be favorably disposed toward each other and ready to cooperate in the most effective way. Custom, trust, and implicit assent emerge as more basic than explicit assent and contractual agreements.—*J.F.*

ADDITIONAL RECOMMENDED READING

Aaron, Richard I. *John Locke.* Oxford: Clarendon Press, 1971. Chapter 2 of Part III, devoted to a discussion of Locke's political theory, not only provides an excellent exposition of Locke's views but also puts them in the setting of contemporary religious and political thinking.

Dunn, John. *The Political Thought of John Locke: An Historical Account of the Argument of the "Two Treatises of Government"*. Cambridge: Cambridge University Press, 1969. A superb analysis of Locke's views by an author who is fully conversant with all the pertinent literature and is not at all hesitant to differ from other leading authorities.

Gough, J. W. *John Locke's Political Philosophy*. Oxford: Clarendon Press, 1973. An extended analysis of eight major themes in Locke's political philosophy, including, among others, the law of nature, individual rights, consent, property, and sovereignty.

Macpherson, C. B. *The Political Theory of Possessive Individualism: Hobbes to Locke*. Oxford: Clarendon Press, 1962. Chapter 5 is devoted to an analysis of Locke's theory of property rights, natural rights, the state of nature, and various other political questions. The essay is in the context of others dealing with Locke's predecessors.

O'Connor, D. J. *John Locke*. London: Penguin Books, 1952. Chapter 9 contains an excellent summary of Locke's political theory, a critical and well-balanced analysis in the tradition of current British analytical philosophy. The book as a whole is excellent, with biographical as well as philosophical information about Locke.

Steinberg, Jules. *Locke, Rousseau, and the Idea of Consent: An Inquiry into the Liberal-Democratic Theory of Political Obligation*. Westport, Connecticut: Greenwood Press, 1978. In Chapter 3, "Locke and the Idea of Consent," the author attempts to demonstrate that Locke used consent theory merely as a means to convey his theory of obligation, consent being equivalent to "what individuals ought to do" or "what is morally right," regardless of whether the persons concerned had consented to anything in the ordinary sense of the word.

THE HISTORICAL AND CRITICAL DICTIONARY

Author: Pierre Bayle (1647-1706)
Type of work: Skeptical criticism of theology
First published: 1695-1697

PRINCIPAL IDEAS ADVANCED

Since reason is useless, man should turn to faith.

The traditional philosophical and theological arguments prove nothing; skeptical criticism can demolish any theory.

By consistently employing the arguments of philosophers we find that we can no longer be certain even of the existence of external objects, to say nothing of their qualities.

Such Christian doctrines as those concerning the Trinity, the Fall, Transubstantiation, and Original Sin, if self-evidently true, contradict other propositions that are also self-evidently true.

There is no faith better established on reason than that which is built on the ruins of reason; the true man of faith accepts beliefs for which he can give no rational justification.

Bayle's *Historical and Critical Dictionary* is a compendium of arguments, tending toward a skeptical view, for and against almost every theory in philosophy and theology. It was called in the eighteenth century the "Arsenal of the Enlightenment," and it played a very important role in intellectual discussions throughout the first half of the eighteenth century. Significant criticisms of the major and minor philosophers and theologians of the time appear throughout the *Dictionary*. Thinkers such as George Berkeley, David Hume, and Voltaire used the work as a source of arguments and inspiration. Remaining in vogue until it was no longer useful as a reference work, the last edition appeared in 1820.

The author was one of the most interesting critical figures of his time. He was born in southern France, the son of a Calvinist pastor. He was sent to a Jesuit school in Toulouse, where he was converted to Catholicism. Shortly thereafter he was reconverted to Calvinism, after which he fled to Geneva to avoid being persecuted. He studied at the Calvinist university there, and then returned to France incognito. For a time he was professor of philosophy at the Calvinist college at Sedan, but when the final persecutions of the Huguenots took place in France, he fled with many of his coreligionists to The Netherlands, where he remained for the rest of his life. He taught first in a high school in Rotterdam and then devoted himself to editing one of the first learned journals, the *Nouvelles de la Republique des Lettres*. He became embroiled in one controversy after another, with the liberal Calvinist theologians, with the orthodox ones, with Catholic spokesmen in France, and with

philosophers of every school. During the last twenty years of his life, he was
a central figure in almost every intellectual debate. He insisted that he was
a Protestant in the true sense of the word; he protested everything that was
said and everything that was done. He fought against religious intolerance
and philosophical dogmatism, and he died with pen in hand, writing another
blast against some hapless opponent. His death was mourned by friend and
foe alike, for he had contributed much to the learned world through his
polemical publications and with his critical acumen, his many and varied
interests, and his many friendships throughout the intellectual world.

At once the greatest and the most notorious of Bayle's achievements is his
Dictionary. It was begun as a series of corrections to a previous biographical
dictionary, but it grew until it became an enormous work in its own right. It
consists, formally, of a series of articles in alphabetical order, giving biographical information and historical data about all sorts of people, places,
and things, some historical, some mythological. Many of the people discussed
are obscure theologians, or philosophers with strange theories. The meat of
the *Dictionary* appears primarily in the footnotes, which occupy most of the
space, appearing below the text on the huge folio pages in double columns
of small print. Many of the footnotes contain digressions which allow Bayle
to bring up all of his favorite disputes. An important, interesting, or exciting
digression can appear almost anywhere. In the article on "Rorarius," for
example, Bayle launches into one of the first and most significant criticisms
of Leibniz. The footnotes are also interspersed with spicy tales about the love
lives and sexual practices of various famous people, and with profane versions
of Bible stories. In the course of the thousands of footnotes, virtually every
theory ever propounded is attacked, and a recurring theme appears—man,
realizing the uselessness of rational endeavors, should turn to faith.

When the work first appeared, it was immediately attacked and banned in
France for its anti-Catholic, antireligious, skeptical views, as well as for its
obscene content. It was similarly criticized in Holland by Bayle's own church,
the French Reformed Church of Rotterdam, which demanded an explanation
for the material contained in the *Dictionary*. The author insisted that he had
been misunderstood. The obscenities, he said, represented reports of actual
historical facts, and he could not be held responsible for the actions of historical personages, many of them long dead. As to the other charges, he
insisted that they were entirely without foundation. His intention was to
support the faith of his church by exposing the weaknesses of all rational
theories, so that people, seeing this, would turn away from philosophy and
science, to faith. His opponents contended that Bayle had made such a mock-
ery of the faith that he could not possibly be seriously advocating it. To answer
the charges, Bayle wrote some appendices to the *Dictionary*, plus additional
footnotes, and incorporated them into the next edition, that of 1702. These
additions were considered so much more dangerous and heretical than his

original work that they produced another storm of attacks, as well as a series of answers on Bayle's part. For the rest of his life, Bayle fought to vindicate his contention that his general, overall view was the same as that of John Calvin and of all of the most orthodox theologians. The liberal and the orthodox Calvinists fought against this claim and tried to unmask their opponent as a true heretic. Bayle kept pointing out that his most extreme orthodox opponents really said the same things as he did. But, as one of them observed, "When I say it, it is serious. When he [Bayle] says it, it turns out comical."

Bayle has been interpreted, by most critics, as being the earliest figure in the Enlightenment to use his scholarship and his critical abilities for the purpose of destroying all confidence in religion, both through undermining the reasons given by theologians for the faith, and through making the faith appear ridiculous. On the other hand, some scholars have argued that Bayle was sincere, that he was actually defending religion rather than opposing it, using the same sort of irrational "defense" later employed by Søren Kierkegaard. Neither the information about Bayle's life, nor an analysis of his writings, results in a definitive solution of the mystery of his *real* intentions. But, regardless of what he may have thought he was trying to accomplish, the impact of Bayle's thought in the eighteenth century caused many thinkers to doubt traditional philosophical and theological arguments, and to doubt the philosophies and religions as well. Bayle also supplied much of the ammunition used by the skeptical philosophers of the Age of Reason.

In the wide range of articles and issues dealt with in the *Dictionary*, some deserve special notice because of either their influence or their content. The longest article, on Spinoza, was notorious in its day because it presented the first defense of Spinoza's character as a saintly human being, in contrast to the grim rumors of the time that Spinoza must have been a villainous person to have advocated the philosophy that he did. But while defending Spinoza's character, Bayle also engaged in his favorite sport, that of decimating other people's theories. The article on "Rorarius" presents the first serious discussion that had appeared in print of Leibniz's novel metaphysical theory. (When Leibniz wrote a lengthy response, Bayle enlarged the footnotes in "Rorarius," in the second edition, to discuss Leibniz's defense as well as some new criticisms of his own.) The philosophies of Father Malebranche, John Locke, and Sir Isaac Newton are all subjected to devastating criticisms in the article on Zeno of Elea. Two of the articles on early religious groups, one on the Manicheans and the other on the Paulicians, deal with the problem of evil, arguing that it is not possible to disprove the Manichean theory that there is an evil as well as a good God, or the theory that God is author of evil. These two articles unleashed a storm of controversy and led to the writing of two famous answers, that of Leibniz, in his *Theodicy* (1710) and that of William King, Archbishop of Dublin, in his *Origins of Evil* (1739). Both Hume and

Voltaire used Bayle's arguments on the subject of evil in their attacks on traditional theology.

In the article on Zeno of Elea, especially in the famous footnotes G and H, Bayle levels his attacks on the modern metaphysical systems. He tries to show that, on the basis of the premises of a philosopher such as René Descartes, no satisfactory evidence can be offered to show that an external world exists, or that it can be consistently described in mathematical terms. First, Bayle argues that the same sort of skeptical evidence that led modern philosophers to doubt that real objects possess the secondary qualities that we perceive, such as color, smell, heat, and so on, should also lead these philosophers to doubt whether real objects possess the primary, mathematical qualities, such as extension. The reality of secondary qualities is denied by almost all seventeenth century philosophers. They all point out that because these qualities are perceived differently at different times, under different conditions, and by different people, the real object cannot possess these variable properties. Bayle then contends that if this argument is considered adequate, it should also be applied to a quality such as extension. The same object appears big to one at one time, small at another. One's perception of its size differs from that of other persons. Hence, extension, like color, is no more than an idea in my own mind, and is not a characteristic of real objects. Further, Bayle gathers together all the arguments from philosophers such as Malebranche to show that there is no genuine evidence that real objects even exist. It cannot be demonstrated that they do. All of the information that is offered as evidence could be due to the actions of God upon us, without requiring the actual existence of objects corresponding to our ideas and feelings, or causing them. If it is answered that God would be deceiving us if he made us believe in the existence of real objects when there really were none, Bayle answers, in the article on Pyrrho of Elis, that God makes peasants think that snow is white, and the philosophers claim this is a delusion, so why cannot God also delude the philosophers into thinking objects exist? To conclude this subject, Bayle endorses Malebranche's view that it is faith only, and not reason, that can justify our beliefs about the real existence of things. Hence, we ought to be content with the light of faith, and give up the hopeless pursuit of truth by means of reason.

The longest and most explicit statement of this theme (and the one that was most often debated in the eighteenth century) occurs in footnotes B and C of the article on Pyrrho. The discussion begins as a comment on the observation in the text that it is fitting that Pyrrhonian skepticism is detested in the schools of theology. Bayle points out that Pyrrhonism, complete skepticism, is a danger only to theology, not to science or politics. Practically every scientist *is* a skeptic, since scientists doubt that it is possible to discover the secret causes and springs of nature. Instead, the scientists look only for descriptive information and probable hypotheses about nature. Regarding politics, the skeptics are not dangerous since they are always willing to follow the laws and customs of society because of the fact that they have no dogmatic moral or legal principles. But skepticism can be a great danger to religion, because religious docrines should be completely certain. If not, there will be no firm conviction. Fortunately, however, Bayle points out, skepticism has little effect on people, either because of the Grace of God, their education, their stupidity, or their natural inclinations.

To show the merits or the dangers of skepticism, Bayle tells a story about a discussion between two abbots. One asserts that it is incomprehensible to him that there are still any skeptics around, since God has given us the Revelation. The other replies that both the "new philosophy" and Christian theology provide excellent ammunition for any skeptic. The philosophy of thinkers such as Descartes leads, as the article on Zeno shows, to a complete skepticism about the nature and existence of the real world. By consistently employing the arguments of seventeenth century philosophers we can no longer be sure whether objects possess *any* qualities, including those of extension and motion, and we cannot even be sure that there are any objects.

Further, Bayle insists, we cannot even be sure of the dogmatic philosophers' contention that something is true, because we cannot be certain of the criterion of truth. Philosophers have said that self-evidence is the sure mark of truth. But, the skeptical abbot declares, if Christianity is true, then there are self-evident propositions which must be false, and so, self-evidence cannot be taken as the standard for measuring what is true. Bayle then argues that the Christian doctrines of the Trinity, Transubstantiation, the Fall, and Original Sin contradict various self-evident propositions of philosophy such as that two things not different from a third are not different from each other, that a body cannot be in several places at the same time, that one ought to prevent evil if one can, and so on. In passing from the shadows of paganism to the light of Scripture, the abbot points out, we have learned the falsity of a great many self-evident notions.

Then the skeptical abbot answers the possible objection that all of the evidence against the criterion of truth depends upon evaluating God and his actions by human standards, and these may not be the correct criteria for some judgments. If this objection is taken seriously, then we are again led to complete skepticism because we are then unable to know what is true in God's world if we cannot employ our own standards to judge by.

The arguments of the skeptics, Bayle contends, cannot be answered by human reason, and they expose the weakness of our rational faculties. Thus we are made to feel the need for a guide different from reason; namely, faith. In footnote C, this point is explored further, first by pointing out that complete skepticism is the greatest achievement of human rationality, but that even so, it is completely self-defeating. One cannot even believe that skepticism is true without ceasing to be a skeptic. The attempt to become completely dubious about everything by means of reason finally leads one to give up reasoning entirely, and to turn to a more secure guide, faith. Skepticism is portrayed as the best preparation for religion because it reveals the total and hopeless inadequacy of reason as a means for finding truth. One is then ready to accept Revelation without question. In a later defense of this theory, Bayle asserts that there is no faith better established on reason than that which is built on the ruins of reason.

This total irrationalism and acceptance of religion on blind faith was bitterly attacked by theologians everywhere. In the second edition of the *Dictionary*, Bayle added a more detailed (and more antirational) exposition of his views in the appendix explaining the article on Pyrrho. Here, he argued that the world of reason and the world of faith are two totally different and opposing realms. If one looks for evidence, one cannot have faith, and the search for evidence will end only in complete skepticism. If one completely abandons the quest for evidence, then faith is possible. In fact, the more irrational one's beliefs are, the more this means that such beliefs cannot be based on any evidence whatsoever (otherwise, there might be some reason for them). The true and complete man of faith, then, according to Bayle's rendition of the case, is the person who accepts a belief for which he can give no justification and no reason of any kind. Bayle, in keeping with the other French skeptics from Montaigne onward, cites as his Scriptural authority for this interpretation of religion St. Paul's antirational pronouncements in the first chapter of his first letter to the Corinthians.

Opponents immediately pointed out that this irrationalism would destroy religion rather than defend it. There would be no reason left for accepting a religion, no standards by which to tell what is true or false, and no way of distinguishing the true religion from all the others. In fact, the critics claimed, Bayle's religion without reason would actually be a form of madness, or superstition, which neither Bayle nor any other "reasonable" man could possibly accept. Bayle fought back during the last years of his life, attacking the reasons his opponents offered for their religious views and for their criticisms, and insisting that all of the most orthodox theologians had said exactly the same thing as he was saying.

Whether Bayle was sincere or not, the arguments he presented to show that religion could not be based on reason became basic ingredients in the deistic, agnostic, and atheistic views developed in the course of the Enlightenment. His arguments against modern philosophy became crucial themes in the theories of Berkeley, Hume, and Voltaire. The *Dictionary* was all-important in transforming the intellectual world from its metaphysical and theological phase to the skeptical and empirical phase of the Age of Reason. —R.H.P.

PERTINENT LITERATURE

Bayle, Pierre. *Historical and Critical Dictionary: Selections*. Translated by Richard H. Popkin. Indianapolis: Bobbs-Merrill, 1965.

This volume contains forty articles from Pierre Bayle's *Dictionary*, translated by Richard H. Popkin. These include selections from some of the most important essays on philosophy and theology, such as "David," "Jupiter," "Leucippus," "Manichaeans," "Paulicians," "Pyrrho," "Rorarius," "Simonides," "Spinoza," "Zeno of Elea," and the four clarifications Bayle wrote to answer charges leveled at him by members of the French Reformed Church. (They had accused him of favoring atheism, and/or Pyrrhonism, of supporting Manichaeanism, and of introducing obscenities into his discussions.)

Popkin's lengthy Introduction first indicates what sort of strange entity Bayle's *Dictionary* was; then it tries to indicate how such a huge reference work could have greatly influenced such important thinkers as George Berkeley, David Hume, Voltaire, Denis Diderot, Gottfried Wilhelm von Leibniz, the Earl of Shaftesbury, and Bernard Mandeville. A detailed biography of Bayle is also presented, culminating in Bayle's defense of the *Dictionary* against his religious brethren and, in his last decade of controversy, against his friend Leibniz and against theologians of all persuasions. Bayle died while finishing the last of these controversial works.

The Introduction closes with ten pages devoted to assessing Bayle's real position in philosophy and theology. Bayle has been judged mainly by the effects of his work on the Enlightenment. Popkin instead tries to evaluate him chiefly in terms of the overall argument that runs through the *Dictionary*, together with Bayle's later defenses of his position. Bayle, like the skeptics before him, challenged all knowledge claims. Using the arsenal of arguments from Sextus Empiricus, Bayle attacked the leading philosophical, scientific, and theological views of the time, showing that the most rational theories become highroads to Pyrrhonism. When one realizes this, Bayle suggested, one should seek another guide to truth—faith or revelation. Whether in discussing secular or sacred matters, Bayle pointed out that reason fails to make the real world intelligible. The revealed world, he insisted, is fundamentally unintelligible to human reason. Many of Bayle's discussions about the content of the Bible try to drive this message home. The antirational theology developed throughout the *Dictionary* and the defenses of it bear much resemblance to the fideism of Søren Kierkegaard or Léon Chestov. Bayle also constantly said that his antirational view was the same as that of his worst enemy—Pierre Jurieu.

Jurieu, in his attacks on Bayle, insisted that no matter how close their views seemed to be in print, their purposes were radically different—in fact, diametrically opposed. Jurieu claimed that he was trying to lead people to faith, whereas Bayle was trying to destroy faith. Some said Bayle was a good

Christian; others doubted it. Bayle's fideism is stated with none of the fervor of Blaise Pascal or Kierkegaard, and his religious outlook seemed to have no emotional content. However, Popkin argues, Bayle may still have had a genuine religious orientation; but if so, it was one that he found he could not justify intellectually. If that was Bayle's situation, he could have been a man of faith, although only of an unemotional religion of the heart. But then what was his faith? Is there an extant religion or belief system that best conforms to Bayle's words? What religion did he actually accept? Popkin explores a wide range of possible answers, among them, that Bayle was a genuine Manichaean, that he was a secret Jew, that he was a Christian. Until we can know what he actually was, Popkin suggests, we cannot tell whether he was sincere or whether his Enlightenment admirers understood him properly.

Labrousse, Elisabeth. *Pierre Bayle, Tome I, Du pays de foix à la cité de Erasme, Tome II, Hétérodoxie et rigorisme*, in *Archives internationales d'historie des idées*. I and VI. The Hague, The Netherlands: Martinus Nijhoff, 1963 and 1964.

These two volumes provide the most complete presentation of the historical background of Pierre Bayle's career and the most complete examination and evaluation of his thought.

Prior to Elisabeth Labrousse's superb biography, the only lengthy one had been written by Bayle's younger contemporary, Pierre Desmaizeaux, fewer than twenty-five years after Bayle's death. Using a wealth of city, church, and personal records supplementing the available published material, Labrousse presented a detailed account of Bayle's development: his early Protestant life in southern France, his brief career as a Catholic, his studies in Geneva, his years as a teacher at the Protestant academy at Sedan, and his tempestuous and fruitful years engaged in many controversies in Rotterdam. Since Bayle fought advocates of almost every theology and philosophy, can one really tell whether he sincerely believed anything? Was he, as he claimed to be, a true and believing follower of John Calvin, or was he a complete skeptic? Labrousse ends her biographical account with a discussion of the last letter Bayle ever wrote—on the day of his death. She suggests that perhaps he died as the last Manichaean in history, or as one of the first deists.

The second volume analyzes Bayle's doctrines. Labrousse traces basic themes as they appear both in the *Dictionary* and in his many polemical works and letters—the latter both published and unpublished. Beginning by examining how Bayle used historical materials as ways of criticizing and challenging ideas, Labrousse shows how he developed a skepticism about the theological and philosophical views of his contemporaries. First to be considered is Bayle's examination of factual truths, then his examination of rational truths, and finally (the most interesting part) his examination of revealed truths. This involves fideism, biblical exegesis, the problem of evil, and the problem of free will. Here are to be found some of Bayle's most notorious paradoxes.

Finally, after showing how the various stages of Bayle's skeptical view were developed—and they represented different kinds of reactions to the dogmatic philosophers and theologicans of the time—Labrousse turns to some of Bayle's practical conclusions. If doubts can be raised about everything, are there any views that we can live by? One, of course, for which Bayle is justly famous, is that of civil and religious toleration. Bayle, more than John Locke, was the leading apostle of complete toleration. From being victimized both by the political intolerance of Louis XIV toward the Hugenots and by the religious intolerance of both Catholic and Protestant bigots, Bayle used his skepticism to erode any standards that could justify intolerance. Each person was left with his own conscience to guide him, and each was entitled to the liberty of conscience.

In a brilliant final section, Labrousse sums up her results by briefly showing Bayle's position in relation to the major currents of thought of his time. Bayle's views are neatly compared with those of René Descartes, Pierre Gassendi, Nicolas de Malebranche, and Pierre Nicole, among others. The lasting influence of Calvinism as well as skepticism is evident in Bayle's views. Labrousse's study is the most thorough available. Based on a rich knowledge of Bayle's Protestant heritage, the study provides the most complete picture of Bayle up to its time.

Dibon, Paul, ed., *Pierre Bayle, le philosophe de Rotterdam*. Amsterdam: Elsevier Publishing Company, 1959.

This volume, a collaborative collection of nine essays in English and French by European and American scholars, marked the beginning of a new stage of Pierre Bayle studies. The editor entitled his Introduction "The Rediscovery of Bayle." Most previous scholarship portrayed Bayle as an irreligious Enlightenment skeptic seeking to destroy Christianity. The authors of these essays, in examining Bayle's views in the light of what was occurring in his actual historical context, began a revolution in the evaluation of Bayle's place in European thought.

Paul Dibon pointed out that it is a myth to imagine Bayle as a skeptic who in his own time was writing as a premature Voltaire, providing the ammunition for future polemicists and *philosophes* to use against the *ancien régime*. In reviewing many previous studies of Bayle, Dibon showed that they ignored the fact that Bayle was a persecuted Calvinist who wrote a great many of his works in order to challenge what was happening to the Hugenots of the time. Bayle lived most of his intellectual life in the French-speaking Reformed circles in Holland.

The articles in this volume are by R. H. Popkin, H. C. Hazewinkel, André Robinet, Leszek Kolakowski, P. J. S. Whitmore, Elisabeth Labrousse, Robert Shackelton, C. Louise Thijssen-Schoute, and Erich Haase. The authors are from the United States, England, The Netherlands, France, Germany, and Poland. Each opened up new areas of Bayle studies. The first article by Popkin tried to show what was unique about Bayle's kind of skepticism in a seventeenth century context. Bayle's constant contrasts between reason and faith, as well as his purported fideism, were considered in terms of the views of other skeptics from Michel Eyquem de Montaigne to Pierre Huet. Bayle was shown to be less antirational than the Montaignians, but more so than his English contemporary, Joseph Glanvill. In this respect Bayle was closer to David Hume than to any of the other skeptics of the time.

Hazewinkel's article (in French) brings together a great deal of old and new material concerning what is known about Bayle's long sojourn in Rotterdam. Robinet (also in French) examines Bayle's critique of Nicolas de Malebranche's philosophy. Kolakowski (again in French) analyzes Bayle's astounding attack on Benedictus de Spinoza's theory, showing that in spite of Bayle's misunderstandings of Spinoza, he wrote the most penetrating criticism of his time. Whitemore (in English) studies Bayle's criticism of the views of his contemporary John Locke, showing the role that these cirticisms played in the history of Locke's influence. The essay by Labrousse (in French) began her presentation of the detailed background of Bayle that was hitherto unknown. Shackleton's essay on Bayle and Charles Montesquieu carefully traces Bayle's influence on the latter. The article by the late Thijssen-Schoute (in French) on the diffusion of Bayle's ideas in Europe shows the many different directions that Bayle's ideas took, as well as the diverse uses to which they were put. The last article (in French), by the late Erich Haase, sheds some light on one aspect of the controversy between Bayle and his onetime protector and later archenemy among the French Reformed theologians, Pierre Jurieu.

This volume shows how new scholarship requires a reevaluation of both Bayle's thought and his role in the pre-Enlightenment. The articles also point to a great deal of serious research that had to be done in order to gain a fuller understanding of Bayle's achievements. Much of the work on Bayle of the last twenty years had been influenced by this ground-breaking volume.
—*R.H.P*

ADDITIONAL RECOMMENDED READING

Brush, Craig B. *Montaigne and Bayle: Variations on the Theme of Skepticism*, in *International Archives of the History of Ideas*. No. 14. The Hague, The Netherlands: Martinus Nijhoff, 1966. Important study of the similarities and differences between the skeptical views of Montaigne and Bayle.

Mason, H. R. *Pierre Bayle and Voltaire*. London: Oxford University Press,

1963. A careful study of the influence of Bayle on Voltaire.

Rex, Walter. *Essays on Pierre Bayle and Religious Controversy*, in *International Archives of the History of Ideas*. No. 8. The Hague, The Netherlands: Martinus Nijhoff, 1965. Places Bayle's views in the context of the religious controversies of the time.

Robinson, Howard. *Bayle the Sceptic*. New York: Columbia University Press, 1931. The standard presentation of Bayle as an unbeliever.

Sandberg, Karl C. *At the Crossroads of Faith and Reason: An Essay on Pierre Bayle*. Tucson: University of Arizona Press, 1966. Attempts to show how Bayle's views on faith and reason are compatible with religious belief.

A TREATISE CONCERNING
THE PRINCIPLES OF HUMAN KNOWLEDGE

Author: George Berkeley (1685-1753)
Type of work: Metaphysics, epistemology
First published: 1710

PRINCIPAL IDEAS ADVANCED

The belief in abstract ideas had led to the supposition that material objects are quite different from sensations; the fact is that material objects are nothing but collections of sensations given a common name.

Esse *is* percipi; *to be is to be perceived—this is a truth concerning all material objects.*

If it be argued that ideas are copies of material objects, consider whether anything could be like an idea but an idea.

The distinction between primary and secondary qualities (between such structural properties as figure, motion, and shape, on the one hand, and color, odor, and sound, on the other) on the ground that the former are objective, the latter subjective, cannot be maintained: the primary qualities depend on the secondary; they are equally subjective.

There is no independently existing material substratum; a distinction between the world of illusion and the world of reality can be maintained by realizing the greater vividness and coherency to be found in veridical sensations.

The order in nature is created and maintained by God, who secures the reality of all things by his perception.

The idea that "all those bodies which compose the mighty frame of the world, have not any subsistence without a mind—that their *being* is to be perceived or known" will hardly seem obvious to anyone unfamiliar with Bishop Berkeley or with idealism. This startling statement has considerable shock value, but it is true to Berkeley's bold metaphysical thesis that reality is mental or spiritual in nature.

The statement's emphasis on perception reveals its author's epistemological and methodological approach: empiricism. While not all empiricists would accept Berkeley's conclusions and not all metaphysical idealists would accept his method, none would deny his importance in the traditions of both empiricism and idealism. That his method and even his immaterialism have influenced some modern physicists and that his analytical technique is valued even by such antimetaphysicians as the logical positivists are proofs of the classical status Berkeley's work still enjoys.

His aims, however, were primarily those of a metaphysician and theologian; he wished to undermine skepticism and atheism by refuting materialism, to demonstrate God's existence and immateriality, to show the immortality of the soul, and to clarify current scientific and philosophical confusions. The latter are due, he claimed, not to inherent defects in man's mental faculties, but to their use: "we have first raised a dust and then complain we cannot see." Berkeley intended to settle this dust and to destroy materialism.

A chief cause of obscurity, he begins, is the doctrine of abstract ideas, the theory that the mind can abstract from particular qualities a clearly conceived notion of what is common to them, but which itself is otherwise like none of them, or that the mind can separate in thought what cannot be separated in reality. An example of the first abstraction would be a notion of color which is neither red, blue, green, and so forth, or of extension which has neither size, shape, line, plane, nor surface; an illustration of the second would be an abstract idea of color or motion without extension.

Berkeley finds such abstraction psychologically impossible and challenges the reader to conceive such an idea as that of a triangle with all of the general and yet none of the specific characteristics of triangles. But must Berkeley then deny the universality of ideas essential to rational demonstration such as geometrical proofs relevant to all triangles? No—ideas may be general without being abstract; we generalize particular ideas by temporarily disregarding their unique features, while our demonstrations concern only features shared. But this universality in *function* must not be mistaken for abstract *conception*; the latter is actually without content and unintelligible.

Berkeley claims that the confused belief in abstract ideas arises from language; we have assumed that general names signify precise abstract ideas indispensable to thinking and communication, but these assumptions are false. Let us then attend not to words but to ideas themselves; since these are perfectly transparent, being known directly, we can avoid merely verbal controversies and errors springing from abstraction. Thus, we will be prepared for a most far-reaching application of the above conclusions to an analysis of the nature and existence of the objects of knowledge.

The objects of knowledge, Berkeley writes, are ideas of three kinds: sensations; ideas originating in the mind's own passions and activities; and those of memory and imagination. Our immediate concern is with "sensible" objects. Through sight we know color; through sight and touch we know size and shape; through touch, hardness; through smelling, odors. Certain constant collections of such ideas are considered one object or thing and accordingly named, such as "apple" or "tree." But obviously perceived ideas require a perceiver, and this is spirit or mind, not itself an idea. Careful examination shows that thoughts and ideas have no existence external to minds; hence "sensible" things or physical objects do not exist apart from their perception in minds—their very "*esse* is *percipi*"; for them to *be* is to be perceived.

The typical reaction to this conclusion is to accuse Berkeley of denying the reality of the physical world and even the evidence of his senses. But Berkeley explains that when we say that a table *exists*, this means that we or some other spirit sees and feels it, or will do so on occasion. The very meaning of "existence" or "being" applied to perceptible objects is exhaustively described in terms drawn from perception—nothing else can meaningfully be said about them. To think that sensible objects or their alleged metaphysical substratum, matter, exist "without" (external to) the mind is to entertain an unintelligible abstraction and a clear contradiction. People commonly think that houses or mountains exist unperceived. But what are these but objects of the senses? Is it not self-contradictory to think that sensations or ideas exist unperceived? When we imagine that we can think of unperceived objects we are merely thinking of objects while forgetting the perceiver, but meanwhile we *are* perceiving or thinking of them. We cannot conceive the inconceivable.

But the common belief that matter exists even when it is unperceived will not die easily, so Berkeley tries to anticipate every possible objection. One of the first arises from the "representative" theory of perception, which grants that ideas occur only in minds but holds that they represent or copy things outside minds. Berkeley's most direct answer is that ideas can resemble nothing but other ideas. How could a color represent something uncolored, or a sound something inaudible?

Both rationalists and empiricists such as Descartes and Locke held that in describing our knowledge of the physical world we must distinguish sensed qualities which are mostly subjective from others which are wholly objective. These philosophers argue that "primary" qualities such as figure, motion, spatial location, and shape inhere in objects themselves and are perceived without distortion or addition by the observer. But "secondary" qualities such as color, sound, and taste are so obviously variable they must be contributed by the subject's mind, though of course originally caused by action upon him of the primary qualities. Thus color qualities are subjective but caused by motion of light—color is "in the mind" but motion is "out there." Since qualities must qualify something (it was assumed), the primary qualities subsist in matter, the reality of which they are the appearances. Thus primary qualities really do represent or copy the external world.

But this theory is fallacious, Berkeley holds; if it admits that secondary qualities are in the mind, it must concede that primary qualities are also, since both types are inseparable actually and conceptually. Can one conceive of an extended, moving body which has no color or temperature? Too, the arguments from their relativity proving that secondary qualities are subjective apply equally to the primary. Consider size; our estimate of size depends on the nature and position of our sense organs. Berkeley's *Three Dialogues Between Hylas and Philonous* (1713) makes this point by noting that what will seem minute to a man may appear mountainous to a mite. Even number varies with point of view, as when a given length is considered as one, three, or thirty-six (yard, feet, or inches). But finally, the copy theory leads to utter skepticism by insisting that ideas represent something wholly unlike ideas, and by distinguishing between "mere appearance" and "reality," for it thus posits an external world forever unknowable.

Still, belief in a material substratum or support of sensed qualities will persist. Yet matter cannot literally "support" qualities, since "support" is itself a spatial term and space is perceptual. Even if there were such a substance, the problem of knowledge would remain. Knowledge stems from either sense or reason; the former yields only immediate objects of perception, or ideas, as even the materialists hold. But reason cannot bridge the gap between ideas and matter, since it would then have to argue from what we know—ideas—to something quite alien; and materialists themselves admit no logically necessary relationship between ideas and matter. Furthermore, it sometimes happens, and conceivably always could happen, that we entertain ideas when no external bodies are supposed present, as in the case of dreams. Finally—and here Berkeley broaches a problem Descartes could not solve—how could matter possibly act on spirit to produce ideas? The more one insists on their substantial differences, the less conceivable is causal interaction.

But if we deny the reality of external bodies, will it not sound very odd to say that we eat and drink ideas? Of course, agrees Berkeley; but his argument is about truth, not terminology. We may use common speech, even the term "matter" itself, as long as we refer only to the sensible world. If an opponent boasts his senses' superiority to any argument whatever, Berkeley is only too glad to join him, for he denies nothing actually perceived. "It were a mistake to think that what is here said derogates in the least from the reality of things." Berkeley intended to refute skepticism and atheism not by denying reality but by showing the impossibility of the materialistic account of it.

Yet if his theory is true, can it distinguish reality from illusion—for example, real from merely imaginary fire—since everything perceived consists only of ideas? If there is any doubt, Berkeley answers, put your hand in the real fire, and you will sense a pain lacking in the imaginary one—but can you suppose pain existing externally to a mind? We differentiate fantasy and illusion from the real world by obvious differences in their ideas; those of the latter are more vivid, constant, and coherent; their regular, predictable order constitutes the laws of nature, and they are independent of our wills as imagination is not. In fact, this independence marks the one legitimate sense in which we speak of "external objects"; sensed qualities are external to finite spirits' wills but not to that of the eternal Spirit, God, of whose will they are a perceptible expression.

Almost every reader objects that if the existence of things depends on perception, they will exist and cease to exist with the occurrence and cessation of perception, and that this theory is absurd. Berkeley counters by asking whether the statement that a table continues to exist when everyone leaves the room means anything more than that *if* one were still there he would perceive it, or if he were to return, he would once again see it. From the reliability of nature's order we can both reconstruct the past and predict the future, in neither of which are there *present* finite minds as perceivers, but this is wholly consistent with saying that objects and events are only what they are perceived to be (in past, present, or future). If no finite minds existed at all, whatever remained would nevertheless be perceived by the omniscient, eternal Spirit. Clearly, the strength of Berkeley's arguments here lies in the difficulty of *describing* an existent known to no mind whatever.

But is this really a plausible account of nature? Must not any scientific explanation of natural events presuppose causal efficacy resident either in matter itself or in primary qualities such as extension and motion? Berkeley says no, he has shown already that the notion of matter explains nothing at all, since it is incomprehensible and the primary qualities are ideas. Ideas are inert or inactive, having no causal power; there is no *idea* of causation in addition to those of successive events. Yet we gain a *notion* of causality from our own volition; we find that we can produce and manipulate some ideas at will. But if action is the prerogative of spirit, and if finite minds could not possibly produce the vast and intricate system of ideas we call nature, it follows that nature is the work of the infinite Spirit.

Suppose, however, that we grant both the existence of this Spirit and the extremely complicated mechanism of nature. To what purpose did God create such a powerless machine if he wished merely to communicate with finite minds? Why not do it directly? Berkeley meets this cavil by observing that if anything were superfluous, it would be an unknowable, ineffectual corporeal substance; it is possible, on the other hand, to give a rationale for nature.

Its orderly mechanism, while not indispensable to God, is still instrumental to man's learning and profit. Observing the conjunction of fire and heat, man learns not that the idea of fire *causes* the idea of heat, but that the former *signifies* that the latter will follow. Single ideas are like words, and the laws of nature like the grammar of a language; however, just as it is unwise to study only grammar and neglect meaning, so it is folly for science to concentrate only on mechanical laws and neglect the final causes (purposes) they express, those determined by God's wisdom and goodness. This does not derogate from science, but redirects it to explication of phenomena as signs rather than as effects of physical causes. Thus the hypothesis of matter is unnecessary even to physics.

Why, then, is belief in matter so pervasive? Partly because men found that objects of sensation seemed to be independent of themselves and thus supposed that such ideas exist externally. Philosophers saw the error of this supposition, but in trying to correct it by positing the external existence of matter they substituted another mistake, unaware of the internal contradictions involved. Furthermore, the operations of the eternal Spirit are so lawful that it was not imagined they were those of a *free* spirit rather than those of rigidly mechanical causes; and while they clearly point to his being, still there is no collection of sensed qualities making God visible or tangible as men are.

In the foregoing considerations the existence of spirit has been assumed on the basis of only one argument—that since ideas are not self-subsistent and matter is a nonentity, ideas can exist only in a different substance, spirit. But if they are inactive and we can thus have no ideas of spirit, how do we *know* that spirit exists? Berkeley says that we have a *notion* of spirit because we understand the terms describing it and its activities, a notion we get "by inward feeling or reflection." Other spirits are known by reasoning from analogy with our own; we perceive their effects and infer other minds as causes. A spirit's existence consists not in being perceived but in perceiving; it is "one simple, undivided, active being—as it perceives ideas it is called the *understanding*, and as it produces or otherwise operates about them it is called the *will*." No more than a notion of matter can be abstracted from sensed qualities can the existence of spirit be abstracted from its cogitation.

An interesting consequence follows from this in conjunction with Berkeley's analysis of time; time cannot be abstracted from the succession of ideas we experience, and so the duration of a spirit depends on the ideas and activities occurring within it. Therefore, Berkeley concludes, the spirit always thinks, the notion of a literally thoughtless mind being unintelligible. He asserts, "*Spirits* and *ideas* are things so wholly different. . . . There is nothing alike or common in them. . . ." Since spirits are indivisible, incorporeal, and unextended, it follows that they are not subject to the laws of nature and hence enjoy immortality.

Berkeley's arguments for God's existence have been given in part; the eternal Spirit must exist as the only sufficient cause of nature. When we consider the lawfulness, perfection, beauty, and design of the whole system, it is obvious that the characteristics of nature suggest the character of God. God's existence is in a sense known more certainly than that of any other spirit, since we constantly perceive his effects, even those ideas by which we communicate with other men. If we do not realize this fact fully, it is because we are "blinded with excess of light."

But granted the existence of God, Berkeley is still faced with the problem of evil. Why does God's universe contain pain, monstrosities, sorrow, death? And is the cumbersome machinery of nature very obviously turned directly by the hand of God? Berkeley answers that natural events occur according to rules of the greatest simplicity and generality; without such regularity there could be no human foresight. What seems like waste from man's viewpoint—countless blighted plants, little fish devoured by parents, and so forth—can be understood as necessary to the riches of God; the apparent defects of nature really augment its beauty, and seeming evil contributes to the good of the whole. Even the mixture of pain with pleasure is necessary for man's guidance. Clear understanding of these truths instills in us that holy fear which is the chief motive to virtue, and indeed "consideration of God and our duty," was Berkeley's chief aim in writing the book.

To what extent did Berkeley achieve his announced aims? The complete answer cannot be given in brief, just as Berkeley himself could not make all the grounds and implications of his philosophy clear at once. Many readers find themselves unable to refute Berkeley's arguments, yet they remain unconvinced by them; and many professional philosophers have given long and profound attention to the problems he raises. A great merit of this book and of the *Three Dialogues* is that Berkeley was thorough and clever in foreseeing and forestalling possible objections. Yet there are criticisms which, while insufficient to prove a diametrically opposite position such as materialism, or even a more moderate realism, nevertheless show that Berkeley's conclusions do not necessarily follow from his premises.

He was probably correct in his insistence on the dangers of abstraction, although he sometimes seems to have confused conception with visualization. Many thinkers today would agree also with his demand that terms and statements describing the physical world be defined and verified by reference to sensory experience. But can one infer from this experience that the world is ultimately mental or immaterial in nature? Berkeley's argument seems either to beg the question or to depend on ambiguous terms. A fair but condensed statement of it seems to be this: (1) Physical objects are objects of knowledge. (2) Objects of knowledge are ideas or sets of ideas. (3) Ideas and sets of ideas are in the mind, or mental. (4) Therefore, physical objects are in the mind, or mental. But "objects of knowledge" is ambiguous, unless one already grants that the world is mental; in the first sentence, it means "nonmental things," but in the second it means "constituents of knowledge." Of course, the constituents of knowledge are ideas by definition, but this fact does not bestow upon knowledge the power to *constitute* the real nature of what would not otherwise have been considered ideal or immaterial. Whether we do or do not perceive or conceive a "physical" object is actually irrelevant to the object itself.

Still, this criticism does not prove that physical objects are independently real or that the term "matter" has a meaning describable in terms not ultimately derived from perception. Berkeley has a strategical advantage in the fact that all men are caught in what Ralph Barton Perry called "the egocentric predicament": in a sense we are forever imprisoned within our own consciousness, since we must always use thought as a bridge to the "outside." But this advantage can also be a liability, for Berkeley's skepticism about external reality can be turned against our knowledge of other minds, the eternal Spirit, and even our own minds considered as substantial entities. Hume and subsequent philosophers, for example, have not agreed that an indivisible, incorporeal self can be discovered by inward reflection. Many of Berkeley's conclusions, such as his account of the self's continuity by saying that the spirit always thinks, have the appearance of absurdities demanded by his premises rather than of facts verifiable by experience. Hence, "spirit" itself may turn out to be an abstraction to be relegated to the company of "matter."

In Berkeley's later writings the purity of his empiricism is diluted by noticeable amounts of rationalism, and even in the present work there are assumptions hardly empirical in origin or confirmation, such as his facile acceptance of the traditional attributes of God—eternal, infinite, omniscient—as obviously pertaining to that Spirit. Berkeley's arguments for God's existence, which are the traditional cosmological and teleological "proofs," would have to meet the devastating criticisms produced by such philosophers as Hume and Kant before they could be acceptable to a modern reader. But even were the being of an infinite, omnipotent, omniscient Spirit granted, the traditional problem of evil posed by comparison of such a Creator with the created universe is one to which Berkeley offers only the usual but ineffective answers. Hume showed in the *Dialogues Concerning Natural Religion* (1779) how ill such answers suit even an empirical theism.

While it is thus doubtful that Berkeley accomplished some of his chief aims, it is certain that he achieved much by the method of his efforts. If he unintentionally undercut his own metaphysics by settling the dust of materialism, philosophy since has been able to learn from his experience.—*M.E.*

PERTINENT LITERATURE

Pitcher, George. *Berkeley*. London: Routledge & Kegan Paul, 1977.

Although it is written in a style that is lucid and easy to read, George Pitcher's *Berkeley* is not a book to be recommended to the novice in philosophy but only to the advanced student. The level of discussion, including both the presuppositions made concerning the history and problems of philosophy and the sophistication of the arguments employed, renders this a book designed for the scholar. In it the author combines a study of the development of George Berkeley's philosophical thought with an exposition and critical analysis of his views, concentrating on his epistemology and metaphysics but containing a chapter, the last, devoted to his moral philosophy.

After a short account of his subject's life, Pitcher turns to Berkeley's first published work, *An Essay Toward a New Theory of Vision* (1709). Three chapters are devoted primarily to this work; in them Pitcher considers Berkeley's views on the visual perception of distance, the visual perception of magnitude, and the heterogeneity of tangible and visible objects. The most important conclusion that Pitcher draws from his analysis of *An Essay Toward a New Theory of Vision* is that Berkeley believes that the metaphysical status of visible objects is quite different from that of tangible objects. The former are nothing more than ideas whose sole existence is in the mind of an observer;

their being consists in their being perceived. Tangible objects, however, are ontologically independent of any observer, having a physical existence in three-dimensional space. Pitcher's description of Berkeley, thus, is of a metaphysical dualist, in that he accepts the existence of both mental and physical reality, although he draws the line between these in an unusual place. As Pitcher hastens to add, however, Berkeley does not persist long in his original dualism, replacing it shortly with his final, idealistic (or mentalistic) conception of reality.

Chapter V is devoted to Berkeley's attack on abstract ideas, which he argues to be the ultimate source of the "opinion strangely prevailing amongst men that houses, mountains, rivers, and in a word all sensible objects have an existence natural or real." Against the theory of abstract ideas, whose chief philosophical spokesman and his main target was John Locke, Berkeley mounted a dual attack, attempting to establish not only that such ideas do not exist but also that they cannot exist. In Chapter VI, Pitcher examines in detail the arguments Berkeley offers, reaching the conclusion that Berkeley does not succeed in his goal of demolishing the theory of abstract ideas since the existence of such entities is necessary to explain the connection between general terms and the range of particular things to which they apply.

With an excursus in Chapter VII, devoted to an examination of Berkeley's attack on Lockean matter, the next five chapters concentrate on the mature Berkeleyan theory of reality and the ways in which it is known, drawing for their sources primarily on *A Treatise Concerning the Principles of Human Knowledge* and *Three Dialogues Between Hylas and Philonous*. Pitcher points out that Berkeley's enterprise consists in commencing with the same assumption about sense perception with which Locke (and also René Descartes) had begun and then going on to construct his own novel and radical metaphysical system from this basis. The assumption is simple and, Berkeley would claim, indisputable: In sense perception, what the perceiver has before his mind in every case is just one or more ideas of sense. In Chapters VI through X, Pitcher outlines and critically assesses the main arguments Berkeley offers in the construction of his world view. On some counts—for example, that the view can be interpreted in a way that would be acceptable to common sense— he supports Berkeley. On others—for example, that Berkeley demolishes Locke's theory of matter—he takes issue with him. On still others—for example, that God knows every object (that is, idea) that exists—he tries to develop an interpretation of Berkeley's thought that is not internally incoherent.

In Chapter XI Pitcher turns to one of the most difficult and controversial aspects of Berkeley's philosophy: his view of the nature of the human mind and the means by which we can know it. This is a rich and rewarding chapter offering a number of insights into Berkeley's developing thought. Pitcher points out that Berkeley originally held the view that the mind is not a real entity but only a "congeries" of perceptions (thus anticipating David Hume) but gradually came to his final theory that it is a mental substance. He also rejects the common interpretation that we have a direct intuitive awareness of our mind, reading Berkeley as advancing the view that our knowledge is gained by a process of reflection. Such an interpretation has an important historical consequence, as Pitcher makes clear. "With the doctrine of reflection . . . Berkeley joins the rationalists in holding that by the use of reason alone, one can arrive at substantial truths about reality."

Pitcher commences his discussion of Berkeley with an appreciation of his philosophy phrased so felicitously that only full quotation can do it justice. He writes: "Berkeley's metaphysics rises in the garden of British thought like some fantastic plant—beautiful and extravagant. Nevertheless, when one digs among its roots, one finds there a sober, well-informed account of that most familiar of processes—sense perception. How these ordinary roots yield such wondrous foliage is the story of Berkeley's philosophy."

Bracken, Harry. *Berkeley*. London: Macmillan and Company, 1974.

In his book *Berkeley*, Harry Bracken is concerned not just with offering an exposition of the views of the philosopher but equally with providing a historical interpretation of them. His objective in the latter is to support a thesis that runs counter to the traditional conception of George Berkeley's work and its place in the modern tradition; according to Bracken, Berkeley is not a British empiricist, to be viewed as the follower of John Locke and precursor of David Hume, but rather a Continental rationalist, the intellectual descendant of René Descartes and Nicolas de Malebranche. As he states his thesis at the outset of his argument: "Berkeley is neither British nor empiricist. If he must be labelled, he might more accurately be called an Irish Cartesian." To support his interpretation Bracken devotes a considerable portion of his discussion to various thinkers in the Western tradition. He directs attention to such diverse figures as Plato, Aristotle, Saint Augustine, Thomas Aquinas, Gottfried Wilhelm Leibniz, Simon Foucher, and Pierre Bayle, as well as Descartes and Malebranche. Thus the book is an invaluable work in the history of ideas, as well as an essay on Berkeley.

Bracken begins his discussion, after a brief summary of Berkeley's life, with a discussion of the philosopher's early views as developed in his first published book, *An Essay Toward a New Theory of Vision* (1709). He concentrates on two arguments. First is Berkeley's theory of *minima sensibilia*, which is a criticism of contemporary mathematical reconstructions of reality based on the contention that a physical "point" cannot be reduced in size beyond a minimum limit in which it can be perceived through one of the senses. Second is the "man-born-blind" thought experiment. This "experiment" concerns a hypothetical individual blind from birth who suddenly can see, and the question turns on his ability to distinguish visually between the shapes of various physical objects he had previously known only through touch. The postulated fact that he cannot do so leads Berkeley to conclude that the ideas gained through sight and touch are radically heterogeneous.

The central portion of the book is devoted to a commentary on Berkeley's famous dictum, *esse est percipi*, concentrating on four consequences he derives from it, which Bracken calls, respectively, antiabstractionism, the likeness principle, the principle of ontological inherence, and the analysis of skepticism. The discussion is based largely on the Introduction and Sections 1-33 of *A Treatise Concerning the Principles of Human Knowledge*.

Berkeley's antiabstractionism, or denial of our ability to form abstract general ideas, is the chief topic of the Introduction to *A Treatise Concerning the Principles of Human Knowledge*. Bracken recognizes Berkeley's view to be a consequence of his empiricistic assumption about the origin of our ideas, but he emphasizes a contrary point to which little attention has been given; namely, that Berkeley's antiabstractionism has roots in Descartes as well. Since Descartes and his followers rested their antiabstractionism on a rejection of empiricism, in siding with them (and against Locke) Berkeley reveals himself, at least in this respect, to be an antiempiricist. In Bracken's summation, "No step that Berkeley could have taken would so clearly have put him within the Cartesian camp than beginning an examination of the principles of human knowledge with a set of arguments against abstractionism." The likeness principle describes one of Berkeley's chief arguments against a belief in the existence of a material world. It attacks representative theories of perception—those that hold that our ideas resemble and hence are representative of physical objects—on the grounds that an idea can be like nothing but an idea. The principle of ontological inherence is closely related to the likeness principle, being the theory that ideas, not having their source in a material world, exist solely in the mind. All three of the consequences just noted support the fourth and most important, Berkeley's analysis of skepticism. A basic motivation behind Berkeley's work was his desire to refute skepticism by showing how it is possible for us to know the nature of reality. This Berkeley believed himself to have accomplished by eliminating the gulf separating knower from known through giving the objects of our knowledge a home within the very mind that knows them.

In the latter portion of his book Bracken turns to Berkeley's ontology, concentrating on the nature of the mind and the way in which it is known. On these and related issues, Bracken believes, Berkeley's debt to the Cartesians is particularly evident. Elements common to both include their views on the contrast between a mind and an idea, the ontological dependence of ideas on minds, the radical difference between ideas as sentiments and ideas as concepts or notions, our knowledge of other minds by analogy with our own, and our belief in God as the only primary cause whose existence is directly evident from a reflection on the objects of knowledge. On all of these counts Berkeley's stand represents a clear continuation of the tradition of rationalism.

After a discussion in the final chapter devoted to several of Berkeley's lesser-known writings, Bracken concludes his book by giving two reasons for offering a Cartesian interpretation of Berkeley's philosophical work: (1) Such an interpretation is supported by the texts and (2) it encourages an appreciation of both philosophers as defenders of the dignity of the human person.—*O.A.J.*

ADDITIONAL RECOMMENDED READING

Armstrong, D. M. *Berkeley's Theory of Vision*. Melbourne, Australia: Melbourne University Press, 1960. A critical examination of Berkeley's *An Essay Toward a New Theory of Vision*.

Bennett, J. F. *Locke, Berkeley, Hume*. Oxford: Clarendon Press, 1971. A comparative study of three central themes in the three philosophers.

Luce, A. A. *Berkeley and Malebranche*. Oxford: Clarendon Press, 1934. A comparative study of the two philosophers.

Ritchie, A. D. *George Berkeley: A Reappraisal*. Manchester: Manchester University Press, 1967. A reinterpretation of Berkeley's thought.

Steinkraus, W. E., ed. *New Studies in Berkeley's Philosophy*. New York: Holt, Rinehart and Winston, 1966. Thirteen essays on topics in Berkeley's thought by various authors.

Warnock, G. J. *Berkeley*. London: Penguin Books, 1953. A survey of Berkeley's thought.

THEODICY

Author: Gottfried Wilhelm von Leibniz (1646-1716)
Type of work: Theology, metaphysics
First published: 1710

PRINCIPAL IDEAS ADVANCED

The truths of philosophy and theology cannot contradict each other.

If God is all-good, all-wise, and all-powerful, how did evil come into the world?

The answer is that some error is unavoidable in any creature less perfect than its creator; furthermore, all possible worlds contain some evil, and evil improves the good by contrast.

Since man has free will, he is responsible for his acts; God's foreknowledge of the course of man's inclinations did not involve predestination.

The soul is coordinated with the body by a preestablished harmony.

In some philosophical circles Leibniz's *Theodicy* has been much neglected. This fact is not strange in view of the lack of interest, until recently, in traditional theological questions. It is strange, however, in view of the centrality of the *Theodicy* in Leibniz's own thinking. A good case could be made out that in his own mind it represented his most important, as well as his most characteristic, work. Without it there is much of importance left to Leibniz, to be sure: the pure metaphysician, the logician, the epistemologist, and the mathematician. Yet a balanced view of Leibniz's thought demands that the *Theodicy* be restored to its rightful place as central in his systematic effort.

For all of the continental rationalists (Descartes, Spinoza, and Leibniz), God occupied a large and a systematic place. Much could be made of all that these men owe to medieval theology, but the point is that all these men were centrally interested in the nature of God and his relationship to the natural world. The way in which this problem is worked out by Leibniz has a great deal to do with his solution to other problems. Moreover, there is evidence that Leibniz looked upon himself (to a considerable extent) as a theologian and was most proud of his contributions there. He wished to bring peace between Catholics and Protestants, and his writing has had some effect along this line. Particularly, Leibniz wanted to give rational solutions to traditional theological issues, and more than almost any other man he made it his major goal to provide a reconciliation between traditional religious views and philosophical thought, through demonstrating their essential harmony.

The *Theodicy* has a unique place among the classical writing in philosophical theology, for it is one of the first attempts to "justify the ways of God to man" in straightforward and philosophical terms. All theological views, to be sure, had dealt with the issue of God's choice and his creation of this particular natural order; but many had bracketed the question as being beyond rational scrutiny, and few had set out to answer it directly and in detail. Theodicy, the discussion of God's orderings insofar as they concern man's purposes, became a major part of philosophical theology after Leibniz's treatise.

Leibniz was among those of his age who considered Christianity's merit to be its rational and enlightened nature, as contrasted with at least some other religions. Along with rationalism went a tendency to minimize the differences in nature between God and man. Leibniz shared in this tendency, stating that the perfections of God are those of our soul, even though he possesses them in boundless measure. Leibniz was also an optimist about the essential goodness of man and the possibility of his perfection, and it is probably this view of the nature of man which more than any other single factor led Leibniz into his "best of all possible worlds" doctrine.

The freedom of man and the justice of God form the object of this treatise, and Leibniz's aim was to support both while minimizing neither. To do this would justify God's ways to man; man would be more content to receive what God has ordained, once the logic and harmony of God's plan were grasped. God does whatever is best, but he does not act from absolute necessity. Nature's laws allow a mean between absolute necessity and arbitrary decrees. In this way both God's and man's actions were to be explained and reconciled.

God (for Leibniz) is deeply involved in the affairs of men, continually creating them, and yet he is not the author of sin. Evil has a source somewhere other than in the will of God; God permits moral evil, but he does not will it. Leibniz hoped that this view would offend neither reason nor faith. Consciously, Leibniz set out to modify the strictness of the necessity he found in Hobbes, Spinoza, and Descartes. These philosophers had not been interested in a Christian doctrine of evil, for such a doctrine requires that man be given greater freedom in order to remove evil from God's immediate responsibility.

In the *Theodicy* Leibniz assumes that the truths of philosophy and theology cannot contradict each other. God acts in creation according to general rules of good and of order. Mysteries may be explained sufficiently to justify belief in them, but one cannot comprehend them. In explaining this, Leibniz distinguishes between logical or metaphysical necessity (whose opposite implies contradiction) and physical necessity. Even miracles must conform to the former although they may violate the latter. Reason is the ultimate norm: no article of faith must imply contradiction or contravene proofs as exact as mathematics.

When we come to consider evil, we do so by asking what just reasons, stronger than those which appear contrary to them, may have compelled God to permit evil. God is subject to the multitude of reasons and is even "compelled" by them. Leibniz infers that God must have had innumerable considerations in mind, in the light of which he deemed it inadvisable to prevent certain evils, for nothing comes from God which is not consistent with goodness, justice, and holiness. God must have been able to permit sin without detriment to his perfections; the weight of the reasons argues for it. Men are essentially in the same circumstance in which God was in finding it necessary to permit certain evils.

Since reason is a gift of God even as faith is, Leibniz argues, contention between them would cause God to contend against God. Therefore, if any reasoned objections against any article of faith cannot be dissolved, then the alleged article must be considered as false and as not revealed. Reason and faith can be reconciled. Yet reason is still faced with its central problem: How could a single first principle, all-good, all-wise, and all-powerful, have been able to allow evil and to permit the wicked to be happy and the good unhappy? Since Leibniz's time, philosophical inquiry into theological problems has often begun with this question.

Leibniz did not attempt to make the connection between God and moral evil an indirect one, which has been the traditional method. An evil will, he says, cannot exist without cooperation. An action, he asserts, is not for being evil the less dependent on God. Thus Leibniz makes the solution to the problem of evil directly a matter of accounting for God's action, since nothing can come to pass without his permission. God is the first reason of things.

The cause of this world, Leibniz writes, must be intelligent, for the first cause has to consider all possible worlds and then fix upon one to create. Such an intelligence would have to be infinite and, united to a goodness no less infinite, it cannot have chosen other than the best of all possible worlds.

It may be, for instance, that all evils are almost as nothingness in comparison with the good things which are in the universe. Whence did evil come then? We must consider that there is some original imperfection, due to the creature's limited nature, in the creature before sin. Leibniz adopts this view of "original sin," that some error is unavoidable in principle in a creature which must be less perfect than the being who creates it.

Other reasons for evil may be given: There is evil in all of the possible worlds, and so no choice could avoid it entirely. Evil often makes us savor good the more because of it—evil in that sense being necessary to any good. Man's will is responsible for its own actions; but this explanation simply leads Leibniz into a consideration of the divine foreknowledge and the question of divine predestination. Here Leibniz indulges in hairsplitting, distinguishing between what is certain and what is necessary. The will is inclined toward the course it adopts, and in that sense its action is and always has been "certain" in God's knowledge. But the action of man's will is not necessary, although this means merely that its opposite does not involve a logical contradiction. Such "contingency" Leibniz allows to remain.

God always chooses the best, but he is not constrained so to do. This is the extent of his freedom. Another natural sequence of things is equally possible, in the logical sense, although his will is determined in the choice it makes by the preponderating goodness of the natural order he chose; that is to say, the natural order that we actually have. Everything is certain and determined beforehand in man's action, although this is not the absolute necessity which would find any alternative logically contradictory. The necessity comes from the goodness of the object chosen.

The prevailing inclination always triumphs. In that sense Leibniz cannot conceive of either God or man acting irrationally, and hence the actions of both God and man are necessary. The whole future is doubtless determined. But since we do not know what it is, nor what it is that God foresees or has resolved, we must still do our duty, according to the reason God has given us and the rules he has prescribed. In the midst of an expansive metaphysical doctrine of possible worlds and the infinity of possible choices open to God, Leibniz adopted as conservative a theological view of predestination as the tradition has seen. A radical in metaphysics, he was almost a reactionary in his view of the fixed relation of God to the world.

Like many conservatives, Leibniz tried—and believed that he had succeeded—to reconcile absolute foreknowledge on God's part with human freedom. His answer is as old as Augustine's. We are free in that our actions flow from our own will, but the action of the will in turn is dependent upon its causes, which ultimately run back to God. Notwithstanding this dependence of voluntary actions upon other causes, Leibniz still believed that the existence within us of a "wonderful spontaneity" is not precluded. This makes the soul independent of the physical influence of all other creatures, although Leibniz was careful not to say that it is also independent of God.

The docrine of preestablished harmony is introduced to reconcile the difficulty. It was predestined from the beginning that God's design and man's volition should coincide: to Leibniz this seems to be a satisfactory solution. It is the typical solution of the rationalist. A reason has been given, and the whole scheme is seen to fit into a logical framework in which there is no contradiction or ultimate disharmony. Whereas a contemporary might begin with the premise that human freedom must at all cost be allowed for, Leibniz begins with the idea that all factors should be accounted for by a rational framework.

Preestablished harmony again accounts for the coordination of the soul and body. Like Spinoza's "parallel attributes," God ordained at the time of creation a logical ordering in which the soul's actions coincide with the body's movements. Like Descartes and Spinoza, Leibniz was thoroughly convinced that there is no interaction but there is a rationally determined plan of agreement. God has arranged beforehand for the body to execute the soul's orders. God has accommodated the soul to the body. Actually, the design of the world is simply an extension of God's perfection. Just as the rationalists of this era saw God and the human soul as being very close by nature, so also they viewed the natural order as an extension of the divine nature through creation. Although it is less than God, the created order essentially exhibits the same qualities as does divinity itself.

God is inclined toward every possible good, in proportion to the excellence of that good. God, before decreeing anything, considered among all the possible sequences of things that one which he afterwards approved. God grants his sanction to this sequence (our present natural order) only after having entered into all its detail. From such a description of God's rational selective activity comes the doctrine of the best of all possible worlds.

In most traditional accounts of ultimate origin (as, for example, in Plato's *Timaeus*), the first cause moves because he is good and outgoing, not grudging. But in all classical and in most medieval schemes such a god has no real choices to make. Leibniz presents a modern metaphysical framework in that he stresses the infinitely wide range of alternatives open to God's choice. The philosophical solution, however, is traditional. God selects according to fixed norms. It makes sense to say that classical thinkers also considered this world to be the best possible, but they believed that God had no alternatives. Leibniz simply set classical theory into a wider context of possibilities, but continued to agree to God's fixed goodness and to his necessary selection and creation.

In the *Theodicy* Leibniz also takes up traditional and primarily theological questions concerning Christ and salvation. His answers here are not startlingly novel, except that Leibniz transferred miracles, belief in the nature of Christ, and a Christian doctrine of salvation into a thoroughly rational framework. Leibniz wanted the doctrines of traditional Christianity to be amenable to his philosophical scheme of metaphysics. In the process of demonstrating this mutual harmony, like all philosophical theologians, he was pushed into giving some rather far fetched accounts of some rather difficult religious notions— for example, the assertion of the existence of all human souls in seed in their progenitors since the very beginning of things. Obviously such an idea would be helpful in establishing a religious notion of original sin in Adam; but it is hardly likely to be confirmable by the microscopic observations Leibniz's rationalism suggests.

It is not in the slightest an exaggeration to say that both Leibniz's questions and his answers are repetitious. The *Theodicy* sets out to refute certain doctrines which Leibniz opposed (particularly those of Pierre Bayle). Leibniz did this partly by reference to and elaboration of certain of his famous theories (preestablished harmony, the essential goodness of God's choice), but primarily his weapon was the repetition of his own position. As a rationalist Leibniz evinced the traditional irritation at finding that someone else did not find his reasoning as persuasive as he himself did and that his opponent continued to hold different theories. Despite this defect, the *Theodicy* illustrates how important works do not always have the technical rigor and logical tightness that one might suppose. Leibniz repeats his maxims and principles; he does little to explore them in detail. Yet Leibniz is dealing with questions of great moment and common interest, and his proposed solutions are interesting and suggestive. More precise and cogent pieces of philosophical analysis have proved to be less interesting over the years, but Leibniz's sometimes tedious and often loose reflections on the crucial issues of theology are still very much alive.—*F.S*

PERTINENT LITERATURE

Russell, Bertrand. *A Critical Exposition of the Philosophy of Leibniz*. London: George Allen & Unwin, 1900.

A Critical Exposition of the Philosophy of Leibniz is one of the most important secondary works on Gottfried Wilhelm von Leibniz's philosophy. The chief value of this work lies in its analyses of Leibniz's logic and metaphysics. According to Bertrand Russell, Leibniz's metaphysics—his monadology—is almost entirely derived from his logic. Russell does not think highly of Leibniz's theodicy; in his mind it represents an unsatisfactory compromise between Christian dogma and the "impieties" to which, Russell claims, Leibniz's own logic should have led him. Still, Russell presents a brief analysis of Leibniz's understanding of evil and its relation to an all-powerful, entirely good, God.

Russell maintains that in Leibniz's system, moral and physical evil (sin and suffering) are necessary results of metaphysical evil (imperfection). According to Leibniz, moral evil (that is, sin) is a consequence of judging wrongly, for if one were to judge rightly one would always act rightly. However, one is bound to judge wrongly since, because one is imperfect, one's perceptions are confused. Pain necessarily accompanies wrong actions. Thus metaphysical evil—imperfection—is the source of moral and physical evil.

Russell maintains that Leibniz's notion that moral and physical evil are necessary results of metaphysical evil is problematic. It stands in opposition to the traditional Christian account of evil and it poses the question whether imperfection is really evil. According to Russell, since imperfection is nothing more than finitude, Leibniz has no basis for asserting that imperfection is a type of evil. If existence is good, as Leibniz states, then everything is good by virtue of its existence. Internal consistency should have precluded the existence of evil in Leibniz's system altogether. Yet for Leibniz to deny that there is real evil in the world is to contradict Christian dogma. In order to stay within the bounds of Christian thought, Leibniz is forced into affirming the existence of something that his system cannot support.

A second problem arises from Leibniz's commitment to the Christian tradition. According to Leibniz, moral evil (sin) is the result of metaphysical evil. One sins because one is finite. According to traditional Christian dogma, sin is not necessary but contingent; that is, it is the result of free action. In Russell's estimation, Leibniz is not successful in his attempt to show that metaphysical necessity and freedom are compatible. Russell states: "The Ethics to which he [Leibniz] was entitled was very similar to Spinoza's; it had the same fallacies and similar consequences. But being the champion of orthodoxy against the decided atheist, Leibniz shrank from the consequences of his view, and took refuge in the perpetual iteration of edifying phrases."

A Critical Exposition of the Philosophy of Leibniz does not devote a great deal of attention to Leibniz's theodicy because Russell does not believe that it merits much attention. Nevertheless, what Russell does have to say is interesting and should be considered.

Lovejoy, Arthur O. *The Great Chain of Being*. Cambridge, Massachusetts: Harvard University Press, 1936.

The Great Chain of Being has an excellent chapter on the philosophies of Gottfried Wilhelm von Leibniz and Benedictus de Spinoza and a chapter on eighteenth century optimism which includes a brief treatment of Leibniz's theodicy. Anyone interested in Leibniz's thought will profit greatly simply from reading these two chapters. However, a complete reading of *The Great Chain of Being* is strongly recommended since the notions of plentitude, continuity, and gradation—notions which are immensely important for Leibniz—have a long history in Western thought. *The Great Chain of Being* is devoted to uncovering that history.

Arthur O. Lovejoy contends that the notion of plentitude—that everything which could possibly exist does exist—can be traced back to Plato, and that the idea of continuity—that there are no gaps in creation—can be deduced from Plato's notion of plentitude and found in some of Aristotle's teachings. The notion of gradation—that there is a hierarchy of being—is present in certain of Plato's writings and, to a larger extent, in Aristotle's works. In Neoplatonism all three of these notions are clearly present and are fully organized into a coherent philosophical doctrine.

According to Lovejoy, Western philosophy up to the nineteenth century is rationalistic in the sense that the questions "Why is there an actual world?" and "What principles determine the number of kinds of beings that make up the actual world?" are meaningful and can be answered. The answer to the second of these two questions usually involves the notions of plentitude, continuity, and gradation. The answer to the first question usually involves the notions of goodness and self-sufficiency, and, for the Christian philosopher, the idea of an omnipotent God.

Leibniz's philosophy illustrates the Christian brand of rationalism. The reason that there is a world at all is that there is a good God and that the principles that characterize the world are plentitude, continuity, and gradation. The world is full, there are no empty niches, and there is a definite hierarchy of being. Leibniz's famous contention that "This is the best possible world" is derived from the principles of God's goodness and of plentitude. Because God is good by definition, God chooses to create the best possible world. Because the world contains as many types of actualities as possible, this is the best possible world. For Leibniz variety is one of the important aspects of the best, and no other possible world could have as many types of actualities as the present world does.

In his *Theodicy* Leibniz addresses the issue of how there can be evil in the world if it is created by an all-powerful God who is entirely good. His solution to this quandary is that (with the exception of metaphysical evil) what is meant by "evil," that is, by sin and suffering, is necessary for the sake of plentitude. Leibniz writes: "It is true that one can imagine possible worlds without sin and suffering, just as one can invent romances about Utopias or about the Sevarambes; but these worlds would be much inferior to ours." Like Plotinus, who said that "the whole earth is full of a diversity of living things, mortal and immortal, and replete with them up to the heavens," Leibniz insists on the necessity of everything that is and on its essential goodness.

The Great Chain of Being is an informative inquest into a set of ideas which have played an important role in Western thought; in the process, it sheds a great deal of light on Leibniz's theodicy.

Griffin, David Ray. *God, Power, and Evil: A Process Theodicy*. Philadelphia: Westminster Press, 1976.

In *God, Power, and Evil: A Process Theodicy*, David Ray Griffin reviews and criticizes the most famous and influential theodicies of the past, concluding with a consideration of a theodicy based on the process philosophy of Alfred North Whitchead. In addition to Gottfried Wilhelm von Leibniz's theodicy, Griffin examines the biblical and Greek sources on the nature of God and the reality of evil and the traditional theodicies of Saint Augustine, Thomas Aquinas, Benedictus de Spinoza, Martin Luther, John Calvin, Karl Barth, John Hick, James Ross, Emil Fackenheim, and Emil Brunner.

Griffin believes that most scholars have misinterpreted Leibniz's theodicy. The dominant interpretation of Leibniz's position is that although there is sin and suffering in this world it is still the best possible world since any other possible world would include even more sin and suffering. God cannot create a world that is better than this world because God is limited by the possibilities that exist, many of which are "incompossible," that is, mutually exclusive. Leibniz does not doubt God's moral perfection—God chose to create the best possible world—but he does question God's omnipotence when "omnipotence" is taken to include the ability to do the impossible. The dominant interpretation of Leibniz's theodicy, then, is that real sin and suffering exist because God is limited by the types of things that can coexist and that sin and suffering are a result of this limitation.

Griffin argues very convincingly against this interpretation. According to Griffin, Leibniz's solution to the problem of evil—the problem of how to reconcile the fact of evil with the existence of an all-good, all-powerful being—is not to deny God's omnipotence but rather to deny the reality of genuine evil. God could have created a world with no sin or suffering (moral and physical evil), but he did not do so because it would not be "proper." A world with sin and suffering in it is better, *all things considered*, than any possible world without sin and suffering. Moral and physical evil add to the overall perfection of the world and hence are not genuinely evil. (Metaphysical evil, Griffin argues, is not genuinely evil since it is nothing more than finitude.)

Griffin is also interested in examining and explicating Leibniz's views on the relation of faith and reason and on contingent events and God's knowledge of the future. Griffin concludes that the difference between Leibniz's claim that faith should never be contrary to reason and the traditional position that faith is often unreasonable is "more verbal than real." Griffin's interest in Leibniz's contention that God knows the future in every detail, even the future of contingent events, is "less with the validity of Leibniz's arguments that this can happen without the contingency of these events being undercut than with the presupposition it requires about the nature of 'actual events.'" Griffin concludes that God could know everything that will happen only if the sufficient reasons for those things precede the occurrence of those things. If some of the sufficient reasons for any event lie within the event itself, then the event cannot be fully known before it occurs.

Griffin's work is scholarly—well-reasoned and well-documented—and accessible. The fact that it presents an alternative "process theodicy" which the author feels is entirely credible in the contemporary world is also significant. Even though Griffin takes exception to Leibniz's solution to the problem of evil, he shares Leibniz's concern that evil be explained in light of God's existence.—*M.F.*

ADDITIONAL RECOMMENDED READING

Carr, Herbert Wildon. *Leibniz*. Boston: Little, Brown and Company, 1929. Carr discusses Leibniz's historical situation, his philosophy, and his influence. He understands Leibniz's theodicy as a corollary of Leibniz's philosophy which may be rejected without damaging Leibniz's philosophical system.

Hick, John. *Evil and the God of Love*. New York: Harper & Row Publishers, 1966. Hick's book is an account of the major Christian theodicies and a statement of his own position. Hick understands Leibniz as compromising God's power and therefore holding to a "sub-Christian" concept of God.

Hostler, John. *Leibniz's Moral Philosophy*. New York: Barnes & Noble, 1975. Hostler's well-written book explores the ethical implications of Leibniz's philosophy.

Rescher, Nicholas. *The Philosophy of Leibniz*. Englewood Cliffs, New Jersey: Prentice-Hall, 1967. This is a systematic introduction to Leibniz's thought. Rescher gives an excellent account of how the various aspects of Leibniz's philosophy, including his theodicy, are related to each other.

CHARACTERISTICS

Author: Anthony Ashley Cooper, Earl of Shaftesbury (1671-1713)
Type of work: Ethics, aesthetics
First published: 1711

PRINCIPAL IDEAS ADVANCED

Metaphysics has little to offer man either in regard to a proof of the nature of the self or concerning his morality; in such matters it is better to count on common sense.

True philosophy is the search for what is just in society and beautiful in nature.

Nature is orderly, and virtue for men consists in following nature and in enthusiastically seeking out the true, the good, and the beautiful.

Conscience and aesthetic judgment are alike in being faculties for the discovery of the beauty of nature, the reflection of an order given to nature by God.

Man must exercise his reason by discussing opinions and by examining himself.

Anthony Ashley Cooper, third Earl of Shaftesbury, was a grandson of the famous Whig statesman of that name. When his own career in politics was cut short by ill health, he turned his liberal and humanitarian efforts into literary channels, bringing to the task, besides a puritan sense of moral responsibility, an aesthetic sensibility disciplined by the study of Greek and Roman models. His assorted essays, published under the title of *Characteristics of Men, Manners, Opinions, and Times*, develop the ideal of man working out the purposes of God through moral and spiritual striving. He opposed the dehumanizing tendencies of the Cartesian and Newtonian philosophies, much in the same way that Socrates had opposed the naturalism of an earlier day, and, like the famous Athenian, he taught his age that man should know himself.

John Locke, who was for many years secretary to the elder Shaftesbury, was tutor to the author of the *Characteristics* and may be credited with imparting to him a liberality of spirit and a general trust in reason. But Shaftesbury rejected Locke's theory of ideas and the whole philosophical enterprise which, beginning with Descartes, pursued the ideal of certitude based on self-evident truths.

Far from putting a stop to skepticism, said Shaftesbury, the attempt initiated by Descartes to demonstrate the rationality of nature and morality played directly into the hands of sophists and triflers. The famous *Cogito, ergo sum* merely stated a verbal identity. It left untouched the real problems, "what constitutes the I," and "whether the I of this instant be the same with that of any instant preceding or to come." We have nothing but memory, he said, to warrant our belief in our own identity; and if one wishes to play the metaphysical game, the question about the "successional I" must remain undecided. ". . . I take my being upon trust. Let others philosophise as they are able: I shall admire their strength when, upon this topic, they have refuted what able metaphysicians object and Pyrrhonists plead in their own behalf."

Indulging the irony or "wit" with which, according to Shaftesbury, persons of breeding habitually respond to the pedantry of scholars, Shaftesbury constructed a metaphysical theory of morals which showed, after the fashion of the Stoics and of Spinoza, that, if one accepts the theory of ideas, man's well-being consists in learning to entertain only those thoughts which will not disappoint. This excursus into "dry philosophy" and the "rigid manner" of metaphysical disputes was, however, only half serious. It was useful, he said, to be able to argue in this way with "moon-blind wits . . . who renounce daylight and extinguish in a manner the bright visible outward world, by allowing us to know nothing beside what we can prove by strict and formal demonstration. . . ." And, in any case, "it is in a manner necessary for one who would usefully philosophise, to have a knowledge in this part of philosophy sufficient to satisfy him that there is no knowledge or wisdom to be learnt from it."

Because it had become engrossed in introspection, Shaftesbury said, philosophy had fallen into ill-repute among men of judgment. The philosopher was now what was formerly intended by the word "idiot"—a person who can attend to nothing except his own ideas. Persons concerned to bring honest reason to bear upon the affairs of life stood "to gain little by philosophy or deep speculations of any kind." "In the main," said Shaftesbury, in a passage which was often appealed to during the eighteenth century, " 'tis best to stick to common sense and go no farther. Men's first thoughts in this matter [morals] are generally better than their second: their natural notions better than those refined by study or consultation with casuists." For, he added, "Some moral and philosophical truths there are withal so evident in themselves that 'twould be easier to imagine half mankind to have run mad, and joined precisely in one and the same species of folly, than to admit anything as truth which should be advanced against such natural knowledge, fundamental reason, and common sense."

But Shaftesbury was unwilling to give up the word "philosophy." A person does not become a philosopher by writing and talking philosophy, he said. In reality, a philosopher is one who reasons concerning man's main interests, and there are good and bad philosophers according as one reasons skillfully or unskillfully. In Shaftesbury's hands, therefore, the bald contrast between philosophy and common sense was not a philistine repudiation of the life of reason but an attempt to vindicate a venerable tradition against the pretensions of "the new learning." Although committed to the political ideals of the rising bourgeoisie, Shaftesbury was alarmed at what appeared to be its want of sound moral foundations. For the greater glory of God, the followers of Luther and Calvin repudiated nature; and for the greater glory of man, the followers of Bacon and Descartes repudiated the past. To remedy these defects, Shaftesbury turned to Plato and Aristotle and to the living tradition of Renaissance Platonism. The aim of philosophy is "to learn what is just in society and beautiful in Nature and the order of the world," and this with a view to enabling man to realize the highest ideal of manhood—what the Greeks called *aner kalos k'agathon*, and the Italians *uomo virtuoso*.

The starting point of Shaftesbury's moral philosophy was the conception of nature as an orderly whole. The daylight philosopher, in contrast to those who fumble among ideas in the cellars of their own minds, recognizes with Plato that nature is a system in which each part is ordered with a view to the perfection of the whole. Shaftesbury was no less impressed than were his contemporaries by the regular motion of the heavens. But even more remarkable, in his opinion, was the microscopic life revealed by the new biology. The latter, in particular, suggested that the world is a self-sustaining whole composed of subordinate wholes, each having a life and nature of its own but so adjusted that while it pursues its private end it also functions in the interest of the systems that comprehend it.

From this point of view, all excellence consists in following nature. Shaftesbury said that he was a realist, holding that virtue or excellence is "really something in itself and in the nature of things; not arbitrary or factitious; not constituted from without, or dependent on custom, fancy, or will; not even on the supreme will itself, which can no way govern it; but being necessarily good, is governed by it and ever uniform with it." The breeder of animals knows what is natural and what is unnatural behavior in a dog or in a horse; he knows a good animal from a mediocre one, and wherein the excellence of the former consists. So it is with men. By a native endowment, each of us knows what is just, fair, and honest in men's character and conduct.

The human soul, as Shaftesbury represented it, is like every other living form in that it has a natural constitution. Within the systems of nature and society, each human being is himself a system in which passions, inclinations, appetites, and affections have their place. Some of these are purely local, such as the appetite for food; others are more comprehensive, such as pride, embracing the individual's general interest; others, such as parental love and friendship, bind the individual to society. Each is good in its proper place. And man is endowed with reason to regulate them.

According to Shaftesbury, reason or reflection is that faculty by which man reviews his mind and actions and passes judgment upon them, either approving or disapproving. It manifests itself in two quite different ways, which may be designated "prudence" and "conscience." By the former, man judges what is to his advantage; by the latter, what is proper and right. Shaftesbury denied that prudence gives adequate direction for a man's life. For this purpose, we have been given conscience. It follows, according to Shaftesbury, that the goal of life does not lie in happiness, whether in this world or that to come, but in the perfection of the soul itself and its harmony with the total order of things.

In opposition to the religious doctrine of human depravity, Shaftesbury maintained that all men are endowed with a sufficient sense of right and wrong to enable them to achieve virtuous lives, and that the only obstacles are passion and vice. Appetite or passion he described as the elder brother of reason, striving to take advantage of reason; but when reason grows strong enough to assert itself, appetite, "like an arrant coward . . . presently grows civil, and affords the younger as fair play afterwards as he can desire." Vicious habits and customs presented a more difficult problem. One source of these, according to Shaftesbury, is "corrupt religion and superstition," which teaches men to regard as praiseworthy practices which are "most unnatural and inhuman." Another is idleness, such as befell the "superior" classes in his day. Without a proper goal in life, men fall, he said, into a "relaxed and dissolute state" in which passions break out.

As Shaftesbury pictured it, conscience or moral insight is all of a piece with aesthetic judgment. There is a "natural beauty of figures," for example, which causes a mere infant to be pleased with the proportions of a ball or a cube or a dye. And if, in more intricate cases, where color, texture, motion, sound, and the like are involved, there is room for dispute as to which is the finer fabric, the lovelier face, the more harmonious voice, it remains as a fundamental assumption "that there is a beauty of each kind." "All own the standard, rule, and measure; but in applying it to things disorder arises, ignorance prevails, interest and passion breed disturbance." Nor is it otherwise, Shaftesbury continues, in matters of conduct. That there is a "fitness and decency in actions" can never be denied as long as men preserve the distinction between "that which interests and engages men as good," and "that which they admire and praise as honest."

Ultimately, for Shaftesbury, the beautiful and the good are the same. If we are speaking of a building or of a picture or of the human body, we call it beautiful. If we are speaking of action, life, or operation, we call it good. There are, according to Shaftesbury, three degrees of beauty. The first is the beauty of "dead forms"—of pictures and statues—which exhibit harmony and proportion, but have "no forming power, no action or intelligence." The second, which possesses all that the former lacks, is a double beauty: it is the beauty of "forming forms"—of artists and craftsmen. But there is a third order of beauty—that which forms the "forming forms." Principally, this is the beauty of nature itself, or of the Mind which informs it. This parent-beauty, because it fashions men's minds, "contains in itself all the beauties fashioned by those minds, and is consequently the principle, source, and fountain of all beauty," even including "architecture, music, and all which is of human invention."

The admiration which we owe to this highest beauty was, for Shaftesbury, the foundation of true religion. He raised no opposition against Christianity, except to question whether it conduced to true worship and piety to dwell upon the evil of creation as contemporary divines were wont to do. He thought of himself as a deist, but he denied that the world is like a machine which the Maker, having completed, could leave to its own operation. He rejected the usual "proofs" of God based upon the necessity for a first cause and he appealed rather to the immanence of a continuing Providence which orders all things well.

Thus, Shaftesbury held morality to be the foundation for belief in God, rather than the contrary. But carried further, true religion, or the apprehension of the divine creativity in nature, raises man's eyes to a higher vocation for himself than he would otherwise know. As the offspring of divinity, he is himself divine and is called upon to be himself a creator—not merely in the sense of imposing form upon matter, but in the sense of forming his own nature and that of other rational creatures. In this way he participates in the highest beauty: "He only is the wise and able man who, with a slight regard to [bodies and outward forms] applies himself to cultivate another soil, builds in a different matter from that of stone or marble; and having righter models in his eye, becomes in truth the architect of his own life and fortune, by laying within himself the lasting and sure foundation of order, peace and concord."

Such wisdom comes only to those who exercise their reason in an extra-ordinary degree. Mere knowledge of the world does not suffice, nor do ordinary deliverances of conscience. A man must find ways of examining opinions which seem true to himself and his generation in order to pass from ignorance into knowledge. Shaftesbury recommended "soliloquy" as the best way for a person to rectify his opinions, especially for those addicted to being "talkers or haranguers" in public. " 'Tis the hardest thing in the world," he said, "to be a good thinker without being a strong self-examiner. . . ." For the same reasons, Shaftesbury wished for more honest discussion "in the way of dialogue, and patience of debate and reasoning, of which we have scarce a resemblance left in any of our conversations at this season of the world." Philosophy, or wisdom, as he conceived it, is not the sort of thing that can be transmitted as information. It is a discipline of the mind, a step beyond good breeding.

Shaftesbury's reaffirmation of design in the world raised in an acute form the problem of evil. His answer was similar to that given by the Stoics and by St. Augustine. Suffering and loss are bound to appear evil to the individual because of his limited perspective. When better instructed, we find cause for admiration in the arrangement by which the individual sacrifices his life for the species, and even in the relentless force of earthquake and fire. Monstrous and abnormal births, he said, do not mitigate against the design of nature, since they result not from any natural failure but from the natural conflict of forces. " 'Tis good which is predominant," says one of the characters in his dialogue; "and every corruptible and mortal nature by its mortality and corruption yields only to some better, and all in common to the best and highest nature which is incorruptible and immortal."

The optimism of Shaftesbury was far from being forced. As opposed to materialists, such as Thomas Hobbes, he found in the conception of nature as a system grounds for rejecting the doctrine of egotism and the war of each against all. He contended that besides the self-regarding passions man also has passions which impel him to act for the interest of others. Both kinds are necessary in the economy of things. Private affections are necessary, not only because they assist the survival of the individual, but also because they contribute to the public good. Similarly, social affections, such as parental love and friendship, further the interests and fill out the happiness of the individual. Shaftesbury argued that the purely selfish man does not, in fact, serve his own interest. On the other hand, it is possible for a person to be too much affected with the needs of others for even the public good. Thus, the happy life coincides with the life of virtue, in which reason is allowed to prevail over impulse.

The foundations of art, like those of mortals, must, according to Shaftesbury, be laid in natural harmonies and proportions which the styles and humors of a particular age cannot brush aside the impunity. True beauty, he said, is not that which appeals to the senses, but that wherein the rational mind may come to rest. Its enjoyment is a disinterested contemplation, totally different from the pleasures which have their seat in desire. Hence the artist should not aim to represent objects which men find enjoyable, but to create new unities analogous to those which make up the fabric of nature. True beauty lies deep. Many things which seem shocking and offensive at first are later known and acknowledged as the highest beauties.

The influence of Shaftesbury's thought was far-reaching. The French Encyclopedists and the early German Romantics were in his debt no less deeply than the moral philosophers of England and Scotland. The fact that in the Age of Reason "philosophy" freed itself from the knottier problems of metaphysics and epistemology, and engaged the attention of poets and economists, statesmen and propagandists, was in the main his doing.—*J.F.*

PERTINENT LITERATURE
Trianosky, Gregory W. "On the Obligation to Be Virtuous: Shaftesbury and the Question, Why be Moral?," in *Journal of the History of Philosophy*. XVI, no. 3 (July, 1978), pp. 289-300.

Gregory W. Trianosky notes that contemporary discussion of the question

"Why be moral?" has given insufficient consideration to an ethics of *being* as distinguished from an ethics of *acting*. Attempts at justification of the claim that one should be moral usually have involved, he says, arguments that the morally right act is—at least, almost always—also the prudent act. But, he continues, one plausibly might say, "Yes, I believe that I am justified in *acting* morally, outwardly; but am I justified in *being* a moral person, inwardly, and not just acting like one?" In his "Inquiry Concerning Virtue and Merit" in the *Characteristics*, Lord Shaftesbury, Trianosky maintains, construes the question "Why be moral?" as a demand for justification of the claim that one has what Shaftesbury calls an "obligation to be virtuous." Trianosky believes not only that an examination of Shaftesbury's arguments for such an obligation can make an important contribution to contemporary thought, but also that Shaftesbury's thought is interesting in its own right.

In support of his claim that it is always or almost always in one's own interest to be moral, Shaftesbury argues, Trianosky says as follows:

(1) It is always in one's own interest to be happy.
(2) Having the natural affections to an appropriate degree is (at least) a necessary condition for being happy.
(3) Therefore, it is always in one's own interest to have the natural affections to an appropriate degree.
(4) Being virtuous ("moral"), however, consists precisely in having the natural affections to such a degree (together with some other conditions which Shaftesbury holds to be satisfied by almost all rational creatures).
(5) Therefore, it is almost always in one's own interest to be virtuous ("moral").

Shaftesbury, Trianosky continues, appears to believe that the truth of step (1) needs no support, but he offers the following definitions and arguments (as Trianosky understands them) in support of (2) and (4) above.

(a) All *affections* are "sentiments" or "passions" (desires, attitudes, or mental states of a certain sort).
(b) An affection has as its *intentional object* that toward which the affection is directed or aimed.
(c) An affection has as its *immediate object* the good of the kind or species just in case the operation of the affection tends to enhance the good of the kind or species.
(d) An affection is *natural* just in case it has as its immediate object (and not necessarily its intentional object) the good of the kind or species. (Shaftesbury countenances, Trianosky notes, *some* natural affections the *intentional objects* of which are the good of the individual self.)
(e) An affection has a *rational* or *mental object* when its intentional object is something on which the mind reflects, such as past actions, character traits, and memories of events; an affection has a *sensible object* when it does not have a mental object.

(f) The *moral sense* (*proper*) is that faculty of only rational creatures which, upon reflection by such a creature, generally will approve of those affections (and their consequences) that are *natural* and disapprove of those which are not (Shaftesbury holds that not all rational creatures need have a *full* moral sense, but that in fact most do.)

(g) The *approving and disapproving attitudes* of the moral sense (proper) are themselves higher-order natural affections the intentional objects of which are moral, rational, or mental objects, not sensible ones.

(h) A *creature* is *virtuous* just in case it has a moral sense, and the intentional object of the approval of the moral sense is the natural affections and their consequences.

(i) An *action* is *virtuous* just in case it is performed out of the natural affections, and they are the intentional objects of the approval of the moral sense. (Trianosky observes that if his reading of the definition of "natural affection" is correct, then Shaftesbury, although he is neither an act-utilitarian nor a rule-utilitarian, plausibly can be considered a *trait-utilitarian*—"one who thinks, roughly, that an affection is virtuous or morally good if and only if its cultivation or operation maximizes utility.")

Shaftesbury's argument is paraphrased as follows. (The theological arguments for the obligation to be virtuous are not discussed since Trianosky believes that they are independent of the "moral sense" issues and arguments with which he is concerned.)

(1) All rational creatures introspect because they are rational.

(2) Upon introspection, one's "unjust" or "foolish" actions either will generate feelings of disapproval or they will not.

(3) (a) Suppose, on the one hand, that they *do* (as Shaftesbury believes in some sense they always do).

(b) Then, to have feelings of disapproval precisely is to manifest either a "prudential" moral sense (that is, a faculty—not a *full* moral sense—which recognizes that one cannot "do ill" without "deserving ill" and, deserving ill, one must fear and expect ill from everyone) or the moral sense "proper" (the faculty which recognizes that the wrong act is "deformed" and "odious" in itself, that it does not contribute to the public good).

(c) In case one possesses either a prudential moral sense or the moral sense proper, (it appears to follow that) it is not in one's self-interest to perform actions that will be disapproved by his or her moral sense.

(d) Therefore, it is in one's own interest to be virtuous.

It follows, Trianosky points out, that even if one rejects the notion of the moral sense proper—which is what Shaftesbury's *doctrine of the moral sense* concerns—the claim can still be made on prudential grounds alone that one has an obligation to be virtuous.

The argument continues:

(4) (a) Suppose, on the other hand, that upon introspection, "unjust" or "foolish" acts do *not* generate feelings of disapproval. (Since Shaftesbury believes that no rational creature lacks the prudential moral sense, this is to suppose that one lacks the moral sense proper.)

(b) Such a creature can be neither virtuous nor wicked and is "absolutely indifferent toward moral Good or Ill."

(c) If he is absolutely indifferent toward moral Good or Ill, then he is altogether incapable of natural affection.

(d) If he is altogether incapable of natural affection, then he will be "most of all miserable in Life."

(e) Therefore, a rational creature who fails to possess the moral sense proper will be most of all miserable in life.

Trianosky admits that step (4) above seems to make the obligation to be virtuous dependent on Shaftesbury's questionable doctrine of the moral sense. However, although Trianosky considers step (4-b) unexceptionable, he takes issue with (4-c). He says it appears that in support of (4-c), Shaftesbury argues as follows:

(i) To say that a creature is absolutely indifferent to moral good or ill is to say that the creature feels neither favorably nor unfavorably inclined toward the good of the kind or species.

(ii) But to have the natural affections *is* to have a favorable inclination or attitude toward the good of the kind or species.

(iii) Therefore, to be absolutely indifferent to moral good or ill entails not having the natural affections.

Trianosky rejects (i) on the ground that a rational creature might find it in his self-interest to cultivate the natural affections but still be without the moral sense *proper*. Such a creature, Trianosky argues, although lacking the moral sense proper, clearly would possess a prudential moral sense. Furthermore, the author contends that Shaftesbury has forgotten in (4-c) and (ii) his distinction between natural affections with *mental* objects and those with *sensible* objects.

Trianosky concludes that Shaftesbury's arguments for the obligation to be virtuous can be formulated independently of his doctrine of the moral sense proper and deserve to be considered on their own merits. In addition, he believes he shows that some of Shaftesbury's arguments which *do* depend on the doctrine of the moral sense can be stripped of tenets which contemporary thinkers generally consider untenable and yet remain interesting and challenging and important to discussions of the question "Why be moral?"

Stolnitz, Jerome. "'The Aesthetic Attitude' in the Rise of Modern Aesthetics," in *The Journal of Aesthetics and Art Criticism*. XXXVI, no. 4. (Summer, 1978), pp. 409-422.

Jerome Stolnitz previously has maintained that the concept of aesthetic disinterestedness, which he says is central to and distinctive of the thinking of the eighteenth and early nineteenth centuries, marked out a new field of study and considerably enlarged the denotation of "aesthetic object." In *Art and the Aesthetic*, George Dickie agrees; but he disagrees with Stolnitz that "the aesthetic attitude," defined in terms of disinterestedness, is employed fully in the work of any eighteenth century British thinker, maintaining instead that it is not so employed until the work of Arthur Schopenhauer. In the paper under consideration, Stolnitz argues that, understanding "aesthetic attitude" as Dickie apparently uses it, the aesthetic attitude figures essentially in Lord Shaftesbury's aesthetic theory.

According to Stolnitz, Dickie has identified "taste theory" (T-theory) and "aesthetic attitude theory" (A-theory). Briefly, A-theory involves "disinterested perception, consciousness or contemplation" and holds that when and only when perception is disinterested does it provide not the ordinary kind of awareness of the world but awareness of aesthetic objects or the aesthetic properties of objects. T-theory involves ordinary perception (of a perceiver who is calm, attentive, and not under the influence of distorting associations), a specific kind of object which alone possesses aesthetic properties, the faculty of taste which reacts to ordinary perception of this kind of object, and the feeling of "disinterested pleasure" which is produced by this reaction. Dickie spells out the fundamental difference between the two theories as follows: T-theory recognizes only ordinary perception, whereas A-theory distinguishes aesthetic (disinterested) perception, thereby rendering unnecessary the T-theory categories of taste, a particular kind of object, and pleasure. Stolnitz contends that Shaftesbury—who Dickie agrees is not a T-theorist as are, he says, later eighteenth century British thinkers—is more clearly an A-theorist than is Schopenhauer, Dickie's paradigm A-theorist.

In Shaftesbury, Stolnitz maintains, "disinterestedness" is defined in contrast to "interestedness" or "self-concern" and is applied to a broad range of human activities. Its meaning in a specific context depends in part on the structure and purpose of the activity of which it is predicated; the moral person is disinterested in that he acts not out of self-interest but out of the love of goodness for its own sake; the disinterested appraiser judges an issue not on the basis of his self-interest but on the merits of the issue.

Dickie has maintained, Stolnitz says, that none of the eighteenth century British philosophers distinguishes ordinary from aesthetic (or disinterested) *perception*. Stolnitz rejects such a claim for the following reason. If Dickie's claim were true, then an account of the nature of perception could not answer the ubiquitous eighteenth century question, "Why does not taste react commonly or universally to beautiful things?" The answer suggested by Dickie's account, that the faculty of taste is largely or completely lacking in many people, is denied by Shaftesbury; Shaftesbury holds that the capacity to respond to aesthetic and moral goodness in objects and people is inherent in, and natural to, all human beings. When Shaftesbury asks himself why most people fail to appreciate beauty, his answer in part is that people generally look at the world *interestedly*; although people are "made for contemplation," perception usually involves anticipatory concern for the self. Contemplation allows one to see that even objects which appear "ghastly and hideous" are "beauteous in themselves."

Stolnitz admits that Shaftesbury's "aesthetic disinterestedness" is not as explicit and official as Schopenhauer's, but, he holds, it is more original; and in both, the idea of the perceiver's devoting himself wholly to contemplation is prominent. (Stolnitz notes that Dickie, appropriately, assigns the term "contemplation" to A-theory.)

So, Stolnitz maintains, with regard to the single respect in which T-theories and A-theories are mutually exclusive, Shaftesbury is an A-theorist. Stolnitz urges, however, that his aesthetic can best be understood by means of a model which incorporates compatible elements of both theories: beauty (aesthetic or moral) is apprehended or enjoyed when and only when we see and hear disinterestedly; it is not, however, apprehended by the external senses but by an "inward eye" common to all human beings. Shaftesbury's "inward eye," Stolnitz points out, is the historical source of "the faculty of taste" in later British thought; but, unlike that taste, it is, in Dickie's terms, "cognitive" as well as "reactive," and its functioning requires a mode of perception described by Shaftesbury as disinterested in precisely the sense of the term which Dickie properly attributes to Schopenhauer.

Stolnitz proceeds to argue strongly against Dickie's claim that Shaftesbury comes close to being a T-theorist in that he limits aesthetic contemplation to one "specific kind" of object, the Platonic Form of Beauty. Stolnitz notes that Shaftesbury nowhere uses the term "the Platonic Form" and gives textual support for his belief that Shaftesbury countenances more than one kind of beauty. According to Stolnitz, there is, for Shaftesbury, the superior beauty of the "beautifying"—the creativity of the supreme Mind and that of human minds—and the lesser beauty of the "beautified," the products of such creativity. Shaftesbury holds, Stolnitz says, that the "sovereign beauty" informs all other minds and progressively informs the universe, and that human beings can exemplify, in their lives and communities, the beauty of the beautifying and the beauty of the beautified.—*B.C.S.*

Additional Recommended Reading

Dickie, George. *Art and the Aesthetic: An Institutional Analysis*. Ithaca, New York: Cornell University Press, 1974. Dickie characterizes Shaftesbury's aesthetic theory as closer to a "taste theory" than an "aesthetic attitude theory."

Shaftesbury, Anthony Ashley Cooper. *The Life, Unpublished Letters, and*

Philosophical Regimen of Anthony, Earl of Shaftesbury. Edited by Benjamin Rand. New York: Macmillan Publishing Company, 1900. A biography of Shaftesbury written by his son, the fourth earl, is included here, together with Shaftesbury's unpublished philosophical notes and letters.

Stolnitz, Jerome. "On the Significance of Lord Shaftesbury in Modern Aesthetic Theory," in *The Philosophical Quarterly*. II, no. 43 (April, 1961), pp. 97-113. Stolnitz argues that Shaftesbury's thought concerning aesthetics is more important and interesting than it usually has been considered.

Toole, Robert. "The Concepts of Freedom and Necessity in Shaftesbury's Philosophy," in *Studia Leibnitiana*. IX, no. 2 (1977), pp. 190-211. It is argued that Shaftesbury's *Philosophical Regimen* makes it clear that he is a necessitarian who holds that human freedom is not incompatible with determinism.

_____ . "Shaftesbury on God and His Relationships to the World," in *International Studies in Philosophy*. VIII (Fall, 1976). Shaftesbury's *Philosophical Regimen* shows, it is contended, that Shaftesbury is a pantheist and genuine Spinozist, rather than a theist or deist, as has been maintained previously.

THREE DIALOGUES BETWEEN HYLAS AND PHILONOUS

Author: George Berkeley (1685-1753)
Type of work: Metaphysics
First published: 1713

PRINCIPAL IDEAS ADVANCED

The universe is composed not of matter but of minds and spirits. Material objects, conceived of as nonmental substances existing outside consciousness, do not exist.

The universe of sensible objects is a projection of the mind. The existence of sensible objects is comparable to that of objects in dreams or hallucinations.

The view that tables, chairs, and other sensible objects exist independently of being perceived leads to skepticism about the existence and nature of such a realm.

Perceptions are not caused by material substances.

An infinite being causes and coordinates all perceptual experiences.

In this book the view is defended that matter does not exist. The universe contains minds or spirits but no realm of atoms and molecules. George Berkeley argues that things which are normally considered material objects—stones, trees, shoes, apples—have no existence outside the minds and experiences of conscious beings. Like an object in a dream, a stone has no existence outside consciousness. If all conscious beings were to stop perceiving some sensible object—the moon, for example—that object would cease to exist. Although Berkeley's book owes its philosophical greatness to the many important arguments which are presented in support of the main thesis, the work is also notable for the simplicity and clarity with which the ideas are conveyed. The ideas are presented in the form of a dialogue between Hylas, a materialist, and Philonous, the representative of Berkeley's idealism.

The main argument in the work centers around an examination of the set of properties of which sensible objects are composed. Berkeley first examines the properties which philosophers have called "secondary qualities" (heat, taste, sound, smell, color) and argues that these properties have no existence outside sensations and perceptions in the minds of perceivers. He then argues that the same sorts of considerations will show that what have been called the "primary qualities" of sensible objects—extension (length and width), shape, hardness, weight, motion and other characteristics—also have no existence outside the perceptions of conscious beings. In arguing that *every* property which a sensible object has exists only as a sensation or a property of a sensation within a mind, Berkeley is showing that the entire sensible object has no existence outside of the mind. For Berkeley a cherry is nothing over and above the sensations experienced in connection with it. "Take away the sensations of softness, redness, tartness, and you take away the cherry," he writes.

Berkeley begins his argument by reference to heat. Intense heat like intense cold is a pain; it is intrinsically unpleasant. Pain, like pleasure, is a kind of experience; it is something which cannot exist outside of someone's consciousness. Therefore, when someone feels intense heat or intense cold, Berkeley reasons, what he feels is in his own mind, not in some inert, unfeeling object existing outside his consciousness. To be aware of intense heat is simply to be aware of a particular kind of pain sensation.

To the objection that intense heat is a *cause* of pain and not itself literally "pain," Berkeley replies that when a person is perceiving intense heat, the heat of which he is aware is not distinguishable from the pain sensation of which he is aware. In perceiving the heat the person is not aware of *two* things, heat *and* a pain sensation, but of only one thing, a painful sensation.

The temperature which an object appears to have differs under different circumstances, Berkeley proceeds. If a person's left hand is hot and his right hand cold and he then immerses both hands into a bowl of water, the water seems cool to the left hand and warm to the right hand. From this fact Berkeley concludes that the heat which the person feels cannot be a feature of some object existing outside his mind. No single object could have the incompatible properties of warmth and coolness at once. Berkeley concludes that the warmth and coolness which the person perceives are sensations within his own experience. What people think of as the "temperature" of the water is simply the sensation experienced in connection with the water. The sensation is in the consciousness of the person perceiving the temperature, not in an unfeeling object outside his consciousness.

These arguments concerning heat can be paralleled for the other secondary qualities of sensible objects. A sweet taste is a form of pleasure; a bitter taste is intrinsically unpleasant or painful. Since pleasure and pain are necessarily mental phenomena, a sweet or bitter taste, because it is a pleasure or pain, must itself be a mental phenomenon, Berkeley reasons. Furthermore, the taste which people perceive in an object varies under different conditions. A food which someone finds sweet at one time he may find bitter or tasteless at another time. The taste a food has to a person when he is sick is different from the taste it has to him when he is well, Berkeley writes. What differs in the two cases, he reasons, is not the alleged external object but the experience had when tasting the food. In each case one has different taste sensations, and these taste sensations, which *are* the taste of the food, exist in the mind of the person doing the tasting. The fact that some people delight in the same food which others find repulsive Berkeley considers further proof that the taste of a food is not a property inherent in the object which allegedly exists outside people's minds but a sensation undergone by the people who taste the food. Similar considerations can be appealed to in support of the claim that odor or smell is a sensation within someone's mind.

As happens with other secondary qualities, the *color* which an object appears to have varies under different conditions. A cloud which appears some shade of white under most conditions may appear red or purple when perceived at sunset, Berkeley writes. Someone who holds that color is an inherent property of the clouds will need to say that not all the colors that may be perceived in an object are the true color of the object and that some of these colors are only apparent.

How then is the true color to be distinguished from the colors which are said to be merely *apparent*? It might be suggested that the true color is the one the object presents when it is viewed under white light. But this suggestion raises problems. An object presents a somewhat different color under candlelight from that which it presents under daylight, Berkeley notes. Indeed, there are many different intensities and shades of what we call "white light," and each of these intensities and shades is as normal and common as the others. Yet each shade and intensity leads to a somewhat different color being perceived in an object.

One might reply that the true color of an object is the color that is perceived when the object is given the most close and careful inspection possible. But this suggestion also runs into serious problems. To examine an object in the closest and most careful manner possible is to examine the object under a microscope, Berkeley writes. However, when an object is examined under a microscope, the microscope does not simply present *one* color to the eye, a color which one could label the true color; rather, the microscope (like the naked eye) presents numerous colors to the eye, and the particular color one sees in an object depends on the magnification one gives to the microscope. To pick out one color from the various colors which are perceived and call it the true color of the object would require a choice which has no justification.

A further problem for someone who maintains that color is a property inherent in objects exterior to minds is the fact that objects under the same conditions present different colors to different perceivers. Objects which appear yellow to people with jaundice appear other colors to people without jaundice, Berkeley writes. Furthermore, given the structural differences between the eyes of animals and those of people, it is probable that some animals perceive colors in objects that are different from those which people perceive, Berkeley reasons. To pick out any of these perceived colors and call it the true color would involve an arbitrary, unjustifiable decision. The view that an object has a true color Berkeley considers untenable in face of the above facts. From these considerations Berkeley concludes that *all* colors perceived in sensible objects are simply visual sensations in the minds of those perceiving the color.

The accounts which scientists give of perception are often consistent with his account of secondary qualities and may even be interpreted as supporting it, Berkeley writes. Although scientists do, of course, believe in a material world existing external to consciousness which causes people to hear sounds and see colors, they often think of hearing or seeing as a matter of having certain auditory or visual *sensations*. Scientists say, for example, that when an object causes air to move in a certain manner and this air strikes the ear drum, a certain neurological activity is produced and the neurological activity causes one to experience *the sensation of sound*. Color is seen, they say, when light rays, after being reflected off some object, enter the eye and stir the optic nerve such that a message is communicated to the brain, upon which the person experiences *the sensation of color*. To say, as these scientists do, that sound and color are *sensations* is to say that they are mental phenomena.

The view that "secondary qualities" are nothing but sensations in the minds of conscious beings, although queer in relation to common sense, did not originate with Berkeley. The view had been previously defended by John Locke. Berkeley's most radical departure from previous philosophical opinion was in his claim that all properties of sensible objects, including the "primary qualities," could be shown to have no existence outside the minds of perceivers.

If the existence of perceptual variation is reason to conclude that the secondary qualities do not exist outside minds, Berkeley reasoned, then philosophers have the same reason to conclude that the primary qualities also lack existence outside minds. Like the secondary qualities, the primary qualities give rise to radical perceptual variations. The extension which an object appears to have varies as the object is perceived from different positions, Berkeley explains. The visible extension which a tree has, the extension which it has in relation to the expanse of a perceiver's field of vision, grows larger as the perceiver approaches the tree and shrinks as the perceiver moves away from the tree. When a perceiver is near, a tree may appear to be a hundred times larger than it does from a great distance. (Imagine how much larger the moon would look if you could see it from a distance of only ten miles.) It does not help to reply that the tree has the same size in *feet* and *inches* whatever one's distance from it. For the visible extension of a foot or an inch itself is not a constant and it too goes through the same variations as one approaches or recedes from it. A twelve-inch ruler looks large from very close but tiny when perceived from a distance. Furthermore, Berkeley argues, a sensible object may present differing visible extensions at one and the same time. The foot of a mouse, which seems tiny to a man, would seem to be of considerable extension to the mouse. An object which extends over a large portion of the field of vision of a mouse would extend over a small portion of the visual field of a man. Berkeley concludes that the extension of a sensible object is not a property of an object which exists outside our consciousness but a property of a sensation in the mind of a perceiver.

The types of considerations which show that the extension of a sensible object has no existence outside a mind also show that shape, hardness, and the other primary qualities are only properties of sensations within the minds of perceivers. The shape, hardness, and motion which an object appears to have also vary from one perceiver to another and vary for a single perceiver when the object is viewed under different conditions.

One might think that the fact that objects are perceived as being *at a distance* from the person perceiving them proves that the objects cannot be inside the perceiver's mind. Berkeley responds to this objection with the observation that even in dreams and hallucinations objects are experienced as being at a distance and outside of the mind, yet in spite of these appearances these imagined objects do not exist outside of the mind of the person imagining them. Thus it clearly *is* possible for an object to be experienced as being at a distance from oneself even when the object is really not outside one's own mind.

Another reason why the primary qualities must be in the mind with the secondary qualities, Berkeley writes, is that all sensible qualities coexist. When a person perceives a table the extension and shape which he perceives are *joined* to the color. The shape outlines the color. If the color which is perceived is in the person's mind, then so are the extension, shape, and motion which are experienced as being together with the color.

It might be supposed that when someone perceives an object he has an image in his mind which *copies* or *mirrors* a material world existing outside his mind—a world which is the cause of the image. Although it is the mental image and not the material world a perceiver is directly aware of, the image provides accurate information about the external, material world, it may be said. Berkeley finds serious problems in this view. First, if it is admitted that all the primary and secondary qualities of objects exist only within minds, then there are no properties remaining for this so-called "material substance" outside the mind to have. Talk of "material substance" in this context becomes meaningless. Furthermore, it is not possible, Berkeley argues, for an image which is continually undergoing radical changes (which our perception of sensible objects is doing) to be a copy of some set of objects which remains unchanged throughout this period (as the alleged material substance is assumed to do).

A further problem with this view, Berkeley argues, is that the model of perception which it presents leads to a severe skepticism about the alleged material world. According to this view a person perceiving a sensible object is not directly aware of the material world but only of the image in his mind. That this image which is said to be a copy of a material world outside the mind does indeed copy or resemble the object alleged to be the original could not be known. If our knowledge of the alleged original is derived entirely from our familiarity with the image which is said to be the copy, there is no independent means of checking that the "copy" is actually like the original.

Indeed, since in this view people are never directly aware of the alleged material world, it follows that it is not possible even to know whether this outside, unexperienced world exists. The existence of a mental image does not itself guarantee that there is an external object causing the image, for it is logically possible for someone to have exactly the same perceptions or mental images even if no world of material objects exists.

If what we consider *real* objects are like objects in dreams and hallucinations in having no existence outside the mind, how then does Berkeley distinguish the former from the latter? Berkeley explains that the perceptions we consider real are vivid and consistent in a way that those which we do not consider real are not.

What then is the cause of people's perceptions of sensible objects if not a world of material substance corresponding to those perceptions? Berkeley reasons that because a person does not cause or coordinate his own sensations, his sensations must have a cause outside himself, and this cause, Berkeley concludes, is an omnipresent infinite spirit. From the order, beauty, and design with which our sensations appear Berkeley concludes that the designer is wise, powerful, and good "beyond comprehension."—*I. G.*

PERTINENT LITERATURE

Hamlyn, D. W. *Sensation and Perception: A History of the Philosophy of Perception.* London: Routledge & Kegan Paul, 1961, pp. 94-116.

In this survey of the various theories which philosophers have had about perception and its relation to objects of perception, D. W. Hamlyn offers various criticisms of the arguments which George Berkeley uses in his attempt to prove that the sensible world has no existence outside the minds of those who perceive it. One of the arguments in *Three Dialogues* Berkeley bases on a claim that secondary qualities sometimes are inherently unpleasant or painful. (To perceive intense heat is to feel a kind of pain, Berkeley writes.) Since pain has no existence outside the mind, Berkeley reasons, the secondary qualities which are pains have no existence outside minds. Because intense heat is a kind of pain, it is nothing but a feeling in the mind of one who perceives it, he concludes. Hamlyn writes that this argument—an argument which Berkeley picks up from John Locke—is invalid. Although people may have certain feelings or sensations while perceiving heat, the warmth or heat which they feel is not just the sensation they experience. Even if it were true that a feeling of intense heat cannot be distinguished from a feeling of pain, *both* feelings, Hamlyn writes, are distinguishable from the heat in the object which causes the feelings. From the fact that a sensation of heat is a mental phenomenon, it does not follow that its cause is a mental phenomenon. To refer to "the heat" is to refer to the *cause* of the sensations and not to the sensations themselves. Hamlyn gives a similar account of the other secondary qualities which Berkeley says may be inherently painful or unpleasant. When people find a certain taste unpleasant or "painful" the taste is the property in the object which causes the unpleasant experience and not the experience itself. The unpleasantness experienced is not itself the taste but an effect of the taste.

Hamlyn explains that Berkeley is wrong to assimilate perceiving to the having of sensations. Like Locke, Berkeley thinks of the pain which someone feels when he perceives intense heat as a part or the whole of his perceiving of the heat. However, perceiving an object is not the same thing as having certain sensations, Hamlyn writes. To have a pain is not in itself to perceive anything, Hamlyn states.

Berkeley based another of his arguments on the fact that our perceptions of objects are variable. That the color, taste, shape, and other qualities that an object appears to have may vary under different conditions Berkeley presents as further proof that it could not be a single (material) object that is being perceived in all these instances. Hamlyn objects that the conclusion Berkeley draws does not follow from the premises. From the fact that an object may appear to have different properties under different conditions it does not follow that none of the properties it appears to have are truly inherent in the object. All that follows is that not all of the properties perceived are inherent in the object. How then can one determine which of the various properties that an object may appear to have are really inherent in the object? The property which is inherent in an object is the one which is perceived when the object is examined under normal conditions, Hamlyn writes.

Hamlyn commends Berkeley for observing that Locke had been inconsistent in failing to notice that the primary qualities are like the secondary qualities in being subject to perceptual variations. If perceptual variation is reason for concluding that secondary qualities have no existence outside minds, then there is the same reason for concluding that primary qualities also have no existence outside minds. However, Hamlyn writes, from the fact that the primary qualities are like the secondary in their perceptual variations it would have been wiser for Berkeley to conclude that both qualities are properties of external objects than it was to conclude that both exist together in the mind.

Moore, G. E. "Proof of an External World," in *Philosophical Papers*. London: George Allen & Unwin, 1959.

In this paper, originally published in 1939, G. E. Moore argues that chairs, stars, mountains, and all the other things which people consider material objects exist outside the minds of conscious beings. Moore does not examine or criticize the arguments which George Berkeley and other philosophers have used in support of the contrary position but simply offers a positive argument in favor of his own position—the position of common sense.

In his attempt to prove the existence of external objects, Moore distinguishes the idea of an object's being "presented in space" from the idea of an object's being such that it may be "met in space." To prove that there are objects of the latter sort is to prove that there are external objects; objects of the former sort are not external objects. After-images and toothaches are objects which are "presented in space" because they are objects having spatial locations. (An after-image appears as being outside one's head, in front of one's eyes; a toothache is experienced as being in or near one's tooth.) But after-images and toothaches are not "to be met with in space." An object that is "to be met with in space" is one which would be seen or felt by any person of normal perceptual apparatus who is in the right position. It is not possible for another person directly to perceive my after-images or pains, but if there are objects that can be perceived by more than one person then these objects are "to be met with in space." If there are objects which are "to be met with in space," then there are objects external to our minds.

External objects, objects which can "be met with in space," are objects which can exist without being perceived, Moore explains. Part of the meaning in the distinction between an object's existing only "in someone's mind" and an object's being "external to people's minds" is that in saying that an object exists only "in someone's mind" we *mean* that it does not exist at times when he is not experiencing it, whereas in describing an object as "external to our minds" we mean that it can exist at moments when it is not being perceived.

To prove that there are external objects, Moore writes, it is sufficient to prove that there are "physical objects." If one can prove that there is a human hand, a soap bubble, a shoe, a sock, or any other "material object," then one has proven that there are things which "are to be met with in space" and which exist "outside us," Moore writes. The sentence "There is a soap bubble" entails "There is a material object" and "There is an external object." The meaning of "soap bubble" is such that an object would not be a soap bubble unless it were something which could in principle be perceived by more than one person. The meaning of the word is such that it is not a contradiction to speak of a soap bubble as existing at times when it is not perceived.

Can one prove that there are soap bubbles, hands, or other material objects? To do so is easy, Moore writes. To prove to another person that there are material objects, one need only hold up a hand and say "Here is a hand." An additional argument could be added by raising one's other hand and saying "Here is another hand." There is no better proof, Moore argues. The statement which is the premise in the argument ("Here is a hand") differs from the statement which is the conclusion ("Here is an object external to our minds"); the premise is known to be true (it would be absurd to suggest that a person does not know that he has two hands, Moore writes), and the conclusion follows from the premise.

Could a person *prove* the premise of this argument (that he is holding up one of his hands)? Moore admits that he is not confident that a person can prove that he is holding up a hand; but even if he cannot prove this, he can know it to be true. Some things one can know to be true without being able to offer a proof for them, Moore writes. It would be absurd to claim of a normal conscious person that he could not know if he is holding up a hand, Moore writes. A philosopher who is dissatisfied with this proof of the external world, merely because the premise has not itself been proven, has no grounds for dissatisfaction.

Moore, G. E. "A Defence of Common Sense," in *Philosophical Papers*. London: George Allen & Unwin, 1959.

George Berkeley's view that there are no material objects and his claim that even if there were material objects we could not know of their existence are among the views G. E. Moore attacks in this article. Other philosophical theses which sharply clash with common sense are also attacked in the paper.

Berkeley's view that there are no external, material objects *must* be wrong, Moore argues, because there are many propositions known to be true which entail that there are material objects. Among the propositions which Moore says he knows with certainty to be true are that he has a body, that his body was smaller when he was a baby than it is at the time of his writing this article, that his body has been in contact with the earth or near the surface of the earth during his whole life, and that during his life his body has been at various distances from other objects such as his bookcase and pen. Moore writes that, first, he knows with certainty that these and other propositions are true and that, second, each of these propositions entails the existence of external objects. The propositions that he has a body and that his body has been in close contact with the earth imply the existence of material things (namely, his body and the earth). Moore writes that he knows that many other people also know with certainty the same propositions about themselves—namely, that they have bodies, that these bodies have been in contact with the earth, and so forth. The reality of material objects is also entailed by these propositions which other people know to be true. A philosopher who denies that there is a material world *must* be wrong, Moore writes, simply because the above propositions and many related propositions are known with certainty to be true.

Philosophers like Berkeley who say that they do not know if there is an external world or who deny the existence of such a world regularly say things inconsistent with these claims, Moore writes. When an Idealist assumes the existence of other philosophers or of the human race he is being inconsistent with his Idealism, since being a philosopher or any other human being entails being a creature with a body. When referring to "we" or to "us," an Idealist is speaking in a way that is inconsistent with his Idealism since he is alluding to other human beings—that is, to other bodily creatures who live on the earth.

Moore is not simply accusing Idealists of being *careless* when they say things which are inconsistent with their thesis. Rather, Moore is saying that a philosopher who maintains that there are no material objects or that we do not know whether there are any such objects is defending a thesis which is inconsistent with many propositions *that he knows to be true.* An Idealist who refers to other philosophers or who speaks in terms of "we" thereby betrays the fact that he, like Moore, *knows* that there are other people (other embodied creatures). When a philosopher claims that "no human being has ever known whether material objects exist" he is making a claim that is not simply about himself. In saying this he is claiming, first, that there *are* in addition to himself other persons (other beings with bodies who live on the earth) and, second, that none of these other persons knows if there are material objects. Thus, the Idealist betrays the fact that he considers it certain that there are other embodied creatures, Moore contends. Since *all* people—even philosophers who deny the existence of a material world—know that they have bodies and that there are other people with bodies, it is inevitable that they will betray their knowledge of these facts, Moore writes, and thus it is inevitable that they will say things inconsistent with their Idealism.

The view that there are no material objects is not self-contradictory, Moore writes. It is logically possible that there might not have existed material objects. Moore explains that his reason for saying that he knows with certainty that there are material objects is the fact that he knows with certainty that his statements "I have a body," "There are other persons with bodies," and similar, related statements are true.—*I. G.*

ADDITIONAL RECOMMENDED READING

Bennett, Jonathan. "Substance, Reality, and Primary Qualities," in *American Philosophical Quarterly.* II, no. 1 (January, 1965), pp. 1-17. An examination of the arguments which Berkeley and Locke use in defending their views on perception.

Broad, C. D. "Berkeley's Denial of Material Substance," in *The Philosophical Review.* LXIII, no. 2 (April, 1954), pp. 155-181. A critical discussion of Berkeley's theory.

Lean, Martin. *Sense Perception and Matter.* New York: Humanities Press, 1953. A detailed critique of the thinking that leads philosophers to skepticism over the existence of material objects.

McGreal, Ian P. *Analyzing Philosophical Arguments.* San Francisco: Chandler Publishing Company, 1967. Contains a detailed examination of Berkeley's argument, including a reconstruction of the argument, premise-by-premise appraisal, and logical analysis. The key to the argument is the ambiguity of the term "sense quality," according to McGreal.

Moore, G. E. "The Refutation of Idealism," in *Philosophical Studies*. London: Routledge & Kegan Paul, 1922. Moore points to certain confusions which he says have had important roles in all defenses of Idealism.

Russell, Bertrand. *The Problems of Philosophy*. London: Oxford University Press, 1912. In a style free from technical words Russell clearly explains the philosophy of Idealism.

Warnock, G. J. *Berkeley*. Harmondsworth, England: Penguin Books, 1953. An illuminating, thorough exposition of Berkeley's philosophy.